Handbook of Energy Governance in Europe

Michèle Knodt • Jörg Kemmerzell
Editors

Handbook of Energy Governance in Europe

Volume 1

With 145 Figures and 78 Tables

Editors
Michèle Knodt
Institute of Political Science
Technical University of Darmstadt
Darmstadt, Germany

Jörg Kemmerzell
Institute of Political Science
Technical University of Darmstadt
Darmstadt, Germany

ISBN 978-3-030-43249-2   ISBN 978-3-030-43250-8 (eBook)
https://doi.org/10.1007/978-3-030-43250-8

© Springer Nature Switzerland AG 2022

This work is subject to copyright. All rights are reserved by the Publisher, whether the whole or part of the material is concerned, specifically the rights of translation, reprinting, reuse of illustrations, recitation, broadcasting, reproduction on microfilms or in any other physical way, and transmission or information storage and retrieval, electronic adaptation, computer software, or by similar or dissimilar methodology now known or hereafter developed.

The use of general descriptive names, registered names, trademarks, service marks, etc. in this publication does not imply, even in the absence of a specific statement, that such names are exempt from the relevant protective laws and regulations and therefore free for general use.

The publisher, the authors, and the editors are safe to assume that the advice and information in this book are believed to be true and accurate at the date of publication. Neither the publisher nor the authors or the editors give a warranty, expressed or implied, with respect to the material contained herein or for any errors or omissions that may have been made. The publisher remains neutral with regard to jurisdictional claims in published maps and institutional affiliations.

This Springer imprint is published by the registered company Springer Nature Switzerland AG
The registered company address is: Gewerbestrasse 11, 6330 Cham, Switzerland

Preface

We started working on the *Handbook of Energy Governance in Europe* in a workshop with the first 15 authors in December 2017, began publishing the first chapters online in March 2019, and have continued to do so ever since. As one can imagine, the project did not remain untouched by the global Covid 19 pandemic. Originally, we had planned to complete the work on this handbook by the end of 2020, but unfortunately, this was impossible due to delays in contributions, authors dropping out, and other issues related to the pandemic. Therefore, we could not realize some of the originally planned chapters, for example on the governance of European energy networks or a couple of additional countries. Among them is the chapter on Ukraine that could not be realized due to the dreadful political circumstances.

We finished working on this handbook in February 2022 with the acceptance of the last chapters. Therefore, we were not able to consider the developments in energy governance caused by the Russian war of aggression against Ukraine beginning in late February 2022 after the completion of the handbook, which will have undoubtedly radical consequences for both the European energy architecture and national energy strategies. Several developments are conceivable. Very likely there will be a vast reduction or a cut in energy relations between most European countries and Russia, which will change the geopolitics of energy significantly. Also likely seems a strengthening of the European Union as a strategic actor. Other developments are more in the balance – e.g., the reduction of natural gas supply may cause an at least temporary comeback of coal in the energy mix of some countries. The expansion of renewable energy generation, green hydrogen, and biofuels will gain pace as nuclear power could be strengthened again. However, concrete developments in energy governance and policy will play out differently in different national contexts. And these contexts are shaped to a great deal, independently of external shocks, by the long-term developments and entrenched institutional structures that are presented in this handbook.

That we have been able to complete the handbook is due to the fruitful and instructive cooperation with more than 100 authors, as well as to the understanding and competent supervision of the project by Barbara Wolf and Esther Niederhammer from Springer. Our special thanks go to them. We would like to thank also the German Federal Ministry of Education and Research, which supported the handbook project within the Kopernikus projects ENavi (funding code: 03SFK4P0) and Ariadne (funding code: 03SFK5LO).

SPONSORED BY THE

Darmstadt, Germany
August 2022

Michèle Knodt
Jörg Kemmerzell
Editors

Acknowledgments

We would like to thank the German Federal Ministry of Education and Research for its financial support of this handbook. It has funded two Kopernikus projects in which the editors were involved: ENavi – Energy Transition Navigation System (funding code 03SFK4P0) and Ariadne – Evidence-Based Assessment for the Design of the German Energy System Transformation (funding code 03SFK5LO).

Contents

Volume 1

Part I Introduction 1

1 Energy Governance in Europe: Introduction 3
   Michèle Knodt and Jörg Kemmerzell

Part II Energy Governance Research: Theories, Issues, and Problems 17

2 Transition of Energy Systems: Patterns of
   Stability and Change 19
   Mario Neukirch

3 Energy Democracy and Participation in Energy Transitions 49
   Cornelia Fraune

4 Energy Poverty 67
   Christoph Strünck

5 Monitoring Energy Policy 77
   Jonas J. Schoenefeld and Tim Rayner

6 Extending Energy Policy: The Challenge of Sector Integration ... 101
   Michael Rodi and Michael Kalis

Part III European Governance 119

7 European Union Energy Policy: A Discourse Perspective 121
   Michèle Knodt and Marc Ringel

8 Energy Policies in the EU: A Fiscal Federalism Perspective 143
   Erik Gawel and Sebastian Strunz

9 The EU in Global Energy Governance 163
   Laima Eicke and Franziska Petri

10	EU Energy Cooperation with Emerging Powers: Brazil, India, China, and South Africa	189
	Michèle Knodt, Roberto Schaeffer, Madhura Joshi, Lai Suetyi, and Agathe Maupin	
11	EU-Russia Energy Relations	237
	Marco Siddi	
12	EU-US and EU-Canada Energy Relations	263
	Petra Dolata	
13	Energy Relations in the EU Eastern Partnership	287
	Katharina Kleinschnitger, Michèle Knodt, Marie Lortz, and Anna K. Stöckl	
14	Energy Relations of the EU and its Southern Neighborhood	315
	Britta Daum	
15	The Energy Charter Treaty: Old and New Dilemmas in Global Energy Governance	347
	Anna Herranz-Surrallés	
16	Sustainable Europe: Narrative Potential in the EU's Political Communication	367
	Natalia Chaban and Jessica Bain	
17	Clean Energy in the European Green Deal: Perspectives of European Stakeholders	383
	Nils Bruch, Marc Ringel, and Michèle Knodt	
18	Cities in European Energy and Climate Governance	411
	Jörg Kemmerzell	

Volume 2

Part IV	**Country Studies**	**429**
19	Energy Governance in Armenia	431
	Shushanik Minasyan	
20	Energy Governance in Austria	455
	Niclas Wenz	
21	Energy Governance in Azerbaijan	483
	Murad Nasibov	
22	Energy Governance in Belgium	511
	Thijs Van de Graaf, Erik Laes, and Aviel Verbruggen	

Contents

23	**Energy Governance in Croatia**	533
	Ana-Maria Boromisa	
24	**Energy Governance in the Czech Republic**	563
	Jan Osička, Veronika Zapletalová, Filip Černoch, and Tomáš Vlček	
25	**Energy Governance in Denmark**	593
	Helene Dyrhauge	
26	**Energy Governance in Finland**	619
	Mikael Hildén and Paula Kivimaa	
27	**Energy Governance in France**	647
	Pierre Bocquillon and Aurélien Evrard	
28	**Energy Governance in Germany**	667
	Jörg Kemmerzell	
29	**Energy Governance in Greece**	709
	Marula Tsagkari	
30	**Energy Governance in Hungary**	737
	John Szabo, Csaba Weiner, and András Deák	
31	**Energy Governance in Ireland**	769
	Diarmuid Torney	
32	**Energy Governance in Italy**	791
	Maria Rosaria Di Nucci and Daniele Russolillo	
33	**Energy Governance in Latvia**	823
	Sigita Urdze	
34	**Energy Governance in Lithuania**	841
	Šarūnas Liekis	
35	**Energy Governance in the Netherlands**	863
	Elisabeth Musch	
36	**Energy Governance in Norway**	897
	Elin Lerum Boasson and Torbjørg Jevnaker	
37	**Energy Governance in the Republic of Poland**	923
	Maksymilian Zoll	
38	**Energy Governance in Portugal**	959
	Luís Guerreiro, Helge Jörgens, and Vicente Alves	
39	**Energy Governance in Romania**	993
	Aron Buzogány and Simona Davidescu	

40	**Energy Governance in Russia: From a Fossil to a Green Giant?** Veli-Pekka Tynkkynen	1019
41	**Energy Governance in Serbia** Stefan Ćetković	1037
42	**Energy Governance in Slovakia** Matúš Mišík and Veronika Oravcová	1055
43	**Energy Governance in Slovenia** Danijel Crnčec	1083
44	**Energy Governance in Spain** Jose M. Campos-Martín, Laura Crespo, and Rosa M. Fernandez	1121
45	**Energy Governance in Sweden** Bengt Johansson	1157
46	**Energy Governance in Switzerland** Andreas Balthasar	1187
47	**Energy Governance in Turkey** Emre İşeri and Tuğçe Uygurtürk	1217
48	**Energy Governance in the United Kingdom** Matthew Lockwood, Catherine Mitchell, and Richard Hoggett	1255

Part V   Comparison and Conclusion **1287**

49	**Energy Governance in Europe: Country Comparison and Conclusion** Jörg Kemmerzell, Nils Bruch, and Michèle Knodt	1289

Index 1319

About the Editors

Michèle Knodt is Professor of Political Science at the Technical University of Darmstadt, Jean Monnet Chair (ad personam) and Director of the Jean Monnet Centre of Excellence "EU in Global Dialogue" (CEDI), Director of the Jean Monnet Centre of Excellence "EU@School," Chair of the COST Network ENTER (EU Foreign Policy Facing New Realities), Co-leader of the Loewe-Excellence Centre "emergenCITY," Co-leader of the DFG Research Training Group "Critical Infrastructures," PI in the Kopernikus Project "Ariadne – Evidence-Based Assessment for the Design of the German Energy System Transformation," and leader of smaller cooperative and interdisciplinary projects. She has published widely on the EU, is especially interested in energy and climate governance, and has received research grants from the German Federal Ministry of Education and Research (BMBF), German Federal Ministry of Economic Affairs and Energy (BMWi), the German Research Council (DFG), the Volkswagen Foundation, and the European Commission.

Jörg Kemmerzell received his Ph.D. in Political Science from the Technical University of Darmstadt, Germany, in 2007. His research interests include energy and climate policy in multilevel systems, comparative politics and methods, and applied theory of democracy. He has published over 50 journal articles, books, and book chapters mostly on energy and climate policy and related topics. After finishing his Ph.D., Jörg Kemmerzell worked as a researcher and lecturer in Political Science at the Technical University of Darmstadt and the University of Hildesheim (Germany). Since 2012, he was a senior researcher in four research projects of the German Research Council (DFG) and the German Federal Ministry of Education and Research (BMBF), focusing on climate policy of cities and the assessment of the German energy transition. He worked also as a consultant for research communication. Since 2021, he is a senior lecturer in Political Science at the Technical University of Darmstadt and a research associate in the Kopernikus project "Ariadne – Evidence-Based Assessment for the Design of the German Energy System Transformation."

Contributors

Vicente Alves CIES_Iscte – Centre for Research and Studies in Sociology, Lisbon, Portugal

Jessica Bain School of Media, Communication and Sociology, University of Leicester, Leicester, UK

Andreas Balthasar University of Lucerne, Lucerne, Switzerland

Elin Lerum Boasson Department of Political Science, Center for International Climate Research, University of Oslo and CICERO, Oslo, Norway

Pierre Bocquillon School of Politics, Philosophy, Language & Communication Studies, University of East Anglia, Norwich, UK

Ana-Maria Boromisa Department for International Economic and Political Relations, Institute for Development and International Relations, Zagreb, Croatia

Nils Bruch Institute of Political Science, Technical University of Darmstadt, Darmstadt, Germany

Aron Buzogány Institute of Forest, Environmental, and Natural Resource Policy (InFER), University of Natural Resources and Life Sciences Vienna (BOKU), Vienna, Austria

Jose M. Campos-Martín Instituto de Catálisis y Petroleoquímica, CSIC, Madrid, Spain

Filip Černoch Center for Energy Studies, Masaryk University, Brno, Czech Republic

Stefan Ćetković Bavarian School of Public Policy, Technical University of Munich, Munich, Germany

Natalia Chaban Department of Media and Communication, University of Canterbury, Christchurch, New Zealand

Laura Crespo Centro de Estudios y Experimentación de Obras Públicas, CEDEX, Madrid, Spain

Danijel Crnčec Faculty of Social Sciences, University of Ljubljana, Ljubljana, Slovenia

Britta Daum Paris, France

Simona Davidescu University of York and ESSCA, Angers, York, UK

András Deák Institute of World Economics, Centre for Economic and Regional Studies, Budapest, Hungary

Institute of Strategic and Security Studies, National University of Public Service, Budapest, Hungary

Maria Rosaria Di Nucci Environmental Policy Research Centre, Freie Universität Berlin, Berlin, Germany

Petra Dolata Department of History, University of Calgary, Calgary, AB, Canada

Helene Dyrhauge Department for Social Sciences & Business, Roskilde University, Roskilde, Denmark

Laima Eicke Energy Systems and Societal Change, Institute for Advanced Sustainability Studies (IASS), Potsdam, Germany

Aurélien Evrard UFR Droit et Sciences Politiques, University of Nantes, Nantes, France

Rosa M. Fernandez Department of Social and Political Science, University of Chester, Chester, UK

Cornelia Fraune Institute of Political Science, Technical University of Darmstadt, Darmstadt, Germany

Erik Gawel Department of Economics, Helmholtz Centre for Environmental Research – UFZ, Leipzig, Germany

Institute for Infrastructure and Resources Management, Leipzig University, Leipzig, Germany

Luís Guerreiro CIES_Iscte – Centre for Research and Studies in Sociology, Lisbon, Portugal

Anna Herranz-Surrallés Faculty of Arts and Social Sciences, Maastricht University, Maastricht, The Netherlands

Mikael Hildén Finnish Environment Institute, SYKE, and the Strategic Research Council, Helsinki, Finland

Richard Hoggett Energy Policy Group, University of Exeter, Penryn, UK

Emre İşeri Department of International Relations, Yaşar University, İzmir, Turkey

Torbjørg Jevnaker Fridtjof Nansen Institute, Lysaker, Akershus, Norway

Contributors

Bengt Johansson Environmental and Energy Systems Studies, Lund University, Lund, Sweden

Helge Jörgens CIES_Iscte – Centre for Research and Studies in Sociology, Lisbon, Portugal

Department of Political Science and Public Policy, Iscte – Instituto Universitário de Lisboa, Lisbon, Portugal

Madhura Joshi Natural Resources Defense Council, Delhi, India

Michael Kalis Institute for Climate Protection, Energy and Mobility (IKEM), Berlin, Germany

Interdisciplinary Centre for Baltic Sea Region Research, University of Greifswald, Greifswald, Germany

Jörg Kemmerzell Institute of Political Science, Technical University of Darmstadt, Darmstadt, Germany

Paula Kivimaa Finnish Environment Institute, SYKE, Helsinki, Finland

SPRU, University of Sussex, Brighton, UK

Katharina Kleinschnitger Institute of Political Science, Technical University of Darmstadt, Darmstadt, Germany

Michèle Knodt Institute of Political Science, Technical University of Darmstadt, Darmstadt, Germany

Erik Laes Sustainable Energy and Built Environment, VITO/EnergyVille, Genk, Belgium

School of Innovation Sciences, University of Eindhoven, Eindhoven, The Netherlands

Šarūnas Liekis School of Political Science and Diplomacy, Vytautas Magnus University, Kaunas, Lithuania

Matthew Lockwood Science Policy Research Unit, University of Sussex, Brighton, UK

Marie Lortz Institute of Political Science, Technical University of Darmstadt, Darmstadt, Germany

Agathe Maupin SAIIA – South African Institute of International Affairs, University of the Witwatersrand, Johannesburg, South Africa

Shushanik Minasyan Institute of Political Studies and Sociology, University of Bonn, Bonn, Germany

Matúš Mišík Department of Political Science, Comenius University in Bratislava, Bratislava, Slovakia

Catherine Mitchell Energy Policy Group, University of Exeter, Penryn, UK

Elisabeth Musch School of Cultural Studies and Social Sciences, University of Osnabrueck, Osnabrueck, Germany

Murad Nasibov Institute of Political Science, Justus-Liebig University of Giessen, Giessen, Germany

Mario Neukirch Institute for Social Sciences, University of Stuttgart, Stuttgart, Baden-Württemberg, Germany

Veronika Oravcová Department of Political Science, Comenius University in Bratislava, Bratislava, Slovakia

Jan Osička Center for Energy Studies, Masaryk University, Brno, Czech Republic

Franziska Petri Leuven International and European Studies, Faculty of Social Sciences, KU Leuven, Leuven, Belgium

Tim Rayner Tyndall Centre for Climate Change Research, University of East Anglia, Norwich, Norfolk, UK

Marc Ringel Nuertingen Geislingen University, Geislingen, Germany

Michael Rodi Institute for Climate Protection, Energy and Mobility (IKEM), Berlin, Germany

Faculty of Public Law, Finance Law, Environmental and Energy Law, University of Greifswald, Greifswald, Germany

Daniele Russolillo Institute for European Energy and Climate Policies, Amsterdam, The Netherlands

Roberto Schaeffer Energy Planning Program, COPPE, Universidade Federal do Rio de Janeiro, Centro de Technologia, Rio de Janeiro, Brazil

Jonas J. Schoenefeld Institute for Housing and Environment, Darmstadt, Germany

Tyndall Centre for Climate Change Research, University of East Anglia, Norwich, Norfolk, UK

Marco Siddi European Union Research Programme, Finnish Institute of International Affairs, Helsinki, Finland

Anna K. Stöckl Institute of Political Science, Technical University of Darmstadt, Darmstadt, Germany

Christoph Strünck Department of Social Sciences, University of Siegen, Siegen, Germany

Sebastian Strunz Department of Economics, Helmholtz Centre for Environmental Research – UFZ, Leipzig, Germany

Lai Suetyi Centre for European Studies of Guangdong University of Foreign Studies, Guangzhou, China

John Szabo Department of Environmental Sciences and Policy, Central European University, Budapest, Hungary

Institute of World Economics, Centre for Economic and Regional Studies, Budapest, Hungary

Diarmuid Torney School of Law and Government, Dublin City University, Dublin, Ireland

Marula Tsagkari Department of Economics, University of Barcelona, Barcelona, Spain

Veli-Pekka Tynkkynen Aleksanteri Institute, University of Helsinki, Helsinki, Finland

Sigita Urdze Institute of Political Science, Technical University of Darmstadt, Darmstadt, Germany

Tuğçe Uygurtürk Deparment of Economics, Yaşar University, İzmir, Turkey

Thijs Van de Graaf Department of Political Science, Ghent University, Ghent, Belgium

Aviel Verbruggen Department Engineering Management, Antwerp University, Antwerp, Belgium

Tomáš Vlček Center for Energy Studies, Masaryk University, Brno, Czech Republic

Csaba Weiner Institute of World Economics, Centre for Economic and Regional Studies, Budapest, Hungary

Niclas Wenz Institute of Political Science, Technical University of Darmstadt, Darmstadt, Germany

Veronika Zapletalová Center for Energy Studies, Masaryk University, Brno, Czech Republic

Maksymilian Zoll Institute of Political Science, Technical University of Darmstadt, Darmstadt, Germany

Part I

Introduction

Energy Governance in Europe: Introduction

Michèle Knodt and Jörg Kemmerzell

Contents

Introduction	4
Energy Systems and the Governance of Transitions	4
Conceptual Topics of Energy Governance	5
European Energy Governance	6
Country Studies on Energy Governance	8
Structures and Legacies	8
Transition of Energy Systems	9
The Transition of Socio-technical Regimes	10
Drivers of Energy Transitions	11
Cross-References	15
References	15

Abstract

Energy Governance has become an issue of growing importance both in the social sciences and in political practice. This introductory chapter gives an overview of the structure, topics, and concepts that are key in the *Handbook of Energy Governance in Europe*. It introduces in brief the three major sections that are concerned with conceptual issues, European energy governance, and national energy governance. The first section covers key concepts of energy governance in Europe, transitional aspects of energy systems, and specific challenges for energy governance. The second section of the Handbook examines the internal and external dimensions of energy governance in the European Union. Finally, country-specific chapters deal with national trajectories of energy policy and analyze the instruments, coordination mechanisms, and adoption of external influences of national energy systems. A central concern of these chapters is the issue of the transition of energy systems toward climate-neutrality. Therefore, the

---

M. Knodt (✉) · J. Kemmerzell
Institute of Political Science, Technical University of Darmstadt, Darmstadt, Germany
e-mail: knodt@pg.tu-darmstadt.de; kemmerzell@pg.tu-darmstadt.de

© Springer Nature Switzerland AG 2022
M. Knodt, J. Kemmerzell (eds.), *Handbook of Energy Governance in Europe*,
https://doi.org/10.1007/978-3-030-43250-8_35

country-specific chapters intend to account for the varying, institutionally embedded, and governing strategies of adopting the challenges related to such fundamental transitions.

Keywords

Energy Governance · Energy Policy · Energy Transition · Europe · Governance · Renewable Energy

Introduction

Energy Governance has become an issue of growing importance both in the social sciences (Sovacool 2014; van de Graaf and Colgan 2016) and in political practice. This handbook provides a full account of energy governance in Europe, in that it examines both the European level of energy governance and the development of energy policy in European countries. Therefore, it first gives an overview of the conceptual issues of energy governance in Europe, transitional aspects of energy systems, and specific challenges for energy governance. Secondly, it examines the internal and external dimensions of energy governance in the European Union. Thirdly, the country-specific chapters analyze national energy policy developments and examine the instruments, coordination mechanisms, and adaptation of national energy systems to external influences. A central concern of the country-specific chapters is the issue of the transition of energy systems. Due to the background of both global and national challenges like climate change or energy security, sustainable energy transitions are on the agenda of many countries. Beyond all differences in terms of the definition of sustainable energy, as well as targets and scopes of transitions, the challenges of energy transition governance are quite similar. The country-specific chapters intend to account for different, institutionally embedded and governing strategies in coping with these challenges. Therefore, they serve two particular purposes: first, to describe the legacies and the state-of-affairs of a country's energy governance; secondly, to capture particular transitional pathways and show options for further development of national energy systems.

Energy Systems and the Governance of Transitions

In a broad sense, governance describes how actors make decisions, share power and competencies, organize responsibility, and assure accountability within a given structure of formal and informal institutions. In an overview of the literature on transformations toward sustainability, Patterson et al. (2017, p. 4) emphasize at least three dimensions of transitional governance. First, governance as a prerequisite for transformations that "creates the conditions for transformation to emerge from complex dynamics in socio-technical-ecological systems"; secondly, governance of transitions, as active steering of transformation processes; and thirdly, transformations in governance, i.e., "transformative change within governance regimes."

Applied to transitions toward climate-neutral energy systems this implies first analyzing the institutional and political (in terms of power) legacies of transitions, including crucial events and decisions, as well as significant external influences. The adoption of long-term goals and strategies also belongs to this dimension. The second dimension refers to the policy of transitions, the consideration of particular transitional pathways, the bargaining processes of political actors, the adoption of instruments, and the implementation of the policy. Thirdly, transitional pathways, by definition, turn out to be dynamic and subject to change at a second and third-order level (Hall 1993). Even if long-term goals remain stable, political power shifts may lead to the adjustment, abandonment, or replacement of policy instruments with far-reaching consequences for the progress of transitional processes.

Conceptual Topics of Energy Governance

The concept of energy governance allows the definition of the interactions, which are taking place in the policy field of energy, as being a kind of functionally confined, institutionalized arena (Schmitter 2002, p. 58). Governance comprises of interactive arrangements, which rest on "horizontal forms of interaction between actors who have conflicting objectives, but who are sufficiently independent of each other so that neither can impose a solution on the other and yet sufficiently interdependent so that both would lose if no solution were found" (Schmitter 2002, p. 53). In governance arrangements, different kinds of actors cooperate. Non-state actors, as well as supranational actors, take part in problem-solving. Within the governance paradigm, power becomes more flexible and ubiquitous, and beyond the constraining capacities, the productive qualities of power gain meaning. These forms of liberal governance arrangements aim at "solving societal problems or creating societal opportunities" (Kooiman, 2002, p.73, Müller et al. 2015, p. 18).

In addition, a distinctive feature of energy governance is its *nexus quality*. Energy as a policy field is an almost classical cross-cutting issue, standing in close connection not only to climate policies but also to development cooperation, research and innovation policies, trade policies, and foreign and security policies. The full consequences and challenges of this nexus quality are seldom taken into account . As a cross-cutting issue, energy governance involves a variety of public and non-state actors that is more complex and more fragmented (Lesage et al. 2010; Keohane and Victor, 2010) when compared to most other policy fields. In this handbook, we will not only stress traditional *government* by politically accountable institutions, which is of crucial importance indeed but will also include those non-state actors that play an undeniable role in energy *governance* arrangements. Non-state actors should be understood as all actors, which are not part of the public administration (public actors) and follow a business, agency, association, or NGO logic. We are aware that defining actors in these two categories is not an easy and uncontestable endeavor. For instance, state-owned companies are organizational hybrids that combine an entrepreneurial for-profit orientation with varying forms and degrees of public ownership and accountability to politicians (Müller et al. 2015, p. 18).

This handbook assembles five chapters on general issues of energy governance. Mario Neukirch examines conceptual aspects of the research in energy system transitions, while Cornelia Fraune discusses a core issue of democratic governance: the participation of citizens in transition processes. Christoph Strünck introduces the discussion on energy poverty, which often accompanies debates on the unpleasant consequences of energy transitions. Jonas Schoenefeld and Tim Rayner analyze surveillance instruments and monitoring processes of energy policy, and Michael Rodi and Michael Kalis take a look ahead at one of the major challenges of energy transitions: the increasing demand for *sector coupling* in energy systems dominated by the use of (renewable) electricity.

European Energy Governance

National energy governance of European countries is increasingly influenced by developments on the EU level, which have brought new requirements for the national energy governance of the EU member states and also impulses for non-member states.

A brief look at European integration history might lead to the conclusion that a common energy policy, alongside trade policy, could be considered as one of the earliest *European* issues. Two of the three European Communities were linked to energy sources: the European Coal and Steel Community (ECSC) and the European Atomic Energy Community (EURATOM). Nevertheless, it took until the Lisbon Treaty 2009 to establish energy policy as a European issue area in primary law. Until the Lisbon Treaty, the European Community, and later Union, carried out energy measures through secondary legislation without regulating energy policy in the primary law. Since the Lisbon Treaty, the energy competence of the EU is regulated in Article 194 TFEU. The energy policy objectives, defined in Art.194(1) TFEU, refer to ensuring energy market functionality and security of energy supply, promoting energy efficiency and energy saving, supporting the development of new and renewable energy, and promoting the interconnection of energy networks. However, the EU competencies do not apply to a Member State's right to determine the conditions for exploiting their energy resources, their choice between different energy sources, or the general structure of their energy supply. This reservation of sovereignty, in favor of the Member States according to Article 194(2) TFEU, limits the EU's ability to steer energy policy. Only, if a measure is based on the environmental competence of Art. 192(1) TFEU, is it decided by majority vote, but in exceptional cases of paragraph 2, the principle of unanimity may apply. The latter is the case, if "measures significantly affect a Member State's choice between different energy sources and the general structure of its energy supply" (Art. 192(2) TFEU).

EU energy policy is characterized by three primary goals: (1) energy security, which contains instruments to ensure a secure supply; (2) competitiveness, integrating the internal energy market to ensure liberalization and competitive prices; and

1 Energy Governance in Europe: Introduction

(3) sustainability, to minimize the environmental impacts of energy consumption, particularly by CO_2 emission reduction. These three goals have received different levels of attention in different periods and were driven by external as well as internal developments (Knodt and Ringel in this Handbook). Also, the member states do not agree on the three targets, so negotiations on target agreements, and the instruments needed to achieve the targets, are an ongoing point of contention.

In 2014, the then newly elected Commission President Jean-Claude Juncker initiated the establishment of an Energy Union, to overcome discord and blockades within European energy policy. To realize the Energy Union, the European Commission developed an ambitious governance strategy in 2016 to successfully achieve its goals of the 2030 targets (Ringel and Knodt 2018) – the EU was expected to achieve a 40% reduction in greenhouse gas emissions, a share of renewable energy of at least 32% of final energy consumption and an increase in energy efficiency of at least 32.5% (Council of the European Union 2018). As the centerpiece of its strategy, the Commission presented the Governance Regulation ((EU) 2018/1999), which entered into force on 24 December 2018. The Governance Regulation is a central element of the legislative package presented under the title "Clean Energy for All Europeans" in November 2016 (Knodt et al. 2020). This regulation introduced a strategy to influence member states' energy policies without shifting more competencies to the European level and without the need for unanimous decisions. The core elements of the Governance Regulation are the National Energy and Climate Plans (NECPs), which Member States are required to present to the Commission, showing their national objectives, targets, and contributions in line with the five dimensions of the Energy Union, their strategies and measures, the current situation, as well as prognoses and impact assessments. The Commission evaluates the submitted NECPs and suggests recommendations with regard to their level of "ambition" to fully achieve the European 2030 framework targets and the method of implementing corresponding measures. Member states must respond to these recommendations to close possible "ambition gaps" or "implementation gaps" within one year. Within the Governance Regulation, the EU inserted some harder elements to these soft governance mechanisms, such as an algorithm to define yet missing national targets for the European 2030 goals, at least in the case of renewable energies expansion.

The incoming European Commission under Ursula von der Leyen in 2019 gave energy governance an even stronger push and launched the European Green Deal (EGD), which envisages a carbon-neutral European economy and society by 2050. The EGD came with an agreed goal of climate neutrality by 2050 and, by 2030, a reduction of 55% of greenhouse gases compared to 1990 levels. With the July legislative package "Fit for 55," the Commission has presented the revision and introduction of several legislative initiatives related to the climate measures of the EGD.

The section on European energy governance in this handbook gives a broad picture, ranging from specific policies to the international dimension of EU energy governance. Therefore, it also provides chapters on external energy relations of the EU to the most important partner regions. The chapters by Michèle Knodt and Marc

Ringel, and Eric Gawel and Sebastian Strunz, both contribute to the development of EU energy governance in general, and specific policies of transition in particular. Laima Eicke and Franziska Petri examine the role of the EU in global energy and climate policy, and set the stage for *outward-looking* chapters that provide deeper insights into the external energy relations of the EU. These include energy relations with emerging powers (by Michèle Knodt et al.), Russia (by Marco Siddi), the USA and Canada (by Petra Dolata), as well as energy cooperation in the Eastern partnership (by Katharina Kleinschnittger, Anna Stöckel, and Marie Lortz), and with its Southern neighbors, the MENA region (by Britta Daum). The chapter on the Eastern energy partnership also contains some information on countries that are not included among the country-specific chapters. Anna Herranz-Suralles discusses the Energy Charter Treaty, a rare example of rule-based international energy governance, which nevertheless became contested because of assumed shortcomings of the treaty in climate change concerns. The three final chapters of the section are rather *inward-looking*. Natalia Chaban and Jessica Bain examine the EU political communication of energy policy using the example of the *Sustainable Europe* narrative. Nils Bruch, Michèle Knodt, and Marc Ringel shed light on stakeholders' views on the European Green Deal agenda. Eventually, Jörg Kemmerzell discusses, by example of cities, the role of the EU in the energy, and climate policy of subnational units.

Country Studies on Energy Governance

The most extensive section of this handbook belongs to national energy systems, country-specific patterns of energy governance, and the various attempts at energy transitions. All country-specific chapters follow a roughly similar structure that nonetheless varies according to particularities of the cases. The chapters pay attention both to country-specific legacies and traditions, as well as interdependencies of national energy governance and the repercussions of European influences. Since the section contains 30 chapters on the most important countries in and outside the EU, it seems inappropriate to introduce all chapters in detail. Instead, in the remainder of this introduction to the handbook, we briefly set out the structure and the main topics of the country-specific chapters.

Structures and Legacies

Energy transitions do not emerge within an open space. Besides universal patterns (Urpelainen and Aklin 2018), national and regional particularities shape transitions a great deal (Smil 2017), and even the same external influences are adapted by national systems differently and lead to varying institutional and policy outcomes (Boasson et al. 2021). At least four crucial *structural conditions and legacies* shape the prospects of sustainable transitions of energy systems. The first legacy refers to particular path dependencies of the energy system. It takes into account developmental patterns of the energy sector (e.g., dependency on fossil or nuclear fuels), topographic conditions (e.g., the traditionally high share of hydropower in Austria, Sweden, or Norway), raw material deposits (e.g., the vast lignite reserves in Germany or Poland), and crucial political decisions which steer the development of the energy sector in a particular direction (e.g., the early phase-out of nuclear power by referendum in Italy).

The second structural condition considers the development and the actual composition of the *energy mix* of power supply and consumption. On the one hand, the energy mix can be understood as a result of past political and economic decisions; on the other hand, it constrains the future decisions and transitional aspirations of political actors. While the first two legacies refer to the material basis of energy governance, the discursive aspects of energy governance as a third structural condition should not be underestimated. Debates related to energy policy revolve around different *Leitbilder* (general principles) and frameworks, which are not easy to reconcile. At least four dominant principles can be distinguished:

- Ecological sustainability- emphasizing a *clean* or *green* energy supply that relies on low-carbon sources.
- Energy security- highlighting the need for a steady supply of energy, that remains independent of foreign countries and depends particularly on domestic sources.
- Competitiveness- stressing the importance of affordable energy as an economic location factor.
- Energy equity- also emphasizing the costs of energy consumption, but concerned with equal access to energy, independent of consumers' social and financial status.

A fourth structural condition relates to the key political institutions in the sector and the distribution of competences between the different governmental levels (national, sub-national/regional, local). Furthermore, it is necessary to be aware of the relationship between public and private actors, particularly as to ownership structures in the energy sector. In the perspective of transitional aspects, it seems useful to analyze political power structures by detecting dominant actors and political entrepreneurs who can shape the development and induce political shifts.

Transition of Energy Systems

We assume that, at least due to European and international obligations, every European country is, to some extent, engaged in the adjustment of its energy sector. Crucial issues of analysis are: the type of transition that evolves in different contexts, the drivers of energy transitions that could be both endogenous and exogenous, and the involvement of the different levels of government in transitional processes.

Since the 1990s, we have observed a global trend toward the expansion of renewable energies, implying a restructuring of energy supply systems that depend on the combustion of fossil fuels (which serve simultaneously as efficient energy stores) and centralized infrastructures. However, the transition of energy systems evolves in a contradictory fashion and is still far from meeting its ecological goals. With regard to the legacies mentioned above, it seems appropriate to distinguish different types of energy transitions.

The Transition of Socio-technical Regimes

The socio-technical regime approach (Geels 2002; Neukirch in this Handbook) represents a good starting point to elaborate on this issue. Energy systems can be understood as socio-technical regimes in a broad sense, encompassing not only the technologies at work but also the communities of producers and consumers, cognitive routines, regulations, and standards, as well as path dependencies of infrastructures (Geels 2002; Lockwood et al. 2017). The stability of such a regime is challenged by both "landscape pressures" (the global technological context) from above and "niche innovations" from below. At least every country in the EU is engaged to some extent in the adjustment of its energy sector away from fossil fuels to a higher share of renewable energies. However, those transitional processes evolve, not straightforwardly, but dependent on general configurations of economic governance (Mikler and Harrison 2012; Ćetković and Buzogány 2016; Rentier et al. 2019), particular infrastructural legacies, on an adherence to principles, the distribution of political power, and political coalitions. Geels and Schot (2007) distinguish different types of sociotechnical change that relate to different transition paths:

- The reproductional path describes a dynamically stable regime that faces no landscape pressure and develops evolutionally. In energy transitions, this could be the case where renewable energies emerged within, and not without or against, the established structures of the energy sector.
- The transformational path indicates moderate landscape pressure and existing but not "sufficiently developed" niche innovations (Geels and Schot 2007: 406). This seems a good description of early adoptions of energy transitions in the 1980s and 1990s. On the one hand, landscape pressure, generated by growing awareness for climate change or the risks of nuclear power, was present but did not gain a regime-changing pace in the short term. On the other hand, niche innovations emerged but did not reach an appropriate state to overthrow the existing regime. The transformational path differs from the reproductional path since innovations take place outside the established regime structures with the consequence of the emergence of parallel, not fully integrated structures. The course of the German energy transition up until 2010 serves as a good example for a transformation; here different forms of power generation coexisted without the old (fossil and nuclear) being substituted by the new (renewables) energy sources. This type of transition bred increasing coordinational challenges, to which the government reacted with adjustments to the most important instrument, the Renewable Energy Law EEG.
- Both the de−/re-alignment path and the substitutional path can be fully applied to energy transitions, since niche technologies are not sufficiently developed to

completely substitute older technologies. A second condition for those transitional pathways is massive landscape pressures, created by specific shocks (e.g., invention of the combustion engine) or fundamental social change (e.g., industrialization). For a complete replacement of the old socio-technical regime, neither the landscape pressure nor the standard of niche innovations has reached a sufficient degree so far. However, fundamental change might emerge within subfields of the regime, like the transportation sector, if gasoline vehicles were removed by regulatory policy (France and the UK proposed the termination of selling fossil fuel-driven vehicles by 2040, Norway by 2025).
- The reconfigurational path combines a steady inclusion of radical niche innovations into the existing regime. The difference to the transformational path is that reconfiguration provokes substantial change in the regime's basic structure and results in a new architecture of the regime. With respect to energy transitions, this would imply a deeper restructuration than the transformational type.

Drivers of Energy Transitions

Developments of the socio-technical landscape and within niches can be understood as drivers of energy transitions. Besides country-specific developments that are undoubtedly related to national legacies, conditions, and niche phenomena, external influences on a particular country originate from international integration of the energy sector or dependencies on energy imports. Of similar interest is the European climate and energy policy as an external driver, since the European Union has become more and more engaged in energy and climate policy. A central question refers to the relationship between European and national policies and the adaptation of national energy sectors to European influences (Solorio and Jörgens 2017). We may distinguish between countries where the transition is merely internally driven and those setting up transitional policies, e.g., for renewable energy support, to fulfill European obligations. Denmark is an example of a country that introduced renewable energies long before the debate on climate change and low-carbon development took off (Eikeland and Inderberg 2016, Dyrhauge in this Handbook). However, being a front-runner does not always guarantee easy adaption to European policies, as indicated by the European Commission's longtime suspicion of the German feed-in-tariffs (Lauber 2017, Kemmerzell in this Handbook). An example of a largely external-driven process is Poland (Szulecki 2017, Zoll in this Handbook), where a significant renewable energy sector developed by the time the country adopted the European climate and energy targets.

Instruments of Energy Governance and Energy Transitions

On an operative scale, the promotion and regulation of energy transitions depend on the adoption of particular policy instruments. Therefore we must first distinguish between long-term strategies and programs, like climate protection plans or national energy concepts, and policy instruments. We are aware of a wide spectrum of instruments promoting the transition toward a greater share of renewable energy sources in the total primary energy supply (Verbruggen and Lauber 2012; Bayer et al. 2016; Gawel et al. 2017; Boasson and Leiren 2021). However, the debate on policies and the *best mix* of instruments is still controversial. While some authors (and political actors) adhere to incentive-based instruments, others do prefer regulatory policies or concentrate on internalizing policies. From a comparative perspective, it seems important to distinguish between different instruments and different sectors (like electricity supply, electricity consumption, heat supply, heat consumption, mobility, etc.). At the level of policy instruments, it is possible to distinguish at least four general categories including several sub-categories:

- *Regulatory policy-making* sets certain standards or prohibits particular technologies. Examples are both large-scale decisions on, e.g., nuclear or coal phase-out and narrower technology-specific regulations on the prohibition of outmoded light bulbs, or energy efficiency standards for new and existing buildings.
- *Incentive-based instruments* for clean energy focus on the expansion of a renewable energy supply. The most common distinction here is between price- and quantity-driven models. The first covers feed-in-tariffs guaranteed for investments in renewables for a pre-defined time frame, while the second comprises quota models based on tender offers. These usually apply auctions that award bidders guaranteeing energy supply at the lowest comparative price. Another quota-based model obliges utilities to offer a particular share of renewables. The choice of a particular instrument has a significant impact on the opportunities of different actors in the market and the distribution of investments between different groups of shareholders.
- *Internalizing instruments* set prices on unfavorable carbon-intensive energy production and support the transition of energy supply systems indirectly. Both the regulation of prices (carbon tax) and quantities (emission cap) belong to this category. The trading of emission rights (e.g., the European ETS) depends on the application of internalizing instruments.
- The last category refers to wide-ranging soft governance. It includes the distribution of best practices, information campaigning, or benchmarking. It should be noticed that the outcomes of soft governance might be a cornerstone for later regulations.

Coordination Mechanisms and Multilevel Governance

A final feature of energy governance relates to the involvement of different governmental levels and sectors in the process. The transformation of the energy sector covers different tasks and issues (energy supply, energy distribution, energy consumption), which requires the coordination of multiple actors. We can further distinguish the coordination of governmental institutions and the coordination between public and private actors.

In the governmental domain, it is necessary to differentiate between the horizontal and vertical governance dimensions. The horizontal dimension refers to the responsibility of departments and ministries for energy issues. The competencies can be fragmented between different branches of government or can be widely centralized within a single department. This has serious effects on the streamlining of policies but also on conflict-management between competing units.

In Germany, for example, the governance of the energy transition changed over time. While responsibilities were shared between the Ministry of the Economy and the Environmental Ministry from 2002 to 2013, the grand coalition managed a re-centralization within the Ministry of the Economy after taking office in 2013 (Lauber 2017), a tendency that has been reinforced by the center-left coalition that took office in 2021. Similarly, vertical differentiation plays a crucial role in the governance of energy transitions. To some extent, uneven developments of transitional processes are due to the vertical differentiation of competencies between the governmental levels. To illustrate one more time using the German case, the development of strategies and long-term planning, as well as decisions on power transmission grids, are highly centralized at the federal level. In contrast, the states (Bundesländer) are mainly responsible for decisions concerning the expansion of renewable energy sources and the energy mix.

A different pattern evolves in rather centralized countries where the national government has a greater share of competencies, and developments mostly occur on a horizontal scale through the shift of competencies between ministries and agencies (Fig. 1).

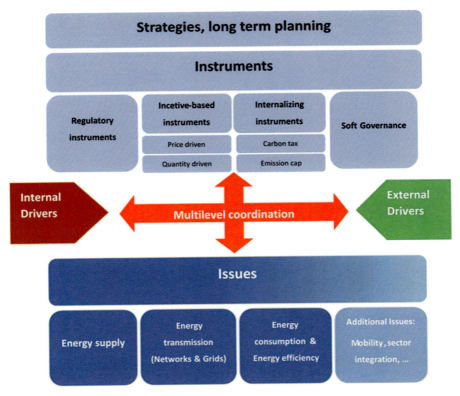

Fig. 1 Analytic framework of National Energy Governance and Energy Transitions

Outcomes, Challenges, and Prospects of Energy Governance

The country-specific chapters conclude with a summary of the outcomes of energy transitions and a discussion of the challenges and the prospects of the respective energy sector. However, as European energy systems face similar challenges on the landscape level, we should be aware that those challenges play out differently in different countries according to a countries' energy mix, political conflicts, and established governance mechanisms and institutions:

- Monitoring and surveillance: An essential prerequisite for the assessment of energy transitions is the application of monitoring mechanisms: every EU member accepted at least fixed climate and energy targets related to the development of renewable energy, the improvement of energy efficiency, and the reduction of GHG emissions. However, monitoring and surveillance of the fulfillment of those targets remain difficult (Schoenefeld et al. 2016, Schoenefeld and Rayner in this Handbook), even more if the global scale is considered.
- Sector coupling and sector integration: In engineering sciences, system or sector integration of renewable energies (i.e., interconnectivity of electricity, heat/cold, and mobility) has been a major topic in recent years (Oberle et al. 2020). From a social science perspective, sector integration causes specific problems that go beyond the technical challenges and require regulatory and coordination activities (Rodi and Kalis in this Handbook).
- Energy conflicts and participation: The conflicts that accompanied the installation of nuclear power plants, but also large-scale conventional energy infrastructures, have been widely acknowledged since the 1970s. Although early proponents of renewable energy emphasized the less conflict-prone nature of renewables, we observe the rise of considerable resistance against the installation of renewable energy infrastructures (Batel and Devine-Wright 2015; Reusswig et al. 2016; Hoeft et al. 2017, Fraune in this Handbook)). A governance perspective asks for different ways to accommodate protests and contributes to the issue of citizen participation in energy transitions.
- Multilevel energy governance: At least the often contradictory influence of European Union energy policy triggers an understanding of energy transition as a multilevel issue. Therefore, empirical analysis may ask more explicitly for the distribution of competencies between governmental levels, including the EU, and deepen insights into the coordination mechanisms of transitions. In this respect, the balancing of centralization and decentralization within multilevel polities is of great interest, since it breeds particular coordination demands.

We conclude the handbook with a comparison of the development of the energy mix and energy governance in European countries. This chapter (by Jörg Kemmerzell, Nils Bruch, and Michèle Knodt) concentrates on the development in EU member countries but also occasionally considers non-EU members. It ends with a plea for a balanced empirical analysis of energy governance that neither is blind to European and international developments nor underestimates the inertia and path dependencies of national regimes.

Cross-References

▶ Energy Democracy and Participation in Energy Transitions
▶ Energy Governance in Denmark
▶ Energy Governance in Germany
▶ Energy Governance in the Republic of Poland
▶ European Union Energy Policy: A Discourse Perspective
▶ Extending Energy Policy: The Challenge of Sector Integration
▶ Monitoring Energy Policy
▶ Transition of Energy Systems: Patterns of Stability and Change

Acknowledgments We gratefully acknowledge funding from the Kopernikus-Projekt ENavi (FKZ 03SFK4P0) and the Kopernikus-Projekt Ariadne (FKZ 03SFK5LO) by the German Federal Ministry of Education and Research.

References

Batel, S., & Devine-Wright, P. (2015). A critical and empirical analysis of the national-local 'gap' in public responses to large-scale energy infrastructures. *Journal of Environmental Planning and Management, 58*(6), 1076–1095.

Bayer, B., Schäuble, D., & Ferrari, M. (2016). *International experiences with tender procedures for renewable energy – A comparison of current developments in Brazil, France, Italy and South Africa.* Retrieved from osf.io/vf84r.

Boasson, E. L., & Leiren, M. D. (2021). Comparing renewable support mixes. In E. L. Boasson, M. D. Leiren, & J. Wettestad (Eds.), *Comparative renewables policy. Political, organizational and European fields* (pp. 219–239). Abingdon, New York: Routledge.

Boasson, E. L., Leiren, M. D., & Wettestad, J. (2021). Comparative assessments and conclusions. In E. L. Boasson, M. D. Leiren, & J. Wettestad (Eds.), *Comparative renewables policy. Political, organizational and European fields* (pp. 219–239). Abingdon, New York: Routledge.

Ćetković, S., & Buzogány, A. (2016). Varieties of capitalism and clean energy transitions in the European Union: When renewable energy hits different economic logics. *Climate Policy, 16*(5), 642–657.

Eikeland, P. O., & Inderberg, T. H. (2016). Energy system transformation and long-term interest constellations in Denmark: Can agency beat structure? *Energy Research & Social Science, 11*, 164–173.

Gawel, E., Strunz, S., & Lehmann, P. (2017). Support policies for renewables: Instrument choice and instrument change from a public policy perspective. In D. Arent et al. (Eds.), *The political economy of clean energy transitions*, pp. 80–99.

Geels, F. W. (2002). Technological transitions as evolutionary reconfiguration processes: A multi-level perspective and a case study. *Research Policy, 31*, 1257–1274.

Geels, F. W., & Schot, J. (2007). Typology of sociotechnical transition pathways. *Research Policy, 36*, 399–417.

Hall, P. (1993). Policy paradigms, social learning, and the state: The case of economic policymaking in Britain. *Comaparative Politics, 25*, 275–296.

Hoeft, C., et al. (Eds.). (2017). *Bürgerproteste in Zeiten der Energiewende Lokale Konflikte um Windkraft, Stromtrassen und Fracking.* Bielefeld: Transcript.

Keohane, R. O., & Victor, D. G. (2010). *The regime complex for climate change. Discussion paper 2010–33.* Harvard project on international climate agreements. Cambridge, MA: Harvard

Kennedy School. Available at: http://belfercenter.ksg.harvard.edu/files/Keohane_Victor_Final_2.pdf.

Knodt, M., Ringel, M., & Müller, R. (2020). 'Harder' soft governance in the European energy union policy. *Journal of Environmental Policy & Planning, 22*(4), 787–800.

Kooiman, J. (2002). Governance: A socio-political perspective. In J. K. Grote & B. Gbikpi (Eds.), *Participatory governance: Political and societal implications* (pp. 71–96). Opladen: Leske + Budrich.

Lauber, V. (2017). Germany's transition to renewable energy. In T. C. Lehmann (Ed.), *The geopolitics of global energy. The new cost of plenty* (pp. 153–182). Boulder/London: Lynne Rienner.

Lesage, D., Van de Graaf, T., & Westphal, K. (2010). *Global energy governance in a multipolar world*. Farnham: Ashgate.

Lockwood, M., Kuzemko, C., Mitchell, C., & Hoggett, R. (2017). Historical institutionalism and the politics of sustainable energy transitions: A research agenda. *Environment and Planning C: Politics and Spa, 35*(2), 312–333.

Mikler, J., & Harrison, N. (2012). Varieties of capitalism and technological innovation for climate change mitigation. *New Political Economy, 17*(2), 179–208.

Müller, F., Knodt, M., & Piefer, N. (2015). Müller challenges of EU external energy governance towards emerging powers. In I. M. Knodt, N. Piefer, & F. (Eds.), *Conceptualizing emerging powers and EU energy governance: Towards a research agenda* (pp. 17–32). Farnham: Ashgate.

Oberle, S., Stute, J., Fritz, M., Klobasa, M., & Wietschel, M. (2020). Sector coupling technologies in gas, electricity, and heat networks. *TATuP – Journal for Technology Assessment in Theory and Practice, 29*, 24–30. https://doi.org/10.14512/tatup.29.2.24.

Patterson, J., Schulz, K., Vervoort, J., van der Hel, S., Widerberg, O., Adler, C., Hurlbert, C., Anderton, K., Sethi, M., & Barau, A. (2017). Exploring the governance and politics of transformations towards sustainability. *Environmental Innovation and Societal Transitions, 24*, 1–16. https://doi.org/10.1016/j.eist.2016.09.001.

Rentier, G., Lelieveldt, H., & Kramer, G. J. (2019). Varieties of coal-fired power phase-out across Europe. *Energy Policy, 132*, 620–632. https://doi.org/10.1016/j.enpol.2019.05.042.

Reusswig, F., et al. (2016). Against the wind? Local opposition to the German 'Energiewende'. *Utilities Policy, 2016*. https://doi.org/10.1016/j.jup.2016.02.006.

Ringel, M., & Knodt, M. (2018). The governance of the European energy union. Efficiency, effectiveness and acceptance of the winter package 2016. *Energy Policy, 112*, 209–220.

Schmitter, P. (2002). Participation in governance arrangements: Is there any reason to expect it will achieve "sustainable and innovative policies in a multi-level context"? In J. K. Grote & B. Gbikpi (Eds.), *Participatory governance: Political and societal implications* (pp. 51–69). Opladen: Leske + Budrich.

Schoenefeld, J. J., et al. (2016). The challenges of monitoring national climate policy: Learning lessons from the EU. *Climate Policy*. https://doi.org/10.1080/14693062.2016.1248887.

Smil, V. (2017). *Energy transitions: Global and National Perspectives*. Santa Barbara, Denver: Praeger.

Solorio, I., & Jörgens, H. (Eds.). (2017). *A guide to EU renewable energy policy: Comparing Europeanization and Domestic Policy Change*. Cheltenham: Edward Elgar.

Sovacool, B. (2014). What are we doing here? Analyzing fifteen years of energy scholarship and proposing a social science research agenda. *Energy Research & Social Science, 1*, 1–29.

Szulecki, K. (2017). Poland's renewable energy policy mix: European influence and domestic soap opera. *CICERO working papers* 1/2017. Retrieved 03/07/2017 https://ssrn.com/abstract=2964866.

Urpelainen, J., & Aklin, M. (2018). *Renewables: The politics of a global energy transition*. Cambridge, MA: MIT Press.

Van de Graaf, T., & Colgan, J. (2016). Global energy governance: A review and research agenda. *Palgrave Communications, 2*, 15047. https://doi.org/10.1057/palcomms.2015.47.

Verbruggen, A., & Lauber, V. (2012). Assessing the performance of renewable electricity support instruments. *Energy Policy, 45*, 635–644.

Part II

Energy Governance Research: Theories, Issues, and Problems

Transition of Energy Systems: Patterns of Stability and Change

2

Mario Neukirch

Contents

Introduction	20
Analyses of Socio-technical Regimes and Transitions	21
Energy Regimes	24
Stability and Change	25
Stabilizing Factors	25
Destabilizing Factors	27
Janus-Faced Factors	30
Variants of Transition	32
Application to the Dynamics of Energy Regimes	35
France: From Fossil Fuels to Nuclear Power (1974–1996)	36
Great Britain: Dash for Gas and the Decline of Coal (1987–1997)	38
Germany: Energy Transition (Since the Mid-1970s)	39
Denmark: Energy Transition (Since the Mid-1970s)	40
Discussion	41
Scope of Transition Pathways MLP 1–4	41
Avoiding Oversimplifications	41
Insufficient or Unclear Conceptualization of Actors	42
Modes of Institutional Change: Low Degree of Selectivity?	42
Summary	43
Cross-References	43
References	44

Abstract

This chapter provides an overview of proven analytical tools, among others, the multilevel perspective, strategic action fields, and modes of institutional change, for a better understanding of the dynamics that lead to change or stability of socio-technical regimes. From a theoretical point of view, a critical issue is the role of

M. Neukirch (✉)
Institute for Social Sciences, University of Stuttgart, Stuttgart, Baden-Württemberg, Germany
e-mail: Mario.neukirch@sowi.uni-stuttgart.de

© Springer Nature Switzerland AG 2022
M. Knodt, J. Kemmerzell (eds.), *Handbook of Energy Governance in Europe*,
https://doi.org/10.1007/978-3-030-43250-8_40

actors in such transitions. In the face of institutions – formal and informal rules that sometimes may define future trajectories completely, like a railway – it is not easy for large companies, governments, or any other large organization to facilitate or even implement fundamental change. In other cases, the path is more like a motorway, which can be exited easily after a few miles. With this ambiguous character of socio-technical transitions in mind, the chapter will present crucial reasons that explain stability or change. Moreover, the analytical tools mentioned above will be applied to either historical or contemporary energy regime transitions. However, the discussion section will show that these tools – which promise consistent and reliable explanations of the empirical world – sometimes fail in practice. The categories are often conceptualized too broadly to make fruitful statements. In other cases, they just do not fit certain real-world contexts. Therefore, the chapter argues for a sensible use of the different approaches.

Keywords

Socio-technical regime · Energy transition · Institutional change · Strategic action fields · Multilevel perspective · Path dependency

Introduction

For several reasons, a transition to renewable energies seems inevitable: to reduce the negative effects of climate change, to stop regional pollution, to decrease the risks of nuclear radiation, to secure the national energy supply, and to overcome the dependence on oil and gas, which may reduce conflicts in the Middle East and parts of Africa.

Spain, Germany, China, and the UK, as well as many other countries, have introduced renewable energy technologies and thus achieved an important first step in the process toward sustainability. Key technologies like onshore and offshore wind power, photovoltaics, and rechargeable batteries have displayed impressive learning curves (Reichardt et al. 2015; Kern et al. 2016; Smith et al. 2014). Considering this, there seem to be good reasons for an optimistic view on whether the transition to sustainability will succeed in the near future. However, in terms of what still lies ahead, a green and bright future is far away. On the international level, the emission of greenhouse gases is still rising (Pbl 2017). Although there is a significant international tendency to decrease the number of new coal power plants – including recent developments in China and India (Wille 2016) – in some countries, like Turkey, Vietnam, and Indonesia, coal is envisioned as playing a major role for the energy supply (Edenhofer et al. 2018). Destruction of the rainforests is ongoing (Müller-Jung 2016), and the emission-intensive (worldwide) production of meat is increasing (Statista 2018).

This incomplete list raises questions: How is this possible? Why are the politicians in charge doing nothing? Why are most large corporations unwilling to change their business practice? What effect can the power of consumers, citizens' initiatives, and social movements have? Are they nonexistent or are they just unable to implement their ideas and visions? What role do structural barriers like institutions, path dependency, and so-called lock-ins play? The STS (Science and Technology Studies) literature has presented crucial insights, numerous detailed case studies, helpful analytical concepts, and powerful heuristics, all dealing with the core issue of stability and change of socio-technical systems. In this chapter I will describe and apply some of these to a few empirical energy regime transition cases. This may contribute to a better understanding of the options and limitations for an active steering of energy system transitions. The chapter will proceed as follows:

First, the notion of *socio-technical regimes* will be introduced and explained (section "Analyses of Socio-technical Regimes and Transitions"). The multilevel perspective (MLP) is of particular importance for the analysis of the dynamics of such regimes. It was introduced by Rip and Kemp (1998) and is well established within the discourse of transition research. It is understood to be a heuristic and an analytical concept, but not a consistent theory (Kuzemko et al. 2015). The MLP will be supplemented by institutionalist as well as actor-centered approaches. In section "Energy Regimes," the notion of socio-technical regimes will be applied to energy systems. After this, the chapter examines factors that contribute to stability or change (section "Stability and Change"). In history, transitions have followed different socio-technical paths, in the course of which they were supported or opposed by incumbent actor groups and reached different levels of radical deviation from the former status quo. Regarding this, section "Variants of Transition" will discuss different concepts used in the classification and interpretation of these variant forms of transition. On this basis, I will illustrate the theoretical approaches to historical and current transitions of European energy regimes (section "Application to the Dynamics of Energy Regimes"). In many cases, plausible theories can seem ambiguous and tricky at first glance. Some theoretical and conceptual pitfalls will be discussed in section "Discussion." The chapter ends with a short summary.

Analyses of Socio-technical Regimes and Transitions

In the context of STS research, the category regime, which can carry a normatively negative meaning elsewhere, serves as an analytical, descriptive category. The notion of socio-technical regimes leads back to the one of socio-technical systems. Both categories seem to be used synonymously (Smith et al. 2010; Kuzemko et al. 2015). They "are understood as being made up of a wide range of analytically separable but dynamically interrelated areas – for example user practices, the environment, infrastructures, technology, corporate groups, civil society, institutions and politics" (Kuzemko et al. 2015). Moreover, a socio-technical regime consists of a wide range of actors: "Not only firms and the activities of engineers but also other social groups, such as users, policy makers, special interest groups and civil society actors" (Geels and Kemp 2012).

Andrews-Speed (2016) highlights the role of institutions as formal and informal rules that reinforce the position of the organizations that embody these rules: "In addition to markets, policies, laws and regulations, a socio-technical regime encompasses the beliefs, values, expectations and cognitive routines of the various actors. (...) The behavior of these actors will be conditioned by the regime and many actors will also build strong political and economic interests in the prevailing regime. The concept of socio-technical regimes recognizes that technology and society are not separate spheres of activity or policy, but are highly interdependent" (Andrews-Speed 2016). Technology can influence peoples' behavior, and individual technologies may have specific cultural symbolic values, e.g., the use of cars is strongly rooted in western societies. The choice for any future mobility technology cannot be understood without taking the cultural role of cars into account. Thus, one central feature of socio-technical regimes is the co-evolvement of society and technology (Andrews-Speed 2016).

Socio-technical regimes are often characterized by "powerful path-dependencies" (Andrews-Speed 2016) and resistance against transition. Araújo (2014) describes lock-ins as a concept to "explain why a new energy technology may not be adopted even if it is superior and/or economically feasible."

Historically, Thomas Hughes (1983) referred to the role of path dependency by emphasizing similarities in the formation process of electrical systems in western societies and, on this empirical basis, introduced the concept of *large technical systems*. In this context, Hughes (1983) explained path dependency as the result of the following reasons: high cost of construction, great extension in space and time, and interdependent components that prevent new products from market entry. Due to increasing returns of scale, the more a system is used, the better its economic performance will be. As a result, large technical systems have an internal tendency toward growth. Once established, they build up a system momentum – something that is a bit more than a force of inertia – that has the tendency to reject any attempts from outside that seek to alter the direction or pace of the system's development (Hughes 1983). Contradicting this approach, Garud and Karnøe (2001) emphasized the ability of actors to create new paths via a *mindful deviation* from the old ones (Beyer 2005). Actors' roles may be seen as big or small, but in any case, these roles ought to be transparent and measurable. To this aim, the categories of *agency* and *capacity* can be useful. Agency refers to the actor's ability to articulate his free will, whereas capacity is the ability to impose this will (Parag and Janda 2014).

Whereas institutionalism, and especially path dependency, explains stability well, the MLP becomes relevant when it comes to understanding why transitions occur (Kuzemko et al. 2015). Generally speaking, a transition indicates a shift from one regime to another. The MLP explains transition as the outcome of interdependent developments that occur on three levels: *niche*, *regime*, and *landscape*. The following paragraphs will deal with the niche and the landscape levels:

The niche is the place where radical innovations emerge (Geels and Schot 2007). In the beginning, these novelties are unstable and exhibit attainments at low techno-economic levels. "Niches act as 'incubation rooms' protecting novelties against mainstream market selection" (Rip and Kemp 1998). The innovative activities, which strive for configurations that work, are carried out by enthusiasts, small networks, and often outsiders and fringe actors (Rip and Kemp 1998; Geels and

Schot 2007; Geels 2010). Frequently, the innovations are not only a threat for the regime due to their superior economic performance or viability for a given purpose but rather because their use represents a new institutional setting that directly contradicts established rules.

Kuzemko et al. (2015) define the landscape as "the external structural context for the regime-level" that "is made up of social and physical factors such as broad political coalitions, socio-cultural norms, paradigms, and economic growth. It forms an exogenous environment beyond the direct influence of niche and regime actors (macro-economics, deep cultural patterns, macro-political developments). Changes at the landscape level usually take place slowly (decades)" (Geels and Schot 2007). New developments or critical incidents taking place on the landscape (e.g., catastrophic disasters, modified trade regulations on international level, or the viability of grand technological innovations) may exert pressure on the regime. Niches will be reinforced and windows of opportunity might open. Facing stormy times now, the prevailing regime may become destabilized and will allow for niche innovation breakthroughs. "Here, disruptive technologies co-evolve with shifts in markets, regulations, infrastructure, user practices, industrial networks, cultural meaning and scientific understanding" (Araújo 2014). The MLP defines transitions as a shift of regimes. Thus, a process of transition never ends with the simple disappearance of the prior dominant regime, but rather with the creation of a new one at the same time. Transitions usually do not come easy but are the result of "subsequent struggles between niches and regimes" (Geels 2010). These struggles "are enacted by interpretive actors that fight, negotiate, search, learn, and build coalitions as they navigate transitions" (Geels 2010). Similarly, Kuzemko et al. (2015) define socio-technical transitions as large-scale transformations within society during which the structure of a socio-technical system fundamentally changes. Sections "Variants of Transition" and "Application to the Dynamics of Energy Regimes" will show that there may also be socio-technical transitions of a smaller scope.

The question of whether actors are sufficiently considered within the MLP or not (Geels 2010; Andrews-Speed 2016) will be left open. However, transitions are also analyzed by other theories and heuristics. Among them is the theory of *strategic action fields* by Neil Fligstein and Dough McAdam (2011), which explicitly focus on actors and agency. They understand strategic action fields as being constituted by actors who seek to defend or improve their position by means of strategic action. In conflictive fields, there often are two basic kinds of actors: *incumbents*, who claim the central position of the field, hold the power, control the major share of the respective resources, and have a strong influence on regulation, and *challengers*, who generally have less privileged positions and few resources. Nevertheless, they wait for their opportunity, which may occur in periods of crises and insecurity (Fligstein and McAdam 2011). It seems evident that the incumbents correspond clearly to the regime level and the challengers – in some cases – with the niche. Will there be a transition or not? The outcome will largely depend on the result of the conflict between the opposing actor groups, following the approach of strategic action fields.

Energy Regimes

In this section, *energy regime* will refer specifically to electrical energy and will not deal with the transport and heating sectors. Energy regimes consist of a wide nexus of interrelated technological components, e.g., power plants, energy grids, and transformer stations. Kuzemko et al. (2015) point out that energy regimes also incorporate a certain set of rules, special skills, and complex engineering practices as well as various actors, like engineers, firms, energy producers, energy consumers, capital banks, and, not least, policymakers (Kuzemko et al. 2015). In this way, the technological infrastructure is embedded in a network of actors and institutions that usually advocate for established solutions that include large base-load fossil fuel and nuclear power plants, big energy companies, and overcapacities (Berlo and Wagner 2015).

It would be hard to determine whether energy regimes differ from other sociotechnical regimes in certain structural ways. Are there stronger path dependencies as compared to the agriculture and mobility regimes? It seems evident that a comparison between these kinds of regime would not be trivial at all. There are always institutions and actors with or without power as well as there are technical infrastructures. What makes the energy regime of special interest for this context is the fact that there is a broad consensus on the necessity for a fundamental change to sustainability.

Most energy regimes are confronted with severe constraints on the sociotechnical landscape that seem to exclude business-as-usual strategies: Mainly, it is the climate change that puts pressure on the regime to reduce the emissions of greenhouse gases. Depending on the national contexts, air pollution, risks of nuclear power use, and import dependency of energy production are further issues. Of course, all these topics are part of an "objective reality." However, for the energy regime, they might represent serious threats only after they become part of public discourse (see section "Discussion").

In the past decades, renewable energy technologies, like wind turbines and photovoltaics, have improved steadily (see above). In combination with base-load-capable power plants or storage technologies, today wind and solar parks can guarantee the security of energy supply just as well as nuclear and fossil power plants, but they generate far fewer negative externalities at the same time. Today, growing niches of renewable energy have been established in many countries and have achieved a considerable size. For example, the share of renewable electricity production in Spain, Portugal, Denmark, and Germany has reached more than 30%.

Thus, there is pressure from both sides, landscape and niche. As seen above, in such cases regime transitions are feasible. At least with respect to the landscape level, the pressure is comparable for every energy regime across the world, more or less. However, numerous national case studies or comparisons have shown a strong heterogeneity among the energy regimes' stability as well as in their willingness for greater reforms (e.g., van d. Vleuten 1999; Hadjilambrinos 2000; Geels et al. 2016; Hermwille 2016). The following section will present more factors and circumstances that support or hinder change.

Stability and Change

For a better understanding of the likelihood of regime transitions, a set of supporting and limiting factors is available. In accordance with the context of the handbook, factors are highlighted that are supposed to be of special relevance for the transitions of energy regimes. Moreover, the factor descriptions will be complemented by examples from this topical background.

It is obvious that there is a variety of factors that either increase or decrease stability of socio-technical regimes. For many of these factors, the literature explicitly indicates the effects. It is suggested that they clearly support stability (4.1) or contribute to destabilization (4.2). For some other factors, the influence on the regime cannot be predicted a priori. The effect of these Janus-faced factors (4.3) depends on the circumstances of the individual case.

It is important not to overestimate the existence of certain constellations of factors. Such constellations, e.g., *factors A, B, and C are given, but factors D and E are missing*, may provide important clues for understanding why transition is occurring or not. However, they never explain complex socio-technical contexts on their own. Thus, the mere existence of factor constellations will never substitute empirical studies. "The understanding of a specific combination of actions, structures, situations and circumstances are, in our view, the result of the investigation rather than pre-defined categories" (Stegmaier et al. 2014). Furthermore, it is crucial to analyze and interpret the meaning of the factors within the specific context. According to Andrews-Speed (2016), "regime transition will be promoted if the selection pressures from different sources are mutually reinforcing and if resources such as factor endowments, capabilities and knowledge are coordinated with these selection pressures."

Stabilizing Factors

Resistance Based on Economic Interests (Geels and Kemp 2012; Haas and Sander 2016)

Although this factor description deals with energy regimes, the statements are also valid for many other regime transitions. The focus is on powerful actors especially, who often seek to defend the old structures because of economic interests.

A notion applicable to power plant owners, stockholders of the large energy corporations, workers in the coal mines, and engineers in nuclear reactors is that, due to sunk costs (like lost investments in regime technologies, devaluation of professional qualifications and knowledge), they all would suffer economic and other disadvantages if transition took place. Therefore, they seek to defend the status quo and apply different strategies, like influencing policy debates and public discourse (Haas and Sander 2016). Lobbying is an important strategy to counteract regime transition. Of course, this strategy can only work if crucial state actors listen to the lobbyists. Usually this is out of the question because in many cases, the crucial state actors are part of the regimes (see below).

Regulation and Laws that Create Market Entry Barriers (Geels and Kemp 2012)

Especially for energy regimes, most state actors have traditionally acted clearly as regime actors (Hennicke and Müller 2005; Neukirch 2018). This does not mean that legislative support for the regime may not originate in direct or indirect corruption (Hennicke and Müller 2005). The most famous example illustrating how the German electric energy regime was historically constituted is the Energy Industry Act (*Energiewirtschaftsgesetz*, EnWG) of 1935. The EnWG guaranteed the monopoly status of the incumbent energy suppliers for many decades and, especially in the 1980s, excluded independent actors who tried to get grid access for their wind turbines or solar panels (Berlo and Wagner 2015). The EnWG had also been crucial for stabilizing central institutions as well as for the predominant understanding of economics of scale.

Institutional Reproduction of the Regime (Geels and Kemp 2012; Andrews-Speed 2016)

Regime actors represent not only the interests of their company or other institutions they may represent. Moreover, within these institutions certain core beliefs are reproduced. To a certain extent, these beliefs are beyond the criterion of right or wrong but are held as self-evident within the regime context. For the energy regime, the criterion that energy has to be cheap and secure is the most salient. That *cheap*, from a holistic point of view, is not cheap at all – because of the externalization of the costs on nature, health, and climate damages – and does not change anything in their view. Energy issues are often complex and hard to understand for people without specific knowledge. Therefore, the majority of people trusts the experts and politicians' statements and adopts their viewpoint. Moreover, the institutional argument is also crucial for consumers' behavior. In this context, Engels (2016) highlights the cultural meaning of certain carbon emission-intensive social practices and behavior as one important reason why climate protection strategies only seem to lead to small successes at most. Good examples of this are the reluctance of consumers to renounce a car, the enthusiasm for long-distance journeys, and the consumption of meat.

Path Dependency and Large Technical Systems: Economics of Scale (Hughes 1983; Unruh 2000; Beyer 2005; Geels and Kemp 2012)

As described above, large technical systems and path dependency have a strong effect on the stability of socio-technical regimes. Infrastructures display certain characteristics that lead to strong path dependencies. Energy transmission lines and power plants are built to last several decades. Such an infrastructure is cost intensive, and it is evident that basic modifications would be implemented only for good reasons.

Another important explanation for path dependency is economics of scale. Its effect can be demonstrated perfectly by looking at energy regimes. The principle that was once a standard decision-making criterion for the power plant sector is prototypical: "degression of costs by progression of size" (Hennicke and Müller 2005).

Due to the target of cheap energy, the power plants that are operated by the regime actors have become larger and larger over the decades. For example, in the 1960s/1970s, new power plants in Germany had to have a minimum size of 300 MW (Hellige 2012). This way, decentralized energy production was forced back step by step. High investment costs blocked market access for small actors anyway (even if grid access for "independent" producers had been permitted).

Large Corporations and Tight Interrelationship Between Economy and the State (Hennicke and Müller 2005; Berlo and Wagner 2015)

As the international diesel scandal around Volkswagen and other automobile producers has shown, questionable practices may persist if there is insufficient distance between industry and the state authorities that control companies' compliance with the law.

This notion is highly relevant not only in the automotive sector but also in the energy sector. With their economic and financial resources, energy corporations often have the ability to influence the political agenda. For the German energy sector, Berlo and Wagner (2015) emphasize the economic dominance that is combined with a strong political influence. The stabilizing effect on the regime stems not only from the pure market power and lobbying from the outside. With special regard to the German energy system, until the mid-1980s, Hennicke and Müller (2005) state that there has been no other sector with such a symbiotic connection between economy and the political sphere.

Emotional Factors (Bakke 2016)

When it comes to making a decision as to whether a sustainable innovation should be introduced or not, emotions can be important. Bakke (2016) points out that emotional factors matter in that, for many decision-makers, it is very important that proposals should come from *the right side*. For example, a regional environmental minister would perhaps reject a proposal for a new bike road, because it came from the local bike-riding initiative (that shamed him 3 years ago for driving a big SUV). Some years later, when the proposal was almost forgotten, he decided to build the bike road and claimed the idea as his own.

Destabilizing Factors

Strong Social Movements (Byzio et al. 2002; Mautz et al. 2008; Neukirch 2010, 2018; Andrews-Speed 2016)

It seems evident that social movements which are founded to challenge the status quo can have a destabilizing effect on socio-technical regimes. To a large extent, it was the merit of environmental movements that the emission of pollutants in many western countries significantly decreased during 1970s and 1980s due to the application of end-of-pipe solutions (Weiland 2007). New policies managed to overcome the death of the forests (*Waldsterben*), to significantly improve the water quality of rivers, and to stop the ozone hole's growth (Weiland 2007). In this case the different industrial regimes were able to react by means of step-by-step innovations. The question of whether the result should be seen as an important step toward a sustainable industry regime or rather as an improvement of the status quo has to be left open in this context.

In contrast, the antinuclear movements that arose in countries like the USA, Denmark, and West Germany during the 1970s challenged the established energy regimes in a more fundamental way (Mautz et al. 2008). Nuclear power plants embody the main characteristics of a socio-technical regime more than any other energy production technology: concerning the power plant size, the promise of cheap and secure energy, the idea of controlling high risks by means of formalized scientific knowledge, and the threat that surrounds large technologies from the public's viewpoint. At least for Denmark and West Germany, it can be clearly said that the antinuclear movements strongly contributed to the market introduction of grid-connected wind turbines that were operated by independent actors (Neukirch 2010). Although they only had a small share of the market, these *new renewable energies* underscore the emergence of three new core institutions that were clearly in contrast to the regime: (1) energy generation by a multitude of producers, no longer by a few monopolists; (2) decentralized, as opposed to centralized, production; and (3) sustainability as the most important target, instead of cheap and secure energy as first criterion (Mautz et al. 2008).

Ecological Pioneers (Mautz et al. 2008; Berlo and Wagner 2015)

Without pioneers who dealt with sustainable energy technologies in their early state, technologies like wind turbines and solar panels would not have taken off: In Denmark, during the 1970s and 1980s, many craftsmen and engineers were involved in the design and construction of small wind turbines (Neukirch 2010). The first reliable wind turbine designs were created in this socio-technical environment and formed one of the main conditions for the creation of a market. The antinuclear movement framed wind turbines as a counter-technology to prevent nuclear power from being introduced (Neukirch 2010).

Active Support by Legislation/Niche Policies (Mautz et al. 2008; Andrews-Speed 2016)

The number of ecological pioneers is limited in every country. Again, this applies to the case of wind power: It is necessary to guarantee a secure product and to achieve an industrial level of production in order to overcome the limits of embryonic markets (Neukirch 2010). This way, the output becomes more predictable, and new buyers are included who are no longer mainly guided by ecological or humanitarian reasons. At this time, the introduction of cost-effective support by the legislative framework would be needed to enable further diffusion of this technology.

While laws supporting wind and solar power may be successful in contributing to the stabilization of the niche and the improvement of these technologies, they probably do not suffice for a transition away from the old energy regime. There are several authors who emphasize the necessity of a policy mix that combines policies of innovation with those of exnovation (Strunz 2014; Kivimaa and Kern

2015; David 2017). It is not enough to strengthen the niche, but at the same time, policies have to support "motors of creative destruction" (Kivimaa and Kern 2015). It seems evident that policy combinations like these would help to accelerate transitions. In retrospect, one may state: *Yes, it was this certain kind of support that enabled the transition (at last)*. Descriptions like these are true in a way, for example, they can be important for policy recommendations. However, they often fail to analyze the dynamics that have led to a certain regulation. Following the MLP, the government and thus its most important institutions are part of the regime. They may support a niche for renewable energies as a strategy supposed to calm down public ecological concerns or as a means of industrial policy. Nevertheless, the niche actors' resources alone would never be sufficient to establish policies to enable creative destruction of the old regime.

Governance of Transition (Meadowcroft 2009; Kuzemko et al. 2015)

A policy mix that includes exnovation policies is crucial for a transition. Active exnovation – like the nuclear phaseout law in Germany – will not usually happen accidentally. On the contrary, they might be the result of long-term controversies within and outside the political arena, in which many actors are involved: politicians, governments on different administration levels, industrial associations (from within and outside the regime), environmental groups and movements, NGOs, and scientists. A transition governance or transition management (Meadowcroft 2009) can only be successful if there are active actors (e.g., social movements, ecological pioneers, and change agents Mautz et al. 2008) who aim to push this process forward.

A prominent example is the German nuclear phaseout debate. For the former conservative-liberal government, it seemed almost out of the question that the old phaseout decision should have to be canceled (what happened in 2010). Perhaps with the strategic aim of framing the old phaseout decision of 2000 as the result of a societal debate, the government of Social Democrats and the Greens established the term *nuclear consent*. In fact, the conservative party, large utilities as reactor owners, and industrial lobby associations had never agreed to it. Thus, the *consent* was modified in 2010 when the shutdown of each reactor was postponed by 12 years on average (since the Social Democrats had left the government in 2009). After the Fukushima nuclear disaster in March 2011, the discursive situation changed again. The antinuclear movement became stronger, and the support for the Green Party increased significantly. Against this background, the oldest reactors were quickly shut down, paving the way for the start of a new policy process this way. The Nuclear Commission, consisting of representatives of different societal groups, was established and – after several months of discourse – pleaded for a phaseout path that returned to the old arrangement in great measure.

It is important to understand a governance process in a broader sense that not only includes so-called stakeholders (e.g., companies and interest associations) but also less formal, unorganized actors, like the antinuclear movement. Without their increased activity after the nuclear consent was rejected and, more importantly, after the disaster in Japan, the Nuclear Commission might have achieved another result. As Berlo and Wagner (2015) emphasize, governance processes can also be fueled by bottom-up developments: Together, local coalitions – constituted by members from several regions – of municipal utilities and local initiatives constitute the core of a *polycentric governance*.

Below, a special type of actor will be considered: the *intermediaries*, located between challengers and incumbents and who cannot be categorized easily as part of the regime or niche. The *middle-out approach* by Parag and Janda (2014) criticizes that both transition paths, top-down (in the case where the regime acts in favor of change) and bottom-up, are insufficient. The regime actors, of course, would have the resources and the power to implement a transition, but they often lack agency (the ability to act in an independent way and make free choices). Thus, their actions are strongly guided by the predominant institutions. Apart from that, the niche actors would be able to act freely but have no power (capacity). In contrast to both niche and regime actors, the so-called intermediaries that are not part of the regime and support the transition may become very important in the transition process – as they have not only agency but also higher capacity than the niche actors (Parag and Janda 2014).

Janus-Faced Factors

The impact of some indicators of transition and stability cannot be anticipated, since it depends on particular circumstances. Narratives, new technologies, external shocks, consumer lifestyles, and adaptive capacities of regime actors – they all can foster or hinder transition. Below, both forms will be briefly described, each illustrated with one example from the energy sector.

Narratives (Hermwille 2016)

It seems evident that the effect of narratives for transition processes can support change or stability. Looking at the German Energiewende, e.g., the narrative about wind power pioneers (Oelker 2005) and charismatic persons like Hermann Scheer (the former head of Eurosolar and member of the German parliament) played a crucial role for the legislation on renewable energy installations (Mautz et al. 2008). On the other hand, there are heroic narratives of the coal sector that gave jobs to thousands of people. Thus, after the World War II, coal was a guarantor for prosperity, growth, and stability. With the ability to deliver electrical energy at any time, coal became a discursive counterpart to the unstable, volatile wind and solar technologies.

New Technologies (Dolata 2013; Fouquet 2016)

Technical innovations surely can assume an important role for socio-technical transitions (Dolata 2013; Fouquet 2016). The effect may support or hinder transitions. The viability of new renewable energy technologies was an important precondition for government actors to decide in favor of their legislative support. On the contrary, there can be technical innovations on the regime level as well. Technologies like carbon capture and storage and efficient filters of pollutant emissions of cadmium, lead, or mercury had strong discursive effects that improved the public reputation of coal-fired power plants. Seen from a more holistic point of view, technology is not a decisive factor within transition processes, especially not in cases of wide transitions. Looking at the German energy sector, there were consistent transition plans available since the mid-1980s (Hennicke et al. 1985). Their foundation was to switch from centralized, large power plants to small, combined heat and power (CHP) systems. CHP was well developed then, but in the given market environment, it hardly had a chance for diffusion. Thus, new technology *is* a factor, but it is very important to look at the social context (e.g., institutional and discursive environment) as well – it usually will play a more important role for transition processes.

External Shocks and Landscape Pressure (Hermwille 2016; Fouquet 2016)

Certain events that are not immediately connected to the regime or niche level may have a major influence on the dynamics of the regime. They can have a destabilizing function (Fouquet 2016) or even contribute to a change in governance structures (Fuchs 2012). In terms of the MLP, those events are located within the socio-technical landscape. For the German energy system, the nuclear disasters of Chernobyl and Fukushima, as well as the oil crises of 1973, were such events (Neukirch 2018). Foremostly, these factors contributed to weaken the public approval and the legitimacy of the regime.

Hermwille (2016) highlighted that a shock may only have an impact if it is transmitted by certain discourses and narratives. The latter not only have an enabling function but also have massive influence on the reception of the shock. Most of the STS literature seems to be more interested in explaining change rather than stability. For this reason, it is less surprising that shocks are usually conceptualized as a factor that contributes to destabilization. However, sometimes the opposite can be true as well. Just imagine what consequences a real European-wide blackout of the energy supply structure in Germany can have on the discourse on the energy transition. It would be easy for the regime actors to argue: *Sorry, but we are responsible for constantly increasing the share of volatile wind and solar power in the system. This unfortunately led to this disaster. Consequently, we will now restrict the share of volatile power. We promise, this won't happen again!* What might happen afterwards is unclear. Who would be held responsible? And who would explain the cause of the blackout? Was it the high proportion of wind and solar power or rather the inability – or even reluctance – of the regime to manage such situations? Thus, the effect of an external shock cannot be predicted in advance and remains subject to retrospective analysis.

Consumer Lifestyles (Geels and Kemp 2012)

The influence of the public on transition or stability has been emphasized in different contexts. Of course, except for possible avant-garde positions, consumer behavior can become crucial in both directions, if a certain behavior is exhibited by a large number of people. Looking at the automobile, nutrition, and tourism sectors, it seems clear that consumers as a whole theoretically would have a great capacity to destabilize existing socio-technical regimes. Notwithstanding the discourse on sustainable consumption that has been going on for several decades now, the vast majority of people do not consider ecological aspects in their consumption decisions consistently. Alternatives to the status quo (e.g., vegetarianism, car sharing, commuting by bike or public transport) – traditionally emphasized by ecologists – fail to receive the support of societal majorities. Hence, there is a strong empirical evidence to support the notion that "consumer lifestyle (is) a reason for stability" (Geels and Kemp 2012).

On the other hand, it is not absurd to suppose that someday this majority, which more or less tacitly rejects a transition to sustainability, will change its behavior. Such a development does not necessarily have to be driven by altruism. Referring to the transitions of energy regimes, Fouquet (2016) pointed out that "consumers may gain from the transition."

Adaptive Capacities and the Role of the Incumbents (Kuzemko et al. 2015; Fouquet 2016)

Usually, the incumbent actors will not play an active role for transition but, rather, will seek to defend the status quo. The rules of the old regime are made mostly in favor of the incumbents' interests and viewpoints (Fligstein and McAdam 2011). Nevertheless, sometimes there are incumbents who actually have rethought their positions and strategies for the sake of a long-term perspective to maintain the established position in the field, but under slightly modified conditions. Kuzemko et al. (2015) state that "under certain circumstances, incumbent energy companies can become part of the progress of change, as has been the case in Denmark and Portugal." Without discussing the precise circumstances here, we should pay attention to the ambivalent character of *progressive* incumbents. By way of controlling techno-economic resources, including specific knowledge, they might become an important accelerator of transition. On the other hand, a proactive role for incumbents may discourage niche actors who, in many cases, have contributed strongly to the initiation of transition processes before. Whereas there is no doubt that the latter pursue an agenda of transition, the motivation of the incumbents is not self-explanatory. Are they really persuaded by the transition, or is their activity a strategic maneuver that would be stopped after they regained control? The more important the role of the incumbents is for a transition, the more it is necessary to pay close attention to determine whether this process is still on track.

This leads to the question of the transition's scope. What does it include, and what will persist? Considering different transition concepts, the following section turns to this issue.

Variants of Transition

This section deals with different approaches to conceptualize transition processes. Since a comprehensive literature review would be impossible, I will concentrate on three approaches that will be applied to energy regime transitions in section "Application to the Dynamics of Energy Regimes": MLP (Geels and Schot 2007), strategic action field crises (Fligstein and McAdam 2011), and modes of institutional change (Streeck and Thelen 2005; Mahoney and Thelen 2010).

Firstly, the MLP defines transition as the process leading from an old regime to a new one (Geels and Schot 2007). Geels and Schot (2007) proposed four transition pathways that were further enhanced by Geels and Kemp (2012) to prove the concepts' endurance:

Transformation (MLP 1): This pathway occurs when there is moderate landscape pressure at a moment when niche-innovations have not yet been sufficiently developed, leading regime actors to respond by modifying the direction of development paths and innovation activities.

De-alignment and re-alignment path (MLP 2): Major landscape pressures first cause big internal problems for regimes leading to their disintegration (de-alignment of elements); this erosion then creates space for various niche-innovations that co-exist for prolonged periods. The variety of niches creates uncertainty and may delay important actors to make full-scale commitments for fear of betting on the wrong horse. Eventually, processes of re-alignment occur around one of the innovations, leading to a new regime.

Technological substitution (MLP 3): This pathway occurs when there is much landscape pressure at a moment when niche-innovations have developed sufficiently, causing the latter to break through and replace the existing regime.

Reconfiguration pathway (MLP 4): Niche-innovations are initially adopted in the regime to solve local problems but subsequently trigger adjustments in the basic architecture of the regime.

Secondly, Fligstein and McAdam (2011) analyzed strategic action fields (SAF) that under certain circumstances may run into heavy crises. They assume four basic outcomes of the crises occur (Fligstein and McAdam 2011):

A *reimposition of the old order with some adjustments (SAF 1)*. This will occur most frequently with the state enforcing whatever new agreements have been reached most often at the expense of the challenger groups.

The SAF breaks down into unorganized social space (SAF 2). If the groups that make up the social space are unable to find a new conception of control and the state is unwilling or unable to impose a new order, the field can become unorganized. This kind of condition is likely by definition to be unstable for the groups that remain and one can expect that they will migrate to other social spaces or else disappear.

The SAF is partitioned into several social spaces (SAF 3). One solution is to break the field down by redefining the activities of the groups in the field so that they are no longer trying to occupy the same social space. Thus, new agreements are possible amongst potentially smaller set of groups.

The challengers can build a coalition to produce a new SAF (SAF 4). Challengers and incumbents can migrate to already existing social space or they can try and colonize new social space.

Thirdly, Mahoney and Thelen (2010) proposed four modes of institutional transition: *layering, conversion, drift,* and *displacement.*

Mahoney and Thelen (2010) characterize the categories as follows:

Displacement occurs when existing rules are replaced by new ones, entailing a radical shift if it happens in an abrupt way. But the transition from old to new institutions may also occur in a more incremental way. If the existing rules are still valid and new rules appear as attached to the status quo, Mahoney and Thelen (2010) define this as layering. In many cases, this kind of transition leads to smaller modifications. Nevertheless, layering may also "bring substantial change if amendments alter the logic of the institution or compromise the stable reproduction of the original 'core' (...) Drift occurs when rules remain formally the same but their impact changes as result of shifts in external conditions. When actors choose not to respond to such environmental changes their very inaction can cause change in the impact of the institution" (Mahoney and Thelen 2010). Finally, if the old rules remain formally but are interpreted and enacted in new ways, this mode is defined as conversion. Thus, the existing rules are not neglected (as would be true for drift). Rather, actors "actively exploit the inherent ambiguities of the institutions" (Mahoney and Thelen 2010).

Which mode will be predominant for a certain political context, according to Mahoney and Thelen (2010), will depend especially on two conditions: First, are the veto possibilities – of the regime actors – low or high? Secondly, is the level of discretion – considering aspects of interpretation and enforcement – low or high (see Table 1)?

At first glance, it looks as if drift, conversion, and displacement are expressions of lacking adaptive capacities. This may but will not always be the case. On the contrary, the incumbent actors might have initiated such developments for strategic reasons as well (Streeck and Thelen 2005). For example, it can be "appealing for the government and economic players to make the social welfare state and the idea of equality of all human beings" appear to be outdated. Conversely, layering does not necessarily have to refer solely to strategies of integration and acceptance: "(...) new institutions are set in motion by political actors working on the margins by introducing amendments that can initially be 'sold' as refinements of (...) existing institutions. Since the new layers (...) do not as such (...) directly undermine existing institutions, they typically do not provoke countermobilization by defenders of the status quo. To the extent, however, that they operate on a different logic and

Table 1 Characteristics of institutional change

Type of institutional change	Veto position of regime actors	Level of discretion in interpretation/enforcement
Layering	Strong	Low
Drift	Strong	High
Displacement	Weak	Low
Conversion	Weak	High

Source: Own composition with regard to Mahoney and Thelen (2010: 19)

grow more quickly than the traditional system, over time they may fundamentally alter the overall trajectory of development as the old institutions stagnate or lose their grip (...)" (Streeck and Thelen 2005).

Thus, in times of crises, the stability of core institutions – or socio-technical regimes – will largely depend on the ability of the incumbents to adopt major reforms and support institutional novelties that are compatible with the old setting.

There seems to be an evident relationship between the adaptive capacities and the role of new actors. If the regime actors are proactive and are able to apply new answers to the *big questions*, niche actors or challengers will not have a chance to gain a dominant position within the field. Otherwise, the more the incumbents stay passive, the more chances new actors will have of taking increasingly significant roles.

Dolata (2013) applied these modes of transition and broadened their scope to the description of the dynamics of socio-technical regimes. Another important difference is that Dolata (2013) focused the modes on incumbent actors' adaptive capacities on the one hand, as well as the role of new technologies on the other. Both make this variant attractive for applications within the context of energy transitions.

It is not the aim of this chapter to discuss the extent to which these concepts – due to different analytical perspectives – are compatible with each other or not. But when applying them to the case of energy regimes that might be in a phase of transition, it is necessary to be aware of these different views: Are we looking at strategic action fields with a special emphasis on actors or rather at transition pathways and different socio-technical levels where a transition might occur? For both perspectives, different types of institutional change as (first) introduced by Streeck and Thelen (2005) and applied by Dolata (2013) are an analytical enrichment.

Application to the Dynamics of Energy Regimes

Three categories of energy regime transition, each with a different scope, will be considered:

1. Transition from one nonrenewable technology to another technology, steered by regime actors or other (energy) corporations (*non-sustainable transition*)
2. Transition of the fossil-nuclear energy regime to a renewable energy regime, steered by regime actors or other (energy) corporations (*sustainable transition*)
3. Transition to renewable energies that is (mainly) steered by outsiders who aim for a decentralization of the energy system (*sustainable transformation*)

It seems clear that categories (1) and (2) will not lead to transitions of a wide scope. Both will integrate new technologies that will be operated by the actors of the old regime or other (energy) corporations. An important difference between both types is that transitions to sustainable energies are, to a large extent, normatively legitimized.

From the perspective of transition research, *sustainable transformations* (3) are of special interest. In this context, a transformation is defined as a transition with a wide scope. The main differences – when dealing with the empirical cases – are

Table 2 Variants of energy transition

Kind of transition	Role of energy corporations after transition	Modes of transition (Mahoney and Thelen 2010)	Transition pathway (Geels and Kemp 2012)	Outcomes of conflict (Fligstein and McAdam 2011)
Non-sustainable transition (1)	Crucial	Layering, conversion, displacement	MLP 1–4	SAF 1
Sustainable transition (2)	Crucial	Layering, conversion, displacement	MLP 1–4	SAF 1
Sustainable transformation (3)	Marginal	Drift, displacement	MLP 1, 2, 4	SAF 3, SAF 4

Source: own

summarized in Table 2. It is important to consider that the transitions on the national level are not completed. Thus, one can speak of transition pathways but full transitions. According to Dolata (2013), processes of transformation usually are characterized by the occurrence of different modes of transition. This statement also seems valid for the MLP. Looking at the time dimension, e.g., in the early phase, a *sustainable transition* may be characterized by the predominance of MLP 1. Due to the maturing of renewable energy technologies, the main pathway switches to MLP 3.

Below is an interpretation of several transitions against the background of the categories defined in Table 2. In this context, the periodization of transitions remains an important issue. For Sovacool (2016), this period refers to the timespan from the market introduction of a new technology or a group of related technologies to their reaching a share of 25% (Smil 2010) and 50% (Grubler 2012) of a national or global market. Without deepening this discussion here, it seems evident that a technology is well established whenever it achieves a market share of 50%. The question of whether this is also true when a government defines the aim of a transition as 100% would be rather academic.

The empirical cases will deal with energy transitions in France, Great Britain, Germany, and Denmark (Table 3). These cases have been chosen because these ideal-typical transitions have already concluded or have reached an advanced stage.

This is not the place for detailed case descriptions. Rather, the aim is to shed light on specific characteristics referring to the reasons for stability and change (section "Stability and Change") as well as the conceptual frames of transition to be addressed in certain contexts (section "Variants of Transition").

France: From Fossil Fuels to Nuclear Power (1974–1996)

Without national resources of oil, gas, or coal during the oil crises in the early 1970s, the extent to which the French energy system was vulnerable became obvious. Facing this landscape pressure that resulted from high dependency on

2 Transition of Energy Systems: Patterns of Stability and Change

Table 3 Historical energy transitions

Transition	Transition type	Transition complete?	Modes of transition	Transition pathways	Outcomes of conflict	Land-scape pressure	Niche dy-namics
France: from fossil to nuclear	(1)	Yes	Displacement	MLP 3	SAF 1	Oil crises	–
Great Britain: from coal to gas	(1)	Yes	Drift, displacement	MLP 3	(SAF 4)	Market liberalization	–
Germany: energy transition	(2), (3)	No	Layering, drift, displacement	MLP 2 MLP 3	Tendency: SAF 1 SAF 3	Oil crises, antinuclear move-ment, climate change	Yes
Denmark: energy transition	(3), (2)	No	Layering, drift, displacement	MLP 2 MLP 3	SAF 1 SAF 3	See German case	Yes

Source: own

imported oil, Prime Minister Pierre Messmer announced in 1974 that the national electricity would be produced by nuclear power plants in the future (Sovacool 2016). As a consequence, between 1974 and 1989, 56 nuclear power plants in total were built. Whereas the market share of electricity produced by nuclear power was 8.2% in 1973, in 1982 it reached a share of 40% and even 77.5% in 1996 (Hadjilambrinos 2000; Sovacool 2016). This development legitimates an interpretation of the French case as being a top-down transition that is restricted to a technical displacement.

To explain the decision for nuclear energy as the most centralistic power technology, Hadjilambrinos (2000) referred to the hierarchic structure of the French state and the history of technocratic approaches. Nuclear technology fits perfectly in the existing energy system. As the technology was available at times of high landscape pressure, this transition followed the pathway of a technical substitution (MLP 3). However, it would be inaccurate to frame nuclear power as niche technology. It was developed in high-security research facilities that were part of the regime. Thus, nuclear power is a regime technology. The incumbent monopolist, EDF (Electricité de France), founded in 1946, kept its position before and after the transition to nuclear power (Hadjilambrinos 2000). Against this background, this transition is only one of a small scope. Rather, a new sub-regime arose around the nuclear power technology, one that had also influenced the main regime (Sovacool 2016). From the perspective of strategic action fields, the nuclear strategy was a strong blow against the OPEC countries that – as challengers in the field of *energy supply of France* – demanded higher prices for oil. Whereas the subfield *fossil energies in France* shrunk, a new field was established around the nuclear technology. This move enabled a stabilization of the old order (SAF 1).

Great Britain: Dash for Gas and the Decline of Coal (1987–1997)

Traditionally, the British energy regime was governed by a large state-owned corporation, the CEGB (Central Electricity Generation Board). After the EU demanded the liberalization by 1987, the CEGB was divided into two large power generation companies, one transmission grid operator and 12 regional distribution companies (RECs) (Rohracher 2007). At that time, the combined cycle gas turbine (CCGT), an innovative gas power plant technology that can provide base-load as well as peak-load power, was available (Rohracher 2007). Directly after the regulation started, the RECs and other new market actors started to invest in CCGT technology. Due to better economics, CCGT displaced the coal-fired power plants that dominated the British power sector for decades. During the 1990s, gas reached a market share of 50%, until the newly elected Labour government stopped new CCGT installations in 1997 in order to defend the remaining coal sector that was tightly organized by unions. For the same reason, the former conservative government supported the *dash for gas* (Rohracher 2007).

Andrews-Speed (2016) considers this development as a change that was driven from within the regime. Whether the liberalization (that was strongly advocated for by the British government) asserted the pressure from the landscape (MLP logic) or from within the regime will be left open for discussion (see below). In contrast to the French case, the new technology was not introduced by the regime but by new actors or challengers. Moreover, this process can be described as drift and displacement: seen from a technical perspective (from coal to CCGT) as well as an institutional perspective (from a corporatist setting to a competitive market environment).

The proposed outcomes of conflicted fields (SAF 1–4) seem not to fit here well. In fact, there is a conflict between old and new actors. However, surely it would be misleading to understand CCGT as a new SAF set up by the challengers. Rather, coal and CCGT still existed within the same action field, but the regulation of this field significantly changed. The transition reached further when compared to France, since not only did the dominant technology change, but also new actors, the RECs, entered the sector of electricity production. Compared to the old energy regime, the dash for gas caused a more extensive transition. Nevertheless, three characteristics limited the scope of the transition: First, it took place within the fossil-nuclear system. Second, it confirmed the old principles that say that energy has to be cheap (compared to coal) and secure (CCGT can deliver base-load power and the UK commands Europe's second largest reserves of natural gas). Third, it was the introduction of market logic in the electricity sector that broke up the corporatist path. Thus, this transition can be seen as a process of adjustment of the energy regime to the overall developments in British policy (austerity, neoliberalism) that exert a strong landscape pressure. Nevertheless, the government of Margaret Thatcher played a key role in increasing this pressure. Overall, this transition can be understood as technical substitution (MLP 3).

Germany: Energy Transition (Since the Mid-1970s)

To sum up the whole process (Mautz et al. 2008; Neukirch 2018) would be impossible here. For this context, it is important to understand that this development cannot easily be interpreted as one story without cracks and inconsistencies over a timespan of more than 40 years. Neukirch (2018) understands this process as a longtime battle between two large coalitions – a challenger coalition that is favor of the transition and the established one that seeks to hinder it. The transition started in the mid-1970s as discursive revolution by ecologic activists, especially the antinuclear movement and the radical left. Even though this attempt failed in the short run, the nuclear path slowed down, and acceptance strategies were introduced (SAF 1).

Pushed by the nuclear accident of Chernobyl in 1986, a socio-technical niche for small renewable energy technologies – wind power in particular – started to grow and increased the pressure on the established regime. Following the theory of strategic action fields, this niche constituted a new SAF with new actors and rules (SAF 3). At least in the beginning, the old regime was not really challenged by these new actors, because the output of electricity produced by renewable energies was rudimentary. Nevertheless, the intruders took a performative role.

Using the MLP terminology, discourses over climate change and the Fukushima disaster (2011) would be seen as landscape factors that increasingly challenged the legitimacy of the fossil-nuclear energy regime during the last years. At the same time, the niche of renewable energies grew up in such a way that it started to become a real threat for this regime. The latter took up this battle again and managed to marginalize the challenger coalition, especially by adopting the aim of the energy transition (Neukirch 2018) and by fighting back the attempts to decentralize the energy system (SAF 1). In 2012, the support for photovoltaics was significantly shortened, destroying hundreds of jobs in this sector. In the following years, the plans for new wind parks were increasingly restricted (Neukirch 2018). At the same time, the offshore wind market that easily enabled the regime actors to enter the renewable sector opened up. Moreover, any attempts at consistent coal phaseout regulation, as well as the integration of the mobility and heating sectors into the transition, were constantly rejected by the established coalition (Neukirch 2018).

Thus, extrapolating from this development, the process will result in a reimposition of the old order (SAF 1). As one looks at the different phases of this development, transition pathways, especially MLP 2 and MLP 3, are occurring, or rather occurred, in the past. Several modes of transition are displayed, especially layering, drift, and displacement.

This transition reaches further than those of the French and British cases. On the one hand, there is a clear commitment that is the result of a governance process to leave the fossil-nuclear regime in favor of green energies. On the other hand, the transition was slowed down and brought under control of the incumbent actors again. Overall, looking at Table 2, Category (2), sustainable transition may be adequate to describe this process.

Denmark: Energy Transition (Since the Mid-1970s)

In a way similar to the German situation, Denmark was concerned by the oil crises, and there was a strong movement that fought against the introduction of nuclear power to counteract the energy scarcity. Already in the late 1970s, a niche for wind power opened up. In contrast to the German case, this niche did not remain at this state, since it became part of a new heterogeneous but sustainable regime. For this, the early regulation in favor of small wind power in 1978/1979 was crucial. Since the beginning of the 1980s, local wind power cooperatives became the dominant owner-operator type (Neukirch 2010). In 2017, the share of wind energy of the total electric energy consumption in Denmark was 44.4% (Wind Europe 2018).

Moreover, the Danish energy plan of 1981 (energiplan 81) fixed the target of a decentralized energy system based mainly on wind power, fossil energy-based CHP, and district heating (Hadjilambrinos 2000; van der Vleuten and Raven 2006). In 2006, the share of CHP in Denmark (district heating and electricity production together) was about 52% (International Energy Agency 2008).

There are also some large coal power plants in operation, together with several offshore wind parks, representing the centralized energy path. In 2014 the government decided to phase out coal by 2030 (State of Green 2017). Thus, a core element of the old energy regime will disappear. In contrast to Germany, in Denmark one can speak of a clear path to a sustainable energy system, however decentralized and centralized, energies. Therefore, it seems adequate to talk of the (original) main SAF as being split into two smaller SAFs (SAF 3). Nevertheless, both – decentralized and centralized – kinds of installations are part of the same national energy system and are technically connected via the same grid. Ørsted (former DONG), the Danish incumbent utility, again in contrast to the German situation, is not an obstacle but rather acts in a proactive way. The utility announced it would shut down all coal-fired power plants by 2023 (DONG 2017). Moreover, it has become the most important player in the field of offshore wind power, not only in Denmark but also in the German market (Neukirch 2018). In Denmark, renewable energies have left the niche long time ago. It would be wrong to argue: *Now, as Ørsted became green, it no longer makes sense to decide between challengers and incumbents.* From the grassroots activists' viewpoint, the energy transition was one target. The other was to introduce a more democratic and non-hierarchic energy system, which could hardly be achieved if a large corporation like Ørsted played a major role. In terms of strategic action fields, the outcome of the conflict over the Danish energy regime has to be located as a mixture of SAF 1 and SAF 3.

Looking at the MLP here, the situation is ambiguous, too. Offshore wind power has been a proven technology for several years, and it has been used by Ørsted, which clearly speaks for MLP 3. But it is also important to look at the niche expansion in order to understand the Danish energy transition. Especially during the early phase of the development, de-alignment and realignment path (MLP 2) seems to describe the situation well.

The Danish energy transition includes more decentralized elements than the German transition. However, especially during the last years, Ørsted became strongly involved in this process. Both small onshore-based wind power and decentralized CHP, on the one hand, and offshore wind power and large CHP (till 2030), on the other, persist. Thus, the Danish tradition of a heterogeneous energy regime (van der Vleuten and Raven 2006) will be continued.

The four illustrative cases display the empirical variety of energy transitions among industrialized western countries. Moreover, the powerful analytical tools, applied to categorize and interpret the transitions adequately, lost much of their clarity and became ambiguous to some extent.

Discussion

The empirical illustrations in section "Application to the Dynamics of Energy Regimes" pointed to ambiguities and shortcomings of the dominant transition theories and left some open questions to be discussed hereafter:

Scope of Transition Pathways MLP 1–4

It seems that radical transition pathways are not conceptualized. Full regime transitions – like Category (3) in Table 3 – are missing. For example, if the Danish transition had occurred without the involvement of an incumbent like Ørsted – as in the early phases of the process – there would have been no appropriate pathway (MLP 1–4). Thus, I propose – as MLP 5 – a new category *transformative transition pathway*, if there is strong pressure from the niche and/or landscape and if there are new actors who claim the central role in the new regime.

Avoiding Oversimplifications

In order to apply the MLP consistently in this context, I understood the antinuclear movement as a part of the landscape (Table 2). In fact, the reasoning is not that straightforward, because the antinuclear movement did not prosper outside the regime. Rather, it was coproduced by the latter and might disappear if the regime were to change. Otherwise, it would also be insufficient to *put* the movements into the niche, especially if they do not take part in developing technical or social innovations that may at some point seriously challenge the regime. When examining transitions of *socio*-technical regimes, it may be problematic to exclude those parts of society that belong neither to the regime nor to the niche. For Geels and Schot (2007), these outsiders primarily have the function of a medium. Things that are happening at the landscape can only unfold pressure if they are framed as critical problems (e.g., climate change). Thus, the parts of society that are involved have no meaning as actors with their own targets, strategies, and resources. For a social science-based analysis, it seems insufficient to reduce some of the actors to an abstract medium that has to *talk about* the landscape. An example is the Fukushima nuclear accident. For all countries (except for Japan), the disaster performed more or less at the same landscape. Whereas in France (with 58 nuclear reactors) – due to a missing medium – there was no pressure on the regime, the German government turned off the oldest reactors immediately and returned mainly to the old nuclear phaseout path. According to this, imagining a landscape that was to display something like a so-called objective reality is misleading. Rather, this notion ought to refer to a discursive order that depends strongly on the given regional or national context.

Insufficient or Unclear Conceptualization of Actors

Of course, the criticism that actors are not sufficiently considered within the MLP is not new. The problem consists not only of a lack of attention to the actors outside the niche, regime, or landscape. The comparison between the French and the British transition cases displays the importance of actors. Whereas the introduction of nuclear power in France did not lead to a change of the incumbents, in the UK, new regime actors conducted mainly the transition from coal to CCGT. This is an important difference between both transitions that can only be put into focus adequately with an actor-based analytical concept. In contrast, strategic action fields even consist of actors. However, it remains unclear whether the new actors are just "market challengers" who are looking for new ways of making a profit or whether there are real "game changers" (e.g., those who help push through the idea of sustainable energy against the institutional dominance of the *cheap-and-secure principle* that – apart from great speeches – still characterizes almost every energy system of today). Thus, it should be considered to differentiate the category of actors. Empirical studies always ought to take special care as to what kind of actors they are dealing with. Otherwise, there is the risk of remaining on the analytical surface of the considered case.

There is another criticism of the SAF concept. Fligstein and McAdam (2011) differentiate between SAFs with state actors and SAFs without state actors. Both actor types can never be inside the same SAF. There are cases where such a separation can be justified (e.g., the dash for gas in the UK). However, in some cases, this would lead to misguiding interpretations and especially to an underestimate of the strength of the networks between the economic and political spheres (s. a.). Thus, this is a plea not to apply theories and heuristics dogmatically but rather as helpful tools that may have to be modified depending on the application.

Modes of Institutional Change: Low Degree of Selectivity?

It is important to consider that usually transition processes are characterized not by one but various different modes (Dolata 2013). The role of certain developments can only be interpreted adequately from a retrospective. Especially when dealing with ambiguous categories like layering, it is difficult to make any binding statements, when processes of transitions are still open. In the early 1980s, it was not ultimately clear whether wind power would remain a small gift to the antinuclear movement or become the door opener for *sustainable transitions* or even *transformations*.

Summary

Several decades ago, there already were good reasons for a transition of the world's energy system toward sustainability. However, only in recent years have countries begun carefully to expand their share of renewable energies.

To understand energy systems as socio-technical regimes means striving for a rejection of those viewpoints that tend to reduce energy supply to a set of technical artifacts. Overoptimistic positions that assume that a transition to sustainability would only require top-down legislation ought to be challenged as well.

A socio-technical regime is a complex entity that consists of actors, institutions, *and* technology. For an adequate conceptualization of the dynamics of such regimes, especially the MLP, strategic action fields and different modes of transition (Mahoney and Thelen 2010) were applied here.

With or without implicit and explicit reference to these concepts, the crucial factors that support or hinder a regime transition were presented. Transitions will be supported by the activity of social movements and niche actors like ecological pioneers and proper legislative rules, especially if these include exnovation policies. Usually, the latter will only occur in the framework of a broader governance process. In contrast, the main constraints of a transition are as follows: economic interests, networks between industrial and political spheres, economics of scale, institutional reproduction, market barriers against new actors, and emotional factors. Finally, some Janus-faced determinants are considered; depending on their alignment, they can either foster or prevent a destabilization: narratives, new technologies, innovations, external shocks, consumer lifestyles, and the adaptive skills of the regime actors.

In section the "Application to the Dynamics of Energy Regimes," some historical energy transitions were illustrated. For a better understanding of these empirical developments, the crucial factors influencing transitions were applied, as were the concepts described. They are helpful for a deeper understanding of socio-technical transitions. However, empirical analysis requires a reflexive, creative, and open application of the presented theoretical approaches to illuminate a given context adequately.

Cross-References

▶ Energy Democracy and Participation in Energy Transitions
▶ Energy Governance in Denmark
▶ Energy Governance in Europe: Country Comparison and Conclusion
▶ Energy Governance in France

▶ Energy Governance in Germany
▶ Energy Governance in the United Kingdom

Acknowledgments The author thanks the German Federal Ministry of Education and Research for financial support. This text was written within the frame of the ENavi project, which pursues a comprehensive inter- and transdisciplinary analysis of the German energy transition. The author is very grateful for many helpful and constructive comments by Angela Pohlmann (University of Hamburg) and coeditor Jörg Kemmerzell (TU Darmstadt). Moreover, he thanks Eduardo X. Fargas, who did the language check.

References

Andrews-Speed, P. (2016). Applying institutional theory to the low-carbon energy transition. *Energy Research & Social Science, 13*, 216–225. https://doi.org/10.1016/j.erss.2015.12.011.

Araújo, K. (2014). The emerging field of energy transitions: Progress, challenges, and opportunities. *Energy Research & Social Science, 1*, 112–121. https://doi.org/10.1016/j.erss.2014.03.002.

Bakke, G. (2016). *The grid: The fraying wires between Americans and our energy future.* New York/London/Oxford/New Delhi/Sydney: Bloomsbury.

Berlo, K., & Wagner, O. (2015). Strukturkonservierende Regime-Elemente der Stromwirtschaft als Hemmnis einer kommunal getragenen Energiewende. Eine Akteursanalyse aus der Multi-Level-Perspektive der Transitionsforschung. *Momentum quarterly. Zeitschrift für Sozialen Fortschritt., 4*(4), 233–253.

Beyer, J. (2005). Pfadabhängigkeit ist nicht gleich Pfadabhängigkeit! Wider den impliziten Konservatismus eines gängigen Konzepts. *Zeitschrift für Soziologie, 34*(1), 5–21.

Byzio, A., Heine, H., Mautz, R., & Rosenbaum, W. (2002). *Zwischen Solidarhandeln und Marktorientierung. Ökologische Innovationen in selbstorganisierten Projekten – autofreies Wohnen, Car-Sharing und Windenergienutzung.* Göttingen: Soziologisches Forschungsinstitut.

David, M. (2017). Moving beyond the heuristic of creative destruction: Targeting exnovation with policy mixes for energy transitions. *Energy Research & Social Science, 33*, 138–146. https://doi.org/10.1016/j.erss.2017.09.023.

Dolata, U. (2013). *The transformative capacity of new technologies. A theory of sociotechnical change.* London/New York: Routledge.

DONG. (2017). *DONG energy to stop all coal use by 2023.* Press release, 07-02-2017. https://stateofgreen.com/en/partners/Ørsted/news/dong-energy-to-stop-all-use-of-coal-by-2023/. Accessed: July 26, 2018.

Edenhofer, O., Steckel, J. C., Jakob, M., & Bertram, C. (2018). Reports of coal's terminal decline may be exaggerated. *Environmental Research Letters, 13*, 024019. https://doi.org/10.1088/1748-9326/aaa3a2.

Engels, A. (2016). Anthropogenic climate change: How to understand the weak links between scientific evidence, public perception, and low-carbon practices. *Energy and Emission Control Technologies, 4*, 17–26. https://doi.org/10.2147/EECT.S63005.

Fligstein, N., & McAdam, D. (2011). Towards a general theory of strategic action fields. *Sociological Theory, 3*, 1–26.

Fouquet, R. (2016). Historical energy transitions: Speed, prices and system transformation. *Energy Research & Social Science, 22*, 7–12. https://doi.org/10.1016/j.erss.2016.08.014.

Fuchs, G. (2012). Zur Governance von technologischen Innovationen im Energiesektor. In S. Bröchler, G. Aichholzer, & P. Scehaper-Rinkel (Eds.), *Theorie und Praxis von technology governance* (ITA-12-02_Sondernummer, pp. 65–78).

Garud, R., & Karnøe, P. (2001). Path creation as a process of mindful deviation. In R. Garud & P. Karnøe (Eds.), *Path dependence and creation* (pp. 1–38). Mahwah: Lawrence Earlbaum Associates.

Geels, F. W. (2010). Ontologies, socio-technical transitions (to sustainability), and the multi-level perspective. *Research Policy, 39*, 495–510. https://doi.org/10.1016/j.respol.2010.01.022.

Geels, F. W., & Kemp, R. (2012). The multi-level perspective as a new perspective for studying socio-technical transitions. In F. W. Geels, R. Kemp, G. Dudley, & G. Lyons (Eds.), *Automobility in transition? A socio-technical analysis of sustainable transport* (pp. 49–79). New York (et al.): Routledge.

Geels, F. W., & Schot, J. (2007). Typology of sociotechnical transition pathways. *Research Policy, 36*, 399–417. https://doi.org/10.1016/j.respol.2007.01.003.

Geels, F. W., Kern, F., Fuchs, G., Hinderer, N., Kungl, G., Mylan, J., Neukirch, M., & Wassermann, S. (2016). The enactment of socio-technical transition pathways: A reformulated typology and a comparative multi-level analysis of the German and UK low-carbon electricity transitions (1990–2014). *Research Policy, 45*(4), 896–913. https://doi.org/10.1016/j.respol.2016.01.015.

Grubler, A. (2012). Grand designs: Historical patterns and future scenarios of energy technological change. Historical case studies of energy technology innovation. In A. Grubler, F. Aguayo, K. S. Gallagher, M. Hekkert, K. Jiang, L. Mytelka, L. Neij, G. Nemet, & C. Wilson (Eds.), *The Global Energy Assessment (chapter 24)*. Cambridge: University Press.

Haas, T., & Sander, H. (2016). Shortcomings and perspectives of the German Energiewende. *Socialism and Democracy, 30*(2), 121–143.

Hadjilambrinos, C. (2000). Understanding technology choice in electricity industries: A comparative study of France and Denmark. *Energy Policy, 28*, 1111–1126.

Hellige, H. D. (2012). Transformationen und Transformationsblockaden im deutschen Energiesystem. Eine strukturgenetische Betrachtung der aktuellen Energiewende. *artec-paper* 185.

Hennicke, P., & Müller, M. (2005). *Weltmacht Energie. Herausforderung für Demokratie und Wohlstand*. Stuttgart: Hirzel.

Hennicke, P., Johnson, J. P., & Kohler, S. (1985). *Die Energiewende ist möglich*. Frankfurt/Main: S. Fischer.

Hermwille, L. (2016). The role of narratives in socio-technical transitions—Fukushima and the energy regimes of Japan, Germany, and the United Kingdom. *Energy Research & Social Science, 11*, 237–246. https://doi.org/10.1016/j.erss.2015.11.001.

Hughes, T. P. (1983). *Networks of power: electrification in western society, 1880–1930*. Baltimore (et al.): John Hopkins University Press.

International Energy Agency. (2008). *Combined heat and power. Evaluating the benefits of greater global investment*. https://www.iea.org/publications/freepublications/publication/chp_report.pdf. Accessed July 26, 2018.

Kern, F., Verhees, B., Raven, R., & Smith, A. (2016). Empowering sustainable niches: Comparing UK and Dutch offshore. *Technological Forecasting and Social Change, 100*, 344–355. https://doi.org/10.1016/j.techfore.2015.08.004.

Kivimaa, P., & Kern, F. (2015). Creative destruction or mere niche support? Innovation policy mixes for sustainability transitions. *Research Policy, 45*, 205–217. https://doi.org/10.1016/j.respol.2015.09.008.

Kuzemko, C., Lockwood, M., Mitchell, C., & Hoggett, R. (2015). Governing for sustainable energy system change: Politics, contexts and contingency. *Energy Research & Social Science, 12*, 96–105. https://doi.org/10.1016/j.erss.2015.12.022.

Mahoney, J., & Thelen, K. (2010). A gradual theory of institutional change. In J. Mahoney & K. Thelen (Eds.), *Explaining institutional change: Ambiguity, agency, and power*. Cambridge: Cambridge University Press.

Mautz, R., Byzio, A., & Rosenbaum, W. (2008). *Auf dem Weg zur Energiewende: Die Entwicklung der Stromproduktion aus erneuerbaren Energien in Deutschland*. Göttingen: Universitätsverlag Göttingen.

Meadowcroft, J. (2009). What about the politics? Sustainable development, transition management, and long term energy transitions. *Policy Sciences, 42*, 323–340. https://doi.org/10.1007/s11077-009-9097-z.

Müller-Jung, J. (2016). Brasilien holzt den Regenwald massiv ab. Faz.net, 30 November 2016. http://www.faz.net/aktuell/wissen/erde-klima/brasilien-holzt-seinen-amazonas-regenwald-massiv-ab-14553093.html. Accessed July 18, 2018.

Neukirch, M. (2010). *Die internationale Pionierphase der Windenergienutzung*. Dissertation. Göttingen: University of Göttingen.

Neukirch, M. (2018). Die Energiewende in der Bundesrepublik Deutschland (1974–2017) – Reform, Revolution, oder Restauration? Makroperspektive auf einen Dauerkonflikt. *sozialpolitik.ch.*, 1/2018, 1–31. https://doi.org/10.18753/2297-8224-102.

Oelker, J. (2005). *Windgesichter: Aufbruch der Windenergie in Deutschland.* Dresden: Sonnenbuch Verlag.

Parag, Y., & Janda, K. B. (2014). More than filler: Middle actors and socio-technical change in the energy system from the "middle-out". *Energy Research & Social Science, 3*, 102–112. https://doi.org/10.1016/j.erss.2014.07.011.

Pbl. (2017). *Trends in global CO2 and total greenhouse gas emissions: Summary of the 2017 report*, 28-09-2017. http://www.pbl.nl/node/64128. Accessed July 16, 2018.

Reichardt, K., Rogge, K. S., & Negro, S. (2015). *Unpacking the policy processes for addressing systemic problems: The case of the technological innovation system of offshore wind in Germany.* Working Paper Sustainability and Innovation, S2/2015, Fraunhofer ISI, Karlsruhe.

Rip, A., & Kemp, R. (1998). Technological change. In S. Rayner & E. L. Malone (Eds.), *Human choice and climate change* (Vol. 2, pp. 327–399). Columbus: Battelle Press.

Rohracher, H. (2007). Die Wechselwirkung technischen und institutionellen Wandels in der Transformation von Energiesystemen. In U. Dolata & R. Werle (Eds.), *Gesellschaft und die Macht der Technik. Sozioökonomischer Wandel durch Technisierung.* Frankfurt/Main: Campus Verlag GmbH.

Smil, V. (2010). *Energy myths and realities: Bringing science to the energy policy debate.* Washington, DC: Rowman and Littlefield.

Smith, A., Voss, J. P., & Grin, J. (2010). Innovation studies and sustainability transitions: The allure of the multi-level perspective and its challenges. *Research Policy, 41*(6), 955–967. https://doi.org/10.1016/j.respol.2010.01.023.

Smith, A., Kern, F., Raven, R., & Verhees, B. (2014). Spaces for sustainable innovation: Solar photovoltaic electricity in the UK. *Technological Forecasting and Social Change, 81*, 115–130. https://doi.org/10.1016/j.techfore.2013.02.001.

Sovacool, B. K. (2016). How long will it take? Conceptualizing the temporal dynamics of energy transitions. *Energy Research & Social Science, 13*, 202–215. https://doi.org/10.1016/j.erss.2015.12.020.

State of Green. (2017). *Denmark to be coal free by 2030.* Press declaration, 16 November 2017. https://stateofgreen.com/en/partners/state-of-green/news/denmark-to-be-coal-free-by-2030/. Accessed July 26, 2018.

Statista. (2018). *Produktion von Fleisch weltweit in den Jahren 1961 bis 2018* (in Millionen Tonnen Schlachtgewicht). https://de.statista.com/statistik/daten/studie/28782/umfrage/die-globale-fleischerzeugung-seit-1990/. Accessed July 18, 2018.

Stegmaier, P., Kuhlmann, S., & Visser, V. R. (2014). The discontinuation of socio-technical systems as a governance problem. In S. Borras & J. Edler (Eds.), *The governance of socio-technical systems* (Eu-SPRI forum on science, technology and innovation policy series) (pp. 111–128). Edward Elgar Publishing. https://doi.org/10.4337/9781784710194.

Streeck, W., & Thelen, K. (2005). Introduction: Institutional change in advanced political economies. In W. Streeck & K. Thelen (Eds.), *Beyond continuity. Intitutional change in advanced political economies* (pp. 1–39). Oxford: Oxford University Press.

Strunz, S. (2014). The German energy transition as a regime shift. *Ecological Economics, 100*(April 2014), 150–158. https://doi.org/10.1016/j.ecolecon.2014.01.019.

Unruh, G. C. (2000). Understanding carbon lock-in. *Energy Policy, 28*, 817–830. https://doi.org/10.1016/S0301-4215(00)00070-7.

Van der Vleuten, E. (1999). Constructing centralized electricity supply in Denmark and the Netherlands: An actor group perspective. *Centaurus, 41*, 3–36. https://doi.org/10.1111/j.1600-0498.1999.tb00273.x.

Van der Vleuten, E., & Raven, R. (2006). Lock-in and change: Distributed generation in Denmark in a long-term perspective. *Energy Policy, 34*(18), 3739–3748. https://doi.org/10.1016/j.enpol.2005.08.016.

Weiland, S. (2007). *Politik der Ideen. Nachhaltige Entwicklung in Deutschland, Großbritannien und den USA*. Wiesbaden: VS Verlag für Sozialwissenschaften.

Wille, J. (2016). Warnung vor Investitions-Blase. Ende des Kohle-Booms in Sicht. *Neue Energie*, 6 April 2016. https://www.neueenergie.net/wirtschaft/markt/ende-des-kohle-booms-ist-in-sicht. Accessed July 17, 2018.

Wind Europe. (2018). *Wind in power 2017. Annual combined onshore and offshore wind energy statistics*. https://windeurope.org/wp-content/uploads/files/about-wind/statistics/WindEurope-Annual-Statistics-2017.pdf. Accessed: November 14, 2018.

Energy Democracy and Participation in Energy Transitions

3

Cornelia Fraune

Contents

Introduction	50
Energy Democracy and Participatory Governance	52
Citizen Participation in Energy Transformation Reviewed	54
Community Energy	55
Participation in the Context of Spatial Planning	57
Participation in Energy Policy-Making at the Large-Scale	59
Conclusion	60
Cross-References	62
References	62

Abstract

The democratization of energy systems by citizen participation has been an important characteristic of the discourse on energy transformation processes. On the one hand, the material features of renewable energy technologies allow for new actors in energy supply. On the other hand, unconventional political participation is discussed as a mean for enhancing the legitimacy and effectiveness of energy transformation processes. But energy transformation processes also seem to be decelerated by democratic procedure. By utilizing both energy democracy and participatory governance as analytical lens, it will be argued that the evolvement of new forms of citizen participation cannot only be traced back to the material features of renewable energy technologies but are also dependent on political decisions and policies. Furthermore, legitimacy as well as effectiveness of democratic decision-making can be decreased by citizen participation if agency and mandate of the latter are not explained transparently.

C. Fraune (✉)
Institute of Political Science, Technical University of Darmstadt, Darmstadt, Germany
e-mail: cornelia.fraune@tu-darmstadt.de

© Springer Nature Switzerland AG 2022
M. Knodt, J. Kemmerzell (eds.), *Handbook of Energy Governance in Europe*,
https://doi.org/10.1007/978-3-030-43250-8_45

Keywords

Energy transformation · Renewable energy · Citizen participation · Energy democracy · Participatory governance · Forms of control and ownership · Democratic decision-making · Protest

Introduction

Participation seems to be a double-edged sword in the context of sustainable energy transformations. On the one hand, the shift of energy systems from large-scale fossil fuel-based energy technologies to decentralized, small-scale renewable energy technologies is not only characterized by a technological transformation but also allows for a transformation of the social dimensions of the energy system (Szulecki 2018, p. 22). In 1976, Amory Lovins introduced the "hard" versus the "soft" path paradigm that integrates technical and social dimensions of energy systems analytically. The hard path relies on energy supply by fossil fuels and nuclear power harnessed by centralized, large-scale technical systems operated by some powerful actors. Energy supply of the soft path is characterized by renewable energy sources harnessed by small-scale and decentralized technologies allowing for new models of ownership and therefore more egalitarian energy systems (Lovins 1976).

Albeit its oversimplification caused by the single dichotomy between hard and soft energy paths, this paradigm is still of analytical value today in order to grasp the technical and social differences of energy sources and related energy systems (Lilliestam and Hanger 2016; Brondi et al. 2014; Szarka 2007). The idea that sustainable energy transformations not only imply a shift in energy sources and technologies but also allow for a social reorganization of energy supply systems lies at the heart of the energy democracy literature (Szulecki 2018; Burke and Stephens 2018; van Veelen and van der Horst 2018). In the context of renewable energy transformations, the notion of energy democracy has gained prominence in order to describe "the normative goal of decarbonization and energy transformation" (Szulecki 2018, p. 23) as well as the process of energy transformation itself. In terms of the latter, a great part of the energy democracy literature assumes "that participation benefits the collective or public" and argues "for a need to reform how decisions are made around energy" (van Veelen and van der Horst 2018, p. 20).

On the other hand, it seems that renewable energy transformation processes are slowed down by democratic procedures (Burke and Stephens 2018, p. 78). For example, in Germany who has been a frontrunner regarding renewable energy capacity, the expansion of renewable energy installations, especially wind energy turbines, has been delayed or even prevented by public protest or by court disputes (Hoeft et al. 2017; Reusswig et al. 2016; Quentin 2019). Therefore, "[i]t would thus appear an unlikely and even poorly considered time to call for greater democratic engagement with the renewable energy transition" (Burke and Stephens 2018, p. 78).

Public protest and resistance against energy generation technologies are not a new phenomenon. For example, there had been fierce protest against nuclear energy in many European countries as well as in the United States (Kitschelt 1986; Knollmann 2018). Against this background, renewable energy technologies have been perceived as socially accepted, an assumption that has been backed by strong support of renewable energy technologies revealed by opinion polls (Wüstenhagen et al. 2007, p. 2683; Setton 2019). Indeed, compared to fossil fuels, renewable energy sources are superior in terms of meeting general public interests like global climate protection as well as reducing risks of energy supply for humans and the environment tremendously. But, the expansion of renewable energy installations, especially wind energy turbines, as part of energy transformations has shown that even renewable energy sources are characterized by trade-offs (Wüstenhagen et al. 2007, p. 2684; Mautz et al. 2008, p. 110). Beyond land use, the utilization of renewable energy sources arouses conflict issues like nature protection, animal protection, landscape preservation, or adverse health effects (Ellis and Ferraro 2016; Mautz et al. 2008; Weber et al. 2017; Leibenath et al. 2016). At large, these individual conflict issues reveal that energy transformation processes are not only a technological challenge but also a social one (Fournis and Fortin 2016, 3f.). The social challenge refers to questions like how to develop a sustainable or renewable system of energy supply, what are the ends of the transition, and how to deal with trade-offs (Mautz et al. 2008, p. 114).

Due to the material features of renewable energy technologies, energy transformation processes not only allow for unconventional citizen participation in collective decision-making processes but also allow for other forms of control and ownership of energy resources. Disregard the different forms of citizen participation, all participatory approaches interpret citizen participation as a mean to overhaul the energy system (van Veelen and van der Horst 2018, p. 22). Renewable energy transitions are not only characterized by a substitution of fuels but also by social challenges. It is not only a matter of techno-scientific policy-making but a matter of collective choice (Szarka 2007; Fournis and Fortin 2016) and therefore democratic decision-making (Szulecki 2018, pp. 29–30). Again, this finding is not new in the context of energy policy-making: "[…] they [grass-roots groups] wanted to avoid becoming an elite of counterexperts and instead wanted to create a political discourse between policymakers and citizens through which the goals of society could be set collectively. Only such a democratic process, they argued, could restore the legitimacy of political institutions" (Hager 1993, p. 43). Moreover, citizen participation has been a legal and political issue in the context of technology and environmental policy at the EU, national and international levels since the 1990s, especially concerning planning, in order to enhance public acceptance of technological change. These ideas and commitments are also applied in the context of energy transformation processes (Lee et al. 2013, p. 37).

Against this background, both the demand for more citizen participation within democratic decision-making and the decreasing legitimacy of renewable energy technologies is puzzling. This contribution addresses this puzzle by exploring different forms of citizen participation in the context of the expansion of renewable energy technologies. Theoretically, energy democracy and participatory governance are concerned with unconventional participation in energy transformation processes.

Energy democracy focuses mainly on the question on how the current political and energy system can be transformed by a shift from fossil to renewable energy sources, while participatory governance addresses the challenge of legitimate and effective decision-making in the context of the energy transformation process. Both concepts share their focus on deliberative democracy. They differ in their overall approach that is rather normative in the case of energy democracy and rather pragmatic in the case of participatory governance. In order to explore different forms of citizen participation, this contribution draws on empirical illustrations from the German Energy Transition. On the one hand, many different participatory innovations have been implemented in the context of the German Energy Transition (Fraune and Knodt 2017; Fraune 2015). On the other hand, the implementation of specific policies and projects like the expansion of wind energy arouses public protest and resistance that delayed or even prevented the realization of energy transformation policies (Reusswig et al. 2016; Hoeft et al. 2017).

Energy Democracy and Participatory Governance

By now, the term energy democracy does not refer to a coherent scientific concept but is rather characterized by an activist agenda (Burke and Stephens 2018, p. 79). Its utilization in the scientific literature refers to both an ideal outcome of renewable energy transition on the one hand and to processes of democratic procedure in order to reach the ideal outcome on the other hand (van Veelen and van der Horst 2018, p. 20). These processes are not "merely about the increasing participation of publics in energy policy-making" but rather about a transformation of the energy system from a capitalist, profit-seeking, and commodity-based centralized one to a public- and community-owned and community-operated one serving the public good (Burke and Stephens 2018, p. 79; Szulecki 2018, p. 35). This normative goal of energy transformation is inspired by the material features of renewable energy technologies, i.e., its scalability and distributed character, that allow for new forms of ownership and involvement within the energy system (Szulecki 2018, p. 22; van Veelen and van der Horst 2018, p. 22).

Theoretically, energy democracy refers mainly to associative democracy, material democracy, and deliberative democracy. The former ones are concerned with new forms of democratic engagement in order to reshape social life, while the latter is about collective opinion-formation. Since energy democracy literature is mainly concerned with the role of community-led associations within the energy system, it focuses on recasting the relationship between the state, the market, and civil society in respect to energy supply: "they see self-governing voluntary bodies as the primary means of both democratic governance and the organization of social life" (van Veelen and van der Horst 2018, p. 23). By not only focusing on new forms of public engagement within the energy system but also on access to and control of socioeconomic resources, energy democracy not only refers to associative but also to material democracy (van Veelen and van der Horst 2018, p. 24). Both concepts inform about the normative goals of energy democracy. Deliberative democracy rather refers to the question on how to achieve these normative goals of societal organization. Beyond the focus on discursive participation, the energy democracy literature is rather sparse concerning the question of how energy transformations could be governed.

New forms of democratic engagement can also be grasped by participatory governance. Against the background of the emergence of complex and ambiguous challenges of sustainable development, traditional forms of democratic collective decision-making, i.e., representative democracy and bureaucratic decision-making, have been called into question. Models of participatory governance have gained popularity, in both theoretical discussion and policy-making (Jäske 2019). Participatory governance is concerned with unconventional forms of political participation within democratic decision-making beyond conventional forms like democratic elections (Newig 2011; Newig and Kvarda 2012). It is argued that participatory governance in contrast to traditional forms of democratic collective decision-making addresses the complex and ambiguous challenges of sustainable development by allowing for collective learning on the one hand and by enhancing the of democratic decision-making on the other (Newig 2011, p. 485; Szulecki 2018, p. 30). It is assumed that the involvement of citizens and stakeholders in democratic decision-making not only facilitates an exchange of information but also advances comprehension of the challenges at hand as well as mutual understanding of different points of views and interests. Fostering individual and collective learning effectivity of policy-making should be enhanced (Newig 2011, p. 492). Legitimacy is rather referred to procedural aspects of participation. It is assumed that models of participatory governance allow for both innovative procedures of collective opinion-formation in terms of policy goals and priorities as well as increased transparency of democratic decision-making and therefore for greater control of political authorities (Newig 2011, pp. 485, 490).

The term "political participation" is used in order to describe all kinds of voluntary actions aimed at influencing collective decision-making (Barnes and Kaase 1979). From a governance perspective, participation is characterized by (Newig 2011, p. 487; Newig and Kvarda 2012, pp. 31–32):

- The mode collective will formation
- By collective decision-making
- By participation of actors in collective decision-making that are not state representatives
- By delegation of power
- By equal representation of legitimate interests

Participation differs from strict sovereign decision-making like administrative acts or court decisions, and therefore, its mode of collective will formation is characterized by a reconciliation of interests and problem-solving. Moreover, participation refers to collective decision-making, i.e., the decisions taken are generally binding and therefore political in nature (Newig 2011, p. 487). Actors need to be involved in collective decision-making that are not mandated officially with this task, i.e., state representatives (Renn 2005, p. 227; Newig 2011, p. 487). Participation is characterized by a delegation of power, i.e., non-state representative actors gain decision-making authority to a certain extent, and is therefore different from mere consultative or information-sharing kinds of involvement (Arnstein 1969, p. 222; Newig 2011, p. 487). Finally, participation from the governance perspective requires equal representation of legitimate interests and is therefore different from lobbying or corporatist policy-making (Newig 2011, p. 487).

While participatory governance requires the involvement of actors that are not state representatives in collective decision-making, the degree of participation can vary by the process, i.e., the mode of collective will formation as well as the delegation of power (Newig and Kvarda 2012, p. 32). Deliberative democracy is seen as the most appropriate mode of collective will formation in terms of participatory governance (Newig 2011, p. 487). According to the deliberative procedure, ideal citizens develop their preferences by democratic talk that is characterized by reasoning and mutual justification (Jäske 2019, p. 604). It is argued that this kind of democratic talk produces meta-consensus as well as intersubjective rationality. The former is defined as "agreement in the domain of relevant reasons or considerations (involving both beliefs and values) that ought to be taken into account, and on the character of the choices to be made" (Niemeyer and Dryzek 2007, p. 500). The latter "results from deliberative procedure in which both agreement and disagreement are possible, but are constrained by a condition of consistency regarding the reasons that produce a particular decision" (Niemeyer and Dryzek 2007, p. 500). A recent study of participatory innovations implemented at the local level in Finland supports these expectations empirically. Citizen participation in democratic decision-making processes seems to enhance perceived procedural fairness and thus enhances legitimacy if deliberative collective opinion-formation is enabled. Moreover, legitimacy is not only enhanced among those who participated in the deliberative procedure but also among the wider public (Jäske 2019, pp. 619–620).

Next, different forms of citizen participation in energy transformations will be as analytical lenses explored by utilizing both energy democracy and participatory governance. Although forms of citizen participation as well as the socioeconomic challenges linked to energy transformation processes are dependent on the specific national context, new forms of participation within in the energy system allowed by the material features of renewable energy technologies are similar—ownership and control of resources (van Veelen and van der Horst 2018, pp. 25, 22). Therefore, community ownership, citizen participation in planning, and collective decision-making will be explored by drawing on empirical illustrations from the German Energy Transition.

Citizen Participation in Energy Transformation Reviewed

In the context of the German Energy Transition, many different participatory innovations have been implemented in the context of ownership of energy generation technologies, spatial planning, as well as policy-making. By drawing on both energy democracy and participatory governance, it will be argued that the evolvement of new forms of citizen participation cannot only be traced back to the material features of renewable energy technologies but are also dependent on political decisions and policies.

Community Energy

Participation of citizens as well as local and regional authorities in energy markets is considered as an important measure to meet the EU's renewable energy targets as well as to realize energy democracy (European Commission 2015, pp. 8–9). Community energy is seen as the "highest level of citizen power as it confers to the control over the decision-making process and its outcomes" (Gorroño-Albizu et al. 2019, p. 1) in energy transition. By now, a common definition of the term community energy does not exist in the literature. Hence, very different empirical phenomena of ownership of renewable energy technologies are addressed by community energy like ownership by individuals, small group of local residents, local authorities, etc. What these different kinds of ownership have in common is that they are different from traditional ownership of energy technologies by privately or state-owned large-scale companies (Gorroño-Albizu et al. 2019, p. 2). In contrast to large-scale fossil fuel-based energy technologies, the material features of renewable energy technologies allow for these new forms of ownership and different forms of investors (Szulecki 2018, p. 22; van Veelen and van der Horst 2018, p. 22).

The energy democracy literature is especially concerned with community energy. It rests on the idea that the material features of renewable energy technologies described above allow for new forms of participation in the energy system, not only but especially in terms of energy-generating technologies (van Veelen and van der Horst 2018, pp. 22–23). Theoretically, the energy democracy literature mainly refers to the idea of associative democracy: "The most clearly identifiable form of democracy that is apparent in the energy democracy literature is associative democracy. [...] both associative democracy and energy democracy proponents extend the notion of participation by focusing on how social life is organized. The associative view advocated by many of those arguing for greater energy democracy thus focuses particularly on recasting the relationship between the state, the market, and civil society through a reorganisation of how and where energy resources are *controlled*. [...] these associative forms of democratic governance are means to link procedural and substantive dimensions of democracy, where the management of social affairs by voluntary and self-governing associations is deemed to ensure that both citizen choice and public welfare are best served" (van Veelen and van der Horst 2018, pp. 23–24). But community energy defined as an increased democratization of the energy system depends on institutional incentives determined by the political process rather than on the material features of renewable energy technologies (Gorroño-Albizu et al. 2019, p. 2; van Veelen and van der Horst 2018, p. 23). By now, community energy is realized rather by citizen ownership than by public control and therefore does not fulfill the ideal of equal participation (Fraune 2015; Yildiz et al. 2015),

From a participatory governance perspective, the increase of community energy can be rather traced back to enhance the effectiveness of renewable energy policy. The main prominent examples of community ownership in Europe are Denmark and Germany that are the two countries with the highest share of community ownership in the European Union (Heinrich Böll Foundation et al. 2018, p. 16). In both countries, the high share of community energy in renewable energy has not been induced by the technical features of renewable energy technologies but by politics (Mendonça et al. 2009; Meyer 2007). In Germany, renewable energy technologies became part of the energy policy agenda in the light of social conflicts about both the use of nuclear energy and about environmental sustainability of energy supply in the 1970s and 1980s (Mautz 2012, p. 153). As a result, research and development programs have been implemented by the German government. Initially, these programs aimed at integrating renewable energy technologies into the existing large-scale system of energy supply. The most prominent project has been the so-called GROWIAN project, an onshore wind energy power plant mainly operated by traditional big energy utilities. The project has been started in 1977 and has been terminated in 1987 due to technical challenges on the one hand as well as due to insufficient interest of the big energy utilities in renewable energy technologies on the other (Mautz 2012, p. 153; Mautz et al. 2008, p. 50). In consequence, the German government changed its research and development policy completely. Governmental policy did not focus on supporting pilot projects invented by professional developers and manufacturers anymore but on supporting private operators (Mautz et al. 2008, p. 52).

The expansion of community energy has been bolstered by the introduction of feed-in tariffs in 1991 (Mautz et al. 2008, 86ff). Against the background of both external pressure by the EU Commission's State Aid Guidelines and domestic debates about the affordability of the energy transition in light of increasing costs of renewable energy deployment, the German government implemented a stepwise shift of the national support scheme for renewable energy from a price-based to a volume-based support scheme in 2014. In consequence, the incentive for private operators to invest in renewable energy generation technologies decreased, and the plurality of actors has been reduced (Tews 2018, 2019). Therefore, community energy expansion in Germany depends rather on the governmental choice of the regulatory mechanism to expand renewable energy, i.e., regulation by the market economy through private investment complemented by a government-financed support scheme (Klagge 2013).

Beyond the expansion of renewable energy technologies, community energy is seen as instrumental for enhancing social acceptance of renewable energy technologies (Tews 2019, p. 291). In the context of the German Energy Transition, empirical research has shown that informative participation is preferred over financial participation, at least in the context of wind energy (Langer et al. 2017, p. 69). Informative participation is realized in the context of spatial planning that will be explored next.

Participation in the Context of Spatial Planning

The rapid expansion of renewable energy technologies revealed that acceptance of renewable energy transformation is dependent on the processes of conflict regulation rather than on the material features of renewable energy technologies (Zoellner et al. 2008, p. 4137). Since the German Energy Transition has always been supported by a large majority of the German population, it is argued that acceptance of the German Energy Transition is rather challenged by specific measures of their implementation like expansion of wind energy technologies or transmission lines (Setton 2019; Sonnberger and Ruddat 2016; Renn 2015) Therefore, the German Energy Transition is primarily perceived as a challenge of infrastructure policy-making that is governed by spatial planning (Fraune et al. 2019, p. 9).

Especially in the context of both the expansion of wind energy technology and the electricity grid, many renewable energy projects aroused protest and resistance (Hoeft et al. 2017; Reusswig et al. 2016; Neukirch 2013). Research on public acceptance usually assumes that the conflicts about renewable energy expansion are mainly characterized by distributional issues. According to the theory of procedural justice, it is hypothesized that public acceptance of specific renewable energy projects mainly depends on a fair distribution of benefits and burdens (Renn 2015, p. 140; Zoellner et al. 2008, p. 4137). This also implies the assumption that renewable energy projects primarily refer to local concerns (Devine-Wright and Batel 2017, p. 111).

For both, the expansion of renewable energy technologies and grid expansion, citizen participation measures are implemented by law in the context of spatial planning (Huge and Roßnagel 2018; Volkert 2013; Schadtle 2013; Schweizer and Bovet 2016). Beyond aims like protection of individual rights, information, or transparency of administrative behavior, another purpose of citizen participation is seen to enhance legitimacy of the actual energy transformation project. The idea is to complement institutions of representative democracy by procedures allowing for conflict regulation not only by voting but also by deliberation (Ziekow 2012, D 18). Against this background, it has turned out that a decent level of public acceptance of energy transition measures will neither be reached by expanding citizen participation measures quantitatively (Volkert 2013, p. 141) or by optimizing individual participation measures (Fraune and Knodt 2019, p. 163) alone. Therefore, research is concerned with processes of conflict regulation by citizen participation (Eichenauer 2018). Beyond processes of conflict regulation, current research also focuses on the contents of conflicts dealt within these processes (Fraune et al. 2019, pp. 8–11).

Research on public protest and resistance in the context of the German Energy Transition shows that these conflicts are about quite fundamental issues like the design and implementation of a renewable energy system (Reusswig et al. 2016, p. 225; Wirth and Leibenath 2017, p. 396). Therefore, although a large majority of the German population supports the energy transition in principal (Setton 2019), the choice of aims, priorities, and policy instruments are a political matter rather than a technical one and are therefore characterized by value conflicts rather than distributional ones (Fournis and Fortin 2016; MacArthur 2016, p. 633). However, citizen participation within the context of spatial planning does not allow for conflict regulation in terms of value conflicts. The reason is the multilevel governance system of the German Energy Transition, which is characterized by two dimensions of governance: political regulation and spatial planning that are interrelated by a hierarchical relationship. The goals and priorities in terms of the specific design of the renewable energy system, in terms of choice of technological options as well as in terms of quantitative measures of renewable energy generation, are determined by political regulation at the national and federal levels. Spatial planning that is governed at the regional and local levels needs to provide the space necessary in order to reach these goals (Klagge 2013).

In consequence, spatial planning does not allow for conflict regulation in terms of value conflicts. There is no space given for the negotiation of emission limit values concerning noise, for example, that yield legally defined priorities in terms of health issues and renewable energy technologies (Leibenath et al. 2016, p. 211). Moreover, there is no space given for the negotiation of issues that are not operationalizable like changes of landscape and related issues like loss in values of property or perceived loss of home (Huge and Roßnagel 2018, p. 616; Ziekow 2012, D 73).

Both concepts, participatory governance and energy democracy, refer to deliberative democracy as adequate form of collective opinion-formation. It is argued that complementing institutions of representative democracy by deliberative democracy enhances the legitimacy of policy-making in the context of large-scale projects like the energy transition that are characterized by noticeable changes for the citizens due to their influence on the economic, social, and cultural future as well as by incongruent cost-benefit structures of different social groups (Ritzi 2013, p. 80): "[...] the implementation of deliberative groups from the perspective of legitimacy seems to be more promising than the increased used of direct democratic referendums, because deliberative modes of consultation are able to build a "second stage" of legitimacy that supplements the legitimacy of representative processes in an adequate way by enhancing its "epistemic procedural legitimacy"'" (Ritzi 2013, p. 78). Normatively, democratic decision-making needs to accomplish the requirements of legitimacy. Democratic legitimacy is a multidimensional concept; it can be distinguished between input legitimacy, output legitimacy, and throughput legitimacy (Scharpf 1972; Schmidt 2013). Different concepts of democracy accomplish each of these dimensions to different extent, no concept can claim to produce more legitimate outcomes than others: "Thus no law, whether made by aggregation, by deliberation to consensus, or by a mixture of the two, is ever fully legitimate. Legitimacy is a spectrum, not a dichotomy" (Mansbridge 2007, p. 263). Although there exist some severe concerns regarding deliberative democracy in terms of its idealization of a common good as well as its realization in large-scale contexts, deliberative democracy seems an appropriate mode of collective opinion-formation in the context of energy transitions.

The difference between energy democracy and participatory governance approaches is the assumption about the goals and priorities in democratic decision-making.

In the energy democracy literature, there exist the assumption about a shared vision of the "future utopia" conflicts are not well acknowledged (van Veelen and van der Horst 2018, p. 24). The participatory governance approach is rather concerned with conflict regulation by unconventional citizen participation. But participation needs to be seen in the context of the governance system (Fraune and Knodt 2017).

Participation in Energy Policy-Making at the Large-Scale

In the context of the German energy transition, citizen participation took also place in the context of political regulation in order to consult policy-makers (Erhard et al. 2013, p. 89). To establish the so-called citizen dialogues (*Bürgerdialoge*) at large-scale had been an aim of the coalition agreement between the Christian Democratic Union, the Christian Social Union, and the Free Democratic Party in 2009. In the light of the Fukushima disaster and the governmental decision to implement a nuclear phase-out until 2022, energy transformation gained salience, and therefore, the Federal Ministry of Education and Research organized a citizen dialogue on the future use of energy technologies that took place between July and September 2011. The citizen dialogue was organized as a bottom-up participatory process consisting of different participatory formats at different scales: citizen workshops at the local scale, citizen conferences at the regional scale, and finally a citizen summit at the national scale (Erhard et al. 2013, pp. 58–59).

Regarding the issues to be discussed, it was guided by two questions defined in accordance with recommendations from the German Ethics Commission for a Safe Energy Supply: (1) "which technologies are needed to implement an energy transition and (2) which requirements must these technologies meet to achieve energy transition goals on the one hand and to be supported by citizens at the local level on the other?" (BMBF 2011). As a result, the citizen dialogue recommended to implement a sustainable energy transformation by a decentralized system of renewable energy supply and by improving energy efficiency through legislation, research, and development as well as education (BMBF 2011).

The citizen dialogue has been the only participatory measure in the context of the German Energy Transition at the national scale. Due to its design features, it has been rather experimental in character. For example, the citizen workshops at the local scale were held in the metropolitan areas across 18 municipalities of different geographical locations rather than in rural areas where renewable energy technologies are deployed (Erhard et al. 2013, p. 59). Moreover, the policy recommendations have not been very specific. It was not made transparent on whether and how the results could be applied to parliamentary decision-making (Erhard et al. 2013, p. 89). Another critical dimension is timing and a lack of repetition (Fraune and Knodt 2017, p. 266). In the initial phase after the governmental decision on the nuclear phase-out, renewable energy projects have been described quite positively in the general discourse and in mass media discourse. Critical arguments have almost remained absent (Reusswig et al. 2016). In most cases, opposition at the local level has formed when specific wind energy projects have been discussed (Eichenauer 2016; Leibenath et al. 2016; Marg 2017; Reusswig et al. 2016; Wirth and Leibenath 2017).

From a perspective of energy democracy, the example of the citizen dialogue shows that "renewable energy transitions [..., are] unavoidably political processes as well as key opportunities for advancing renewable energy and democracy together" (Burke and Stephens 2018, p. 80). However, the example also exhibits that the conflicts within energy transition processes are not only characterized by socioeconomic challenges, i.e., a reordering of social and political relations (Burke and Stephens 2018, p. 80), but also involve conflicts about technical features as well as further aims and priorities in order to develop a sustainable energy system. As mentioned above, the use of renewable energy sources arouses conflict issues like nature protection, animal protection, landscape preservation, or adverse health effects (Mautz et al. 2008, p. 110; Weber et al. 2017, p. 227; Leibenath et al. 2016, p. 211). Although the energy democracy agenda mainly focuses on a "future utopia" of renewable energy systems, it also claims for greater inclusion of communities and local levels within energy transformation policies: "a massive shift of technologies within the modern energy sector present innumerable challenges as well as potential benefits. Greater democratic engagement would offer communities a means to steer energy transitions and shape the development of renewable energy futures" (Burke and Stephens 2018, p. 79).

Again, participatory governance complements the energy democracy literature by elaborating on how citizen participation can be realized. The example of the citizen dialogue shows that participation needs to be carefully designed in order to fulfill the goals of participatory governance, i.e., enhancing the legitimacy and effectiveness of democratic decision-making. Beyond establishing a deliberative process of collective opinion-formation, the integration of citizen participation within the multilevel governance system as well as the integration of citizen participation into the institutions of representative democracy is challenging (Fraune and Knodt 2017, 2019). Generally, the feasibility of implementing deliberative participatory processes at a large-scale and across different governance levels is questioned. But there exist some examples of bottom-up, large-scale deliberative processes. Informed by the National Public Policy Conferences in Brazil as empirical model, Thamy Pogrebinschi proposed a conceptual framework of institutional design criteria allowing for bottom- up deliberation across scales. These criteria address challenges of procedure, participation, and representation (Pogrebinschi 2013). Although this approach seems to be fruitful, it has not been realized in participatory energy governance so far (Fraune and Knodt 2017).

Conclusion

Concerning participation, both energy transition processes and energy transition literature yield puzzling results. Although different kinds of unconventional political participation have been realized in the context of energy transition processes, there is still a call for enhancing democratic engagement. This call is even more puzzling against the background of many examples of slowing down renewable energy transformation processes by democratic procedure. This chapter has explored existing forms of citizen participation within the German Energy Transition by using energy democracy and participatory governance as analytical lenses. It has been shown that energy democracy rather deals with the question on how both the current political and energy systems can be transformed by renewable energy transformation characterized by more distributed energy technologies allowing for new collective while participatory approaches in energy supply (van Veelen and van der Horst 2018), participatory governance is rather concerned with legitimate and effective decision-making in the context of the energy transformation process.

Energy democracy literature is especially concerned with describing an agenda for a renewable energy transition, i.e., the outcome or normative goal of such transformation processes (Szulecki 2018; van Veelen and van der Horst 2018). "The energy democracy agenda seeks to advance democratization and participation through democratically-planned and public- and community-owned and -operated renewable energy systems that serve the public interest and deliver tangible community benefits, [...]" (Burke and Stephens 2018, p. 79). Energy democracy is focusing on democratizing both energy and political systems by a reordering of social and political relations within the system of energy supply that are allowed by the specific technological characteristics of renewable energy (Burke and Stephens 2018, p. 80; van Veelen and van der Horst 2018, p. 22). But the energy democracy literature also discusses barriers for implementing their agenda (Burke and Stephens 2018, p. 79). The basic tensions of renewable energy transition are seen as a challenge that needs to be addressed by energy democracy: "The question of democratic outcomes also deserves attention, especially related to environmental protections and the concerns over pace of transition. How does energy democracy ensure a sufficiently rapid energy transition while protecting local and global ecosystems?" (Burke and Stephens 2018, p. 87).

While energy democracy rather deals with the question on how current political and energy systems can be transformed by renewable energy transformation (van Veelen and van der Horst 2018), participatory governance is rather concerned with legitimate and effective decision-making in the context of energy transformation processes. The analysis of participation measures implemented in the context of the German Energy Transition has shown that participation needs to be carefully designed in order to enhance both the legitimacy and effectiveness of democratic decision-making. Even more important in this respect is that legitimacy as well as effectiveness of democratic decision-making can be weakened by participatory governance if it is not well established. For example, in case of the German Energy Transition, empirical research reveals that opportunities of participatory governance rather increase than decrease resistance and protest against renewable energy policies (Eichenauer 2018, p. 329; Reusswig et al. 2016, p. 226). These findings can be explained by the concept of self-efficacy. Participatory governance increases people's belief in their agency to influence the decision-making process and therefore decreases their inclination to accept political decisions fatalistically. This is not to say that fatalism is a feasible strategy for gaining public acceptance of political decisions. On the contrary, fatalism destroys trust and increases disenchantment with politics (Renn 2015, p. 137). In order to enhance effectiveness and legitimacy of democratic decision-making by participatory governance, transparency of mandate of decision-making power is important. Citizens need to be informed about the degree of delegation by participatory governance measures in order to gain realistic expectations about their agency to influence the decision-making process (Schroeter et al. 2016, p. 122; Geßner and Zeccola 2019). By now, citizen participation in the context of the German Energy Transition does not allow for a public discourse about its aims and priorities neither at the local nor at the national level. In order to solve the puzzle of a call for enhancing democratic participation on the one hand and a deceleration of renewable energy transformation processes by democratic procedure on the other, innovative measures of unconventional political participation need to be established that allow for bottom-up deliberation across all governance levels.

Beyond the assumed positive effects of citizen participation on energy transformation processes by both energy democracy and participatory governance, empirical research on procedures of citizen participation in energy transitions also reveals its selectivity and inequalities determined by individual resource endowment among others (Kemmerzell and Selk 2020; Fraune 2015, 2018).

Cross-References

► Energy Governance in Denmark
► Energy Governance in Germany
► Transition of Energy Systems: Patterns of Stability and Change

Acknowledgments The work on this chapter has been financially supported by the German Federal Ministry of Education and Research (Bundesministerium für Bildung und Forschung, BMBF) in the context of the funding initiative Kopernikus Projects for the German Energy Transition (Project ENavi, grant number: 03SFK4P0).

References

Arnstein, S. R. (1969). A ladder of citizen participation. *Journal of the American Institute of Planners, 35*, 216–224.
Barnes, S. H., & Kaase, M. (Eds.). (1979). *Political action: Mass participation in five western democracies*. Beverly Hills: Sage.
BMBF. (2011). Der BMBF Bürgerdialog Energietechnologien für die Zukunft. Bundesministerium für Bildung und Forschung. http://www.forum-netzintegration.de/uploads/media/Brass_BMBF_27032012.pdf. Accessed 27 Apr 2017.
Brondi, S., Armenti, A., Cottone, P., Mazzara, B. M., & Sarrica, M. (2014). Parliamentary and press discourses on sustainable energy in Italy: No more hard paths, not yet soft paths. *Energy Research & Social Science, 2*, 38–48.
Burke, M. J., & Stephens, J. C. (2018). Political power and renewable energy futures: A critical review. *Energy Research & Social Science, 35*, 78–93.

Devine-Wright, P., & Batel, S. (2017). My neighbourhood, my country or my planet? The influence of multiple place attachments and climate change concern on social acceptance of energy infrastructure. *Global Environmental Change, 47*, 110–120.

Eichenauer, E. (2016). Im Gegenwind – Lokaler Widerstand gegen den Bau von Windkraftanlagen in Brandenburg: Ergebnisse einer Onlinebefragung. Potsdam-Institut für Klimafolgenforschung e.V. http://energiekonflikte.de/fileadmin/template/Daten/Ergebnisse/Arbeitspapiere/Eichenauer_2016_Arbeitspapier_Waldkleeblatt.pdf. Accessed 28 Apr 2017.

Eichenauer, E. (2018). Energiekonflikte – Proteste gegen Windkraftanlagen als Spiegel demokratischer Defizite. In J. Radtke & N. Kersting (Eds.), *Energiewende* (pp. 315–341). Wiesbaden: Springer Fachmedien Wiesbaden.

Ellis, G., & Ferraro, G. (2016). The social acceptance of wind energy: Where we stand and the path ahead. https://publications.jrc.ec.europa.eu/repository/bitstream/JRC103743/jrc103743_2016.7095_src_en_social%20acceptance%20of%20wind_am%20-%20gf%20final.pdf. Accessed 10 Dec 2019.

Erhard, J., Lauwers, S., & Schmerz, S. (2013). Do unconventional forms of citizen participation add value to the quality of democracy in Germany? A case study of the Bürgerdialog Energietechnologien für die Zukunft. In A. Römmele & H. Banthien (Eds.), *Empowering citizens: Studies in collaborative democracy* (pp. 17–105). Baden-Baden: Nomos.

European Commission. (2015). The European Union leading in renewables. https://ec.europa.eu/energy/sites/ener/files/documents/cop21-brochure-web.pdf. Accessed 20 Oct 2019.

Fournis, Y., & Fortin, M.-J. (2016). From social 'acceptance' to social 'acceptability' of wind energy projects: Towards a territorial perspective. *Journal of Environmental Planning and Management, 60*, 1–21.

Fraune, C. (2015). Gender matters: Women, renewable energy, and citizen participation in Germany. *Energy Research & Social Science, 7*, 55–65.

Fraune, C. (2018). Bürgerbeteiligung in der Energiewende – auch für Bürgerinnen? In L. Holstenkamp & J. Radtke (Eds.), *Handbuch Energiewende und Partizipation* (pp. 759–767). Wiesbaden: Springer VS.

Fraune, C., & Knodt, M. (2017). Challenges of citizen participation in infrastructure policy-making in multi-level systems – The case of onshore wind energy expansion in Germany. *European Policy Analysis, 3*(2), 256–273.

Fraune, C., & Knodt, M. (2019). Politische Partizipation in der Mehrebenengovernance der Energiewende als institutionelles Beteiligungsparadox. In C. Fraune, M. Knodt, S. Gölz, & K. Langer (Eds.), *Akzeptanz und politische Partizipation in der Energietransformation* (pp. 159–182). Springer Fachmedien Wiesbaden: Wiesbaden.

Fraune, C., Knodt, M., Gölz, S., & Langer, K. (2019). Einleitung: Akzeptanz und politische Partizipation – Herausforderungen und Chancen für die Energiewende. In C. Fraune, M. Knodt, S. Gölz, & K. Langer (Eds.), *Akzeptanz und politische Partizipation in der Energietransformation* (pp. 1–26). Springer Fachmedien Wiesbaden: Wiesbaden.

Geßner, L., & Zeccola, M. (2019). Akzeptanzfaktoren in der Energiewende und ihre Übertragbarkeit in das Recht. In C. Fraune, M. Knodt, S. Gölz, & K. Langer (Eds.), *Akzeptanz und politische Partizipation in der Energietransformation* (pp. 133–158). Springer Fachmedien Wiesbaden: Wiesbaden.

Gorroño-Albizu, L., Sperling, K., & Djørup, S. (2019). The past, present and uncertain future of community energy in Denmark: Critically reviewing and conceptualising citizen ownership. *Energy Research & Social Science, 57*, 1–12.

Hager, C. (1993). Citizen movements and technological policymaking in Germany. *The Annals of the American Academy of Political and Social Science, 528*, 42–55.

Heinrich Böll Foundation, Friends of the Earth Europe, European Renewable Energies Federation, & Green European Foundation. (2018). Energy Atlas: Facts and figures about renewables in Europe 2018. https://www.boell.de/en/european-energy-atlas-2018. Accessed 20 Oct 2019.

Hoeft, C., Messinger-Zimmer, S., & Zilles, J. (2017). Einleitung. In C. Hoeft, S. Messinger-Zimmer, & J. Zilles (Eds.), *Bürgerproteste in Zeiten der Energiewende: Lokale Konflikte um Windkraft, Stromtrassen und Fracking* (pp. 9–39). Bielefeld: Transcript.

Huge, A., & Roßnagel, A. (2018). Möglichkeiten der Öffentlichkeitsbeteiligung in Planungs- und Genehmigungsverfahren von Windenergieanlagen. In L. Holstenkamp & J. Radtke (Eds.), *Handbuch Energiewende und Partizipation* (pp. 613–625). Springer Fachmedien Wiesbaden: Wiesbaden.

Jäske, M. (2019). Participatory innovations and maxi-publics: The influence of participation possibilities on perceived legitimacy at the local lelve in Finland. *European Journal of Political Research, 58*, 603–630.

Kemmerzell J., & Selk, V. (2020). Three responses to democracy problems of energy transitions. In Political Studies, in press. https://doi.org/10.1177/0032321720907556.

Kitschelt, H. P. (1986). Political opportunity structures and political protest: Anti-nuclear movements in four democracies. *British Journal of Political Science, 16*, 57–85.

Klagge, B. (2013). Governance-Prozesse für erneuerbare Energien – Akteure, Koordinations- und Steuerungsstrukturen. In B. Klagge & C. Arbach (Eds.), *Governance-Prozesse für erneuerbare Energien* (pp. 7–16). Hannover: ARL Akad. für Raumforschung und Landesplanung.

Knollmann, D. (2018). *Gescheiterte Kernenergiepolitik: Politische Veränderungsprozesse in Deutschland und den USA*. Baden-Baden: Nomos.

Langer, K., Decker, T., & Menrad, K. (2017). Public participation in wind energy projects located in Germany: Which form of participation is the key to acceptance? *Renewable Energy, 112*, 63–73.

Lee, M., Armeni, C., Cendra, J. d., Chaytor, S., Lock, S., Maslin, M., et al. (2013). Public participation and climate change infrastructure. *Journal of Environmental Law, 25*, 33–62.

Leibenath, M., Wirth, P., & Lintz, G. (2016). Just a talking shop?: – Informal participatory spatial planning for implementing state wind energy targets in Germany. *Utilities Policy, 41*, 206–213.

Lilliestam, J., & Hanger, S. (2016). Shades of green: Centralisation, decentralisation and controversy among European renewable electricity visions. *Energy Research & Social Science, 17*, 20–29.

Lovins, A. B. (1976). Energy strategy: The road not taken. *Foreign Affairs, 55*(1), 65–96.

MacArthur, J. L. (2016). Challenging public engagement: Participation, deliberation and power in renewable energy policy. *Journal of Environmental Studies and Sciences, 6*, 631–640.

Mansbridge, J. (2007). "Deliberative democracy" or "democratic deliberation"? In S. W. Rosenberg (Ed.), *Deliberation, participation and democracy* (pp. 251–271). London: Palgrave Macmillan UK.

Marg, S. (2017). "Ich kann einfach nicht mehr vertrauen." Demokratie- und Legitimitätsvorstellungen. In C. Hoeft, S. Messinger-Zimmer, & J. Zilles (Eds.), *Bürgerproteste in Zeiten der Energiewende: Lokale Konflikte um Windkraft, Stromtrassen und Fracking* (pp. 207–220). Bielefeld: Transcript.

Mautz, R. (2012). Atomausstieg und was dann? Probleme staatlicher Steuerung der Energiewende. *Der moderne Staat – Zeitschrift für Public Policy, Recht und Management, 5*(1), 149–168.

Mautz, R., Byzio, A., & Rosenbaum, W. (2008). *Auf dem Weg zur Energiewende; die Entwicklung der Stromproduktion aus erneuerbaren Energien in Deutschland; eine Studie aus dem Soziologischen Forschungsinstitut Göttingen (SOFI)*. Göttingen: Universitätsverlag Göttingen.

Mendonça, M., Lacey, S., & Hvelplund, F. (2009). Stability, participation and transparency in renewable energy policy: Lessons from Denmark and the United States. *Policy and Society, 27*, 379–398.

Meyer, N. I. (2007). Learning from wind energy policy in the EU: Lessons from Denmark, Sweden and Spain. *European Environment, 17*, 347–362.

Neukirch, M. (2013). Ausbau der Stromnetze – Konflikte und Perspektiven der deutschen EnergiewendeExtension of power grids – A contested area in the German Energy Transition. *GAIA – Ecological Perspectives for Science and Society, 22*, 138–139.

Newig, J. (2011). Partizipation und neue Formen der Governance. In M. Groß (Ed.), *Handbuch Umweltsoziologie* (pp. 485–502). VS Verlag für Sozialwissenschaften: Wiesbaden.

Newig, J., & Kvarda, E. (2012). Participation in environmental governance: Legitimate and effective? In K. Hogl, E. Kvarda, R. Nordbeck, & M. Pregernig (Eds.), *Environmental governance* (pp. 29–45). Cheltenham: Edward Elgar Publishing.

Niemeyer, S., & Dryzek, J. S. (2007). The ends of deliberation: Meta-consensus and intersubjective rationality as ideal outcomes. *Swiss Political Science Review, 13*, 497–526.

Pogrebinschi, T. (2013). The squared circle of participatory democracy: Scaling up deliberation to the national level. *Critical Policy Studies, 7*, 219–241.

Quentin, J. (2019). Hemmnisse beim Ausbau der Windenergie in Deutschland: Ergebnisse einer im 2. Quartal 2019 durchgeführten Branchenumfrage in Zusammenarbeit mit dem Bundesverband WindEnergie. https://www.fachagentur-windenergie.de/fileadmin/files/Veroeffentlichungen/Analysen/FA_Wind_Branchenumfrage_beklagte_WEA_Hemmnisse_DVOR_und_Militaer_07-2019.pdf. Accessed 13 Nov 2019.

Renn, O. (2005). Partizipation – ein schillernder Begriff: Reaktion auf drei Beiträge zum Thema "Partizipation" in GAIA 14/1 (2005) und GAIA 14/3 (2005) Partizipation – ein schillernder Begriff: Reaktion auf drei Beiträge zum Thema "Partizipation" in GAIA 14/1 (2005) und GAIA 14/3 (2005). *GAIA – Ecological Perspectives for Science and Society, 14*, 227–228.

Renn, O. (2015). Akzeptanz und Energiewende: Bürgerbeteiligung als Voraussetzung für gelingende Transformationsprozesse. In M. Heimbach-Steins (Ed.), *Ethische Herausforderungen der Energiewende* (pp. 133–154). Münster: Aschendorff.

Reusswig, F., Braun, F., Heger, I., Ludewig, T., Eichenauer, E., & Lass, W. (2016). Against the wind: Local opposition to the German Energiewende. *Utilities Policy, 41*, 214–227.

Ritzi, C. (2013). A second stage: The revitalization of democratic legitimacy with the help of deliberative forums. In A. Römmele & H. Schober (Eds.), *The governance of large-scale projects: Linking citizens and the state* (pp. 77–97). Baden-Baden: Nomos.

Schadtle, K. (2013). Neue Leitungen braucht das Land – und Europa!: Die Neuregelung der TEN-E-Leitlinien und deren Konsequenzen für das deutsche Planungs- und Genehmigungsrecht für Höchstspannungsleitungen unter besonderer Berücksichtigung der Vorschriften über Öffentlichkeitsbeteiligung. *Zeitschrift für Neues Energierecht, 17*(2), 126–132.

Scharpf, F. W. (1972). *Demokratietheorie zwischen Utopie und Anpassung*. Konstanz: Univ.-Verl.

Schmidt, V. A. (2013). Democracy and legitimacy in the European Union revisited: Input, output and 'throughput'. *Political Studies, 61*, 2–22.

Schroeter, R., Scheel, O., Renn, O., & Schweizer, P.-J. (2016). Testing the value of public participation in Germany: Theory, operationalization and a case study on the evaluation of participation. *Energy Research & Social Science, 13*, 116–125.

Schweizer, P.-J., & Bovet, J. (2016). The potential of public participation to facilitate infrastructure decision-making: Lessons from the German and European legal planning system for electricity grid expansion. *Utilities Policy, 42*, 64–73.

Setton, D. (2019). *Soziales Nachhaltigkeitsbarometer der Energiewende 2018: Kernaussagen und Zusammenfassung der wesentlichen Ergebnisse*. Potsdam: Institute for Advanced Sustainability Studies.

Sonnberger, M., & Ruddat, M. (2016). *Die gesellschaftliche Wahrnehmung der Energiewende: Ergebnisse einer deutschlandweiten Repräsentativbefragung*. Stuttgarter Beiträge zur Risiko- und Nachhaltigkeitsforschung, Nr. 34/Dezember 2016. Stuttgart. https://elib.uni-stuttgart.de/bitstream/11682/9035/1/Sonnberger%20%26%20Ruddat%20%282016%29%20-%20Die%20gesellschaftliche%20Wahrnehmung%20der%20Energiewende%20-V2.pdf. Accessed 30 Oct 2017.

Szarka, J. (2007). *Wind power in Europe: Politics, business and society* (Energy, climate and the environment series). New York: Palgrave Macmillan.

Szulecki, K. (2018). Conceptualizing energy democracy. *Environmental Politics, 27*, 21–41.

Tews, K. (2018). The crash of a policy pilot to legally define community energy. Evidence from the German Auction Scheme. *Sustainability, 10*, 1–12.

Tews, K. (2019). Privilegierte Marktzugangschancen für Bürgerenergie als Akzeptanzinstrument? Lehren aus dem Scheitern des deutschen Ausschreibungsdesigns für Windenergie. In C. Fraune, M. Knodt, S. Gölz, & K. Langer (Eds.), *Akzeptanz und politische Partizipation in der Energietransformation* (pp. 275–298). Springer Fachmedien Wiesbaden: Wiesbaden.

van Veelen, B., & van der Horst, D. (2018). What is energy democracy? Connecting social science energy research and political theory. *Energy Research & Social Science, 46*, 19–28.

Volkert, D. (2013). Legitimität und Legitimation von Partizipation: Zur Frage der Notwendigkeit einer Ausweitung der Öffentlichkeitsbeteiligung im Verwaltungsverfahren für das Gelingen der

Energiewende. In K. Töpfer, D. Volkert, & U. Mans (Eds.), *Verändern durch Wissen: Chancen und Herausforderungen demokratischer Beteiligung: von "Stuttgart 21" bis zur Energiewende* (pp. 133–147). München: oekom.

Weber, F., Roßmeier, A., Jenal, C., & Kühne, O. (2017). Landschaftswandel als Konflikt. In O. Kühne, H. Megerle, & F. Weber (Eds.), *Landschaftsästhetik und Landschaftswandel* (pp. 215–244). Springer Fachmedien Wiesbaden: Wiesbaden.

Wirth, P., & Leibenath, M. (2017). Die Rolle der Regionalplanung im Umgang mit Windenergiekonflikten in Deutschland und Perspektiven für die raumbezogene Forschung. *Raumforschung und Raumordnung, 75*, 389–398.

Wüstenhagen, R., Wolsink, M., & Bürer, M. J. (2007). Social acceptance of renewable energy innovation: An introduction to the concept. *Energy Policy, 35*, 2683–2691.

Yildiz, Ö., Rommel, J., Debor, S., Holstenkamp, L., Mey, F., Müller, J. R., et al. (2015). Renewable energy cooperatives as gatekeepers or facilitators? Recent developments in Germany and a multidisciplinary research agenda. *Energy Research & Social Science, 6*, 59–73.

Ziekow, J. (2012). *Neue Formen der Bürgerbeteiligung?: Planun und Zulassung von Projekten in der parlamentarischen Demokratie* (Gutachten D zum 69. Deutschen Juristentag). München: C.H. Beck.

Zoellner, J., Schweizer-Ries, P., & Wemheuer, C. (2008). Public acceptance of renewable energies: Results from case studies in Germany. *Energy Policy, 36*, 4136–4141.

Energy Poverty

Christoph Strünck

Contents

Introduction 68
How to Define and Measure Energy Poverty 68
Main Drivers of Energy Poverty 70
Income and Energy Poverty 71
Policy Instruments and Their Effectiveness 73
Energy Poverty and Social Rights 74
Future Directions 75
Cross-References 75
References 75

Abstract

Households need energy for everyday activities. Energy enables people to participate in society. However, access and affordability of energy are not equally distributed. If people are not able to use an appropriate amount of energy, or if energy bills push them below the poverty line, pundits phrase this phenomenon energy poverty. Energy poverty is a multidimensional phenomenon, cutting across different policy areas. This chapter scrutinizes how energy poverty can be defined, what the main drivers are, and which policies have been put in place. Internationally, there is no consensus how to measure energy poverty, nor is there comprehensive policy. Yet the debate on energy poverty touches on crucial issues of climate policy. Carbon tax initiatives will have to pay more attention to social inequality in private energy consumption if they are to be successful.

C. Strünck (✉)
Department of Social Sciences, University of Siegen, Siegen, Germany
e-mail: christoph.struenck@uni-siegen.de

Keywords

Poverty · Deprivation · Low income/high cost · Cutoffs · Thermal efficiency · Retrofitting · Winter fuel payments · Vulnerable consumers · Right to energy · Energy justice

Introduction

To most people, access to energy is essential for a decent living. Households need energy to heat or cool their shelter, to prepare food, or to wash clothes and dishes. One in ten persons does not have access to electricity, globally. Electric light or centralized heating does not only enable people to lead a social life. Modern grids also avoid risks that occur when people resort to candlelight or open fire. Thus, access to energy at home can be considered a basic social right such as access to clean water, although it is not yet part of the international bill of right. People are denied this right if they are not provided with the infrastructure, if they are cut off, or if they simply cannot afford energy. If people lack access to energy, it is a clear sign of poverty. There are major consequences: people can get ill; they can even starve.

You can also get poor by using energy. This is another dimension of energy poverty. There are multiple reasons for it: high energy prices, poor housing quality, inefficient household devices, and specific needs are crucial factors. People react differently when facing the risk of energy poverty: They might abstain from using adequate energy to save income. Or they spend the money which pushes them below the poverty line. Thus, access and affordability are two different dimensions of energy poverty. Which groups have limited access to energy? Who cannot afford the appropriate amount of energy? Which policies can ensure that energy is equally accessible? Those questions are guidelines for this contribution on energy poverty. Traditionally, energy poverty is a term applied to developing countries, whereas fuel poverty has long since used in the European debate. This chapter uses energy poverty as catch-all-term.

How to Define and Measure Energy Poverty

Due to the complexity of energy poverty, it is not easy to define the phenomenon, let alone to define who is affected. It starts with the term itself: Does energy cover electricity, heating, as well as mobility? Usually, energy poverty excludes expenditure for mobility. Thus, this chapter does not touch on mobility outside households.

Energy poverty is a multidimensional phenomenon. There are different approaches how to measure it (Castaño-Rosa et al. 2019). First of all, you can directly measure whether households are able to sufficiently heat and light their place. This takes original empirical work because established surveys do not include this kind of information. Secondly, you can check expenditure and relate it to standard costs as well as disposable income. Most prominent is the low income/ high cost indicator (LIHC) by John Hills (2012). Both the national median energy bill and the threshold of less than 60% of median income are combined to measure the share of energy poor. Thirdly, subjective indicators apply, asking people about their energy usage, their well-being, etc.

Eurostat provides data on the inability to keep one's home adequately warm or arrears in utility bills (Bouzarovski 2018). Each of these approaches faces different problems of gathering data, of calculating costs, and of constructing indices, let alone fundamental methodological problems. If you apply the low income/high cost indicator, you are likely to exclude those households with fairly low amounts of expenditure. However, a reasonable share of those households might miss out on appropriate use of energy just because they lack resources. So, the data you use for your indicator might be flawed. Additionally, any threshold to define vulnerable groups is arbitrary and to some extent subject of political judgment. It is no wonder, then, that the percentage of people affected can vary between 10% and 30%, depending on the indicator used (Berry 2018).

Measuring energy poverty takes data on income, expenditure, housing, energy use, as well as subjective data on attitudes and behavior. It also takes standards on necessary use of energy in households. In most countries, data on income are easiest to achieve. However, energy use in households is not monitored representatively; matching data on housing quality are often lacking. The quality and range of data are thus generally poor. For instance, there is no official survey of energy poverty; there is no consensus or standard on energy expenditure in private households. Consequently, there is no comparable date available, aside from some subjective assessments on heating, such as the Eurobarometer data for EU countries (Bouzarovski 2014).

There is no official definition at international level, either. There are several concepts, both qualitative and quantitative. The French government, for instance, applies a qualitative approach:

> A person suffers from energy poverty if he/she encounters particular difficulties in his/her accommodation in terms of energy supply related to the satisfaction of elementary needs, this being due to the inadequacy of financial resources or housing conditions. (Thomson and Snell 2016)

If you want to measure energy poverty based on this qualitative definition, you would ask people about their experiences and attitudes. There are governments that aim at quantitative definitions which lead to different indicators of energy poverty. The UK was among the first countries to develop policies against energy poverty. The current official approach reads:

> A household is considered to be fuel poor where they have required fuel costs that are above average (national median level). Were they to spend that amount, they would be left with a residual income below the official poverty line. (Department of Energy and Climate Change 2013)

Plenty of governments apply a simple indicator that relates to the pioneering work by Brenda Boardman (1988). When households spend more than 10% of their income on energy, they mostly belong to financially poor households. This is what she found in her empirical work. Thus, she created an indicator that is accessible yet methodologically flawed.

Aside from definition and indicators, policies are diverse, as well. In developing countries, energy poverty is a matter of access or disputable sources of energy (Sagar 2005). Large amounts of the population may be continuously or temporarily cut off from energy. This is a topic of exclusion and neglect. If governments are not capable of providing affordable energy through infrastructure, people might resort to individual solutions. Some of them, like petroleum heating or gas ovens, come with high risks to neighborhoods. They might cause environmental problems, as well. Fighting energy poverty in developing countries takes different policies. It is less about social policies but more about economic policy and infrastructure. However, a global understanding of energy poverty is unfolding (Bouzarovski and Petrova 2015).

In industrialized countries, tackling energy poverty can be an issue of energy policy, environmental policy, housing policy, and social policy. Policy instruments range from social benefits to subsidized tariffs or targeted housing schemes. Some governments see energy poverty as a specific policy challenge. Other governments assume that energy poverty is just another dimension of income poverty. Public debates on energy poverty have different reasons, too. One classic topic is winter mortality. The "paradox of excess winter mortality" is a well-established finding in early research on energy poverty (Healy 2003). It states that people living in areas with mild winters face the biggest risks of winter deaths. This is because insulation and quality of dwelling are getting worse toward Southern countries. However, the topic of winter deaths fueled the debate in the UK, too. Along with poor thermal insulation, the issue of energy poverty centered around heating (Bridge et al. 2018). In Germany, it was rising prices of electricity, due to government policies supporting renewable energy. This has sparked a debate about social inequality and energy transition (Großmann et al. 2017). Prices for electricity are among the highest worldwide.

Different policies reflect different national contexts of energy poverty. They also reveal different interests involved in setting the agenda for energy poverty. Some social movements blame big energy providers for blowing up the bills. Consequently, they expect a more decentralized system of renewable energy to safeguard against energy poverty. Other pundits and their constituencies argue just the other way: Funding renewables would rip off low-income households without yielding the benefits of cheaper energy from nature. Thus, energy poverty is a divisive issue in environmental and energy policy.

From a scientific point of view, there are three crucial questions that relate to each other: What are main factors that cause energy poverty? What is the link between income poverty and energy consumption? Which policy instruments are effective to tackle energy poverty?

Main Drivers of Energy Poverty

Low income, high energy costs, and poor housing are main drivers of energy poverty. Those factors aside, there are specific causes such as household structure, household energy needs, or regulatory issues. Looking at income, poor households have to spent large parts of their disposable income on food and energy. Statistically, those persons have less than 50% of the median household income or less. Reasons for income poverty are manifold, and they go far beyond the subject of energy poverty.

However, income poverty always relates to prices, expenditure, and household structure. If people live in cheap areas, their purchasing power might be well enough. If people can switch to cheaper products, this will have a similar effect. Yet in the case of energy, prices play a specific role. Theoretically, competitive markets might keep prices low. Overall, this has been the case in the USA or Japan. Contrary, the European Union saw steep rises in energy prices. Between 2005 and 2011, the average price for electricity in the EU rose by 29% (Jeliazkova 2014). People in post-Soviet countries in the EU have been facing dramatic increases, due to privatization. Especially in the EU, energy has a big price tag from governments. There are taxes, environmental schemes, and other variables that have effectively increased energy prices.

At the same time, poor households do not benefit from competitive markets as much as households that are better off. On the one hand, this is a behavioral trap, due to lack of information, energy literacy, or awareness. On the other hand, it is an issue of regulatory policy. In countries such as Germany, you might be handcuffed to expensive tariffs once you have a negative record with a rating agency. So, switching the energy provider is no option for those who would benefit most from cheaper tariffs.

There is another comparative disadvantage of poor households. Most of them live in buildings whose thermal efficiency is low. Rents might be affordable at first glance. However, energy costs per square meter are significantly higher. If landlords invest in thermal isolation, rents will be rising. This is a big financial burden for poor households. Energy efficient devices are expensive, and most poor households use dated technology that is energy-consuming.

Sociologically, poor households show different behavioral patterns when it comes to energy. If people are unemployed, they will stay home more often, using energy more intensely than people in full-time work. This leads to higher expenditure. On the other hand, poor households often miss out on using appropriate energy for heating or lighting to save costs. This is an issue of "deprivation," and it can even do harm to health (Tod and Hirst 2014). Poor households resort to strategies to compensate for their low income. As for energy, there is a lack of alternative strategies, though. Heating systems, thermal insulation, or household devices cannot be changed at all or only at higher costs.

Income and Energy Poverty

In industrialized countries, governments usually provide universal access to energy. However, daily energy is not a public good. Access is guaranteed, but no basic amount of energy is provided for free. Thus, energy poverty can be considered just another aspect of income poverty. Low-income households cannot adapt their tight budget. This is why they miss out on using energy or on using their money for other essential goods just to pay for energy. If people cannot afford enough energy, they are just lacking income. Following this perspective, there is no difference between not having enough money for energy and not having enough money for clothes or food. This approach denies that energy poverty is a phenomenon beyond income poverty (Kakwani and Silber 2014).

However, poverty is multidimensional. Even if social security provides a decent income, energy might cause challenges. Households that receive social benefits face specific challenges. Benefits might not be adjusted as fast as energy prices are rising. At least, expenditure for energy is partly compensated for in most countries. Low-income households that fall through the cracks of social security are worse off. They do not get compensation for energy spending, nor will they get advice by social administration. Thus, social security does not avert energy poverty per se (Strünck 2017).

Rising energy prices hit low-income households hardest (Templet 2001). Low-income households spend most of their disposable income on everyday consumption. Costs for housing represent the biggest share, including energy. And energy prices in the European Union have increased more than wages. This is because most European countries tax energy heavily. Additionally, households fund energy transition through redistributive schemes and tax-like instruments. Thus, even in an era of low inflation, higher prices for inevitable goods such as energy can do severe harm to low-income groups.

In some countries, energy poverty is predominantly a problem of low income not high expenditure. This might be the case in continental Europe, for instance, where the average thermal insulation and technical standards of buildings are in relatively good shape. However, even in those countries, low-income households are refined to older buildings with dated heating technology and energy-wasting devices (Buzar 2007). Additionally, indebted households are often banned from switching energy providers to save money. So even in countries with a decent housing quality, low-income households do not benefit as much from energy efficiency as middle-class households.

Low-income households are more likely to face cutoffs, too. Cutoffs result in absolute energy poverty, even in wealthy countries. If people cannot afford paying their energy bills, it might pile up an even bigger debt. Energy providers levy fines, and finally they can cut off households temporarily. Getting plugged into the network again will cost additional fees, feeding a vicious cycle of debt. There is no comprehensive regulation on cutoffs in the EU, for example (Bouzarovski et al. 2012).

Again, data and disclosure on this fundamental dimension of energy poverty are poor. For instance, EU member states are legally obliged to monitor and publish temporary disconnections. They are also urged to define vulnerable consumers that are exempted from cutoffs. Neither regulation is fully enforced throughout the EU (ACER 2018). Cutoffs are not necessarily a sign of energy poverty. Usually, cutoffs reveal lasting problems of indebted households. Considering energy a basic good, indebted households might stop paying their energy bills first, without anticipating huge additional costs that will follow. So, cutoffs can accelerate the spiraling threat of debt in low-income households.

Policy Instruments and Their Effectiveness

Only few governments recognize energy poverty as a distinctive policy issue. Furthermore, tackling energy poverty is often dealt with as an issue of social policy not energy policy. Indeed, energy poverty cuts across different policy areas such as energy policy, environmental policy, housing policy, social policy, and consumer policy. Prominent policy instruments range from financial support, over efficiency programs, to consumer protection and education. Most of them are tailored to the needs of "vulnerable" households (Csiba 2016). In the OECD area, especially in the EU, countries are urged to protect vulnerable consumers in energy markets. The European watchdog ACER regularly compiles data on those policies.

Financial support has different faces, and it can be linked to income or expenditure. As for income, measures start with means-tested welfare that might include energy-sensitive top ups. There are specific direct payments, too, such as winter fuel payments that may be even restricted to a smaller group of households such as the elderly. As for expenditure, social tariffs by energy providers are another tool. Regulated tariffs contradict competitive private energy markets, however. It does not come as a surprise that social tariffs largely occur in countries with large public energy providers. From an environmental perspective, subsidized tariffs are no sound policy. Households have to conceive the negative external effects of energy, so prices should be even higher. The selective impact could be compensated for by extra financial support for low-income households.

Increasing energy efficiency is another policy instrument (Dobbins and Pye 2016). It can be targeted to vulnerable consumers. Most measures are linked to retrofitting of buildings, focusing on deprived areas. Scandinavian countries have focused on energy-efficient social housing, implementing high standards that tenants do not have to pay for. There are local solutions, too. For instance, mini-contracting projects are popular throughout Europe. Energy providers offer cheap loans to finance efficient devices such as refrigerators. Those policies offer quick help, but they add to debts low-income households may already have piled up.

Consumer protection and education refer to averting cutoffs and saving energy, mainly. Energy providers can be obliged to advise consumers and to offer special support. Additionally, indebted consumers can be allowed to switch suppliers to save costs. Low-income households get advice on saving energy at home, provided by nonprofits. A prominent technological path is prepaid metering. It cannot completely avoid disconnection, but it can help to manage energy bills. Yet it does not effectively reduce costs. Consumer protection and education best work if they come as a precautionary measure. However, there is no comprehensive policy to reach out to vulnerable consumers in advance.

The UK is one of the pioneering countries in tackling energy poverty. Scientists and policy-makers put energy poverty on the agenda back in the 1990s. The UK has significantly more days with heating than any other European country (Schumacher et al. 2015). At the same time, scientists predict more than 125,000 people dying from inappropriate heating between 2015 and 2030 (NEA 2015). Accordingly, the focus has been on poor housing and thermal inefficiency. The affordable warmth scheme and winter fuel payments for the elderly are most prominent examples. Britain's regulatory body Ofgem is one of the rare agencies that have come up with defining vulnerable consumers (Ofgem 2019).

Targeting vulnerable households through energy efficiency is controversial. Pundits claim that only half of all deserving households benefit from retrofitting (Platt et al. 2013). Prepaid meters are ambivalent, too. They shift the burden to household's energy management without touching on structural issues such as bad housing. Generally, the effectiveness and efficiency of targeting are on doubt. Without having comprehensive monitoring, a lot of policy instruments might create windfall profits and leave others unprotected.

Belgium blurred the boundaries of energy policy most when some of its regions introduced a free basic provision of energy. This approach treated energy as a basic good, undermining the concept of privatized, competitive energy markets. It was cancelled in 2013, due to its high costs and efficiency problems (Strünck 2017).

Despite remarkable differences between countries, some policy features look similar. First of all, social security is supposed to better safeguard against rising energy prices. Secondly, schemes improving thermal efficiency figure prominently. Thirdly, low-income households are given advice on saving energy. This policy mix captures specific problems in industrialized countries. Energy poverty in the less developed world is a question of absolute poverty, lacking adequate access to basic energy. This is clearly an issue of infrastructure, energy policy, or economic policy.

Energy Poverty and Social Rights

As for industrialized countries, the debate on energy poverty sheds light on the social costs of energy transition. High-energy prices hit low-income households hardest. At the same time, technologies that help to raise energy efficiency do often benefit middle classes most. This is why some policy advocates urge an "inclusive agenda" of energy transition (N. Healy and Barry 2017). A lot of policy measures featuring renewable energy, electric cars, or insulating homes have had a strong middle-class bias. The EU and other bodies have long ago started to turn an eye to vulnerable consumers when it comes to using energy at home. However, there is no comprehensive approach toward energy poverty in the industrialized world. There is not even consensus that energy poverty is an issue of its own. However, NGOs and some grassroots movements have been drumming up support for a right to affordable and clean energy.

As for less-industrialized countries, energy poverty is an issue of social rights and basic infrastructure. A lack of universal grids, threats of permanent blackouts, and other obstacles leave poor people even more unprivileged. A right to energy is not yet enshrined in the international bill of rights, contrary to a right to water, food, and shelter. This might change, due to a growing global movement (Hui et al. 2017). This movement invokes Amartya Sen's Nobel Prize winning capability approach: The right to energy and the right to use energy are not just individual capabilities. They need a stable and equally accessible infrastructure; they need opportunities.

The debate on the right to energy is subject of lobbying, too. Governments as well as companies in developing countries seek their own right to roll out carbon-intensive industry (Bickerstaff et al. 2013). Thus, the right to energy is a contentious policy instrument in international environmental and energy policy, as well.

Future Directions

Modern societies are energy-driven. Given the overall impact of digitalization, this will even grow stronger. However, social inequality is also reflected in energy consumption. This is why the debate on energy poverty fuels approaches that seek to define and regulate basic goods, such as education, banking accounts, shelter, or access to clear water.

Additionally, international attempts to tax carbon will further drive up prices for energy. This might put more people at the risk of getting poor. So environmental policies have to be bolstered by social policy and compensating schemes. This is the broader context of energy poverty.

Scientists and policy-makers might not agree on indicators and policy measures for the time being. So, in a narrow sense, energy poverty is still a murky issue, lacking data and comprehensive policies. However, the social dimension of energy prices and energy infrastructure is looming big. Political terms such as the right to energy or energy justice might impact climate policy more than the clumsy expression of energy poverty.

Cross-References

▶ Energy Democracy and Participation in Energy Transitions
▶ Energy Governance in Germany
▶ Energy Governance in the United Kingdom
▶ Monitoring Energy Policy

References

ACER. (2018). *Annual report on the results of monitoring the internal electricity and natural gas markets in 2017 – Consumer empowerment volume*. Belgium: Brussels.

Berry, A. (Mars 2018). *Measuring energy poverty: Uncovering the multiple dimensions of energy poverty*. Working papers/CIRED. http://www2.centre-cired.fr/IMG/pdf/cired_wp_2018_69_berry.pdf

Bickerstaff, K., Walker, G., & Bulkeley, H. (2013). *Energy justice in a changing climate: Social equity and low carbon energy. Just Sustainabilities*. Zed Books. http://gbv.eblib.com/patron/FullRecord.aspx?p=1426381

Boardman, B. (1988). *Fuel poverty*. London: Belhaven Press.

Bouzarovski, S. (2014). Energy poverty in the European Union: Landscapes of vulnerability. *Wiley Interdisciplinary Reviews: Energy and Environment, 3*(3), 276–289.

Bouzarovski, S. (2018). *Energy poverty: (Dis) Assembling Europe's infrastructural divide* (1st ed. 2018). Cham, Switzerland: Springer.

Bouzarovski, S., & Petrova, S. (2015). A global perspective on domestic energy deprivation: Overcoming the energy poverty–fuel poverty binary. *Energy Research & Social Science, 10*, 31–40. https://doi.org/10.1016/j.erss.2015.06.007.

Bouzarovski, S., Petrova, S., & Sarlamanov, R. (2012). Energy poverty policies in the EU: A critical perspective. *Energy Policy, 49*, 76–82.

Bridge, G., Barr, S., Bouzarovski, S., Bradshaw, M., Brown, E., Bulkeley, H., & Walker, G. (2018). *Energy and society: A critical perspective*. Routledge. https://ebookcentral.proquest.com/lib/gbv/detail.action?docID=5405519

Buzar, S. (2007). *Energy poverty in Eastern Europe: Hidden geographies of deprivation*. Aldershot: Ashgate.

Castaño-Rosa, R., Solís-Guzmán, J., Rubio-Bellido, C., & Marrero, M. (2019). Towards a multiple-indicator approach to energy poverty in the European Union: A review. *Energy and Buildings, 193*, 36–48. https://doi.org/10.1016/j.enbuild.2019.03.039.

Csiba, K. (Ed.). (2016). *Energy poverty handbook*. European Union: Brussels. https://publications.europa.eu/en/publication-detail/-/publication/5e2b1b12-c03d-11e6-a6db-01aa75ed71a1/language-en/format-PDF/source-69560451. https://doi.org/10.2861/094050.

Department of Energy and Climate Change. (2013). *Fuel poverty report – Updated August 2013*. London: Department of Energy and Climate Change.

Dobbins, A., & Pye, S. (2016). Member State level regulation related to energy poverty and vulnerable consumers. In K. Csiba (Ed.), *Energy poverty handbook* (pp. 119–148). Brussels: European Union.

Großmann, K., Schaffrin, A., & Smigiel, C. (2017). *Energie und soziale Ungleichheit*. Wiesbaden: Springer Fachmedien Wiesbaden. https://doi.org/10.1007/978-3-658-11723-8.

Healy, J. D. (2003). Excess winter mortality in Europe: A cross country analysis identifying key risk factors. *Journal of Epidemiology and Community Health, 57*, 784–789.

Healy, N., & Barry, J. (2017). Politicizing energy justice and energy system transitions: Fossil fuel divestment and a "just transition". *Energy Policy, 108*, 451–459. https://doi.org/10.1016/j.enpol.2017.06.014.

Hills, J. (2012). *Getting the measure of fuel poverty: Final report of the fuel poverty review*. London: Department of Energy and Climate Change.

Hui, A., Day, R., & Walker, G. (Eds.). (2017). *Demanding energy: Space, time and change* (1st ed. 2018). Cham: Springer.

Jeliazkova, M. (2014). *Energy poverty: The three pillars approach*. Belgium: Brussels.

Kakwani, N., & Silber, J. (Eds.). (2014). *Many dimensions of poverty* (1st ed. 2007). London: Palgrave Macmillan

NEA. (2015). *UK fuel poverty monitor 2014–2015*. Newcastle Upon Tyne: National Energy Action.

Ofgem. (2019). *Consumer vulnerability strategy 2025*. London: Open Government Licence.

Platt, R., Aldridge, J., & Washan, P. (2013). *Help to heat: A solution to the affordability crisis in energy*. London: Institute for Public Policy Research.

Sagar, A. D. (2005). Alleviating energy poverty for the world's poor. *Energy Policy, 33*(11), 1367–1372. https://doi.org/10.1016/j.enpol.2004.01.001.

Schumacher, K., Cludius, J., Förster, H., Greiner, B., Hünecke, K., Kenkmann, T., & van Nuffel, L. (2015). *How to end energy poverty? Scrutiny of current EU and member states instruments*. Belgium: Brussels.

Strünck, C. (2017). *Energiearmut bekämpfen – Instrumente, Maßnahmen und Erfolge in Europa*. Bonn: Friedrich-Ebert-Stiftung Abteilung Wirtschafts- und Sozialpolitik.

Templet, P. H. (2001). Energy price disparity and public welfare. *Ecological Economics, 36*(3), 443–460. https://doi.org/10.1016/S0921-8009(00)00243-3.

Thomson, H., & Snell, C. (2016). Definitions and indicators of energy poverty across the EU. In K. Csiba (Ed.), *Energy poverty handbook* (pp. 99–115). Brussels: European Union.

Tod, A. M., & Hirst, J. (2014). *Health and inequality: Applying public health research to policy and practice*. Taylor and Francis. http://gbv.eblib.com/patron/FullRecord.aspx?p=1675908

Monitoring Energy Policy

Jonas J. Schoenefeld and Tim Rayner

Contents

Introduction	78
Policy Monitoring: Administrative Task or Political Exercise?	81
Steering and Control	82
Monitoring Costs	84
Cases in Energy Policy Monitoring	85
Monitoring at the International Level: The UNFCCC and Beyond	85
The Emergence and Significance of Monitoring Energy Policy in Europe	87
Monitoring at the Member State Level: United Kingdom and Germany	90
Future Directions	93
Cross-References	94
References	94

Abstract

Policy monitoring has been gaining importance in energy and climate governance. It is currently being heralded as a key solution for coordinating energy governance not only regionally in the emerging Energy Union in the European Union (EU), but also globally in the Paris Agreement on climate change. The core idea is that transparency through monitoring will incentivize actors to adopt policy pathways toward mutually agreed long-term energy and climate policy goals. In addition, monitoring of key indicators (e.g., use of certain kinds of energy), in particular, sectoral contexts, may be a necessary precursor to

---

J. J. Schoenefeld (✉)
Institute for Housing and Environment, Darmstadt, Germany

Tyndall Centre for Climate Change Research, University of East Anglia, Norwich, Norfolk, UK
e-mail: j.schoenefeld@iwu.de

T. Rayner
Tyndall Centre for Climate Change Research, University of East Anglia, Norwich, Norfolk, UK
e-mail: tim.rayner@uea.ac.uk

© Springer Nature Switzerland AG 2022
M. Knodt, J. Kemmerzell (eds.), *Handbook of Energy Governance in Europe*,
https://doi.org/10.1007/978-3-030-43250-8_43

evaluation and improved regulation. This chapter unpacks the concept of monitoring, reviews the emergence of energy and climate policy monitoring in the EU, and then details experiences with concrete monitoring regimes in different settings related to energy and climate policy, ranging from the United Nations (UN) to the EU, as well as nation states and nongovernmental actors. In so doing, it highlights various strands of emerging research and knowledge on monitoring structures, steering effects and costs, but also the need for further work, especially regarding usage and impact. Issues related to politics, coordination, and resources are likely to challenge monitoring regimes; further investigation should focus on the efficacy of monitoring systems, which many assume, but few have researched.

Keywords

Policy monitoring · Energy policy · Climate policy · UNFCCC · EU · Transparency

Introduction

A combination of rising needs for international coordination in energy and climate policy, and a receding willingness of many countries to share their sovereignty over energy matters due to diverging priorities, has precipitated a turn toward softer steering mechanisms. For example, European countries were unable to agree on binding renewable energy targets for the new 2030 package (Bürgin 2015; Ringel and Knodt 2018). One form of softer governance put forward to address such issues is policy monitoring, which many hope will be a key factor in overcoming tough political differences and enabling a low-carbon future. There is, however, no clear agreement on a definition of policy monitoring, nor common expectations of what it entails. The OECD (2002), for instance, discusses monitoring in terms of "a continuous process of collecting and analyzing [sic] data to compare how well a project, program, or policy is being implemented against expected results" (30). By contrast, Vedung (1997: 303) insists that monitoring is a checking device purely to assess implementation, rather than ultimate outcomes. Menon et al. (2009) respond that the Vedung approach falls short, and advocate that monitoring should not only assess implementation, but also gauge progress against extant policy goals. Other definitions, which have emerged over time, differ in their scope; while some authors focus on monitoring broader public policy efforts, others have in mind more limited projects and potentially their stakeholders when discussing policy monitoring. Table 1 provides an overview of definitions from different authors and approaches. Rather than using one particular definition, this chapter reviews the emergence of energy policy monitoring in various different governance settings, demonstrating how monitoring systems play out in practice.

Monitoring has a decades-long history in the area of energy and climate policy as countries, for example, started systematically tracking their greenhouse gases

5 Monitoring Energy Policy

Table 1 Monitoring Definitions

Publication/ authors	Term/concept	Description (all quotations)
Aldy (2018)	Policy surveillance	The generation and analysis of information on the existence and performance of GHG mitigation policies and measures, such as emission levels and estimated reductions, costs and cost-effectiveness, potential cross-border impacts and ancillary benefits (210–211)
Annecke (2008)	Monitoring	Monitoring usually implies a continuing operation conducted by project staff during project implementation to ensure that the project stays on track to achieve its objectives (2840)
Ausubel and Victor (1992)	Monitoring	Monitoring here means the process of acquiring information used to facilitate decision-making and implementation of an agreement (14)
Bisset and Tomlinson (1988)	Monitoring	Monitoring is defined as an activity undertaken to provide specific information on the characteristics and functioning of environmental and social variables in space and time (117)
Menon et al. (2009) (UNDP)	Monitoring	Monitoring can be defined as the ongoing process by which stakeholders obtain regular feedback on the progress being made towards achieving their goals and objectives (8)
OECD-DAC (2002)	Monitoring	A continuing function that uses systematic collection of data on specified indicators to provide management and the main stakeholders of an ongoing development intervention with indications of the extent of progress and achievement of objectives and progress in the use of allocated funds (27–28)
OECD-DAC (2002)	Performance monitoring	A continuous process of collecting and analysing [sic] data to compare how well a project, program, or policy is being implemented against expected results (30)
Sabel (1993)	Monitoring	Monitoring is the periodic review of performance to ascertain its conformity with the agreement (21)
Tosun (2012)	Monitoring	The term "monitoring" summarizes various screening operations and actions for gathering information about whether the regulatees comply with environmental regulation, that is, whether they modify their behaviour in accordance with the legal requirements (438)
UNEP (2017)	Monitoring, reporting and verification	A process/concept that potentially supports greater transparency in the climate change regime (ix)
Vedung (1997)	Monitoring	The process of checking what is happening in the implementation and results stages of the evaluand without raising questions about intervention impact on outcomes. The five steps of monitoring are: 1. Reconstruct intervention theory; 2. Select where empirical checks could be set in; 3. Collect and

(continued)

Table 1 (continued)

Publication/authors	Term/concept	Description (all quotations)
		analyze data; 4. Apply merit criteria and performance standards to the findings, and 5. Analyze evaluand and its intended implementation from a general governance perspective (303)
Waterman and Wood (1993)	Policy monitoring	Policy monitoring involves 4 steps: 1. Qualitative evidence on substantive issues involved in the policy-related question (interviews, etc.) 2. Collection & management of a database on actual outputs 3. Quantitative statistical analysis 4. Re-examination of government records and qualitative data in order to eliminate rival explanations (summary 687–690)

following the creation of the United Nations Framework Convention on Climate Change (UNFCCC) in 1992 (Yamin and Depledge 2004). At that time, the EU was particularly keen to persuade others to establish energy and climate policy monitoring at the international level, to ensure at least some progress in the face of its own inability to adopt more concrete policy measures at home (e.g., a carbon tax), a failure which left it unable to advocate such concrete measures in UN-based negotiations (see Haigh 1996). At the very minimum, negotiators felt that agreement on consistent monitoring of emissions of greenhouse gases was needed. As Feldman and Wilt (1996) explain:

> ... international climate change agreements and many national action plans encourage goals that are to be universally adopted by countries and, in the case of the latter, by every region within a country. *To ensure that states and other regional jurisdictions can be equivalently evaluated on their progress in achieving these goals, some means must be developed to collect valid energy and emissions data across jurisdictions and—equally important—to ensure that these data measure the same things in the same way.* (49; emphasis added)

However, Niederberger and Kimble (2011: 48) point out that "[...] national greenhouse gas inventories are poorly suited as a means of identifying the most promising opportunities, mobilizing the required resources and tracking the effectiveness of individual national or subnational mitigation actions." As aggregate numbers, they simply do not provide enough detail to make finer, policy-based judgments on the efficacy of different public policy approaches in order to reduce greenhouse gas emissions.

Responding to such issues, monitoring *public policies*, which aims to track policy development and effects over time, is a somewhat younger activity than the more long-standing approaches to reporting on energy flows and greenhouse gases. According to the Oxford English Dictionary (online version), a (public) policy may be understood as "a principle or course of action adopted or proposed as desirable, advantageous, or expedient; esp. one formally advocated by a government, political party, etc.," even though one should note that the meaning of public policy remains contested in academic literatures (Hill and Varone 2017: 15–23). Well-known examples of energy policies in the EU include legislation to stimulate energy efficiency or renewable energy sources such as wind or solar power (see below).

As Dunn (2018) explains, there are numerous ways in which one could potentially monitor public policies. On the one hand are a set of methodologies including monitoring through "social systems accounting" by focusing on headline indicators such as unemployment; "policy experimentation" by detecting policy effects in experimental settings; "social auditing," which considers the relation of policy inputs and impacts; "research practice and synthesis," which conducts monitoring through case studies and research reports; or "systematic reviews and meta-analyses," which systematically bring together quantitative and qualitative data from existing studies. On the other hand, more specific sets of indicators may be used to track policies, such as greenhouse gas emissions or energy prices (see Lehtonen 2015). In their early ground-breaking book, Guba and Lincoln (1981) argued that measurement and evaluation were originally (i.e., in the 1950s) thought to be same thing. But over time, the two practices diverged, with measurement turning more toward the use of indicators (which may be composites of various variables in order to measure some underlying dimension, the creation of which is, by nature, also potentially a political and thus contentious, interest-infused task – see Lehtonen 2015), and evaluation becoming a practice of policy analysis, with wide-ranging debates on methods and "valuing" policy outputs (Vedung 1997). Today, this distinction is widely accepted – indeed the European Court of Auditors (2018: 25) argues that monitoring generates crucial information for "*ex post*" legislative reviews.

In this chapter, section "Policy Monitoring: Administrative Task or Political Exercise?" focuses on key characteristics of monitoring, including its administrative elements, but also political conflicts over the financial and other burdens associated with maintaining monitoring infrastructures, as well as (political) control as a function of the policy knowledge that monitoring invariably generates. Section "Cases in Energy Policy Monitoring" elaborates on three broad cases of energy policy monitoring reflecting practices at the international level, the EU level, as well as the national level. In doing so, it pays particular attention to the (historical) emergence and significance of monitoring energy policy in Europe over time. Section "Future Directions" concludes with some thoughts on future directions including, for example, further exploring policy monitoring in the real world in the areas of renewables and energy efficiency.

Policy Monitoring: Administrative Task or Political Exercise?

In the early days, policy monitoring tended to be presented as a purely administrative task, and was therefore purposefully "depoliticized" (see Hildén et al. 2014). However, as theorizing and empirical research has built up to investigate policy monitoring "*in situ*" (as opposed to its theoretical functions), it became increasingly clear that monitoring itself has at times become a site of political conflict and struggle. Niederberger and Kimble (2011: 47) explain that monitoring, reporting, and verification (MRV) "has proven to be one of the most intractable issues in reaching a global climate deal" in 2009 (for a related argument, see Gupta et al. 2012). This section focuses on two particular reasons why monitoring has become overtly political, namely its relationship with control and steering and the cost and administrative burdens that it may entail.

Steering and Control

One of the stated aims of policy monitoring is to enable some level of steering – and therefore control (see Schoenefeld and Jordan 2019). In the EU, this has the potential to enable energy policy coordination and strengthen the EU's role, given that decisions on the energy mix remain, by and large, with the Member States as per the Lisbon Treaty (Article 194, Treaty on the Functioning of the European Union [TFEU]). While some definitions are explicit that monitoring relates to checking on the progress, *ex post* (i.e., retrospective), of implemented policies, according to others monitoring could also precede and indeed lay the necessary groundwork for the future development of policy instruments (Aldy 2018: 212). Putting in place a new system of monitoring could, by itself, have a significant steering effect. For example, in the case of regulating the climate impacts of international shipping, the International Maritime Organization (IMO) has prioritized improved monitoring of ship fuel use as part of a three-step approach, moving from data collection, to analysis, then potentially to further regulations to reduce emissions from the sector (International Maritime Organization 2015). It is not clear yet whether the new system will be voluntary or compulsory (Austria et al. 2015). Creating such monitoring capacities in the shipping sector could ultimately lead to further policy action, such as forms of emissions trading.

The extent to which monitoring may be necessary in order to enable steering is also a function of the nature of the problem it seeks to address. As Oberthür et al. (2017: 18) have highlighted, "coordination problems" do not require strong transparency measures (because countries are prone to play by the commonly agreed roles), while "cooperation problems" call for much stronger transparency arrangements as there are incentives to "free ride." Furthermore, the "intrinsic" transparency of certain activities varies – on a technical level, it is, for example, easier to check whether vessels carrying oil have installed pollution-reduction technology, than whether that technology is actually used at sea (Oberthür et al. 2017).

But as knowledge on policy efforts and effects (including their shortcomings) builds up, actors may resist efforts by higher-level entities to using such information in order to seek influence over policy trajectories. As Waterman and Wood (1993) explain, the idea of monitoring at its core derives from agency theory, where there are at least two actors, one of whom is monitoring the other. They go on to argue that agents may seek to "convince the[ir] principal[s] that their policy goals are being achieved, when in fact they are not. Since various agents themselves probably would

5 Monitoring Energy Policy

be evaluated on the basis of this faulty but complimentary information, *agents possess not only the means but also the incentive to provide misleading information to political principals*, who are often the actual decisionmakers or clients" (687; emphasis added).

An example of this phenomenon has recently emerged in the area of transport policy. Here, car manufacturers have been revealed to have "gamed" official tests of fuel economy over many years by creating artificially favorable laboratory test conditions, by, for example, removing equipment in order to make test cars lighter (Carrington 2018). According to some estimates, the gap between test and actual performance may have increased from 9% in 2000 to 42% in 2016 (International Council on Clean Transportation 2017). Deliberately presenting overly favorable data is not necessarily illegal, but it implies that despite fuel economy and emission control regulations, there has been minimal to no real-world improvement in CO_2 emissions (International Council on Clean Transportation 2017). But while this discussion focuses on particular private sector companies, whole EU Member States may also face incentives to provide only a minimum level of information on energy and climate policy development, seek to limit possibilities for comparison, or, in other cases, even actively mobilize "counter-expertise" (Gupta et al. 2012). In other words, because monitoring may entail political costs (because it may, for example, highlight shortcomings in government programs), it has at times become a site of political struggle.

One way in which EU Member States may avoid control is to resist standardization of monitoring procedures and outcomes (see Schoenefeld and Jordan 2017). Judging from ADAM project meta-analysis (Huitema et al. 2011), a review of other literature (see, for example, Gijsen and Lohuis (2005)), and evidence from practitioners (see Schoenefeld et al. 2018), the practices through which quantification of emission savings occur are far from being standardized. "As no unequivocal method for policy evaluation has been established, a broad distribution of effects can be obtained depending on the method chosen. The differences arise from the algorithm used for determining the separate effects on the level of emissions, as they cannot be measured" (Gijsen and Lohuis 2005: 47). This may be considered problematic and has led some political actors to attempt to bring about more consistency. For example, concerns over the inadequacy of capacity and variability in methods for "*ex post*" evaluation have prompted the European Commission's Environment Directorate General (DG) to sponsor efforts to improve the quality of climate policy evaluation, in particular a 1-year project on "Quantification of the effects on greenhouse gas emissions of policies and measures" (AEA et al. 2009; see also Öko-Institut et al. 2012). However, the success of such initiatives at methodological harmonization remains an open question (Schoenefeld et al. 2018).

Lack of standardized approaches to monitoring and evaluation is striking, but not necessarily surprising – climate change is a "super wicked problem" (Levin et al. 2012), and what are categorized for reporting purposes as climate policies were often developed for other reasons, including many on energy policy:

> National climate change programmes will generally build upon, rather than replace, existing legislation in the energy, industry and land use sectors, and given the differences that exist

between national policies in these areas, it is almost inevitable that systems for quantifying emission reductions will differ significantly from country to country. (ECCM 2003: 14)

But issues with data quality and inconsistencies may also relate to the fact that policies themselves may have an internal lack of clarity, including with regards to monitoring:

> Several programmes, plans, policies etc. are not very explicit as to how the mechanisms for climate change aims are supposed to work. In addition, goals are often very general, like national reduction targets. If the goal is not subdivided into more specific goals – e.g. for different sectors – it becomes more difficult to plan a reporting procedure, and later, *ex post*, to assess successes and failures. It is essential, however, not to evaluate goal achievement per se, but to evaluate the means – strategies, instruments, changed practices etc. – by which to reach them. (Mickwitz et al. 2009: 78)

Taken together, there are both political and technical reasons that challenge steering via monitoring.

Monitoring Costs

Monitoring – if understood as a process of data collection and collation – tends to be a costly activity, particularly when it involves multiple institutions and governance levels (see Dunn 2018; Leeuw 2010). The costs emerge from the material and personnel resources involved in data collection, preparation, and ultimately transmission to other institutions, as well as data analysis. As a consequence, related political conflict has centered on the scope of reporting, its frequency, and the distribution of the costs among different actors (Schoenefeld et al. 2018). If monitoring happens across different governance levels and countries with different characteristics (see Schoenefeld and Jordan 2017), the distribution of the costs of monitoring may be subject to political debate. Reflecting this phenomenon, countries agreed at the international level that developing countries need financial support and flexibility in order to conduct monitoring, review, and verification (MRV) (Niederberger and Kimble 2011; Stefanini 2018). Similarly, in the case of the EU Emissions Trading System (EU ETS), it was determined in the early stages of its development that (decentralized) emissions monitoring by Member States and therefore monitoring of individual installations should be as accurate as possible, but *without* generating unreasonably high costs (see Peeters 2006a, b). A 95% confidence interval around the estimated emissions value is seen as a sufficient level of accuracy (Peeters 2006b). However, even today, aspects of monitoring the EU ETS such as data on the use of revenues from auctioning emission allowances, remain patchy across the Member States (WWF 2016: 5). In sum, monitoring costs can generate political conflict, especially when it happens across governance levels and multiple actors.

Cases in Energy Policy Monitoring

The section focuses on three broad "cases," or realms, of energy and climate policy monitoring: the international level, the EU level, as well as the national level by considering two large Member States, namely the United Kingdom (UK) and Germany. It reviews key trends in our knowledge, but also spots gaps in the current understanding of the relevant monitoring practices.

Monitoring at the International Level: The UNFCCC and Beyond

At the international level, the UN compiled its first publication on "World Energy Supplies in Selected Years, 1929–1950" in 1952 (Statistical Office of the United Nations 1952). Much of the more recent reporting on energy and climate policies centers on the UNFCCC. Created at the Rio Earth Summit in 1992 and in line with the Intergovernmental Panel on Climate Change (IPCC), the UNFCCC first obliged its Member States to collect, compile and report data on greenhouse gas emissions, before it also demanded reporting on the impact of individual policies (Yamin and Depledge 2004). Over time, the IPCC has emerged as an important standard setter in reporting, but has had less influence on the institutional setup for monitoring (Feldman and Wilt 1996). A mixture of technical difficulties, capacity issues, but also political conflict has long plagued reporting under the UNFCCC (Aldy 2018: 214; Wettestad 2007). Importantly, differentiation (i.e., putting different demands on developed and developing countries) has historically not only been applied to emissions reduction targets, but also to monitoring and reporting, with developed countries having to report more data, and more frequently, than developing countries (Aldy 2018; Stefanini 2018).

China's critical role in efforts to reduce emissions means that accurate monitoring and reporting is particularly important. Monitoring of greenhouse gas has been especially sensitive there, epitomized by the fact that China has only reported emissions twice, namely for 1994 (in its 2004 report to the UN) and for 2004 (in its 2012 report to the UN) (Aldy 2018). It has thus been slow to publicly acknowledge its stunning growth in carbon emissions (Hsu 2015), and some questions also remain regarding the quality of the data provided (Hsu et al. 2015). While other emerging countries have submitted a similarly low number of reports, countries such as Mexico and Brazil have done somewhat more (Wong 2017).

With the emerging implementation of the 2015 Paris Agreement, this system is now slowly changing. Each party has a legally binding obligation under Article 13.7(b) to regularly provide "[i]nformation necessary to track progress made in implementing and achieving" its Nationally Determined Contribution (NDC): the document in which countries pledge their targets to reduce emissions. The NDC needs to include carbon emissions and policies and measures in place. The standards underpinning this information, negotiated as part of the Paris "Rulebook" that was largely agreed at the Katowice conference in 2018, are due to apply to both developed and developing countries. This new approach contrasts with the more differentiated system that has applied hitherto, although developing countries insisted on retaining some flexibility given different levels of capacity (Stefanini 2018). The new standards also seek to avoid double counting (Harvey 2018; Stefanini 2018). This move to a more uniform, global system was made possible by an apparent shift in the position of China (Harvey 2018; Stefanini 2018). The review processes now embodied in the Rulebook will not only allow to check each country's performance against its NDC, but also enable learning about the efforts and successes of others – especially because international experts can provide recommendations without impinging upon national sovereignty (see Yamide and Cogswell 2018). Ultimately, the effectiveness of the Paris Agreement in limiting global temperature rise depends on its ability to bring about a rapid upward "ratcheting" of ambition levels over time. This in turn requires enhanced transparency through accurate and timely reporting.

There have been various additional monitoring efforts around and outside the UNFCCC that deserve attention. Nongovernmental organizations (NGOs) are one type of organization that have stepped into the breach when countries have been reluctant to make their energy and climate policy-related activities transparent (and monitoring has thus been a way for them to enter the debates, see Schoenefeld and Jordan 2019). For example, as Whitley et al. (2018) demonstrate, although countries agreed in numerous fora to phase out fossil fuel subsidies, notably in the G-7 and the G-20 (see also Skovgaard and van Asselt 2018), monitoring of the related efforts with a view to goal achievement remains scarce, even though the G-20 leaders called for both self-reporting and assessments by international organizations (see Aldy 2017). As a response, various NGOs, including the Overseas Development Institute (ODI), the International Institute for Sustainable Development (IISD), and Oil Change International have taken monitoring into their own hands in order to hold the countries to account. Their work makes clear that in 2015 and 2016, more than 50 countries still paid out $100 billion per year in order to support fossil fuels (Gençsü et al. 2017; Whitley et al. 2018). While the G-20 has signaled the need to remove "inefficient" fossil fuel subsidies and facilitated voluntary peer review, struggles to even agree on a common definition of fossil fuel subsidies have hampered progress (Asmelash 2017), so much so that scholars have recommended building an international working group in order to resolve these issues (Koplow 2018).

Aside from NGOs, particular sectors and industries have also taken some (but often limited) action. Among the energy-intensive industries, the Cement Sustainability Instrument (CSI) and the International Council of Chemical Associations (ICCA) have set up mechanisms that aim to account for greenhouse gas emissions, although the sector as a whole remains rather opaque (Rayner et al. 2018). Similarly, the International Civil Aviation Organization (ICAO) has created accounting systems for airline emissions (WWF-UK 2017). In the international shipping sector, the International Marine Organization (IMO) has introduced the obligatory Ship Energy Efficiency Management Plans (SEEMP) in order to identify existing and possible future features to enhance efficiency and monitor progress. In order to track maritime fuel consumption, the IMO has introduced a "three-step approach," which involves collecting data, analyzing it, and potentially regulating these activities at a later stage (International Maritime Organization 2015). There are also other private initiatives in order to track ship emissions, but their efforts are currently not standardized and their influence remains by and large limited (Gençsü and Hino 2015; Scott et al. 2017). In sum, we observe a panoply of international monitoring activities related to energy and climate policy. Time will tell to what extent the Paris Agreement and associated efforts can bring these efforts together more systematically.

The Emergence and Significance of Monitoring Energy Policy in Europe

Tracking developments in energy production, trade, and use has a relatively long history in the countries making up the EU, which began with their first attempts to gather statistical information on coal and petroleum production, as well as electricity, in the middle of the nineteenth century in various European countries (see Mitchell 2007). The creation of the European Community with the Treaty of Rome in 1957 stimulated further monitoring, such as, for example, through the rise of the Euratom Supply Agency, which was tasked with monitoring the European market for nuclear materials and advising national agencies on creating long-term supplies of nuclear fuels. In other words, much like the activities in a range of other fields such as coal, the initial monitoring activities of European-level actors related very much to monitoring energy-related activities in the European community and eventually in the emerging common market. The oil crises in the 1970s also led to an increased feeling that more monitoring had become necessary; for example, Hoerber (2013: 88–89) demonstrates that as a consequence of increasing scarcity of oil, the Commission intensified its monitoring of oil imports and exports, including from/to non-EU member countries.

Since these early beginnings and building up over time, statistical collection has grown and become more systematic. Today, Regulation (EC) 1099/2008 on energy statistics governs the respective data collection in the EU (for an overview of energy statistics and related regulation, see Eurostat 2018). The preamble of the regulation notes that:

> The Community needs to have precise and timely data on energy quantities, their forms, sources, generation, supply, transformation and consumption, for the purpose of monitoring the impact and consequences of its policy work on energy.

In other words, energy statistics are seen as part and parcel of monitoring the impact of European energy policies. The preamble furthermore details that there are a range of additional pieces of legislation that require energy data collection at the European level, including the Monitoring Mechanism (EU Regulation 525/2013) for greenhouse gases and policies and measures, as well as directives on renewables (EU Directive 2009/28/EC) and energy efficiency (EU Directive 2012/27/EU).

Notwithstanding these more long-standing efforts to collect general energy statistics, endeavors to specifically monitor *public policies* in the energy sector have a shorter history, especially legally binding approaches. Over the last decade or so, policy monitoring has become more commonplace in Europe, and revisions of energy and climate legislation typically meant an insertion of monitoring clauses (see also Bussmann 2005; Wirths et al. 2017). As a result, there are now over 100 individual monitoring, reporting, and/or planning streams listed in the impact assessment in preparation for the emerging Energy Union (European Commission 2016). One of the aims of the Energy Union is to streamline reporting and reduce the burden on Member States arising from these many different – and in some cases overlapping – monitoring and reporting obligations (Ringel and Knodt 2018). This section focuses on three specific energy *policy* monitoring efforts that have gathered strength and become more established in the 2000s: policy monitoring under the EU's Monitoring Mechanism for greenhouse gases and policies and measures, as well as the more specific requirements emerging from the directives promoting renewable energy sources and energy efficiency.

The Monitoring Mechanism

The EU created a Monitoring Mechanism for greenhouse gases and policies and measures in 1993 (after several revisions now EU Regulation 525/2013) in order to comply with the new monitoring requirements that had emerged from the 1992 Earth Summit in Rio de Janeiro, where the UNFCCC was created (Hyvarinen 1999). While the mechanism originally focused on accounting for greenhouse gases, in the 2000s, the Commission managed to extend the emphasis on policies and measures, with grudging agreement from EU Member States, who had to agree on the new reporting requirements (Hildén et al. 2014). In practice, Member States report their greenhouse gas emissions yearly and their policy efforts every other year to the European Environment Agency (EEA), which in turn compiles the data, checks them for quality, and then provides them to the European Commission. The Commission then uses them in the communications to the UNFCCC (Schoenefeld et al. 2018). The EEA also publishes the data in a freely available database on the Internet (see European Environment Agency 2018).

Aside from monitoring national greenhouse gases for the preparation of the inventories, at the policy level, the Monitoring Mechanism requires Member States to provide lists of all implemented or planned policies and chiefly assesses predicted greenhouse gas emissions reductions linked to individual policies, as well as other metrics, such as costs. Given decentralized data collection, there have been long-standing issues with data quality and plausibility in the Monitoring Mechanism (Gupta and Ringius 2001; Wettestad 2000), which have become especially acute in the policy-level data that were published in more recent years (Hildén et al. 2014; Schoenefeld et al. 2018). Furthermore, the policy-focused data from the Mechanism are lopsided, with most Member States focusing on the (legally mandated) "*ex ante*" (i.e., prospective) predictions of policy impact, and a general neglect of "*ex post*" (i.e., retrospective) assessments (Schoenefeld et al. 2018). There are also important data gaps, notably with regard to maritime emissions that are currently not included in the inventory, which has led to the EU's efforts to integrate shipping efforts into monitoring and ultimately policy-making activities. As noted in section "Monitoring at the International Level: The UNFCCC and Beyond," efforts to improve the monitoring and regulation of energy use and greenhouse gas emissions from shipping have faced resistance at global-level institutions, but the EU has to some extent been able to force the pace by taking its own regulatory steps.

The technical issues of reporting on the policy level have certainly contributed to heterogeneous data (see Gijsen and Lohuis 2005), and some of them have become political. For example, in the early days, the Commission and the Member States preferred a 1995 baseline in order report progress on the Kyoto Protocol targets; the European Parliament wanted to be more flexible, and eventually the baseline was set for 1990 (Farmer 2012). But even though the Monitoring Mechanism has contained a quality control procedure in order to check Member State submissions from 2006 onwards (Farmer 2012), concerns over increased control for EU-level institutions, as well as debates on cost and administrative burden have inhibited decisive steps in increasing reporting frequency and quality in a 2013 revision of the regulation that underwrites the Monitoring Mechanism (Schoenefeld et al. 2018).

Monitoring Renewable Energy Policy
As a separate policy track (though arguably included in the Monitoring Mechanism data discussed above), the renewable energy directive also includes more specific requirements in order to observe renewables policy in the Member States with a view to the European targets. Following earlier unsuccessful attempts to achieve nonbinding renewable targets (see Kanellakis et al. 2013), both the targets (a 20% share for renewables by 2020), as well as their monitoring became mandatory in the new renewable energy directive (2009/28/EC), where "National Renewable Energy Action Plans" now contain most of the prospective and retrospective reporting (Howes 2010). Member States are required to report yearly to the Commission on their progress (Kanellakis et al. 2013). However, there is currently comparatively little knowledge of the operation of these reporting endeavors in action, for example, regarding data quality and potential conflicts.

Monitoring Energy Efficiency Policy
Energy efficiency policy at the EU level has traditionally been nonbinding in the EU (see Jordan and Rayner 2010). More concerted monitoring first found its way into the directives in 2006, and the Commission has at times been asked to define methodological standards, although Member States have no obligation to use these (Ringel 2017). This has created heterogeneous application of energy efficiency reporting across the Member States, even though they have all implemented some monitoring, but generally with no homogeneous reporting tool, little quantification, and by and large top-down (rather than bottom-up) monitoring approaches (Iatridis et al. 2015). The most recent version of the Energy Efficiency Directive (2012/27/EU) obligates Member States to define national targets in order to achieve the overall goal of reducing EU energy consumption by 20% compared to business-as-usual projections by 2020. By and large, the decentralized monitoring of energy efficiency efforts around the EU has often produced inconsistent data, and therefore issues with comparison and challenges in tracking policy development over time (e.g., Rosenow

et al. 2015). Researchers have therefore recommended building a central institution that coordinates the monitoring, developing bottom-up methods in order to generate better data and setting up central databases with clear standards with a view to collecting the monitoring data (Tourkolias and Iatridis 2016), and there are ongoing efforts to bring together knowledge on monitoring and evaluating efficiency policy more systematically (e.g., Breitschopf et al. 2018). Further research should shed additional light on the operation of energy efficiency policy monitoring in practice – especially the efficacy of the reporting schemes vis-à-vis policy impact remains a key knowledge gap (Iatridis et al. 2015).

Monitoring at the Member State Level: United Kingdom and Germany

The previous sections demonstrate that the lion's share of energy policy monitoring in Europe happens at the Member State, that is, the national level. With a view to the country chapters elsewhere in this handbook, this section carefully reviews examples of energy policy monitoring in the UK and in Germany. We have chosen these two countries because they are large Member States where both energy/climate policy development and related monitoring and evaluation activities have been especially dynamic in recent decades (see AEA et al. 2009; Jordan et al. 2010). However, they also differ substantially on account of their governance structure, with the UK being more of a unitary and Germany a federal state. They thus provide two exemplary cases in energy and climate policy monitoring. This overview is by no means comprehensive; rather, we focus on particularly salient and evolving monitoring initiatives that have emerged more recently and drawn significant scholarly and – in some cases – public attention.

United Kingdom

The UK contains, in many ways, a relatively sophisticated monitoring and evaluation community, featuring a range of actors based in government, parliament, and nongovernmental spheres. Some, such as the National Audit Office (NAO), are long established and enjoy a strong reputation for independence and quality of analysis (Contact Committee of the Supreme Audit Institutions of the European Union 2016). The NAO was established in 1983 and is the UK's supreme audit institution (SAI). As such it participates in international networks of equivalent bodies in other countries, including the European Organization of Supreme Audit Institutions (EUROSAI) and the International Organization of Supreme Audit Institutions (INTOSAI). The NAO's role is to scrutinize the effectiveness, efficiency, and economy of government spending, helping Parliament to hold government to account and improve public services. The NAO regularly tackles energy and climate policy-related topics, and its reports have, at times, been strongly critical, for example, regarding decision-making over the proposed new Hinkley Point C nuclear power station (National Audit Office 2017), or government's failure to anticipate that subsidies to promote renewable electricity investment would exceed the envisaged limit for them (National Audit Office 2013). NAO's work supports that of a range of cross-party Parliament Select Committees that also provide a policy scrutiny function, each dedicated to tracking the work of a particular government department or, in the case of the Environmental Audit Committee (EAC), looking across the whole of government (Russel et al. 2013). The EAC has also frequently taken on energy- and climate-related inquiries, and been critical, for example, of government's lack of transparency over fossil fuel subsidies (Environmental Audit Committee 2013). Other analyses revealed that a relatively high number of evaluation studies conducted in the UK present a quantification of the emission reductions achieved by a particular instrument or package of instruments (see Huitema et al. 2011). Of these, more than half are government-commissioned, many associated with the Climate Change Programme Review of 2006 overseen by the Department of Environment, Food and Rural Affairs (DEFRA). Increasing volume and formalization of climate policy evaluation is evident, with prescribed methods set by government for consultants to apply during Climate Change Programme Review (CCPR) (National Audit Office 2007). Clear guidance on monitoring and evaluation practice and a supporting infrastructure across the government made for greater consistency and formalization in the UK compared to, for example, Germany, where assessments could be politicized when particular ministries sought to defend or attack particular policy instruments. Nevertheless, powerful UK actors, and in particular the Treasury, have managed to evade formal mechanisms including those for peer review.

In more recent years, the Climate Change Act (2008) has brought an overhaul to monitoring and evaluation practice in the area of energy policy, introducing an independent Committee on Climate Change (CCC), which advises government on the meeting of legally binding greenhouse gas emission targets set by the Act, and issues annual progress reports to Parliament. The Committee also reports on Scotland's progress against its annual carbon targets. The CCC has developed a set of indicators to track emissions, progress in low-carbon investments, and the development of government policies, allowing early identification of areas where targets may be missed. These indicators cover, for example, the size of onshore and offshore wind farms at various stages of the project cycle, emissions from new cars and the rate of development in the market for electric vehicles, and progress of policies such as grants for electric vehicles and electricity market reform.

There are signs (in 2017–2018) that the Committee is prepared to offer increasingly blunt, more politically inconvenient advice, for example, highlighting particularly serious policy gaps in the transport and buildings sectors where emissions continue to rise and threaten the achievement of carbon budgets (see Climate Change Committee 2018). This is arguably a bold move by the Committee, which risks provoking certain politicians who might be looking for a pretext to undermine the UK's climate commitments, including by abolishing the committee.

Germany

Since the need for alternative forms of energy forcefully entered European political agendas in the wake of the 1970s' oil crises (see Hoerber 2013; Knodt 2018), the *Energiewende*, or the national switch away from nuclear and fossil energy toward renewables, has been the most significant development on the German energy policy landscape (Lauber 2017; Neukirch 2018). Soon after its introduction in the 1990s and surely in the early 2000s, elements of monitoring started to emerge. As Schumacher et al. (2014: 384) emphasize:

> Consistent monitoring and evaluation of policies and measures under the German energy transition is essential to promote the effectiveness and efficiency of these measures, to redesign if needed and to keep on track for reaching Germany's goal to move to a sustainable economy.

This section therefore focuses on the monitoring of the *Energiewende*, as well as related policy initiatives, such as the *Nationale Klimainitiative* (NKI). While policy monitoring and evaluation has typically been more secretive in Germany than in other countries, on the *Energiewende*, the federal government agreed on a monitoring process where ministry reports are subjected to (public) expert judgment on a regular basis (Wörlen et al. 2014). Indeed, following a federal government decision in 2011, the "Energy of the Future" Monitoring Process was created under the auspices of the Federal Ministry for Economic Affairs and Energy (Federal Ministry for Economic Affairs and Energy 2018). As part of the process, the relevant ministries (environment, energy) prepare an annual monitoring report – six published to date – as well as a progress report, every 3 years (Ziesing 2014), of which there has been so far only one in 2014 at the time of this writing (Federal Ministry for Economic Affairs and Energy 2014). All reports are publicly available and scrutinized by an independent expert commission which then issues recommendations; the government can take these recommendations into account but cannot change the text and has to publish them as an annex to its own reports (Ziesing 2014).

Methodologically, the reporting collates statistics on numerous policy areas linked with the *Energiewende*, including greenhouse gases, efficiency, buildings, transport, and renewables as well as descriptions of the policy efforts undertaken in order to accomplish the overall targets. To do so, it draws on official energy statistics, as well as data from several federal government agencies, industry, as well as the "Working Group on Renewable Energy Statistics" (Federal Ministry for Economic Affairs and Energy 2018). Reporting from 2012 and 2014 shows that the government reports are somewhat less critical than the expert reports; the expert commission has also recommended reforming the relevant German energy statistics legislation in order to provide better data for the *Energiewende* monitoring processes (Ziesing 2014). But the system has also been criticized for using no hierarchy of indicators (Wörlen et al. 2014). Others have highlighted that its indicators miss core aspects of sustainability, such as the distribution of benefits and costs, as well as participation, and have in turn developed alternative indicator systems (see Rösch et al. 2017). It should also be noted that while the monitoring includes both indicators and descriptions of concrete measures, the report does not explore (potential) causal links between the policies and the indicators in all cases, thus often leaving open important questions on the efficacy of the policies in place. Overall, Germany has been successful in various aspects of the NKI, but there remain key shortcomings, not least in the area of policy monitoring (Schumacher et al. 2014).

Future Directions

Monitoring and evaluation are on the rise in energy and climate governance in Europe and well beyond, for example, in the context of the Paris Agreement and the emerging Energy Union. Multiple authors have pointed to their importance in enabling the transition toward a low-carbon future (see also Tosun 2012). The previous sections have highlighted conceptual debates and discussed empirical examples of monitoring efforts in the real world. Taking these insights together reveals various important points about monitoring energy policy in Europe.

First, there is currently no clear agreement on what policy monitoring precisely entails, notably whether it involves solely data collection or whether it does/should also involve an assessment and evaluation of the data it generates. The empirical examples above reveal mixed realities – whereas, for example, the Monitoring Mechanism at the EU level indeed focuses to a considerable degree on collecting and collating data, energy policy monitoring processes in the UK (Climate Change Act) and in Germany (National Climate Initiative) very much include both data collection, collation, and assessment, in these cases with the help of independent experts. Varying understandings of monitoring have furthermore crystallized in different ways of organizing monitoring systems and related debates on their costs and burdens (see Schoenefeld and Jordan 2017); overall, there appears to be a general trend toward more monitoring of energy and climate policy, which is assisted by experts, and whose results are placed in the public domain.

Second, the growing multiplicity of monitoring efforts both in Europe, as well as internationally, has generated some challenging questions regarding their coordination. As Dagnet et al. (2017: 19) warn, in highlighting the provisions of the Paris Agreement:

> Undertaking the technical review of more than 190 transparency reports every two years (in addition to the yearly review of developed country GHG inventories) will pose a burden to the system, especially the UNFCCC Secretariat and available experts. There is no precedent for conducting such a massive number of technical reviews because the submission of reports by developing countries under the Convention is not yet regular. The current system needs to be adapted to handle the biennial reporting envisioned by the Paris Agreement.

In Europe, where there are arguably more available resources and capacity, as well as experience, with conducting policy monitoring (Schoenefeld et al. 2018) than in many developing countries, the implementation of the Paris Agreement is generating significant change. Monitoring obligations emerging from various pieces of legislation, including, for example, renewables, energy efficiency, or greenhouse gas reporting, will likely be more streamlined and in some cases trimmed under the umbrella of the emerging "Energy Union" (see Ringel and Knodt 2018). Overall, we observe centralizing tendencies in policy monitoring around the EU – often responding to what were perceived to be ineffective decentralized approaches (for another example, see reporting in the EU ETS in Verschuuren and Floor 2014: 23–30). However, such changes may also lead to power shifts and steering effects, particularly when "harder" elements are added to the "softer" governance, as the European Commission has been attempting (Knodt and Ringel 2018).

As new institutions (for example those governing international aviation and shipping sectors) increasingly adopt climate policy commitments, the growing need to coordinate the monitoring that they undertake with more established systems under the auspices of the UNFCCC is also worth highlighting as a significant challenge. Without close coordination, the risk will be that emission reductions are double-counted, potentially presenting an overly rosy picture of policy effectiveness (Rayner et al. 2018). With multifarious monitoring efforts, the use of monitoring data is an especially key area for future research, where little is currently known, but much rests on its assumed efficacy.

In sum, policy monitoring has a relatively long history in the energy sector, where the first endeavors to collect systematic statistics on coal, petroleum, and later electricity had commenced by the middle of the nineteenth century. The emergence of new ways of using energy, as well as the ever-growing pressure of climate change and a wide variety of public policies in order to address it, have in many ways put policy monitoring center stage. Never has policy monitoring been as extensive, complex, and at times politicized as today. Policy-makers will be well-advised to keep these points in mind while deliberating over different options for setting up monitoring systems (see Schoenefeld and Jordan 2017), such as the implementation of the "Paris Rulebook " or in the context of the emerging Energy Union.

Cross-References

► Energy Governance in Germany
► Energy Governance in the United Kingdom
► Energy Policies in the EU: A Fiscal Federalism Perspective
► European Union Energy Policy: A Discourse Perspective

Acknowledgments We thank the participants of the 2018 UACES Annual Conference in Bath, UK, and especially Dr. Tomas Maltby, for constructive comments. Feedback from the handbook editors has considerably strengthened this chapter. Nils Bruch provided very helpful research assistance. JS acknowledges support from the German Federal Ministry of Education and Research (Reference: 03SFK4P0, Consortium ENavi, Kopernikus) and TR from the Horizon 2020 COP21 RIPPLES project (Reference: 730427).

References

AEA, ECOFYS, Fraunhofer, & ICCS. (2009). *Quantification of the effects on greenhouse gas emissions of policies and measures: Final Report* (No. ENV.C.1/SER/2007/0019). Brussels: European Commission.
Aldy, J. E. (2017). Policy surveillance in the G-20 fossil fuel subsidies agreement: Lessons for climate policy. *Climatic Change, 144*(1), 97–110.

Aldy, J. E. (2018). Policy surveillance: Its role in monitoring, reporting, evaluating and learning. In A. Jordan, D. Huitema, H. van Asselt, & J. Forster (Eds.), *Governing climate change: Polycentricity in action?* (pp. 210–227). Cambridge: Cambridge University Press.

Annecke, W. (2008). Monitoring and evaluation of energy for development: The good, the bad and the questionable in M&E practice. *Energy Policy, 36*(8), 2839–2845.

Asmelash, H. B. (2017). Phasing out fossil fuel subsidies in the G20: Progress, challenges, and ways forward. Retrieved from http://www.greengrowthknowledge.org/sites/default/files/downloads/resource/Phasing%20Out%20Fossil%20Fuel%20Subsidies%20in%20the%20G20_Progress%2C%20Challenges%2C%20and%20Ways%20Forward.pdf. Accessed 18 Jan 2019.

Austria, Belgium, Bulgaria et al. (2015). *Development of a global data collection system for maritime transport* (No. IMO Doc MEPC 68/4/1). London: International Maritime Organization, MEPC 68th Session.

Ausubel, J. H., & Victor, D. G. (1992). Verification of international environmental agreements. *Annual Review of Energy and the Environment, 17*(1), 1–43.

Bisset, R., & Tomlinson, P. (1988). Monitoring and auditing of impacts. In P. Wathern (Ed.), *Environmental impact assessment: Theory and practice* (pp. 117–128). London: Unwin Hyman.

Breitschopf, B., Schlomann, B., Voswinkel, F. & Broc, J. S. (2018). Identifying current knowledge, suggestions and conclusions from existing literature. Retrieved from https://epatee.eu/sites/default/files/epatee_t3.1_report_on_the_knowledge_base_vfinal.pdf. Accessed 18 Jan 2019.

Bürgin, A. (2015). National binding renewable energy targets for 2020, but not for 2030 anymore: Why the European Commission developed from a supporter to a brakeman. *Journal of European Public Policy, 22*(5), 690–707.

Bussmann, W. (2005). Typen und Terminologie von Evaluationsklauseln. *LeGes, 16*(1), 97–102.

Carrington, D. (2018). Carmakers' gaming of emissions tests 'costing drivers billions'. Retrieved from https://www.theguardian.com/environment/2018/aug/29/carmakers-gaming-of-emissions-tests-costing-drivers-billions. Accessed 18 Jan 2019.

Climate Change Act. (2008). Retrieved from https://www.legislation.gov.uk/ukpga/2008/27/pdfs/ukpga_20080027_en.pdf. Accessed 3 May 2019.

Climate Change Committee. (2018). Reducing UK emissions – 2018 progress report to Parliament. Retrieved from https://www.theccc.org.uk/wp-content/uploads/2018/06/CCC-2018-Progress-Report-to-Parliament.pdf. Accessed 18 Jan 2019.

Contact Committee of the Supreme Audit Institutions of the European Union. (2016). 2016. Retrieved from https://www.eca.europa.eu/sites/cc/en/Pages/Meetings_2016.aspx. Accessed 18 Jan 2019.

Dagnet, Y., van Asselt, H., Cavalheiro, G., Rocha, M. T., Bisiaux, A. & Cogswell, N. (2017). Designing the enhanced transparency framework, part 2: Review under the Paris Agreement. Retrieved from https://www.wri.org/sites/default/files/designing-enhanced-transparency-framework-part-2-review-under-paris-agreement.pdf. Accessed 18 Jan 2019.

Dunn, W. N. (2018). Monitoring observed policy outcomes. In W. N. Dunn (Ed.), *Public policy analysis* (6th ed., pp. 250–319). Oxon: Routledge.

ECCM. (2003). *Policy audit of UK climate change policies and programmes: Report to the Sustainable Development Commission*. Edinburgh: Edinburgh Centre for Climate Change Management.

Environmental Audit Committee. (2013). Energy subsidies. Retrieved from https://publications.parliament.uk/pa/cm201314/cmselect/cmenvaud/61/61.pdf. Accessed 18 Jan 2019.

European Commission. (2016). *Impact assessment accompanying the document 'Proposal for a regulation of the European Parliament and the Council on the governance of the Energy Union* (No. SWD (2016) 394 final). Brussels: European Commission.

European Court of Auditors. (2018). *Ex-post review of EU legislation: A well-established system, but incomplete* (No. 16/2018). Luxembourg: European Union.

European Environment Agency. (2018). EEA database on climate change mitigation policies and measures in Europe. Retrieved from http://pam.apps.eea.europa.eu. Accessed 18 Jan 2019.

Eurostat. (2018). Energy statistics – Annual, monthly, & short-term monthly. Retrieved from http://ec.europa.eu/eurostat/web/energy/legislation. Accessed 18 Jan 2019.

Farmer, A. M. (2012). Monitoring and limiting greenhouse gases. Retrieved from https://ieep.eu/uploads/articles/attachments/3c5e75f4-7292-42a7-b8f4-26473c5a9f3d/3.4_Monitoring_and_limiting_greenhouse_gases_-_final.pdf?v=63664509872. Accessed 18 Jan 2019.

Federal Ministry for Economic Affairs and Energy. (2014). Die Energie der Zukunft: Erster Fortschrittsbericht zur Energiewende. Retrieved from https://www.bmwi.de/Redaktion/DE/Publikationen/Energie/fortschrittsbericht.pdf?__blob=publicationFile&v=15. Accessed 18 Jan 2019.

Federal Ministry for Economic Affairs and Energy. (2018). Monitoring the energy transition. Retrieved from https://www.bmwi.de/Redaktion/EN/Artikel/Energy/monitoring-implementation-of-the-energy-reforms.html. Accessed 18 Jan 2019.

Feldman, D. L., & Wilt, C. A. (1996). Evaluating the implementation of state-level global climate change programs. *Journal of Environment & Development, 5*(1), 46–72.

Gençsü, I., & Hino, M. (2015). Raising ambition to reduce international aviation and maritime emissions. Retrieved from http://newclimateeconomy.report/workingpapers/wp-content/uploads/sites/5/2016/04/NCE-Aviation-Maritime_final.pdf. Accessed 18 Jan 2019.

Gençsü, I., McLynn, M., Runkel, M., Trilling, M., van der Burg, L., Worrall, L., ... Zerzawy, F. (2017). Phase-out 2020: Monitoring Europe's fossil fuel subsidies. Retrieved from https://www.odi.org/sites/odi.org.uk/files/resource-documents/11762.pdf. Accessed 18 Jan 2019.

Gijsen, A., & Lohuis, J. O. (2005). From reference to reality: Methods for explaining emission trends. *Environmental Sciences, 2*(1), 47–55.

Guba, E. G., & Lincoln, Y. S. (1981). *Effective evaluation*. San Francisco: Josey-Bass Limited.

Gupta, J., & Ringius, L. (2001). The EU's climate leadership: reconciling ambition and reality. *International Environmental Agreements, 1*(2), 281–299.

Gupta, A., Lövbrand, E., Turnhout, E., & Vijge, M. J. (2012). In pursuit of carbon accountability: The politics of REDD measuring, reporting and verification systems. *Current Opinion in Environmental Sustainability, 4*(6), 726–731.

Haigh, N. (1996). Climate change policies and politics in the European Community. In T. O'Riordan & J. Jäger (Eds.), *Politics of climate change: A European perspective* (pp. 155–185). New York: Routledge.

Harvey, F. (2018). Progress and problems as UN climate change talks end with a deal. Retrieved from https://www.theguardian.com/environment/2018/dec/15/progress-and-problems-as-un-climate-change-talks-end-with-a-deal. Accessed 18 Jan 2019.

Hildén, M., Jordan, A. J., & Rayner, T. (2014). Climate policy innovation: Developing an evaluation perspective. *Environmental Politics, 23*(5), 884–905.

Hill, M., & Varone, F. (2017). *The public policy process*. Oxon: Routledge.

Hoerber, T. C. (2013). *The origins of energy and environmental policy in Europe: The beginnings of a European environmental conscience*. London: Routledge.

Howes, T. (2010). The EU's new renewable energy Directive (2009/28/EC). In S. Oberthür, M. Pallemaerts, & C. Roche Kelly (Eds.), *The new climate policies of the European Union: Internal legislation and climate diplomacy* (pp. 117–150). Brussels: Brussels University Press.

Hsu, A. (2015). Data transparency: New dynamic at COP-21 in Paris. Retrieved from http://datadriven.yale.edu/china/data-transparency-new-dynamic-at-cop-21-in-paris/. Accessed 18 Jan 2019.

Hsu, A., Xu, K., & Moffat, A. (2015). Carbon statistics: China should come clean on emissions. *Nature, 523*(7559), 158.

Huitema, D., Jordan, A. J., Massey, E., Rayner, T., Van Asselt, H., Haug, C., ... Stripple, J. (2011). The evaluation of climate policy: Theory and emerging practice in Europe. *Policy Sciences, 44*(2), 179–198.

Hyvarinen, J. (1999). The European Community's Monitoring Mechanism for CO2 and other greenhouse gases: The Kyoto Protocol and other recent developments. *Review of European Community & International Environmental Law, 8*(2), 191–197.

Iatridis, M., Tourkolias, C., Jamek, A., Pickl, N., Andersen, J., Kjaer, T., ... Struss, B. (2015). Synthesis report on M&V schemes and coordination mechanisms in EU countries. Retrieved from https://multee.eu/system/files/D%201.2_Synthesis_Report_M%26V_schemes_%26_coordination_Mechanisms_0.pdf. Accessed 18 Jan 2019.

International Council on Clean Transportation. (2017). From laboratory to road: A 2017 update of official and "real world" fuel consumption and CO2 values for passenger cars in Europe. Retrieved from https://www.theicct.org/sites/default/files/publications/Lab-to-road-2017_ICCT-white%20paper_06112017_vF.pdf. Accessed 18 Jan 2019.

International Maritime Organization. (2015). Emissions from fuel used for international aviation and maritime transport. Retrieved from http://www.imo.org/en/OurWork/Environment/PollutionPrevention/AirPollution/Documents/Third%20Greenhouse%20Gas%20Study/IMO%20SBSTA%2043%20submission.pdf. Accessed 18 Jan 2019.

Jordan, A. J., & Rayner, T. (2010). The evolution of climate change policy in the EU: An historical overview. In A. J. Jordan, D. Huitema, H. van Asselt, T. Rayner, & F. Berkhout (Eds.), *Climate change policy in the European Union: Confronting the dilemmas of mitigation and adaptation?* (pp. 52–80). Cambridge: Cambridge University Press.

Jordan, A. J., Huitema, D., Van Asselt, H., Rayner, T., & Berkhout, F. (2010). *Climate change policy in the European Union: Confronting the dilemmas of mitigation and adaptation?* Cambridge: Cambridge University Press.

Kanellakis, M., Martinopoulos, G., & Zachariadis, T. (2013). European energy policy – A review. *Energy Policy, 62*, 1020–1030.

Knodt, M. (2018). EU energy policy. In H. Heinelt & S. Münch (Eds.), *Handbook of European policies: Interpretive approaches to the EU* (pp. 224–240). Cheltenham: Edward Elgar.

Knodt, M., & Ringel, M. (2018). The European Commission as a policy shaper–harder soft governance in the energy union. In J. Ege, M. W. Bauer, & S. Becker (Eds.), *The European Commission in turbulent times* (pp. 181–206). Baden-Baden: Nomos.

Koplow, D. (2018). Defining and measuring fossil fuel fubsidies. In J. Skovgaard & H. van Asselt (Eds.), *The politics of fossil fuel subsidies and their reform* (pp. 23–46). Cambridge: Cambridge University Press.

Lauber, V. (2017). Germany's transition to renewable energy. In T. C. Lehmann (Ed.), *The geopolitics of global energy: The new cost of plenty* (pp. 153–182). London: Lynne Rienner Publishers.

Leeuw, F. L. (2010). Benefits and costs of evaluation: An essay. *Zeitschrift für Evaluation, 9*(2), 211–227.

Lehtonen, M. (2015). Indicators: Tools for informing, monitoring or controlling? In A. Jordan & J. Turnpenny (Eds.), *The tools of policy formulation: Actors, capacities, venues and effects* (pp. 76–99). Cheltenham: Edward Elgar.

Levin, K., Cashore, B., Bernstein, S., & Auld, G. (2012). Overcoming the tragedy of super wicked problems: Constraining our future selves to ameliorate global climate change. *Policy Sciences, 45*(2), 123–152.

Menon, S., Karl, J., & Wignaraja, K. (2009). *Handbook on planning, monitoring and evaluating for development results*. New York: UNDP Evaluation Office.

Mickwitz, P., Aix, F., Beck, S., Carss, D., Ferrand, N., Görg, C., ... Kuindersma, W. (2009). *Climate policy integration, coherence and governance*. Helsinki: Partnership for European Environmental Research.

Mitchell, B. R. (2007). *International historical statistics: Europe 1750–2005*. London: Palgrave Macmillan.

National Audit Office. (2007). Cost-effectiveness analysis in the 2006 climate change programme review. Retrieved from https://www.nao.org.uk/wp-content/uploads/2007/01/Climate_Change_analysis.pdf. Accessed 18 Jan 2019.

National Audit Office. (2013). The levy control framework. Retrieved from https://www.nao.org.uk/wp-content/uploads/2013/11/10303-001-Levy-Control-Framework.pdf. Accessed 18 Jan 2019.

National Audit Office. (2017). Hinkley Point C. Retrieved from https://www.nao.org.uk/wp-content/uploads/2017/06/Hinkley-Point-C.pdf. Accessed 18 Jan 2019.

Neukirch, M. (2018). Die Energiewende in der Bundesrepublik Deutschland (1974–2017) –Reform, Revolution, oder Restauration? *Sozialpolitik.Ch, 1*(1), 1.3.

Niederberger, A. A., & Kimble, M. (2011). MRV under the UN climate regime: Paper tiger or catalyst for continual improvement? *Greenhouse Gas Measurement and Management, 1*(1), 47–54.

Oberthür, S., Hermwille, L., Khandekar, G., Obergassel, W., Rayner, T., Wyns, T., ... Melkie, M. (2017). Key concepts, core challenges and governance functions of international climate governance. Project Ripples (COP21: Results and implications for pathways and policies for low emissions European societies). Retrieved from https://www.cop21ripples.eu/wp-content/uploads/2017/02/Deliverable-4.1-Ripples-Final2.pdf. Accessed 3 May 2019.

OECD-DAC. (2002). *Glossary of key terms in evaluation and results based management*. Paris: DAC Network on Development Evaluation, OECD.

Öko-Institut, Cambridge Economics, AMEC, Harmelink Consulting, & TNO. (2012). Ex-post quantification of the effects and costs of policies and measures (No. CLIMA.A.3/SER/2010/0005). Berlin: Öko-Institut.

Peeters, M. (2006a). Enforcement of the EU greenhouse gas emissions trading scheme. In M. Peeters & K. Deketelaere (Eds.), *EU climate change policy: the challenge of new regulatory initiatives* (pp. 169–187). Cheltenham/Northampton: Edward Elgar.

Peeters, M. (2006b). Inspection and market-based regulation through emissions trading-the striking reliance on self-monitoring, self-reporting and verification. *Utrecht Law Review, 2*, 177.

Rayner, T., Shawoo, Z., Hermwille, L., Obergassel, W., Mersmann, F., Asche, F., ... Zamarioli, L. (2018). Evaluating the adequacy of the outcome of COP21 in the context of the development of the broader international climate regime complex. Retrieved from https://www.cop21ripples.eu/wp-content/uploads/2018/07/RIPPLES_D4.2-Final.pdf. Accessed 18 Jan 2019.

Ringel, M. (2017). Energy efficiency policy governance in a multi-level administration structure – Evidence from Germany. *Energy Efficiency, 10*(3), 753–776.

Ringel, M., & Knodt, M. (2018). The governance of the European Energy Union: Efficiency, effectiveness and acceptance of the Winter Package 2016. *Energy Policy, 112*, 209–220.

Rösch, C., Bräutigam, K., Kopfmüller, J., & Stelzer, V. (2017). Indikatorensystem zur Bewertung des deutschen Energiesystems und der Energiewende. In J. Schippl, A. Grunwald, & O. Renn (Eds.), *Die Energiewende verstehen-orientieren-gestalten* (pp. 351–370). Baden-Baden: Nomos.

Rosenow, J., Forster, D., Kampman, B., Leguijt, C., Pato, Z., Kaar, A., & Eyre, N. (2015). Study evaluating the national policy measures and methodologies to implement Article 7 of the Energy Efficiency Directive. Study for the European Commission. Retrieved from https://ec.europa.eu/energy/sites/ener/files/documents/final_report_evaluation_on_implementation_art._7_eed.pdf. Accessed 3 May 2019.

Russel, D., Turnpenny, J., & Rayner, T. (2013). Reining in the executive? Delegation, evidence, and parliamentary influence on environmental public policy. *Environment and Planning. C, Government & Policy, 31*(4), 619–632.

Sabel, C. F. (1993). Learning by monitoring: The institutions of economic development. In N. J. Smelser & R. Swedberg (Eds.), *The handbook of economic sociology* (pp. 137–165). Princeton: Princeton University Press.

Schoenefeld, J. J., & Jordan, A. J. (2017). Governing policy evaluation? Towards a new typology. *Evaluation, 23*(3), 274–293.

Schoenefeld, J. J., & Jordan, A. J. (2019). Environmental policy evaluation in the EU: Between learning, accountability, and political opportunities? *Environmental Politics, 28*(2), 365–384.

Schoenefeld, J. J., Hildén, M., & Jordan, A. J. (2018). The challenges of monitoring national climate policy: Learning lessons from the EU. *Climate Policy, 18*(1), 118–128.

Schumacher, K., di Nucci, M. R., Görlach, B., Grünig, M., Heldwein, C., Repenning, J., ... Ziesing, H. J. (2014). Evaluation as a cornerstone of policies and measures for the Energiewende. In A. Brunnengräber & M. R. di Nucci (Eds.), Im Hürdenlauf zur Energiewende: Von Transformationen, Reformen und Innovationen (pp. 369–385). Wiesbaden: Springer.

Scott, J., Smith, T., Rehmatulla, N., & Milligan, B. (2017). The promise and limits of private standards in reducing greenhouse gas emissions from shipping. *Journal of Environmental Law, 29*(2), 231–262.

Skovgaard, J., & van Asselt, H. (2018). The politics of fossil fuel subsidies and their reform: An introduction. In J. Skovgaard & H. van Asselt (Eds.), *The politics of fossil fuel subsidies and their reform* (pp. 3–20). Cambridge: Cambridge University Press.

Statistical Office of the United Nations. (1952). *World energy supplies in selected years, 1929–1950*. New York: United Nations.
Stefanini, S. (2018). China open to 'uniform' climate rules, sidestepping old allies. Retrieved from http://www.climatechangenews.com/2018/12/13/china-open-uniform-climate-rules-sidestepping-old-allies/. Accessed 18 Jan 2019.
Tosun, J. (2012). Environmental monitoring and enforcement in Europe: A review of empirical research. *Environmental Policy and Governance, 22*(6), 437–448.
Tourkolias, C., & Iatridis, M. (2016). Policy recommendations on Monitoring & Verification schemes in EU. Retrieved from https://multee.eu/system/files/multEE_Policy_Brief_MV2017.pdf. Accessed 18 January 2019.
UNEP. (2017). *The emissions gap report 2017 – A UN environment synthesis report*. Nairobi: UNEP.
Vedung, E. (1997). *Public policy and program evaluation*. New Brunswick: Transaction Publishers.
Verschuuren, J., & Floor, F. (2014). Report on the legal implementation of the EU ETS at Member State level. Retrieved from https://pure.uvt.nl/ws/portalfiles/portal/4822572/ENTRACTE_Deliverable_TSC_SEPT2014FINAL_1.pdf. Accessed 18 Jan 2019.
Waterman, R. W., & Wood, B. D. (1993). Policy monitoring and policy analysis. *Journal of Policy Analysis and Management, 12*(4), 685–699.
Wettestad, J. (2000). The complicated development of EU climate policy. In J. Gupta & M. J. Grubb (Eds.), *Climate change and European leadership* (pp. 25–45). Dordrecht: Kluwer.
Wettestad, J. (2007). Monitoring and verification. In D. Bodansky, J. Brunnée, & E. Hey (Eds.), *The Oxford Handbook of International Environmental Law* (pp. 974–994). Oxford: Oxford University Press.
Whitley, S., Chen, H., Doukas, A., Gençsü, I., Gerasimchuk, I., Touchette, Y., & Worrall, L. (2018). G7 fossil fuel subsidy scorecard. Retrieved from https://euagenda.eu/upload/publications/untitled-149669-ea.pdf. Accessed 18 Jan 2019.
Wirths, D., Rosser, C., Horber-Papazian, K., & Mader, L. (2017). Über die gesetzliche Verankerung von Evaluation: Die Verteilung von Evaluationsklauseln und deren Auswirkungen auf kantonaler Ebene. In F. Sager, T. Widmer, & A. Balthasar (Eds.), *Evaluation im politischen System der Schweiz* (pp. 155–188). Zürich: NZZ Libro.
Wong, E. (2017). China wants to be a climate change watchdog, but can it lead by example? Retrieved from https://www.nytimes.com/2017/01/10/world/asia/china-wants-to-be-a-climate-change-watchdog-but-cant-yet-lead-by-example.html. Accessed 18 Jan 2019.
Wörlen, C., Rieseberg, S., & Lorenz, R. (2014). *A national experiment without evaluation or monitoring and evaluating the Energiewende?* Berlin: International Energy Policy and Programme Evaluation Conference.
WWF. (2016). Smart cash for the climate: Maximising auctioning revenues from the EU Emissions Trading System. Retrieved from http://ec.europa.eu/environment/life/project/Projects/index.cfm?fuseaction=home.showFile&rep=file&fil=MAXIMISER_Technical-report_EN.pdf. Accessed 18 Jan 2019.
WWF-UK. (2017). Grounded: Ten reasons why international offsetting won't solve Heathrow's climate change problem. Retrieved from https://www.wwf.org.uk/sites/default/files/2017-05/WWF_Grounded_report_FINAL_1.pdf. Accessed 18 Jan 2019.
Yamide, D., & Cogswell, N. (2018). At COP24 in Poland, negotiators must lay down ground rules for the Paris Agreement. Retrieved from https://www.wri.org/blog/2018/11/cop24-poland-negotiators-must-lay-down-ground-rules-paris-agreement. Accessed 18 Jan 2019.
Yamin, F., & Depledge, J. (2004). *The international climate change regime: a guide to rules, institutions and procedures*. Cambridge, UK: Cambridge University Press.
Ziesing, H. J. (2014). Monitoring der Energiewende – Ist Deutschland schon auf dem Zielpfad? In A. Brunnengräber & M. R. di Nucci (Eds.), *Im Hürdenlauf zur Energiewende: Von Transformationen, Reformen und Innovationen* (pp. 353–368). Wiesbaden: Springer.

Extending Energy Policy: The Challenge of Sector Integration

Michael Rodi and Michael Kalis

Contents

Introduction	102
Definition	104
Definition of Sector Coupling	104
Analysis of Concept Development Based on Existing Definitions	105
Governance Structures for "Good" Sector Coupling	108
Purpose and Objectives of Sector Coupling	108
Principles of "Good" Sector Coupling	110
Summary – Normative Governance for "Good" Sector Coupling	114
Conclusion	115
Cross-References	115
References	115

Abstract

Sector coupling has become a well-known term and is seen as playing a crucial role in shifting away from fossil fuels and thus as a decisive factor in the success of the energy transition. The European Green Deal and the Climate Action Plan 2050 also address the concept. However, there is still a lack of a definitive, generally accepted definition of sector coupling. This also means that the discourse has not yet considered the purposes, goals, and principles of sector

---

M. Rodi (✉)
Institute for Climate Protection, Energy and Mobility (IKEM), Berlin, Germany

Faculty of Public Law, Finance Law, Environmental and Energy Law, University of Greifswald, Greifswald, Germany
e-mail: michael.rodi@uni-greifswald.de

M. Kalis
Institute for Climate Protection, Energy and Mobility (IKEM), Berlin, Germany

Interdisciplinary Centre for Baltic Sea Region Research, University of Greifswald, Greifswald, Germany
e-mail: michael.kalis@ikem.de

© Springer Nature Switzerland AG 2022
M. Knodt, J. Kemmerzell (eds.), *Handbook of Energy Governance in Europe*,
https://doi.org/10.1007/978-3-030-43250-8_44

coupling. This chapter examines the issue at an abstract level. To this end, the concept of sector coupling was analyzed and criteria for "good" sector coupling were established. Criteria are the purpose, objectives, and principles of "good" sector coupling. To those belong in particular the contribution to existing national and international commitments and additionality of the energy used. Based on the purpose, objectives, and principles of "good" sector coupling, this chapter offers a valid instrument for assessment and review by legislators, stakeholders, and the public of sector coupling measures and regulation.

Keywords

Sector coupling · Good sector coupling · Sector integration · Renewable energy · Additionality · Flexibility and efficiency

Introduction

"Sector coupling" has become a well-known term in academia (Hoffrichter and Beckers 2018; Gea-Bermúdez et al. 2021; Buttler and Spliethoff 2018; Pavičević et al. 2020; Emonts et al. 2019; Fridgen et al. 2020; Brown et al. 2018; Gils et al. 2021; Jarke-Neuert and Perino 2019; Lichtenwoehrer et al. 2021; Oberle et al. 2020; Ramsebner et al. 2021; Robinius et al. 2017a; Wietschel et al. 2020a, Olczak and Piebalgs 2018), in the energy industry (GEODE 2020; ENTSO-E 2019), and in politics (Van Nuffel et al. 2018; EU Parliament 2019; EU Commission 2019; BMWi 2016) and plays a crucial role in shifting away from fossil fuels and thus as a decisive factor in the success of the energy transition. The Climate Action Plan 2050 identifies sector coupling as an important topic in the German energy policy debate (BMU 2016). The European Green Deal also addresses the concept, albeit with the slightly different terminology "(smart) sector integration" (EU Commission 2019).

At a certain level of abstraction, it is possible to make general statements about the challenges of sector coupling, despite the existence of clear differences between the energy systems of individual states. The essence of these challenges can be summed up in the following question:

How Does Renewable Energy Move from One Sector to Another?

At this level of abstraction, the solution seems relatively simple, if not obvious: systems for the generation of energy from renewable sources, systems for transmission or transport, and facilities for conversion or usage – in short, a suitable infrastructure. However, if we take a closer look at the challenges in concrete terms, we quickly find ourselves bogged down in the complexity of individual issues that are nearly impossible to untangle: support for renewable electricity generation plants when the energy generated is used in a sector other than the energy sector itself; passing on the green attribute – and thus the verifiable and creditable greenhouse gas reduction effect – of renewable energy; the use of (electricity) Guarantees of Origin (GOs), the distinction between natural gas grids and hydrogen grids; the charges, levies, and other electricity price components; technology neutrality and technology promotion; quotas for blending, use, and greenhouse gas reduction; power-to-X and direct electrification; flexibility incentives; and many other areas of discussion.

The challenges for the different sectors do not necessarily seem to overlap. Rather, challenges vary based on certain sector-specific characteristics. The example of hydrogen shows this very clearly. The challenges for the production and transport of hydrogen are identical or at least comparable for the different sectors – except for any hydrogen purity levels that must be considered. However, decisive differences emerge on certain issues, at least for usage technologies and additional infrastructure. The conversion of a mineral oil refinery, for example, poses far fewer challenges than does the conversion of a district heating system. There are certainly entirely different challenges for (energy-intensive) industries and the management of volatile energy supply there. The European Union and the Member States – in this case, Germany – are responding to these challenges with a large number of regulations that typically address specific factors or a specific obstacle to sector coupling. For example, in the revised Renewable Energy Directive (RED II) 2018/2001/EU, the European legislature addresses the credit eligibility criteria for hydrogen in the transport sector, produced from electricity from renewable energy sources and drawn from the public supply grid (cf. Article 27 (3) (6) RED II). In Germany, an exemption from the otherwise applicable EEG levy for companies producing green hydrogen is now regulated (Sections 64a, 69b EEG 2021). However, this support for the industrial production of hydrogen does not alter the fact that different requirements are placed on hydrogen for specific uses in different sectors, such as the feeding of renewable hydrogen into gas supply networks or as a renewable fuel in transport (cf. Section 3 (10f) EnWG as well as Section 3 in conjunction with Annex 1 37th BImSchV).

Even from this cursory overview, it is clear that sector coupling poses many different challenges. No single solution can resolve all of these issues. Thus far, however, attempts to identify solutions have revealed the absence of any coherent overall strategy. There is already a lack of a definitive, generally accepted definition of sector coupling. This opens up opportunities for criticism of sector coupling as a political buzzword (Jarke-Neuert and Perino 2019). It also means that the discourse has not yet considered the purposes, goals, and principles of sector coupling. The following chapter is intended to fill this gap.

In contrast to previous approaches in practice and research, which have produced quite convincing proposals for reducing and overcoming individual obstacles and hurdles to sector coupling, this chapter examines the issue at a more abstract level – that is, a metalevel. To this end, the concept of sector coupling will be analyzed and criteria will be established for "good" sector coupling. Based on the definition of good sector coupling and the corresponding benchmarks, a suitable and overarching control instrument for sector coupling measures will be developed. The aim is to propose a working basis for the legal policy development and evaluation of sector coupling approaches that will be necessary in the future. This analysis begins by establishing a clear, interdisciplinary understanding of the term (B.). On this foundation, principles of and requirements for (future) sector coupling are derived to develop criteria for "good" sector coupling (C.).

Definition

Requirements for, and principles of, sector coupling can be developed only after the term "sector coupling" is clearly defined. In this context, the definition of sector coupling must also be strictly separated from that of "good" sector coupling. The latter is derived from the principles of the former and does not itself contribute to a critical justification of such principles.

The working basis for this discussion will be a definition of sector coupling developed by the authors. This will be analyzed in relation to, and based on, existing definitions of the concept.

Definition of Sector Coupling

In our understanding, sector coupling should be defined as follows:

> "Sector coupling" describes the interconnection and interlocking of sectors, i.e. the unimpeded flow of energy and the cooperation of infrastructures. "Sectors" describes energy production and (end) consumption categories, such as electricity, buildings and mobility. Sector coupling leads to the interdependence of otherwise independent sectors and aims at creating unhindered energy flows in an integrated energy system.

The term "sector coupling" was chosen deliberately. Other terms can also be found in the literature. For example, at least in the German-speaking world, a distinction is drawn between the "coupling of sectors" and "sector coupling" (Wietschel et al. 2018, 2020a). Elsewhere in the discourse, "integration" is used in place of "coupling" (GEODE 2020, EU Commission 2019; Ramsebner et al. 2021; Robinius et al. 2017a; Van Nuffel et al. 2018).

First, it should be noted that the term "coupling of sectors," as opposed to "sector coupling," more clearly refers to the interconnection of multiple sectors $(2 + x)$ with and among each other (Fridgen et al. 2020; Jarke-Neuert and Perino 2019; Ramsebner et al. 2021; Scorza et al. 2018; Gils et al. 2021). Therefore, at least in German, the plural "sectors" should be used (i.e., *Sektorenkopplung* rather than *Sektorkopplung*) for a more precise definition. To be precise, in English the term "coupling of sectors" should be used. For convenience, the usage of the English term "sector coupling" seems appropriate and will be used hereinafter.

Regarding the question of a distinction between "coupling" and "integration," it is sometimes argued that the latter is preferable in the sense of a holistic approach because it implies a broader systemic interplay between different sectors and energy sources beyond "mere" coupling (GEODE 2020). However, the term "coupling" can also be understood from a systemic perspective – as a description of (plastic) relationships that are characterized in certain respects by autonomy, in other respects by a lack of autonomy, and by dependence on the environment. The concept of coupling is therefore not incompatible with a holistic perspective. In contrast, the concept of integration requires the existence of an initial or core sector, into which other sectors are inserted. This is likely based on a perception of the energy sector as the starting point for sector coupling. This is probably true to the extent that sector coupling was at least originally aimed at electrifying other end-use sectors (Van Nuffel et al. 2018). However, sector coupling has since evolved from this limited understanding of the term. Sector coupling can also exist without such a core sector and, in particular, without the energy sector – as is accurately indicated by the term "coupling," though not by "integration" (Lichtenwoehrer et al. 2021; Ramsebner et al. 2021). Examples include the use of biomass from the agricultural sector to provide heat or the use of waste heat from industrial processes to provide heat for buildings.

Analysis of Concept Development Based on Existing Definitions

As the above formulation makes clear, sector coupling is defined here as broadly and comprehensively as possible. A detailed discussion and justification of this definition will follow to account for this divergence from previous interpretations. It should be noted at the outset that a uniform conceptual basis for sector coupling has not yet been established (Lichtenwoehrer et al. 2021; Ramsebner et al. 2021). This is due in particular to the fact that the terminology used generally reflects a specific perspective in the relevant field of interest (above all technology or systemic infrastructure) (Ramsebner et al. 2021; Wietschel et al. 2018; Wietschel et al. 2020a). A normative approach has likely been used only once so far (Wietschel et al. 2018).

The Origin and Purpose of Sector Coupling as the "Driving Force" of the Definition

To approach the concept of sector coupling, it is first worth examining the origins of the term in scientific and political discourse. Sector coupling is a term associated with the more recent debate and is closely linked to the increasing share of volatile renewable energy in the electricity sector (Fridgen et al. 2020; Ramsebner et al. 2021; Robinius et al. 2017a). The term probably originated in the German-speaking world and is a part of an extension of the energy transition (BMWi 2016; Fridgen et al. 2020, Van Nuffel et al. 2018; Ramsebner et al. 2021; Robinius et al. 2017a). Because of this, many publications consider sector coupling a key tool to manage the fluctuating generation of renewable energy and facilitate their full integration into the energy system (Fridgen et al. 2020, Van Nuffel et al. 2018; Ramsebner et al. 2021; Robinius et al. 2017a, 2018; Wietschel et al. 2018, Bruckner and Kondziella 2021, Schaber et al. 2013, Roach and Meeus 2020; Gils et al. 2021, Schaber et al. 2012; Hansen et al. 2019).

In this context, sector coupling is above all associated with, and derived from, the goal of decarbonizing the energy system and thus of making progress toward climate policy targets (Fridgen et al. 2020; Van Nuffel et al. 2018; Jarke-Neuert and Perino 2019; Ramsebner et al. 2021; Robinius et al. 2017a; Wietschel et al. 2018, Bruckner and Kondziella 2021, Brear et al. 2020).

In addition, other aspects of sector coupling, sometimes described as secondary goals or cobenefits, are integrated into the understanding of the term (Wietschel et al.

2018; Brown et al. 2018; Van Nuffel et al. 2018; Olczak and Piebalgs 2018; Robinius et al. 2018). According to Wietschel et al. (2018), for example, a secondary objective of sector coupling is to contribute to flexibility and energy efficiency improvements in the energy system. In addition, it is argued that sector coupling makes it possible to optimize the degrees of freedom (Wietschel et al. 2018).

However, there is just partial consideration of a more far-reaching, overarching goal of linking all sectors into an integrated overall system that can contribute to greenhouse gas reduction. The European Union, in particular, refers to an "Energy System Integration – the coordinated planning and operation of the energy system "as a whole," across multiple energy carriers, infrastructures, and consumption sectors" as part of the Green Deal (EU Commission 2020; Van Nuffel et al. 2018). "Multi-energy system" is sometimes used, likely with little difference in meaning (Fridgen et al. 2020).

It is questionable whether describing the purpose and goals of sector coupling is useful in producing a definition of the term. Integrating the goal or underlying purpose into the definition of the term thus mixes a descriptive element with a normative claim. In order to define clear principles and requirements for "good" sector coupling in our understanding, the concept must be clearly distinguished from the descriptive meaning of sector coupling. This must be considered from an overall systemic perspective that focuses on the fundamental conceptual meaning of sector coupling. From this perspective, sector coupling is predominantly a process of transforming the conceptualization of the energy system from a collection of isolated sectors to a linked system. The core elements of the definition are thus the interlinkage and reciprocity that characterize an integrated energy system. Embedding certain climate objectives (such as increasing flexibility and efficiency) in the term does not help to develop a broadly useful definition that captures the essence of sector coupling. An interdisciplinary definition of sector coupling must therefore detach itself from the political "origin" of the term and, at least initially, from goals such as decarbonization. This is in no way intended to give the impression that sector coupling and the transformation process addressed here are ends in themselves. Rather, it is an intermediate step in the development of a definition and the conceptualization of good sector coupling. The next step considers the specific ways in which "good" sector coupling should contribute to climate change mitigation.

The Concept of Sectors

In addition to the question of whether sector coupling should be defined by its purpose and objectives, a decisive factor is how broadly the system to be integrated is interpreted. This must start with the word itself and its components. In contemporary linguistic, sector (Latin: sector = *tailor/cutter*) means a subsection, a section of a whole. Thus far, the specific subsections of the energy system included in sector coupling and the definition of such subsections have varied widely (Ramsebner et al. 2021; Scorza et al. 2018). From an energy industry perspective, the subsections cited are the typical consumption sectors – households; trade, commerce, and services; industry; and transport – which are to be supplied with electricity from renewable sources in different ways (BMWi 2016; Ramsebner et al. 2021). This is supported by the argument that it enables a technology-neutral approach that does not differentiate according to the energy source used (electricity, gas, or heat) (Ramsebner et al. 2021). The electricity sector itself – consisting of generation and original electricity demand – is often regarded as a sector associated with other areas of application (Scorza et al. 2018). These consumption sectors vary in turn. For example, the German government's climate protection plan refers to the heating, mobility, and industrial sectors (BMU 2016). At the same time, however, the Climate Action Plan, like the Federal Climate Protection Act, bases its determination of sectoral targets for greenhouse gas (GHG) emissions on a differentiation between the energy, building, mobility, industrial and commercial, agriculture, and land use, and forestry sectors (BMU 2016). The European Parliament takes such distinctions even further, differentiating not only between end-use sectors ("end-use sector coupling") but also between generation sectors themselves (especially electricity, gas, and so-called "cross-vector integration") in its plans for sector coupling (Van Nuffel et al. 2018; Wietschel et al. 2018; DENA 2018; Fridgen et al. 2020; Ramsebner et al. 2021).

One reason for the partial limitation to, or focus on, certain sectors (most notably mobility and heat) is that these are the central areas in which fossil energy sources are still very widespread; as a result, the potential for sector coupling is considered to be particularly high here (Wietschel et al. 2018). However, if the aim is not only to look at central fields of action, especially climate policy, from a specific perspective but also to establish a general foundation for sector coupling, a more comprehensive understanding is required. The concept should encompass not only the consumption sectors that are typically based on fossil fuels but also the possible synergies within these sectors or in relation to energy generation. Central to this concept is an understanding of sector coupling as a future-oriented transformation process that is open to various linkages. A broad interpretation of the term sector, as proposed by the European Parliament, should thus be selected in reference to this concept of transformation and is the understanding applied here (Van Nuffel et al. 2018; Wietschel et al. 2018; EU Commission 2020).

The Concept of Coupling

However, there is virtually no explicit discussion of the concept of coupling (DENA 2018; Brown et al. 2018; Hoffrichter and Beckers 2018; Fridgen et al. 2020). Still, the various definitions used reveal how coupling, and thus the "stages" of sector coupling, is understood. Particularly from a technological perspective, some definitions and interpretations in use focus primarily on the direct or indirect electrification of the sectors and regard this as a sufficient understanding of "coupling" (Ramsebner et al. 2021; Scorza et al. 2018). In such cases, the coupling of sectors functions as a "one-way street" (Ramsebner et al. 2021), which is significantly oriented toward the transfer of (surplus) electricity to other sectors. Different approaches, on the other hand, interpret a coupling of sectors from a systemic point of view. In these cases, coupling (even if not explicitly referred to as such) denotes a holistic interlinkage of the entire energy system with diverse, multidimensional interactions in all directions (Fridgen et al. 2020; Fridgen and Körner 2019; Ausfelder et al. 2017).

As described above, the concept of coupling refers precisely to a coordinated relationship characterized by aspects of both autonomy and a lack of autonomy. Approaches that describe sector coupling primarily in terms of a one-dimensional pathway are typically guided, above all, by the potential for decarbonization and by the origin of the debate on sector coupling. They, therefore, fall short of more comprehensive and foundational approaches and do not consider the potential of a fully integrated overall energy system.

In this context, it is also important to note that infrastructures are only sporadically included in the concept of sector coupling (DENA 2018; Wietschel et al. 2018, 2020a; Fridgen et al. 2020; Lichtenwoehrer et al. 2021; Olczak and Piebalgs 2018; Guelpa et al. 2019). According to Fridgen et al. (2020), any attempt to define sector coupling without including infrastructures neglects aspects beyond the inter-sectoral energy flow and thus represents only a subpart of a holistic sector coupling. The inclusion of infrastructures is essential if sector coupling is understood in as integrative a sense as possible – that is, as an overall concept for a future energy system.

Summary

The above explanations make it clear that no uniform, interdisciplinary, basic understanding has been established to date. An interpretation of sector coupling that is as far-reaching and open to transformation as possible can serve as a foundation for the concrete principles and requirements that characterize "good" sector coupling. From this perspective, the definition is deliberately selected at the outset to capture the comprehensive concept of coupling in the sense of an overall energy system and should then make it possible to identify specific principles of sector coupling. Such a broad interpretation also remains technology-neutral and can encompass future coupling options.

Governance Structures for "Good" Sector Coupling

Starting from a broad, open, and systemic perspective on sector coupling, it is possible to consider the criteria for a "good" sector coupling of the future and the basic principles applicable to it. An initially descriptive term must thus take on a normative designation based on its role in the overall system. Principles are the general rules against which actions taken to achieve the goals of sector coupling must be measured. Typically, principles are linked primarily to the specific purposes and objectives of the relevant subject matter, which must therefore be examined first in greater detail (cf. B.II.1 above).

Purpose and Objectives of Sector Coupling

Sector coupling is not an end in itself, but an aspect of climate change mitigation and the energy system, as is clear from the fact that the term originated in the *Energiewende* (BMWi 2016; Fridgen et al. 2020, Van Nuffel et al. 2018; Ramsebner et al. 2021; Robinius et al. 2017a, Bruckner and Kondziella 2021). However, the literature contains no clear differentiation between the purpose and goals of sector coupling.

Based on the definition applied here, the goal of sector coupling can be understood as the achievement of an "end state" in which the energy system is interpreted not as a collection of isolated sectors, but as an integrated energy system (EU Commission 2020; DENA 2018; Ausfelder et al. 2017; Fridgen et al. 2020; Ramsebner et al. 2021).

What is sought, however, are further-reaching, normative deductions about a "sector coupling of the future" that reflect the expectations placed on it. The purpose of such "good" sector coupling is to contribute to climate change mitigation and the climate targets and commitments associated with it (EU Commission 2020, 2019; Wietschel et al. 2018, 2020a). On this basis, the key objective of "good" sector coupling is to accelerate reductions in GHG, i.e., the decarbonization of the energy industry (Fridgen et al. 2020; Wietschel et al. 2018; Ramsebner et al. 2021; Van Nuffel et al. 2018; Lichtenwoehrer et al. 2021). It is debatable whether the substitution of fossil energy sources and the integration of renewable energy in this context constitute a specific goal of sector coupling, based on this interpretation. These contribute significantly to decarbonization but are not a mandatory precondition for it. For example, reductions in GHG emissions through increased use of combined heat and power (CHP) applications from fossil energy or the use of (fossil-based) electricity in the transport sector are also possible and, in this sense, are applications of sector coupling that reduce GHG. In light of the historical origin of sector coupling (i.e., as the coupling of an energy sector already fed by renewable energy with other sectors and thus as a logical progression from the electricity transition to a holistic energy transition), the classification of renewable energy integration as a mere instrument is not persuasive. Moreover, the purpose of climate change mitigation will not be fully served without the use, and thus the increasing integration, of renewable energy. Therefore, the integration of renewable energy is an independent goal of sector coupling (Fridgen et al. 2020; Ramsebner et al. 2021; Wietschel et al. 2018, 2020a; Robinius et al. 2017b).

In addition to the central goals of GHG reduction and renewable energy integration, the literature cites certain secondary goals or cobenefits, such as the contribution to increasing flexibility and energy efficiency in the energy system and the potential to optimize the degrees of freedom (Wietschel et al. 2018, 2020a; Van Nuffel et al. 2018). Furthermore, sector coupling can contribute to the avoidance of overcapacity in infrastructure, and existing infrastructure can be used for the necessary decarbonization (Fridgen and Körner 2019; Fridgen et al. 2020; Robinius et al. 2018). It could also ultimately increase the resilience of the energy system in the face of disruptions (Van Nuffel et al. 2018). However, classifying these aspects as genuine goals of sector coupling does not seem appropriate. If a goal is a desired state that, if valid, cannot allow for deviations, then such aspects represent possible advantages or benefits of sector coupling (Wietschel et al. 2018, 2020a). These are not the desired states that every sector coupling technology necessarily seeks to achieve; at best, such states thus represent principles against which corresponding instruments must be measured.

Principles of "Good" Sector Coupling

The purpose described above (i.e., climate change mitigation and climate goals) gives rise to certain principles. Others can arise from more general principles, such as those of the energy law.

Common principles cited in the context of sector coupling include flexibility (Ramsebner et al. 2021; Wietschel et al. 2018, 2020a; Scorza et al. 2018, Muenster et al. 2020, Bruckner and Kondziella 2021, Roach and Meeus 2020, Gils et al. 2021), energy efficiency (Wietschel et al. 2018, 2020a; Lichtenwoehrer et al. 2021; Ausfelder et al. 2017, Bruckner and Kondziella 2021), and additionality (Agora Verkehrswende et al. 2018; Adelphi 2019; Matschoss and Nishimura 2019).

Flexibility

The term "flexibility" is widely used in energy law, but there is no standard legal definition. The German Federal Network Agency (BNetzA) defines the term as the change in feed-in or withdrawal in response to an external signal (price signal or activation) to provide a service in the energy system (BNetzA 2017).

The principle of flexibility is linked to and embedded in the general principles of the German Energy Industry Act (Sect. 1a (3) EnWG) as well as in the Internal Electricity Market Directive (Sect. 3 Directive 2009/72/EC). Flexibility takes into account the balancing of feed-in and withdrawal of electricity from the electricity grid at all times and thus primarily serves the purpose of security of supply.

With regard to sector coupling, the flexibility potential of certain technologies is repeatedly highlighted (Fridgen et al. 2020, Van Nuffel et al. 2018; Ramsebner et al. 2021; Robinius et al. 2017a, Bruckner and Kondziella 2021). For example, extensive storage flexibilities can be exploited through heat storage or power-to-X (PtX) applications in the context of sector coupling. In addition, aspects of demand flexibility continue to be a key consideration. Such flexibility may consist, for example, in the adjustment of the electricity demand of flexible consumption facilities to electricity generation ("demand-side management"), as in the case of charging points for electric vehicles.

The German legislature has also – at least to some extent – incorporated the flexibility potential of sector coupling technologies into the principles of the electricity market, according to Section 1a EnWG. In addition, individual legal regulations privilege flexibility options associated with certain sector-coupling technologies. In the context of examples cited above, Section 118 EnWG provides for a temporary exemption from grid charges for electricity storage facilities that generate hydrogen or synthetic gases from electricity.

The increasing importance of flexibility and pointed emphasis on sector coupling is closely linked to the increasing share of volatile renewable energy generation in total electricity feed-in. Publications highlighting flexibility as a goal or central benefit of sector coupling are largely based on this finding (Ramsebner et al. 2021; Wietschel et al. 2018; Fridgen et al. 2020, Van Nuffel et al. 2018; Robinius et al. 2017b, Bruckner and Kondziella 2021).

The question of flexibility as a principle of "good" sector coupling again raises the question of its relationship to renewable energy integration (see C.I.). If the substitution of fossil energy sources and the integration of renewables is understood as the goal of sector coupling, flexibility, too, emerges as a central original principle.

In any case, flexibility, as described above, is a general principle of the energy law. It is therefore also relevant to questions of sector coupling and must be taken into account.

Energy Efficiency

Energy efficiency describes the ratio of a certain benefit or a certain yield of performance, services, goods, or energy to given energy input. Energy efficiency is a subcategory of "energy conservation," in the sense that energy is saved by reducing (as opposed to forgoing) the energy input.

The principle of efficiency is also a general principle of the Energy Industry Act under Sect. 1 EnWG. In the context of the Energy Union, energy efficiency is also part of the framework strategy (recital 1 Directive 2018/2002/EU). In this context, efficiency primarily means energy efficiency and thus the conservation of primary energy sources. Ultimately, energy efficiency, as a contribution to energy conservation, serves the overarching goals of climate change mitigation.

The term energy efficiency is also increasingly used and discussed in relation to sector coupling (Wietschel et al. 2018, 2020a; Lichtenwoehrer et al. 2021; Ausfelder et al. 2017). In this context, energy efficiency refers to the imperative to minimize both quantitative and qualitative energy losses.

In the energy policy debate in general, the concept of demand-side efficiency is becoming increasingly important. Moving away from an approach focused primarily on the expansion of renewable energies, greater consideration of energy efficiency is intended to significantly reduce the costs of the energy transition. This has given rise to the political principle of "efficiency first," which in general involves being more attentive to efficiency measures on the demand side and giving preference to these measures over the supply side if they are more cost-effective in macroeconomic terms (Article 1 Directive 2018/2002/EU (Energy Efficiency Directive)). In concise terms, there is no need for energy supply where consumption can be spared (BMWi 2016).

With regard to the use of sector-coupling technologies, the "efficiency first" principle also leads to certain conclusions for different technologies. A fundamental distinction can be drawn between the direct application of generated energies in another sector (e.g., the use of renewable electricity in cars) and indirect or conversion applications (e.g., the production of electricity-based, synthetic fuels). From the perspective of efficiency, a principle of sector coupling must therefore be the priority of direct sector-coupling technologies (Wietschel et al. 2018; Bracker 2017). Additional conversion steps introduce large energy losses, which are contrary to the idea of energy efficiency (Wietschel et al. 2018; Bracker 2017). As a result, synthetic fuels, for example, may only be used if another more efficient measure (direct electrification) is ruled out.

Like flexibility, this principle is rooted in the general energy law. Nevertheless, it claims significance as a requirement for "good" sector coupling due to its overriding function, which is confirmed in a legal sense in Article 1 Energy Efficiency Directive.

Additionality

The purpose of "good" sector coupling is to contribute to climate change mitigation, and the goal is to reduce GHG emissions. In this respect, climate change and the increasing concentration of GHG in the atmosphere represent a global problem. The purpose and goal are therefore not served by merely contributing to Germany's climate change mitigation goals or reducing GHG emissions within the borders.

The same also applies to the relationship between the sectors of a possible sector coupling. The mere shifting of electricity or a climate-protecting contribution from one sector to another does not serve the interest of climate change mitigation and does not lead to a global reduction in GHG. Rather, a corresponding measure must be taken to produce farther-reaching effects. In particular, when using PtX technologies, care must be taken to ensure that widespread use does not lead to an increase in electricity generation from fossil fuels (UBA 2016; Agora Verkehrswende et al. 2018; Adelphi 2019; Matschoss and Nishimura 2019). Due to the "merit order effect" on the electricity market, there is a risk that additional electricity demand, e.g., from electrolyzers, will be met with electricity from fossil plants (Bracker 2017).

This topic is addressed under the term "additionality." This has become particularly important as a result of the European Union's Renewable Energy Directive (RED II). Recital 90 of the RED II Directive addresses "additionality" in a broader discussion of the proof of renewable electricity use in the production of liquid or gaseous fuels of nonbiogenic origin in the transport sector, as well as in the eligibility of these substances for credit. In addition to other criteria that ensure the actual purchase of renewable electricity, an element of additionality in the form of additional capacity or additional financing of renewable energies must be established as a prerequisite.

Additionality, in the sense of further expansion capacity, covers electricity purchase under a contract with a newly constructed plant. Furthermore, additional capacity could also be assumed for existing plants if it could be demonstrated that this would make it unnecessary to dismantle the plant. The "additional" capacity understood in this context could be secured by a guaranteed minimum period of continuous operation.

Financial additionality requires that a generation plant does not receive any further financial support during the electricity procurement for the production of corresponding fuels. This is already satisfied if the plant does not participate in a support regime or tender market during the term of the power purchase agreement. Other privileges, such as grid access or feed-in priority, remain unaffected.

Even if the existing legal framework addresses the characteristic of "additionality" only for the transport sector, it follows from the overarching purpose of "sector coupling of the future" that the principle of additionality must be valid beyond the individual sector (Agora Verkehrswende et al. 2018; Adelphi 2019; Matschoss and Nishimura 2019; Robinius et al. 2017a). Indeed, sector coupling measures only contribute to the purpose and goal of "good" sector coupling if they do not merely shift emissions and climate impacts, but also explicitly promote additional GHG emission reductions in the overall system.

"Additionality" is therefore one (and indeed the original) principle of "good" sector coupling and is the standard against which corresponding measures and instruments should be measured.

Other Principles

Additional general principles of the energy law – as expressed in Sect. 1 of the German Energy Industry Act (EnWG) – may apply. The principles of affordability and security of supply should be noted in this context, although the latter was already partly addressed in the discussion of flexibility.

In addition, it is noticeable that the current legal framework often focuses on individual technologies, in particular PtX technologies (Wietschel et al. 2018). An example of this is the privileged exemption from the electricity tax for companies in the manufacturing sector that use electricity for electrolysis (Sect. 9 StromStG). The exemption from grid charges for storage technologies in the form of PtG also addresses a specific technology (Sect. 118 EnWG). The same applies to the exemption from the EEG surcharge that has been introduced for companies producing green hydrogen (Section 69b EEG 2021). However, the general principle of the energy law is precisely the promotion of a free market and undistorted competition (cf. Section 1 EnWG). This also includes competition between innovations or technologies. The technology-neutrality of an instrument can thus also be included in an assessment of "good" sector coupling as one aspect of the general energy law principle of "free market and competition."

Sector Coupling in the Broader Context of Sustainability

"Good" sector coupling is primarily oriented toward climate change mitigation and GHG reduction. In contrast to general sector coupling, it also operates in the broader context of sustainability. The term "sustainability," which is not uniformly or clearly defined, encompasses a basic ecological understanding of the protection and preservation of natural systems through the (long-term) careful use of the resources available in such systems (Ekardt 2020).

A corresponding classification in the context of sustainability and the development of binding sustainability criteria seems indispensable against the background of the energy transition since the mere use of corresponding technologies alone does not guarantee sustainable use of resources. The sustainability criteria at the European level for biofuels provide some orientation for possible sustainability criteria. Under Article 29, RED II imposes further sustainability-related requirements on the corresponding substances, which must be met to be counted toward the objectives of the directive and the mandatory use of renewable energy under Article 25 RED II and to be taken into account in public funding rules.

These also include the obligation to achieve corresponding reductions in GHG reductions compared to certain target years (Article 29 (10) RED II). It follows from the calculation method in Annex V of the Directive that all emissions – from the production of the substance to the transport and use – must be taken into account for this purpose. This reflects an overarching guiding principle that expands the issue of GHG reduction in the context of sustainability to include a consideration of all life-cycle greenhouse gas emissions (Bracker 2017). In addition, the RED II requirements explicitly distinguish between GHG mitigation and other sustainability criteria in paragraphs 2–7, which primarily focus on land-use conflicts and the chosen feedstock (Kalis and Langenhorst 2020; Wietschel et al. 2020b). This delineation shows that sustainability is "more" than GHG mitigation and that mitigation cannot be achieved at any price. Thus, the ecological and social sustainability of the material, as well as the land used, can play a role as general sustainability criteria due to possible competition.

It seems appropriate to transfer these aspects and criteria to measures for sector coupling (Kalis and Langenhorst 2020; Wietschel et al. 2020b). In particular, hydrogen – representing one of the most promising developments in the *Energiewende* – can create tension with sustainability goals, both in terms of the origin of the input materials water and electricity and in terms of land competition; this shows that the consideration of such factors is necessary (Kalis and Langenhorst 2020; Wietschel et al. 2020b). The former, for example, is closely linked to questions of social and ecological sustainability in the case of imports from countries with less available drinking water. In this respect, this technology-specific example shows that relevant sustainability aspects should also be taken into account to achieve the goals of "good" sector coupling. Depending on the technology used, other conflicts and other sustainability aspects could be of importance.

Summary – Normative Governance for "Good" Sector Coupling

The following principles can thus constitute a "canon" for evaluation and review in the sense of normative governance for good sector coupling:

- Purpose: climate change mitigation and contribution to existing national and international climate commitments.
- Objective: GHG reduction in an integrated energy system and the integration of renewable energy.
- Principles:
  – Additionality of the energy used/of the climate-protecting effect.
  – Efficiency and flexibility as general principles of energy management must be taken into account.
  – In addition, other general energy law principles apply, such as security of supply, low prices, a free market and free competition, and transparency.
- In the context of sustainability, GHG emissions must be considered against the background of the entire life cycle, and general sustainability requirements for input materials, and land use must be taken into account.

The considerations thus outline a normative framework for "good" sector coupling. Regulations in energy law that address sector coupling technologies must be measured against the purpose, objective, and principles mentioned here. However, principles should not be understood as dogmas: Deviations are conceivable, even if only in exceptional cases and for objective reasons. An example of this is lorries operating on overhead contact line systems, which are not flexible but may be more efficient than lorries powered by fuel-cell systems (Wietschel et al. 2018).

Conclusion

Sector coupling will shape the energy policy debate soon, particularly concerning the production of renewable hydrogen, and will gradually find its way into the existing legal framework. As an instrument for assessment and review by legislators, stakeholders, and the public, the normative governance requirements for "good" sector coupling developed in this chapter can offer a substantive contribution to future regulations.

Cross-References

▶ The EU in Global Energy Governance

References

Adelphi. (2019). The role of clean hydrogen in the future energy systems of Japan and Germany. https://www.adelphi.de/de/system/files/mediathek/bilder/The%20role%20of%20clean%20hydrogen%20in%20the%20future%20energy%20systems%20of%20Japan%20and%20Germany%20-%20Study.pdf

Agora Verkehrswende, Agora Energiewende, & Frontier Economics. (2018). The future cost of electricity-based synthetic fuels. https://www.agora-energiewende.de/fileadmin/Projekte/2017/SynKost_2050/Agora_SynKost_Study_EN_WEB.pdf

Ausfelder, F., Fischedick, M., Münch, W., Sauer, J., Themann, M., Wagner, H.-J., Drake, F.-D., Henning, H.-M., Pittel, K.; Schätzler, K., Umbach, E., Wagner, U., Erlach, B., Kost, C., Rehtanz, C., Stephanos, C., Wagemann, K. (2017). Sektorenkopplung - Untersuchungen und Überlegungen zur Entwicklung eines integrierten Energiesystems. file:///C:/Users/user/Downloads/ESYS_Analyse_Sektorkopplung.pdf

Bracker, J. (2017). An outline of sustainability criteria for synthetic fuels used in transport. https://www.oeko.de/fileadmin/oekodoc/Sustainability-criteria-for-synthetic-fuels.pdf

Brear, M., Baldick, R., Cronshaw, I., & Olofsson, M. (2020). Sector coupling: Supporting decarbonisation of the global energy system. *The Electricity Journal, 33*, 106832.

Brown, T., Schlachtberger, D., Kies, A., Schramm, S., & Greiner, M. (2018). Synergies of sector coupling and transmission reinforcement in a cost-optimised, highly renewable European energy system. *Energy, 160*, 720–739.

Bruckner, T., & Kondziella, H. (2021). Sector coupling the next stage of the energiewende. http://library.fes.de/pdf-files/wiso/17593.pdf

Bundesministerium für Umwelt, Naturschutz und nukleare Sicherheit. (2016). Klimaschutzplan 2050. https://www.bmu.de/fileadmin/Daten_BMU/Download_PDF/Klimaschutz/klimaschutzplan_2050_bf.pdf

Bundesministerium für Wirtschaft und Energie. (2016). What exactly is meant by 'sector coupling'? https://www.bmwi-energiewende.de/EWD/Redaktion/EN/Newsletter/2016/13/Meldung/direkt-answers.html

Bundesnetzagentur. (2017). Flexibilität im Stromversorgungssystem. https://www.bundesnetzagentur.de/SharedDocs/Downloads/DE/Sachgebiete/Energie/Unternehmen_Institutionen/NetzentwicklungUndSmartGrid/BNetzA_Flexibilitaetspapier.pdf?__blob=publicationFile&v=1

Buttler, A., & Spliethoff, H. (2018). Current status of water electrolysis for energy storage, grid balancing and sector coupling via power-to-gas and power-to-liquids: A review. *Renewable and Sustainable Energy Reviews, 82*, 2440–2454.

Deutsche Energie-Agentur GmbH (dena). (2018). Dena-Leitstudie Integrierte Energiewende. https://www.dena.de/fileadmin/dena/Dokumente/Pdf/9262_dena-Leitstudie_Integrierte_Energiewende_Ergebnisbericht.pdf

Emonts, B., Reuß, M., Stenzel, P., & Welder, L. (2019). Flexible sector coupling with hydrogen: A climate-friendly fuel supply for road transport. *International Journal of Hydrogen Energy, 44*, 12918–12930.

Ekardt, F. (2020). *Sustainability – Transformation, governance, ethics, law*. Springer Verlag. https://doi.org/10.1007/978-3-030-19277-8.

ENTSO-E. (2019). Position on sector coupling through power to gas and sector integration. https://eepublicdownloads.entsoe.eu/clean-documents/Publications/Position%20papers%20and%20reports/Sector_coupling_integration_PositionPaper.pdf

European Parliamentary Research Service. (2019). Energy storage and sector coupling – Towards an integrated, decarbonised energy system. https://www.europarl.europa.eu/RegData/etudes/BRIE/2019/637962/EPRS_BRI(2019)637962_EN.pdf

European Commission [Communication]. (2019). The European green deal. https://eur-lex.europa.eu/legal-content/EN/TXT/HTML/?uri=CELEX:52019DC0640&from=EN

European Commission [Communication]. (2020). Powering a climate-neutral economy: An EU strategy for energy system integration. https://eur-lex.europa.eu/legal-content/EN/TXT/HTML/?uri=CELEX:52020DC0299&from=EN

Fridgen, G., Keller, R., Körner, M., & Schöpf, M. (2020). A holistic view on sector coupling. *Energy Policy, 147*, 111913.

Fridgen, G., & Körner, M. (2019). Sektorenkopplung als ganzheitlicher Ansatz für das Energiesystem: Potentiale und Herausforderungen. In J. Gundel & K. W. Lange (Eds.), *10 Jahre Energierecht im Wandel: Tagungsband der Zehnten Bayreuther Energierechtstage 2019* (pp. 33–48). Tübingen: Mohr Siebeck, 2020.

Gea-Bermúdez, J., Jensen, I., Münster, M., Koivisto, M., Kirkerud, J., Chen, Y., & Ravn, H. (2021). The role of sector coupling in the green transition: A least-cost energy system development in northern-Central Europe towards 2050. *Applied Energy, 289*, 116685.

GEODE. (2020). The role of Sector integration in decarbonising Europe. https://www.geode-eu.org/wp-content/uploads/2020/06/20200603-GEODE-PP-SECTOR-INTEGRATION.pdf

Gils, H. C., Gardian, H., & Schmugge, J. (2021). Interaction of hydrogen infrastructures with other sector coupling options towards a zero-emission energy system in Germany. *Renewable Energy, 180*, 140–156.

Guelpa, E., Bischi, A., Verda, V., Chertkov, M., & Lund, H. (2019). Power-to-gas: Electrolyzers as an alternative to network expansion – An example from a distribution system operator. *Energy, 184*, 2–21.

Hansen, K., Breyer, C., & Lund, H. (2019). Status and perspectives on 100% renewable energy systems. *Energy, 175*, 471–480.

Hoffrichter, A., & Beckers, T. (2018). Cross-border coordination as a prerequisite for efficient sector coupling in interconnected power systems. https://www.wip.tu-berlin.de/fileadmin/fg280/forschung/publikationen/2018/hoffrichter_beckers_2018-cross-border_coordination_in_interconnected_power_systems_sc-v56.pdf

Jarke-Neuert, J., & Perino, G. (2019). Understanding sector coupling: The general equilibrium emissions effects of electro-technology and renewables deployment. https://papers.ssrn.com/sol3/papers.cfm?abstract_id=3326407

Kalis, M., & Langenhorst, T. (2020). Nachhaltigkeits- und Treibhausgaseinsparungskriterien für Wasserstoff. *ZNER - Zeitschrift für neues Energierecht, 2*, 72–78.

Lichtenwoehrer, P., Abart-Heriszt, L., Kretschmer, F., Suppan, F., Stoeglehner, G., & Neugebauer, G. (2021). Evaluating spatial interdependencies of sector coupling using spatiotemporal modelling. *Energies, 14*, 1256.

Matschoss, P., & Nishimura, K. (2019). Analysis of framework conditions for foundation of green retailers in Japan. https://www.izes.de/sites/default/files/publikationen/EM_18_014.pdf

Münster, M., Bramstoft, R., Sneum, D., & Bühler, F. (2020). Sector coupling: Concepts, state-of-the-art and perspectives. https://www.researchgate.net/publication/339365854_Sector_Coupling_Concepts_State-of-the-art_and_Perspectives

Oberle, S., Stute, J., Fritz, M., Klobasa, M., & Wietschel, M. (2020). Sector coupling technologies in gas, electricity, and heat networks. *TATuP – Journal for Technology Assessment in Theory and Practice, 29*, 24–30. https://www.tatup.de/index.php/tatup/article/view/6812/11494.

Olczak, M., & Piebalgs, A. (2018). Sector coupling: The new EU climate and energy paradigm? *Robert Schuman Centre Policy Brief, 17*. https://cadmus.eui.eu/bitstream/handle/1814/59294/PB_2018_17.pdf?sequence=1&isAllowed=y.

Pavičević, M., Mangipinto, A., Nijs, W., Lombardi, F., Kavvadias, K., Jiménez Navarro, J. P., Colombo, E., & Quoilin, S. (2020). The potential of sector coupling in future European energy systems: Soft linking between the Dispa-SET and JRC-EU-TIMES models. *Applied Energy, 267*.

Ramsebner, J., Haas, R., Ajanovic, A., & Wietschel, M. (2021). The sector coupling concept: A critical review. *WIREs Energy and Environment, 10*. https://wires.onlinelibrary.wiley.com/doi/epdf/10.1002/wene.396.

Roach, M., & Meeus, L. (2020). The welfare and price effects of sector coupling with power-to-gas. *Energy Economics, 86*, 104708.

Robinius, M., Raje, T., Nykamp, S., Rott, T., Müller, M., Grube, T., Katzenbach, B., Küppers, S., & Stolten, D. (2018). Power-to-gas: Electrolyzers as an alternative to network expansion – An example from a distribution system operator. *Applied Energy, 210*, 182–197.

Robinius, M., Otto, A., Heuser, P., Welder, L., Syranidis, K., Ryberg, D., Grube, T., Markewitz, P., Peters, R., & Stolten, D. (2017a). Linking the power and transport sectors – Part 1: The principle of sector coupling. *Energies, 10*, 956. https://www.mdpi.com/1996-1073/10/7/956.

Robinius, M., Otto, A., Heuser, P., Welder, L., Syranidis, K., Ryberg, D., Grube, T., Markewitz, P., Peters, R., & Stolten, D. (2017b). Linking the power and transport sectors—Part 2: Modelling a sector coupling scenario for Germany. *Energies, 10*, 957. https://www.mdpi.com/1996-1073/10/7/957.

Schaber, K., Steinke, F., Hamacher, T. (2013). Managing temporary oversupply from renewables efficiently: Electricity storage versus energy sector coupling in Germany. International Energy Workshop 2013 Paris. https://www.internationalenergyworkshop.org/docs/IEW%202013_4E3paperSchaber.pdf

Schaber, K., Steinke, F., & Hamacher, T. (2012). Transmission grid extensions for the integration of variable renewable energies in Europe: Who benefits where? *Energy Policy, 43*, 123–135.

Scorza, S., Pfeiffer, J., Schmitt, A., & Weissbart, C. (2018). Kurz zum Klima: „Sektorkopplung" – Ansätze und Implikationen der Dekarbonisierung des Energiesystems. Ifo Schnelldienst, 71, 49–53.

Umweltbundesamt. (2016). Integration von Power to Gas/Power to Liquid in den laufenden Transformationsprozess. https://www.umweltbundesamt.de/sites/default/files/medien/1/publikationen/position_power_to_gas-power_to_liquid_web.pdf

Van Nuffel, L., Gorenstein Dedecca, J., Smit, T., Rademaekers, K. (2018). Sector coupling: how can it be enhanced in the EU to foster grid stability and decarbonise? https://www.europarl.europa.eu/Regdata/etudes/STUD/2018/626091/IPOL_STU(2018)626091_EN.pdf

Wietschel, M., Plötz, P., Pfluger, B.; Klobasa, M., Eßer, A., Haendel, M., Müller-Kirchenbauer, J., Kochems, J., Hermann, L., Grosse, B., Nacken, L., Küster, M., Pacem, V., Naumann, D., Kost, C., Kohrs, R., Fahl, U., Schäfer-Stradowsky, S., Timmermann, D., & Albert, D. (2018). Sektorkopplung – Definition, Chancen und Herausforderungen. https://www.ikem.de/wp-content/uploads/2018/02/WP_Sustainability-and-Innovation_Sektorenkopplung_S01-2018.pdf

Wietschel, M., Held, A., Pfluger, B., & Ragwitz, M. (2020a): Energy integration across electricity, heating & cooling and the transport sector – Sector coupling. https://publica.fraunhofer.de/eprints/urn_nbn_de_0011-n-5971244.pdf

Wietschel, M.; Bekk, A., Breitschopf, B., Boie, I., Edler, J., Eichhammer, W., Klobasa, M., Marscheider-Weidemann, F., Plötz, P., Sensfuß, F., Thorpe, D., & Walz R. (2020b). Opportunities and challenges when importing green hydrogen and synthesis products. https://www.isi.fraunhofer.de/content/dam/isi/dokumente/cce/2020/policy_brief_hydrogen.pdf

Part III

European Governance

European Union Energy Policy: A Discourse Perspective

7

Michèle Knodt and Marc Ringel

Contents

Introduction	122
Discourses and Frames Within EU Energy Policy	123
EC Energy Policy: Born in the Frame of Competitiveness	124
International Energy Threats and the Framing of Security in EC Energy Policy	126
The Emergence of the Sustainability Frame in the 1990s	127
The Security of Supply and Solidarity Nexus in an Enlarged EU	130
The Cleavage Between the Northern and Western and (Middle) Eastern Member States: Security of Supply Versus Sustainability	133
"Harder Soft Governance" Within the Energy Union and the European Green Deal as Backup for the Sustainability Frame	135
Conclusions	138
Cross-References	139
References	139

Abstract

In the history of European integration, common energy policy seems, in addition to trade policy, to be one of the earliest "European" issues, as exemplified by the European Coal and Steel Community (ECSC) and the European Atomic Energy Community (EURATOM). Instead, energy policy entered the treaties as a policy area of its own only with the Lisbon Treaty 2009, which did not entail substantial transfers of competences to the supranational level. In this development the discourse on energy policy was shaped by three frames – security (of supply), sustainability, and competitiveness, which guided European energy policy in different ways. This chapter will analyze the development of the energy policy

M. Knodt (✉)
Institute of Political Science, Technical University of Darmstadt, Darmstadt, Germany
e-mail: knodt@pg.tu-darmstadt.de

M. Ringel
Nuertingen Geislingen University, Geislingen, Germany
e-mail: marc.ringel@hfwu.de

© Springer Nature Switzerland AG 2022
M. Knodt, J. Kemmerzell (eds.), *Handbook of Energy Governance in Europe*,
https://doi.org/10.1007/978-3-030-43250-8_50

within the integration process up to the latest development of the European Energy Union. The Energy Union is characterized by a new governance system which installs a soft governance with harder elements in order to steer member states' energy policy with regard to the European energy transformation targets.

Keywords

Energy governance · Energy policy · European Union

Introduction

In the history of European integration, common energy policy seems, in addition to trade policy, to be one of the earliest "European" issues, as exemplified by the European Coal and Steel Community (ECSC) and the European Atomic Energy Community (EURATOM). These early supranational integrational steps should not be misunderstood as first efforts to create a common energy policy. Instead, energy policy entered the treaties as a policy area of its own only with the Lisbon Treaty 2009, which did not entail substantial transfers of competences to the supranational level. Nevertheless, over time, the European Commission acquired at least a partial energy profile. Thus, the Commission was able to extend its energy competences (1) into the new integrated environmental competences in the 1980s; (2) via the development of a single European Market for electricity, petroleum, and natural gas; and (3) through appending cross-border construction of energy infrastructure such as "trans-European networks" (see Fischer 2009; Knodt et al. 2015a, p. 57). The Commission is now seeking to implement its newest concept of an Energy Union in the face of massive conflicts between the Northern/Western and the Central and Eastern European member states.

This chapter will analyze the development of EU energy policy against the background of the debate over energy policy within the EU. The discourses are analyzed by their different frames. Three frames have been used in the debates on security (of supply), sustainability, and competitiveness. The three frames received different levels of attention over time. They were elaborated and discussed throughout a set of EU documents that form the "strategic backbone of the EU energy policy" (Van Vooren 2012, p. 268) and will be discussed in detail below. Different stages of European integration in energy policy exhibit varying compositions of these frames, which are supported by different discourse coalitions. This chapter will show that the energy discourse is highly politicized, both within the EU and among the member states. Thus, the following questions will be addressed: Which composition of frames shapes EU energy policy discourses in different integration periods? Which actors and actor coalitions support which policies and frames in the European energy discourse? What are the consequences for the integration process?

The chapter begins with an overview of the three different frames in EU energy policy and some methodological remarks. The subsequent sections present the dominant framing within the discourse on energy policy in the EU in different time periods. The chapter ends with concluding remarks on the main finding of competition between the energy security and sustainability frames, which has produced the present deadlock in EU energy policy.

Discourses and Frames Within EU Energy Policy

The three frames were first jointly elaborated in the 2006 Commission Green Paper "A European Strategy for Sustainable, Competitive and Secure Energy" (European Commission 2006). The Green Paper states that European energy policies should strive to fulfill the three main objectives (Knodt et al. 2015a, pp. 64–65):

- Sustainability: (i) developing competitive renewable sources of energy and other low carbon energy sources and carriers, particularly alternative transport fuels, (ii) curbing energy demand within Europe, and (iii) leading global efforts to halt climate change and improve local air quality.
- Competitiveness: (i) ensuring that energy market opening brings benefits to consumers and to the economy as a whole, while stimulating investment in clean energy production and energy efficiency, (ii) mitigating the impact of higher international energy prices on the EU economy and its citizens and (iii) keeping Europe at the cutting edge of energy technologies.
- Security of supply: tackling the EU's rising dependence on imported energy through (i) an integrated approach – reducing demand, diversifying the EU's energy mix with greater use of competitive indigenous and renewable energy, and diversifying sources and routes of supply of imported energy, (ii) creating the framework which will stimulate adequate investments to meet growing energy demand, (iii) better equipping the EU to cope with emergencies, (iv) improving the conditions for European companies seeking access to global resources, and (v) making sure that all citizens and business have access to energy. (European Commission 2006, pp. 17–18)

The Lisbon Treaty represents the first time a contractual basis for energy policy, which was included in the European treaties and regulates the frames in the following ways (see Fig. 1).

Although the three norms are treated equally in the Lisbon Treaty, they have attracted different levels of attention over the history of integration and led to different actions. The present effort to reconstruct the discourses on energy policy follows discursive institutional research on energy policy (Herranz-Surrallés 2015; Selianko and Lenschow 2015; Knodt et al. 2015b).

To analyze this process, we must identify how actors give meaning to a situation or problem within a specific discourse, frame it, and communicate it. The process of framing can be defined by referring to Entman: 'To frame is to select some aspects of a perceived reality and make them more salient in a communicating text, in such a way as to promote a particular problem definition, causal interpretation, moral evaluation, and/or treatment recommendation' (Entman 1993, p. 52). Entman

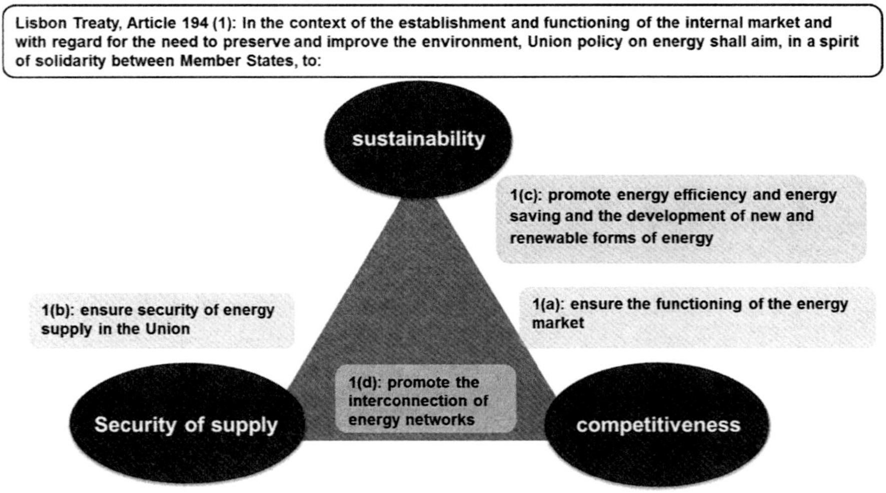

Lisbon Treaty, Article 194 (1): In the context of the establishment and functioning of the internal market and with regard for the need to preserve and improve the environment, Union policy on energy shall aim, in a spirit of solidarity between Member States, to:

- sustainability
- 1(c): promote energy efficiency and energy saving and the development of new and renewable forms of energy
- 1(b): ensure security of energy supply in the Union
- 1(a): ensure the functioning of the energy market
- 1(d): promote the interconnection of energy networks
- Security of supply
- competitiveness

Fig. 1 Frame triangle of EU energy policy. (Source: own, inspired by Knodt et al. 2015a, p. 65)

notes that framing, as the "central process by which government officials and journalists exercise political influence over each other and over the public" (Entman 2003, p. 417) is a political process with the aim of influencing policymaking. A frame does not reflect reality and a problem in a neutral way but (re-)constructs meaning. "The result is an argumentative struggle in which actors frame issues to increase or decrease attention to them, mobilize actors or demobilize them, and direct policymakers towards solutions" (Bomberg 2015, p. 6). Actors who are framing issues and problems form groups of actors in which framing and social construction is shared. They form discourse coalitions in the sense of Hajer (1993, p. 45). Regarding the focus of this chapter, discourse coalitions are formed by member states and supported by European institutions. The aim of this chapter is to delineate the three energy frames. It documents their use in different periods of European integration and analyzes the discourse coalitions supporting different frames and their consequences for political action within the EU.

The data used to analyze the different frames of European energy policy are derived primarily from documents that the EU has published on its energy policy. In addition, selected media articles, public statements from various institutions and politicians, and secondary literature were used to reconstruct discourse coalitions.

EC Energy Policy: Born in the Frame of Competitiveness

In the history of European integration, common energy policy seems, alongside trade policy, to be one of the earliest "European" issues. Two of the three European Communities were linked to energy sources: the ECSC and EURATOM. The competitiveness frame was crucial for the formation of both communities, although they also served to establish peaceful cooperation among European member states after World War II. As Herranz-Surallés notes, "EU energy policy was thus born with the main *goal* of eliminating the barriers to free and fair competition in the energy markets" (Herranz-Surrallés 2015, p. 4).

The ECSC treaty created a common market for coal and steel among its member states, with the aim of avoiding militant competition among the European nations over national resources. In the 1950s, coal covered 80% of the Community's energy supply. The ECSC treaty regulated the Community Market for all coal products via mechanisms ranging from market regulations and prices to the modernization of products and external trade. Thus, a high share of energy resources within the Community was covered by the regulations on the European coal market. Article 3 of the ECSC Treaty (1951) contains those positive regulations. The negative regulations are presented in Article 4 of the ECSC Treaty, which forbids import and export duties between member states, measures that discriminate among producers, subsidies or state assistance, and restrictive practices tending toward the division of markets or consumer exploitation.

The same logic applied to the creation of the EURATOM Treaty, which was also a sectorial treaty. The EURATOM Treaty focuses on nuclear energy and was meant to create good conditions for the establishment and growth of the European nuclear industries and create a special market for nuclear power within the Community. The preamble of the treaty stresses EURATOM's importance for the European Community: "REALISING that nuclear energy constitutes the essential resource for ensuring the expansion and invigoration of production and for effecting progress in peaceful achievement" (EURATOM Treaty, Preamble). It clearly demonstrates that the member states founded the Community "to create the conditions required for the development of a powerful nuclear industry" (EURATOM Treaty, Preamble). The EURATOM Treaty also includes positive measures to create a common nuclear market (article 2, EURATOM Treaty) and negative obligations such as not establishing national external tariffs (article 92, EURATOM Treaty), but there was no prohibition of subventions or government aid.

The European Economic Community (EEC 1957) presents a different picture. As a comprehensive treaty that does not focus on one or two sectors, it does not mention the word energy. Beyond a protocol on mineral oil and mineral oil products and a clarification of the boundaries of the ECSC and EURATOM treaties, it contains no energy-specific regulations. Nevertheless, the treaty includes many regulations that employ the competitiveness frame and in the event of an emergency could have been executed on energy matters, such as special measures that "shall apply also in the event of difficulties arising in connection with the supply of certain products" (article 103, 4 EEC treaty 1957). In this vein, article 18 states that member states declare "their willingness to contribute to the development of international commerce and the reduction of barriers to trade" (article 18, EEC treaty 1957). This chapter includes measures that could be executed in the area of energy policy. These regulations paved the way for future regulations on energy policy, which would authorize the community to realize a common energy policy.

The three communities inaugurated an "interexecutive working group, energy" in 1959, which prepared a study on the future of energy policy within the Communities.

The main message was to create a common market for oil and equal competitive conditions. Based on this, the executives of the three communities signed the "Protocol of Agreement on Energy Problems" (Council of Ministers of the ECSC 1964), stating the necessity of a common energy market.

Especially with the establishment of the Single Market Program in the 1980s, the competitiveness frame was re-focused to justify energy measures. The measures were based on a commission working document "The Internal Energy Market" (Commission of the European Communities 1988). The competition frame appears to have been shared by all member states when addressing energy policy during the 1980s. At the Council meeting in June 1987, the member states expressed their will to eliminate existing obstacles to an internal energy market before the end of 1992. The European Parliament and the Economic and Social Committee expressed their interest in this endeavor, as the Commission noted in one of its documents (Commission of the European Communities 1988, p. 2).

However, neither these efforts nor the Single European Act of 1987 resolved the lack of energy policy regulations within European primary law. Nevertheless, those efforts show that, in the early years, the discourse on energy centered on a common energy market and the competitiveness of European industry.

International Energy Threats and the Framing of Security in EC Energy Policy

The discussion on energy security has been influenced less by the internal dynamics or formulations of the treaty and more by the perception of international energy threats (McGowan 2011). In 1968, energy security first became an issue within the European Community as a direct result of the Six-Day War in the Middle East, which affected oil supply (Fischer 2011, p. 112). In response, the debates on energy security within the Community resulted in a directive that imposed an obligation on member states to maintain minimum stocks of crude oil and/or petroleum products (Council of the European Community 1968). The directive obligated member states to store crude oil and/or petroleum products at a level equal to at least 65 days' average daily internal consumption in the preceding calendar year. As an outcome of the dramatic oil crisis of 1973/1974, the European regulation was superseded by an international regulation issued by the International Energy Agency (IEA), founded in 1974 within the framework of the OECD, which slightly changed the details of the regulation – extending the requirement on stocks to last up to 90 days.

In September 1974, the Commission urged the Council to develop the "Resolution Concerning a New Energy Policy Strategy for the Community" (Council 1974a) and the "Resolution Concerning Community Energy Policy Objectives for 1985" (Council 1974b) to cope with the challenges posed by the energy crisis. For the first time, the member states agreed to work toward a common policy on energy production and energy demand. In this early statement, the Council established guidelines for a common strategy for reducing energy demand and measures to secure the energy supply.

The relative calm in the oil markets in the aftermath of the crisis removed the pressure to pursue more detailed work on the energy security frame and allowed the

European Commission to make only slight changes to regulations on storing crude oil and/or petroleum products until the end of the 1990s. In 2000, the European Commission reacted to the EU's growing dependence on external energy sources in a "Green Paper on Energy Security" (European Commission 2000). By this year, the EU's external energy dependence had already increased, and the EU met up to 50% of its energy needs through imports. At the time, 45 % of its oil was imported from the Middle East, and 40% of its natural gas imports came from Russia. The European Commission noted that the EU did not have the power to influence international markets and that this "weakness" was "highlighted by the sharp rise of oil prices at the end of 2000" (European Commission 2000). This prompted the European Commission to begin a debate on energy security, thereby stressing the importance of the security frame for European energy policy. The Council and European Parliament were unwilling to frame the issue in the same way. The growing dispute is reflected in the discussion of a 2002 Commission proposal to strengthen stock regulation to secure oil and gas supplies, which far exceeded IEA requirements. Member states and parliamentarians criticized the Commission's proposal by advancing the narrative that, at that time, there was a very low risk of supply disruptions. A member of parliament stated, "I see such a situation [referring to the interruption of supply] as highly unlikely" (Linkohr (EP debate 2003), quoted in Herranz-Surrallés 2015, p. 10). Both the Council and the European Parliament, which criticized the growing influence of the Commission in energy policy, rejected the Commission's proposal.

As energy security gained importance with the accessions of the East European member to the EU (see below), the EU reinforced the regulation in 2006 (2006/67/EC) but still did not harmonize the different stocking procedures. The Commission sought to further harmonize EU and IEA procedures in 2007, which resulted in a 2009 Council Directive (2009/119/EC). In addition to better harmonization with the mechanism existing under the IEA, the regulation called for more comprehensive reporting by the member states, a better examination of the required reserve capacities, and better coordination in the event of an emergency.

The desire for a secure energy supply obviously inspired the entire discussion and the resulting regulations. Viewed through this frame, the European member states were demonstrably vulnerable. In this interpretation, the storage of crude oil and petroleum represented a form of preparedness to avoid energy shortages and provide energy security. The oil supply shortage due to international threats encouraged the interpretation of European energy policy as a problem of security of supply. This framing was taken up again by the new Eastern European member states directly after their accession in 2006 (see below).

The Emergence of the Sustainability Frame in the 1990s

In its resolution concerning a new energy policy strategy for the Community in 1974, for the first time, questions of environmental protection were mentioned as marginalia but not taken up to form a separate frame. Throughout the 1980s, the environmental protection aspect of energy policy constantly ranked after the "integration of the Community energy markets," "energy security," and "environmental impact," as listed in the communication "New Community Energy Objectives" of the Commission to the Council in 1985 (Commission of the Communities 1985, p. 2).

Throughout the 1990s, environmental issues gained increasing prominence, and discussions on sustainability as a concept were held at the international level with the work of the Brundtland Commission of the UN and the UN conference on environment and development in 1992. This international debate and environmental movements in several member states catapulted the sustainability frame into European discourses.

Thus, in the 1990s, the environmental aspects of energy became the third frame that formed the energy triangle. The 1994 Green Paper of the Commission (Commission 1995a) for the first time established the triangle of energy frames in part II of the paper. The three frames were introduced as objectives in this paper, starting with "overall competitiveness," followed by "security of supply" and "environment," which already revealed a hierarchy of the frames within the triangle due to the market orientation (Single Market) of the time. The importance accorded to the competitiveness objective was justified as follows: "it gives companies in the sector the international dimension necessary for security of supply" and "ensures the development of the whole economy" (Commission 1995a, p. 16). According to the Green Paper, the contribution of energy to the overall competitiveness of the Community was determined by two factors: "its availability in various forms and its price" (Commission 1995a, p. 19). The Green Paper elaborated on the influence of energy competitiveness on European industry, markets, and individuals. "Security of supply" was defined by the Commission as "ensuring that future essential energy needs are satisfied by means of a sharing of internal energy resources and strategic reserves under acceptable economic conditions and by making use of diversified and stable, externally accessible sources" (Commission 1995a, p. 24). In the Green Paper, the "environment" was linked with the sustainable growth objective in the Maastricht Treaty. The Commission stated clearly that "synergies between the objectives of competitiveness, energy security and environmental protection" needed to be developed (Commission 1995a, p. 28), well knowing that the objectives are "contradictory" and that it would be difficult "to balance the different elements in such a way that the essential objects can be satisfied" (Commission 1995a, p. 5). Within the broad debate on the Green Paper, the Council supported the establishment of new energy policy guidelines focused on the rapid completion of the internal market and the security of supply. The sustainability frame for energy policy was particularly promoted by the European Parliament. The three frames were elaborated in a White Paper on "An Energy Policy for the European Union" (Commission 1995b) that was published in the same year as the Green Paper, reflecting the discourse on the three frames. Again, the internal market and the competitiveness objective were placed at the top of the agenda. Environmental protection was mentioned as a second-tier goal and interlinked with the competitiveness frame. Thus, environmental issues were framed in terms of market logic.

If the Commission is to continue to work on fiscal instruments by helping the member states to restructure their own taxation policies with a view towards convergence while talking account of the aim of reducing taxation pressure on business; this must not undermine efforts to meet environmental challenges by taking into account energy efficiency at consumer-product level, [...]. (Commission 1995b, p. 4)

Approximately 10 years later, the Green Paper on "A European Strategy for Sustainable, Competitive and Secure Energy" (European Commission 2006) lists all three frames, but the order was revised. Sustainability had reached the top of the list. The document stresses that the EU should strive to fulfill the three following main objectives: (1) sustainability with respect to renewable sources of energy and other low-carbon energy sources to combat climate change and improve local air quality; (2) competitiveness to open the energy market, which should ensure benefits for consumers; and (3) security of supply, which should address the EU's growing dependence on imported energy (European Commission 2006, pp. 17–18).

The sustainability frame had gained increasing prominence by the end of the 2000s due to the discourse on climate change. As the international discourse on the greenhouse effect and global warming grew, energy policy also began to be debated under the heading of climate policy.

This focus was advanced even further during the German presidency in the first half of 2007. As the German government stated at the beginning of its presidency, "A focus of the European Spring Council 2007 during the German EU Council Presidency will be the adoption of an action plan on an 'Energy Policy for Europe' containing measures categorized in the order of their priority importance" (German Government 2007). Within the statement, the German government explicitly linked energy measures with the challenges of climate change. It stated, "the European Council will therefore conduct an integrated debate on energy and climate policy" (German Government 2007). The March 2007 summit was shaped by the ambitions of Chancellor Merkel to advance the EU's efforts to combat climate change. Merkel's ambitious initiative was also driven by high expectations for the upcoming G8 summit in Heiligendamm (Germany), where climate change was at the top of the agenda. Thus, the European Council decided to "develop a sustainable integrated European climate and energy policy" (European Council 2007, p. 1). The focus of this new turn was to take seriously the crosscutting nature of energy policy and link it closely to climate policy focused on emissions reduction, the expansion of renewable energies, and energy efficiency. The targets for these three main objectives of the EU were established under the slogan of "20-20-20 by 2020." This should be read as a reduction of at least 20% in greenhouse gases by 2020 compared to the year 1990, a 20% share of renewable energies in EU energy consumption by 2020, and reducing primary energy use by 20% in comparison with projected levels – to be achieved through energy efficiency. The 20-20-20 objectives provided a strategic superstructure for policies and measures in the energy and climate field that had progressively been developed in all three areas since the early 2000s (e.g., the Effort Sharing Decision, the Renewable Energy Directive or regulation in the field of energy efficiency such as the Labelling Directive, the Energy Performance of

Buildings Directive or the Energy Service Directive). In 2008, the Council invited the Commission to prepare an additional package of internal measures to implement these objectives. In addition, it was agreed that the member states would pursue a 30% reduction if a global agreement with comparable commitments by other countries were successfully negotiated (Oberthür and Pallemaerts 2010, p. 45). With this step, the European Council prepared the EU to take the lead in the forthcoming UN climate negotiations. To implement the European Council's March 2007 decision, the Commission prepared a suite of legislative proposals, which were termed the "climate and energy package" on 23 January 2008. They include measures to promote renewable energies, regulations for the EU emissions trading system (see European Commission 2015 for details), and the development of low-carbon and carbon capture and storage technologies. In addition, binding targets for member states were agreed upon. Both the Council and the European Parliament rapidly approved the package. The remaining controversial issues – especially on CO_2 reduction – had to be decided at the EU summit in December 2008. The discussion at this summit showed the beginnings of opposition by the new Central and Eastern European member states to sustainability-dominated energy policy (see below). French president Nicolas Sarkozy, then holding the EU presidency, was negotiating lower CO_2 reduction targets, and the inclusion of exceptions for affected industries secured an agreement. In addition to the opposition by the Central and Eastern European member states, the German government also no longer supported ambitious action in this respect. Chancellor Merkel argued for exceptions in favor of German industry. Thus, the ambitious energy and climate commitments from March 2007, which shaped EU energy policy following the sustainability frame, had already been diluted. Higher targets were linked to the framework of a UN global agreement on climate change to be signed in Copenhagen and to apply to the period after 2012 (European Council 2008). This also constituted part of the compromise, as the Central and Eastern European countries did not expect Copenhagen to achieve substantial results, whereas most of the Northern and Western EU member states placed their hopes in this international agreement. The 2009 Copenhagen summit was disappointing for the Northern and Western member states of the European Union with respect to the agreed climate reduction targets. In addition, the financial and economic crisis had begun and shifted attention away from environmental issues. Thus, the sustainability frame lost prominence relative to the frames of competitiveness and security in the subsequent years (Fischer 2014, p. 1), and EU energy policy became deadlocked.

The Security of Supply and Solidarity Nexus in an Enlarged EU

However, only 3 years later, the EU had to face the "unlikely" scenario of potential interruptions of supply. Disputes over gas deliveries between Ukraine and Russia (2006) and between Belarus and Russia (2007) challenged the security of the EU's supply. The cuts of Russian gas affected the European Union more than in previous years because the Eastern Enlargement, especially the accession of Poland, had changed the situation. The fossil fuel energy supplies of Poland and many other Central and Eastern European member states depended to a very high degree on Russian gas and oil. Conflicts between Russia and Ukraine or Belarus over gas supply immediately jeopardized Poland's supply. Thus, in debates on energy leading up to the then-forthcoming revision of the Lisbon Treaty, Poland emphasized the energy security frame. Poland linked the security frame with a demand for solidarity by other European member states in the event of supply disruptions to ensure energy security for Polish citizens.

This external threat and Poland's efforts increased European energy activities (Geden 2007). Thus, the Commission took up the issue in its March 2005 Green Paper on "A European Strategy for Sustainable, Competitive and Secure Energy" (European Commission 2006), a Commission communication on "An Energy Policy for Europe" (European Commission 2007), and a comprehensive Energy Action Plan for the period 2007–2009 (European Council 2007).

With respect to the security of supply frame, the Russia-Ukraine gas conflict represented an emerging topic and an initial indicator of an energy crisis in the Green Paper of 2006. It introduced the Strategic EU Energy Review, which was intended to offer a clear European framework for national decisions on the energy mix to avoid supply crises and ensure the energy security of the EU. This review process was tasked with regularly analyzing all of the advantages and disadvantages of various energy sources based on a standard methodology (European Commission 2006, p. 9), starting with the first Strategic Energy Review, the communication on "An Energy Policy for Europe" (European Commission 2007). In this communication, the Commission framed minimizing the EU's vulnerability with respect to imports, shortfalls in supply, and possible energy crises as its clear priority because such vulnerability "carries political and economic risks" (European Commission 2007, pp. 3–4).

Together with its dependency on a small number of third countries, the Commission highlighted "expected exponential increases in global demand; rising and volatile prices; and climate change" (Van Vooren 2012, p. 268) as additional threats to the energy security of the EU. Nevertheless, this communication was clearly written under the influence of the gas conflict between Russia and Ukraine in 2006 and its impact on Europe, without addressing this issue explicitly. Nevertheless, the precarious situation was highlighted implicitly when the Commission maintained the following: "In addition, the mechanisms to ensure solidarity between member states in the event of an energy crisis are not yet in place and several member states are largely or completely dependent on one single gas supplier" (European Commission 2007, p. 4). Thus, in its communication, the Commission reminds readers that "it remains important for the EU to promote diversity with regard to source, supplier, transport route and transport method" and calls for the establishment of effective mechanisms to "ensure solidarity between member states in the event of an energy crisis" (European Commission 2007, p. 10). To stress the importance of the security frame and allay the Eastern member states' fears, the Commission explicitly included the security and solidarity nexus in its communication.

The linkage between the solidarity and energy security frames can also be found in the Energy Action Plan for the period 2007–2009 devised by the European Council (2007). The presidential conclusion notes that the action plan was established not only to complete the EU's internal market for gas and electricity and to achieve a more interconnected and integrated market but also to "address the crucial issue of security of energy supply and the response to potential crisis" (European Council 2007, p. 14). Even if the solidarity frame was listed in connection with all three frames in the introduction of the section on climate and energy policy, it is only made explicit in the subsection on "security of supply." The European Council underlined "the need to enhance security of supply for the EU as a whole as well as for each Member State" through various measures, such as effective diversification of energy sources and transport routes and effective crisis mechanisms including data collection, review, and assessment (European Council 2007, p. 18). The action plan is linked and refers to measures proposed in the energy strategy of the Commission from 2007. Following the security frame, the priority has been on important infrastructure measures, especially to link the Central and Eastern European countries and the Iberian Peninsula (European Commission 2007, p. 9). In addition, linked to the security frame, the communication stressed the necessity to prioritize the external dimension of the EU's energy policy. The action plan especially highlighted relations with Russia, Central Asia, Africa, and the BICs (Brazil, India, and China). It also linked energy policy to the European Neighbourhood Policy and its instruments and to the implementation of the Energy Community Treaty with a view toward its possible extension to Norway, Turkey, Ukraine, and Moldova (European Council 2007, p. 19).

The discourse coalition around Poland pressed successfully not only to strengthen the security frame but also to insert energy policy and the security and solidarity nexus into the Lisbon Treaty. The treaty, for the first time, delivered a contractual basis for energy policy within the European treaties (see above). The priority of the energy security frame and the strong link with the solidarity frame is also obvious in the Commission's Second Strategic Energy Review, launched in November 2008, on "An EU Energy Security and Solidarity Action Plan" (European Commission 2008). Therein, the Commission proposes a five-point EU Energy Security and Solidarity Action Plan that again listed (1) infrastructure needs and the diversification of energy supplies, (2) external energy relations, (3) oil and gas stocks and crisis response mechanisms, (4) energy efficiency, and (5) making the best use of the EU's indigenous energy resources (European Commission 2008, p. 3).

The diversification of energy supply in conjunction with infrastructure measures was highly discussed within the EU. The issue flared up again because of a new Russia-Ukraine gas conflict. On 1 January 2009, Russia cut off its gas supply to Ukraine because of unresolved disagreements over payments from the Ukrainian gas company Naftogaz to the Russian natural gas company Gazprom. The Czech Prime Minister, Mirek Topolanek, whose country held the EU's 6-month rotating presidency at that time, pushed for a European solution to diversify energy supply. Thus, while the presidency together with the Commission announced support for the Nabucco pipeline project (bringing gas from the Caspian to Central Europe), member states such as Germany were also pushing the EU to support pipeline projects, including the North Stream and South Stream pipeline projects carried out by Russia with participation by Germany (Nord Stream) and Italy (South Stream). In January 2009, the dispute culminated in a letter from German Chancellor Angela Merkel to Commission President Jose Manuel Barroso and Topolanek. Merkel also used the energy security frame to support her argument that diversifying the energy supply does not simply mean relying on the EU's own projects and withdrawing from joint ventures with Russia. It is of "great significance" that the Nabucco, Nord Stream, and South Stream pipelines should be "politically desired and supported by all EU member states," she wrote in her letter (cited according to Spiegel international online, 01/29/2009). The European Parliament supported the European Commission, which reinforced the Nabucco project to prevent continued dependence on Russia (Herranz-Surrallés 2015, p. 11).

The advocacy in favor of the security frame by the discourse coalition surrounding Poland led to energy policy being anchored in the primary law of the EU and a nexus with the solidarity frame within the Lisbon Treaty, which creates a responsibility for all EU member states to ensure energy security. The discussion on the security and solidarity nexus paved the way for a rivalry with the sustainability frame, which led to the present-day cleavage and sometimes deadlock in energy policy.

The Cleavage Between the Northern and Western and (Middle) Eastern Member States: Security of Supply Versus Sustainability

The forthcoming rivalry between the Northern and Western and (Middle) Eastern member states slowed the progress toward the previously agreed targets in energy policy. The Commission's November 2011 communication complained that "the price of failure is too high," "despite the importance of energy policy aims, there are serious gaps in delivery," and "more European action" is required (European Commission 2010). In its Roadmap 2050, the Commission addresses the shortcomings of its 2020 framework implementation and presents different scenarios for European energy policy (European Commission 2011). However, there was no real move forwards toward the successful implementation of the agreed goals. Only in 2013 did the Commission begin another initiative on those targets agreed upon in 2008 and 2009. It published a Green Paper and launched a public consultation on the content of a 2030 framework (European Commission 2013).

In January 2014, the Commission proposed the EU 2030 framework for its energy policy, which contained an emission reduction target of 40% compared to 1990 levels by 2030 and a share of renewable energy on the order of 27% by 2030. Some months later, in July 2014, the Commission also proposed a new energy efficiency target on the order of 30% by 2030 (European Commission 2014). This communication began a highly controversial discussion on the EU's climate and energy policy and especially the sustainability frame. In the European Council, two discourse coalitions formed along the lines of the 2008 discussion. On the one side, member states such as Germany and Denmark led a group of environmentalist and climate-friendly governments within the EU and pushed for the package proposed by the Commission. On the other side, the Visegrád states (Poland, Slovakia, the Czech Republic, and Hungary), along with Bulgaria and Romania and under the leadership of the Polish government, opposed the new targets and insisted on national sovereignty over decisions on their national energy mix and a limited role for the EU. The latter camp pleaded for greater emphasis on the security frame rather than pushing for sustainability targets (Fischer 2014, p. 2–3). To settle this compromise, the Central and Eastern European states made a highly strategic move. The Polish government, which had been forced onto the defensive because of its obstructionist attitude, developed a new concept. Donald Tusk, then Polish Minister President and the current president of the European Council, launched the concept of an Energy Union. Tusk revisited an old idea of Jacques Delors and then-president of the European Parliament Jerzy Buzek from 2010, who pleaded unsuccessfully for a European Energy Community to integrate the Central and Eastern European member states into a system of common energy security. The concept pushed the energy security frame to the center of the European discussion. The Central and Eastern European member states united in a discourse coalition held together by the narrative of how Central and Eastern European households would be left without heat in the winter due to Russian gas policy. They linked the discussion with the European solidarity frame, and Tusk asked for a new policy under the umbrella of a European Energy Union. The Central and Eastern European member states' problem definition quickly attracted sympathizers due to the Ukraine crisis, which accompanied the discourse even without being mentioned explicitly (Fischer and Geden 2015a). The cleavage deepened between the Northern and Western sustainability-oriented member states in one discourse coalition and the Central and Eastern European member states asking for solidarity in energy supply in another. A final agreement could only be secured because of the substantial ambiguity in the formulation of the conclusions. The targets for 2030 that were agreed upon were an "at least" 40% cut in greenhouse gas emissions compared to 1990 levels, as proposed by the Commission, an "at least" 27% share of renewable energy consumption, and "at least" 27% energy savings compared with the business-as-usual scenario – thus, failing to satisfy the Commission's in plea for 30%. Moreover, the extent to which the decision could be revised was ambiguously framed. The European Council's conclusions included a review of the framework after the climate conference in Paris in December 2015. The two discourse coalitions interpreted this in different ways. Whereas the Northern and Western member states hoped for greater greenhouse gas reductions, the Central and Eastern member states expected an unsuccessful outcome of the international negotiations. Thus, both sides were willing to agree. In addition, the European Council, at the direction of the Eastern camp, stated that "these targets will be achieved while fully respecting the member states' freedom to determine their energy mix. Targets will not be translated into nationally binding targets" (European Council 2014, p. 5). To achieve consensus, extensive concessions were also made to the governments of Central and Eastern Europe in the form of financial compensation and exemptions from the regulations (Fischer 2014, pp. 3–5).

The newly elected president of the European Commission, Jean-Claude Juncker, adopted the idea of the Energy Union after his election in 2014 and asked Vice-Commissioner Maroš Šefčovič (responsible for the Energy Union) and the Commissioner for Climate Action and Energy, Miguel Arias Cañete, to draft a framework for the Energy Union (Fischer and Geden 2015). Note that new directorate general on climate action and energy underlines the close relationship between the climate and energy topics and, thus, is committed to the sustainability frame. Obviously, the Commission and Juncker were pursuing the project to work toward developing broader mutual consent on all three frames within the Energy Union and sought to bridge the cleavage between the discourse coalitions.

"Harder Soft Governance" Within the Energy Union and the European Green Deal as Backup for the Sustainability Frame

Already in February 2015, the Commission composed a communication called the "Energy Union Package. A Framework Strategy for a Resilient Energy Union with a Forward-Looking Climate Change Policy" (European Commission 2015). In the communication, the Commission presents its vision of a European energy system, which unites all three of the existing frames – being secure, sustainable, and competitive – while also producing affordable energy. The Commission makes explicit that "achieving this goal will require a fundamental transformation of Europe's energy system" (European Commission 2015, p. 2) away from the 28 different national regulatory frameworks toward one common European framework. The Commission's strategy contains five dimensions that were adopted by the European Council in March 2015: (1) energy security, solidarity, and trust; (2) a fully integrated European energy market; (3) energy efficiency contributing to moderation of demand; (4) decarbonizing the economy; and (5) research, innovation, and competitiveness (European Council 2015, p. 1). The wide range of the Energy Union reflects the effort of the Juncker Commission to integrate all three energy frames to bridge the gap between member states.

To implement the Energy Union, the European Commission's November 2016 package for "Clean and Secure Energy for All Europeans" (the so-called Winter Package) comprised a set of legislative measures to define European energy and climate policies with a 2030 perspective (Turner 2015; Umpfenbach 2015; Turner et al. 2015). The package codifies the politically agreed energy and climate targets of the EU and proposes a set of both regulatory and non-regulatory measures to reach the overall Energy Union objectives (EC 2016). The regulatory measures notably comprise (i) energy efficiency policies via the recast directives on energy efficiency in buildings (Energy Performance in Buildings Directive, EPBD) and the Energy Efficiency Directive (EED); (ii) the recast Renewable Energy Directive; (iii) directives and regulations on the internal energy markets, which are still in the negotiation phase; and (iv) the Governance Regulation. Whereas the sectorial policy directives update the existing EU energy policy acquis, the Governance Regulation is designed to enforce the coordination of member states' energy and climate change policies through soft governance mechanisms that are peppered with harder elements (Knodt and Ringel 2017, 2018; Ringel and Knodt 2018). With the political agreement of June 2018 between the European Commission, Council, and European Parliament on energy efficiency, renewable energy support, and Governance Regulation, the strategic EU energy policy framework for 2030 has been fixed.

The coordinating mechanisms of the Governance Regulation align the post-2020 energy and climate change monitoring and reporting (European Commission 2018; Karakas 2015). The regulation synchronizes the energy governance process with the macroeconomic coordination of the European Semester and the stocktaking exercises under the Paris Agreement. The Commission continues to follow the open method of coordination, using iterative processes and feedback loops to track progress toward the EU's headline targets. A structured dialogue is established between the Commission and member states through the means of planning and reporting obligations. The coordination follows (i) strategic long-term energy and climate policy planning and (ii) short-term reporting (see Ringel and Knodt 2018 for details): The cornerstones of the long-term planning are integrated National Energy and Climate Plans (iNECPs) with a 10-year perspective, covering national objectives, strategies, and policies in the clean energy and climate fields. The Governance Regulation asks the Commission to comment on the plans regarding the level of ambition of objectives, targets, and contributions as well as on specific policies and measures included in the plan (Regulation 2018). However, the originally strong form of open coordination foreseen in article 28 of the regulation (member states "shall take the utmost account of any recommendations from the Commission when finalising their integrated national energy and climate plan") has been watered down to taking "due account," thus limiting the sanctioning potential of the Commission. Details in the governance mechanisms vary within the different issue-related directives of the Winter Package.

The Governance Regulation and the recast Renewable Energy Directive (Council of the European Union 2018a) set out a series of obligations on member states to track progress toward clean energy objectives. The regulation sets a binding target at the EU level of at least 32% renewable energy in gross final consumption by 2030. Member states support this EU objective by setting indicative national contributions. To track member states' efforts to increase the share of renewable energy, the national contributions must be complemented by an indicative trajectory for the increase of these forms of energy. The trajectory starts at the level of either the binding national 2020 renewable energy target or the real value of renewable energy shares in gross final consumption, in the event that the real value surpasses the 2020 target. The regulation foresees achieving three reference points: 18% of the national contribution has to be met by 2022, 43% by 2025, and 65% by 2027 (Council of the European Union 2018c). The sum of these national reference points defines the EU reference points and simultaneously allows the Commission to evaluate whether the EU objective is met.

The co-legislators have agreed on a "gap-filler mechanism," in the event that the EU share of renewable energies is below the reference points and thus at risk of not meeting the 2030 objective. Annex Ia of the Governance Regulation (Regulation 2018) installs an algorithm that defines the allocation of the missing percentage points to the member states. Member states falling below their national reference points will have to cover the gap by implementing additional measures within 1 year. This mechanism brings the missing binding national targets back through the backdoor and enables the Commission pressure member states. Member states have to react within 1 year and take measures to fill the gap. Alternatively, member states can also contribute to a financial platform. This contribution is voluntary, in contrast to the Commission proposal with its obligatory financial contribution in the event of noncompliance. It can be seen as a first attempt to introduce a harder form of soft governance (Knodt et al. 2021).

In legislating an "energy efficiency" objective (usually defined as energy intensity, that is, energy consumption divided by GDP) rather than a consumption reduction target, the European Council (European Council 2014) has opted for a weak target formulation. While striving for a minimum 32.5% energy efficiency improvement, growing GDP will contribute to reaching this overall objective (Kuebler 2018; Grillingham et al. 2009; Ringel et al. 2016). Whereas both the renewable target and the climate objectives are referred to as "binding" at the EU level, this specification is missing for energy efficiency. In this sense, the target formulation is weaker than the specification of the original EED of 2012 (European Commission 2012), which clarified that the 20% energy efficiency objective for 2020 was to be understood as aiming for an absolute reduction of the EU's energy consumption. The recast of the EED (Council of the European Union 2018b; Sajn 2017) in part rectifies this. It proposes clear energy consumption levels for 2030. Linked to the Governance Regulation, the EED asks member states to define indicative national energy efficiency contributions to reach the EU headline target. These contributions must both be formulated at the absolute level of primary and final energy consumption and include an indicative trajectory for reaching the 2030 contribution levels. Analogous to the Renewable Energy Directive, the Commission reviews the overall progress toward the EU headline target in 2023. However, no reference points are fixed, and the co-legislators fell short of establishing a gap-filling mechanism in this policy field. If the EU falls short of its energy efficiency headline target, the Commission has to propose additional legislation in the building, product, and transport sectors at the EU level (Council of the European Union 2018b).

The introduction of harder elements of soft governance in the latest legislative acts on the Energy Union is closely linked to the sustainability frame. It reflects the efforts, especially of the Commission, to back soft governance mechanisms with some obligatory features.

However, the first analysis of the implementation of the Commission's recommendations on ambition gaps in the NECPs by the Member States speaks a clear language. During the drafting phase, a clear "European" ambition gap was identified in both areas. The national plans to increase the share of renewables reached 33 %, which is just above the old target of 32 %. In the case of energy efficiency, current target of 32.5 % was not reached, the ambition ended up at only 30 % after revising the NECPs on the basis of Commission's recommendations. Thus, it could be stated, that the Commission's subsequent recommendations on national NECPs were largely implemented by only a minority of Member States.

In 2019, the President of the European Commission, Ursula von der Leyen, presented the European Green Deal (EGD), which envisages a climate-neutral European economy and society by 2050. The new EU climate law aims to set a legally binding climate target for 2030 of at least 55% net greenhouse gas reduction compared to 1990 and a binding target to achieve climate neutrality by 2050 at the latest. With the July legislative package "Fit for 55," the Commission will present the revision and introduction of a number of legislative initiatives related to the climate measures of the European Green Deal.

The Commission has learned from the experience of drawing up the NECPs. The proposal for the revision of the energy efficiency directives is now based on the existing regulations for renewable energies. The Commission proposed that in future, national minimum contributions are to be calculable by means of a formula, which the member states are to take into account when calculating their contribution. Likewise, national indicative target paths are to be introduced in order to identify deviations and to be able to address them within 1 year. The agreement of binding national targets is dispensed with. However, the aim is to make them binding at the European level. These additions to the existing regulation should help to improve the poor performance of the energy efficiency measures of the member states and harden the soft governance of the energy efficiency directive.

Conclusions

This chapter showed that the framing of European energy policy – security of supply, sustainability, and competitiveness – varies over time. While the competitiveness frame and a market orientation were initially dominant, the security of supply has gained prominence during periods featuring energy supply crises. The ecological movement of the 1990s provided the impetus for the growth of the sustainability frame within European energy policy.

The different framing of the EU energy policy throughout the history of integration also demonstrates that European policies are closely linked to the international level. Supply crises and global discourses, such as on sustainability and climate change, affected the framing of discourses within the EU. The latter increased the prominence of the sustainability frame within EU energy policy.

The reinvigorated security framing after the enlargement of the EU demonstrates that intra-European developments could affect the discourse coalitions and, in turn, the framing of energy policy. Thus, enlargement returned the security frame to the top of the agenda, driven by the efforts by the newly acceded Central and Eastern member states. Most obviously, the Central and Eastern accession states advanced the narrative of possible supply shortages due to the disputes between Russia and Ukraine. In contrast, the Northern and Western member states were especially supportive of the sustainability frame, which linked energy with the challenges of climate change. While Germany and Denmark led a group of environmentally and climate-friendly governments, shaping the sustainability frame, the Visegrád states in particular (Poland, Slovakia, the Czech Republic, and Hungary), but also Bulgaria and Romania, advanced the energy security frame. Between the two discourse coalitions, a deep gap emerged within the energy policy decision-making process in the highly politicized context of the last 10 years taking.

By introducing the Energy Union and the European Green Deal, the Commission attempts to bridge the gap between the member states and to secure greater acceptance for the coexistence of the three frames. As the EU does not hold competences with respect to European member states' energy mix, the Commission reacted with its new governance mode, which resembles the "open method of coordination" (OMK) but was extended with the inclusion of harder instruments to enhance its leverage.

Cross-References

▶ Energy Policies in the EU: A Fiscal Federalism Perspective
▶ Extending Energy Policy: The Challenge of Sector Integration

References

Bomberg, E. (2015). Shale we drill? Discourse dynamics in UK fracking debates. *Journal of Environmental Policy and Planning, 1–17*(2015). https://doi.org/10.1080/1523908X.2015.1053111.
Commission of the European Communities. (1985). New community energy objectives, COM (85) 245 final, Brussels, 28 May 1985.
Commission of the European Communities. (1988). The internal energy market, COM (88) 238 final, Brussels, 2 May 1988.
Commission of the European Communities. (1995a). For a European Union Energy Policy, Green Paper, COM (94) 659, final 2, Brussels, 23 February 1995.
Commission of the European Communities. (1995b). An energy policy for the European Union, COM (95) 682 final, Brussels, 13 December 1995.
Council of Ministers of the European Coal and Steel Community. (1964). Protocol of agreement on energy problems, Reached between the governments of the member states of the European communities at the 94th meeting of the special Council of Ministers of the European coal and steel community, Luxembourg, 21 April 1964, OJ 69, 30 April 1964, 1099–1100.
Council of the European Community. (1968). Directive imposing an obligation on member states to maintain minimum stocks of crude oil and/or petroleum products, (68/414/EEC), No. L308/14, Brussels, 23 December 1968.
Council of the European Community. (1974a). Council resolution concerning a new energy policy strategy for the community, 17 September 1974, official journal C 153/1, 9 July 1975.
Council of the European Community. (1974b). Council resolution concerning community energy policy objectives for 1985, 17 December 1974, official journal C 153/2, 9 July 1975.
Council of the European Union. (2018a). *Proposal for a directive of the European Parliament and of the council on the promotion of the use of energy from renewable sources – Analysis of the final compromise text with a view to agreement* (Document 10308/18). Brussels: Council of the European Union.

Council of the European Union. (2018b). *Proposal for a directive amending directive 2012/27/EU on energy efficiency* (Council interinstitutional file 206/0376 (COD)). Brussels: Council of the European Union.

Council of the European Union. (2018c). Governance of the Energy Union: Council confirms deal reached with the European Parliament. Press Release 424/18. http://www.consilium.europa.eu/en/press/press-releases/2018/06/29/governance-of-the-energy-union-council-confirms-deal-reached-with-the-european-parliament/pdf. Accessed 25 July 2018.

ECSC Treaty. (1951). Treaty establishing the European Coal and Steel Community, Paris, 18 April 1951. https://eur-lex.europa.eu/LexUriServ/LexUriServ.do?uri=CELEX:11951K:EN:PDF. Accessed 12 Nov 2019.

EEC. (1957). Treaty of Rome, Rome 25 March 1957. https://ec.europa.eu/romania/sites/romania/files/tratatul_de_la_roma.pdf. Accessed 12 Nov 2019.

Entman, R. (1993). Framing – Toward clarification of a fractured paradigm. *Journal of Communication, 43*(4), 51–58. https://doi.org/10.1111/j.1460-2466.1993.tb01304.x.

Entman, R. (2003). Cascading activation: Contesting the white house's frame after 9/11. *Political Communication, 20*(4), 415–432. https://doi.org/10.1080/10584600390244176.

European Commission. (2000). Towards a European strategy for the security of energy supply, Green Paper, COM (2000) final, Brussels, 29 November 2000.

European Commission. (2006). A European strategy for sustainable, competitive and secure energy, COM (2006) 105 final, 8 March 2006.

European Commission. (2007). An energy policy for Europe, communication from the commission to the European council and the European Parliament, COM (2007) 1 final, 10 January 2007.

European Commission. (2008). Second strategic energy review: An EU energy security and solidarity action plan, communication from the commission to the European Parliament, the council, the European economic and social committee and the committee of the regions, COM (2008) 781 final, Brussels, 13 November 2008.

European Commission. (2010). Energy 2020. A strategy for competitive, sustainable and secure energy, communication form the commission to the European Parliament, the council, the European economic and social committee and the committee of the regions, COM (2010) 639 final, Brussels, 10 November 2010.

European Commission. (2011). Energy roadmap 2050, communication from the commission to the European Parliament, the council, the European economic and social committee and the committee of the regions, COM (2011) 885 final, Brussels, 15 December 2011.

European Commission. (2012). Energy efficiency, directive 2012/27/EU of the European Parliament and of the council of 25 October 2012 on energy efficiency, amending directives 2009/125/EC and 2010/30/EU and repealing directives 2004/8/EC and 2006/32/EC, Official Journal of the European Union, L315/1–56, 14 November 2012.

European Commission. (2013). A 2030 framework for climate and energy policies, Green Paper, COM (2013) 169 final, Brussels, 27 March 2013.

European Commission. (2014). A policy framework for climate and energy in the period from 2020 to 2030, communication from the commission to the European Parliament, the council, the European economic and social committee and the committee of the regions, COM (2014) 15 final, Brussels, 22 January 2014.

European Commission. (2015). Energy union package. A framework strategy for a resilient Energy Union with a forward-looking climate change policy, communication from the commission to the European Parliament, the council, the European economic and social committee and the committee of the regions, COM (2015) 80 final, Brussels, 25 February 2015.

European Commission. (2016). Fitness check. Reporting, planning and monitoring obligations in the EU energy acquis. SWD (2016) 397 final. European Commission, Brussels.

European Commission. (2018). The Energy Union gets simplified, robust and transparent governance: Commission welcomes ambitious agreement. http://europa.eu/rapid/press-release_IP-18-4229_en.htm. Accessed 25 July 2018.

European Council. (2007). Presidency conclusions, 7334/1/07, REV 1, CONCL 1, Brussels, 9 March 2007.

European Council. (2008). Presidency conclusions, 17271/08, CONCL 5, Brussels, 12 December 2008.
European Council. (2014). Presidency conclusions, EUCO 169/14, co EUR 13, CONCL 5, Brussels, 24 October 2014.
European Council. (2015). Presidency conclusions, EUCO 11/15, CO EUR 1, CONCL 1, Brussels, 20 March 2015.
Fischer, S. (2009). Die Neugestaltung der EU-Klimapolitik: Systemreform mit Vorbildcharakter? *Internationale Politik und Gesellschaft, 2*, 108–126.
Fischer, S. (2011). *Auf dem Weg zur gemeinsamen Energiepolitik. Strategien, Instrumenteund Politikgestaltung in der Europäischen Union*. Baden-Baden: Nomos.
Fischer, S. (2014). The EU's new energy and climate policy framework for 2030. SWP comments, 55, Berlin. https://www.swp-berlin.org/fileadmin/contents/products/comments/2014C55_fis.pdf. Accessed 10 Sept 2018.
Fischer, S., & Geden, O. (2015). Die Grenzen der ,Energieunion. SWP-Aktuell, 36, Berlin. https://www.swp-berlin.org/fileadmin/contents/products/aktuell/2015A36_fis_gdn.pdf. Accessed 10 Sept 2018.
Fischer, S., & Geden, O. (2015a). Europäische Energieunion. Für jeden ist was dabei. Neu Zürcher Zeitung, 2 December 2015. https://www.nzz.ch/meinung/kommentare/fuer-jeden-ist-etwas-dabei-1.18655960. Accessed 10 Sept 2018.
Geden, O. (2007). Energiesolidarität im EU-Reformvertrag. SWP-Aktuell, 34, Berlin. 2007. https://www.swp-berlin.org/fileadmin/contents/products/aktuell/2007A34_gdn_ks.pdf. Accessed 10 Sept 2018.
German Government. (2007). German presidency. Statement on energy policy. http://www.eu2007.de/en/Policy_Areas/Transport_Telecommunications_and_Energy/Energy.html. Accessed 20 Mar 2016.
Grillingham, K., Newell, R. G., & Palmer, K. (2009). Energy efficiency economics and policy. *Annual Review of Resource Economics, 1*, 597–620.
Hajer, M. (1993). Discourse coalitions and the institutionalization of practice: The case of acid rain in Britain. In F. Fischer & J. Forester (Eds.), *The argumentative turn in policy-analysis and planning* (pp. 43–76). Durham/London: Duke University Press.
Herranz-Surrallés, A. (2015). An emerging EU energy diplomacy? Discursive shifts, enduring practices. *Journal of European Public Policy, 17*. https://doi.org/10.1080/13501763.2015.1083044), https://doi.org/10.1080/13501763.2015.1083044).
Karakas, C. (2015). Economic governance framework: Stocktaking and challenges. European Parliamentary Research Service, 2015, 1. http://www.europarl.europa.eu/RegData/etudes/ATAG/2015/559515/EPRS_ATA%282015%29559515_EN.pdf. Accessed 3 Mar 2017.
Knodt, M., & Ringel, M. (2017). Governance der Energieunion: Weiche Steuerung mit harten Zügen? *Integration, 40*(2), 125–140.
Knodt, M., & Ringel, M. (2018). The European commission as a policy shaper – Harder soft governance in the energy union. In M. W. Bauer, J. Ege, & S. Becker (Eds.), *The European commission in turbulent times* (pp. 181–204). Wiesbaden: Nomos.
Knodt, M., Mueller, F., & Piefer, N. (2015a). Explaining European Union external energy governance with emerging powers. In M. Knodt, N. Piefer, & F. Mueller (Eds.), *Challenges of EU external energy governance towards emerging powers* (pp. 57–74). Farnham/Burlington: Ashgate.
Knodt, M., Piefer, N., & Mueller, F. (Eds.). (2015b). *Challenges of EU external energy governance towards emerging powers*. Farnham/Burlington: Ashgate.
Knodt, M., Ringel, M. & Müller, R. (2021). 'Harder' soft governance in the European energy union policy. In M. Knodt, & J. Schönefeld (eds.), *Special Issue, 'Harder' soft-governance" in European climate and energy policy: Following a new trend? Journal of Environmental Policy & Planning, 22*(4), 787–800 https://doi.org/10.1080/1523908X.2020.1781604.
Kuebler, K. (2018). Energieeffizienz und Energieeinsparung: Politik beginnt mit dem Betrachten derRealität. Energiewirtschaftliche Tagesfragen, 68, 23–27. http://et-energie-online.de/Portals/0/Bilder/Ausgabe2018-06/et-201806-Kuebler.pdf. Accessed 10 Sept 2018.
McGowan, F. (2011). Putting energy insecurity into historical context: European responses to the energy crises of the 1970s and 2000s. *Geopolitics, 16*(3), 486–511. https://doi.org/10.1080/14650045.2011.520857.

Oberthür, S., & Pallemaerts, M. (2010). The EU's internal and external climate policies: An historical overview. In S. Oberthür & M. Pallemaerts (Eds.), *The new climate policies of the European Union* (pp. 27–64). Brussels: Brussels University Press.

Regulation (EU). 2018/1999. Regulation of the European Parliament and of the Council of 11 December 2018 on the Governance of the Energy Union, amending Directive 94/22/EC, Directive 98/70/EC, Directive 2009/31/EC, Regulation (EC) No 663/2009, Regulation (EC) No 715/2009, Directive 2009/73/EC, Council Directive 2009/119/EC, Directive 2010/31/EU, Directive 2012/27/EU, Directive 2013/30/EU and Council Directive (EU) 2015/652 and repealing Regulation (EU) No 525/2013 of the European Parliament and of the Council.

Ringel, M., & Knodt, M. (2018). The governance of the European energy union. Efficiency, effectiveness and acceptance of the winter package 2016. *Energy Policy, 112*, 209–220.

Ringel, M., Schlomann, B., Krail, M., & Rohde, C. (2016). Towards a green economy in Germany? Therole of energy efficiency policies. *Applied Energy, 179*, 1293–1303.

Sajn, N. (2017). Revised energy efficiency directive. *European Parliamentary research service*, 1–8.

Selianko, I., & Lenschow, A. (2015). Energy policy coherence from an intra-institutional perspective: Energy security and environmental policy coordination within the European Commission. In C. Neuhold & S. Vanhoonacker (Eds.), *Dynamics of institutional cooperation in the European Union: Dimensions and effects*, European Integration online Papers (EIoP), Special issue, 19(1), 1–29.

Spiegel International Online. (2009). http://www.spiegel.de/international/europe/europesplit-over-energy-security-merkel-calls-on-eu-to-support-baltic-gas-pipeline-a-604277.html. Accessed 3 June 2016.

Turner, S. (2015). Embedding principles of good governance into the 2030 climate & energy framework. https://www.foeeurope.org/sites/default/files/renewable_energy/2015/turner_2015-six_principles_of_good_governance.pdf. Accessed 24 June 2017.

Turner, S., Genard, Q., Roberts, J., & Luebbke, I. (2015). Four key messages for the governance of the European climate and energy policies after 2030. https://www.e3g.org/docs/E3G_Four_Key_Messages_for_the_governance_of_EU_climate_and_energy_policies_after_2020_V2.pdf. Accessed 24 June 2017.

Umpfenbach, K. (2015). Streamlining planning and reporting requirements in the EU Energy Union framework. http://ecologic.eu/sites/files/publication/2015/planning_reporting_ecologic_institute_final_20150908_2.pdf. Accessed 24 June 2017.

Van Vooren, B. (2012). *EU external relations law and the European neighbourhood policy. A paradigm for coherence*. London/New York: Routledge.

Energy Policies in the EU: A Fiscal Federalism Perspective

8

Erik Gawel and Sebastian Strunz

Contents

Introduction 144
The Theory of Fiscal Federalism 146
   Decision-making: Centralized or Decentralized? 146
   Policies: Homogeneous or Heterogeneous? 148
   Beyond Harmonization: The Case of Convergence 148
   A Brief Positive Overview of Energy Policies in the EU 151
Case Study: Renewable Energy Policies 153
   Decision-making on RES Policies: Centralized or Decentralized? 153
   RES Policies: Homogeneous or Heterogeneous? 155
   Is There Convergence of RES Policies in the EU? 156
Conclusion 157
Cross-References 158
References 159

Abstract

In this chapter, we apply the theory of Fiscal Federalism to energy policies in the EU. Centralization of decision-making power and homogeneity of policies incur both costs and benefits. We look at the case of renewable energy sources (RES) policies in more detail to specify the relevant pros and cons. Finding that neither full and imminent centralization/homogenization nor complete

---

E. Gawel
Department of Economics, Helmholtz Centre for Environmental Research – UFZ, Leipzig, Germany

Institute for Infrastructure and Resources Management, Leipzig University, Leipzig, Germany
e-mail: erik.gawel@ufz.de

S. Strunz (✉)
Department of Economics, Helmholtz Centre for Environmental Research – UFZ, Leipzig, Germany
e-mail: Sebastian.strunz@ufz.de

© Springer Nature Switzerland AG 2022
M. Knodt, J. Kemmerzell (eds.), *Handbook of Energy Governance in Europe*,
https://doi.org/10.1007/978-3-030-43250-8_51

fragmentation would be desirable, we explore whether bottom-up convergence might offer a feasible way to sensibly balance the trade-off. From an empirical perspective, there is some evidence for (temporary and conditional) convergence of RES policies. Overall, the efforts of the EU Commission to steer national policies more directly promise to reap some more of the possible benefits of cooperation. The analysis, however, also makes clear that there exist not only politico-economic obstacles but also economic rationales against fully harmonizing all aspects of EU energy policy.

Keywords

Centralization · Convergence · Decentralization · Energy Union · Fiscal federalism · Harmonization · Heterogeneity

Introduction

Energy cooperation historically forms part of the European integration project: Indeed, the European Coal and Steel Community, founded in 1951, was a forerunner of the European Union (EU). Then again, energy policy has not been among the main legal competencies of the EU: only in 2009 the Lisbon treaty for the first time explicitly stipulated that the EU is co-responsible for initiating, devising, and implementing energy policy, besides the member states' respective policies. Lately, the EU Commission pushes towards an "Energy Union" (see also Buchan and Keay 2016; Andersen et al. 2017), which refers to the vision of resilient, clean and affordable energy provision within an integrated European market. More specifically, the Commission in 2016 released the so-called "Winter Package," a number of regulative proposals aiming to streamline energy governance within the EU (cf. Ringel and Knodt 2018). Overall, then, the status of the "Energy Union" is somewhat ambiguous: on the one hand, the impact of EU directives and guidelines on national energy policies is clearly observable (e.g., consider Germany's switch from feed-in tariff as main support scheme for renewables towards tender schemes, Tews 2015). On the other hand, member states have repeatedly declined to make any substantial concessions in terms of transfer of decision-making power to the EU. Thus, the recent efforts to promote the "Energy Union" might also be interpreted as a sign of crisis in that the list of stalled integration projects, such as the vision of a common and continent-wide electricity market, is long (Fischer and Geden 2015).

In the following, it is useful to distinguish two (nevertheless related) dimensions of conflict. First, a general conflict revolves around the allocation of decision-making power. This boils down to a constant wrangling between member states and supranational institutions on who calls the shots on energy policy. This general cleavage, second, cuts across a range of more policy-specific controversies that do not sort along the divide member-state/supranational institutions but that include cleavages between different blocs of member states or ideological faultlines within member states and within EU institutions. What is more, all of these issues are debated in the scientific as well as the political arena.

For instance, as regards the first conflict dimension, there is a scientific debate about the benefits or downsides of centralization of decision-making in energy policy: some authors, often from an economic perspective, emphasize the merits of centralized and harmonized policy-making (e.g., Bigerna et al. 2016; Tagliapietra 2014). By contrast, some authors, often from a political science perspective highlight the downsides of centralization, favoring more decentralized approaches (e.g., Burger and Weinmann 2013; Tews 2015). Both within the economic and the political sciences, however, balanced views are to be found as well (e.g., Söderholm 2008; Strunz et al. 2015; Bausch et al. 2017). This debate also spills over into the political arena, for instance, with regard to Germany's energy transition: the *Energiewende* is regularly criticized for being "unilateral" (e.g., Hübner et al. 2012; Weimann 2012).

As regards the second conflict dimension, consider the East vs. North/West cleavage within the EU. The member states exhibit strongly diverging policy priorities and, in consequence, alternative interpretations of what the "Energy Union" is about: Eastern European member states, such as the Visegrád bloc, put security of supply, particularly with respect to gas, first. Hence, their preferred "Energy Union" essentially represents an instrument to pool buying power (Austvik 2016). In this view, sustainable energy provision refers to guaranteed long-term availability of fossil resources rather than decarbonization. By contrast, the member states in Northern and Western Europe aim for increasingly stringent climate policy (Schreurs and Tiberghien 2007). From this perspective, the point of the "Energy Union" is to initiate a coordinated transition towards renewable energy sources. The pretense of the EU Commission, of course, is that one can resolve all these differences in the form of a "resilient energy union with a forward-looking climate change policy" (EU Commission 2015). Yet the deeply ambivalent status quo of EU energy policy raises the question whether such a reading is more glossing over existing cleavages than realistic description.

Against this background, this chapter explores the following specific issues: To start with, we review the rationales for (de)centralization of policies and apply it to energy policy making in the EU. The theory of Fiscal Federalism (seminal: Musgrave 1959; Olson 1969; Oates 1972) contrasts the arguments for both centralization vs. decentralization as well as heterogeneous vs. homogeneous policies. In other words, the theory of Fiscal Federalism thus allows us to balance different rationales about the desired future development energy policies in the EU. Since energy policy actually subsumes a range of aspects (e.g., technology-specific policies, security of supply, climate policies), we then focus on RES policies for a more detailed discussion of the normative debate about (de)centralization. Furthermore, a brief look at the current status quo of RES policies in the EU suggests that top-down harmonization of RES policies on EU level will not be politically available in the near future (and neither would they be desirable, see below). Consequently, we review the empirical evidence for bottom-up convergence of RES policies; to this end, we also sketch important conceptual characteristics of convergence: depending on the exact operationalization of convergence, one may or may not conclude that policies converge. This is also the case for RES policies in the EU, with some but restricted (temporal, conditional) evidence for RES policy convergence.

The remainder of this chapter is structured as follows. In section "The Theory of Fiscal Federalism," we introduce the theory Fiscal Federalism, discuss the conceptual properties of policy convergence and give brief snapshot of energy policy in the EU. Subsequently, in section "Case Study: Renewable Energy Policies," we apply this conceptual set-up to RES policies: we contrast the arguments for more centralized decision-making and more homogeneous policies on the EU level with the arguments for decentralized decision-making and heterogeneous policies. Furthermore, we summarize some empirical results on whether RES policies are converging. Finally, we discuss implications from our argument and draw policy conclusions in section "Conclusion."

The Theory of Fiscal Federalism

Following the seminal contributions from Musgrave (1959), Olson (1969), and Oates (1972, 1999), the theory of Fiscal Federalism discusses the benefits and downsides of centralized, homogenous policies as compared to decentralized, heterogeneous policies. This chapter outlines the theory of Fiscal Federalism and its application to energy policy in the EU. To start with, we conceptually distinguish two dimensions and demonstrate which trade-offs arise within each dimension. The first dimension concerns the degree of centralization of decision-making structures: how centralized should decision making be (see section "Decision-making: Centralized or Decentralized?")? The second dimension concerns the degree of homogeneity of policies: how homogeneous should policies be (see section "Policies: Homogeneous or Heterogeneous?")? As becomes clear from Fig. 1, both dimensions may, but need not align: in particular, the case of convergence, where policies become more homogeneous while decision-making stays decentralized, is of interest here (see section "Beyond Harmonization: The Case of Convergence"). Finally, we provide a brief overview of energy policy in the EU as seen through the lens of the Fiscal Federalism perspective (section "A Brief Positive Overview of Energy Policies in the EU").

Decision-making: Centralized or Decentralized?

The theory of Fiscal Federalism aims to balance the benefits and costs from (de) centralization. The two most prominent arguments for centralization of decision-making are economies of scale and scope in production. Economies of scale imply that the centralized provision of public goods incurs lower average costs than the decentralized provision. Consider, for example, the centralized deployment of RES in the EU as compared to national deployment of RES: a centralized RES support scheme would entail less administrative costs than a diversity of twenty-eight schemes and it would allow for cost-effective – that is, geographically optimized – deployment of RES

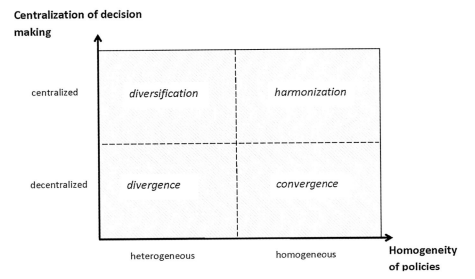

Fig. 1 Two dimensions of "Europeanization." (Source: own illustration)

(see section "Decision-making on RES Policies: Centralized or Decentralized?"). Generally, centralization of decision making serves to internalize spill-over effects between different regions. Economies of scope, in turn, arise when centralized production of several outputs is cheaper than decentralized production, leading to lower joint costs of production per unit of output (Bailey and Friedlaender 1982).

By contrast, the arguments for decentralized decision-making involve "the fact that most public goods are local, that their production does not exhibit important economies of scale," as well as the goal of "avoiding the inefficiency of imposing a uniform national standard in the face of locally different marginal costs of provision" (e.g., Dalmazzone 2006, p. 459). In other words, in contexts where spill-over effects between regions are low and economies of scale and scope in production are negligible, decentralization is more efficient than centralization. Yet, there exists a further argument for decentralization of decision making which goes beyond the mere absence of grounds for centralization. Indeed, an influential strand of the Fiscal Federalism literature highlights "laboratory federalism" (Oates 1999), the merits of decentralized problem-solving. From this perspective, decentralization gives the opportunity for policy experimentation, thereby enabling trial-and-error problem solving. Since policy experiments can be conducted on smaller scales (compared to a centralized approach), more policy alternatives can be applied, tested, and evaluated with respect to their advantages and downsides. In consequence, the chances to find even better overall solutions to a given policy problem increase. As environmental problems give rise to a range of uncertainties, decentralization may be sensible if spill-over effects are negligible (Anderson and Hill 1997). Moreover, the transition towards sustainable energy provision certainly faces numerous challenges, such as the question how to incentivize the system integration of

RES; thus, the "laboratory federalism" call for policy experimentation may be particularly relevant for the adaptation of RES policies from niche support to system integration (see also Gawel et al. 2017).

Policies: Homogeneous or Heterogeneous?

A core theme of the theory of Fiscal Federalism relates to the costs and benefits from centralized provision of public goods – that is, uniform and homogeneous policies to provide public goods (Oates 1972, 1999). On the one hand, uniform approaches may solve coordination failure among smaller units of governance and increase the overall provision of a public good. On the other hand, public goods are often local in nature and there is no reason to assume that the population's preferences over these public goods should be homogeneous. Thus, Oates's (1972) "decentralization theorem" states that, in the absence of spill-over effects and economies of scale, the level of welfare achieved via the decentral provision of these public goods will be typically higher than a uniform approach with homogenous policies. The main reason for this superiority has been termed "the preference-matching argument" (Lockwood 2006): the output of public goods may be better tailored according to the diversity of preferences – optimally, the provision of public goods exactly matches the heterogeneous geographical distribution of preferences.

Consequently, for our purposes, the crucial issue is whether preferences are distributed heterogeneously across Europe. For instance, are attitudes towards different energy technologies and their external effects (e.g., air pollution from coal, nuclear risks, increasing bird mortality due to wind power) homogeneous or heterogeneous? How diverse is Europeans' valuation of security of supply? The whole spectrum of energy-related preferences, as well as intra-Member State heterogeneity, should be considered here. Clearly, the *political* preferences are distributed heterogeneously. So assuming that political preferences more or less reflect the population's preferences, different energy policies across the EU could find their normative economic justification in this preference-matching argument: diverging technology choices such as nuclear phase-outs in Belgium or Germany as compared to the continued reliance on nuclear power in other Member States such as France or the UK might, at least to some extent, reflect heterogeneous risk preferences.

Having reviewed the basics of the theory of Fiscal Federalism, we now turn to policy convergence as the intersection of homogeneous policies with decentralized decision-making structures in Fig. 1. As we will demonstrate, discussing policy convergence is useful to shed some light on the context of energy policies in the EU, particularly RES policies.

Beyond Harmonization: The Case of Convergence

Most commonly, policy convergence is understood as the "increase of policy similarity over time" (Holzinger et al. 2008, p. 24); and this increase in similarity is driven by voluntary decentralized decisions, rather than coercion from higher governance levels. In other words, convergence refers to the bottom-up alignment of policies. Yet apart from this general understanding, there arise a number of conceptual issues when we intend to operationalize, measure, and explain policy convergence in specific settings. In the following, we distinguish four aspects of policy convergence (see Strunz et al. 2018 for an extended presentation of the conceptual framework). This allows to appreciate the more clearly which mechanism lead to convergence, and the different understandings one may have of convergence.

First, the *object* of convergence. When we say that policies converge – do we refer to targets, to instruments or to outcomes? In principle, each of these may represent a reasonable objective of convergence research. For instance, from a climate justice perspective, one might be interested in whether per capita carbon emissions converge – whatever the specific national policy instrument. Then again, some economists argue that an EU-wide harmonized scheme of RES support would be preferable for reaping the benefits of more coordinated RES deployment (e.g., Unteutsch and Lindenberger 2014, see also section "Decision-making on RES Policies: Centralized or Decentralized?"). Yet such an alignment of policies would rather lead to *diverging* RES deployment: indeed, the main point of such approaches is to geographically concentrate RES production following natural conditions – which implies divergence of outcomes. In sum, it should be noted that convergence of policy instruments does not necessarily imply convergence of policy outcomes (and vice versa).

Second, the *benchmark* for convergence measurement may be absolute or conditional – that is, we may acknowledge background differences between countries (such as Gross Domestic Product per capita) or we may choose not to do so (e.g., Barro and Sala-i-Martin 2004). In a way, conditional convergence is "weaker" because it allows denoting movements in the same direction as convergence, even if convergence in absolute terms is very low.

Third, the *drivers* of policy convergence include both economic and political drivers. Economic drivers explain the demand that certain issues are addressed and solved. In a nutshell, the basic idea is that economic convergence leads to converging preferences such as more local environmental protection and cleaner technologies (cf. Brock and Taylor 2010). Thus, economic drivers are a necessary condition for policy convergence. However, they are not sufficient for explaining why problems should be solved in similar ways. Genuinely political drivers are also necessary to account for states implementing the same policies. The literature has pointed to "policy diffusion," triggered by transnational communication or regulatory competition, as the main mechanism here (Tews 2005).

Fourth, policy convergence should be conceived of as a *directed process*. Convergence has a dynamic connotation – "otherwise, the concept becomes a synonym for similarity" (Bennet 1991, p. 230). When policies develop over time in a way that makes them more similar (given the different possible operationalizations as outlined above), we may refer to this as convergence. Nevertheless, such processes may also lead to more than one and generally different final states: policies may align in clearly distinguishable clusters, convergence processes may come to an end before absolute convergence is reached or they may even reverse. In other words, referring to a directed process should not mislead us to assume a single, inevitable, and predestined final state.

Summing up, policy convergence has multiple facets. These aspects have to be considered whenever the question "is there convergence?" shall be answered for a specific context (see section "Is There Convergence of RES Policies in the EU?"). Before that, however, we argue that convergence may be especially relevant in the case of EU RES policies.

What is the rationale for exploring convergence in the context of energy policies in the EU? Before the Lisbon Treaty became effective, that is, before 2009, the EU had no formal legislative competency with respect to energy policy. Thus, only the Lisbon treaty provided EU institutions with a mandate to conduct energy policy. And, to be sure, Member States have not relinquished their sovereignty over their national energy mixes (Article 194(2), Treaty on the Functioning of the European Union). So referring to Fig. 1 above, decision-making on energy policy is far from being centralized at EU level. Yet, the overlap of competencies also implies that decision-making is not any more completely decentralized. In particular, the EU commission tries to influence Member States' energy policies even though its coercive means are limited. As Callies and Hey (2013, p. 88) argue: the "EU impact on the national energy mix is predominantly indirect, yet powerful." The common EU climate and energy framework represents an *indirect* way of top-down steering. From the Member States' point of view, the EU directives, guidelines, and communications from the Commission create a similar problem context (such as "how to increase the share of RES in line with the 2020 targets?"). Member States still retain the right to choose specific instruments; nevertheless, the Commission increasingly influences national policy making, for instance via the State Aid Guidelines on Environmental Protection and Energy from 2014 to 2020 (EU Commission 2014). Specifically, the Commission pushes Member States to adopt competitive auctions to determine the level of RES support (see Strunz et al. 2016). Note that Art. 194 (TFEU) still grants the Member States a last word on their national energy portfolios. So for the foreseeable future, there will be no general transfer of sovereignty to the EU level as regards energy policy. But one might also see it this way: since top-down efforts to fully harmonize policies at once can be expected to meet strong national resistance, bottom-up processes of coordination and convergence are *more* likely to yield homogeneous policies not *less*.

For instance, the Open Method of Coordination (OMC) traditionally is a very useful tool for the Commission to influence Member States: the OMC relies on agenda setting, moderating the intergovernmental discourse, proposing benchmarks for policy evaluation, and supporting national policy makers on the issues at hand. Thereby, the OMC intends to slowly but steadily steer national policies (cf. Ania and Wagener 2014; Borrás and Jacobsson 2004; Kitzing et al. 2012). So even if decision-making power formally rests with the Member States, the latter are under pressure to take both binding and nonbinding legislation into account. And the EU Commission is very clear in that it would prefer a more homogeneous policy pattern across the EU in order to support its internal market agenda (i.e., the vision of an integrated electricity market with strong policy coordination to increase cost-effectiveness).

Hence, energy policy represents an important field for convergence research. Before addressing the case of RES policies in more detail (section "Case Study: Renewable Energy Policies"), it seems useful to provide a short overview of the energy policy landscape in the EU: why does the Commission see the need for more homogeneity in the first place?

A Brief Positive Overview of Energy Policies in the EU

"Energy policy" actually comprises a number of subfields. Table 1 provides an overview of how centralized decision-making is and how homogeneous policies are with respect to the following categories: technology policies (nuclear power, RES), energy efficiency, security of supply, internal market/transnational transmission lines, and climate policy.

This overview demonstrates that the subfields differ on both dimensions (in a way, energy policy just replicates the overall pattern of "differentiated integration" (Leuffen et al. 2013) in the EU on a smaller level): for instance, while climate policy decisions are partly centralized and climate policies partly homogeneous, nuclear policies are decentralized and heterogeneous. While decisions on RES policies are mostly decentralized, the policies themselves are partly homogeneous (see section "Is There Convergence of RES Policies in the EU?"). From a Fiscal Federalism perspective, the trade-off between the advantages and the downsides of centralization need to be evaluated specifically for each subfield (see Strunz et al. 2015). Two points seem noteworthy: first, it might indeed be efficient to keep different degrees of heterogeneity and of centralization in different subfields. For instance, the risk preferences towards nuclear power are clearly heterogeneous and there is no rationale for centralizing decision making on nuclear policies on the EU level or to expect bottom-up homogenization for the foreseeable future. By comparison, the internal market is a genuinely integrative project and hence the rationale for a careful and stepwise centralization is clearer (keeping possible trade-offs with diverse requirements across Member States in mind). For instance, some aspects of the transition towards sustainability may contradict the Commission's internal market agenda. Amongst others, the calls for a more decentralized, locally rooted energy provision run counter the perspective of integrated markets with continent-wide electricity trade (e.g., Tews 2015).

Second, the "long road" towards an Energy Union (Buchan and Keay 2016) may be passing another turn into this direction with the "Winter Package: Clean and Secure Energy for all Europeans," an array of legislative proposals the EU Commission published in November 2016 that comprises over 4500 pages of text. A main impetus of the Winter Package is to streamline procedures such as reporting responsibilities of the Member States for different aspects of energy policy. Thus, from 2019 on, Member States are required to submit so-called "integrated National Energy and Climate Plans" (iNECP) rather than diverse reports for energy related-issues and climate protection

Table 1 Characteristics of different areas of energy policy

Area		Centralization of decision making	Homogeneity of policies	
			Aims	Instruments
Climate protection		Partly centralized	2020 and 2030: EU-overall aim for ETS-sectors, Diversified aims of the MS for non-ETS-sectors In addition, partly national climate protection aims	Partly homogeneous: ETS on EU-level, but national exemptions and/or additional instruments Heterogeneous for non-ETS-sectors
Internal market and transnational transmission lines		Partly centralized	Internal market: finalization in 2014 as EU-aim	Partly homogeneous: binding rules (e.g., unbundling, network codes), guidelines for transnational transmission lines Heterogeneous for national transmission lines
Security of supply		Mostly decentralized	No specific EU-aim	Heterogeneous Nonbinding guidelines on "appropriate production capacities"
Technology	**Nuclear power**	Decentralized	No EU-aim, heterogeneous aims of the MS	Heterogeneous
	RES	Mostly decentralized	2020: EU-aim, diversified aims for the MS 2030: EU-aim without diversified aims for the MS	Partly homogeneous
Energy efficiency		Decentralized	2020: EU-aim requiring MS to implement national action plans with efficiency targets (sectors: transport, households, industry) 2030: EU-aim	Heterogeneous

Source: adapted from Strunz et al. 2015, p. 146; Information for 2030 based on EU Council (2014)
MS Member States, *ETS* Emissions Trading Scheme

activities as before. These iNECPs can be expected to serve as a "dynamic governance tool" (Ringel and Knodt 2018, p. 213) for the EU Commission – that is, the iNECPs promise to be more than mere reporting obligations, and to allow the Commission stronger leeway in steering national policies: Member States would have to justify wtheir actions with respect to specific recommendation from the Commission, and "this clearly surpasses the original concept of the OMC" (Ringel and Knodt 2018, p. 215). If the Commission's legislative proposals will be accepted by the EU Council (in other words, by the Member States), the Commission's overall grip on all energy policy matters would increase. With regards to the conceptual framework of Fig. 1 and the thematic overview in Table 1, the EU Commission would gain decision-making power and the different subfields of energy policy could become more homogeneous.

Case Study: Renewable Energy Policies

In the following, we apply the Fiscal Federalism perspective to the case of RES policies. First, we assess the rationales for (de)centralization on decision-making power in this case (section "Decision-making on RES Policies: Centralized or Decentralized?"). Second, we review the respective arguments for heterogeneity and homogeneity of RES policies (section "RES Policies: Homogeneous or Heterogeneous?"). Third, we take an empirical look at the question whether RES policies in the EU are converging (section "Is There Convergence of RES Policies in the EU?").

Decision-making on RES Policies: Centralized or Decentralized?

The main arguments for centralized decision making, economies of scale and scope, also relate to the case of RES policies in the EU (e.g., Busch and Ortner 2019). The characteristic feature of economies of scale, namely that higher output is associated with lower costs, also applies to RES technologies: capital costs represent the main share of RES production costs, so when large-scale units rather than small distributed modules are built, average investment costs decline. Furthermore, centralized decision-making would not only increase the opportunities for large-scale generation capacities, but would also help optimize location-decisions: the geographical allocation of RES capacities could be optimized with respect to natural, particularly meteorological conditions around the EU (e.g., solar PV in Southern Europe, wind power along the coasts). A continent-wide spatial allocation would also lower the overall need for generation capacities because continent-scale weather patterns could be taken into account: for instance, this would imply a geographical focus of new wind farms along the coasts of the Balkans in order to exploit the complementary wind patterns between the North Sea and the Eastern Mediterranean – this would effectively yield a "pan-European wind power system" providing "stable output across a wide range of large-scale weather conditions" (Grams et al. 2017, p. 5).

Economies of scope, in turn, arise when the EU instead of single Member States organizes the administrative issues of RES support (and the necessary co-developments such as transnational transmission lines). Moreover, systemic costs such as the scale of required back-up generation capacities are lower if the fluctuating RES output is centrally managed (Hirth et al. 2015; Neuhoff et al. 2013). Finally, economies of scope arise when the financing risk for potential investments in RES installations decline under a jointly organized EU instrument. Consider that the cost of equity for RES installations in countries such as Greece, Croatia, or Bulgaria is very high compared to the perceived investment risk in Germany or Denmark (DiaCore 2016). A collective EU-wide support instrument would strongly decrease the contingency risks from RES investments in these Member States – the credibility of an EU scheme would be certainly higher and the chances of a payment default for RES correspondingly lower. For instance, in 2012 the Spanish government temporarily suspended its support scheme due to the financial and economic crisis. Also, note the analogy of a hypothetical EU-wide RES support scheme's effect on perceived risks to the European Central Bank's monetary policy lowering the interest (i.e., perceived risks) for bonds of highly indebted EU Member States on the capital market. By implication, the incentives for capital owners to invest more in RES installations in high-cost countries increase.

Besides the opportunities to exploit cost saving potential from these more spatial aspects, centralizing decision-making might also help optimize the timing of RES deployment. For instance, the existing infrastructure (transmission and distribution grids, conventional production capacities) exhibits limited adaptability and therefore gives rise to path dependencies (Dangerman and Schellnhuber 2013) which might hamper the timely scale-up of RES deployment. Moreover, innovation and technology markets often fail to adequately diffuse new technologies (cf. Gallagher et al. 2012). Against this background, coordinated intervention on an EU-wide scale may be less costly and more effective than national interventions to overcome such path-dependencies. Overall, centralization of decision-making may lend itself to optimize RES deployment both as regards timing and as regards the spatial allocation.

What about the benefits from decentralization? As already introduced in section "Decision-making: Centralized or Decentralized?," one of the main arguments of the theory of Fiscal Federalism is that decentralized decision-making provides room for policy experimentation, thereby promoting innovation and learning potential (e.g., Saam and Kerber 2013). Generally, the OMC in the EU has been described as a case of laboratory federalism (Kerber and Eckardt 2007; Ania and Wagener 2014). Within the fields of climate and energy policy, such policy laboratories may be of particular relevance: decentralization enables frontrunners who aim for initiating a transformation to sustainable energy provision to opt for ambitious policy experiments (Bausch et al. 2017; Tews 2015). As a result, Member States such as the Visegrád states who currently prioritize energy security over climate protection can learn from the frontrunners' experience and later adopt those climate and energy policies that have yielded the best results.

The above conceptual framework (cf. Fig. 1) noted that regulatory diversification might, in principle, also unfold under centralized decision-making – however, the experience of EU climate and energy policy shows that, in practice, a harmonized framework rather tends to represent the lowest common denominator (since the EU Council/all Member States need to consent to the Commission's legislative proposals). Consider the evolution of RES in the EU: early efforts of the EU Commission to introduce a harmonized quota scheme on EU level failed (see Lauber and Schenner 2011; Jacobs 2012, 25 ff.). Instead, national policy experiments with feed-in tariffs (for instance, frontrunners included Denmark or Germany) resulted in learning and adaptation processes (see Jacobs 2012 for detailed study on France, Spain and Germany). The outcome attests to the effectiveness of this policy process: the RES share at gross electricity consumption in the EU-28 increased from 14.3% in 2004 to 29.6% in 2016 (Eurostat 2018). It is debatable whether an EU-wide quota scheme would have enabled equal results; while this cannot be categorically ruled out, the rationale for flexibility and experimentation as a prerequisite for the development of effective policies is strong (Bausch et al. 2017). Again, it might be instructive to look at the case of the EU ETS – from a global perspective, the ETS was a policy experiment which allowed followers such as California and China to learn from mistakes in the set-up of Europe's trading scheme (Ranson and Stavins 2014; Fialka 2016).

Overall, there are clear cases for both centralization and decentralization of decision making with respect to RES policies in the EU. The resulting trade-off may not have a clear-cut, objective solution. There are those who highlight the centralization (e.g., Bigerna et al. 2016; Unteutsch and Lindenberger 2014) and those who highlight decentralization (e.g., Burger and Weinmann 2013; Tews 2015). Our – necessarily subjective – balance of the arguments reads as follows: the potential benefits of more coordinated RES support notwithstanding, the remaining challenges of system integration of RES still call for further policy experiments and should caution against premature centralization of decision-making (see Gawel et al. 2017).

RES Policies: Homogeneous or Heterogeneous?

Compared to the balancing of different theoretical arguments in the issue of (de) centralization, the trade-off homogeneity vs. heterogeneity is rather simple: it boils down to the empirical question how homogeneous/heterogeneous preferences with respect to RES policies are distributed across the EU. RES entail negative externalities from renewables (e.g., bioenergy production leading to reduced biodiversity and wind power yielding NIMBYism) on the local and regional level; the more heterogeneous the populations' preferences with respect to RES externalities, the more heterogeneous policies should be. There seems to be not much empirical evidence on this issue. The existing literature suggests that the evaluation of technology-specific externalities is not homogeneous across the EU (EU Commission 2007; Welsch and Biermann 2014). Consequently, EU-wide homogeneous RES policies would be less efficient than national policies – certainly, there is no reason to expect that preferences are homogeneous on Member State-level; rather some heterogeneity within Member States is also likely (consider supporters of Wind Power on the one hand and citizen initiatives against Wind Power on the other hand). Therefore, regulatory diversity in the form of national

RES policies does not deliver perfect preference matching either. Yet, barring possibilities to achieve overall efficient preference matching, national solutions may represent a feasible second-best option.

In sum, while a full and immediate centralization and homogenization of renewables policies would probably be inefficient (due to preference heterogeneity and laboratory federalism), more cooperation between Member States seems advisable because of the expected gains in terms of production-cost efficiency.

Is There Convergence of RES Policies in the EU?

So far, we have argued that a completely centralized, homogeneous approach to RES is neither preferable, nor likely to emerge any time soon because of the Member States' fallback option to draw Art. 194 TFEU when justifying national exceptions. Also, Member States do not make much use of the existing cooperation mechanisms of the RES directive (Klinge Jacobsen et al. 2014). Yet, we also pointed to the Commission's growing influence on Member States' policies and the downsides of a fragmentation of RES policies. Hence, it seems worthwhile to ask whether there is any empirical evidence of bottom-up convergence of RES policies.

Following the conceptual outline of section "Beyond Harmonization: The Case of Convergence," evaluations of convergence may differ depending on the object and the benchmark of analysis. This is also the case for RES policies in the EU. There is some empirical evidence for bottom-up convergence of RES support *instruments*: for instance, Jacobs (2012) demonstrates how the support schemes of France, Germany, and Spain converged up to 2012. On the EU-level, Kitzing et al. (2012, p. 200) conclude that "[t]here is certain reason to expect a further development into the direction of a bottom-up convergence of RES-E policy supports [...]." Then, again this trend towards ever more similar feed-in tariffs seems to have stopped in the 2010s – and may even have reversed. Recently, there seems to be an overall trend towards tender schemes (competitive auctions) or combinations of feed-in premiums or tariffs with auctions to determine the support level (see Strunz et al. 2018). This trend can be expected to foster since the Commission's State Aid Guidelines on Environmental Protection and Energy compel Member States to move into this direction. Thus, one might sum up that there is evidence for (temporary) convergence of RES instruments. As regards the *outcome* of RES policies (i.e., RES shares), we need to differentiate between conditional and absolute measures of convergence: while the absolute shares of RES at national electricity consumption still widely diverge, we also find that growth rates of frontrunners are much lower than growth rates of laggards (Fig. 2). In other words, there is convergence of RES shares conditional on the "initial level" (or conditional on the geographical conditions, since frontrunners such as Sweden of Austria heavily rely on hydro power).

Furthermore, the evolution of RES policies in the EU also demonstrates that both economic and political drivers of convergence need to be considered. Around 2010, every indication seemed to suggest that absolute convergence towards feed-in tariffs would continue; the political processes of diffusion and emulation were clearly

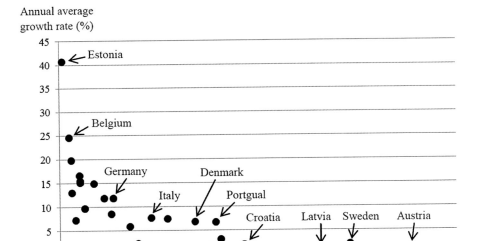

Fig. 2 EU Member States' RES shares in 2004 and growth rates to 2014. (Source: Strunz et al. 2018, p. 19)

observable (see Jacobs 2012). But then the economic crisis hit the EU and suddenly reducing the costs of RES support was a priority for Member States facing budgetary problems. Spain's drastic temporary shut-down of its RES scheme in 2012 constitutes a prime example here. From an analytical perspective, we may conclude that economic drivers of convergence must not be neglected – both political and economic drivers form prerequisites of successful and sustained policy convergence.

Finally, convergence does not mean that there exists some a priori given final state to which different policies converge. Rather, bottom-up convergence means that policy makers often face similar challenges and that transnational communication and regulatory competition may lead to them employing similar solutions. Nevertheless, RES policies may well converge towards different rather than a single final state – there is no automatism here: even if the Commission pushes towards tender schemes, national circumstances may call for, and from a legal point of view may also justify differentiated policy solutions, the State Aid guidelines notwithstanding (Gawel and Strunz 2014).

Conclusion

The theory of Fiscal Federalism provides tools to analyze the trade-offs between centralized/homogeneous policy-making on the one hand and decentralized/heterogeneous policy-making on the other hand. Applying these tools to energy policies in the EU, the following results stand out: first, a uniformly "Europeanized" approach towards all aspects of energy policy would not be desirable. Different aspects call for different solutions to the trade-off. For instance, highly diverse technology preferences (e.g., nuclear power) justify heterogeneous policies and decentralized decision-making power. Then again, other aspects (e.g., grid integration) would benefit from more centralized decisions and more homogeneous policies. Second, this also implies that the current diversity of the energy landscape in the EU, with some areas more integrated than others, probably reflects this requirement for case-based balancing of the trade-off well. Third, in the case of RES policies, clear rationales for both decentralized and heterogeneous but also centralized and homogeneous policies exist. We might, therefore, find the optimal balance somewhere in between fully harmonized and fully fragmented approaches – however, a single, exact, and objective solution of the trade-off does not exist because of numerous uncertainties and contested normative issues. Fourth, empirically, there is some evidence for bottom-up convergence of RES policies in the past. Yet these convergence processes were temporary and conditional. Hence, it is unclear where this process leads; in particular, RES policies need not converge towards a single final state but might also converge to different clusters, for instance, depending on the countries geographical conditions.

What can we infer from our analysis for the further path of energy policies in the EU? The Commission's vision of an "Energy Union," where all national differences have been resolved and a common internal market for energy provides secure, cheap, and sustainable energy for all, lies surely far afield. That said, the indirect influence of the Commission on national policies, such as via the State Aid guidelines, should not be underestimated. Some empirical evidence for bottom-up convergence has already been observed – assuming that the Commission's relative standing will further grow, more such convergence might be expected. Whether such a development should be welcomed, depends on how exactly the influence unfolds: if Member States sufficiently possess opportunities to experiment with policies ("laboratory federalism"), Member States might be nudged to reap some of the benefits of coordination without incurring the costs of centralization.

Cross-References

▶ Energy Governance in Belgium
▶ Energy Governance in Denmark
▶ Energy Governance in France
▶ Energy Governance in Germany
▶ Energy Governance in Spain
▶ Energy Governance in the United Kingdom
▶ European Union Energy Policy: A Discourse Perspective
▶ Monitoring Energy Policy

References

Andersen, S., Goldthau, A., & Sitter, N. (Eds.). (2017). *Energy Union – Europe's new Liberal Mercantilism?* London: Palgrave Macmillan.

Anderson, T. L., & Hill, P. J. (Eds.). (1997). *Environmental federalism.* Lanham: Rowman and Littlefield.

Ania, A., & Wagener, A. (2014). Laboratory federalism: The open method of coordination (OMC) as an evolutionary learning process. *Journal of Public Economic Theory, 16*(5), 767–795.

Austvik, O. G. (2016). The Energy Union and security-of-gas supply. *Energy Policy, 96*, 372–382.

Bailey, E. E., & Friedlaender, A. F. (1982). Market structure and multiproduct industries. *Journal of Economic Literature, 20*, 1024–1048.

Barro, R. J., & Sala-i-Martin, X. (2004). *Economic growth* (2nd ed.). Cambridge, MA: The MIT Press.

Bausch, C., Görlach, B., & Mehling, M. (2017). Ambitious climate policy through centralization? Evidence from the European Union. *Policy Analysis, 17*(1), 32–50.

Bennet, C. J. (1991). What is policy convergence and what causes it? *British Journal of Political Science, 21*(2), 215–233.

Bigerna, S., Bollino, C. A., & Micheli, S. (2016). Renewable energy scenarios for cost reductions in the European Union. *Renewable Energy, 96*, 80–90.

Borrás, S., & Jacobsson, K. (2004). The open method of coordination and new governance patterns in the EU. *Journal of European Public Policy, 11*, 185–208.

Brock, W. A., & Taylor, M. (2010). The Green Solow model. *Journal of Economic Growth, 15*(2), 127–153.

Buchan, D., & Keay, M. (2016). *Europe's long energy journey: Towards an energy union?* Oxford: Oxford University Press.

Burger, C., & Weinmann, J. (2013). *The decentralized energy revolution. Business strategies for a new paradigm.* Basingstoke: Palgrave Macmillan.

Busch, S., & Ortner, A. (2019). From national to cross-border support of renewable electricity in the European Union. In E. Gawel, S. Strunz, P. Lehmann & A. Purkus (Eds.), *The European dimension of Germany's energy transition – Opportunities and conflicts.* Cham: Springer, pp. 207–225.

Callies, C., & Hey, C. (2013). Multilevel energy policy in the EU: Paving the way for renewables. *Journal for European Environmental and Planning Law, 10*(2), 87–131.

Dalmazzone, S. (2006). Decentralization and the environment. In E. Ahmad & G. Brosio (Eds.), *Handbook of fiscal federalism* (pp. 459–477). Cheltenham: Edward Elgar.

Dangerman, A. J., & Schellnhuber, H. J. (2013). Energy systems transformation. *Proceedings of the National Academy of Sciences, 110*, E549–E558.

DiaCore (2016). The impact of risks in renewable energy investments and the role of smart policies. https://www.ecofys.com/files/files/diacore-2016-impact-of-risk-in-res-investments.pdf

European Commission (Ed.) (2007). Eurobarometer 262. Energy technologies: Knowledge, perception, measures. http://ec.europa.eu/commfrontoffice/publicopinion/archives/ebs/ebs_262_en.pdf

European Commission (2014). Communication from the commission: Guidelines on state aid for environmental protection and energy 2014–2020, April 2014. http://ec.europa.eu/competition/sectors/energy/eeag_en.pdf

European Commission (2015). Communication from the commission: A framework strategy for a resilient energy union with a forward-looking climate change policy, February 2015. http://eur-lex.europa.eu/resource.html?uri=cellar:1bd46c90-bdd4-11e4-bbe1-01aa75ed71a1.0001.03/DOC_1&format=PDF

European Council (2014). Conclusions on 2030 climate and energy policy framework. Brussels, 23 October 2014. http://www.consilium.europa.eu/uedocs/cms_data/docs/pressdata/en/ec/145356.pdf

Eurostat (2018). 30% of electricity come from renewable sources. https://ec.europa.eu/eurostat/statistics-explained/index.php?title=Renewable_energy_statistics#of_electricity_generated_come_from_renewable_sources

Fialka, J. (2016). China will launch the world's largest carbon trading market. The Scientific American. May 16, 2016. https://www.scientificamerican.com/article/china-will-start-the-world-s-largest-carbon-trading-market/
Fischer, S., & Geden, O. (2015). Die Grenzen der „Energieunion". SWP-Aktuell 36, April 2015. Berlin: Stiftung Wissenschaft und Politik.
Gallagher, K. S., Grübler, A., Kuhl, L., Nemet, G., & Wilson, C. (2012). The energy technology innovation system. Annual Review of Environment and Resources, 37, 137–162. https://doi.org/10.1146/annurev-environ-060311-133915.
Gawel, E., & Strunz, S. (2014). State aid Disput on Germany's support for renewables. Is the commission on the right course? Journal of European Environmental and Planning Law, 11, 137–150.
Gawel, E., Strunz, S., & Lehmann, P. (2017). Support policies for renewables – Instrument choice and instrument change from a public choice perspective. In D. Arent, C. Arndt, M. Miller, F. Tarp, & O. Zinaman (Eds.), The political economy of clean energy transitions (pp. 80–99). Oxford: Oxford University Press.
Grams, C., Beerli, R., Pfenninger, S., Staffell, I., & Wernlie, H. (2017). Balancing Europe's wind-power output through spatial deployment informed by weather regimes. Nature Climate Change, 7(8), 557–562.
Hirth, L., Ueckerdt, F., & Edenhofer, O. (2015). Integration costs revisited – An economic framework for wind and solar variability. Renewable Energy, 74, 925–939. https://doi.org/10.1016/j.renene.2014.08.065.
Holzinger, K., Jörgens, H., & Knill, C. (2008). State of the art – Conceptualising environmental policy convergence. In K. Holzinger, C. Knill, & B. Arts (Eds.), Environmental policy convergence in Europe (pp. 7–29). Cambridge: Cambridge University Press.
Hübner, M., Schmidt, C. M., & Weigert, B. (2012). Energiepolitik: Erfolgreiche Energiewende nur im europäischen Kontext. Perspektiven der Wirtschaftspolitik, 13(4), 286–307.
Jacobs, D. (2012). Renewable energy policy convergence in the EU: The evolution of feed-in tariffs in Germany, Spain and France. London: Ashgate.
Kerber, W., & Eckardt, M. (2007). Policy learning in Europe: The open method of co-ordination and laboratory federalism. Journal of European Public Policy, 14, 227–247.
Kitzing, L., Mitchell, C., & Mothorst, P. E. (2012). Renewable energy policies in Europe: Converging or diverging? Energy Policy, 51, 192–201.
Klinge Jacobsen, H., Pade, L. L., Schröder, S. T., & Kitzing, L. (2014). Cooperation mechanisms to achieve EU renewable targets. Renewable Energy, 63, 345–352.
Lauber, V., & Schenner, E. (2011). The struggle over support schemes for renewal electricity in the European Union: A discursive-institutionalist analysis. Environmental Politics, 20(4), 508–527.
Leuffen, D., Rittberger, B., & Schimmelfennig, F. (2013). Differentiated integration. Explaining variation in the European Union. Basingstoke: Palgrave Macmillan.
Lockwood, B. (2006). The political economy of decentralization. In E. Ahmad & G. Brosio (Eds.), Handbook of fiscal federalism (pp. 33–60). Cheltenham: Edward Elgar.
Musgrave, R. A. (1959). The theory of public finance. New York: McGraw Hill.
Neuhoff, K., Barquin, J., Bialek, J. W., Boyd, R., Dent, C. J., Echavarren, F., Grau, T., Von Hirschhausen, C., Hobbs, B. F., Kunz, F., et al. (2013). Renewable electric energy integration: Quantifying the value of design of markets for international transmission capacity. Energy Economics, 40, 760–772.
Oates, W. E. (1972). Fiscal federalism. New York: Harcourt Brace Javanovich.
Oates, W. E. (1999). An essay on fiscal federalism. Journal of Economic Literature, 37, 1120–1149.
Olson, M. (1969). The principle of "fiscal equivalence". The division of responsibilities among different levels of government. The American Economic Review, 59(2), 479–487.
Ranson, M. R., & Stavins, R. N. (2014). Linkage of greenhouse gas emission trading systems: Learning from experience. FEEM working papers 2014–7. https://www.econstor.eu/bitstream/10419/101992/1/NDL2014-007.pdf
Ringel, M., & Knodt, M. (2018). The governance of the European energy union: Efficiency, effectiveness and acceptance of the winter package 2016. Energy Policy, 112, 209–220.

Saam, N. J., & Kerber, W. (2013). Policy innovation, decentralised experimentation, and laboratory federalism. *Journal of Artificial Societies and Social Simulation, 16*(1), 7.

Schreurs, M., & Tiberghien, Y. (2007). Multi-level reinforcement: Explaining European Union leadership in climate change mitigation. *Global Environmental Politics, 7*(4), 19–46.

Söderholm, P. (2008). Harmonization of renewable electricity feed-in laws: A comment. *Energy Policy, 36*, 946–953.

Strunz, S., Gawel, E., & Lehmann, P. (2015). Towards a general "Europeanization" of EU Member States' energy policies? *Economics of Energy & Environmental Policy, 4*(2), 143–159.

Strunz, S., Gawel, E., & Lehmann, P. (2016). The political economy of renewable energy policies in Germany and the EU. *Utilities Policy, 42*, 33–41.

Strunz, S., Gawel, E., Lehmann, P., & Söderholm, P. (2018). Policy convergence as a multi-faceted concept: The case of renewable energy policies in the EU. *Journal of Public Policy, 38*(3), 361–387.

Tagliapietra, S. (2014). Building tomorrow's Europe. The role of an "EU Energy Union" (November 13, 2014). Review of Environment, Energy and Economics (Re3). https://papers.ssrn.com/sol3/papers.cfm?abstract_id=2529005

Tews, K. (2005). The diffusion of environmental policy innovations: Cornerstones of an analytical framework. *European Environment, 15*, 63–79.

Tews, K. (2015). Europeanization of energy and climate policy: The struggle between competing ideas of coordinating energy transitions. *Journal of Environment & Development, 24*(3), 267–291.

Unteutsch, M., & Lindenberger, D. (2014). Promotion of electricity from renewable energy in Europe post 2020 – The economic benefits of cooperation. *Zeitschrift für Energiewirtschaft, 38*(1), 47–64.

Weimann, J. (2012). Atomausstieg und Energiewende: Wie sinnvoll ist der deutsche Alleingang? *Energiewirtschaftliche Tagesfragen, 62*(12), 34–38.

Welsch, H., & Biermann, P. (2014). Electricity supply preferences in Europe: Evidence from subjective Well-being data. *Resource and Energy Economics, 38*, 38–60.

The EU in Global Energy Governance

Laima Eicke and Franziska Petri

Contents

Introduction	164
The Legal and Political Foundation of the EU's External Energy Governance	165
EU Competences on External Energy Policies over Time	166
The Role of EU Institutions in External Energy Policies	169
EU External Energy Instruments	173
The EU in the Global Energy Governance Landscape	174
Energy Security	176
Environmental Sustainability	178
Competitiveness	179
Challenges to EU External Energy Action in a Fragmented Global Landscape	181
Conclusion	182
Cross-References	183
References	184

Abstract

This chapter gives an overview on the European Union (EU)'s role in global energy governance. It argues that the EU's capacity to influence the global energy arena is determined by the complex internal design of EU (external) energy policy making on the one side, and the complex role the EU plays as a nontypical global actor in the fragmented landscape of global energy governance on the other side. The first part of the chapter gives an overview of the legal and political foundations shaping the EU's internal and external policy making. It outlines the status

---

L. Eicke (✉)
Energy Systems and Societal Change, Institute for Advanced Sustainability Studies (IASS), Potsdam, Germany
e-mail: laima.eicke@iass-potsdam.de

F. Petri
Leuven International and European Studies, Faculty of Social Sciences, KU Leuven, Leuven, Belgium
e-mail: franziska.petri@kuleuven.be

© Springer Nature Switzerland AG 2022
M. Knodt, J. Kemmerzell (eds.), *Handbook of Energy Governance in Europe*,
https://doi.org/10.1007/978-3-030-43250-8_41

of energy polices in EU treaties and the evolution of EU (external) energy policy ambitions over time and illustrates the role of various intra-EU institutions and instruments in shaping the EU's external energy output. The second part of the chapter situates the EU within the fragmented global energy governance landscape, mapping the various regional and international organizations that address the EU's triangular energy objectives – energy security, environmental sustainability, competitiveness – and reflects upon the EU's status within these various institutions. The chapter closes by reflecting upon current challenges for the EU as an actor aiming at shaping global energy governance.

Keywords

European Union · Global energy governance · Energy actorness · External energy policy · Energy diplomacy · EU institutional setup · Energy transition · Energy security · Energy trilemma

Introduction

"The EU will continue to promote and implement ambitious environment, climate and energy policies across the world" (EC 2019a, p. 20). The European Union (EU) aims to play the role of a global leader in global climate and energy politics, as expressed here in the new European Commission's Communication on the "European Green Deal," proposed in December 2019. The crucial role of energy policies, and by extension their external dimension, takes up a central role in the deal, which notes "a need to rethink policies for clean energy supply across the economy, industry, production and consumption, large-scale infrastructure, transport, food and agriculture, construction, taxation and social benefits" (ibid., p. 4). With ambitions set this high, the key question is to what extent the European Union as a nontraditional actor in global energy politics will be able to deliver on its goals of shaping global energy policies and being a force for change in the global energy transition.

This chapter gives an overview on the EU's role in global energy governance. It argues that the EU's capacity to influence the global energy arena is determined by two factors: (a) the complex internal design of EU (external) energy policy making and (b) the fragmented landscape of global energy governance, in which the EU tries to shape policies. This chapter reflects upon the various literatures addressing the question of what kind of actor or power the European Union aims to be and its role in global energy politics (Goldthau and Sitter 2015; Kustova 2017; Batzella 2018). A key challenge for situating the EU in global energy governance, however, lies not only in the fragmented nature of both the global energy landscape and EU competences, actors, and instruments, but also the fragmented state of the literature on this topic. This both concerns the definition of global energy governance in the nexus between international relations and global governance (Hughes and Lipscy 2013;

Van de Graaf and Colgan 2016) and the complex definition of the EU's external energy policies ("external energy action," "energy cooperation," "external governance," "energy diplomacy," etc.), with definitions even diverging among intra-EU actors. The endeavor of situating the EU in global energy governance is further complicated by the fact that energy policies are inherently crosscutting issues that involve other fields such as climate, development, and trade policies. This chapter addresses these challenges by first disentangling the complexities of EU's internal preconditions for external action on energy policies, and then exploring the EU's various involvements in global energy politics in different dimensions of external energy objectives.

This chapter is structured accordingly: The first section gives an overview of the legal and political foundations shaping the EU's internal and thereby external policymaking. It outlines the status of energy polices in the EU treaties, the evolution of EU (external) energy policy ambitions over time, and analyses the role of various intra-EU institutions and instruments in shaping the EU's external energy output. The second section situates the EU within the fragmented global energy governance landscape by mapping the various regional and international organizations that exist addressing the EU's triangular energy objectives (energy security, environmental sustainability, competitiveness). It then reflects upon the EU's status within these various institutions and discusses challenges to realign global energy governance in the changing reconfiguration of these partly synergetic, partly competing objectives. In closing, the chapter reflects upon current challenges for the EU as an actor aiming at influencing and shaping global energy governance, and outlines future research potentials.

The Legal and Political Foundation of the EU's External Energy Governance

This section will lay out the legal and political framework which enables the European Union (EU) to act as an actor in external relations and in the international energy arena. The EU's external energy *actorness*, a concept commonly defined as "the capacity to behave actively and deliberately in relation to other actors in the international system" (Sjöstedt 1977, p. 16), can thereby provide a useful avenue for understanding the inherent limitations and contextual factors for the EU to play a global role. While the aim of this contribution is not to reflect upon the various conceptualizations of EU energy actorness (for a discussion of this see for example Kustova 2017; Batzella 2018; Herranz-Surrallés 2015; Schunz and Damro 2020), the question of the EU's "capacity" to act externally on energy policies specifically is a useful starting point to help understand EU external energy capacity. The remainder of this section looks at EU capacity from three perspectives: first, the question of competences on the European level to act on external energy policies; second, the role of the various EU institutions involved in EU external policy making; and third, the various energy tools and instruments available for the EU to act externally.

EU Competences on External Energy Policies over Time

To understand the evolution of EU external energy policies, one first has to consider the internal dynamics of EU competences on energy policies. The idea of coordinated European action on (internal) energy policies was part of the original foundation of today's EU. Among the three foundation treaties of the European project signed during the 1950s, two were concretely related to energy policies: the 1951 Treaty of Paris which established the European Coal and Steel Community (ECSC) and the 1957 Treaty establishing the European Atomic Energy Community (Euratom). As such, energy policies have been part of the European integration project since its very inception. Yet, for the remainder of the century, legal competences on energy remained unformalized, scattered, and mostly based on other integration steps. For example, the Single European Act (SEA), which entered into force in 1987, expanded environmental competences and set the basis for completing the internal market with important consequences for the energy sector (for an extensive overview of the historic development of EU energy competences, see Schubert et al. 2016, pp. 92–126). The Treaty of Lisbon, entering into force in 2009, was the first substantial legal footing for EU internal, and by extension, external energy competences (Title XXI – Energy, Art. 194 TFEU (OJEU 2012a), see below). Reflecting the importance of this milestone in European energy integration, Knodt et al. (2017, p. 85) term the Lisbon Treaty the "pioneering attempt to introduce a contractual basis into energy policy within the European Treaties."

In today's post-Lisbon EU, energy belongs to the category of policy areas among the *shared competences* between the EU and its Member States (Art. 4, (2) f, TFEU). This means that while the EU has the right to legislate on energy policies, EU Member States still exercise own competences on energy policies, when the EU does not exercise this right. This gives a first indication of one of the key characteristics of EU internal and external energy policy making: the crucial need for coordination of energy policies between the EU and national levels, since next to common European level action, parallel and sometimes even conflicting national actions can continue. The key role of Member States is also explicitly reiterated in Articles 194 and 192, TFEU, the prior being the main article setting out the EU's energy ambitions and policy making. As such, while emphasizing the sovereign rights of Member States (Art. 194 (2)) and laying out the decision-making mode for EU action under the ordinary legislative procedure (OLP), it also enshrines the gradually developed "strategic backbone of the EU energy policy" (Van Vooren 2012, p. 268), the three goals of competitiveness ("(a) ensure the functioning of the energy market"), energy security ("(b) ensure security of energy supply in the Union"), and sustainability ("(c) promote energy efficiency and energy saving and the development of new and renewable forms of energy").

Importantly, Article 194 does not explicitly refer to the external dimension of EU energy policy (as, for example, Article 191, TFEU, on environmental policies does). Yet, due to the principle of parallelism and implicit powers, a doctrine originating from a 1971 European Court of Justice ruling (Keukeleire and Delreux 2014, p. 95), EU external competences can be derived from internal competences. Furthermore,

9 The EU in Global Energy Governance

Article 21 (1) and (2), TEU (OJEU 2012a), forms another point of reference for EU external action on energy, since it sets out the EU's general external ambition to "seek to develop relations and build partnerships with third countries," to "promote multilateral solutions to common problems" (paragraph 1), as well as the goal to "improve the quality of the environment and the sustainable management of global natural resources, in order to ensure sustainable development" (paragraph 2 f), all of which are factors which also impact EU external energy policies.

While this overview demonstrates the limited footing on which EU external energy policy stands in legal terms, EU treaties are of course only one side of the story: In terms of policy developments and legislative acts, there has been a considerable extension of the EU *acquis* on energy over the past decades, and past 10 years in particular. Figure 1 below illustrates the most important milestones in EU policy proposals on internal/external energy (Knodt et al. 2015, pp. 57–58; Schubert et al. 2016, pp. 92–126; EC 2020a). The following paragraphs provide a detailed account of relevant policy developments over the past decades.

One of the first influential EU policy documents containing clear ideas on an external energy policy was the Commission Green Paper "A European Strategy for Sustainable, Competitive and Secure Energy" (EC 2006). The Green Paper laid out six key areas of action on energy, the sixth one being external policy. The Paper noted that "the EU needs to have a clearly defined external energy policy and to pursue it, at the same time at both national and Community level, with a single voice" (p. 19). To that end, the Green Paper made six concrete proposals, including identifying common European priorities, new energy partnerships, and the deepening of energy relations with major producers. Importantly, some of the Green Paper's ideas were taken up in a European Council document (Consilium 2007) 1 year later, adopting the "European Council Action Plan (2007–2009) Energy Policy for Europe." This document called for "the development of a common approach to external energy policy" (p. 16) based on eight essential elements, including deepened energy relationships and partnerships with third parties, the implementation of the Energy Community, etc. In a similar vein, "Energy 2020 – A Strategy for competitive, sustainable and secure energy" (EC 2010) called for more effective coordination among Member States and identified the "strengthening [of] the external dimension of the EU energy market" as a key priority, laying out four concrete actions (energy regulation export, privileged partnerships, global role promotion, and nuclear standards export). While the 2030 Climate and Energy Framework (EC 2014a) was comparatively less focused on the external dimension, the Energy Security Strategy (EC 2014b) proposed key actions for both the European Commission as well as for Member States to "improv[e] coordination of national energy policies and speaking with one voice in external energy policy," including an emphasis on the newly established information exchange mechanism (OJEU 2012b, 2017) on intergovernmental agreements between Member States and third countries.

The Juncker Commission (2014–2019) gave new momentum to the energy portfolio, most importantly through the Energy Union project. Specifically designed as "not an inward-looking project," the Energy Union Communication (EC 2015)

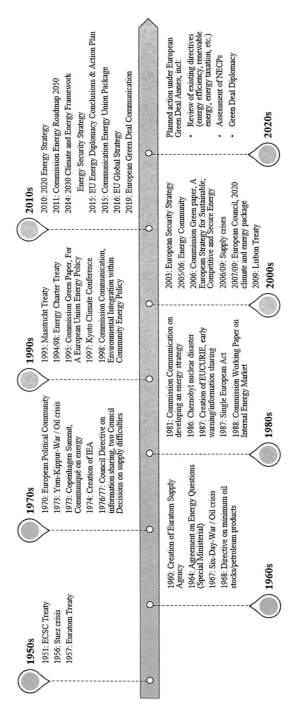

Fig. 1 Timeline of external energy integration. (Own illustration based on Knodt et al. (2015, p. 58), Schubert et al. 2016 (pp. 85–126) and EC 2019a, b, 2020a)

called for the EU to "improve its ability to project its weight on global energy markets" (ibid., p. 6). As part of the proposed Action Points, the Communication calls for the EU to "use all external policy instruments" (ibid., p. 21), including EU energy diplomacy. This diplomacy was formalized only a few months later through Foreign Affairs Council (FAC) conclusions including a new "Energy Diplomacy Action Plan" (Consilium 2015). While in principle, the conclusions could be considered an advancement for foreign energy ambitions, concrete messages, and instruments on energy diplomacy are only to be "develop[ed]" through coordination processes (ibid., p. 3). In addition, while key priorities are outlined – i.e., diversification of sources, suppliers, and routes; energy partnerships and dialogues; nuclear safety; and energy architecture and multilateral initiatives – the concretely proposed actions remain comparatively vague. Most importantly, there have not been follow-up conclusions on the actions proposed, which stands in contrast to the momentum of the FAC's climate diplomacy. The new von der Leyen Commission, which came into office in December 2019, has announced a number of energy-related initiatives, including on the international level, in the European Green Deal Communication and Roadmap (EC 2019a, b); yet, their concrete implementation remains to be seen.

Overall, this overview of milestones in the EU's external policy development illustrates two points: first, the past decade in particular has seen increased ambitions for an EU external energy policy. Second, there is a certain consistency over time in both calls for improved internal coordination, and the need for strengthened and more joined-up use of external tools to achieve the EU's external objectives. As such, the "EU external energy policy matured substantially in the early twenty-first century" (Schubert et al. 2016, p. 215), yet, the "consensus has remained that EU actorness hardly exists in international energy relations" (Kustova 2017, p. 98).

The Role of EU Institutions in External Energy Policies

This section will focus on the "polyphonous structure" (Knodt et al. 2015, p. 63) of EU external energy policy making: for each relevant EU institution, we will illustrate its role within the overall EU architecture and identify key substructures' contribution to energy policy making. At the end of the section, Fig. 2 offers an overview of the main institutional structures.

Since EU Member States continue to play a key role in EU external energy policy making, we start on the intergovernmental side of the EU's institutional spectrum: the two councils representing the voices of EU Member States governments directly. The *European Council* is the forum in which the Heads of States and Governments of all Member States meet at least four times per year. It was established as a fully-fledged EU institution in the Treaty of Lisbon and its role in steering EU politics from an "intergovernmental logic" has increased considerably in the post-Lisbon period (Fabbrini and Puetter 2016, p. 493). It is not directly involved in daily EU legislative processes, but it "defines the EU's overall political direction and priorities" (Consilium 2020a; Nugent 2010, p. 177). As Thaler (2016, p. 571) puts it: "the European Council has been paramount in the development of a common European

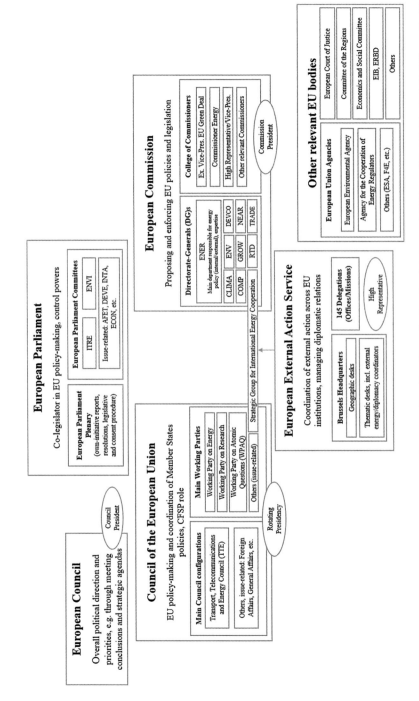

Fig. 2 The EU's complex institutional setup on external energy policy. (Own illustration based on Schubert et al. 2016, pp. 126–143; Knodt et al. 2015, pp. 61–64)

energy policy." It sets strategic priorities for future EU policies through regular conclusions relating to (external) energy policies as well as through its 5-year strategic agenda. The most recent strategic agenda included external aspects on the priority of "[b]uilding a climate-neutral, green, fair and social Europe" (Consilium 2019a, p. 5). Furthermore, the role of the permanent President of the European Council as an agenda-setter and mediator between divergent Member States interests should not be underestimated. As Szulecki et al. (2016, p. 549) show, former office holders Donald Tusk (2014–2019) and former Commission President Juncker were "major policy entrepreneur[s]" in setting the agenda for the Energy Union project.

Another major intergovernmental institution in EU policy making, the *Council of the European Union,* merits closer attention as the forum in which Member States exchange views, reach compromises, and draft conclusions, as well as approve EU legislation on a ministerial and working level. The Council of the EU is not a unitary institution, but consists of multiple Council configurations and working parties. The key configuration at ministerial level is the *Transport, Telecommunications and Energy* (TTE) formation, as its energy composition is "responsible for adopting, together with the European Parliament, legislation on the functioning of energy markets, to ensure that energy supplies are secure, to promote energy efficiency, new and renewable energies, and to promote the interconnection of energy networks" (Consilium 2020b). Since 2014, the energy minister formation has officially met two to four times per year; next to these formal meetings, it is "customary" (Maltese Council Presidency 2017) for the Rotating Presidencies of the Council of the EU to organize informal meetings of energy ministers during their mandate, adding one to two additional yearly meetings of the formation (Consilium 2020c). Other configurations such as the *Foreign Affairs Council* (FAC) or the *General Affairs Council* can also play a role in shaping external energy policies. One example is the FAC conclusions on energy diplomacy (Consilium 2015) and on joined-up climate and energy diplomacies (Consilium 2017). Below the ministerial level, there are the COREPER I and II formations, preparing compromises for the TTE, FAC, etc. Among the Council's numerous Working Parties (WP), three deserve special mention: the *Working Party for Energy,* "considered to be one of the most influential working groups" (Schubert et al. 2016, p. 133), the WP on *Atomic Questions,* and on *Research.* Other WPs can, however, equally deal with external energy matters on a case basis; this as, for example, true for the various region-specific ones (COELA group on the Western Balkans, COAFR on Africa, etc.). Another substructure relevant on the Member States side is the *Strategic Group for International Energy Cooperation* (SGIEC), established in 2012, which aims at enhancing coordination between EU services and Member States representatives on external energy policies (Schubert et al. 2016, p. 217).

On the supranational side of EU institutions, the *European Commission* plays a crucial role in agenda setting through Green Papers or Communications (see Fig. 1), in initiating legislative proposals in the OLP, and in enforcing the implementation of EU policies. The European Commission and its role in shaping (external) energy policies over the past decades have also received considerable attention in the relevant literature (see, for example, Mayer 2008; Maltby 2013; Knodt and Ringel 2018).

Again, one has to differentiate between the various relevant substructures. The *Commission Presidency* takes an important task in agenda setting, as the Juncker Agenda and Energy Union initiative (EC 2015) or the von der Leyen Green Deal announcement (EC 2019a) illustrate. Furthermore, the President steers action within the College of Commissioners and decides on the various Commissioner's portfolios and working groups, which have seen some relevant restructuring also in the area of climate and energy policies during the past terms (see Böttner 2018; Bürgin 2018). The role of individual *Commissioners* can also be crucial in shaping external energy policies, since they are known to "establish their own focal points" within their portfolio (Knodt et al. 2017, p. 102). On the working level, various *Directorates-Generals* (DGs), as the EU's main "organizational units" or "specialized agencies" (Nugent 2010, p. 117), shape EU external energy policies due to the crosscutting nature of such policies. The most central among them is *DG Energy* (ENER), which holds "the main responsibility for all energy related issues" (Knodt et al. 2015, p. 61). It serves as a major hub of energy expertise, drafts energy legislation and major strategic policy documents, and leads on energy exchanges with third partners (in forums such as bilateral energy dialogues or the Energy Community). Considering the strong interlinkages of energy and sustainability portfolios, the DGs *Climate Action* (CLIMA) and *Environment* (ENV) can be additionally relevant interlocutors for external energy policies. In a similar vein, DGs with relevant economic- and innovation-oriented portfolios can add to ENER's expertise and outreach activities, such as *DG Trade* (TRADE), *DG Research and Innovation* (RTD), *DG Competition* (COMP), and *DG Internal Market, Industry, Entrepreneurship and SMEs* (GROW). Depending on the interactions with specific regional interlocutors, relevant DGs are also those for *Neighbourhood and Enlargement Negotiations* (NEAR) and for *International Cooperation and Development* (DEVCO), as these DGs hold not only region-specific expertise and contacts but also control the main area-specific financial instruments.

One of the most recent additions to the EU's institutional system was the *European External Action Service* (EEAS), established in 2010 as the new "cornerstone in the EU's foreign policy system" (Keukeleire and Delreux 2014, p. 81). The *High Representative of the Union for Foreign Affairs and Security Policy/Vice-President of the European Commission* (HR/VP) steers the overall work of the service within the EEAS' Brussels headquarters. In addition, there is the coordination work of the diplomats working on specific countries/regions, the so-called *geographic desks*, as well as those working on the *thematic desks* dealing with energy diplomacy as part of the "Human rights, global and multilateral issues" section. Equally part of the EEAS are the more than 140 EU Delegations and Offices located all around the world, which can perform important outreach functions toward third countries on energy policies, collect relevant intelligence, and even partly deploy energy-specialized staff (for example, in important producer or transit countries). The new role of the EEAS and its energy diplomacy efforts in particular have been the subject of more recent scholarly research, situating the new coordinating service within the EU's external (energy) policy making machinery (see, for example, Knodt et al. 2015, p. 63; Chaban and Knodt 2015; Herranz-Surrallés 2016; Stoddard 2017).

While the *European Parliament*'s (EP) influence on energy policy processes has increased with recent EU Treaties, in particular through the expansion of the ordinary legislative procedure (OLP), its powers generally remain largely limited in areas of external action (Keukeleire and Delreux 2014, pp. 85–88). Yet it still has some tools available to influence external energy policy processes: next to its role as a co-legislator in the OLP, it can use its institutional control powers, the consent procedure in cases of international agreements as well as own-initiative reports on external energy policies. Within the Parliament, a number of committees are relevant input-givers, including the standing committees on *Industry, Research and Energy* (ITRE); *Environment, Public Health and Food Safety* (ENVI); and, depending on issue, and region, others such as the *Committee on Foreign Affairs* (AFET) or the *Committee on Development* (DEVE).

Finally, there are a number of other EU institutions and bodies with limited, yet still potential relevance for external energy processes. Other relevant EU institutions include the *European Court of Justice*, which has developed significant jurisdiction on both internal and external policies (Keukeleire and Delreux 2014, p. 89), as well as the *Committee of the Regions* and the *Economics and Social Committee*. Furthermore, issue-related EU agencies, such as the *European Environmental Agency* (EEA), the *Agency for the Cooperation of Energy Regulators* (ACER), etc., can be useful providers of expertise in external energy efforts. Last but not least, the *European Investment Bank* (EIB) and the *European Bank for Reconstruction and Development* (EBRD) can provide financial measures and expertise.

EU External Energy Instruments

The complex underlying structure of competences and institutions is reflected in the setup of the diverse tools available for the EU to exert influence on its external environment in the energy arena, which can vary substantially depending on the issue-area nexus and the third country or region.

First, there are a number of *diplomatic tools* available to the EU. This includes high-level outreach in *multilateral* frameworks, such as the promotion of EU external energy objectives in formats such as the G7/8 and G20 as well as active outreach toward and within international organizations such as the International Atomic Energy Agency, the International Renewable Energy Agency, etc. In such cases, however, EU participation always depends on the specific rules of engagement within such multilateral fora considering the EU's complex actorness (Jorgensen and Laatikainen 2012). Furthermore, there is *bilateral* outreach toward third countries through the activities of local EU Delegations, bilateral visits of high-level EU actors, and through holding energy dialogues (or dialogues including energy agenda points). The format of bilateral energy dialogues can be an important tool for upholding or promoting special (energy) relationships, for example, with Russia (Aalto 2008), the BICS countries (Knodt et al. 2017), and the United States (first EU-US Energy Council held in 2018 (EC 2019a, c)).

Second, there are instruments of *energy cooperation* channeled through the EU's various *bilateral and regional partnership and association formats*. The EU's relevant formats range from pure trade, partnership and cooperation, and association agreements to strategic partnerships and broader regional frameworks. These may not only establish and nurture economic relations with third countries and regions, but also uphold political relations and strengthen cooperation on sectoral issues such as energy. Examples for such formats include the European Neighbourhood Policy, Economic Partnership Agreements negotiated with countries of the African, Caribbean, and Pacific region, and (Stabilization and) Association Agreements with countries of the Balkan and neighborhood region. Bilateral and regional cooperation arrangements like the afore listed include regular policy dialogues; region-specific financial instruments (like the Instrument for Pre-Accession for accession countries), which can be used to specifically fund energy-related projects in third countries or regions; and economic provisions (such as agreements over a Deep and Comprehensive Free Trade Area, for example, in the case of Ukraine) with relevant dimensions for EU external energy interests and investment. As the wide range of tools related to such specific cooperation formats shows, the various expert DGs with DG Energy at the forefront play a crucial role for these bilateral or regional instruments including available bilateral association funding for financial/development aid; pipeline investments or trade agreements for market access; expertise-based technical dialogues for technical assistance/exchanges; and even rules export.

Third, there are more direct instruments of *rule export*, which deserve special attention despite their interrelatedness with the previous two types of instruments. On the one hand, through negotiations on behalf of EU climate and energy standards, the EU can try to export its rules and its own energy objectives into trade agreements with third countries and regions. On the other hand, rule export through policy harmonization can also take place in association and accession processes. In that sense, the Energy Community deserves special attention. As an international organization founded in 2005 combining the European Union and nine southern neighbors as Contracting Parties (Albania, Bosnia and Herzegovina, Kosovo, North Macedonia, Georgia, Moldova, Montenegro, Serbia, and Ukraine) as well as three observer states (Armenia, Norway, Turkey) (Energy Community 2020), it is inherently dedicated to EU rule export, seen by some as a "diplomatic success story for the EU" in external energy policy (Schubert et al. 2016, p. 221).

The EU in the Global Energy Governance Landscape

In line with its competences, the EU makes use of its external energy instruments when engaging in the global energy governance landscape. There is not one international energy regime as a sector-specific institutional framework that is comprehensive in its scope, cogency, and robustness (Dubash and Florini 2011). Instead, the global energy governance landscape is shaped by various state and nonstate actors and the institutions defining the "rules according to which they behave" (Goldthau and Witte 2010). This fragmented set of organizations with limited scope and capacity was created around specific governance problems and is shaped until today by the key actors and historical circumstances under which it emerged. Several experimental regulatory processes are on the rise, although their legitimacy and efficacy has been questioned (Dubash and Florini 2011).

To address the question "who governs global energy," several attempts have been made to map the global energy governance landscape. Van de Graaf and Colgan (2016) offer a meta-analysis of these mapping exercises and find that the number of identified key actors ranges between 6 (Keppler and Kérébel 2009) and 50 (Florini and Sovacool 2011). This number depends on the scope of the mapping (e.g., whether its focus is on one sector versus all energy sources) and the categories of actors considered (e.g., formalized intergovernmental institutions vs. hybrid semi-private entities, transnational NGOs, or loose networks like summits (Van de Graaf and Colgan 2016, p. 4)). Therefore, no single approach grasps the total complexity of actors (Van de Graaf and Colgan 2016). Accordingly, this chapter abstains from an exhaustive list of organizations, but rather aims to highlight key institutions of the global energy governance landscape in the areas of strategic interest of the EU.

Since 2006, the Commission repeatedly highlighted the importance of the energy policy triangle of energy security, sustainability, and competitiveness for its external energy governance. These three objectives are often referred to as the "energy trilemma" among scholars and policy makers (e.g., World Energy Council 2019; Gunningham 2013; Song et al. 2017). This trilemma describes energy governance as the challenge to balance three competing objectives, with some variations: whereas there is agreement on energy security (sometimes also referred to as reliability) and environmental sustainability (whereby climate change mitigation plays a major role) as two key objectives, the third part is often named energy equity (also referred to as social justice or affordability). The EU highlighted competitiveness as the third objective dimension in its external energy governance instead. This does of course not mean that affordability and equity concerns remain unmentioned in the EU context – for example, the Energy Union Communication highlights the goal to reach "secure, sustainable, competitive and affordable energy" (EC 2015, p. 2) and the commission created an EU Energy Poverty Observatory, bringing together various institutions to collaborate on the topic (EPOV 2020). Yet in the external arena, equity concerns have received less attention (see, for example, Council conclusions on energy diplomacy, Consilium 2015).The lines between these objectives become blurry when synergies exist. In this context, many institutions widened their mandate to address various objectives simultaneously. Yet, many institutions still have a stronger focus on one of these objectives, sometimes at the expense of others. Several key institutions in global energy governance and their work toward these objectives are summarized below. They are characterized along their main funding source (public, private, or semiprivate) by their functions, including (1) correcting market failures, (2) lowering transaction costs, (3) setting rules and standard, and by their enforcement mechanisms (Goldthau and Witte 2010). Furthermore, the following section considers the EU's approach toward these objectives and its relations within these institutions.

Energy Security

Most institutions in the global energy governance landscape include the provision of energy security in their mandates (see Fig. 3). It has been argued that in case of conflict among the three objectives, energy security has often been prioritized (Van de Graaf and Zelli 2016, p. 60). Most commonly, energy security refers to ensuring access to fossil fuel reserves in order to always provide stable energy supply to all domestic consumers. The EU's oil import dependency was 87% in 2017 with around 566 million tons of crude oil imported, mainly from Russia, Norway, Iraq, Kazakhstan, and Saudi Arabia. However, the variation among the member states is high, with the share of net imports in gross available energy varying between −3.9% in oil-exporting Denmark and 115% in Estonia, which bunkered oil beyond its consumption in 2017 (Eurostat 2020).

The first oil crisis in 1973 raised concerns about the security of supply for oil consumer nations. In reaction, the United States fostered the foundation of the *International Energy Agency* (IEA) in 1974 among the major oil importing OECD member states. Its main function was to prevent market failures in the global oil market by coordinating oil reserves among the member states. Furthermore, the IEA lowered transaction costs through the collection and provision of energy market data, most prominently in their annual world energy outlook reports (Goldthau and Witte 2010). Especially in the past decade, the IEA has slowly broadened its perspective toward the promotion of an energy transition for the objective of sustainability. The IEA's headquarters are in Paris, in the EU. Among the EU member states, energy security is mainly seen as a question of national sovereignty, and the EU, consequently, has no competence for the governance of external energy trade. Therefore, the EU's role as an actor in the global governance of oil and gas markets is thus limited. In the IEA, the EU member states act as individual countries

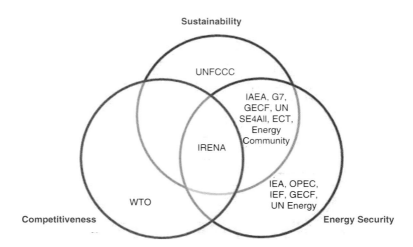

Fig. 3 Institutions of global energy governance and their mandate. (Own illustration)

and hold, like all others, reserves, which reflect their net import shares. However, the EU regulates and supervises oil and gas supplies by its member states: the European Energy Security Strategy requires countries to prepare risk assessments, preventive action plans, and emergency plans, which take into account neighboring countries in a regional approach toward security of supply; these measures are reviewed and supervised by the EC and partly also expands the common regulatory space with the Energy Community (EC 2014b).

Oil exporting states have been cooperating since the 1960, within the intergovernmental *Organization of the Petroleum Exporting Countries* (OPEC), which is often depicted as a counterpart to the IEA. Today, its 13 member countries account for 40% of the world's oil supply (OPEC 2019). Its main objective is the prevention of instability and price volatility in global energy market, which would not only affect these countries' energy security, but also their economic stability. Therefore, the main area of cooperation has been the coordination of oil extraction volumes in order to ensure price stability. OPEC is located in the EU, in Vienna. While the EU is not a member of OPEC, it aims at maintaining a close relationship, among others through holding regular EU-OPEC high-level meetings (EC 2020b). Like OPEC, gas-exporting countries are organized within the *Gas-Exporting Countries Forum* (GECF), but their impact is considerably smaller. In contrast to global oil markets, a global gas market remains "in the making," while most trade still occurs at a regional level (Goldthau and Witte 2010). The future globalization of gas markets will depend on different factors, such as progress on liquefied natural gas (LNG) technologies. Likewise, discussions on green hydrogen, produced by renewable energies, as a potential substitute for natural gas within industrial processes and/or transportation will further change the landscape and require additional global governance.

The EU gas supply is currently mainly organized within a Eurasian gas market with Russia as the main trading partner to most EU member states (Goldthau and Witte 2010, p. 6). The fragmentation of trade agreements, price discrimination, and transit regulations between individual EU member states and Russia have been a source of internal and bilateral conflict. The EU's second largest gas supplier in 2017 was Norway, followed by Algeria and Qatar (Eurostat 2020). With the rising importance of liquefied natural gas (LNG), the diversity of supply has been increasing. Furthermore, the European Commission actively fosters the development of green hydrogen within the "European Clean Hydrogen Alliance," bringing together industries and investors, to speed and scale up applications (EC 2020d).

The EU member states are part of the global *International Energy Forum* (IEF), which fosters the coordination between producer and consumer states through biannual dialogue formats since 2001. While initially antagonistic, consumer and producer states nowadays often join forces (Van de Graaf and Zelli 2016, p. 58). The IEF's main function is to lower transaction costs. While the EU is not a formal member of the IEF, it engages with IEF, for example, through IEF–EU Energy Days, an annual format of expert exchanges that began in 2017 (IEF 2017, 2020).

Furthermore, the EU employs various instruments of external energy governance to increase its security of supply which also shape the global energy landscape.

These include bilateral partnerships with supply and transit countries (such as the strategic energy partnership with Egypt since in 2018) and multilateral political dialogues (for example, with North African and Eastern Mediterranean countries in order to create a Mediterranean gas hub). Additionally, the EU finances infrastructure projects in order to diversify the oil and gas supply sources and routes. Recent examples are the construction of LNG Terminals and the Trans-Adriatic-Pipeline (TAP) to transport gas from Azerbaijan to Italy via Georgia, Turkey, Greece, Albania, and the Adriatic Sea (EC 2020c).

With the unfolding energy transition, security of supply no longer just refers to the access to fossil fuels. Instead, the term is increasingly used to refer to a reliable supply of electricity, which becomes central for more and more sectors. As the shares of renewable energy sources and therefore the volatility of electricity production increases, the further interconnection of electricity markets not only within the EU, but also with external partner countries, improves energy security. Electricity trade is in the process of being fully liberalized within the EU, with common regulatory frameworks. EU approaches to govern energy, and foremost electricity, also spread beyond EU borders: for example, the now-defunct interregional electricity project Desert-Tech failed, which was supposed to increase energy security via the transportation of renewable electricity from Northern Africa. In addition, the *Energy Community* brings the EU together with neighboring countries and aims at creating a pan-European energy market. Its functions include lowering transaction costs through exchange and common standards which are often transferred from EU regulations. The role of the Energy Community has been particularly influential in liberalizing electricity markets within countries that aim to apply for EU membership (Bianco et al. 2019).

Environmental Sustainability

The objective of environmental sustainability has become increasingly important throughout the past decades, and has been interpreted as efforts to mitigate carbon emissions in order to prevent dangerous climate change. The energy sector is responsible for two-thirds of global emissions and must be completely decarbonized within the next decades in order to limit global warming to 1.5 °C (IPCC 2018). After the United States and China, the EU is still the third largest carbon emitter worldwide, making up 9% of global carbon emissions in 2019 (Global Carbon Project 2020). It plays an active role within the global institutions that govern sustainable energy, which are explained in more detail below.

The *United Nations Framework Convention on Climate Change* (UNFCCC), adopted in 1992, is the main global institution uniting all countries for annual negotiations in order to combine greenhouse gas mitigation measures worldwide. The *Paris Agreement*, agreed upon at COP21 in 2015, marks the first time all countries worldwide committed to fulfill nationally determined contributions (NDCs) to the prevention of climate change, often including renewable energy targets. The main function of the institution can be seen in setting rules and standards when it comes to monitoring carbon emissions worldwide, but also investments in climate change mitigation and adaptation. Furthermore, networks have been built among smaller groups of member states, such as the *High Ambition Coalition* established around the COP21 or the *Powering Past Coal Alliance* established in 2017 to exchange best practices and foster ambitious policies. The Secretariat of the Organization is located in Bonn, Germany. Especially within the past 5 years, EU countries hosted and sponsored a majority of climate conferences. Within the UNFCCC negotiations, the EU has its own seat and manages to coordinate positions among the member states, which each have their own seats, but nevertheless mostly speak with one voice (Van Schaik 2013; Oberthür and Groen 2018). On many occasions, the EU has been an active promoter of ambitious target, rule, and standard setting. The EU committed to reduce emissions by 40% in comparison to 1990 levels by 2030, and to increase its shares of renewable energy up to 32% of final energy consumption (EU 2015). Some scholars argue that with the EU's declining share in global greenhouse gas emissions (from 20% in 1990 to 9% in 2019), its bargaining power equally decreased, leading to a change in strategy toward a leadership role based on mediator techniques (Bäckstrand and Elgström 2013). However, bargaining power stems from different sources. Although the UNFCCC does not (in contrast to the former Kyoto-Protocol) include any enforcement mechanisms beyond naming and shaming, the EU itself created such a mechanism among the member states: the National Energy and Climate Plans (NECPs). This "leading by example" approach in internal governance of climate and energy ambitions aimed at strengthening the EU's credibility within the global climate and energy governance landscape, exemplifying important feedback mechanisms between these two spheres.

As several IEA member states increasingly criticized the IEA for not engaging enough within the promotion of renewable energies, the *International Renewable Energy Agency* (IRENA) was founded in 2009 (Van de Graaf and Colgan 2016). Several EU Member States, most prominently Spain, Denmark, and Germany, were very active within the founding process of IRENA and have been strongly engaged in the governance of renewable energy within the organization. In contrast to IEA, whose members are limited to individual OECD countries, IRENA has a more comprehensive, global scope, representing 161 members (including the EU as a member on its own and EU states). Furthermore, its mandate is formulated much more broadly, focusing on all the three strategic areas (see Fig. 3). IRENA therefore serves as an important dialogue forum, provides data on renewable energy markets, technological, and regional developments, and encourages the adoption of energy transition policies.

Competitiveness

Energy policy can have strong impacts on the economic competitiveness of industrial products on global markets. Energy prices vary significantly among countries, based on the electricity mix, domestic resource endowment, taxes, subsidies, and the electricity market design. A global governance of competition in energy-related trade is therefore mostly concerned with the provision of an equal level playing field of rules and regulations.

Economic competition in international trade has been strongly influenced by the *World Trade Organization* (WTO), since its foundation in 1995. Under its leadership, a system of trade rules has been negotiated and agreed upon by 164 member states representing 98% of global trade (WTO 2020). Its main objective is the promotion of free trade, reliability, and predictability of trade relations within an equal level playing field, without unjustifiable discrimination. Its comprehensive framework includes dispute settlement provisions. The EU has been a WTO member since 1995, and EU Member States are also WTO members in their own right. As the EU is a single customs union with a single trade policy and tariff toward third parties, the European Commission speaks for all member states at almost all WTO meetings.

Many trade regulations contained in the General Agreement of Tariffs and Trade (GATT) as well as the Agreement on Trade-Related Aspects of Intellectual Property Rights (TRIPS) govern trade in fossil resources, processed goods and services related to electricity provision, as well as research and innovation in the (renewable) energy sector (Marceau 2020). Going even further, the Energy Charter Treaty protects investments in the energy sector and establishes nondiscriminatory conditions for trade in energy materials, products, and energy-related equipment based on WTO rules, among Eurasian countries. Like the WTO, it also contains regulations for dispute settlement procedures.

The EU has been involved in energy-related dispute settlement procedures of the WTO, e.g., in filing a case against Chinese subsidies for solar panels, which might have influenced the competitiveness of European solar panels on international markets (Meyer 2013). At the same time, China criticized domestic content requirements in the renewable energy sector in Italy and Greece as violating the GATT (Meyer 2013). Although a peaceful agreement could be reached, these incidents highlight that in the past decades, the EU has started to compete for industrial leadership in renewable energy sources. The EU strategically strengthens and develops its capacities in this regard, e.g., by funding research and innovation programmers in the battery and storage sector such as the *European Battery Alliance (EBA)* in 2019. These ambitions bear potential for further conflicts with WTO regulations. At the same time, the WTO conflict settlement procedures, if applied, could gain renewed relevance as institutions for de-escalation, especially in times of increasing trade conflicts among the US and China.

In cases where a global agreement is difficult to achieve, countries agree on multilateral regulations of energy-related regulations with strong implications for trade in bilateral trade agreements. The EU has put increasing emphasis on energy and climate targets within trade agreement negotiations. Another example of multilateral agreement among smaller country groups is the regulation of subsidies for fossil fuels, which are prevalent in many parts of the world. For example, the heads of states of seven advanced economies including France, Germany, and Italy (G7) jointly declared to phase out fossil fuel subsidies by 2025 (G7 2016). Within the *G20* format, similar initiatives have been promoted including at the latest G20 Leaders'

Summit in Osaka, Japan, at which heads of state and government committed to "promoting and leading energy transitions (...) while promoting sustainable growth" (Consilium 2019b, p. 9). EU representatives in particular have been pushing this agenda, which is meant to foster the energy transition as well as competition.

However, it can be argued that despite the existence of G7 and G20 initiatives and WTO regulations, a level playing field will not exist until carbon is priced globally. The EU has been among the first to introduce its own internal carbon pricing scheme (the EU ETS), despite warnings that this might negatively influence its global competitiveness. Now the discussions being taken to the next level: the European Commission suggested to make an institutional adjustment with external implications on its own in the form of carbon border adjustment as part of the European Green Deal (EC 2019a). This measure could have implications for global governance, highlighting the importance of a decarbonization of entire economies as the carbon content of all production matters for trade relations with the EU. Suddenly, the question of decarbonization would no longer be a question of being "green or sustainable" for image reasons, but it has become clear that it can be a competitive advantage. This ties into Nobel prize winner William Nordhaus's idea of climate clubs (2015): by penalizing carbon intensive production, an equal playing field could be created, nationalizing internal efficiency standards (Keohane et al. 2017). Whether or not such a policy would be in line with WTO regulation would depend on its design, and its success would depend on building a stable coalition of like-minded allies. It remains open whether the regulation across traditional institutional barriers between UNFCCC, energy institutions, and WTO will have a cascading effect fostering the introduction of carbon prices worldwide or result in a new area of mercantilist trade barriers.

Challenges to EU External Energy Action in a Fragmented Global Landscape

The EU faces various challenges when it comes to balancing its external energy policy objectives of energy security, sustainability, and competitiveness due to its need for internal need coordination and the fragmentation of the global energy governance landscape.

Internally, energy objectives have long been conceptualized as a trilemma causing trade-offs. Especially in the 1990s and early 2000s, striving for sustainability and an energy transition was criticized as a threat to energy security; renewable energy sources would not be reliable and increase network instabilities due to their volatile generation. At the same time, critics feared that the energy transition would increase energy prices and limit competitiveness of European industries. This perspective has changed throughout the last decade. Increasing shares of renewable energies have proven to be manageable; new storage and sector coupling technologies opened up new ways to balance volatility. Furthermore, dramatically increasing efficiency of renewable energy technologies enables the provision of renewable electricity at low costs (Lachapelle et al. 2017). Accordingly, the European Green Deal does not mention tough trade-offs, but highlights the synergies and cobenefits of sustainability within the other two realms: the energy transition is to limit the EU's import dependency and thereby to increase energy security; global leadership in sustainability is supposed to lead toward international economic competitiveness, create jobs, and further social cobenefits.

The success of creating such synergies will highly depend on the coordination of the EU institutions governing external energy relations. This might be a necessary, but yet not sufficient condition for successful synergy creation. Different EU institutions are involved in external policies for these objectives, which are not fully aligned (e.g., DG Trade in WTO regulations concerning competitiveness, DG Energy in matters regarding energy security, and DG Climate Action in the preparation of UNFCCC negotiations). As such, the various institutional actors' involvement in third-party interactions can lead to competitive priorities and hinder a coherent EU external action in the energy arena.

The fragmentation of the global governance landscape along the lines of the three objectives of security, sustainability, and competitiveness in the EU external energy policy poses further challenges for comprehensive action. Meyer (2013) describes the dilemma of a "systemic governance risk" in which effective cooperation within one institution increases the chances for failure in cooperation within another institution. For example, successful cooperation on energy security within the IEA might in fact be functionally linked to climate change cooperation and "crowd out" cooperation within the UNFCCC. A situation in which these functional linkages could arise would be if both institutions tried to influence prices of fossil fuels in different directions. Whereas the IEA is interested in keeping energy supply stable at low price levels, the climate regime would prefer to raise prices with mechanisms like carbon caps, tariffs or taxes in order to foster a shift toward low-carbon energy (Meyer 2013). Overcoming these "rebound effects" in international energy governance would require the identification of these interlinkages and a prioritization. Furthermore, Meyer (2013) suggests that especially successful institutions like the IEA, OPEC, or IEF could broaden their mandate in order to include sustainability within their decision-making processes. The European Green Deal with its unilateral approach toward carbon border adjustment taxes seems to pursue a different strategy, which might foster uneven energy transition patterns. These could increase the risks of economic instability, limited competitiveness in international markets for late decarbonizing countries, and also the risks of climate change and conflict for the global community (Eicke et al. 2019).

Conclusion

This chapter gives an overview of the EU's role in global energy governance, aiming to balance the three key objectives of sustainability, energy security, and competitiveness. It argues that the EU's capacity to influence the global energy arena is determined by two factors: the complex internal design of EU (external) energy policy making and the fragmented landscape of global energy governance, in which the EU tries to shape policies.

The chapter demonstrates that EU external energy action is based on a complex legal and political foundation. In terms of EU *acquis*, EU external energy action stands on an originally internal policy designed treaty basis. Despite significant developments in policy documents over the past two decades in particular, key competences of external energy action still remain with Member States rather than giving the EU an extensive, concrete toolbox of instruments to play an unlimited role in the global energy landscape. As such, external energy policies are developed, negotiated, influenced, and implemented by a variety of actors within the EU. The two most important actors are the intergovernmental Councils setting the priorities (European Council) and concrete framework for EU action (Council of the EU's energy and foreign policy formations) and the supranational European Commission on the other side (the Commission President and College as agenda setters and the various Commission DGs, with DG Energy at the forefront, implementing policies and providing expertise). Overall, the EU disposes of a diverse combination of instruments to influence global energy politics, ranging from a number of powerful instruments such as partnerships with third countries like the Energy Community to a bystander role in some energy-related multilateral frameworks (such as the IEF where it does not have observer status). This clearly impacts the EU's potential to play a role in the global energy governance landscape, since different dynamics from within and the outside can limit or enable it across policy areas, across energy objectives, across regions, and across multilateral frameworks.

Despite this mixed potential, the EU sets its ambition to act as a meaningful actor in global energy governance very high, as the recent announcement on the EU's global leadership ambitions in the European Green Deal (EC 2019a) clearly shows. Among the Green Deal's policy objectives are overcoming trade-offs and to enhancing synergies. However, these efforts are limited due to the fragmented institutional landscape of global energy governance. Furthermore, the EU's capacity as a non-traditional actor of global politics is challenged by the potential parallel or counter efforts of Member States, a limited political and legal basis to act globally, and the diversity of bilateral and multilateral settings in which the EU is a more or less recognized actor for various third parties. Its potential to influence global energy politics and global energy governance developments will therefore remain limited unless or until more significant internal steps on turning the EU's ambitions into actual legal competences and a clear toolbox of instruments to be used in the various global settings are taken.

Cross-References

- ▶ Energy Governance in Europe: Introduction
- ▶ Energy Relations in the EU Eastern Partnership
- ▶ Energy Relations of the EU and its Southern Neighborhood
- ▶ Energy Poverty

- EU Energy Cooperation with Emerging Powers: Brazil, India, China, and South Africa
- European Union Energy Policy: A Discourse Perspective
- EU-Russia Energy Relations
- EU-US and EU-Canada Energy Relations
- Sustainable Europe: Narrative Potential in the EU's Political Communication
- The Energy Charter Treaty: Old and New Dilemmas in Global Energy Governance

Acknowledgments The authors would like to thank the Handbook editors and Silvia Weko (Institute for Advanced Sustainability Studies (IASS), Potsdam Germany) for useful comments on earlier versions of this manuscript.

References

Secondary Literature

Aalto, P. (2008). *The EU-Russian energy dialogue: Europe's future energy security*. Farnham: Ashgate.

Bäckstrand, K., & Elgström, O. (2013). The EU's role in climate change negotiations: From leader to 'leadiator'. *Journal of European Public Policy, 20*(10), 1369–1386.

Batzella, F. (2018). Work in progress: The development of EU external engagement on energy. In C. Damro, S. Gstöhl, & S. Schunz (Eds.), *The EU's evolving external engagement – Towards new sectoral diplomacies?* (pp. 107–125). Abingdon: Routledge.

Bianco, E., Brown, A., Hafner, M., Eicke, A., Eicke, L., & Uherova Hasbani, K. (2019). *Renewable energy market analysis* (153 p). Southeast Europe, Abu Dhabi: International Renewable Energy Agency (IRENA).

Böttner, R. (2018). The size and structure of the European Commission: Legal issues surrounding project teams and a (future) reduced College. *European Constitutional Law Review, 14*, 37–61.

Bürgin, A. (2018). The impact of Juncker's reorganization of the European Commission on the internal policy-making process: Evidence from the Energy Union project. *Public Administration, 2018*, 1–18.

Chaban, N., & Knodt, M. (2015). Energy diplomacy in the context of multistakeholder diplomacy: The EU and BICS. *Cooperation and Conflict, 50*(4), 457–474.

Dubash, N. K., & Florini, A. (2011). Mapping global energy governance. *Global Policy, 2*, 6–18.

Eicke, L., Weko, S., & Goldthau, A. (2019). Countering the risk of an uneven low-carbon energy transition. *IASS Policy Brief*.

Fabbrini, S., & Puetter, U. (2016). Integration without supranationalisation: Studying the lead roles of the European Council and the Council in post-Lisbon EU politics. *Journal of European Integration, 38*(5), 481–495.

Florini, A., & Sovacool, B. K. (2011). Bridging the gaps in global energy governance. *Global Governance, 17*, 57–74.

Goldthau, A., & Sitter, N. (2015). *A liberal actor in a realist world. The European Union regulatory state and the global political economy of energy*. Oxford: Oxford University Press.

Goldthau, A., & Witte, J. M. (2010). The role of rules and institutions in global energy: An introduction. In *Global energy governance: The new rules of the game* (pp. 1–21). Washington, DC: Brookings Press.

Gunningham, N. (2013). Managing the energy trilemma: The case of Indonesia. *Energy Policy, 54*, 184–193.

Herranz-Surrallés, A. (2015). European external energy policy: Governance, diplomacy and sustainability. In K. E. Jorgensen, K. Aarstad, & E. Drieskens (Eds.), *The SAGE handbook of European foreign policy* (pp. 913–927). London: SAGE.

Herranz-Surrallés, A. (2016). An emerging EU energy diplomacy? Discursive shifts, enduring practices. *Journal of European Public Policy, 23*(9), 1386–1405.

Hughes, L., & Lipscy, P. Y. (2013). The Politics of Energy. *Annual Review of Political Science, 16*, 449–469.

Jorgensen, K. E., & Laatikainen, K. V. (2012). *Routledge handbook on the European Union and international institutions. Performance, policy, power*. London: Routledge.

Keohane, N., Petsonk, A., & Hanafi, A. (2017). Toward a club of carbon markets. *Climatic Change, 144*(1), 81–95.

Keppler, J. H., & Kérébel, C. (2009). *La Gouvernance mondiale de l'énergie* (No. 123456789/141). Paris Dauphine University.

Keukeleire, S., & Delreux, T. (2014). *The foreign policy of the European Union* (2nd ed.). Basingstoke: Palgrave Macmillan.

Knodt, M., & Ringel, M. (2018). Chapter 8: The European Commission as a policy shaper – Harder soft governance in the Energy Union. In J. Ege, M. W. Bauer, & S. Becker (Eds.), *The European Commission in turbulent times. Assessing organizational change and policy impact* (pp. 181–206). Baden-Baden: Nomos.

Knodt, M., Müller, F., & Piefer, N. (2015). Explaining European Union external energy governance with emerging powers. In M. Knodt, N. Piefer, & F. Müller (Eds.), *Challenges of European external energy governance with emerging powers* (pp. 57–74). Abingdon: Routledge.

Knodt, M., Chaban, N., & Nielsen, L. (2017). *Bilateral energy relations between the EU and emerging powers. Mutual perceptions of the EU and Brazil, China, India and South Africa*. Baden-Baden: Nomos.

Kustova, I. (2017). Towards a comprehensive research agenda on EU energy integration: Policy making, energy security, and EU energy actorness. *Journal of European Integration, 39*(1), 95–101.

Lachapelle, E., MacNeil, R., & Paterson, M. (2017). The political economy of decarbonisation: From green energy 'race' to green 'division of labour'. *New Political Economy, 22*(3), 311–327.

Maltby, T. (2013). European Union energy policy integration: A case of European Commission policy entrepreneurship and increasing supranationalism. *Energy Policy, 55*, 435–444.

Marceau, G. (2020). The WTO in the emerging energy governance debate. https://www.wto.org/english/res_e/publications_e/wtr10_forum_e/wtr10_marceau_e.htm. Accessed 20 Feb 2020.

Mayer, S. (2008). Path dependence and Commission activism in the evolution of the European Union's external energy policy. *Journal of International Relations and Development, 11*, 251–278.

Meyer, T. (2013). *Energy subsidies and the World Trade Organization*. American Society of international law Insights (ASIL) (17/22).

Nordhaus, W. (2015). Climate clubs: Overcoming free-riding in international climate policy. *American Economic Review, 105*(4), 1339–1370.

Nugent, N. (2010). *The government and politics of the European Union* (7th ed.). Basingstoke: Palgrave Macmillan.

Oberthür, S., & Groen, L. (2018). Explaining goal achievement in international negotiations: The EU and the Paris Agreement on climate change. *Journal of European Public Policy, 25*, 708–727.

Schubert, S. R., Pollak, J., & Kreutler, M. (2016). *Energy policy of the European Union*. London/New York: Palgrave Macmillan.

Schunz, S., & Damro, C. (2020). Expanding actorness to explain EU external engagement in originally internal policy areas. *Journal of European Public Policy, 27*(1), 122–140.

Sjöstedt, G. (1977). *The external role of the European Community*. Farnborough: Saxon House.

Song, L., Fu, Y., Zhou, P., & Lai, K. K. (2017). Measuring national energy performance via energy trilemma index: A stochastic multicriteria acceptability analysis. *Energy Economics, 66*, 313–319.

Stoddard, E. (2017). Tough times, shifting roles: Examining the EU's commercial diplomacy in foreign energy markets. *Journal of European Public Policy, 24*(7), 1048–1068.

Szulecki, K., Fischer, S., Gullberg, A. T., & Sartor, O. (2016). Shaping the 'Energy Union': Between national positions and governance innovation in EU energy and climate policy. *Climate Policy, 16*(5), 548–567.

Thaler, P. (2016). The European Commission and the European Council: Coordinated Agenda setting in European energy policy. *Journal of European Integration, 38*(5), 571–585.

Van de Graaf, T., & Colgan, J. (2016). Global energy governance: A review and research agenda. *Palgrave Communications, 2*(1), 1–12.

Van de Graaf, T., & Zelli, F. (2016). Actors, institutions and frames in global energy politics. In T. Van de Graaf, B. K. Sovacool, A. Ghosh, F. Kern, & M. T. Klare (Eds.), *The Palgrave handbook of the international political economy of energy* (pp. 47–71). London: Palgrave Macmillan.

Van Schaik, L. G. (2013). *EU effectiveness and unity in multilateral negotiations. More than the sum of its parts?* London: Palgrave Macmillan.

Van Vooren, B. (2012). *EU external relations law and the European Neighbourhood Policy. A paradigm for coherence.* Oxon/New York: Routledge.

Primary (EU) Sources

Consilium. (2007). European Council action plan (2007–2009). Energy Policy for Europe (EPE). https://www.consilium.europa.eu/uedocs/cms_data/docs/pressdata/en/ec/93135.pdf. Accessed 6 Feb 2020.

Consilium. (2015). Council conclusions on energy diplomacy. http://data.consilium.europa.eu/doc/document/ST-10995-2015-INIT/en/pdf. Accessed 6 Feb 2020.

Consilium. (2017). Implementing the EU global strategy – Strengthening synergies between EU climate and energy diplomacies and elements for priorities for 2017 – Council conclusions (06 March 2017). http://data.consilium.europa.eu/doc/document/ST-6981-2017-INIT/en/pdf. Accessed 6 Feb 2020.

Consilium. (2019a). A new strategic agenda 2019–2024. https://www.consilium.europa.eu/en/press/press-releases/2019/06/20/a-new-strategic-agenda-2019-2024/. Accessed 6 Feb 2020.

Consilium. (2019b). G20 Osaka Leaders' Declaration. https://www.consilium.europa.eu/media/40124/final_g20_osaka_leaders_declaration.pdf. Accessed 6 Feb 2020.

Consilium. (2020a). The European Council. https://www.consilium.europa.eu/en/european-council/. Accessed 6 Feb 2020.

Consilium. (2020b). Transport, Telecommunications and Energy Council configuration (TTE). https://www.consilium.europa.eu/en/council-eu/configurations/tte/. Accessed 6 Feb 2020.

Consilium. (2020c). Meeting calendar. https://www.consilium.europa.eu/en/meetings/calendar/. Accessed 6 Feb 2020.

Energy Community. (2020). About us. https://www.energy-community.org/aboutus/whoweare.html. Accessed 6 Feb 2020.

European Commission/EC. (2006). GREEN PAPER. A European strategy for sustainable, competitive and secure energy. https://eur-lex.europa.eu/legal-content/EN/TXT/HTML/?uri=LEGISSUM:l27062&from=EN. Accessed 6 Feb 2020.

European Commission/EC. (2010). Energy 2020. A strategy for competitive, sustainable and secure energy. https://eur-lex.europa.eu/legal-content/EN/TXT/HTML/?uri=CELEX:52010DC0639&from=EN. Accessed 6 Feb 2020.

European Commission/EC. (2014a). A policy framework for climate and energy in the period from 2020 to 2030. https://eur-lex.europa.eu/legal-content/EN/TXT/HTML/?uri=CELEX:52014DC0015&from=EN. Accessed 6 Feb 2020.

European Commission/EC. (2014b). European Energy Security Strategy. https://eur-lex.europa.eu/legal-content/EN/TXT/HTML/?uri=CELEX:52014DC0330&from=EN. Accessed 6 Feb 2020.

European Commission/EC. (2015). A framework strategy for a resilient energy union with a forward-looking climate change policy. https://eur-lex.europa.eu/legal-content/EN/TXT/HTML/?uri=CELEX:52015DC0080&from=EN. Accessed 6 Feb 2020.

European Commission/EC. (2019a). Annex – Roadmap and key actions. https://ec.europa.eu/info/sites/info/files/european-green-deal-communication-annex-roadmap_en.pdf. Accessed 6 Feb 2020.

European Commission/EC. (2019b). Communication on The European Green Deal. https://ec.europa.eu/info/sites/info/files/european-green-deal-communication_en.pdf. Accessed 6 Feb 2020.

European Commission/EC. (2019c). Annual activity report 2018 – Energy. https://ec.europa.eu/info/publications/annual-activity-report-2018-energy_en. Accessed 6 Feb 2020.

European Commission/EC. (2020a). Previous energy strategies. https://ec.europa.eu/energy/en/topics/energy-strategy/previous-energy-strategies. Accessed 6 Feb 2020.

European Commission/EC. (2020b). Organisation of petroleum exporting countries. https://ec.europa.eu/energy/topics/international-cooperation/international-organisations-and-initiatives/organisation-petroleum-exporting-countries_en?redir=1. Accessed 6 Feb 2020.

European Commission/EC. (2020c). Key partner countries and regions. https://ec.europa.eu/energy/topics/international-cooperation/key-partner-countries-and-regions_en. Accessed 13 March 2020.

European Commission/EC. (2020d). Communication from the Commission to the European Parliament, the European Council, the Council, the European Economic and Social Committee and the Committee of the Regions: A new industrial strategy for Europe. https://ec.europa.eu/info/sites/info/files/communication-eu-industrial-strategy-march-2020_en.pdf. Accessed 23 March 2020.

European Energy Poverty Observatory (EPOV). (2020). https://www.energypoverty.eu/. Accessed 20 Feb 2020.

European Union. (2015). Intended nationally determined contribution of the EU and its member states. Submission by Latvia and the European Commission on behalf of the European Union and its Member States to the UNFCCC. https://www4.unfccc.int/sites/ndcstaging/PublishedDocuments/European%20Union%20First/LV-03-06-EU%20INDC.pdf. Accessed 20 Feb 2020.

Eurostat. (2020). Oil and petroleum products – A statistical overview. https://ec.europa.eu/eurostat/statistics-explained/index.php?title=Oil_and_petroleum_products_-_a_statistical_overview&oldid=448293#Oil_imports_dependency. Accessed 20 Feb 2020.

G7. (2016). G7 Ise-Shima Leaders' Declaration. *G7 Ise-Shima Summit*, 26–27 May 2016. https://www.mofa.go.jp/files/000160266.pdf. Accessed 20 Feb 2020.

Global Carbon Project. (2020). Global Carbon Atlas. http://www.globalcarbonatlas.org/en/CO2-emissions. Accessed 20 Feb 2020.

International Energy Forum. (2017). IEF-EU energy day. https://www.ief.org/events/1st-ief-eu-energy-day. Accessed 20 Feb 2020.

International Energy Forum. (2020). 4th IEF-EU energy day: The green new deal and circular economy. https://www.ief.org/events/4th-ief-eu-energy-day-the-green-new-deal-and-circular-economy. Accessed 20 Feb 2020.

IPCC. (2018). *Global warming of 1.5°C. An IPCC special report on the impacts of global warming of 1.5°C above pre-industrial levels and related global greenhouse gas emission pathways, in the context of strengthening the global response to the threat of climate change, sustainable development, and efforts to eradicate poverty* [Masson-Delmotte, V., P. Zhai, H.-O. Pörtner, D. Roberts, J. Skea, P.R. Shukla, A. Pirani, W. Moufouma-Okia, C. Péan, R. Pidcock, S. Connors, J.B.R. Matthews, Y. Chen, X. Zhou, M.I. Gomis, E. Lonnoy, T. Maycock, M. Tignor, and T. Waterfield (Eds.)]. Geneva: World Meteorological Organization.

Maltese Council Presidency. (2017). Informal Meeting of Energy Ministers (TTE). https://www.eu2017.mt/en/Events/Pages/Informal-Meeting-of-Energy-Ministers-TTE.aspx. Accessed 6 Feb 2020.

Official Journal of the European Union/OJEU. (2012a). Consolidated versions of the Treaty on European Union and the Treaty on the Functioning of the European Union. http://data.europa.eu/eli/treaty/tfeu_2012/oj. Accessed 6 Feb 2020.

Official Journal of the European Union/OJEU. (2012b). Decision No 994/2012/EU. Information exchange mechanism. https://eur-lex.europa.eu/legal-content/EN/TXT/HTML/?uri=CELEX:32012D0994&from=EN. Accessed 6 Feb 2020.

Official Journal of the European Union/OJEU. (2017). Decision No 684/2017/EU. Information exchange mechanism. https://eur-lex.europa.eu/legal-content/EN/TXT/HTML/?uri=CELEX:32017D0684&from=en. Accessed 6 Feb 2020.

OPEC. (2019). Annual Statistical Bulletin. https://asb.opec.org/. Accessed 6 Feb 2020.

World Energy Council. (2019). World Energy Trilemma Index 2019. https://www.worldenergy.org/transition-toolkit/world-energy-trilemma-index. Accessed 6 Feb 2020.

World Trade Organisation. (2020). Who we are. https://www.wto.org/english/thewto_e/whatis_e/who_we_are_e.htm. Accessed 6 Feb 2020.

EU Energy Cooperation with Emerging Powers: Brazil, India, China, and South Africa

10

Michèle Knodt, Roberto Schaeffer, Madhura Joshi, Lai Suetyi, and Agathe Maupin

Contents

Introduction	190
Theoretical and Methodological Framework	191
EU-BICS Bilateral Energy Dialogues	193
EU-Brazil Energy Dialogue	194
EU-India Energy Dialogue	203
EU-China Energy Dialogue	210
EU-South Africa Energy Dialogue	220
Conclusions	228
Cross-References	229
Annex 1: Network Actors	230
EU Actors for All Four Dialogues	230
Brazil-EU Energy Dialogue	230

M. Knodt (✉)
Institute of Political Science, Technical University of Darmstadt, Darmstadt, Germany
e-mail: Knodt@pg.tu-darmstadt.de

R. Schaeffer
Energy Planning Program, COPPE, Universidade Federal do Rio de Janeiro, Centro de Technologia, Rio de Janeiro, Brazil
e-mail: roberto@ppe.ufrj.br

M. Joshi
Natural Resources Defense Council, Delhi, India
e-mail: madhura.u.joshi@gmail.com

L. Suetyi
Centre for European Studies of Guangdong University of Foreign Studies, Guangzhou, China
e-mail: cherlai1212@yahoo.com.hk

A. Maupin
SAIIA – South African Institute of International Affairs, University of the Witwatersrand, Johannesburg, South Africa
e-mail: agathe.maupin@gmail.com

© Springer Nature Switzerland AG 2022
M. Knodt, J. Kemmerzell (eds.), *Handbook of Energy Governance in Europe*,
https://doi.org/10.1007/978-3-030-43250-8_53

India-EU Energy Dialogue 231
China-EU Energy Dialogue 231
South Africa-EU Energy Dialogue 232
References 232

Abstract

Governance of scarce energy resources is one of the great global challenges for a multipolar world. The contribution addresses the EU's energy governance with key emerging powers – Brazil, India, China, and South Africa. It has a specific focus on the bilateral energy dialogues within the strategic partnerships regarding energy cooperation. It asks how the EU and the emerging powers interact? Who are the important actors? Which roles do non-state actors play? How do they perceive themselves and others in the dialogue? How do they frame the energy dialogue? The empirical analysis is based on quantitative and qualitative data from an international, interdisciplinary project. The contribution demonstrates that the four energy dialogues considerably differ from each other in terms of interactions, actors' performance, mutual perceptions, the framing of energy policy (sustainability, competitiveness, security of supply), and the overall prominence that the dialogues have acquired in the EU with the emerging powers' cooperation.

Keywords

Energy governance · Energy policy · European Union · Emerging powers · Brazil · China · India · South Africa · Energy dialogue · Strategic partnership

Introduction

In an increasingly multipolar world with a growing demand for energy, including newly emerging powers, such as India and China, European policymakers understand the potential for cooperating with rising powers. This contribution analyzes the interaction between the EU and Brazil, India, China, and South Africa (BICS) in the field of energy policy within bilateral energy dialogues. We identify energy dialogues as the most important arena of interaction and cooperation. These dialogues were developed under the umbrella framework of strategic partnerships. The main guiding questions for this analysis are the following: How do the EU and the emerging powers interact? Who are the important actors? Which roles do non-state actors play? How do they perceive themselves and others in the dialogue? How do they frame the energy dialogue?

To analyze the interaction between the EU and BICS, this study focuses on expert networks that have evolved as a result of dense cooperation on energy issues. Thus, we can provide evidence of the frequency and density of the actors' networks by assessing the importance of the different actors within the dialogue as well as their interactions. To shed light on the differences among the respective dialogues, we draw on the methodological approaches of network analysis, qualitative interviews, and document analysis.

We demonstrate that the four energy dialogues considerably differ from each other in terms of interactions, actors' performance, mutual perceptions, the framing of energy policy (sustainability, competitiveness, security of supply), and the overall prominence that the dialogues have acquired in the EU with the emerging powers' cooperation. With this design, we endeavor to contribute to a two-sided and mutually complementary analysis of the energy dialogues between BICS and the EU. To avoid Eurocentrism, our research is driven by a strong focus on the mutual perceptions of the relationship between the two partners.

This study begins with methodological remarks. Then, the EU-BICS bilateral energy dialogues and their embeddedness within the European system are introduced, and the individual bilateral dialogues between the EU on one side and China, India, Brazil, and South Africa on the other are presented. For each case, findings on the interactions within the dialogue are presented. Then, the mutual perceptions of the EU and the respective BICS actors within the dialogue are analyzed. Finally, we present the results of the guiding energy norms (sustainability, security of supply, or competitiveness) as ranked by interviewees. The conclusion presents the main findings comparing the four dialogues.

Theoretical and Methodological Framework

Understanding the external governance of the EU requires a systematic comparative and empirically informed consideration of the EU's actions and interests as well as values, ideas, norms, and identities. Scholars in the field of EU foreign policy and international relations also increasingly call for a non-Eurocentric bias and the inclusion of a multifaceted inquiry into EU communication with a reception by global partners. Thus, this contribution focuses on informed systematic research reflections on dialogue, cooperation, and collaboration within the EU's external energy governance through the lens of mutual perceptions. The analysis is based on a constructivist approach, which accentuates the idea of reality being socially constructed and international relations being a product of human interactions in a social world. Perceptions, social values, and norms play a crucial role because they shape us and help us understand changes in world structures (Fierke 2010, pp. 179–180; Knodt et al. 2017, p. 18f.).

The methodological framework represents a mixed-method approach of qualitative and quantitative methods: semi-structured expert interviews, a cross-country survey based on a structured questionnaire, a network analysis, and document analysis.

Qualitative, semi-structured expert interviews with the key actors from Europe (the EU and Member States) and BICS provided insights into elite perceptions of the content, structures, highlights, and challenges of energy cooperation. Within the study 150 interviews were conducted from February 2012 to December 2013 and involved EU officials in Brussels and the EU Delegations in BICS; officials from EU Member States (mainly from Denmark, Germany, Spain, and the UK); Chinese, Indian, Brazilian, and South African government officials; and representatives of business associations, NGOs, chambers of commerce, development agencies, other European and emerging powers' business actors, and representatives of state-owned enterprises. The interviews were conducted in Bangalore, Beijing, Berlin, Brasilia, Brussels, Cape Town, Copenhagen, Eschborn, Johannesburg, Hannover, London, Madrid, Mumbai, New Delhi, Pretoria, Rio de Janeiro, and São Paulo by 15 researchers of the project team. Interview questions focused on institutional knowledge of governance structures and emphasized the importance of constructivist thinking of such perceptions as "decision makers act in accordance with their perception of reality, not in response to reality itself" (Brecher 1968, p. 298; Knodt et al. 2017, p. 50).

The survey contained 25 closed and open questions. The survey comprised five sections, which asked respondents for their personal views on (1) participation in EU-emerging powers cooperation on energy issues, (2) procedural aspects of EU-emerging powers' cooperation on energy issues, (3) the importance of events and fora during EU-emerging powers' cooperation on energy issues, (4) the EU and BICS as dialogue partners, and (5) secure, competitive, and sustainable energy policy. A pilot survey was conducted in India and Brussels. The survey was sent to participants of BICS' four energy dialogues with the EU. We have identified all relevant participants who were engaged in the energy dialogues on a regular basis. In addition to the English version, the questionnaire was translated into Portuguese and Mandarin. Overall, 143 questionnaires were filled out, with an average response rate of 52% (Müller et al. 2015, p. 27).

To show the interaction structure of the energy dialogue, we conducted a network analysis that asked about the importance of all the actors participating and about their exchange behavior. To analyze the network data, relational data were processed with the help of social network analysis (SNA). For each bilateral dialogue, this analysis produced networks containing confirmed and unconfirmed connections, in the sense of reciprocal (bold ties in the graphs) and unilateral ties of reputation (thin ties). The mapping of relevant actors combined with insights into the structure of information exchange allows important conclusions to be drawn regarding the form of EU-emerging powers' energy cooperation. Furthermore, comparing the different country networks allows interpretations to be made regarding which actors occupy central positions in the respective structure, who in fact is "the spider in the web," and who are the most prominent gatekeepers or brokers in energy cooperation. Concerning the information on individual institutions and organizations, such as these actors' positions in terms of indegree and betweenness centrality, we have considered all ties in our networks independent of whether they are unilateral or reciprocal. The results of these calculations can be found in the respective tables. In a final step, we submitted our data to a procedure of block modelling to understand more about the relational performance across different types or categories of organizations. To do so, the data matrices were regrouped according to the affiliation of our network members to one of four categories: BICS public, BICS non-state, EU public, and EU non-state actors. We then partitioned the matrix and calculated the density values for each of the resulting four sub-matrices. Each partition obtaining a density value equal to or higher than the density of the respective overall network was attributed a "1" entry so that the resulting 4 × 4 image matrices could now be re-drawn in the form of very simple graphic representations (block matrix graphs) (Müller et al. 2015, pp. 27–29).

EU-BICS Bilateral Energy Dialogues

Within the new polycentric world, the EU is in search of a new role to affect its self-image, institutional structure, and its relations with other major powers (Keukeleire and Bruyninckx 2011). To enhance its global profile, the EU uses its strategic partnerships as a "privileged mode" of interactions. Nevertheless, it has been widely noted that the EU still has no single, concise definition of what a "strategic" partner is (Gratius 2011, p. 1). Meanwhile the EU has identified ten countries as strategic partners and engaged in deeper cooperation with them, including BICS countries: Brazil, Canada, China, India, Japan, Mexico, Russia, South Africa, South Korea, and the United States. For BICS, the recognition of a multipolar world order and, thus, their status as major powers in it might have been a primary motivation to engage in strategic partnerships with the EU (Keukeleire et al. 2011).

In this light, bilateral relations between the EU and BICS attract increasing scholarly attention. This dynamic research field is informed by a view that the EU's individual strategic partnerships with BICS are the most complex in terms of common goals, interests, and global strategies (Gratius 2013, p. 2). Although the EU's respective strategic partnerships with BICS have been explored in various studies, there is a lack of comprehensive comparative in-depth analyses of these relationships. In addition, the energy area of cooperation has been overlooked in the relevant literature (please see Knodt et al. 2015a, 2017 for a comprehensive literature review).

China and India were the first to be identified by the EU as important partners in the European Security Strategy (2003), and strategic partnerships were established at summits in 2003 and 2004. In the case of Brazil, when trade relations with Mercosur began to stagnate, the Portuguese EU Presidency of 2007 expressed great interest in strengthening ties with Brazil, leading to the initiation of the EU-Brazil Strategic Partnership. In South Africa, former President Thabo Mbeki was decisive in seeking stronger cooperation with the EU in 2007.

Strategic partnerships represent a relatively flexible instrument that allows for intensifying cooperation and opening dialogic arenas to facilitate communication between the two partners. Furthermore, these partnerships serve as an "umbrella" for deeper issue-specific cooperation in numerous thematic dialogues, such as the energy dialogues. Energy dialogues are then again split into different working groups focusing on specific technical issues.

Over the years, energy dialogues have been able to connect political actors and promote a regular exchange of ideas. They have resulted in the creation of bilateral policy networks, which have been successful in (re)framing the political agenda and introducing new topics to the field of international energy policymaking. Energy represents a cross-cutting issue that involves more than one EU Commission Directorate General (DG) as well as the European External Action Service (EEAS) (Knodt et al. 2015b, pp. 61–64). The leading actor in the field is "DG Energy," which has the main responsibility for all energy-related issues. *DG Energy* has established a number of activities to strengthen relations with third countries and transnational energy companies. DG Energy has limited budgets for cooperation programs with third countries and thus depends particularly on DG Development and Cooperation (see below) for funding. *DG Climate Action* and *DG Environment* would seem like natural partners for DG Energy because there are considerable overlaps in policies and discourses. However, our survey has interestingly shown that DG Environment is not especially central within the dialogues. DG Climate is slightly more prominently visible due to the strong links between climate and energy policies. For *DG Trade*, energy issues are one of the few topics that are not yet part of a consistent liberalization strategy. *DG Research* has a strong focus on emerging powers and partly shares goals with DG Trade, especially regarding intellectual property rights and the possibilities of technology transfer. *DG Development and Cooperation (DevCo)* is generally responsible for all funded energy projects implemented under the development heading in emerging powers because of budget constraints. It is important to note that within the current financial framework (2014–2019), development cooperation with BICS is phasing out, and new financial strategies must be identified. The *European External Action Service (EEAS)* was created under the Lisbon Treaty and aims at becoming the overall coordinator of EU energy governance. As a strategy, it frames energy relations as "energy diplomacy" in all its facets and thus tries to streamline energy into general external relations, which is not accepted by the other EU actors. In an internal non-paper on energy and EU foreign policy (EEAS 2012), the EEAS acknowledges changing dynamics and power relations in energy governance and aims at supporting EU external energy relations by ensuring policy coordination. Thus far, the EEAS lacks issue-specific competencies and knowledge to develop a clear role in the EU's institutional system (Knodt et al. 2015b, pp. 61–63).

This institutional mapping shows that the governance network of European institutions is rather fragmented and fosters concurrence among the various EU actors involved, which somehow hampers cooperation with the EU's strategic partners (Knodt et al. 2015b, p. 63). Within the newest development of the EU toward an Energy Union, as well as with European ambitions under the Paris agreement, the EU tries to partially overcome the horizontal fragmentation of the EU by, e.g., closely linking energy and climate policy (see Knodt and Ringel, ▶ Chap. 7, "European Union Energy Policy: A Discourse Perspective").

EU-Brazil Energy Dialogue

Cooperation between Brazil and the EU dates back to the exchange of formal diplomatic missions in the 1960s. The bi-regional agreement with Mercosur was the cornerstone of EU-Brazil relations until the initiation of the strategic partnership in 2007, and it was limited on commercial issues. Bilateral summits are now held annually, including several sectoral dialogues – among them energy. The terms of reference of the dialogue focus on areas of mutual interest, such as energy supply, renewable energies, energy efficiency, technology, and infrastructure (European Commission 2007).

Among BICS, Brazil has an exceptional status, which is also reflected in the EU-Brazil Energy Dialogue. Despite the current economic recession and the recent political crisis since 2015, this largest South American country has been showing impressive economic growth rates in recent decades. These rates are inevitably linked to increasing energy demands in Brazil. Brazil's energy consumption rose 40% in 2005–2015, making Brazil the seventh largest energy consumer in the world (BP 2015, 2016; Enerdata 2016). Remarkably, Brazil also shows its strong engagement in fighting climate change and achieving an international climate agreement. Brazil is responsible for less than 1.3% of the world's total CO_2 emissions from fuel combustion and from energy use (Ribas and Schaeffer 2015, p. 174). In Paris COP 21, Brazil played a key role in the negotiations and formulation of the 2015 agreement, which affirmed its commitment to high reductions of greenhouse gas emissions (WBG 2016a).

Since the 1970s, Brazil has undergone immense changes concerning its energy mix and production. Once, it was largely dependent on oil imports. Today, it has largely turned into an independent energy actor due to its own energy production (particularly oil and renewable energy). Hydroelectric power plants, sugarcane-based power plants, ethanol, and biodiesel largely supply energy to Brazil's electric and transport sector, and newly discovered pre-salt oil reserves add to Brazil's energy independence (Ribas and Schaeffer 2015, p. 173). Currently, oil accounts for nearly 50% of Brazil's energy consumption (Knodt et al. 2017, p. 119). Today Brazil is an "important oil-exporting nation with one of the cleanest energy matrices" (Ribas and Schaeffer 2015, p. 178, see Fig. 6). However, these encouraging advances have slowed down because of Brazil's current weak economic growth and the most recent corruption scandal involving Brazil's largest oil company, Petrobras (described below) (IEA 2017).

Brazil began to use renewable energy as a reaction to the oil crises in the 1970s. To reduce its exposure to oil prices and oil imports, Brazil developed one of the largest ethanol fuel-production sectors, ranking second after the USA. The ethanol strategy was solving two problems simultaneously. On the one hand, it reduced Brazil's dependence upon oil imports (the country was importing 80% of its oil in the 1970s). Conversely, it offered an alternative to Brazil's sugar industry as a main export commodity. When sugar prices had collapsed worldwide, sugarcane-based ethanol production offered a new opportunity for Brazil's sugar producers. In 1975, the Brazilian government launched the National Ethanol Fuel Programme (Pro-alcool), aimed at subsidizing the national gasoline supply with Brazilian ethanol production (Hira and de Oliveira 2008). Accompanied by other governmental strategies – such as providing tax exemptions on ethanol-fuelled cars and subsidies to finance a distribution network and pegging the ethanol prices at the gas stations – the government enabled the development of a solid market for ethanol. With improvements in the production chain, sugarcane-based ethanol production increased 6% per year on average from 1980. Hence, costs decreased significantly and became fully competitive with gasoline on the international markets by 2004 (Goldemberg 2007; Goldemberg et al. 2008). Although government interventions have not occurred since the late 1990s, the industrial production of sugarcane-based ethanol has increased significantly (Ribas and Schaeffer 2015, p. 174f). As a side product, Brazilian sugar mills previously combined their production with biomass facilities for power generation, both for self-consumption in the mills themselves and for exports to the grid. Biofuels may be regarded as the main topic and simultaneously the main controversy of the dialogues at the times of our survey, which is consistent with the great priority that Brazil attributes to biofuels in its external energy relations (Interviews Brasilia, December 2013; Piefer et al. 2015b, p. 34f). In the beginning of the 2000s, Brazil took steps to introduce or enlarge capacities for what it calls the "new" or "alternative" renewables – wind, solar, biomass, and small hydropower – into its electricity matrix. By adding the attribute of new or alternative, Brazil distinguishes them from the country's large hydroelectric power plants (Hochstetter 2017, p. 11). Among those technologies, wind power constitutes the fastest-growing source of electrical power in Brazil as part of the most recent 10-Year Energy Expansion Plan of the Brazilian Ministry of Mines and Energy (published December 2015) (MME and SPE 2015). Brazilians hope to emulate their success in wind industry development in the solar sector as well. In both sectors, state-society relations have been largely cooperative, and no blocking coalitions have emerged (Hochstetter 2017, p. 47).

The Brazilian government has implemented two important policies to push forward renewable energies. The first innovative strategy, starting in 2002, was the PROINFA Programme (Incentive Programme for Alternative Electric Generation Sources), which was installed in response to heavy blackouts in 2001 caused by overreliance on the large hydropower systems and extreme dry seasons. The first phase was primarily a feed-in tariff system. The second policy was establishing the auction system in 2003, in which generators can bid to supply a given amount of renewable electricity in exchange for long-term purchasing contracts (Lucas et al. 2013). This instrument allows the government to intervene in technologies that will be allowed to participate as suppliers in the auctions (IRENA 2015, p. 3). Brazilian auctions partly included local content requirements, which established a minimum percentage of locally manufactured inputs, enforced as a condition for connection to the grid, receiving higher payments for electricity and access to subsidized credits from the Brazilian Development Bank (BNDES).

Brazil is also a forerunner in hydropower, with 65% of the total installed capacity in the power sector from hydro sources. Hydropower currently accounts for 12% of Brazil's final energy consumption and 68% of electricity production. The hydropower plants are located all over the country, including in the Amazon region, whereas electricity demand is quite concentrated in the south and southeast, leading to a coordinated, large interconnected transmission network that can be called upon on short notice to react to demand changes. The networks thus provide a certain degree of flexibility to the energy supply (IEA 2013, p. 309f). However, the construction of hydropower dams remains a controversial issue challenged socially and environmentally. Nevertheless, the current National Energy Plan 2030 outlines the government's commitment to further advances in hydroelectric power generation. Construction of new power plants in the Amazon rainforest region has become difficult, however, due to the many socio-environmental restrictions. The new hydroelectric power plants tend to be smaller and hence more susceptible to the effects of rainfall (Knodt et al. 2017, p. 120).

In the first meeting of the EU-Brazil energy dialogue in November 2009, both sides agreed to exchange experiences and technical consultations on regulatory issues for competitive energy markets, including investment opportunities, energy efficiency, and demand management (Council of the European Union 2009). The latter should be realized in particular by participation in the multilateral International Partnership for Energy Efficiency Cooperation (IPEEC). An important topic of the cooperation is joint efforts in second-generation biofuels and the promotion of EU-Brazil industrial cooperation on low-carbon technologies, including inter alia clean coal, research on nuclear energy, and cooperation on nuclear safety; 2.6% of Brazil's domestic electricity supply depends on nuclear energy. Furthermore, indirect land-use change and other topics of renewable energies and climate change are discussed, and three new areas have been included over the years: offshore safety, ocean energy, and trilateral cooperation with African (Mozambique and Kenya) countries on bioenergy (Piefer et al. 2015b, p. 34).

In the following, we analyze the interaction and exchange of the actors involved in the Brazil-EU energy dialogue network. The network of the Brazil-EU energy dialogue is the most dense and most central network of our four energy dialogue networks. Ranking with a density of 0.29 in importance and 0.14 in the exchange network, in both networks it is at the top of our four countries. In addition, the centrality of 25.8 in the importance network is the highest in our sample. The results of our network analysis illustrate a wide range of public and non-state actors from Brazil and the EU being involved in Brazil-EU energy cooperation.

The two most important Brazilian actors in the importance network as shown in Fig. 1 are the Ministry of External Relations (MRE) and the Ministry of Mines and Energy (MME) in addition to Planalto/the Brazilian Presidency.

The *Ministry of External Relations (MRE)*, Department of Energy, is formally responsible for the dialogue in cooperation with the *Ministry of Mines and Energy (MME)*. The latter has an interesting position in the institutional setup. As the name implies, its responsibilities include mines and energy. MME formulates the guidelines and policies for the national energy sector. Thus, it is the key ministry responsible for energy policies, which explains its great importance and central position in the network, although it is less engaged in the dialogue than MRE (Piefer et al. 2015b, p. 35f).

MME is supported by two regulatory federal agencies: the *Agency for Electric Energy (ANEEL)* for the electricity sector and the *Agency for Oil, Gas, and Biofuels (ANP)* in the oil gas and biofuels sector. ANEEL, created in 1996, is financially and politically independent. As such, the agency addresses all electricity topics delegated to it by the MME and the federal government (ANEEL 2016). ANEEL is listed in the

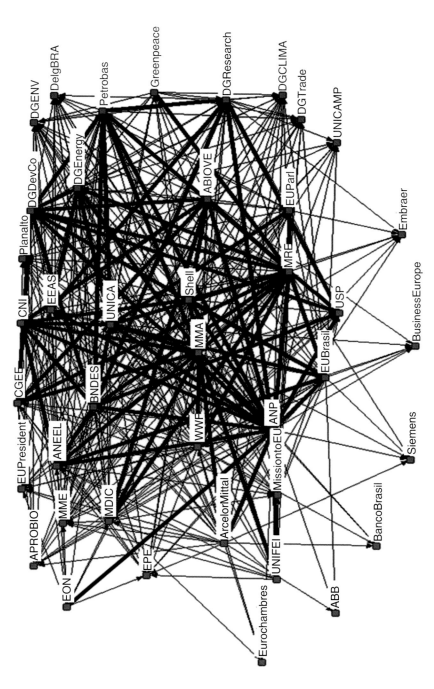

Fig. 1 Importance network for Brazil-EU energy cooperation. (Source: EnergyGov 2014, Darmstadt, Piefer et al. 2015b, p. 35, for actors abbreviation, see annex

network as one of the five most important brokers. ANP, created in 1997, addresses issues related to the assurance of oil, natural gas, and biofuels supply and establishes technical standards (ANP 2016). Moreover, the *Ministry of the Environment (MMA)* is also involved in renewable energy policymaking. Although not formally the primary responsible partner, the MMA is one of the key actors in the Brazil-EU energy dialogue on issues of renewable energies and energy efficiency. MMA ranks sixth in the betweenness centrality and is thus also one of the brokers in the network.

Brazil's energy governance is thus quite fragmented. To better coordinate, the National Council for Energy Policy (CNPE) was created in 1997 as an advisory body to the President on national policies and strategies for overall energy policy in Brazil to better coordinate the different actors. The Council comprises eight ministers and three representatives appointed by the President of Brazil and is chaired by MME.

As in all four dialogues, EU actors are not as relevant as the BICS actors – with DG Energy being the exception (see Table 1). In the EU-Brazilian dialogue, DG Energy was mentioned among the top 5 as the only EU actor in the importance network. The European External Action Service (EEAS) and DG Trade are not among the top 5, but are located more centrally than all other European actors except for DG Energy. This result can be explained by the historic focus (before the strategic partnership was signed in 2007) on trade diplomacy within the scope of the EU-Mercosur dialogue. Interestingly, DG Development and Cooperation (DevCo) and the Delegation of the European Union to Brazil (DelBRA) are not considered as important as the other three EU actors. Until the phasing out of the bilateral development cooperation of the EU and Brazil, all energy-related activities were financed by DG DevCo and not by DG Energy. The Brazilian partners mentioned in interviews in Brasilia (December 2013) that this was at times confusing because of internal incoherence within the EU Commission. At times, DG Energy said "yes," while DG DevCo said "no" to project proposals and vice versa. From 2014 onward, all new activities are being funded by the new Partnership Instrument and the Industrial Cooperation+ Instrument (ICI+) (Piefer et al. 2015b, p. 36f).

The position and role of non-state actors are also interesting. The Brazilian energy sector comprises a large number of private, national, and international companies. Two large, state-owned enterprises are linked to the MME: *PETROBRAS* for oil and gas and *ELETROBRAS* for the power sector (Ribas and Schaeffer 2015, p. 181).

Table 1 Top five actors in Brazil-EU energy dialogue

Importance network	Exchange network	Broker function (exchange)
Five most important actors (indegree centrality)	Five most important actors (indegree centrality)	Five most important actors (betweenness centrality)
MME 53.7	PETROBRAS 27.5	MDIC 14.6
MRE 51.2	MDIC 25.0	UNICA 8.5
UNICA 48.8	UNICA 25.0	MRE 5.6
DG Energy 46.3	MRE 25.0	ANEEL 5.1
Planalto 46.3	MME 22.5	PETROBRAS 3.6

Source: EnergyGov 2014, Darmstadt, Piefer et al. (2015b), p. 36

PETROBRAS, as the country's largest state-owned energy company, naturally plays an important role, especially with the country's recent pre-salt oil discoveries. PETROBRAS appears to be the most important actor in the exchange network. Since 2014, PETROBRAS has been involved in a corruption scandal. Construction companies are accused of overcharging on orders from PETROBRAS and transferring the surpluses to PETROBRAS executives and politicians. Investigations also involve ELETROBRAS. The Brazilian electric sector has faced a deep crisis since 2015, not least due to the problems challenging ELETROBRAS and PETROBRAS in their role in Brazilian energy governance. In addition, the important position of the *Brazilian Confederation of National Industries (CNI)* as representative of the private sector can be explained by the role the private sector plays in most issues in the dialogue on biofuels, renewables, offshore safety, energy efficiency, etc. Moreover, the role of the *Sugarcane Producers' Union (UNICA)* and PETROBRAS as brokers seems noteworthy. However, UNICA was rated at the top of the most important actors. Due to the strong focus on biofuels in the Brazil-EU energy dialogue, this is not surprising (Piefer et al. 2015b, p. 37).

In the case of the Brazil-EU energy dialogue, our data clearly reveals one important broker – the *Ministry for Development, Industry and Commerce (MDIC)*. The reason for this seems to be that MDIC is responsible for cross-cutting issues dealing with energy and foreign investment (Piefer et al. 2015b, p. 37; Knodt et al. 2017, p. 115).

The aggregated data of the network block matrices (see Fig. 2) on importance and exchange present interesting observations about the EU's role and behavior in energy cooperation with Brazil. In terms of both the "sending" and the "receiving" of information, Brazilian actors are clearly the most active, which may be because of the specific time of our survey. As previously mentioned, from 2012 until end of 2013, Brazilian actors attempted to engage with the EU on the certification of Brazil's second generation

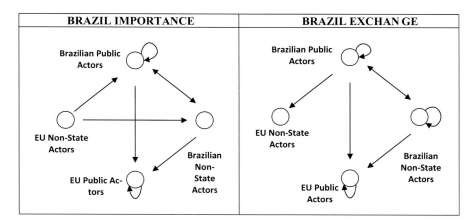

Fig. 2 Importance and exchange network block matrices (Brazil-EU). (Source: EnergyGov 2014, Darmstadt, Piefer et al. 2015b, p. 38)

of biofuels according to EU standards – or else an equivalence agreement. Public EU actors obtain the most choices in terms of information exchange and also exchange among themselves, while non-state actors at the level of the EU merely receive some information by Brazilian actors without exhibiting any noteworthy activity themselves. The EU is in quite a remote position of mainly cooperating internally and not even with the European private sector. A good reciprocal relationship exists between Brazilian public and non-state actors, which is not surprising as some of the main Brazilian energy companies are partially state-owned and the others also maintain close connections to ministries. European non-state actors seem better connected than public actors (Piefer et al. 2015b, p. 38f).

The above networks, our survey data, and results from our qualitative interviews in Brussels and Brazil create the impression that Brazil-EU energy cooperation has not developed overall prominence and remains below its potential. Generally, the EU is not the most important partner for Brazil, and bilateral relations with EU Member States have always been more important. However, Brazil has reoriented its foreign policy – traditionally between the US and the EU – now leading to an increasing "BRICSalization" and South-South cooperation (Gratius 2012). Thus, an important factor in the EU-Brazilian energy dialogue is the evaluations Brazil and the EU assign each other in their perceptions of one another. Brazil is a very self-confident cooperation partner for the EU with clear visions of how the energy dialogue can serve broader national interests. Both groups saw Brazil as being open to mutual learning in the dialogue, possessing compromise-building qualities, and acting with an open agenda. The EU actors perceived Brazil as more of an agenda-setter than Brazil perceived itself (Ribas and Schaeffer 2015, p. 186f; Piefer et al. 2015b, p. 68).

As depicted in Fig. 3, Brazilian public actors had a very positive self-image of Brazil's role as a dialogue partner in energy cooperation. That self-image appears to derive from the country's growing role in international arenas and its status as a regional power, which is reflected in the perceptions of the Brazilian actors of their

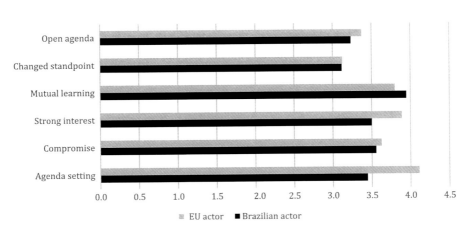

Fig. 3 Perception of Brazil's properties as a dialogue partner. (Means of all answers; 1 = "strongly disagree"; 5 = "strongly agree." Source: EnergyGov, Darmstadt, 2014, Knodt et al. 2017, p. 137)

openness to mutual learning in bilateral cooperation and their strong interest in the EU's perspectives. European actors shared these perceptions. The same holds true for the Brazilian compromise-building qualities and open agenda. Interestingly, the EU actors shared the perception of Brazil's contributions to the dialogue. They even asserted a more active role than Brazil did in initiating topics and placing them on the agenda (Ribas and Schaeffer 2015: 186). In the perception of the EU's properties as a dialogue partner, the Brazilian and European actors did not converge similarly. In particular, the Brazilian actors perceived the EU as not playing with an open agenda. There appears to be a degree of mistrust from the Brazilian side (Knodt et al. 2017, p. 36f).

Brazilian actors perceive the EU as being less open to mutual learning (see Fig. 4). However, the greatest discrepancy is the perception of the open agenda. The EU sees itself as having a rather open agenda; in contrast, Brazil views the EU as acting with a "hidden agenda" (Knodt et al. 2015b, p. 68). Such different perceptions of how the EU acts in the dialogue, particularly if Brazil is examining the EU suspiciously, can hinder further cooperation (Knodt et al. 2017, p. 137).

Energy policy is driven by the three fundamental normative frames of sustainability, competitiveness, and energy security. The survey revealed that different energy frames were prioritized by policy- and decision-makers. The majority of Brazilian actors valued security of supplies as the most important frame in Brazil-EU energy cooperation. Sustainability was considered the second most important frame, whereas only 10% valued competitiveness as the most important frame. Although the EU frames renewable energies, one of the key areas of cooperation in the dialogue is sustainability; Brazil sees it as security of supplies. It is, however, also important to add that security of supplies was largely interpreted as access to energy

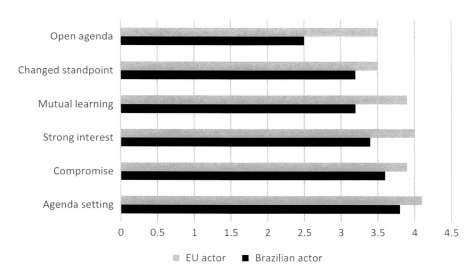

Fig. 4 Perception of the EU's properties as a dialogue partner. (Means of all answers; 1 = "strongly disagree"; 5 = "strongly agree." Source: EnergyGov, Darmstadt, 2014, Knodt et al. 2017, p. 138)

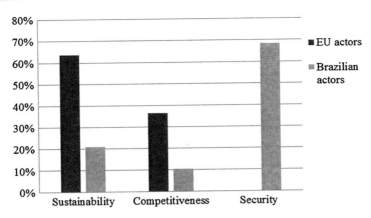

Fig. 5 Energy frames of Brazil-EU cooperation by Brazilian and EU stakeholders. (Percentage of respondents ranking the respective frame highest in energy dialogues. Source: EnergyGov, Darmstadt, 2014, Knodt et al. 2017, p. 134)

technology (Ribas and Schaeffer 2015, p. 185) and less as access to energy autonomy, which is the interpretation by European actors (Knodt et al. 2015c, p. 334). This interpretation can be explained by the fact that Brazil is considered to be much less dependent on energy imports than the EU.

As shown in Fig. 5, European actors value sustainability as the most important norm in their cooperation with Brazil, followed by competitiveness; security of supplies was not chosen at all as an important norm in bilateral cooperation. Although security of supplies is interpreted in different ways by the EU and Brazilian actors, competitiveness and sustainability are both understood similarly. In particular, the threefold understanding of sustainability (social, ecological, and economic) by actors involved in the dialogue promises to provide an important basis for the development of common narratives (Knodt et al. 2015c, p. 334).

EU-India Energy Dialogue

The EU and India signed a Strategic Partnership Agreement in 2004. The earlier attempts to negotiate an India-EU Association Agreement failed due to the EU's classification of all South Asian countries as "non-association" partners (Abhyankar 2009, cited in Joshi and Gansehsan 2015, p. 153). In 1980, two commercial cooperation agreements were signed between the EU and India. The early 1990s brought a more active political dialogue, with the signing of a political cooperation statement (1993), a political statement (1994), and a cooperation agreement (1994), all of which helped to broaden the relations between the two partners (Joshi and Gansehsan 2015, p. 153; Knodt et al. 2017, p. 185). According to Jaffrelot (2006), EU-India relations were slow-moving for a long time, perhaps because of India's experiences from the colonial and post-independence times (Indian Government

2018). Recently, the EU has become more aware of India's role as a strategic partner. Energy and climate change are among the main fields of cooperation of the strategic partnership agreement (see Bava 2007; Noronha and Sharma 2009); thus, in November 2004, the political decision was made to start an energy dialogue (DG Energy 2010).

The EU-India Energy Panel was created as the formal instrument of cooperation in 2005. Since its inception in 2006, regular meetings of the panel and its working groups have been held. The four working groups on coal/clean coal technology, renewable energy/energy efficiency, petroleum/natural gas, and fusion/ITER (an international organization on nuclear energy) report directly back to the panel, and proceedings are discussed jointly. Since coal production is the main source of energy in India, great importance is attributed to this working group, and it has held more frequent meetings than the others. The focus on coal can be explained by India's energy mix. India relies heavily on its vast coal reserves. Coal makes up 64% of the primary commercial energy supply (as of March 2017) (MoSPI 2018) and approximately 60% of installed power capacity (as of March 2018) (CEA 2018a). This reliance on coal is likely to continue in the near future. The argument for continued coal use is often couched in terms of abundantly available domestic coal resources with better security and relatively competitive prices (Knodt et al. 2010; Joshi and Khosla 2016). However, renewables have rapidly gained importance in India's electricity mix. Although renewables' share of India's total primary energy consumption is low, its importance to the electricity sector in India and the Indian economy is critical, particularly in the recent past. Renewables as a whole have a 20% share of the installed electricity mix. India has established ambitious renewable energy targets, aiming to reach 175 GW of installed renewable energy capacity by 2022. The National Electricity Plan 2018 reaffirms this figure and projects a further expansion to 275 GW by 2027. Renewable energy in India has quadrupled from 16 GW of installed power capacity in 2010 to over 71 GW in 2018 and accounts for approximately 20% of India's installed electricity capacity. Hence, for the Indian government, it is critical to engage in clean coal technologies and clean energy.

India is a net importer of energy. India's energy consumption has nearly doubled since 2000, bringing India into the group of the world's largest energy consumers. This consumption is linked to India's rapid economic increase. Despite some decline in recent years, the GDP growth rate remained at 7.6% in 2015 (WBG 2016b). Hence, the potential for further rapid growth in energy consumption is enormous (IEA 2015b, p. 11). India is targeting 8–10% growth per annum in its GDP and is thus in desperate need of substantial growth in primary energy and electricity supply to meet this high target.

The Working Group on Renewable Energy and Energy Efficiency in the dialogue exhibited less activity in the early years of the partnership. Although both India and the EU emphasize the importance of sustainability in the rhetoric of their energy dialogue, this emphasis has hardly been reflected in the working group's activities, with only sporadic meetings having occurred. In addition, renewable energy as a topic in EU-India cooperation is primarily situated in the development cooperation portfolio, which has been phased out. Moreover, cooperation in these fields traditionally occurs through strong cooperative ties between India and several EU Member States, such as Germany, France, the UK, and Spain. However, the domestic importance of clean energy, both for India and the EU, is reflected in the recent developments in the partnership. The EU and India agreed on a Joint Work Programme on Energy, Clean Development, and Climate Change adopted at the EU-India Summit held in Marseille in 2008. Most recently, these issues have been enhanced by the success of COP 21. In a "Joint Declaration between the EU and India on a Clean Energy and Climate Partnership," the two partners stated that they recognize their common interest in promoting clean energy generation and increased energy efficiency for climate action and the positive contribution these can make to global energy security (European Council 2016b,p. 1; Knodt et al. 2017, p. 187). Ultimately, the EU-India energy dialogue was less active than the EU-China dialogue, although there have been encouraging stimuli.

Paris gave the dialogue a new boost. At the 2016 EU-India Summit in Brussels, both partners strengthened their commitment to revitalize bilateral energy relations. Both parties declared their mutual vision of being "global partners and the world's largest democracies" and "reaffirmed their commitment to strengthen the EU-India Strategic Partnership based on shared values and principles" (European Council 2016b, p. 1). The Summit also represented a breakthrough in EU-India energy relations: both partners adopted the "Joint Declaration between the EU and India on a Clean Energy and Climate Partnership" (European Council 2016c; Knodt et al. 2017, p. 181). This engagement was underlined by the 14th India-EU Summit 2017 in New Delhi where partners adopted a Joint Statement on Clean Energy and Climate Change and acknowledged the progress on the Clean Energy and Climate Partnership, which was adopted at the 2016 the EU-India Summit. In addition, the EU and India signed a "Joined Declaration on Smart and Sustainable Urbanization' in October 2017. With regard to energy and climate change, the partners highlighted several areas of interest, including stepping up cooperation on achieving climate targets, low-carbon energy security, development of renewable energy, and energy efficiency (of products, in industrial processes, and in buildings) (European Council 2017, p. 8).

In the case of interaction within the EU-India energy dialogue, the contribution will only present the aggregated data of the importance and exchange networks. Our Indian respondents asked to remain anonymous so that we can draw from the rich qualitative interview data and background information but will not display the network graphics. The Indian importance and exchange networks are among the less dense networks of the four cases. The density of the importance network is only 0.14 compared with Brazil with 0.29. The density of the exchange network is 0.10 and thereby the second lowest after China. The centrality of the importance network is low and ranks in last place with South Africa (15.4). The degree of centrality in the importance network is 13.7 and ranks in a middle position. The low density and centrality of the Indian network can be explained by the fragmentation of the Indian energy governance system. The four Indian ministries, the Ministry of Power (MoP), Ministry of Coal (MoC), Ministry of New and Renewable Energies (MNRE), and Ministry of Petroleum and Natural Gas (MoPNG), are playing an important role in the Indian energy policy.

To explain this fragmented system, political scientists have described the development of the power sector in India as a complex process of institutional layering (Chatterjee 2017, p. 5).

According to van der Heijden, layering is used to describe institutional changes in which new organizational elements are superimposed onto the old institutions without eliminating preexisting structures as much as is reasonable (van der Heijden 2011). Nevertheless, India's government tries to create and execute a more coherent energy policy. A Cabinet Resolution on January 1, 2015 replaced the Planning Commission with the National Institution for Transforming India (NITI Aayog). In its first 1st year of existence, on 1 October 2015, NITI Aayog submitted India's Intended Nationally Determined Contribution (INDC) to advance India's energy and environmental policies. The INDC clearly aims at pursuing a more climate-friendly and cleaner path for India, including commitments to increase the share of non-fossil fuel power sources to 40% and to reduce emissions intensity by 33–35% (measured against the 2005 baseline), both by 2030. The INDC also oversees the India Energy Security Scenarios launched in 2015 (Knodt et al. 2017, p. 196f).

In addition to horizontal coordination, India tries to solve the vertical coordination problems in energy governance. India is a federal system in which regional and local entities play an important role in energy policy. Responsibility for the power sector after India's independence was shared between the center and provincial states. The center is responsible for the broad policy direction, whereas regional authorities controlled the "last mile" of distribution (Chatterjee 2017, p. 4). The key institutions on the state level were the State Electricity Boards (SEBs), "vertically integrated monopolies under the politicized control of State governments, which controlled nearly three-quarters of generation and virtually all distribution by 1991" (Chatterjee 2017, p. 4). In the energy area, the central government has exclusive oversight over mineral and oil resources and nuclear energy. States have jurisdiction over natural gas infrastructure, water issues, taxation on mineral rights, and the consumption/sale of electricity. Both national and federal actors share power over electricity. Since 2014, the new administration has promoted a model of cooperative federalism – also used in Germany's federal energy system – to coordinate these different levels. The system includes devolution developments, which accompany a higher regional share of hydrocarbon revenues in some cases to enable the regional level to participate financially in energy transformation processes. This system also introduces a wider set of regional responsibilities to speed up implementation and approval of the state-level clearances required for investment projects (IEA 2015b, p. 42; Knodt et al. 2017, p. 197).

State-owned enterprises (SOEs) are important actors in Indian energy policies with Coal India Limited, the national Oil and Natural Gas Commission, and the State Electricity Boards being the most important. State-owned Coal India Limited is the largest coal-producing company in the world, the second-largest employer in the world, and the largest employer in the country (Coal India 2012; Knodt et al. 2012). Within the dialogue, the most important industrial actors are the Confederation of Indian Industry and the Federation of Indian Chambers of Commerce and Industry. As in the Brazilian case, the Federation of Indian Chambers of Commerce and Industry (FICCI) is playing a central role in the dialogue, whereas its European counterpart is only marginal in the network.

With regard to the European actors, we can again observe that no European actor is among the five most important actors in the importance network. DG Energy is seen as the second most important actor within the exchange network, which is quite similar to the Chinese example. The EU Delegation in India and DG Energy are rated among the five most important brokers in the exchange network, with the EU Delegation also being the most important broker.

The results of the aggregated network analysis, as shown in Fig. 6, point to much less exchange among actors of different groups than in the other three dialogues. In terms of importance, the picture is more balanced, but the EU public actors nevertheless seem to be in a rather remote position. They regard the Indian public actors as important, and the EU non-state actors perceive the EU to be important, but the reverse is not true. All sides seem to regard the Indian public actors as important and try to gain access to them (Piefer et al. 2015b, pp. 48–50).

In our interviews in New Delhi (September 2013), respondents from both sides emphasized that more concrete cooperation projects should result from the dialogue. Currently, from their perception, the dialogue resembles more of a talk shop, especially when comparing it to bilateral Member States initiatives. The reason for a lack of joint projects such as in the Chinese case, according to the interviewees, is that in addition to personnel constraints, "the EU expects concrete inputs on what India would want; and India expects the EU to come up with concrete proposals of what it could offer" (Interview New Delhi Sept. 2013). For the energy dialogue to remain relevant, this stalemate needs to be overcome, especially since from the Indian side, there is great willingness to contribute funds for projects. The partnership, however, has been working toward addressing this problem. The EIB opened a regional office in New Delhi in March 2017 and is giving out project-specific loans for such projects as metros and solar parks (EEAS 2018). In addition, both sides share the challenge of having to coordinate with 28 Member States, federal states with differing needs, and their governments. In addition, dispersed ministerial structures in India and the complex structure of European Directorates General and

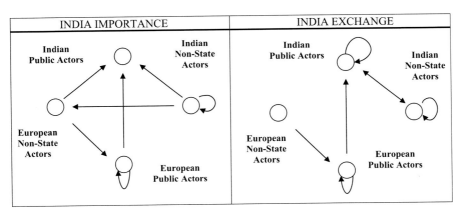

Fig. 6 Importance and exchange network block matrices (India-EU). (Source: EnergyGov 2014, Darmstadt, Piefer et al. 2015b, p. 49)

agencies add to the coordination challenges. Furthermore, it seems to be unclear which value-added cooperation the EU brings compared with its Member States. This aspect is also not unique to the dialogue with India, but Indian interviewees were clearly asking for the specific EU value added (Piefer et al. 2015b, p. 50).

The analysis of the data also included mutual perceptions of the actors in the dialogue. A number of critical differences between the views of the two partners were observed. The main difference was how the EU and Indian stakeholders perceived India as a dialogue partner. Although Indian respondents considered India to be acting with an open agenda in this dialogue, the EU actors perceived India to be acting with a hidden agenda. The same is true for the perception of India being open to mutual learning. European actors perceived the Indian side to be less willing to engage in learning processes. In contrast, Indian respondents saw themselves as open to mutual learning. Interestingly, the EU actors also viewed Indian interlocutors as not insisting on their point of view but as changing their stance, whereas the Indian dialogue partners did not perceive themselves to be changing positions (Knodt et al. 2017, p. 209).

Concerning the perceptions of the EU by both European and Indian actors, European actors saw the EU as challenging India's position and increasing pressure on Indian partners in the dialogue and negotiations (see Fig. 7). They also saw themselves as having more influence on setting the agenda in contrast to how Indian stakeholders perceived it. At the same time, the EU actors perceived themselves to be more willing to compromise than the Indian actors would admit. Surprisingly, the Indian actors attributed to the EU more willingness and openness to mutual learning than the EU actors perceived about themselves. Overall as depicted in Fig. 8, the perceptions between European and Indian actors did not differ as much when they

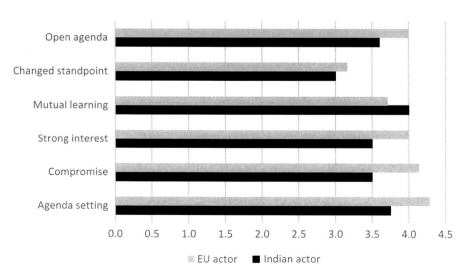

Fig. 7 Perception of the EU's properties as a dialogue partner in the EU-India energy dialogue. (Means of all answers; 1 = "strongly disagree"; 5 = "strongly agree." Source: EnergyGov, Darmstadt, 2014, Knodt et al. 2017, p. 222)

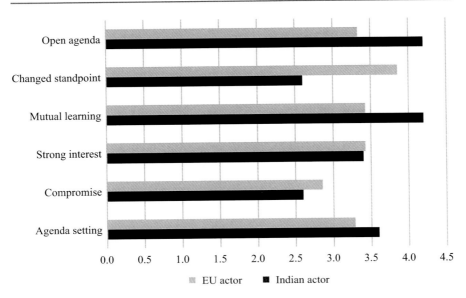

Fig. 8 Perception of India's properties as a dialogue partner in the EU-India energy dialogue. (Means of all answers; 1 = "strongly disagree"; 5 = "strongly agree." Source: EnergyGov, Darmstadt, 2014, Knodt et al. 2017, p. 221)

judged the EU's properties as a dialogue partner vis a vis when they considered India as a dialogue partner (Knodt et al. 2017, p. 209f.).

Our analysis leads to the conclusion that rather negative perception of India exists from the European side. This perception might potentially hinder promising cooperation between the two partners (Knodt et al. 2017, p. 210).

We now turn to how India and the EU frame the dialogue in terms of the three normative energy frames: sustainability, security of supplies, and competitiveness.

Indian participants within the dialogue ranked both sustainability and competitiveness as important (see Fig. 9). This balanced perception may indicate an early reflection of the emerging orientation toward renewables in India. The first steps in this direction were policy instruments in the first decade of the century, such as the "National Tariff Policy of 2006," which mandates that State Electricity Regulatory Commissions purchase "a minimum percentage of electricity from renewable sources" and launch "the Jawaharlal Nehru National Solar Mission in 2009" (Joshi and Ganeshan 2015, p. 163). The emphasis on sustainability is argued here to be not only connected to the expansion of renewables in India but also indirectly connected to the low value attributed to securing energy supplies visible in our survey data. However, in the qualitative interviews, security of supply was highlighted much more than in the survey data (Knodt et al. 2017, p. 205).

Thus, energy security seems to be a strong guiding norm of India's energy governance as such outside the dialogue. India's striving for self-reliance is apparent in its push to advance renewable energy, explore domestic oil and gas sources, expand coal production, and build new nuclear plants. There is ongoing controversy over whether

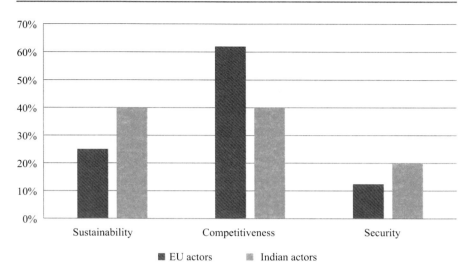

Fig. 9 Energy frames of India-EU cooperation by Indian and EU stakeholders. (Percentage of respondents ranking the respective frame highest in energy dialogues. Source: EnergyGov, Darmstadt, 2014, Knodt et al. 2017, p. 206)

India's goal should be "energy independence" or "energy security" (Betz and Hanif 2010, pp. 12–14). Both appear difficult to fulfil as India is becoming more vulnerable and dependent on foreign energy sources because of its strong economic growth (Knodt et al. 2010). The overall aims of energy security are being increasingly interwoven into clean energy and creating institutional opportunities (Dubash 2011, p. 66; Knodt et al. 2017, p. 184).

Within the sustainability goal, there is a close link between discussions of energy access and development, especially in light of India's economic growth, which results in discussions on energy poverty. Energy poverty "can be defined as lack of access to modern energy services, including both electricity and clean cooking facilities (that is, fuels and stoves that do not cause indoor air pollution) (Jaeger and Michaelowa 2015, p. 236). In India, approximately 25% of the population continues to lack access to electricity, and 66% use traditional biomass for cooking (Jaeger and Michaelowa 2015, p. 237). The country seeks to guarantee a secure, affordable, and sustainable supply of energy to meet the needs within its social development.

EU-China Energy Dialogue

The energy dialogue between China and the EU has a long tradition and is quite advanced compared with other EU energy dialogues. This dialogue is based on nearly 30 years of cooperation history enshrined in the EU-China Trade and Economic Cooperation Agreement (1985) and started with cooperation in basic energy science. As early as 1994, the EU and China initiated biannual energy conferences between the European Commission and the Chinese Ministry of Science and Technology. In 2005 the energy dialogue was initiated with the National Energy Administration (NEA), and the following six priority areas have since been identified for cooperation between the EU and China: renewable energy, smart grids, energy efficiency in the building sector, clean coal, nuclear energy, and energy law (DG Energy 2013; Knodt et al. 2015b, p. 39).

The EU-China energy dialogue is the only EU-BICs dialogue that has resulted in the joint implementation of projects. One example was the EU-China Clean Energy Centre (EC2), which was initiated in 2010 by the European Commission, the National Energy Administration (NEA), and the Ministry of Commerce of China (MOFCOM). The primary goal of EC2 was to offer support to Chinese government officials in the clean energy sector through capacity building, policy advisories and the provision of services in technologies in the focus areas of clean coal technology, sustainable biofuels, renewable energy sources, energy efficiency in energy consumption, and sustainable and efficient distribution systems (Knodt et al. 2015b, p. 39f).

Energy efficiency is a central topic; in recent years, China's energy consumption has increased substantially. In 1993 and 2006, China became a net importer of oil and natural gas, respectively. Today, China's energy consumption makes up over one-fifth of the world's total, of which industrial use accounts for 70%. Therein, China's infrastructure development relies heavily on energy-intensive industries such as steel and cement (IEA 2016, p. 22). Since 1990, this "energy-intensive industrial activity has been the single most important source of growth in final energy" (IEA 2016, p. 62). China is now the largest coal consumer and importer – even though China has the third largest coal reserves worldwide (IEA 2013, pp. 55, 61, 62, 67). Such heavy reliance on fossil fuels contributes to China's extensive greenhouse gas emissions, and China has become the world's largest emitter of CO_2. Because of the acknowledgment of the serious air pollution problems in recent years, China eased off its coal consumption, having achieved a standstill and even a reduction since 2014 (IEA 2015a). "We estimate that only about 2 per cent of the population in China breathes air with a level of fine particulate matter (PM2.5) concentrations that complies with the World Health Organization (WHO) guideline, and only 64 per cent of the population breathes air that meets the standards of even the most modest WHO interim target-1" (IEA 2017, p. 496). The Chinese economy is gradually shifting to being based more on services and less on energy-intensive industries (IEA 2017, p. 471). The IEA in its World Energy Outlook 2016 even calculates that this trend will decrease China's industrial coal use. In 2040, the share of coal in the power mix will be less than 45% (IEA 2016, p. 22). Nevertheless, energy efficiency and the debate over clean coal are at the top of the agenda of the energy dialogue with the EU.

The turn to renewables is also driven by the high costs of air pollution problems. In the last few years, China has taken the lead in expanding renewables-based power generation capacity (IEA 2017, p. 471). The renewables are dominated by hydropower. If we consider hydropower separately, the rest of the renewables, such as solar, biomass, wind, etc., only compose up to 2% of the energy mix. Nevertheless,

Solar PV has experienced strong growth. China's installed capacity increased by more than 75 GW between 2010 and 2016. China's COP21 commitment will continue this path, indicating that "wind capacity is to be expanded to 200 gigawatts (GW) by 2020 and solar power to 100 GW. WEO-2015 highlighted the scope for China to push beyond these levels and there are clear signs that some higher targets for 2020 are being considered" (IEA 2016, p. 405). Thus, in recent years, renewables have played a growing role in the dialogue.

China subsumes nuclear under renewables and is among the leaders in new nuclear power generation, even if it only accounts for 1% of the energy consumption. "Almost half of global nuclear capacity under construction today is in China" (IEA 2017, p. 477). Nevertheless, the trend seems to have passed its peak.

At the 2015 EU-China Summit, the two sides agreed on the Statement on Climate Change, which included their willingness to take steps toward the development of low-carbon emissions and cooperation on emissions trading (European Commission 2015). Positioning their cooperation in the discourse on the then-upcoming UN Climate Summit in Paris, China and the EU stressed that they "commit to work together to reach an ambitious and legally binding agreement" (European Council 2015, p. 2). Notwithstanding the promising rhetoric during the 2015 Summit, reality indicates that close cooperation in energy and climate sectors between the two remains wishful thinking: "Despite the imperative for closer collaboration on energy and climate change, EU-Chinese relations have ebbed and flowed much since 2007" (Lee et al. 2015, p. 6). However, in June 2016, the EU and China agreed to strengthen their energy cooperation up to 2020. European Commissioner for Climate Action and Energy Miguel Arias Cañete and Nur Bekri, Director of the Chinese National Energy Administration, agreed on the EU-China Energy Roadmap (2016–2020). The road map focuses on common energy and climate challenges, including security of energy supply, energy infrastructure, and market transparency. In June 2017, the 2017–2018 Work Plan was signed to implement the EU-China Roadmap on Energy Cooperation. China's most recent official policy papers on EU-China cooperation pay only minimal attention to this area vis a vis other issue areas such as economic and financial cooperation (Suetyi and Zhiqin 2017). This deficit of attention in the energy sector could be emblematic; some scholars argue that over time, the EU is attracting less attention from China. This change is not only a result of EU crises and changes in Chinese foreign policy priorities; China is choosing to focus less on multilateralism and more on bilateral ties (Lee et al. 2015, p. 3).

Turning to the interaction within the EU-China energy dialogue, the network structure depicted in Fig. 10 shows that the Chinese actors are considered to be the most important actors in the network, whereas the EU actors are mostly marginal.

The most important Chinese actors in the network are the National Development and Reform Commission (NDRC), the National Energy Administration (NEA), and the Ministry of Commerce (MOFCOM). The Ministry of Foreign Affairs (MFA) is also an important actor because of its competence in foreign policy as in all the dialogues.

In 2003 the NDRC was founded. The NDRC was the successor to the State Planning Commission (SPC) founded in 1952, which was renamed the State

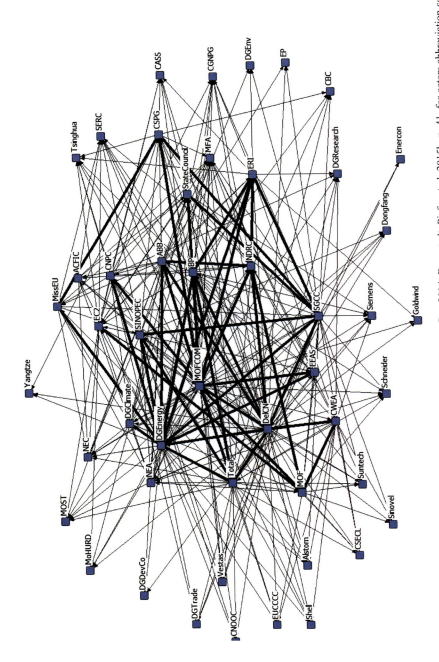

Fig. 10 Importance network for China-EU energy cooperation. (Source: EnergyGov 2014, Darmstadt, Piefer et al. 2015b, p. 41, for actors abbreviation see annex)

Development Planning Commission (SDPC) in 1988. The NDRC is an agency that reports directly to the State Council in different policy areas regarding economic and social development, including energy. Within the NDRC, the Energy Bureau was created to centralize planning and control energy policy under one institutional framework. The Energy Bureau, however, could not act as a central authority for energy affairs as the Ministry of Energy did; the Ministry of Energy was abolished in 1993. Hence, in 2005, the National Energy Leading Group (NELG) was formed to take charge of energy policy and key energy issues. The NELG comprised 13 members from the NDRC and other relevant ministries and was led by then-Premier Wen Jiabao. Notably, the Development Research Centre of the State Council and the NDRC Energy Research Institute have served as internal think tanks, producing leading reports on the main priorities for China's energy policy at the request of leaders, such as the Medium- and Long-Term Energy Conservation Plan (Beijing: NDRC 2004; Knodt et al. 2010).

The *National Energy Administration (NEA)* was established in 2008 under the jurisdiction of the NDRC as part of the reform effort to improve energy governance. The NEA's mandate covers the formulation and implementation of energy development plans and industrial policies, regulation of energy sectors, and promotion of energy system reform; it also leads China's participation in international energy cooperation (Zha and Lai 2015, p. 132). The NEA is one of the main partners in the energy dialogues, and the European Commission calls the NEA its "natural partner in energy cooperation" (European Commission 2014).

The *Ministry of Commerce (MOFCOM)* is responsible for all trade related to energy issues. MOFCOM was founded as a major broker in the network. An additional actor is the *Ministry of Science and Technology (MOST)*, which is in charge of the technology, innovation, and areas related to energy research and development. DG Energy called MOST its oldest Chinese partner in energy cooperation (European Commission 2014), but it seems to be losing importance in external energy affairs.

The State Administration of Coal Mine Safety is responsible for regulating and monitoring the safety of coal mining, which creates an overlap of competence in many areas with the NEA and NDRC. The *Ministry of Housing and Urban Rural Development (MoHURD)* is also part of the network as the partner in the EU-China Urbanization Partnership.

Clearly, national energy governance in China is complex and fragmented, with overlapping competences (Downs 2008; Vaclav 1981; Leung 2011). The Chinese government has made several attempts to streamline its institutional energy policy among other measurements, such as the creation of a Ministry of Energy (1988–1993), which was closed because of ineffective coordination. An effort to re-establish that ministry in 2008 failed, and the initiative in March 2018 has not yet been decided upon. Between 1993 and 2003, the fragmentation of the national energy administration was extensive and particularly enhanced after the National Coal Industry Bureau and the National Petrochemical Industry Bureau were revoked, and responsibilities were distributed to other ministries (Zhao 2001, p. 9f). In January 2010, another attempt to overcome the fragmentation was made, and the *National Energy Commission (NEC)* was created, headed by the Premier. The connection to the NEA occurs by considering the head of the NEA as the NEC deputy. The other 19 members are mostly different Chinese ministers. The NEC's main goal is to formulate a comprehensive and coordinated national energy strategy. The NEC meets every 1 or 2 years. Its daily work was assumed by the NEA. Thus far, however, NEC has functioned on a crisis-driven basis (Zha and Lai 2015, p. 132). Another attempt to overcome fragmentation was made by the 12th Five-Year Plan on Energy Development published by the State Council in January 2013, which included a "division of labor" table in which the NDRC remained the main leader (Zha and Lai 2015, pp. 133–135). However, the NDRC succeeded in preventing an Energy Ministry from being set up. It will be interesting to see what will happen to the 2018 initiative. The 13th Five-Year Plan on National Energy Development (2016–2020) was released in December 2016 by the NDRC and NEA. The 13th Five-Year Plan defines efforts to shift from central planning to policy guidance and regulation, trying again to streamline governance structure and procedures.

Evaluating the responses to the survey question about the importance of the EU, COM's DG Energy was mentioned among the top 5 as the only EU actor (see Table 2). DG Energy was not only appearing within the importance network but also in the exchange network and served as a broker. DG Energy was even considered the most important actor in the exchange network. Considering regular exchange in the network, the Delegation of the European Union to China and DG Energy (DelCN) are key actors within the broker function. DG Climate is also mentioned here. The broker role of the DelCN seems quite reasonable. As a physical representation in Beijing, the Delegation might often be the first contact with the EU, which could then introduce further contact in Brussels (Piefer et al. 2015b).

Since business and market access are central to EU-China energy cooperation, the private sector naturally plays an important role and is prominently represented in the network. Furthermore, business summits are organized parallel to the leaders' meetings (Piefer et al. 2015b, p. 42). In the Chinese case, state-owned companies (SOCs) are central actors. They generally are more competitive than private companies because they are backed by public money and have government support to operate in third-world countries. As energy business is in the hands of state-owned firms, they also play an important role in China's energy governance, especially the

Table 2 Top five actors in China-EU energy dialogue

Importance network	Exchange network	Broker function (exchange)
Five most important actors (indegree centrality)	Five most important actors (indegree centrality)	Five most important actors (betweenness centrality)
NEA 33.3	DG Energy 18.8	MOFCOM 9.0
MOFCOM 29.2	Tsinghua 16.7	DelCN 8.8
NDRC 29.2	CSPG 14.6	CSPG 4.5
MFA 29.2	ACFIC 14.6	DG Energy 2.9
DG Energy 22.9	MFA 14.6	CNPC 2.5

Source: EnergyGov (2014), Darmstadt, Piefer et al. (2015b), p. 41

State Grid Corporation of China (CSPG); the three Oil Giants, China National Petroleum Corporation (CNPC), China Petrochemical Corporation (Sinopec), and China National Offshore Oil Corporation (CNOOC); and the major power generators, China Huaneng, China Datang Corporation (CDT), China Guodian Corporation, China Huadian Corporation, and China Power Investment Corporation (CPI) (Zha and Lai 2015, p. 133). They are supervised by the State-owned Asset Supervision and Administration Commission (SASAC), which is located directly under China's State Council (IEA 2017, p. 499). CSPG and CNPG have been among the primary actors in the exchange network. Interestingly, according to our interviews, the EU Chamber of Commerce in China (EUCCC) in Beijing is a primary representative of European non-state actors' interests, although it was not featured as prominently in the network analysis as its Chinese counterpart, the All-China Federation of Industry and Commerce (ACFIC), which has served as an important broker in the network. It seems that within the working groups, the EUCCC has been serving as a gatekeeper for European companies, through which they gain access to the dialogue and can shape lobbying activities. The EUCCC informs its members of developments concerning market access and its energy-working group and provides advice on the best strategies with which to engage the Chinese authorities (Interviews Brussels, February 2012; Beijing, March 2012).

Interestingly, actors such as Tsinghua University appeared among the most important exchange network actors as an important broker. Meidan explained this as a special way of policymaking and inserting knowledge. The major change in China's energy governance came with the shift in government in 2003, when President Hu Jintao and Premier Wen Jiabao took over power and brought a new vision and policy approach to China's governance. "[. . .] [after] the Third Generation of leaders came to power, the scope and importance of information providers and interest groups affecting problem representation has grown considerably. For the Fourth Generation, the creation of study groups and seeking informed advice has become something of a trade mark" (Meidan et al. 2009, p. 592; Knodt et al. 2010).

The Chinese governance system stretches across several levels (central, province, and municipal). Decisions regarding goals and regulations concerning energy are made at the highest level by the central government. Provincial and municipal governments are responsible for implementation, although implementation at those levels suffers delays and discontinuity due to local priorities such as budget and industry protection (Zha and Lai 2015, p. 133). Nevertheless, all levels are involved when China is setting up its Five-Year Plans, key instruments of its planned economy. Both central and local governments formulate sectoral and regional plans on different issues, including energy. Based on these plans, the National Development and Reform Commission and the National Energy Administration formulated the aforementioned 13th Five-Year Plan on Energy Development, which delegated decision-making authority for energy infrastructure and production capacities to the provincial level and abolished the national-guided approval procedures (IEA 2017, p. 494; Hu and Guan 2017, p. 122).

As shown in Fig. 11, the network block matrices on importance and exchange indicated the EU's great interest in cooperating with China. The EU regarded the

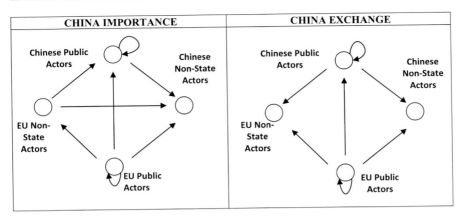

Fig. 11 Importance and exchange network block matrices (China-EU). (Source: EnergyGov 2014, Darmstadt, Piefer et al. 2015b, p. 43)

Chinese public and non-state actors as well as European non-state actors as important and exchanged information with them. However, the Chinese public actors attributed greater importance to the Chinese non-state actors and exchanged information mainly with them and the European non-state actors. From this observation, it is assumed that Chinese interest is very high in technology transfer and exporting its renewable energy technologies to other world regions, including the European market. Thus, private sector cooperation is favored over public sector cooperation and exchange (Piefer et al. 2015b).

All in all, indications of increased interest from both sides were observed. The prominence of the EU-China energy dialogue is greater than EU's dialogues with other BICS countries. However, cooperation with EU Member States is often preferred and referred to as "another cup of tea." When more concrete results and financial flow are expected, China has been dealing more with the EU Member States than with the EU as the former have more to offer (Interviews in Beijing and Brussels, February–May 2012) (Knodt et al. 2015b, p. 42f). The EU-China energy dialogue is the only one considering the importance of Member States in its setup. The EU-China Partnership on Urbanization and the Joint Declaration on Energy Security were the first documents that were agreed to by all 27 Member States plus the European Commission with the Chinese side (Knodt et al. 2015b, p. 39f).

An important aspect of the dialogue is the mutual perception of the actors involved. The self-perceptions of the EU were observed to be positive (Fig. 12). The EU actors themselves viewed the EU as an active agenda-setter and emphasized the EU's strong compromise-building qualities. They also saw the EU as taking an interest in other negotiation partners, i.e., being open to learning (Knodt et al. 2017, p. 174).

Chinese interviewees noted that in the energy sphere, China has more to learn from the EU than vice versa, a point especially pertinent in the areas of technology, energy management, and regulation (see Fig. 12). Several respondents mentioned misunderstandings and misperceptions between China and the EU. The EU side was

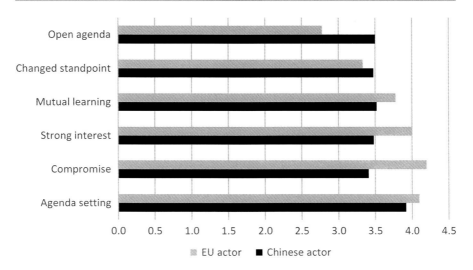

Fig. 12 Perception of the EU's properties as a dialogue partner in the EU-China energy dialogue. (Means of all answers; 1 = "strongly disagree"; 5 = "strongly agree." Source: EnergyGov 2014, Darmstadt, Knodt et al. 2017, p. 187)

seen questioning China's long-term strategic intentions and viewing Chinese enterprises as competitors. The solar panel trade dispute was the most telling example. The various communication mechanisms established were viewed as positive attempts to help the situation. However, the interviewees demanded more and better communication (Zha and Lai 2015, p. 140; Knodt et al. 2017, p. 188).

Perceptions of China in the EU-China energy dialogue between the Chinese and European actors diverged in some areas. Chinese elites saw China's involvement in the bilateral energy dialogue as being rather transparent. In contrast, the EU side considered China to be playing with a "hidden agenda." China saw itself as willing to compromise, whereas the EU considered China to be an actor less inclined to compromises (see Fig. 13). Such divergent perceptions may undermine trust building between the two actors (Zha and Lai 2015, p. 139; Knodt et al. 2017, p. 187).

As mentioned above, energy policy is driven by the three fundamental normative frames of sustainability, competitiveness, and energy security. The survey showed that the visions of normative orientations in the energy dialogue did not match between the EU and Chinese elites (see Fig. 14).

Security of supply was the frame widely preferred by the Chinese respondents, whereas the EU respondents focused on the sustainability frame. The focus on security of supply in China indeed fit with its official political discourse on energy policy and reflected the high priority given to energy security. Notably, both the 13th Five-Year Plan on Energy Development and the 2017 Energy Production and Consumption Revolution Strategy, guided by President Xi Jinping, call for an "energy revolution" as a long-term goal of China's energy policy. Within the "energy revolution," China defines its energy goals: "to build a more secure, sustainable,

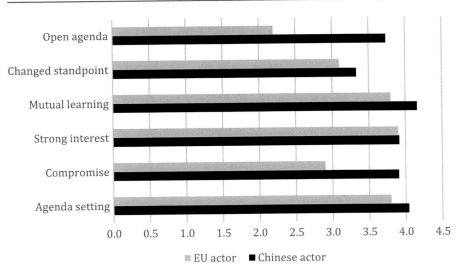

Fig. 13 Perception of China's properties as a dialogue partner in the EU-China energy dialogue. (Means of all answers; 1 = "strongly disagree"; 5 = "strongly agree." Source: EnergyGov, 2014, Darmstadt, Knodt et al. 2017, p. 188)

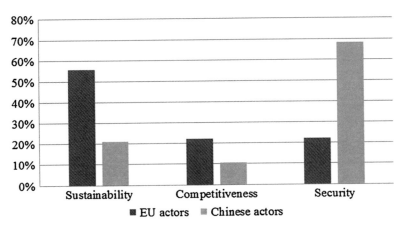

Fig. 14 Energy frames of China-EU cooperation by Chinese and EU stakeholders. (Percentage of respondents ranking the respective frame highest in energy dialogue. Source: EnergyGov, Darmstadt, 2014, Knodt et al. 2017, p. 171)

diverse and efficient energy future" (IEA 2017, p. 471) to address the three traditional primary objectives of energy policy. Partly, this can be explained by the different interpretations of the frames. Our findings noted that European actions in the energy field were guided by a liberal understanding of energy governance, which increasingly interpreted sustainability as energy efficiency, whereas China would categorize energy efficiency under the security norm. These findings suggested that the EU might feature China's priorities on the security of the supply in the EU-China energy dialogue if it is committed to establishing more common ground. For instance, the EU might strengthen its message on a heightened relevance of renewable energy sources in the context of how these sources will guarantee Chinese security of supply. Encouragingly, the EU-China negotiations provide evidence of a long-standing cooperation with a strong focus on sustainability issues (Knodt et al. 2015c, pp. 332–333), especially in the current developments.

EU-South Africa Energy Dialogue

The energy dialogue between South Africa and the EU was established in 2008 during the first high-level summit between the two partners, together with 12 other sectorial dialogues. Again, dialogue is embedded in the strategic partnership, which was signed in 2007 and remains the only one that the EU has signed with an African country. The strategic partnership was and remains funded under the EU's Development Cooperation Instrument (DCI), although with a significantly reduced amount, by the EU under the new financial framework (2014–2020). Thus, South Africa is the only one of the four cases that continues to receive bilateral development assistance. After the bilateral dialogue in 2008's promising beginning, "a period of missed opportunities started" (Piefer et al. 2015b, p. 44). The reasons for this slow progress in cooperation – described in Brussels as "negotiation fatigue" (EnergyGov, Interview Brussels, May 2012) – are manifold. There are serious difficulties in entering the South African energy market due to Eskom's monopolistic role. Moreover, a lack of offers from the South African side made it less attractive for foreign energy providers to invest in joint projects. In addition, the EU-South Africa dialogue is embedded in the regional energy cooperation of the EU with the Southern African Development Community (SADC), which does not always push the bilateral dialogue forward (Interview Brussels, February 2012; Piefer et al. 2015b, p. 44).

The EU's dialogue is most active in areas relating to coal and CCS, with the working group on clean coal being the only one actively holding meetings in recent years (Piefer et al. 2015b, p. 44), because of South Africa's high reliance on coal as its primary energy source after the end of Apartheid. Coal is the main pillar of the South African energy system, comprising nearly 70% of the country's energy consumption. On the supply side, it accounts for over 90% of the domestic electricity supply. However, the position of coal in the energy mix is not as dominant as one might suspect (IEA 2014, p. 146). South Africa is exporting a large share of its coal to international markets; it is the sixth-largest coal exporter in the world. In the past, South Africa was the main supplier of coal to Europe. However, in 2013, South Africa supplied only 6.8% of solid fuels (hard coal, lignite, peat, and derived fuels) to the EU, shifting its coal exports toward the Asia-Pacific area with its growing demand. India is one of the new export priorities for South Africa (IEA 2014, p. 115), which benefits from fast-growing maritime trade in the Indian Ocean. In 2012, a Clean Coal Programme was set up between the EU and South Africa. This focus corresponds to one of the main objectives of South African energy polices, which has to cope with the reliance on coal and the related CO_2 emissions. Among sub-Saharan African states, South Africa is by far the most important contributor of CO_2 emissions (IEA 2014, p. 117). The carbon intensity of the country's electricity production is high because coal is used as the primary energy source for electricity production.

In addition, in 2015, 25% of South African energy consumption came from oil. South Africa imports its oil primarily from Saudi Arabia (38%), Nigeria (32%), and Angola (12%) (2014) (Observatory of Economic Complexity 2014). Recently, substantial shale gas resources have been identified in South Africa in the Karoo Basin (Hedden et al. 2013). Shell, Australia-based Challenger Energy and a number of other companies have been awarded exploration licenses (IEA 2014, pp. 52, 101).

A debate on nuclear energy – framed in the context of renewable energies and positioned within South Africa's decarbonization strategy – is also taking place. South Africa is the only country in sub-Saharan Africa with a nuclear power plant. In 2015, nuclear energy had a share of approximately 2% of the country's total energy consumption (BP 2016). South Africa has stated its intention to expand nuclear power capacity. As South Africa is one of the ten largest uranium resource holders in the world, it would be able to use its own resources to achieve this increase (IEA 2014, p. 60). The signing of the European Atomic Energy community (EURATOM)-South Africa Agreement in July 2013 represented a milestone in this discourse, concluding years of negotiations in this field (European External Action Service 2013). The agreement laid the foundation for enhanced nuclear cooperation between the EU and South Africa, including research and development.

Renewable energy has experienced a lack of financial support due to South Africa's coal legacy since the Apartheid era. To address the domestic energy crisis, the focus was on the long-term expansion of the coal industry (Sebitosi and Pillay 2008, p. 2514). South Africa's options for a decarbonization scenario are also limited because of significant path dependencies and the relatively low cost of electricity produced by coal, which "remains an asset in societies concerned about the affordability of electricity" (IEA 2014, p. 15). At the beginning of the 2000s, competitive costs remained too high to offer an alternative to fossil fuels because of the necessarily large investments in basic transmission infrastructure (Sebitosi and Pillay 2008, p. 2514). However, in the 2003 White Paper on Renewable Energy published by the South African government, a target of 21% of renewable energy production by 2013 was established; this goal has since been increased to 30% by 2030 (Maupin 2015, p. 196). The White Paper triggered remarkable policy transitions such as feed-in tariffs, which were announced in 2009 by South Africa's National Energy Regulation Agency (NERSA) for solar, wind, and biomass energy. Meanwhile, South Africa has also turned to the auction system. In 2011 two large-scale initiatives to unlock the great potential for renewables were begun. First, the South African Renewables Initiative (SARi) was initiated (an international partnership between South Africa, Denmark, Germany, Norway, the UK, and the European Investment Bank) to enhance renewable energy in South Africa. SARi is an example of the importance of the EU Member States to South Africa as stressed in

South African interviews. SARi was designed to solve the funding issue and bridge energy, climate, and industrial policy to create synergies in promoting, developing, and deploying renewable energy capacities (SARi 2011). In addition, the Renewable Energy Independent Power Producer Procurement Programme (REI4P) was initiated in 2013. Within its framework, potential bidders are to produce 3725 MW from renewable sources (Maupin 2015).

However, solar and wind energy combined do not compose even 1% of South Africa's 2015 energy consumption. Nevertheless, the solar sector is particularly promising in large parts of South Africa, while there is promising potential for wind energy in the Western and Eastern Capes; an increase in renewables was noted in 2015 over the previous year (BP 2016). Growth in the solar sector in South Africa is strong, whereas growth in wind is more modest (IEA 2014, p. 79). With its Integrated Resource Plan to 2030, the South African government has plans to increase its solar and wind capacity. To increase capacity, auctions are already occurring. Only 0.2% of energy consumption in South Africa comes from hydropower, and the government does not plan to significantly increase its hydropower capacity. In contrast, it imports increasing volumes of hydropower from other parts of Southern Africa (IEA 2014, p. 105). As in the other examples, the Paris agreement had an impact on the dialogue. On 22 April 2016, the two parties signed the Paris Agreement on Climate Change at the opening ceremony for signatures in New York (Department of Environmental Affairs 2016/European Council 2016).

Our analysis of the interaction within the dialogue shows that the South African importance and exchange networks are the second densest networks (0.17 importance/0.11 exchange) after Brazil, with a very high distance. Nevertheless, the South African exchange network has the highest degree of centrality (14.8) among our four (Piefer et al. 2015b, p. 45).

As shown in Fig. 15, the network analysis provides evidence that it is primarily South African actors who are considered important in the importance and exchange networks. On the topic of energy cooperation, five South African actors were considered to be at the top of the importance network: the Department of Energy (DE), the Development Bank of Southern Africa (DBSA), the Parliamentary Portfolio Committee on Energy (PPCE), Eskom, and the NERSA. In addition, the NECSA and Sasol have prominent places in the perceived importance network and in the exchange network.

Since 2009, energy governance in South Africa has been situated in the then-established *Department of Energy* (DE). The department was created as a reaction to the power crisis of the year 2008. Large increases in energy delivery addressed the historical lack of access of the South African population post-Apartheid (see below), and the energy system has struggled with such fast growth. This rapid electrification was not supported by sufficient investment in the supply structures and generation capacity, leading to frequent nationwide power cuts, which occurred primarily in winter and posed a serious challenge to both private households and industry. Thus, the new DE was created, and the governance of energy and mineral resources was separated. The DE was installed as the main political actor of the South African government. The DE sets out the energy policy as well as the strategic planning for

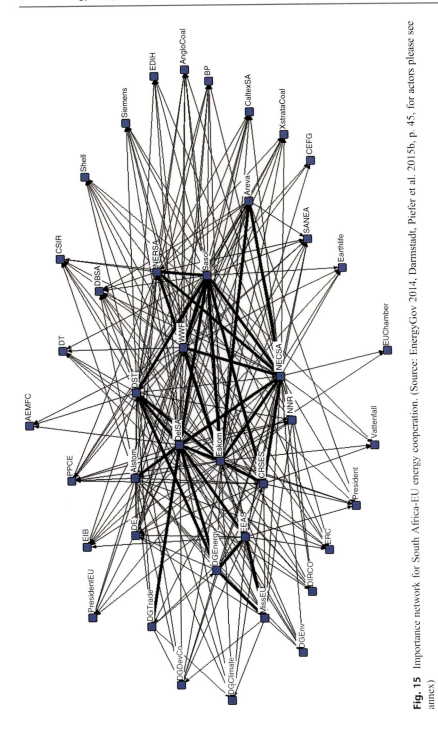

Fig. 15 Importance network for South Africa-EU energy cooperation. (Source: EnergyGov 2014, Darmstadt, Piefer et al. 2015b, p. 45, for actors please see annex)

the energy sector. Within the government, it works closely with the Department of Public Enterprises (DPE) where ESKOM, as a state-owned company, is located. "Since 2010, the DE has gradually imposed more control over energy governance. Its 2010–2030 Integrated Resource Plan (IRP) for electricity (Government of South Africa 2011) and the IRP's 2013 revisions (Government of South Africa 2013) are now generally considered to set the framework for future electricity building, and the various departments and actors, such as ESKOM, need to accommodate their planning to it and/or influence it to affect electricity outcomes" (Hochstetter 2017, p. 34). DE is seconded by two regulators: the National Energy Regulator of South Africa (NERSA) in charge of energy-infrastructure price control and the National Nuclear Regulator (NNR). NERSA is the primary economic regulator and licensing body of the energy sector.

Interestingly, the *Parliamentary Portfolio Committee on Energy (PPCE)* appeared under the most important actors in the importance as well as the exchange networks. This committee is the only parliamentarian committee that occupied an important place in the dialogue in all four networks. It also seems that in the South African energy policy, this committee possesses an important control function with the DE reporting to it regularly.

The South African electricity sector is dominated by the "semi-independent parastatal" (Hochstetter 2017, p. 30) enterprise *ESKOM*, which over the years has produced 96% of South Africa's electricity (Eberhard et al. 2014, p. 5), while private companies were left with the rest, only 2%. In 2001, it was decided that ESKOM's share in power generation should be reduced to 70%, leaving the remaining 30% for private sector participation (Maupin 2015, p. 196). In addition, Eskom owns and operates the national transmission system (Pegels 2010, p. 4946). Links between the Department of Energy and ESKOM remain strong, but they are eroding after corruption scandals concerning the enterprise. There is a strong interest from European companies in entering the South African energy market; however, it "is not an overnight operation" (Maupin 2015, p. 199) because ESKOM's monopolistic position obstructs others from entering that market (Piefer et al. 2015b, p. 44). In addition, the South African Nuclear Energy Corporation (NECSA), a state-owned nuclear company, and South Africa's national oil company, Petro SA, are important actors in South African energy governance.

DG Energy, similar to the three other cases, is viewed as an important actor in the exchange network (see Table 3), whereas – as in Brazil – no European actor can be seen in the importance network. The EU Delegation to South Africa is viewed as playing an important role as a broker in the majority of the dialogues. These findings emphasize that issues of competitiveness and market entry are perceived to gain importance. It is followed – at a great distance – by the EEAS and DG Trade. DG Trade maintains regular contact with a wide range of South African actors. All other European actors occupy marginal positions.

Examining these results from the more abstract level of the network density block matrices, the remote position of EU actors becomes even clearer (see Fig. 16). In terms of the importance network, South African public and EU public actors mutually considered one another to be important. Neither the EU nor the

Table 3 Top five actors South Africa-EU energy dialogue

Importance network	Exchange network	Broker function (exchange)
Five most important actors (indegree centrality)	Five most important actors (indegree centrality)	Five most important actors (betweenness centrality)
DE 32.5	DE 25.0	Eskom 8.1
DBSA 25.0	PPCE 20.0	DelSA 6.6
PPCE 25.0	DST 20.0	EEAS 2.2
Eskom 22.5	CSIR 20.0	DG Trade 1.8
NERSA 22.5	DG Energy 17.5	WWF 1.5

Source: EnergyGov (2014), Darmstadt, Piefer et al. (2015b, p. 46)

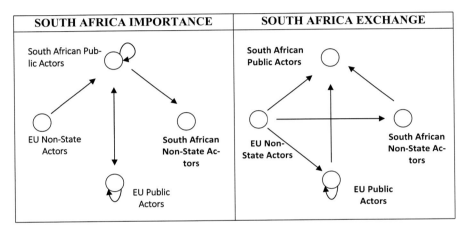

Fig. 16 Importance and exchange network block matrices (South Africa-EU). (Source: EnergyGov 2014, Darmstadt, Piefer et al. 2015b, p. 47)

South African non-state actors attributed importance to the EU and vice versa, suggesting that the EU must find and project its role when cooperating with political and private sectors. In terms of the exchange network, the EU public actors saw themselves addressing South African public actors, but this consideration did not appear to be reciprocated by South African public actors.

Within the dialogue, South African actors and the EU actors assessed the perceptions of each other's roles in the energy dialogue. Importantly, South Africa sees itself as being an agenda setter – more so than the EU perceives South Africa to be as shown in Fig. 17. The same holds true for policy trade-offs, in which South Africa considers itself to trade off energy policy issues against issues in other policy areas (Maupin 2015, p. 204).

Both actors perceive the EU to be a strong agenda-setter in the dialogue (see Fig. 18). However, whereas EU actors perceived the EU to have an open agenda, South African actors stated that the EU was playing with a hidden agenda (Knodt et al. 2015c, p. 68). Although the EU actors perceived the EU to be willing to change positions during negotiations, South African actors agreed less on this aspect. Such

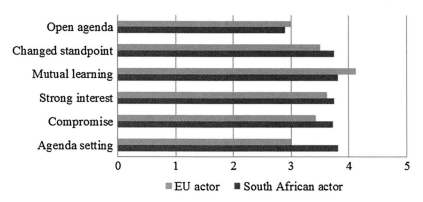

Fig. 17 Perception of South Africa's properties as a dialogue partner. (Means of all answers; 1 = "strongly disagree"; 5 = "strongly agree." Source: EnergyGov, Darmstadt 2014)

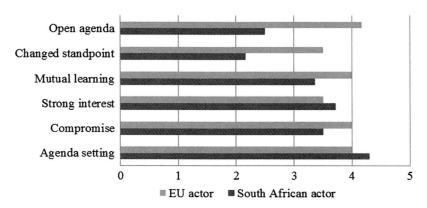

Fig. 18 Perception of the EU's properties as a dialogue partner. (Means of all answers; 1 = "strongly disagree"; 5 = "strongly agree." Source: EnergyGov, Darmstadt 2014)

differences in their perceptions of one another as dialogue partners can hinder a fruitful dialogue. Of major concern are the differing visions of agenda setting, particularly with respect to open vs. hidden agendas. Such perceptions can lead to mistrust among dialogue partners.

Perceptions of the EU-South African energy dialogue analyzed in terms of normative frames revealed that both EU and South African actors ranked the security of the energy supply as the most important frame in EU-South Africa energy cooperation (see Fig. 19). This finding is underlined by the 2013 EU-South African Summit, which showed that the EU understands and supports the priority placed by South Africa on the security of the energy supply. Energy security as such is very much framed as energy access in South Africa. In 1992 after the end of the apartheid regime, the distribution of electricity remained extremely skewed, both racially and socially. In townships, access to electricity was intermittent, and electricity tariffs for

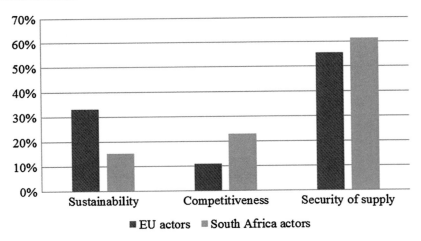

Fig. 19 Energy frames of South Africa-EU cooperation by South African and EU stakeholders. (Percentage of respondents ranking the respective frame highest in the energy dialogue. Source: EnergyGov, Darmstadt, 2014, Knodt et al. 2017, p. 239)

neighborhoods with predominantly black populations were much higher than in white areas. Only 15% of farmworker households had access to electricity (Eberhard and van Horen 1995, p. 49). All in all, the apartheid regime had only brought one third (white part) of the population to the grid (Hochstetter 2017, p. 29). Thus, the immediate post-Apartheid aim was to implement countrywide electrification schemes and to restructure state-owned energy companies (of which Eskom is by far the largest). South Africa succeeded in rapidly electrifying its households. The current electrification rate is approximately 85%, the highest in mainland sub-Saharan Africa (IEA 2014, p. 32). Only approximately 11% of households lack access to electricity, and approximately "4 per cent rely on illegal access (non-paying) or obtain access informally (from one household to another but paying)" (Statistics South Africa 2013, cited in: IEA 2014, p. 32).

The other frames, such as sustainability and competitiveness, were perceived to be in distant second and third places. Whereas the EU actors ranked sustainability as their second choice, the South African actors ranked competitiveness as the second most important frame. The monopolistic role of Eskom in the South African energy market can be one explanation for why competitiveness featured relatively low among EU actors. It is expected that the importance of this frame will grow over time as European interests in entering the renewable energy market in South Africa increase (Knodt et al. 2015c, p. 333).

Interpretations of the competitiveness frame reveal that both South African and EU actors consider the role of the renewable energy sector to be the most important. However, South Africa also highly values energy-intensive industry. This is due to its heavy industry and the minerals sector (Knodt et al. 2015c, p. 334). South African and EU actors both referred to sustainability in the threefold understanding of social, ecological, and economic sustainability (Ibid.), whereas security of supply is, to some extent, interpreted differently. All South African respondents considered access to energy technology to be an important aspect, followed by security of supply for industry and agriculture. Conversely, EU public actors valued security of supply for individual households highest, thus revealing discrepancies in interpretations. Despite some differences, the gap between the EU and South Africa's mutual perceptions in terms of normative frames is not particularly significant, with both actors perceiving technology transfer as an important area for bilateral cooperation (Knodt et al. 2017, p. 239).

Conclusions

The findings presented here allow for commenting on the quality of EU-BICS bilateral energy cooperation and suggest recommendations to develop strategies to optimize energy cooperation. Each of the energy dialogues has developed in a unique manner, representing the highly diversified mix of motivations, interests, perceptions, and normative orientations held by its members.

Nevertheless, all EU-BICS energy dialogues have some characteristics in common. For example, EU Member States are seen as very important partners by the BICS but are not regularly institutionally involved in the dialogues. Furthermore, EU actors try to reach out to and communicate with the respective BICS actors rather than vice versa. Empirical data in the case of Brazil explained that their exception in this regard was related to events at that particular time. In all four dialogues, the BICS public actors and sometimes also the non-state actors play a more important role than the EU actors and dominate the network. Only in the China-EU dialogue was DG Energy considered to be the most important actor in the network. Differences in the four dialogues include the role European actors play, their position in the network, and the density and centrality of the network. Furthermore and unsurprisingly, the political agendas have developed in each case according to the interests and priorities of the dialogue partners.

An important dimension in our analysis is tracing the mutual perceptions of the partners undertaking the dialogue. Across all four cases, problems of latent mistrust and diverging mutual perceptions between the cooperation partners were detected. In their self-perception, the EU public actors tend to view the EU as an active agenda-setter. In particular, they emphasize the EU's strong compromise-building qualities and recognize the EU's interest in the other negotiation partner, a property that is also visible in their openness to mutual learning. Certainly, this is a very noble and elevated self-image, but in reality, it must be juxtaposed with BICS' perceptions of the European actors. BICS actors mostly agree that the EU acts as an agenda-setter but also hope that the EU is willing and able to learn from the BICS side. Although they generally do not consider the EU a dominant promoter of interests, they also note that the EU is not exceptionally flexible in terms of compromise seeking or changing a stand. They do perceive the EU as acting with a hidden agenda. Reciprocating this vision from BICS, European actors showed a lack of trust toward the BICS partners (Knodt et al. 2015c, pp. 336–337), which poses severe challenges for the dialogue.

Concerning normative orientations, we asked our interviewees to rank the aspects of sustainability, security of supply, and competitiveness. Comparing the normative orientations of the EU and BICS actors, we observed a similar pattern for India and South Africa but a complete mismatch in the cases of Brazil and China. Obviously, the EU does not perform as a coherent normative actor promoting the same energy norm in each of the four dialogues. The norm hierarchy of the EU changes according to the context of the respective dialogue.

For the EU as a normative actor at the global level, energy policy is an interesting case because this policy is characterized by extreme institutional segmentation and fragmentation. In the foreseeable future, the EU's bilateral energy-related interactions with third states will be the place to project normative visions on the global level. The EU is sending different normative messages in the dialogues depending on the cooperation partner and the context. In adapting to respective contexts, the EU does not seem to be listening to its partners; however, because a dialogue is a two-way process, it is important not to have the EU be the only norm "exporter." BICS have their own domestic agendas, demands, and pride. Increasingly, they request not to be treated as passive norm receivers but as equal partners. Only through a true dialogue based on respectful and attentive listening can the EU identify common interests with its partners. The EU must learn to speak "with" its partners instead of "at" them (Chaban et al. 2016).

The research presented here concludes that successful cooperation requires primary identification and understanding of the areas of common interest. The EU's energy outreach toward BICS should be informed by the recognition of BICS' desires for substantial cooperation instead of "talk shop." Notably, BICS prefers state-to-state cooperation with individual EU Member States because reaching bilateral agreements with an individual EU country and implementing these agreements as concrete actions are easier and faster (Piefer et al. 2015c, pp. 350–351).

The insights into the self-perceptions of BICS could be instrumental when (and if) the EU revises its strategic partnerships with the respective countries to address true strategic values. Our research suggests that the energy sector is an area in which the EU can carve out added value. The perceptions analysis advocated by this contribution could be helpful in identifying BICS' demands and priorities, what the EU can offer, what perceptions of European demands exist in BICS, and what BICS think they can offer to the EU. If the EU is serious about horizontal, equal, and strategic partnerships that open up creative space for innovative cooperation modalities, then openness to mutual learning and the building of trust are essential.

Cross-References

▶ European Union Energy Policy: A Discourse Perspective
▶ The EU in Global Energy Governance

Acknowledgments The research presented in this contribution is the outcome of a collaborative effort within the international interdisciplinary research project "Challenges of the EU's External Energy Governance." The project was funded by the Volkswagen Foundation led by TU Darmstadt. All data cited as EnergyGov 2014, Darmstadt.

Annex 1: Network Actors

EU Actors for All Four Dialogues

DG Climate	European Commission, Directorate-General for Climate Action
DG DevCo	European Commission, Directorate-General for Development and Cooperation
DG Env	European Commission, Directorate-General for Environment
DG Trade	European Commission, Directorate-General for Trade
DG	Energy European Commission, Directorate-General for Energy
DG	Research European Commission, Directorate-General for Research and Innovation
EC President	President of the European Commission
EEAS	European External Action Service
EIB	European Investment Bank
EP	European Parliament

Brazil-EU Energy Dialogue

ABIOVE	Brazilian Vegetable Oil Industry Association
ANEEL	Brazilian Agency for Electric Energy
ANP	Brazilian Agency for Oil, Gas, and Biofuels
APROBIO	Brazilian Biodiesel Association
BNDES	Brazilian National Development Bank
BRA Mission	Mission of Brazil to the European Union
CGEE	Centre for Strategic Studies
CNI	National Confederation of Industries
Del BRA	Delegation of the European Union to Brazil
EPE	Energy Research Company
MDIC	Ministry of Development, Industry, and Foreign Trade
MMA	Ministry of Environment
MME	Ministry of Mines and Energy
MRE	Ministry of External Relations
Planalto	Brazilian Presidency
UNICA	Sugarcane Producers Union
UNICAMP	University of Campinas
UNIFEI	University of Itajuba

USP   University of São Paulo
WWF   World Wildlife Fund

India-EU Energy Dialogue

CII   Confederation of Indian Industry
CIL   Coal India Limited
CMPDIL   Central Mine Planning and Design Institute Limited
DAE   Department of Atomic Energy
Del IND   Delegation of the European Union to India
EU Chamber European Union Chamber of Commerce in India
FICCI   Federation of Indian Chambers of Commerce and Industry
MC   Ministry of Coal
MCI   Ministry of Commerce and Industry
MEA   Ministry of External Affairs
MEF   Ministry of Environment and Forests
MNRE   Ministry of New and Renewable Energy
MP   Ministry of Power
MPNG   Ministry of Petroleum and Natural Gas
NTPC   National Thermal Power Corporation
ONGC   Oil and Natural Gas Cooperation
RIL   Reliance Industries Limited

China-EU Energy Dialogue

ACFIC   All-China Federation of Industry and Commerce
CASS   Chinese Academy of Social Sciences
CBC   Central Bank China
CGNPG   China Guangdong Nuclear Power Group
CN Miss EU Mission of China to the European Union
CNOOC   China National Offshore Oil Corporation
CNPC   China National Petroleum Corp
CSECL   China Shenhua Energy Company Limited
CSPG   China State Grid Corporation
CWEA   Chinese Wind Energy Association
Del CN   Delegation of the European Union to China
Dongfang   Dongfang Electric
EC2   EU-China Clean Energy Centre
ERI   Energy Research Institute at NDRC
EUCCC   European Union Chamber of Commerce in China
MFA   Ministry of Foreign Affairs

MOF	Ministry of Finance
MOFCOM	Ministry of Commerce
MoHURD	Ministry of Housing and Urban-Rural Development
MOST	Ministry of Science and Technology
NDRC	National Development and Reform Commission
NEA	National Energy Administration
NEC	National Energy Commission
SERC	State Electricity Regulatory Commission
SGCC	State Grid Corporation China
Yangtze	China Yangtze Power Co.

South Africa-EU Energy Dialogue

AEMFC	African Exploration, Mining and Finance Corporation
CEFG	Central Energy Fund Group
CRSES	Centre for Renewable and Sustainable Energy Studies
CSIR	Council for Scientific and Industrial Research
DBSA	Development Bank of Southern Africa
DE	Department of Energy
Del SA	Delegation of the EU to South Africa
DIRCO	Department of International Relations and Cooperation
DST	Department of Science and Technology
DT	Department of Transport
ERC	Energy Research Centre, University of Cape Town
EUChamber	EU-Africa Chamber of Commerce
NECSA	Nuclear Energy Corporation of South Africa
NERSA	National Energy Regulator of South Africa
NNR	National Nuclear Regulator
PPCE	Parliamentary Portfolio Committee on Energy
President	President of the Republic of South Africa
SA Miss	EU Mission of South Africa to the European Union
SADC	Southern African Development Community
SANEA	South African National Energy Association
WWF	World Wildlife Fund
Xstrata	Coal Xstrata Coal

References

Agência Nacional de Energia Elétrica (A ANEEL). (2016). A ANEEL. http://www.aneel.gov.br/. Accessed 13 Oct 2016.

Bava, U. S. (2007). *New powers for global change? India's role in the emerging world order* (FES briefing paper 4). New Delhi: Friedrich Ebert Foundation.

Betz, J., & Hanif, M. (2010). The formation of preferences in two-level games: An analysis of India's Domestic and Foreign Energy Policy. GIGA Working Paper No. 142.

Brecher, M. (1968). *India and world politics, Krishna Menon's view of the world*. New York/Washington: Frederick A. Praeger Publishers.

British Petroleum (BP). (2015). BP statistical review of world energy, 10 June 2015. https://www.bp.com/content/dam/bp/pdf/speeches/2015/statistical-review-of-world-energy-2015-bob-dudley-speech.pdf. Accessed 10 Aug 2015.

British Petroleum (BP). (2016). BP statistical review of world energy, 20 July 2016. http://www.bp.com/content/dam/bp/pdf/energy-economics/statistical-review-2016/bp-statistical-review-of-world-energy-2016-full-report.pdf. Accessed 14 Oct 2016.

Central Electricity Authority (CEA). (2018a). Ministry of Power, Government of India. Installed capacity. http://www.cea.nic.in/installed_capacity.html. Accessed 29 Oct 2018.

Chaban, N., Knodt, M., & Verdun, A. (Eds.) (2016). External images of the EU – Energy power across the globe. *Comparative European Politics*, published online first. http://www.springer.com/social+sciences/political+science/journal/41295. Accessed 1 Oct 2016.

Chatterjee, E. (2017). Electricity and India's weak-strong state. Paper presented at the Workshop on 'Energy and state capacities in BRIC countries' Technische Universität Darmstadt. 21–22 Sept 2017.

Coal India. (2012). https://www.coalindia.in/index-hi.html. Accessed 10 May 2019.

Council of the European Union. (2009). Third European Union-Brazil Summit. Joint Statement. 6 Oct 2009. http://www.consilium.europa.eu/uedocs/cms_Data/docs/pressdata/en/er/110440.pdf. Accessed 11 Nov 2017.

Department of Environmental Affairs, South Africa. (2016) South Africa signs Paris Agreement on Climate Change in New York, 22/4/2016 https://www.environment.gov.za/mediarelease/southafricasignsparisagreementonclimate. Accessed 8 April 2019.

Directorate General Energy (DG Energy). (2010). EU-India relations. http://ec.europa.eu/energy/international/bilateral_cooperation/india_en.htm. Accessed 28 Oct 2014.

DG Energy. (2013). https://ec.europa.eu/energy/en. Accessed 10 May 2019.

Downs, E. S. (2008). China's new energy administration: China's National Energy Administration will struggle to manage the energy sector effectively. *China Business Review, 35*(6), 42–45.

Dubash, N. K. (2011). From norm taker to norm maker? Indian energy governance in global context. *Global Policy, 2*(S1), 66–79.

Eberhard, A., & Van Horen, C. (1995). *Poverty and power-energy and the South African state*. Cape Town/London: UCT Press/Pluto Press.

Eberhard, A., Kolker, J., & Leigland, J. (2014). *South Africa's renewable energy IPP procurement program: Success factors and lessons*. Washington, DC: World Bank Group. http://www.gsb.uct.ac.za/files/PPIAFReport.pdf. Accessed 20 May 2017.

Enerdata. (2016). Global energy statistical yearbook. https://yearbook.enerdata.net. Accessed 11 Aug 2016.

European Commission. (2007). An energy policy for Europe, Communication from the Commission to the European Council and the European Parliament, COM(2007), 1 final, Brussels, 10 Jan 2007.

European Commission. (2014). Energy from abroad. Stakeholders for EU-China Energy Cooperation. http://ec.europa.eu/energy/international/bilateral_cooperation/china/stakeholders_en.htm. Accessed 5 Nov 2014.

European Commission. (2015). EU-China Summit. Press release.

European Council. (2015). EU-China Summit joint statement, Brussels, 29 May 2015.

European Council. (2016). Climate change: EU signs the Paris Agreement, Press release, 22 April 2016. https://www.consilium.europa.eu/en/press/press-releases/2016/04/22/paris-agreement-global-climate-action/. Accessed 12 Dec 2018.

European Council. (2016a). EU-India agenda for action-2020. EU-India Summit. Brussels, 30 Mar 2016.

European Council. (2016b). Joint statement 13th EU-India Summit, Brussels, 30 Mar 2016. http://www.consilium.europa.eu/en/meetings/internationalsummit/2016/03/20160330-joint-statement-eu-india_pdf. Accessed 23 May 2016.

European Council. (2016c). Joint declaration between the European Union and the Republic of India on a clean Energy and Climate Partnership, Brussels, 30 Mar 2016, https://www.consilium.europa.eu/media/23673/20160330-joint-declaration-energy-climate.pdf. Accessed 23 May 2016.

European Council. (2017). Joint statement 14th EU-India Summit, New Delhi, 6 Oct 2017. http://www.consilium.europa.eu/media/23515/eu-india-joint-statement.pdf. Accessed 10 Oct 2017.

European External Action Service (EEAS). (2012). Joint declaration for enhanced cooperation on energy between the European Union and the Government of India, Brussels/Delhi.

European External Action Service (2013) Agreement between the European Atomic Energy Community (Euratom) and the Government of the Republic of South Africa for cooperation in the peaceful uses of nuclear energy. http://ec.europa.eu/world/agreements/prepareCreateTreatiesWorkspace/treatiesGeneralData.do?step=0&redirect=true&treatyId=9881. Accessed 2 Jun 2019.

European External Action Service (EEAS). (2018). EU India relations, factsheet, https://eeas.europa.eu/sites/eeas/files/eu_india_factsheet.pdf. Accessed 29 Oct 2018.

Fierke, K. M. (2010). Constructivism. In T. Dunne, M. Kurku, & S. Smith (Eds.), *International relations theories. Discipline and diversity* (pp. 177–194). Oxford: Oxford University Press.

Goldemberg, J. (2007). Ethanol for a sustainable energy future. *Science, 315*(5813), 808–810.

Goldemberg, J., Coelho, S. T., & Guardabassi, P. (2008). The sustainability of ethanol production from sugarcane. *Energy Policy, 36*(6), 2086–2097.

Government of South Africa. (2011). Integrated Resource Plan for Electricity, 2010–2030. Department of Energy.

Government of South Africa. (2013). Integrated Resource Plan for Electricity (IRP) 2010–2030 Update Report 2013, 30 November 2013. Pretoria: Department of Energy.

Gratius, S. (2011). *The EU and the "special ten": Deepening or widening strategic partnerships?* (Policy Brief, 76). Madrid: FRIDE.

Gratius, S. (2012). Brazil and the European Union: between balancing and bandwagoning, ESPO working paper No. 02 June 2012.

Gratius, S. (2013). *The EU and its "strategic partnerships" with the BRICS*. Berlin: Konrad-Adenauer-Stiftung.

Hedden, S., Moyer, J.D., & Rettig, Jessica. (2013). Fracking for shale gas in South Africa: Blessing or Curse?, Institute for Security Studies, African future papers, No. 9, December.

Hira, A., & de Oliveira, L. G. (2008). No substitute for oil? How Brazil developed its ethanol industry. *Energy Policy, 37*(6), 2450–2456.

Hochstetter, K. (2017). Green industrial policy and the renewable energy transition: Can it be good industrial policy. Paper presented at the Workshop on 'Energy and state capacities in BRIC countries' Technische Universität Darmstadt, 21–22 Sept 2017.

Hu, A., & Guan, Q. (2017). *China: Tackle the challenge of global climate change*. London/New York: Routledge.

Indian Government. (2018). Indian government's brief of EU-India relations. https://www.indianembassybrussels.gov.in/pdf/Revised_Brief_Unclassifiedmar19_2018.pdf. Accessed 29 Oct 2018.

International Energy Agency (IEA). (2013). *World energy outlook 2013*. Paris: IEA.

International Energy Agency (IEA). (2014). *Africa energy outlook. A focus on energy prospects in Sub-Saharan Africa*. Paris: IEA.

International Energy Agency (IEA). (2015a). *Medium-term coal market report 2015. Market analysis and forecast to 2020*. Paris: IEA.

International Energy Agency (IEA). (2015b). *India energy outlook, world energy outlook special report*. Paris: IEA. http://www.worldenergyoutlook.org/me dia/weowebsite/2015/IndiaEnergyOutlook_WEO2015.pdf. Accessed 23 May 2016.

International Energy Agency (IEA). (2016). *World energy outlook 2016*. Paris: IEA.

International Energy Agency (IEA). (2017). *World energy outlook 2017*. Paris: IEA.

Jaeger, M. D., & Michaelowa, K. (2015). Energy poverty and policy coherence in India: Norms as means in strategic two-level discourse. In M. Knodt, N. Piefer, & F. Müller (Eds.), *Challenges of European external energy governance with emerging powers* (pp. 235–247). Farnham: Ashgate.

Jaffrelot, C. (2006). *Indien und die EU: Die Scharade einer strategischen Partnerschaft* (GIGA Focus 5). Hamburg: German Institute of Global and Area Studies.

Joshi, M., & Ganeshan, S. (2015). India-EU energy relations: Towards closer cooperation? In M. Knodt, N. Piefer, & F. Müller (Eds.), *Challenges of European external energy governance with emerging powers* (pp. 149–171). Farnham: Ashgate.

Joshi, M., & Khosla, R. (2016). India: Meeting Energy Needs for Development While Addressing Climate Change. In *Sustainable energy in the G20: Prospects for a global energy transition* (IASS Study; December 2016, pp. 57–63). Potsdam: Institute for Advanced Sustainability Studies (IASS).

Keukeleire, S., & Bruyninckx, H. (2011). The European Union, the BRICs, and the emerging new world order. In C. Hill & M. Smith (Eds.), *International relations and the European Union* (pp. 380–403). New York: Oxford University Press.

Keukeleire, S., Mattlin, M., Hooijmaaijers, B., Behr, T., Jokela, J., Wi-gell, M., & Kononenko, V. (2011). The EU foreign policy towards the BRICS and other emerging powers: Objectives and strategies (Ad Hoc study), European Parliament. Brussels: Directorate General for External Policies.

Knodt, M., Müller, F., & Piefer, N. (2010). Challenges of European external energy governance with emerging powers: Meeting tiger, dragon, lion and jaguar. Panel on "a new mode of European external energy governance. 7th SGIR (Study Group on International Relations) Pan-European international relations conference, 9–11 Sept 2010.

Knodt, M., Müller, F., Piefer, N. (2012). Rising powers in international energy governance. Paper presented at the DVPW Konferenz "Politik und Ökonomie in globaler Perspektive: Der (Wieder) Aufstieg des Globalen Südens", Frankfurt, 05–07 Mar 2012.

Knodt, M., Müller, F., & Piefer, N. (2015a). *Challenges of European external energy governance with emerging powers*. Farnham: Ashgate.

Knodt, M., Müller, F., & Piefer, N. (2015b). Explaining European Union external energy governance with emerging powers. In M. Knodt, N. Piefer, & F. Müller (Eds.), *Challenges of European external energy governance with emerging powers* (pp. 57–74). Farnham: Ashgate.

Knodt, M., Müller, F., & Piefer, N. (2015c). Understanding EU-emerging powers energy governance: Form competition towards cooperation? In M. Knodt, N. Piefer, & F. Müller (Eds.), *Challenges of European external energy governance with emerging powers* (pp. 327–343). Farnham: Ashgate.

Knodt, M., Chaban, N., & Nielsen, L. (2017). *Bilateral energy relations between the EU and emerging powers: Mutual perceptions of the EU and Brazil, China, India and South Africa*. Baden-Baden: Nomos.

Lee, B., Mabey, N., Preston, F., Froggat, A., & Bradley, S. (2015). Enhancing engagement between China and the EU on Resource Government and Low Carbon Development, Research Paper, Chatman House.

Leung, G. C. K. (2011). China's energy security: Perception and reality. *Energy Policy, 39*(3), 1330–1337.

Lucas, H., Ferroukhi, R., & Hawila, D. (2013). Renewable energy auctions in developing countries. IRENA (International Renewable Energy Agency). www.irena.org/Publications. Accessed 24 Aug 2016.

Maupin, A. (2015). South-Africa-EU energy governance: Tales of path dependency, regional power and decarbonization. In M. Knodt, N. Piefer, & F. Müller (Eds.), *Challenges of European external energy governance with emerging powers* (pp. 195–216). Farnham: Ashgate.

Meidan, M., Andrews-Speed, P., & Xin, M. (2009). Shaping China's energy policy: Actors and processes. *Journal of Contemporary China, 18*(61), 591–616.

Ministry of Mines and Energy (MME)/Secretariat of Energy Planning and Development (SPE). (2015). Energy expansion in Brazil – 2024 investment opportunities; Office of Strategic Energy Studies. http://www.mme.gov.br/documents/10584/ 3642013/03+-+Energy+Expansion+in+Brazil+Investiment+Opportunities+ (PDF)/97e49acb-ee22-4c98-ad80-c70056288e89;jsessionid= EA174D8159C21B7 C94B25A59F05C52EC.srv155?version. Accessed 24 Aug 2016.

Ministry of Statistics and Programme Implementation (MoSPI). (2018). *Government of India*. New Delhi: Energy Statistics. http://mospi.nic.in/sites/default/files/publication_reports/Energy_Statistics_2018.pdf. Accessed 29 Oct 2018.
Müller, F., Knodt, M., & Piefer, N. (2015). Conceptionalizing emerging powers and EU energy governance: Towards a research agenda. In M. Knodt, N. Piefer, & F. Müller (Eds.), *Challenges of European external energy governance with emerging powers* (pp. 17–32). Farnham: Ashgate.
National Development and Reform Commission (NDRC). (2004). Medium and Long Term Energy Conservation Plan. http://en.ndrc.gov.cn/. Accessed 12 Aug 2018.
Noronha, L., & Sharma, D. (Eds.). (2009). *Energy, climate and security: The interlinkages* (Proceedings of the 2nd conference jointly organized by TERI and KAF). New Delhi: Konrad-Adenauer-Foundation.
Observatory of Economic Complexity (OEC). (2014). Countries. South Africa. https://atlas.media.mit.edu/en/profile/country/zaf/. Accessed 12 Aug 2018.
Pegels, A. (2010). Renewable energy in South Africa: Potentials, barriers and options for support. *Energy Policy, 38*(9), 4945–4954.
Piefer, N., Knodt, M., & Lai, S. (2015a). Perceptions and challenges of China-EU energy cooperation. Paper presented at the UACES conference 2015, Bilbao.
Piefer, N., Knodt, M., & Müller, F. (2015b). EU and emerging powers in energy governance: Exploring the empirical puzzle. In M. Knodt, N. Piefer, & F. Müller (Eds.), *Challenges of European external energy governance with emerging powers* (pp. 33–53). Farnham: Ashgate.
Piefer, N., Knodt, M., & Müller, F. (2015c). Policy recommendations for enhanced EU-emerging powers energy cooperation. In M. Knodt, N. Piefer, & F. Müller (Eds.), *Challenges of European external energy governance with emerging powers* (pp. 345–354). Farnham: Ashgate.
Ribas, A., & Schaeffer, R. (2015). Brazil-EU energy governance: Fuelling the dialogue through alternative energy sources. In M. Knodt, N. Piefer, & F. Müller (Eds.), *Challenges of European external energy governance with emerging powers* (pp. 173–194). Farnham: Ashgate.
Sebitosi, A. B., & Pillay, P. (2008). Grappling with a half-hearted policy: The case of renewable energy and the environment in South Africa. *Energy Policy, 36*(7), 2513–2516. https://doi.org/10.1016/j.enpol.2008.03.011.
South African Renewable Initiative (SARi). (2011). The Southern African renewable initiative. https://sarenewablesinitiative.files.wordpress.com/2011/12/sari_declaration_of_intent_011211-as-printed.pdf. Accessed 29 Oct 2018.
Suetyi, L., & Zhiqin, S. (2017). How China views the EU in global energy governance: Norm exporter, partner or outsider? *Comparative European Politics, 15*(1), 80–98. https://doi.org/10.1057/cep.2016.14. Published online first.
The Brazilian National Agency of Petroleum, Natural Gas and Biofuels (ANP). (2016). Competências da ANP. http://www.anp.gov.br/. Accessed 03 May 2016.
The International Renewable Energy Agency (IRENA). (2015). *Renewable energy policy brief: Brazil*. Abu Dhabi: IRENA.
Vaclav, S. (1981). Energy development in China: The need for a coherent policy. *Energy Policy, 9*(2), 113–126.
Van der Heijden, J. (2011). Institutional layering: A review of the use of the concept. *Politics, 31*(1), 9–18.
World Bank Group (WBG). (2016a). Brazil. Overview. http://www.worldbank.org/en/country/brazil/overview. Accessed 22 Feb 2016.
World Bank Group (WBG). (2016b). GDP growth (annual %). Overview per country. India. http://data.worldbank.org/indicator/NY.GDP.MKTP.KD.ZG?locations=IN. Accessed 9 Aug 2016.
Zha, D., & Lai, S. (2015). China-EU energy governance: What lessons to be drawn. In M. Knodt, N. Piefer, & F. Müller (Eds.), *Challenges of European external energy governance with emerging powers* (pp. 129–147). Farnham: Ashgate.
Zhao, J. (2001). Reform of China's energy institutions and policies: Historical evolution and current challenges. BCSIA Discussion Paper 2001-20, Energy Technology Innovation Project, Kennedy School of Government, Harvard University.

EU-Russia Energy Relations

11

Marco Siddi

Contents

Introduction	238
Recent Scholarly Research and Debates	239
EU-Russia Energy Relations in a Historical Perspective	241
EU-Russia Energy Trade and the Ukraine Crisis	242
Recent Developments in EU-Russia Gas Trade	245
New Projects for EU-Russia Gas Trade: Yamal LNG and TurkStream	246
The Nord Stream 2 Controversy	247
Ukraine's Current and Future Role in EU-Russia Energy Trade	250
Settling Disputes: The Antitrust and WTO Cases	252
Nuclear Power	254
Renewable Energy	255
Conclusion	256
Cross-References	258
References	258

Abstract

Energy trade is a long-standing pillar of European Union (EU)-Russia relations. Russia is the main provider of oil, gas, and solid fuels to the EU. The EU's demand for reliable energy supplies from abroad and Russia's desire to capitalize on its vast fossil fuels resources have led to strong interdependence in the energy sector. However, within the EU, assessments of the energy relationship with Russia have become more controversial since the late 2000s, and particularly after the Ukraine crisis. The chapter explores the main scholarly debates concerning the EU-Russia energy relationship. It puts the relationship in a historical context and discusses the consequences of the Ukraine crisis, including the measures taken by each side to diversify their partners. The chapter argues

M. Siddi (✉)
European Union Research Programme, Finnish Institute of International Affairs, Helsinki, Finland
e-mail: Marco.Siddi@fiia.fi

© Springer Nature Switzerland AG 2022
M. Knodt, J. Kemmerzell (eds.), *Handbook of Energy Governance in Europe*,
https://doi.org/10.1007/978-3-030-43250-8_54

that the existing path dependencies in the EU-Russia energy relationship, together with market forces, continue to drive bilateral trade. While the focus is mostly on gas trade and geopolitics, the growing relevance of nuclear power and of renewable energy sources is also analyzed.

Keywords

Russia · European Union · Energy · Gas · Oil · Nuclear · Renewable energy · Ukraine · Nord Stream 2 · Energy Union

Introduction

Energy trade is a long-standing pillar of European Union (EU)-Russia relations. Russia is the main provider of oil, gas, and solid fuels to the EU. For some EU member states, Russia is also a supplier of uranium and an important partner in the nuclear energy sector. Soviet Russia began to export fossil fuels to European countries on a large scale during the Cold War. Indeed, some scholars have labelled the emergence of East-West energy networks at this time as the "hidden integration" of Europe in the Cold War era (Högselius 2013, p. 3). The end of the Cold War paved the way for the further expansion of energy trade between EU member states and Russia. The EU's demand for reliable energy supplies from abroad and Russia's desire to capitalize on its vast fossil fuels resources led to strong interdependence in the energy sector.

Up until the mid-2000s, this interdependence was broadly regarded as a positive example of post-Cold War cooperation between Russia and the EU. However, within the EU, assessments of the energy relationship with Russia became more controversial after the gas transit crises between Russia and Ukraine in 2006 and in 2009. With the onset of the Ukraine crisis in 2014 and the ensuing deterioration of EU-Russia relations, some member states (such as Poland and Lithuania) have framed energy trade with Russia as a security issue. Nonetheless, and despite serious disagreements between Brussels and Moscow in the security, legal, and normative arenas, EU-Russia energy trade has experienced a considerable rise since 2016, particularly with regard to gas (Henderson and Sharples 2018). This shows that the EU and Russia have remained interdependent in the sphere of energy, which is thus one of the few sectors where a substantial level of cooperation has continued after the Ukraine crisis (Siddi 2018a).

This chapter explores the current state of EU-Russia energy relations, with reference to recent scholarly works and debates on this topic. The analysis proceeds as follows. It begins by addressing some of the main scholarly debates concerning the EU-Russia energy relationship. It then puts the relationship in a historical context and discusses the relevant consequences of the Ukraine crisis, including the measures taken by each side to diversify their energy partners. At the same time, the chapter shows that the existing path dependencies in the EU-Russia energy relationship, together with market forces, continue to drive bilateral trade. While relations in the field of oil, nuclear power, and renewable energy are briefly discussed, most of the analysis focuses on gas. Gas has been the most politically sensitive commodity due to the vulnerability of some East-Central EU member states (such as Bulgaria or the Baltic States) to potential supply disruptions in the flow of Russian gas. However, such risks are now decreasing as new interconnections among EU countries are being built.

The chapter adopts the premise that energy policy is a complex field where numerous factors play a role. Within the EU, it is an area of shared competence between the Union and its member states (as specified in Article 194 of the Treaty on the Functioning of the European Union), many of which have very different national energy portfolios and diverging attitudes toward Russian energy imports (for an overview of the complexities of EU energy policy, see Schubert et al. 2016). EU and national legal frameworks exist, which are generally oriented toward promoting the competitiveness and liberalization of energy markets. In Russia, the state retains closer control of energy production and supply, but different and at times conflicting interests exist also in the Russian energy sector. Moreover, commercial actors contribute to shaping energy policy and play an essential role in EU-Russia energy trade.

Recent Scholarly Research and Debates

Scholarly literature on EU-Russia energy relations is vast and cross-disciplinary. Recent studies have adopted an international political economy (IPE) perspective (Belyi 2015; Godzimirski 2019) or a framework based on security studies, securitization theory, and constructivist international relations (IR) theory (Szulecki 2018). Other publications have welcomed contributions from economists, political scientists, and geographers in order to provide a comprehensive picture of the topic's complexities (Oxenstierna and Tynkkynen 2014). After the Ukraine crisis in particular, EU-Russia energy relations have (re)attracted the interest of neorealist scholars of international relations, as well as of academics who have applied more nuanced conceptualizations drawn from this IR school, such as geoeconomics (Wigell and Vihma 2016).

While it is not possible to offer an exhaustive and overly schematic account of the recent relevant literature, some overarching trends can be identified. Scholars such as Andreas Goldthau and Nick Sitter (2019) have analyzed EU-Russia relations predominantly from an IPE perspective. They argued that the European Union has approached the relationship mostly as a liberal actor, using regulatory and market power rather than hard economic or geopolitical power (which, in their view, would be more controversial and of dubious benefit to the EU) (Geopolitics of Energy). In practice, this means that the EU has envisaged its energy relations with Russia primarily as a trade relationship within a well-regulated framework. This has led to a high degree of interdependence in EU-Russia energy relations which, as Stulberg (2015) and Siddi (2018a) have noted, persisted or even increased despite political crises. At the same time, Boersma and Goldthau (2017) have noted a trend toward the securitization of EU-Russia energy relations, which could eventually undermine the EU's liberal posture and unravel EU-Russia path dependencies.

While Goldthau, Sitter, and Boersma appear wary of this development, scholars adopting a neorealist perspective have criticized EU-Russia energy interdependence and argued that the EU should take a more strategic approach to relations with Russia. Andrej Krickovic (2015) has claimed that interdependence in the energy sphere has exacerbated security tensions between the two sides. According to him, both the EU and Russia have been worried that in the future interdependence may become asymmetrical; their ensuing efforts to reduce dependence undermine the trust of the other side, thus creating a classical security dilemma. Some studies (cf. Blank and Kim 2016) have argued that energy is an instrument in Russia's aggressive foreign policy – the so-called energy weapon – and described Russia's new pipeline projects as hostile attempts to divide the EU. Many policy papers and popularized analyses echoed this view.

However, many scholars have criticized such "reductionist" interpretations of EU-Russia energy relations. Judge et al. (2016) have highlighted how these interpretations oversimplify the complexity of the relationship by reducing it to the objectives of specific governmental actors, to the diktats of power politics, or to a narrow geopolitical reading of energy security. Similarly, Casier (2016, p. 763) has criticized approaches that frame "highly complex energy relations between the EU and Russia in terms of simple, exclusive geopolitical intentions." Moreover, Van de Graaf and Colgan (2017) have shown that there are strict limits to the efficacy of the "energy weapon," whoever attempts to use it. As Sharples (2016) has noted, the existence of a system of long-term energy contracts, commercial relationships with customers, and long-standing production and transportation arrangements between EU and Russian actors increase enormously the cost of using energy as a "weapon" for political goals.

While Russia tends to be described as a geopolitical actor in energy policy (driven by *Realpolitik* and zero-sum thinking), and the EU as a liberal one, recent analyses have added some nuance to these descriptions. Romanova (2016) has shown that different actors shape energy policy in Russia, and, despite the dominant geopolitical paradigm in decision-making, they usually rely on legal and technocratic instruments that are compatible with the EU's normative approach to energy policy. Siddi (2018a) has argued that Russia predominantly deploys geopolitical power in its external energy policy, while the EU resorts to regulatory power. However, he notes that the policies of both sides have recently become more nuanced, with Russia resorting to normative approaches and the EU adopting a geopolitical stance in some aspects of its external energy policy. This interpretation is consistent with recent studies of EU actorness in energy policy, which highlight the evolution of the EU from being a mere regulator into a "catalytic" actor that can intervene strategically in energy policy (Prontera 2019).

Another significant strand of research on EU-Russia energy relations has adopted a constructivist perspective, emphasizing the role of ideas, identities, and discourses. Kuzemko (2014) has explained divergences between the EU and Russia as a function of different ideas regarding the societal role of energy. Whereas in the

EU, energy is seen primarily as a commodity, in Russia it is also conceptualized as a strategic asset that, if managed correctly, can play a central role in strengthening the country's political and economic performance. By focusing on the role of history and identities, Siddi (2017) and Casier (2011) have attempted to explain why EU member states have often taken different stances with regard to the energy partnership with Russia. For instance, this literature has argued that the skeptical stance of many Eastern European member states vis-à-vis the energy partnership with Moscow is deeply influenced by their conflictual historical relationship with Russia. Furthermore, through an analysis of EU-level and Russian discourses, Tichý (2019) has highlighted the influence of norms, ideas, values, and rules in both actors' formulation of their energy policy (▶ Chap. 7, "European Union Energy Policy: A Discourse Perspective").

EU-Russia Energy Relations in a Historical Perspective

Before turning to recent developments in EU-Russia energy relations, it is important to understand how the current EU-Russia interdependence in the energy sector originated. Today's path dependencies and energy trade patterns are the result of a long historical process. Substantial exports of Soviet oil and gas to Europe began between the 1960s and the early 1970s. In 1964, the Druzhba oil pipeline became operational and started exporting Soviet oil to countries of the Council for Mutual Economic Assistance (Comecon), notably Czechoslovakia, Hungary, Poland, and the German Democratic Republic. Further pipelines were built to transport gas. In the late 1960s, the attenuation of tensions between the Eastern and the Western blocs allowed Western European states to develop economic relations with the Soviet Union. In 1966, the Urengoy gas field – the largest in the world, with a deposit of 9.9 trillion cubic meters – was discovered in the Soviet Union. These gas reserves proved particularly appealing to Central and Western European industry, which was overly dependent on energy imports from the Middle East (Belyi 2015, pp. 76–77). Following intense negotiations, several Western European countries concluded supply agreements with Moscow, and a transcontinental pipeline network was built to transport Siberian gas to Western Europe (Högselius 2013, p. 3).

In 1968, Austria was the first non-Comecon state to receive gas deliveries from the Soviet Union. West Germany signed a large supply contract the year after, followed by Italy, Finland, and France. Economic incentives for the import of Soviet energy increased after the 1973 oil crisis, when the Organization of Arab Petroleum Exporting Countries proclaimed an oil embargo on sales to several Western states due to their support of Israel in the Yom Kippur War. Meanwhile, other gas fields were discovered in the Soviet Union, which became the world's largest gas producer in 1984 (Belyi 2015, p. 76). Despite the concerns and opposition of the Reagan administration in the United States, energy trade between the Soviet Union and Western Europe continued to increase, thereby challenging the confrontational logic of the Cold War. Most notably, the Urengoy-Uzhgorod pipeline, which was essential for the expansion of Soviet gas exports to Europe, was commissioned in 1984, during a peak of military tensions between the Eastern and Western blocs (Högselius 2013, pp. 105–134). The volumes of Soviet gas exports rose from 29 billion cubic meters (bcm) in 1983 to 60 bcm in 1989 (Belyi 2015, p. 77).

After the end of the Cold War, energy trade continued to expand rapidly and became the cornerstone of EU-Russia interdependence. During the 1990s, even states that were suspicious of Russia's foreign policy intentions took a positive stance toward Moscow-led energy projects. In 1993, Polish policy makers hailed an agreement with Russia for the construction of the Yamal-Europe pipeline and long-term gas supplies as "the contract of the century" (Gorska 2010, pp. 107–114). The pipeline, shipping Russian gas to Germany and Poland via Belarus, became operational in 1997 and reached its maximum capacity of 33 bcm/year in 2005. Moreover, in the 1990s and 2000s, several Western European energy companies strengthened their partnership and launched new projects with Russian state company Gazprom. In 2001–2002, a joint venture including Gazprom and the Italian company ENI built the Blue Stream pipeline, which carries Russian gas to Turkey across the Black Sea. Most significantly, in 2005 Gazprom and its German partners BASF and E.ON (later joined by the Dutch Gasunie and the French ENGIE) initiated the Nord Stream pipeline project, with the capacity to transport 55 bcm of gas per year from Russia to Germany across the Baltic Sea. Around the same time, several major European importers of Russian gas (including German, Italian, and French companies) extended their long-term contracts with Gazprom.

However, in the second half of the 2000s, political developments had negative repercussions on EU-Russia energy trade. In 2006 and 2009, disputes between Russia and Ukraine concerning the price and the transit of gas caused temporary disruptions in Russian gas supplies to Europe (approximately 80% of these supplies reached Europe via Ukraine; see Pirani et al. 2009). New geopolitical frictions between Moscow and the West accompanied these developments, leading to the growing securitization of political discourses on energy (▶ Chap. 7, "European Union Energy Policy: A Discourse Perspective"). The prospect of further NATO enlargement, the Russian-Georgian war of August 2008, and Russia's increasingly assertive foreign policy fueled tensions (for detailed discussion, see Forsberg and Haukkala 2016). The Ukraine crisis of 2014 turned these tensions into open confrontation and also affected the EU's and Russia's posture toward their energy trade.

EU-Russia Energy Trade and the Ukraine Crisis

When the Ukraine crisis escalated in early 2014 and the EU imposed sanctions on Russia, energy security was one of the main concerns among policy makers in Brussels. Russian energy supplies covered approximately 40% of the gas, 33% of the crude oil, and 29% of the solid fuels imported by the EU (Eurostat 2018). Although oil is the most lucrative component of EU-Russia energy trade, gas was seen as the most politically sensitive commodity. This is because gas transportation is technically more difficult and diversifying suppliers requires large, long-term investments into pipelines or liquefied natural gas (LNG) terminals.

As approximately half of the EU's imports of Russian gas were channeled via Ukraine, it was feared that EU energy security would fall victim to the political crisis and that Europe would experience gas shortages such as those caused by the Russian-Ukrainian gas transit crisis of January 2009 (see Pirani et al. 2009). This concern was particularly strong in Eastern European countries that were more dependent on Russian gas supplies, such as Latvia, Bulgaria, and Slovakia.

In this context, the EU and its member states agreed to draft the 2014 European Energy Security Strategy and the 2015 Energy Union framework, which included among their goals the diversification of energy suppliers and strengthening resilience against supply shock-induced energy crises. The implementation of the Energy Union was made into a priority of the newly appointed European Commission presided by Jean-Claude Juncker. The Energy Union focused on increasing energy security and solidarity, creating an integrated EU energy market, improving energy efficiency, decarbonizing the economy, and supporting innovation and competitiveness. In order to strengthen energy security, the Energy Union envisaged the construction of new pipelines – most notably the Southern Gas Corridor (Siddi 2019) – and of LNG terminals to import non-Russian gas. With regard to Russia, the Energy Union framework adopted a cold and wary approach, arguing that "when the conditions are right, the EU will consider reframing the energy relationship with Russia based on a level playing field in terms of market opening, fair competition, environmental protection and safety, for the mutual benefit of both sides" (European Commission 2015; for an analysis of the strategy, see Siddi 2016).

On the other hand, Russia adhered to its Energy Strategy up to 2030, which it had launched in 2010 (Ministry of Energy of the Russian Federation 2010; see Gromov and Kurichev 2014 for a full analysis). According to the strategy, the goal of Russia's energy policy was to maximize the use of domestic energy resources in order to support economic growth, improve the quality of life of the people, and strengthen Russia's position in the global economy. The strategy also stated that the European market will remain the main destination of Russia's energy exports until 2030. At the same time, it envisaged an increase in energy exports to East Asia: by 2030, one quarter of Russian oil exports and one fifth of gas exports were expected to go to East Asia. Arguably, tensions with the West following the Ukraine crisis have increased Russia's urgency to progressively reorient its exports toward Asia. In 2014, Gazprom signed a deal to export 38 bcm/year of gas to China over a 30-year period; construction of the Power of Siberia pipeline, which will transport the agreed volumes, is nearing completion as of late 2019 (Geopolitics of Energy). However, as Sharples (2016) has noted, gas exports to China tap into different gas fields and rely on different infrastructure from the ones used for exports to Europe. Hence, competition between China and Europe to secure Russia's gas resources is only apparent, and the EU will remain the main importer for the foreseeable future.

In 2014–2019, a Russian-Ukrainian gas transit crisis comparable to that of 2009 was avoided thanks to successful trilateral negotiations between the EU, Russia, and Ukraine, as well as to Russian and Ukrainian willingness to shelter their lucrative gas trade from the political crisis (Stulberg 2015). As during the Cold War, EU-Russia gas trade continued and even intensified amidst political tensions. Part of the reason why trade continued is that Russia is at least as dependent as the EU on this energy relationship. Most of Russian oil and gas exports, which are vital to the Russian state budget, are sold in the EU market and cannot easily be reoriented toward other markets. Indeed, the oil and gas pipelines themselves are a physical manifestation of path dependency, given the time and investment necessary to build new pipelines to alternative markets. During the summer of 2015, Western European companies and Russian state company Gazprom even developed a new large-scale project to export Russian gas to the EU, the Nord Stream 2 pipeline. Nord Stream 2 is part of Gazprom's long-term strategy to diversify its export routes to Europe, together with TurkStream (see below). As the European market will continue to be the most important for Gazprom, the company is trying to limit its exposure to potential transit disruptions in Ukraine. This strategy is also functional to the Kremlin's goal of diminishing Ukraine's political leverage over Russia and EU-Russia energy relations.

Nevertheless, the political climate around energy cooperation has remained difficult. Eastern EU members such as Poland and the Baltic States have been fiercely critical of further energy trade with Russia and attempted to shape EU policy accordingly (Siddi 2018b) (► Energy Governance in the Republic of Poland). In 2015, the European Commission proceeded with an antitrust investigation against Gazprom, which it had launched in 2012 upon Lithuania's request and claim that Gazprom was abusing its monopolistic position in East-Central European markets (see below).

In the last 5 years, the EU made considerable progress in reducing its vulnerability to disruptions in Russian gas supplies while at the same time continuing energy trade with Russia. Some of the most dependent countries have developed alternative routes. Lithuania opened an LNG terminal in late 2014; Latvia expanded its gas storage capacity; Slovakia, Hungary, and Poland have built interconnecting pipelines; and further interconnections have been planned. The possibility of reverse flows of gas from West to East strengthened the energy security of Eastern members; Ukraine benefitted from this technology too. As the Energy Union framework is implemented, interconnections between the energy systems of member states have improved, and the possibility of external supply shocks affecting one or a group of countries has diminished.

At the same time, the EU-Russia gas relationship has been rendered more predictable by the resolution of long-standing disputes, most notably the European Commission's antitrust investigation concerning Gazprom and Russia's complaint at the World Trade Organization (WTO) against some key EU market regulations (the third energy package). As we shall see below, the settlement of the antitrust case between the European Commission and Gazprom has reduced the potential for legal conflict in EU-Russia gas trade and contributed to the integration of the EU gas market. However, disagreements persist among EU member states regarding the desirable EU stance vis-à-vis Russian energy exports, and particularly new infrastructural projects such as Nord Stream 2. The pipeline has caused heated debates within the EU, where some East-Central member states staunchly oppose the project. Conversely, Russia's main import partners in Western Europe seem keen to continue and even increase their energy purchases from Russia. The United States has intervened in the debate too by threatening to sanction European companies that are involved in Nord Stream 2 and advocating its prospective LNG exports as an alternative. Moreover, the geography of Russian gas deliveries to Europe may partly change in the future. Although Russia and Ukraine signed a new gas transit agreement for another 5 years in December 2019, a gradual shift in gas transit from the Ukrainian route to the Nord Stream and TurkStream routes can be expected in the next years.

Recent Developments in EU-Russia Gas Trade

Russian gas exports to Europe rose to unprecedented records from 2016 to 2018. According to Gazprom's data, around 201 bcm of gas were exported to Europe and Turkey in 2018, compared to 192.2 bcm in 2017 and 158.6 in 2015 (Gazprom 2019). This performance may appear surprising, given the context of political crisis and reciprocal sanctions between the EU and Russia (however, the sanctions only cover restricted and currently marginal areas of the energy sector, such as technology for offshore oil exploration and production in deep Arctic waters). The rise in Russian gas supplies to Europe is due to commercial and contextual factors that are unrelated to politics. From 2015 to 2017, EU gas demand grew considerably to 548 bcm/year in 2017. This is 76 bcm higher than in 2014 (even though it is still below the peak of 585 bcm reached in 2010; see Honoré 2018, p. 1). The economic recovery in Europe, decreasing gas production in the EU, lower Russian gas prices, and the limited availability of non-Russian liquefied natural gas (LNG) in the European market were among the main commercial reasons. Cold winter temperatures and increased coal to gas switching in some European countries (partly due to the growing carbon price in the EU's Emissions Trading Scheme in 2017–2019) also boosted gas demand.

Growing gas demand has been accompanied by decreasing indigenous production in the EU, which was 120 bcm in 2018 (approximately a 40% decrease in the last 10 years; see European Commission 2019a, p. 9). This was mostly due to the progressive depletion of North Sea resources and cuts in production in Groningen, the Netherlands, because of related seismic activity. Europe's growing demand for external gas supplies has been satisfied primarily by Russian gas. Following pressure from the European Commission and its customers, Gazprom has partly renegotiated the terms of its supply contracts by adopting market-based pricing instead of oil-linked prices. Together with the ruble's weakness (which reduces the domestic cost base for Gazprom in US dollar terms), this has made Russian gas more competitive (Henderson and Sharples 2018, pp. 3–5).

The availability of sufficient reserves and spare infrastructural capacity have also played a significant role. While Gazprom was able to sustain increased supplies of gas to the EU, other exporters such as Algeria (the third largest external supplier of gas to the EU after Russia and Norway) saw a 14% decline in pipeline exports in 2017. Not only did Gazprom use the Nord Stream and Yamal-Europe (via Poland/Belarus) pipelines at near full capacity, it also increased the gas it exported via Ukraine, reaching a total volume of 93.5 bcm in 2017, the highest ure since 2011 (Interfax Ukraine 2018). Despite the continuation of political tensions with the EU, Russian companies felt confident enough to implement new infrastructural projects for the export of gas to Europe and beyond. This included the launch of the Yamal LNG project in December 2017 and the construction of the TurkStream and Nord Stream 2 pipelines.

Furthermore, the competition of LNG with Russian gas has been weaker than expected. This was the result of delays in some LNG projects and especially of higher LNG demand in Asia (particularly China), which remains the primary market for LNG due to higher demand and prices. The availability of LNG in the European market began to increase from 2017 and may continue to do so in the next 5 years depending on demand in Asia. In a scenario of lower Asian demand, LNG from the United States (the closest prospective large supplier to Europe) could compete with Gazprom and other pipeline suppliers for some shares of the European market (Henderson and Sharples 2018, pp. 11–16). Russian gas shipped via pipeline tends to be cheaper than LNG, which explains why European commercial actors have preferred and may continue to prefer additional imports of Russian gas. Growing EU imports of Russian gas do not necessarily have a negative impact on European energy security thanks to the possibility of using the large spare capacity in LNG terminals in order to switch to LNG imports from other countries, depending on the commercial or political circumstances.

New Projects for EU-Russia Gas Trade: Yamal LNG and TurkStream

While EU-Russia energy trade has increased, new large-scale energy projects led by Russian companies have generated controversy within the EU. The different perspectives of member states on Russia, particularly its reliability as an energy supplier, have played an important role in the controversy (Siddi 2018b). The broader political crisis in EU-Russia relations has influenced discussions, sometimes overshadowing considerations on the functioning of energy markets and trade. While some politicians and commentators continue to fear the deployment of a hypothetical Russian "energy weapon," the availability of different suppliers, the integration of the EU's internal energy market, and Russia's dependence on this market for its national budget have strengthened considerably the EU's resilience and decreased its exposure to "energy blackmail" (Van de Graaf and Colgan 2017).

The new projects – the Yamal LNG project and the TurkStream and Nord Stream 2 pipelines – aim primarily to uphold or increase the shares of Russian companies in the European market in the face of growing competition. They also serve the purpose of diversifying export routes and of bypassing transit countries where gas trade with Russia has become heavily politicized (such as Ukraine) – largely as a result of Russia's foreign policy. According to the European companies that support them, these projects are commercial endeavors that contribute to European energy security. According to their detractors, they are political instruments to increase Russia's leverage over Ukraine and Eastern Europe. While the projects are significant also from a strategic viewpoint, it is unlikely that they will coerce Ukraine or other countries into a Russian sphere of influence or undermine the EU's energy security. The main risk for the EU is that if member states take incompatible and intransigent stances vis-à-vis the projects, and exaggerate their political significance, the EU's internal coherence will be undermined.

In 2018, the first large project that can export Russian LNG to the European market was launched – even though most of its gas might in fact go to Asia. Yamal LNG is expected to produce 16.5 million tons of LNG per year from 2019. The project was developed by a consortium including the Russian Novatek, the French Total, the China National Petroleum Corporation, and the Silk Road Fund. Yamal LNG is also significant because Novatek, the Russian consortium leader, is a private company, unlike state giant Gazprom. The project was completed on time and within budget despite being targeted by US sanctions. This was possible thanks to Chinese lenders, who swiftly replaced Western investment, and the switching of financing from dollars to euros (Siddi 2018c).

The TurkStream project is also nearing completion. Together with the Nord Stream pipelines, TurkStream is part of Gazprom's strategy to reduce drastically gas transit in Ukraine. It will transport 31.5 bcm/year of gas to Turkey and the EU along a route that goes from Russia's Black Sea coast to European Turkey under the Black Sea. In November 2018, the laying of the offshore part of the pipeline was completed. The pipeline began shipping gas to Turkey in January 2020. Most likely, the first string of TurkStream (with half the total capacity) will replace Russian gas exports to Turkey that are currently transported via Ukraine and the Balkans. The second string of the project is intended for exports to Southeast and Southern Europe. This section of the project would end at the Turkish-EU border, where it will be linked to the EU's system via a Turkey-Bulgaria interconnector and an onward pipeline from Bulgaria to Hungary through Serbia (Sharples 2019, p. 6).

The Nord Stream 2 Controversy

Nord Stream 2 is the new Gazprom-led project that has aroused more controversy in the EU. With a capacity of 55 bcm/year, it will carry gas from the Russian Baltic Sea coast to Germany via an offshore route running parallel to the already existing Nord Stream pipeline. Following its completion, the total capacity of the Nord Stream route will rise to 110 bcm/year, making it the main export corridor for Russian gas to Europe (Goldthau 2016, Lang and Westphal 2017). The project was announced in the summer of 2015 by a consortium including Gazprom, German companies Uniper and Wintershall, France's ENGIE, Austria's OMV, and Dutch/British Shell. Its proponents argued that Nord Stream 2 will connect Gazprom's newer gas fields in the Yamal Peninsula to its bigger customers in Western Europe through a shorter route without transit-related risks and fees. However, the project swiftly attracted criticism. Opponents argued that it will consolidate Gazprom's position in the European energy market and weaken Ukraine's role as a gas transit country, and thus Ukraine's strategic leverage vis-à-vis Moscow in the ongoing political crisis.

Poland, the Baltic States, Romania, and Slovakia have consistently opposed the project. Their opposition tends to be explained by a number of factors including strategic reasons (notably the loss of their current role as transit countries), the intention to diversify energy imports away from Russia, and concerns about being bypassed by the main flows of East-West energy trade (Lang and Westphal 2017, pp. 28–34; Strachota 2015). Long-standing fear of Russia, and of German-Russian cooperation, also plays a role in Poland and the Baltic states (Siddi 2018b). Slovakia sees its substantial revenues from transit fees as being endangered.

On the other hand, Germany and Austria have emerged as the main advocates of the project. France and the Netherlands appear acquiescent to it as well due to the involvement of domestic corporate interests. The main argument that has been put forward to support the project is that it follows commercial logic by linking supplier and customers with competitively priced gas (cf. Hecking and Weiser 2017). It has been argued that Nord Stream 2 can provide cheap gas to compensate for dwindling North Sea gas production. It will also meet further demand that will stem from the closure of nuclear power plants in Germany and the need to switch energy consumption from more polluting coal and oil to gas (▶ Energy Governance in Germany). The controversy around Nord Stream 2 reflects the tension, within the EU, between economic-driven and politically driven approaches to energy relations with Russia. On the one hand, the economic drivers of the relationship advocate the construction of the pipeline, citing commercial reasons. On the other hand, opponents argue against the project by focusing on political arguments, such as solidarity with Ukraine and Russia's aggressive foreign policy. Some scholars also argue that the project will be unprofitable (Neumann et al. 2018).

Caught between opposing views at member state level, EU institutions have taken different stances toward Nord Stream 2 (see also Siddi 2018d). The European Commission opposed the project. In June 2017, it requested a mandate from the Council of the EU to negotiate an agreement with Russia concerning the operation of Nord Stream 2, arguing that it was necessary to define a legal framework. The request seemed to respond to pressure by member states opposing Nord Stream 2 and had the apparent goal of limiting Gazprom's ability to use the pipeline's capacity. However, the Legal Service of the Council concluded that there was no legal basis for an EU-Russia agreement concerning the project. It also stated that the third energy package does not apply to the Nord Stream 2 pipeline (Yafimava 2017). The reasoning of the Legal Service of the Council reflected existing precedents: pipelines reaching the EU from third countries have been built in accordance with the United Nations Convention on the Law of the Sea, whereas the third energy package applied to pipelines on land within EU territory (▶ Chap. 9, "The EU in Global Energy Governance"). Based on this practice, in the case of Nord Stream 2, the package would apply to adjoining, land-based pipelines in the EU. Moreover, the EU energy market has been built around the principles of liberalization and competition, and political attempts to block new projects run counter to this logic.

However, the Commission – with the support of some Eastern members – insisted that a legal void existed. It partly adjusted its argument to claim that, following the introduction of the third energy package in 2009, its prescriptions concerning ownership unbundling and third party access applied not just to EU territory but also to the territorial waters of EU member states. This contradicted the earlier practice of applying the United Nations Convention on the Law of the Sea to regulate offshore pipelines until they reached land in the EU. In order to enforce its reasoning, the Commission proposed amending the Gas Directive, which is part of the third energy package, to make sure it would also apply to new offshore pipelines in member states' territorial waters. This stratagem would create uncertainty and hinder the operations of Nord Stream 2, thereby delaying the project (Yafimava 2019).

In order to become law, the amendment of the Gas Directive required the support of a qualified majority of member states (i.e., 55% of member states voting in favor and representing at least 65% of the total EU population). In 2017 and 2018, this seemed highly unlikely, as the opposition of Germany, France, and several other smaller EU members ensured the existence of a blocking minority. A turning point was reached in February 2019, when France suddenly voiced its support for amending the Gas Directive. The reasons for the change in the French position are unclear and have been described by some as a strategy to obtain concessions from Germany on other, unrelated EU-level issues (FAZ 2019). The French stance urged Germany to seek bilateral negotiations with France in order to achieve a compromise. Eventually, a common text was agreed that made the Gas Directive applicable to EU territorial waters but left the member state where the pipeline first lands in charge of implementation and of authorizing exemptions (which, however, have to be agreed upon by the European Commission). The Franco-German compromise was then endorsed by EU institutions (Gurzu 2019). The amendments became EU law, and member states are expected to transpose them into national law by May 2020.

To complicate matters further, the United States has intervened in the Nord Stream 2 debate through both Congress legislation and President Trump's fiery rhetoric. Legislation passed by Congress in the summer of 2017 threatened to sanction European companies involved in Nord Stream 2 and in other energy projects with Russian involvement. This led to a diplomatic argument with the German and Austrian governments. Berlin and Vienna argued that the US extraterritorial sanctions were illegal and that "Europe's energy supply network is Europe's affair, not that of the United States of America" (German Foreign Office 2017). Following negotiations with European diplomatic envoys, the 2017 legislation was softened with the addendum that sanctions would be imposed at the US president's discretion in coordination with US allies (US Congress 2017). In 2018, however, the US Congress passed a new draft law that could make the sanctions mandatory without requiring the approval of the US president or other coordination. Opponents of Nord Stream 2 saw the law as a powerful instrument to stop the project. Conversely, supporters of the pipeline consider the proposed extraterritorial sanctions as an illegal attempt to interfere in EU energy policy and promote US LNG exports as an alternative, regardless of their potentially higher cost for the EU and uncertainty about available volumes (Geopolitics of Energy).

Despite the risk of US sanctions, construction of the Nord Stream 2 pipelines started during the summer of 2018 and progressed in the following year and a half.

Following US-Russia negotiations in the fall of 2018, US punitive measures appeared less likely. However, in December 2019 the US Congress approved sanctions against Nord Stream 2, leading the Swiss constructor Allseas to suspend the laying of the pipeline in the Baltic Sea, when nearly all the work had been completed. US sanctions will probably fall short of the objective of preventing the project but will delay it by several months because Gazprom was forced to find another vessel with the capability of laying pipes in deep-sea waters (Platts 2019b). US sanctions also soured relations between Washington, on the one hand, and Germany, Russia, and other European countries on the other. The main reason is that, through their extraterritorial sanctions, the United States have interfered in European energy security and political affairs and violated international law (cf. European Parliament 2020).

The international controversy surrounding Nord Stream 2 and the opposition of some member states and the European Commission may thus lead to delays in its implementation, with gas deliveries starting well after January 2020, the date that was initially planned by Gazprom. Denmark delayed its permission to lay the pipeline in the Danish continental shelf for several months but eventually granted its authorization in late October 2019. In November 2019, Russian Deputy Prime Minister Dmitry Kozak stated that Nord Stream 2 will start shipping gas to Germany in mid-2020 (cited in Platts 2019a). This means that Gazprom will have to continue to export large volumes of gas via Ukraine into the 2020s (Pirani 2018).

Ukraine's Current and Future Role in EU-Russia Energy Trade

Many EU politicians consider the preservation of Ukraine's gas transit role as the most politically pressing issue in the light of Gazprom's new projects. Preserving gas transit in Ukraine would contribute to EU energy security because Russian gas would continue to be channeled to the EU via a commercially and strategically important route, in addition to those prioritized in Gazprom's export strategy (Nord Stream, TurkStream, and Yamal-Europe). While the ongoing conflict between Moscow and Kiev raised the risk of transit disruptions, the flow of gas to the EU has in fact continued and even increased. Moreover, the EU insists on upholding this transit route out of solidarity with Ukraine. Ukraine has earned $2–3 billion a year from transit revenues, which are important to its economy. The construction of alternative pipelines could deprive Kiev of this income, weakening it both financially and strategically vis-à-vis Russia. Ukrainian leaders fear that their country will lose its transit role in the 2020s.

Ukrainian concerns increased in February 2018 when Gazprom stated that it would start a termination procedure for its supply and transit contracts with Ukraine. Gazprom's statement was made in response to the outcome of a long-standing arbitration process concerning contracts with Ukraine's state company Naftogaz. After 2014, Gazprom and Naftogaz had filed claims against each other at the Arbitration Institute of the Stockholm Chamber of Commerce. The claims concerned the implementation of supply and transit contracts. A series of pronouncements left Gazprom with a net debt of $2.56 billion – a considerable sum but only a fraction of what the two companies were claiming from each other. Gazprom stated that it wished to terminate the current gas transit agreement with Ukraine in this context, before arguing that it would use all legal means to challenge the outcome of the arbitration (Eyl-Mazzega 2018). However, Gazprom's statement appears unlikely to have any concrete effects before additional infrastructure becomes available for its gas exports. Both in 2017 and in 2018, Gazprom channeled around 90 bcm/year via Ukraine. In order to maintain these export volumes, Ukrainian transit pipelines are indispensable at present.

Most likely, Ukrainian transit capacity will also be necessary after Nord Stream 2 and TurkStream are operational. Certainly, when these projects become fully operational, gas volumes via Ukraine will diminish markedly, but they will not disappear. Following Chancellor Angela Merkel's request that Ukrainian pipelines remain operational, in April 2018 Gazprom itself stated that at least 10–15 bcm/year will be exported via Ukraine. In fact, a larger export capacity via Ukraine will have to be maintained both to meet higher wintertime demand and to face the possibility of technical issues along the other routes. Additional Ukrainian transit will be necessary during the maintenance periods of the Nord Stream and TurkStream pipelines. Southern European customers of Gazprom have also expressed a desire to continue their imports via Ukraine (Pirani 2018, pp. 14–16). Furthermore, as long as the regulatory restrictions imposed by the EU on Gazprom's use of the OPAL pipeline remain in force, it will be more difficult to redirect gas flows from the Ukrainian to the Nord Stream route.

In 2019 Russia, Ukraine and the European Commission conducted negotiations on the transit of gas in Ukraine from January 2020. A breakthrough was achieved in December 2019. Gazprom and Naftogaz signed a 5-year transit contract, in which the Russian company agreed to ship a minimum of 65 bcm of gas in 2020 and a minimum of 40 bcm/year in 2021–2024, including a ship-or-pay clause (meaning that Gazprom would have to pay for the minimum contracted volumes even if it ships less). As part of these negotiations, Gazprom also agreed to pay the net debt resulting from the Stockholm arbitration, while Naftogaz promised to release the Gazprom assets it had seized in Europe in order to enforce the Stockholm arbitration court ruling. Both companies also agreed to drop reciprocal court claims that have not concluded, with the exception of those concerning assets in Crimea (Isachenkov 2019).

Hence, gas transit in Ukraine will certainly continue after 2019, but with smaller volumes than in the 2000s and 2010s. While transit volumes will diminish, it is also important to note that Ukraine is no longer as exposed to disruptions in gas supplies from Russia as it was in the past. Ukraine's gas demand has fallen from around 65 bcm in 2011 to approximately 35 bcm in 2017. Most of the current demand is covered by domestic gas production and imports from the EU (even though the latter include reverse flows of Russian gas). This means that while Ukraine will probably lose most of its leverage as a key transit country, Russia has also lost much of its leverage over Ukraine's energy security.

From the perspective of the EU's energy security and resilience, Ukrainian gas transit is a more complex and multifaceted matter than may appear from mainstream political debates. On the one hand, the EU feels obliged to show solidarity with Ukraine, which is also a fellow member of the Energy Community, an international organization that aims at extending the EU's energy *acquis* (Schubert et al. 2016, pp. 220–222) (▶ Chap. 9, "The EU in Global Energy Governance"). As argued, maintaining Ukrainian transit will contribute to the diversification of import routes. On the other hand, the Ukrainian pipeline network is old, with large parts of it dating back to Soviet times, and requires extensive investments. The new Russian gas fields are located further north than the West Siberian fields that have traditionally supplied gas to Europe and where production is now declining. These factors make the Nord Stream route to the large North-Western European markets shorter and thus more competitive in terms of transportation costs (Pirani 2018, p. 8, 16). Furthermore, for the EU, maintaining reliance on Ukrainian transit means remaining hostage to the heated Russian-Ukrainian relationship for its gas supplies, which is a controversial strategy from a commercial and energy security perspective.

Settling Disputes: The Antitrust and WTO Cases

Agreement on the rules regulating energy trade is particularly important for EU-Russia energy relations, where the two sides have developed partly different approaches and priorities. The EU has focused on the liberalization of its energy market, promoting competition between energy importers in order to achieve security of supply and cheaper prices for domestic consumers (Goldthau and Sitter 2019). On the other hand, as a major energy exporter, Russia has focused on the security of demand by minimizing price volatility, countering the competition of other suppliers, and concluding long-term contracts with its customers, which help cover the costs of building and maintaining the necessary export infrastructure (Siddi 2018a, pp. 1556–1557).

The different priorities of the EU and Russia regarding energy trade have complicated the pursuit of shared practices and norms. In East-Central Europe, Gazprom has been accused of monopolistic behavior, which led the European Commission to investigate the company's practices. In 2011, the Commission launched an antitrust investigation and subsequently accused Gazprom of abusing its dominant market position in Eastern Europe. According to the Commission, Gazprom's contracts in the region hindered the cross-border flow of gas, which resulted in the fragmentation of the regional market and different prices from country to country. However, in the ensuing negotiations, Gazprom committed to removing contractual barriers to the cross-border flow of gas (Stern and Yafimava 2017). It also linked gas prices in Eastern EU members to benchmark prices in Western European hubs. Gazprom's commitments will likely adjust prices in Eastern European markets that are isolated due to the lack of infrastructure to market-based prices in Western Europe. As a result, in May 2018 the European Commission ended its antitrust case against Gazprom, stating that it had secured substantial commitments from the

Russian company on more competitive prices and greater market integration for Eastern European member states (European Commission 2018).

By making these commitments, Gazprom has avoided a fine being imposed by the European Commission. However, the Russian company had to make important concessions and essentially change its marketing strategy from oil-linked contracts to more market-based and, at present, lower prices. Failure to honor the commitments could still lead to Gazprom being fined over the period until 2026. The resolution of the antitrust investigation on terms that are favorable to the EU, and are also accepted by Russia, has removed a major source of contention in EU-Russia energy relations. The EU's competition policy has led Gazprom to adapt its *modus operandi* in the European market in a way that is functional to market integration and competition.

Moreover, in mid-August 2018, the WTO published its ruling on Russia's complaint against the EU concerning certain provisions of the third energy package (see WTO 2018) (▶ Chap. 9, "The EU in Global Energy Governance"). The European Commission introduced the third energy package in 2009 with the aim of integrating the EU's energy market and increasing competition. One of its central requirements is unbundling the ownership of energy production and supply from that of energy transportation. In April 2014, Russia filed a complaint with the WTO about this legislation, arguing that it treated Russian gas and gas transportation services unfairly. However, the WTO ruled that the main principles of the third energy package are lawful. On the other hand, it also stated that some of its aspects were not in line with WTO norms. Most notably, this concerned a 50% cap imposed by the EU on the utilization capacity of the OPAL pipeline, a land-based continuation of the Nord Stream pipeline, which de facto artificially constrained the use of the latter. The WTO ruling also stated that the EU's Trans-European Networks for Energy (TEN-E) strategy, which aims at linking the infrastructure of EU members, was inconsistent with WTO law because it provided most favorable conditions for the transportation of natural gas of any origin other than Russian (thus discriminating against the latter).

While both the EU and Russia have appealed to the WTO's Appellate Body some legal interpretations of the WTO ruling, the latter has helped clarify the rules of EU-Russia gas trade. The EU was satisfied with the overall WTO assessment of the third energy package. In the years after Russia filed the complaint, Gazprom had largely adjusted its strategy to this new legislation. For the Russian company, the WTO pronouncement on the TEN-E strategy and the OPAL pipeline are seen as the main achievements. The WTO's view on OPAL strengthens the case for fuller utilization of the Nord Stream pipeline and can constitute a precedent for the Nord Stream 2 project. However, some EU member states – notably Poland – criticized this interpretation and challenged the Commission's decision to allow Gazprom to use OPAL's full capacity at the European Court of Justice (ECJ). In September 2019, the ECJ ruled in Poland's favor, thus reinstating a cap on OPAL's capacity used by Gazprom (for details, see General Court of the EU 2019). The ECJ's judgments seem to contradict the WTO ruling, which may again increase uncertainty concerning the regulatory framework of EU-Russia gas trade.

Nuclear Power

While fossil fuels, and gas in particular, have been at the center stage of debates on EU-Russia energy relations, nuclear power also plays a significant and growing role. There are several reasons for this. First, the Russian State Atomic Energy Corporation (Rosatom) is an important provider of enriched uranium to European customers. In 2017, it was the second largest supplier of uranium to the EU after Canada, providing 15% of EU imports (WNA 2018). Russia owns approximately half of the world's uranium enrichment capacity and is therefore a major provider in enrichment services (Oxenstierna 2014, p. 158). Second, several Soviet-built nuclear reactors and nuclear power plants are operational in EU member states, including the Czech Republic, Slovakia, Hungary, Bulgaria, and Finland (as well as 15 nuclear reactors in neighboring Ukraine). Russia supplies fuels to these reactors, and, in some cases, it also repatriates spent fuel (Oxenstierna 2014). Third, and most significant from a political perspective, Rosatom plans to build new reactors in Hungary and Finland. It is also building a new nuclear plant in Belarus and another one in Russia's Kaliningrad region, both near the border with Lithuania (with the goal of exporting part of the electricity production to the EU market).

Rosatom's new projects are part of a broader strategy to expand nuclear power production domestically and export Russian nuclear technology abroad. Rosatom's strategy dates back to 2006, when the Russian government launched an ambitious program to increase nuclear and reduce gas power generation. Rosatom has already secured contracts to build about 20 reactors abroad over the next two decades, mostly in Asia and the Middle East (see WNA 2019). The company's portfolio includes over one quarter of globally ongoing civilian nuclear power projects, making Rosatom the largest provider in this strategic sector (Aalto et al. 2017).

While Russia had not built a nuclear reactor for over two decades after the 1986 Chernobyl accident, the nuclear power industry remains one of the country's main high technology industries and has been considered a priority sector in the modernization policy launched in 2009 (Oxenstierna 2014, p. 150). Contrary to developments in some EU members such as Germany, the accident at Japan's Fukushima nuclear power plant in 2011 has not led to a revision of Russia's plans in the nuclear sector. Russia has a competitive advantage in this sector due to its low costs of producing uranium and the availability of state funding for new projects, both domestically and abroad. The main type of reactor currently produced and installed by Rosatom is the VVER, which is comparable to Western pressurized-water reactors (whereas production of RBMK reactors – the type installed at Chernobyl – stopped after the 1986 accident).

Rosatom's planned reactors in Hungary and Finland are significant for several reasons. Both projects were contracted relatively recently, in 2013–2014, and have remained practically unaffected by the political tensions surrounding the Ukraine crisis. They are expected to become operational in the 2020s. Both projects are taking place in EU member states that rely considerably on nuclear power for electricity production (35% of domestically produced electricity in Finland and 53% in Hungary). Rosatom committed to arranging a €10 billion loan, repayable until 2044, for the construction of the two new reactors in Hungary, which would cover most of the related costs (Aalto et al. 2017, p. 402).

Moreover, Rosatom's contracts in Finland and Hungary provide a key EU-area reference for its international activities (▶ Energy Governance in Finland). They represent a diplomatic triumph for Russia, as they increase political cooperation with the host countries due to the long-term nature and strategic significance of the contracts. Rosatom and advocates of the proposed reactors in the EU argue that they are functional to EU plans to decrease greenhouse gas emissions because they will allow replacing electricity generation from fossil fuels (Aalto et al. 2017, pp. 388–395).

Renewable Energy

Both the European Union and Russia have agendas to increase domestic production and consumption of non-hydrocarbon energy sources. The EU's targets for 2030 include a 40% reduction of fossil fuel emissions compared to 1990 levels, 32% of energy consumption from renewable sources, and an improvement of energy efficiency by 32.5% (European Commission 2019b). The targets set in Russia's Energy Strategy up to 2030 are much more modest (▶ Chap. 40, "Energy Governance in Russia: From a Fossil to a Green Giant?"). The strategy only limits carbon dioxide emissions in order not to exceed the level of 1990 by 2030. The target for electricity production from renewables was 4.5% for 2020 excluding large hydropower (and 20% including it) but was later revised to a more realistic 2.5% (IRENA 2017, p. 25). Support schemes were also introduced for renewable energy (Smeets 2018).

Improving energy efficiency has become a priority of the Russian government due to the high energy intensity of the Russian economy. The government is also promoting the productive utilization of associated petroleum gas in order to curb the practice of gas flaring (burning raw gas that comes to surface during crude oil extraction). Gas flaring volumes in Russia are very high, but the government has planned a 50-fold increase in related emission fees, which should lead to the productive utilization of 95% of associated petroleum gas by 2030 (Gromov and Kurichev 2014, pp. 27–30). Improving the energy intensity of industrial production and curbing gas flaring would considerably limit Russia's greenhouse gas emissions and improve its energy efficiency.

Moreover, Russia is planning to limit domestic consumption of fossil fuels for two main reasons: improving environmental security and freeing part of its oil and gas production for more lucrative sales in foreign markets. To increase non-hydrocarbon energy production, Russia's 2030 Energy Strategy envisaged the development of nuclear power plants (mainly) in European Russia and hydroelectric power plants in Eastern Siberia and the Far East, as well as other renewable energy sources. So far, Russia lags behind developed countries in the use of renewable energy. However, in many remote Russian regions, renewables would offer the best solution for decentralized consumers. Some limited positive steps have been made in the last 10 years. In 2010, the RusHydro company received the official status as head state company in the field of renewable energy and developed a few hydropower, wind power, and geothermal power plants (Gromov and Kurichev 2014, p. 35).

More recently, Russian institutions appear to have become more concerned about climate change and the urgency of the energy transition. In 2018, the Ministry of Natural Resources and Environment published a report highlighting the catastrophic environmental and economic consequences of climate change for Russia, including droughts, epidemics, food shortages, and the release of radioactive substances from melting permafrost. This refuted the argument according to which Russia would benefit economically from a warmer climate. Despite concerns that the energy transition will reduce Russia's income from fossil fuel exports (cf. Smeets 2018), Russia ratified the Paris climate agreement in September 2019 (Digges 2019a).

EU-Russia cooperation in the field of renewable energy sources is still limited (Khrushcheva and Maltby 2016). A promising area appears to be that of biofuels, where Russia can significantly increase its exports to the EU (Tynkkynen 2014). Moreover, the North-West of Russia boasts a large renewable energy resource base in geographic proximity to the EU. Developing this resource base could offer win-win prospects for both Russia and the EU: Russia could develop its renewable energy industry with Western technology at a lower cost, whereas EU member states could achieve their 2030 renewable energy targets by importing electricity produced from these sources in Russia (Boute and Willems 2012). EU companies have already become involved in the development of Russian wind power. Notably, Italian energy company Enel is building Russia's largest wind park in the Murmansk region and developing two more in the Stavropol and Rostov regions (Digges 2019b).

In terms of resources, Russia has the potential to become a leader in renewable energy production and consumption, including solar, wind, hydro, geothermal, and bioenergy (Tynkkynen 2014). The traditional forms of EU-Russia energy cooperation and existing path dependencies lead to a focus on the hydrocarbon sector. However, with the energy transition in Europe advancing, and the vast challenges posed by climate change, we can expect a partial and progressive shift of energy cooperation toward renewables. Russia's vast renewable sources offer bright prospects for cooperation and the involvement of Western companies and technologies, which would also shift EU-Russia energy cooperation toward a more sustainable framework.

Conclusion

Energy trade with Russia is one of the EU's largest and most strategic commercial relationships. For Russia, energy exports to the EU are the most significant component of its foreign trade. Current energy flows from Russia to the EU originated during the Cold War and grew exponentially since the 1980s. Fossil fuels, particularly oil and gas, are the most important energy sources in the relationship. Nuclear technology and fuel also play a significant and growing role. Moreover, Russia's vast and currently unexploited renewable energy sources offer new avenues for potential EU-Russia energy cooperation in the coming years. The nefarious effects of climate change, which are acknowledged by both EU and Russian institutions, could induce them to gradually shift the focus of their energy trade from fossil fuels to renewable energy.

For the time being, however, the EU and Russia have to manage their dependence on the import (for the EU) or export (for Russia) of fossil fuels. This trade has become more sensitive from a political perspective with the beginning of the Ukraine crisis and the broader confrontational trend in EU-Russia relations. The interdependent nature of EU-Russia energy relations, which was previously portrayed as a success of post-Cold War cooperation, is now seen by some politicians and scholars alike as a source of vulnerability for either side. This perception is particularly strong in some East-Central European members of the EU (Poland, the Baltic States), where the current political leadership tends to view EU-Russia energy trade as an instrument of Russian political pressure.

However, the path dependencies that have been forged over decades made the EU-Russia energy relationship resilient even to the deep political crisis that began in 2014. The necessity to preserve trade flows from Russia led the EU to take an active role in relevant negotiations. The European Commission successfully negotiated transit and supply agreements between Russia and Ukraine in 2014–2015. Despite the political crisis, EU-Russia energy trade continued and even reached new record volumes in 2017 and 2018. At the same time, the European Commission managed to settle an antitrust dispute with Gazprom through talks, thereby enforcing EU rules for commercial operations in the internal market. The fact that Gazprom has an interest in preserving its lucrative exports to the EU, and that it was put under pressure by other prospective suppliers (such as LNG producers), contributed to the EU's goals.

The main outstanding issue in EU-Russia energy relations concerns the routes through which Russian gas will be exported to the EU in the future, particularly the fate of Ukrainian transit pipelines. The EU has supported Ukraine politically and financially since Russia's annexation of Crimea in 2014, and preserving imports via Ukraine would be consistent with the strategy adopted thus far. Ukrainian transit pipelines constitute an important and currently indispensable corridor for EU gas imports from Russia. However, they are in need of renovation, and their commercial use is exposed to political crises between Kiev and Moscow. The completion of Nord Stream 2 and TurkStream could make them largely (but not completely) redundant within a few years.

Tripartite talks between Russia, Ukraine, and the European Commission have taken place in 2018–2019 and have secured the continuation of substantial gas transit in Ukraine in 2020–2024. The new 5-year transit deal meets the economic interests of all sides involved in the negotiations. Gazprom needs substantial Ukrainian transit capacity to satisfy the demand of its European customers and defend its shares of the EU market from competing suppliers. Ukraine needs to prove that it remains a reliable transit country in order to secure both a profitable business and continued EU support. Furthermore, the EU greatly benefits from the unhindered flow of competitive Russian energy through several routes, including Ukraine. If the EU and Russia intend to improve their relationship, energy cooperation can play a significant role thanks to existing networks and the potential for further mutually beneficial interaction.

Cross-References

▶ Energy Governance in Finland
▶ Energy Governance in Germany
▶ Energy Governance in Russia: From a Fossil to a Green Giant?
▶ Energy Governance in the Republic of Poland
▶ European Union Energy Policy: A Discourse Perspective
▶ The EU in Global Energy Governance

Acknowledgments I would like to thank Dr. Jack Sharples for his comments on an earlier draft of this chapter.

References

Aalto, P., Nyyssönen, H., Kojo, M., & Pal, P. (2017). Russian nuclear energy diplomacy in Finland and Hungary. *Eurasian Geography and Economics, 58*(4), 386–417.
Belyi, A. (2015). *Transnational gas markets and Euro-Russian energy relations*. Basingstoke: Palgrave Macmillan.
Blank, S., & Kim, Y. (2016). Economic warfare à la Russe: The energy weapon and Russian National Security Strategy. *The Journal of East Asian Affairs, 30*(1), 1–39.
Boersma, T., & Goldthau, A. (2017). Wither the EU's market making project in energy: From liberalization to securitization? In S. S. Andersen et al. (Eds.), *Energy union: Europe's new liberal mercantilism?* (pp. 99–113). Basingstoke: Palgrave.
Boute, A., & Willems, P. (2012). RUSTEC: Greening Europe's energy supply by developing Russia's renewable energy potential. *Energy Policy, 51*, 618–629.
Casier, T. (2011). The rise of energy to the top of the EU-Russia agenda: From interdependence to dependence? *Geopolitics, 16*(3), 536–552.
Casier, T. (2016). Great game or great confusion: The geopolitical understanding of EU-Russia energy relations. *Geopolitics, 21*(4), 763–778.
Digges, C. (2019a, September 6). Russia to sign Paris Accord as ministry forecasts climate change calamities. *Bellona*. https://bellona.org/news/climate-change/2019-09-russia-to-sign-paris-accord-as-ministry-forecasts-climate-change-calamities. Accessed 8 Nov 2019.
Digges, C. (2019b, October 14). Russia's largest wind park opens near Murmansk. *Bellona*. https://bellona.org/news/renewable-energy/2019-10-russias-largest-wind-park-opens-near-murmansk. Accessed 8 Nov 2019.
European Commission. (2015, February 15). A framework strategy for a resilient energy union, COM(2015) 80 final. https://eur-lex.europa.eu/legal-content/EN/TXT/?uri=COM%3A2015%3A80%3AFIN. Accessed 11 March 2020.
European Commission. (2018, May 24). *Antitrust: Commission imposes binding obligations on Gazprom to enable free flow of gas at competitive prices in Central and Eastern European gas markets*. Press Release. https://europa.eu/rapid/press-release_IP-18-3921_en.htm. Accessed 8 Nov 2019.
European Commission. (2019a). *Quarterly Report Energy on European Gas Markets 4/2018*. https://ec.europa.eu/energy/sites/ener/files/quarterly_report_on_european_gas_markets_q4_2018.pdf. Accessed 8 Nov 2019.
European Commission. (2019b). 2030 climate & energy framework. https://ec.europa.eu/clima/policies/strategies/2030_en. Accessed 8 Nov 2019.
European Parliament. (2020, February 4). Written answer of the European Commission to European Parliament enquiry. https://www.europarl.europa.eu/doceo/document/E-9-2019-002880-ASW_EN.pdf. Accessed 7 Feb 2020.

Eurostat. (2018). Main origin of primary energy imports, EU-28. https://ec.europa.eu/eurostat/statistics-explained/index.php?title=File:Main_origin_of_primary_energy_imports,_EU-28,_2006-2016_(%25_of_extra_EU-28_imports).png&oldid=398029. Accessed 8 Nov 2019.

Eyl-Mazzega, M. (2018). *The Gazprom-Naftogaz Stockholm arbitration awards: Time for settlements and responsible behaviour*. Paris: IFRI.

FAZ (Frankfurter Allgemeine Zeitung). (2019, March 25). Altmaier opfert Start-ups im Urheberrecht. https://www.faz.net/aktuell/wirtschaft/mehr-wirtschaft/wie-peter-altmaier-start-ups-im-urheberrecht-opfert-16107784.html. Accessed 11 March 2020.

Forsberg, T., & Haukkala, H. (2016). *The European Union and Russia relations*. Basingstoke: Palgrave.

Gazprom. (2019). Delivery statistics, http://www.gazpromexport.ru/en/statistics/. Accessed 8 Nov 2019.

General Court of the EU. (2019, September 10). Judgment in Case T-883/16 Poland v Commission, Luxembourg. Press Release no. 107/19. https://curia.europa.eu/jcms/upload/docs/application/pdf/2019-09/cp190107en.pdf. Accessed 8 Nov 2019.

German Foreign Office. (2017, June 15). Press Release. https://www.auswaertiges-amt.de/en/newsroom/170615-kern-russland/290666. Accessed 8 Nov 2019.

Godzimirski, J. (Ed.). (2019). *New political economy of energy in Europe: Power to project, power to adapt*. Basingstoke: Palgrave.

Goldthau, A. (2016). *Assessing Nord Stream 2: Regulation, geopolitics and energy security in the EU, Central Eastern Europe and the UK* (EUCERS strategy paper 10). London: King's College.

Goldthau, A., & Sitter, N. (2019). Regulatory or market power Europe? EU leadership models for international energy governance. In J. Godzimirski (Ed.), *New political economy of energy in Europe: Power to project, power to adapt* (pp. 27–47). Basingstoke: Palgrave.

Gorska, J. A. (2010). *Dealing with a Juggernaut: Analyzing Poland's policy toward Russia, 1989–2009*. Plymouth: Rowman & Littlefield.

Gromov, A., & Kurichev, N. (2014). The energy strategy up to 2030. In S. Oxenstierna & V. P. Tynkkynen (Eds.), *Russian energy and security up to 2030* (pp. 16–40). Abingdon: Routledge.

Gurzu, A. (2019, February 13). Nord Stream 2: Who fared best. *Politico*. https://www.politico.eu/article/the-winners-and-losers/. Accessed 8 Nov 2019.

Hecking, H., & Weiser, F. (2017). *Impacts of Nord Stream 2 on the EU natural gas market*. Cologne: Institute of Energy Economics. https://www.ewi.research-scenarios.de/cms/wp-content/uploads/2017/09/EWI-1163-17-Studie-Impacts-of-Nord-Stream-2-web.compressed.pdf. Accessed 27 Nov 2018.

Henderson, J., & Sharples, J. (2018). *Gazprom in Europe – Two "Anni Mirabiles", but can it continue?* Oxford: Oxford Institute for Energy Studies.

Högselius, P. (2013). *Red gas: Russia and the origins of European energy dependence*. Basingstoke: Palgrave.

Honoré, A. (2018). *Natural gas demand in Europe in 2017 and short term expectations*. Oxford: Oxford Institute for Energy Studies.

Interfax Ukraine. (2018, January 2). Ukraine sees 13.7% rise in gas transit in 2017. https://en.interfax.com.ua/news/economic/474366.html. Accessed 8 Nov 2019.

IRENA (International Renewable Energy Agency). (2017). Renewable energy prospects for the Russian Federation. Working Paper. https://www.irena.org/-/media/Files/IRENA/Agency/Publication/2017/Apr/IRENA_REmap_Russia_paper_2017.pdf. Accessed 8 Nov 2019.

Isachenkov, A. (2019, December 31). Russia, Ukraine finalize deals for gas transit to Europe. Associated Press. https://apnews.com/4615057928c343afb421a24cdd0bedf1. Accessed 7 Feb 2020.

Judge, A., Maltby, T., & Sharples, J. (2016). Challenging reductionism in analyses of EU-Russia energy relations. *Geopolitics, 21*(4), 751–762.

Khrushcheva, O., & Maltby, T. (2016). The future of EU-Russia energy relations in the context of decarbonisation. *Geopolitics, 21*(4), 799–830.

Krickovic, A. (2015). When interdependence produces conflict: EU–Russia energy relations as a security dilemma. *Contemporary Security Policy, 36*(1), 3–26.

Kuzemko, C. (2014). Ideas, power and change: Explaining EU–Russia energy relations. *Journal of European Public Policy, 21*(1), 58–75.

Lang, K., & Westphal, K. (2017). *Nord Stream 2 – A political and economic contextualization* (SWP research paper 3). Berlin: Stiftung Wissenschaft und Politik.

Ministry of Energy of the Russian Federation. (2010). Energy Strategy of Russia for the Period up to 2030. http://www.energystrategy.ru/projects/docs/ES-2030_(Eng).pdf. Accessed 8 Nov 2019.

Neumann, A., Göke, L., Holz, F., Kemfert, C., & Von Hirschhausen, C. (2018). Natural gas supply: No need for another Baltic Sea pipeline. DIW Weekly Report 27/2018. Berlin: Deutsches Institut für Wirtschaftsforschung. https://www.diw.de/documents/publikationen/73/diw_01.c.593663.de/dwr-18-27-1.pdf. Accessed 27 Nov 2018.

Oxenstierna, S. (2014). Nuclear power in Russia's energy policies. In S. Oxenstierna & V. P. Tynkkynen (Eds.), *Russian energy and security up to 2030* (pp. 150–168). Abingdon: Routledge.

Oxenstierna, S., & Tynkkynen, V. P. (2014). *Russian energy and security up to 2030*. Abingdon: Routledge.

Pirani, S. (2018). *Russian gas transit through Ukraine after 2019: The options* (Oxford energy insight 41). Oxford: Oxford Institute for Energy Studies.

Pirani, S., Stern, J., & Yafimava, K. (2009). *The Russo-Ukrainian gas dispute of January 2009: A comprehensive assessment*. Oxford: Oxford Institute for Energy Studies.

Platts. (2019a). Russia expects to delay Nord Stream 2 launch to mid-2020: Report. https://www.spglobal.com/platts/en/market-insights/latest-news/natural-gas/112119-russia-expects-to-delay-nord-stream-2-launch-to-mid-2020-report. Accessed 28 Nov 2019.

Platts. (2019b, 21 December). Nord Stream 2 pipelayer Allseas suspends operations on US sanctions. https://www.spglobal.com/platts/en/market-insights/latest-news/natural-gas/122119-nord-stream-2-pipelayer-allseas-suspends-operations-on-us-sanctions. Accessed 7 Feb 2020.

Prontera, A. (2019). *Beyond the EU regulatory state: Energy security and the Eurasian gas market*. Colchester: ECPR Press.

Romanova, T. (2016). Is Russian energy policy towards the EU only about geopolitics? The case of the third liberalisation package. *Geopolitics, 21*(4), 857–879.

Schubert, S., Pollak, J., & Kreutler, M. (2016). *Energy policy of the European Union*. Basingstoke: Palgrave.

Sharples, J. (2016). The shifting geopolitics of Russia's natural gas exports and their impact on EU-Russia gas relations. *Geopolitics, 21*(4), 880–912.

Sharples, J. (2019). European geopolitical forum – Gazprom Monitor 95, April.

Siddi, M. (2016). The EU's energy union: A sustainable path to energy security? *The International Spectator, 51*(1), 131–144.

Siddi, M. (2017). *National Identities and foreign policy in the European Union: The Russia policy of Germany, Poland and Finland*. Colchester: ECPR Press.

Siddi, M. (2018a). The role of power in EU–Russia energy relations: The interplay between markets and geopolitics. *Europe-Asia Studies, 70*(10), 1552–1571.

Siddi, M. (2018b). Identities and vulnerabilities: The Ukraine crisis and the securitization of the EU-Russia gas trade. In K. Szulecki (Ed.), *Energy security in Europe: Divergent perceptions and policy challenges* (pp. 251–273). Basingstoke: Palgrave.

Siddi, M. (2018c, May 9). The Arctic route for Russian LNG opens. WE – World Energy. https://www.aboutenergy.com/en_IT/topics/arctic-route-for-russian-lng-opens.shtml. Accessed 8 Nov 2019.

Siddi, M. (2018d). *Russia's evolving gas relationship with the European Union: Trade surges despite political crises* (Briefing paper 246). Helsinki: Finnish Institute of International Affairs.

Siddi, M. (2019). The EU's botched geopolitical approach to external energy policy: The case of the southern gas corridor. *Geopolitics, 24*(1), 124–144.

Smeets, N. (2018). The green menace: Unraveling Russia's elite discourse on enabling and constraining factors of renewable energy policies. *Energy Research and Social Science, 40*, 244–256.

Stern, J., & Yafimava, K. (2017). *The EU competition investigation of Gazprom's sales in central and eastern Europe: A detailed analysis of the commitments and the way forward* (OIES paper NG 121). Oxford: Oxford Institute for Energy Studies.

Strachota, A. L. (2015, November 23). The case against Nord Stream 2. *Energy Post.* https://energypost.eu/case-nord-stream-2/. Accessed 8 Nov 2019.

Stulberg, A. (2015). Out of gas?: Russia, Ukraine, Europe, and the changing geopolitics of natural gas. *Problems of Post-Communism, 62*(2), 112–130.

Szulecki, K. (Ed.). (2018). *Energy security in Europe: Divergent perceptions and policy challenges.* Basingstoke: Palgrave.

Tichý, L. (2019). *EU-Russia energy relations*. Cham: Springer.

Tynkkynen, V. P. (2014). Russian bioenergy and the EU's renewable energy goals: Perspectives of security. In S. Oxenstierna & V. P. Tynkkynen (Eds.), *Russian energy and security up to 2030* (pp. 95–113). Abingdon: Routledge.

US Congress. (2017). Countering America's adversaries through Sanctions Act. https://www.treasury.gov/resource-center/sanctions/Programs/Pages/caatsa.aspx. Accessed 8 Nov 2019.

Van de Graaf, T., & Colgan, J. D. (2017). Russian gas games or well-oiled conflict? Energy security and the 2014 Ukraine crisis. *Energy Research & Social Science, 24*, 59–64.

Wigell, M., & Vihma, A. (2016). Geopolitics versus geoeconomics: The case of Russia's geostrategy and its effects on the EU. *International Affairs, 92*(3), 605–627.

WNA (World Nuclear Association). (2018). Nuclear power in the European Union. https://www.world-nuclear.org/information-library/country-profiles/others/european-union.aspx. Accessed 8 Nov 2019.

WNA (World Nuclear Association). (2019). Nuclear power in Russia. https://www.world-nuclear.org/information-library/country-profiles/countries-o-s/russia-nuclear-power.aspx. Accessed 8 Nov 2019.

WTO (World Trade Organization). (2018). European Union and its member states – Certain measures relating to the energy sector. https://www.wto.org/english/tratop_e/dispu_e/cases_e/ds476_e.htm. Accessed 8 Nov 2019.

Yafimava, K. (2017). *The council legal service's assessment of the European Commission's negotiating mandate and what it means for Nord Stream 2*. Oxford: Oxford Institute for Energy Studies.

Yafimava, K. (2019). *Gas directive amendment: Implications for Nord Stream 2* (Energy insight 49). Oxford: Oxford Institute for Energy Studies.

EU-US and EU-Canada Energy Relations

12

Petra Dolata

Contents

Introduction	264
Historical Developments: Creating Path Dependencies	266
United States	266
Canada	270
Rivalry and Partnership	272
Transatlantic Energy Relations: Multiple Issues and Levels of Engagement	273
The Nature of Transatlantic Energy Relations	273
The United States	275
Canada	278
The United States, Canada, the European Union, and Multilevel Energy Governance	281
Future Directions	283
Cross-References	283
References	283

Abstract

Transatlantic energy relations cover various areas of engagement: energy governance, energy markets, and energy diplomacy. While not always prominent, energy has formed an integral part of American, and to a lesser extent Canadian, involvement with Europe and the European integration project ever since the end of the Second World War. During the Cold War, these energy relations went well beyond economic considerations and took on political and strategic significance, creating path dependencies for today's transatlantic interactions in the energy issue area. The historical entanglement of political or even strategic goals and economic objectives makes it difficult to establish the exact nature of transatlantic energy relations. Historically, these interactions oscillated between complementarity and competition as energy policy goals were either shared or diverged. More recently, the nexus between energy and climate has added a new direction to

P. Dolata (✉)
Department of History, University of Calgary, Calgary, AB, Canada
e-mail: pdolata@ucalgary.ca

© Springer Nature Switzerland AG 2022
M. Knodt, J. Kemmerzell (eds.), *Handbook of Energy Governance in Europe*,
https://doi.org/10.1007/978-3-030-43250-8_55

transatlantic energy relations. To understand the European Union's energy relations with the United States and Canada, it is essential to outline historical developments and examine direct bilateral or trilateral energy diplomacy in addition to multilateral energy governance structures, which include all three players.

Keywords

EU · Canada · United States · Transatlantic relations · EU-US energy relations · EU-Canada relations · Energy diplomacy

Introduction

Energy is foundational to human life and fuels prosperous economies. Because hydrocarbon energy resources – coal, natural gas, and especially oil, which makes up the majority of internationally traded energy carriers to date – are finite and unevenly spread over the world, energy is a highly politicized issue area, which has been defined by intense international competition between countries and regions, including at times across the Atlantic Ocean (Deni and Smith Stegen 2014). Despite energy's centrality and the potential for conflict, global energy governance remains fragmented, dispersed, and underdeveloped (Lesage et al. 2010: Chap. 4; Florini and Sovacool 2009; Leal-Arcas 2016), even dysfunctional (Dubash and Florini 2011). Mirroring this lack of comprehensive energy governance on a regional level, with the exception of separate communities for coal (European Coal and Steel Community, ECSC 1952) and nuclear power (European Atomic Energy Commission, EURATOM 1958), European integration did not include energy for a long time. The European communities lacked explicit jurisdiction over oil and instruments to pursue a common energy policy. Despite some decisions and regulations in the 1990s and early 2000s, which aimed at liberalizing internal EU electricity and gas markets and included the establishment of energy policy as a separate policy field through the Maastricht Treaty in 1993, it was not until 2007 that the Lisbon Treaty established EU competences in energy in December, which came into effect in 2009. Earlier that year, the Commission had presented "An Energy Policy for Europe" and a "New Energy Policy for Europe" was adopted by the European Council (Andoura and Vinois 2015; Duffield and Birchfield 2011; Van der Linde 2007).

Article 194(1) of the Treaty on the Functioning of the European Union postulates that EU energy policy should aim to "(a) ensure the functioning of the energy market; (b) ensure security of energy supply in the Union; (c) promote energy efficiency and energy saving and the development of new and renewable forms of energy; and (d) promote the interconnection of energy networks" (European Union 2012). Based on these desiderata and following the 2014 decision by the European Council to make the Energy Union a strategic EU objective, the European Commission presented the Energy Union strategy in 2015, which rests on five pillars, namely energy security; integrated internal energy market; energy efficiency; decarbonizing the economy; and research and innovation. The inclusion of energy efficiency and decarbonization as separate goals highlights the interlinkages between energy and climate policy, which have become apparent since the late 1990s but only entered a comprehensive European energy agenda in 2007 with climate policy's remit extending well beyond the geographical confines of the European Union, affecting its international role as a norm entrepreneur. The nexus between climate and energy also highlights divergent competencies between the EU Commission and EU member states. While energy policy within the European Union and climate policies are supranational competencies, external energy relations, like EU foreign and security policy more generally, remain intergovernmental (Buchan 2009; Youngs 2020). The European External Action Service (EEAS) was established in late 2010 as a separate institution to pursue external policies. And while the EEAS has been very active in signing energy agreements and launching energy dialogues with third countries and within producing regions, the above-quoted article of the Lisbon Treaty also specifies that "measures shall not affect a Member State's right to determine the conditions for exploiting its energy resources, its choice between different energy sources and the general structure of its energy supply" (European Union 2012). As a result, and regardless of the increasing institutionalization of the Energy Union internally and the introduction of an Energy Diplomacy concept by the EEAS in 2015 (Youngs 2020), pursuing a common foreign energy policy has remained difficult and is still characterized by a lack of coherence as national approaches and energy mixes as well as bilateral agreements undermine a collective foreign EU energy policy (Focken 2015; Georgiou and Rocco 2017; Maltby 2013). Finally, oil remained outside a common EU energy policy as it is internationally traded and available on international markets while its transportation, unlike natural gas, is more flexible (Andoura and Vinois 2015; Goldthau and Witte 2010).

These challenging conditions have also affected transatlantic energy relations, which cover various areas of engagement: energy governance, energy markets, and energy diplomacy (Chaban and Knodt 2015). While not always prominent, energy has formed an integral part of American, and to a lesser extent Canadian, involvement with Europe and the European integration project ever since the end of the Second World War. During the Cold War, these energy relations went well beyond economic considerations and took on political and strategic significance, creating path dependencies for today's transatlantic interactions in the energy issue area. From the early beginnings of European integration in the late 1940s, the United States played a significant role as facilitator. In addition to integrating coal and steel markets, early US attempts at rebuilding Western Europe through the European Recovery Program, better known as the Marshall Plan, also had some clear energy-related objectives. The historical entanglement of political or even strategic goals and economic objectives has made it difficult to establish the exact nature of transatlantic energy relations. Historically, these interactions oscillated between complementarity and competition as energy policy goals were either shared or diverged. The fact that the United States and Canada were at various times net oil and gas producers and exporters while European countries quickly became net consumers further complicates these relations, as have the more recent linkages between energy and climate policy goals (Dubash and Florini 2011). To understand the European Union's energy relations with the United States and Canada, it is essential to outline historical developments and examine direct bilateral or trilateral energy diplomacy in addition to multilateral energy governance structures, which include all three players.

Historical Developments: Creating Path Dependencies

United States

From the late 1940s onwards, the United States was involved in European integration as they helped bring about its first institution, the European Coal and Steel Community (ECSC), which came into force in 1952 (Neuss 2000). The immediate post-war years brought major energy crises to war-torn Western Europe due to shortages of coal, which still fueled more than 80% of ECSC economies and kept Europeans warm during cold winters (Duffield and Birchfield 2011). In order to address these shortcomings and jumpstart Western Europe's reconstruction, production in the most important European coal region located in the West German Ruhr valley needed to be ramped up. In US decision-makers' views, providing energy for daily necessities and keeping the population warm and fed would also fortify a democratic West Germany against potential Communist propaganda as the Cold War unfolded. At the same time, French-German rapprochement and an integrated coal and steel industry were seen as more than just economic necessities. To sustain peace in Europe, German coal and steel industries needed to be folded into a supranational regime ensuring that these strategic resources were not misused for future German rearmament. While proposed by French foreign minister Robert Schuman and based on plans by economist Jean Monnet who envisaged a sectoral institution around French-German economic ties (Diebold 1959), the successful establishment of the European Coal and Steel Community was also a political bargain between the United States and West Germany (Lovett 1996).

Geir Lundestad has coined the expression "empire by invitation" to denote this intricate relationship involving American support for European integration, which allowed for self-organization as well as military containment of Germany and the Soviet Union. As a consequence, "European economies were integrated into an Atlantic framework" (Lundestad 2012). This was especially true for energy. While early approaches by the United States to facilitate the rebuilding and fortification of Western Europe against the Communist East included deliberate strategies to help these European countries, which often relied on coal, to strengthen their existing coal production, these efforts were soon replaced by not entirely altruistic attempts to facilitate the transition of Western European countries to modern petroleum-based economies. With the help of the Marshall Plan and later investment programs administered by the Organisation for Economic Co-operation and Development (OEEC), Western European countries were able to use US dollars to pay for Middle Eastern oil produced by US multinationals and build an extensive network of refineries (Painter 2009). In addition, US domestic energy policy led to a redirection of Middle Eastern oil exports from North America to Europe, when the Eisenhower administration gave in to domestic interest group pressure and curtailed the flow of Middle Eastern oil into the United States through the implementation of a Mandatory Oil Import Program in 1959. In 1963 the European Economic Community abolished import duties on crude oil. As a result, "cheap oil flooded European markets," drastically increasing its share of total primary energy consumption in Western Europe from 10% to almost 50% in the two decades after 1945 (Kander et al. 2013).

The main benefactors were US multinationals who produced oil in the Middle East. Western European societies became increasingly dependent on oil and it was mainly delivered from the Middle East, where until the 1970s it was produced under the auspices of seven leading multinational companies, the so-called Seven Sisters, five of which were based in the United States. This transatlantic energy connection was challenged as events in the oil-producing regions wedded political, strategic, and economic issues. The 1956 Suez Crisis, during which the Egyptian government closed the Suez Canal to tankers shipping oil to Europe, highlighted Europe's increasing dependence on oil shipments from the Middle East, which also gave the United States power over its European allies. In an attempt to coerce Britain and France during the crisis to withdraw their forces from the region, the Eisenhower administration threatened to withhold replacement oil deliveries from the Western hemisphere to Europe (McDermott 1998).

The oil shortage during the Suez Crisis was one of the many reasons why calls to expand the powers of the ECSC to include other forms of energy, especially oil, became louder during the discussions that led to the signing of the Treaty of Rome in 1957. However, while the treaty established the European Economic Community (EEC) and the European Atomic Energy Community (EURATOM), no equivalent community for oil was formed as negotiations had already progressed too far at this stage. Nor did a common energy market emerge in the following decades, despite the creation of the Inter-executive Working Party on Energy in the early 1960s, its 1962 political memorandum, a 1968 Commission publication proposing a framework for action to create a Community energy policy, and various other attempts by the Commission in the 1970s and early 1980s to align member states' energy policies (Duffield and Birchfield 2011; Stingelin 1975; Van der Linde 2007).

As a result, until recently, two of the most important energy carriers, oil and natural gas, remained outside community jurisdiction. At the same time, oil became an important linchpin across the Atlantic as the United States functioned as a swing producer, who could easily increase production if needed and provide oil in times of supply crises until the 1970s. Beginning with the 1956 Suez Crisis, Western Europe could count on oil deliveries from the Western hemisphere whenever regular supplies were turned off due to political events in the Middle East, including during the 1967 Arab oil embargo. Thus, the impacts of various oil supply crises on Western Europe's economies were significantly softened. Until the 1970s, the site of these coordinated transatlantic attempts to ensure Western European economic and political stability during the Cold War was the Oil Committee of the Organization for Economic Co-operation and Development (OECD), which was founded in 1948 as the Organisation for European Economic Co-operation (OEEC) to administer the Marshall Plan and was reorganized into a transatlantic institution in 1961, when Canada and the United States joined (Türk 2014b).

However, limitations of this OECD Oil Committee to deal with major disruptions became obvious during the 1973 oil price crisis. This historic energy crisis, which resulted from the double impact of another oil embargo by Middle Eastern producers and a price hike on posted prices instituted by the Organization of the Petroleum Exporting Countries (OPEC), exposed far-reaching transformations in the international oil order. Not only did the United States cease to function as a swing producer, but it also became a net consumer of oil itself. No longer could it protect its allies in Western Europe by providing alternative supplies whenever regular shipments from the Middle East were stalled for political reasons. At the same time, the Seven Sisters were losing their dominant role as national governments in oil-producing countries in the Middle East took control of production both through raising posted prices and royalties and through nationalizing the oil industry (Venn 1999, 2002). The European Community reacted to the new situation by proposing a new energy policy strategy and direct engagement with the Middle East, making it the priority of the newly established European Political Co-operation (Miller 2014; Noor 2004; Stingelin 1975). The United States did not accept such a unilateral approach and insisted that the West needed to work together as it faced the energy crisis and producers in the Middle East. Now that the transatlantic partners shared similar energy vulnerabilities, and with the OECD Oil Committee insufficiently addressing them, a new institution was needed and proposed by the United States. Following an energy conference in Washington D.C. in February 1974, the International Energy Agency (IEA) was founded later that year. Except France, all Western European OECD members joined the IEA along with Canada and the United States, and the European Community also took part in its work. However, it was difficult to present a joint European position. France was opposed to the establishment of the IEA, and the UK, which had only joined the EEC in 1973, was on the verge of becoming a significant oil and gas producer through its North Sea reserves and did not share the same priorities as oil-dependent member states. Guided by US philosophies and designs, the IEA created an emergency oil share system, collected energy data, and provided a framework for energy cooperation among consumer states (Türk 2014a, b).

Increasingly, the goal of the United States to achieve energy security determined their international energy diplomacy. Encapsulated by the 1980 Carter Doctrine, the United States would even defend its energy (supply) security militarily, turning an internationally traded commodity into a strategic good. Not surprisingly, in the early 1980s energy and energy security were also introduced and discussed within NATO, another intergovernmental forum in which North American and European partners would meet. However, European member states resisted a more formal inclusion of energy security into a modified NATO agenda. Once oil prices plummeted in the 1980s, the urgency of designing a concerted strategy to address energy security within NATO vanished. It resurfaced again when the end of the Cold War and the two Gulf Wars (1991, 2003) brought back the geopolitical debate about oil, and increasingly natural gas, in the 1990s and early 2000s. In a dramatically changing world and during a time period when trade liberalization played a significant role, the relationship between the United States and the European Union became an important strategic partnership in a changing world. At the same time, the energy sector provided potentially the easiest area in which Europe and Russia could collaborate and build trust in the post-Cold War 1990s. In order to agree on rules of engagement a European Energy Charter was established in 1991 and a legally binding Energy Charter Treaty was signed in 1994 (Axelrod 1996).

Events in the strategic oil-producing ellipsis of Russia, the Middle East, and the Caspian region not only brought oil to the fore of international politics once again but also highlighted the shared oil dependence across the Atlantic and facilitated closer transatlantic cooperation. This also included a renewed focus on energy transport infrastructure both at sea and, more importantly, on land and specifically through pipelines. Pipeline politics became an important aspect of American foreign energy diplomacy from the mid-1990s as Washington hoped to open up new oil fields in the Caspian region and transportation possibilities that circumvented Russia. The geopolitical and commercial competition between a Russian-Italian pipeline joint venture (South Stream) and an EU-backed pipeline project (Nabucco) to bring Caspian oil to Europe dominated energy headlines during the first two decades of the twenty-first century (Abbasov 2014; Conley et al. 2016). However, comparing the rivalry to the New Great Game, media coverage may have overemphasized the geopolitical dimension (Baev and Øverland 2010). In the meantime, both the Nabucco and South Stream projects were canceled, in 2013 and 2014 respectively. Generally, the United States responded with irritation whenever European partners would cooperate too closely with Russian energy companies, fearing that this would jeopardize Europe's energy security. Based on an understanding of oil as a strategic good, the United States did not condone what some European countries saw as commercial relations. This divergent view of energy relations with the Soviet Union/Russia had already begun during the Cold War when West Germany concluded oil supply deals with the Soviet Union (Bösch 2014). More recently, in December 2019, tensions resurfaced when the United States sanctioned companies and governments involved in the Nord Stream 2 pipeline, an underwater gas pipeline in the Baltic Sea which directly connects Russia with Germany, circumventing transit through Ukraine.

In the mid-2000s discussions around peak oil and increasing oil demand of large economies such as the United States, China, and India led to fears of depleting global supplies and a renewed focus on the strategic significance of oil. Institutions such as the G8 and NATO but also the European Union put energy security on their meeting agendas. Russia's pipeline disputes with Ukraine and Belarus in 2006 and 2007 had forced European leaders to address their import dependence and discuss a common approach. Such discussions became even more urgent as new EU and NATO member states in Central and Eastern Europe, whose dependence on Russian supplies was significant, saw these developments as a matter of national security. As a consequence, the Lisbon Treaty not only devoted an entire chapter to energy policy but also explicitly mentions energy security as one of its goals. However, while the urgency of addressing climate change intensified toward the end of the decade, energy security became less of an issue as the price of oil, which had peaked just short of $150 in July 2008, fell again and the shale revolution in the United States brought more unconventional oil and gas on the market. The 2014 Ukrainian crisis rekindled a sense of urgency, but EU energy policy had begun to champion diversification of supply as key to ensuring energy security. This diversification was not to be achieved through focusing on new producing regions but through switching to clean energy technologies and emphasizing energy efficiency, and culminated in the passing of the European Green Deal in 2019.

Discussions on energy security were closely linked to another major development since the turn of the century, namely the increasing urgency of climate action. The EU had already paid attention to the issue of climate change in the 1990s and became increasingly vocal about the linkages of climate, energy, and security in the early 2000s (Dubash and Florini 2011). Instituting climate regulations and policies early on, it considered itself a leader and normative entrepreneur in the issue area. By the end of the decade, climate and energy policy were considered together and viewed as two sides of the same coin, as climate change and competition for energy resources were inextricably linked (Vogler 2013). In 2008, the European Union adopted the Climate and Energy Package which introduced binding legislation to ensure that by 2020 EU emissions would be reduced by 20% from 1990 levels, 20% of EU energy consumption would be met by renewables, and the European Union's energy efficiency would be improved by 20% (the so-called 20-20-20 target). Most recently, the European Union, Canada, and the United States all proposed net-zero emissions goals to address the impact of climate change on the economic and environmental well-being of societies all over the globe.

Canada

With a few important exceptions, Canada joined the United States in many of its transatlantic energy relations described above. A founding member of NATO and equally interested in pacifying and reconstructing Western Europe, Canada shared the US policy priorities of the Marshall Plan, to which it also provided separate funding. It joined the OECD in 1960, the IEA in 1974, and the G7 in 1976 along with its closest ally, the United States. While not always sharing the energy vulnerability of its European partners as it became a considerable energy producer, Canada acknowledged the strategic significance of oil and the Middle Eastern region and agreed on the necessity of a joint transatlantic approach to dealing with energy security. Because Canada's energy production relies on carbon dioxide-intensive oil sands and due to different priorities of various Canadian governments, the country's commitments to the Kyoto Protocol and Paris Agreement have been uneven in the past, although more recently Canada has joined the United States and EU in committing to similar net-zero goals. There are, however, two significant specific historical developments that had an enduring impact on Canada-EU relations and that were distinct from broader transatlantic relations between North America and the European Union. Both have to do with the country's significance as a resource-rich economy.

Canada is one of the world's leading producers of uranium making it an important partner for countries pursuing civil use of nuclear power and a significant player in nuclear politics internationally in the 1970s. In response to the 1970s oil price crisis and until nuclear accidents such as the one at Three Mile Island (1979) made it more controversial, nuclear power was considered a viable and desirable alternative to petroleum. Already in the fall of 1959 and as the first third country, Canada had concluded an agreement with the European Atomic Energy Commission (EURATOM) to supply uranium and collaborate on the peaceful use of nuclear power. After India, which had purchased a Canadian heavy water reactor model in the 1960s, detonated a nuclear bomb in 1974, Canada focused even more on nuclear safeguards to ensure that its nuclear technology and uranium would not be used for military purposes. The absence of sufficient safeguards in the 1959 EU-Canada EURATOM agreement constituted a problem for Canada, who did not want to discriminate against other customers in the Global South, but also feared that France, a nuclear power who had not acceded to the 1968 Non-Proliferation Treaty until 1992, could use Canadian uranium for non-peaceful purposes since EURATOM allowed for free movement of nuclear material within the Community. Canada's tightening of restrictions coincided with the increased demand for nuclear power in the wake of the 1973/74 energy crisis and created tensions with the European Economic Community when Ottawa imposed an embargo on uranium exports in early 1977 which lasted until early February. At this time Canada supplied about 30–35% of uranium used in the Community, although most of it was natural and not in enriched form, partly because Canada was still hoping that some European member states would be interested in Canada's nuclear reactor technology (CANDU) which used natural uranium. Because West Germany had contractual obligations to provide uranium to Soviet facilities which would enrich the uranium, it created major dissonances between Canada and the Community. It also ran counter to the institutionalization of Canada-EEC relations which had only been achieved in 1976. Fortunately for both sides, in early 1978 an interim solution was reached and various amendments to the 1959 Canada-EURATOM agreement were added in the following years (Boardman 1981; Bratt 2006).

Energy also played an integral part in facilitating closer relations between Canada and the communities in the 1970s. During the 1973/74 oil price crisis which highlighted Western Europe's dependence on oil and more generally natural resources, Canada became a highly sought-after supplier country for the EEC. Famous for its abundance in raw materials it was coveted as an ideal and complementary partner. The EEC hoped that through institutionalizing relations with Canada it would obtain guaranteed access to these raw materials, including energy resources. Canada, on the other hand, was more interested in diversifying its economic relations away from the United States as well as nuclear safeguards and adding value before exporting any resources. A "contractual link" was finally achieved in July 1976, when Canada and the EEC signed a Framework Agreement for Commercial and Economic Cooperation, which came into force in October 1976. It was the first formal agreement of its kind between the European Economic Community and an industrialized third country (Barry 2004; Potter 1999). Under this agreement, Canada and the EEC committed "to develop and diversify their reciprocal commercial exchanges and to foster economic co-operation." However, it only established a more formal forum for discussing economic relations, including resource diplomacy between the two signatories. During the disagreement over nuclear safeguards and Canada's uranium export embargo, the Joint Cooperation Committee created by the Framework Agreement functioned as a negotiation site (Boardman 1981). At least the agreement facilitated trust and provided opportunities for open discussions in its first years. However, in the long run, bilateral trade disputes were managed through direct high-level contacts or in multilateral fora such as the World Trade Organization (WTO) or in the case of the 1996 turbot war the Northwest Atlantic Fisheries Organization (Barry 1998).

Rivalry and Partnership

As this historical overview has shown, transatlantic energy relations were embedded within larger historical developments, whether these were of a geopolitical (Cold War, Middle East conflict), socio-economic (high modernism, globalization, third industrial revolution, high-energy societies), or even planetary nature (climate change). Transatlantic energy relations, like global, regional, and national energy governance, have been structured around specific energy sources and markets and include market and public policy mechanisms to address questions of energy supply, affordability and, more recently, sustainability (Dubash and Florini 2011; Florini and Sovacool 2009). While energy relations between Europe and North America have been shaped by global energy events and developments, they also have the power to shape global energy markets since they include leading energy consumers and more recently energy producers such as Canada and the United States. Historically, due to fundamental energy transitions from coal to oil and distinct national energy choices and energy mixes, these relations covered various energy carriers, although until recently it was mainly oil that figured prominently. In the case of oil and because it is an internationally traded commodity, they were also influenced by switches from global sellers' (1970s, late 1990s, and 2000s) to buyers' markets (mid-1980s, 1990s). Energy diplomacy across the Atlantic has been defined by both rivalry and partnership, although the rivalry was one among close friends who share values and norms (Haglund 2012; Risse-Kappen 1995; Tuschhoff 2006). Partnership was driven by the necessity to coordinate policy responses to global energy developments and during times of dependence on Middle Eastern producers. It was often achieved within multinational institutions such as the OEEC/OECD, IEA, or NATO and not through direct transatlantic relations. However, within these multinational institutions the United States, Canada, and the European Union would often coordinate their positions. At the same time, a multitude of bilateral energy relations between the United States, Canada, and individual member states rendered a common European external energy policy difficult to achieve. These multilevel entanglements were further complicated by transatlantic rivalry, which was focused on commercial questions of energy trade, different sensibilities with regard to energy security, and, until recently, different commitments to addressing climate change through energy policy. The fragmented and variegated nature of transatlantic energy governance is currently put to the test as future energy relations will move away from traditional hydrocarbon producers and focus on net-zero emissions goals. The Paris Agreement on climate change and the UN Sustainable Development Goal 7 (SDG7) which calls for "affordable, reliable, sustainable and modern energy for all" by 2030 highlight the importance of increasing the share of renewable energy as well as energy justice.

Transatlantic Energy Relations: Multiple Issues and Levels of Engagement

The Nature of Transatlantic Energy Relations

Energy policy transcends the boundaries between foreign and domestic policy and interlinks different levels of jurisdiction. Transatlantic energy relations are complicated by these different levels of authority with regard to energy policy. In the EU context, where energy matters constitute shared competencies between the European Union and its member states, it is difficult to speak with one voice as energy mixes, energy sectors, and import dependencies among member states vary significantly. As a result, different vulnerabilities and approaches toward energy issues exist. For example, Germany has decided to phase out nuclear energy while France relies heavily on electricity generation from nuclear power. In the meantime, there is disagreement among environmentalists as to whether nuclear power is necessary for achieving net-zero greenhouse gas emissions and helps facilitate decarbonization of high-energy economies. In addition to the difficulty of arriving at a common approach within, the European Union also has a legitimacy problem when it comes to its external energy relations, even though energy trade is the one area where competencies clearly rest with EU institutions. As in other foreign policy fields and due to its supranational character, the European Union struggles with its "actorness" in international energy politics and may not always be considered the first point of contact and direct counterpart for the United States or Canada. This energy diplomacy of a supranational actor is further complicated by the European Union's claims to be a normative power, especially in the area of climate change. Finally, as the historical overview has shown, often transatlantic diplomacy is not mainly dealing with bilateral commercial and economic relations but is designed to support mutual political and strategic interests. Thus, negotiations over closer economic cooperation are often primarily about exhibiting Western solidarity and cooperation in a changing world, in which new economic centers and powers emerge. The more recent search by the European Union for strategic energy partnerships with similar international players such as the United States and Canada highlights the political nature of transatlantic energy relations and how the energy transition requires cooperation in science and technology, innovation, and regulatory areas. The linkage of climate and energy policy may also facilitate cohesion as member states have found it easier to agree on climate policy and this consensus may spill over to EU external energy policy (Van der Linde 2007).

While the United States and Canada do not share these legitimacy problems as foreign policy actors, their political systems and federal makeup equally create multilevel setups for energy decision-making. In both countries, substate units have jurisdiction over energy production while competencies over foreign trade reside at the federal level. However, there are instances of direct energy relations between substate actors and the European Union. For example, in 1990 the Canadian province of Quebec and the European Commission agreed on the Euro-Quebec hydro-hydrogen pilot project with participation from European and Canadian industry (Gretz et al. 1990; Wurster 1990). In light of current discussions of hydrogen technology and the adoption of a hydrogen strategy by both the European Union and Canada in 2020, we have seen a revival of such cooperation. The Quebec-Europe Research and Innovation Circle, which is supported by the provincial government, promotes further collaboration in this area, as do Canada and Germany, who agreed on a Memorandum of Understanding on the Establishment of an Energy Partnership in March 2021. Similar connections exist between some US states and the European Union. In 2017 California agreed to strengthen bilateral collaboration with the European Union on carbon markets. Such paradiplomacy mostly relates to collaboration in the area of energy research and technology as well as regulatory regimes because public actors play a more visible role in these fields. Commercial relations remain much less structured and can also be characterized by competition, especially in an emerging clean energy technology market (Andoura and Vinois 2015). Because these new technologies create much-needed jobs, they also have the potential to create tensions between the United States, Canada, and the European Union, whose innovation and industrial policies may support national champions in this technological race to reach net-zero goals.

Based on existing discussions on the nature of energy governance (Leal-Arcas 2016; Cherp et al. 2011; Dubash and Florini 2011), there are different ways to systematically look at transatlantic energy relations covering a wide range of issues including energy trade and investment, energy transit, energy security, and climate change. The respective US-EU and Canada-EU energy relations are impacted and overlayed by trilateral connections, in which all three sides interact. In addition, transatlantic energy relations are embedded in national, supranational/regional, and global governance structures. While the European Union pursues an Energy Union internally, Canada and the United States have a long history of informally and formally integrated energy markets. The Canada-United States Free Trade Agreement, which came into effect in 1989, included a separate energy chapter, which remained in place when Mexico joined to broaden the bilateral agreement into the North American Free Trade Agreement (1994), which was recently revised and renamed the Canada-United States-Mexico Agreement (2020). In the past, these two regional blocs in North America and Europe found themselves at times rivals in a global competition over scarce or unevenly distributed energy sources. At other times, as the European Union aimed to diversify its energy resources and supply regions, energy trade with Canada and the United States, two Western energy suppliers, took on renewed significance. Currently, both the United States and Canada are net exporters of oil, natural gas and coal, and while these commercial activities are covered by existing WTO regulations, there was until recently a lack of a joint transatlantic investment strategy or trade incentives to support the trade in new energy technologies. There is no transatlantic energy trade agreement (Khakova 2019; Leal-Arcas 2016).

Finally, energy security constitutes another aspect of transatlantic energy relations. Europe's dependence on energy imports constituted a security risk during the Cold War and thus became an important aspect of strategic thinking among its North American allies: Canada and the United States. However, such deliberations were confined to NATO, which dealt with transatlantic security. Also, unlike the United States, who until recently shared similar energy patterns of increasing demand, decreasing production, and increasing import dependency with Western Europe, Canada quickly became a significant energy producer and less dependent on energy imports. In addition, the United States and EU addressed their shared vulnerabilities differently. Energy security, or more specifically oil and natural gas security, may have been a constant in transatlantic energy relations since the 1950s (Nemeth 2014), but Europeans only explicitly addressed energy security in the 2000s as they mostly relied on market mechanisms to deal with their dependence. In 2000, the European Commission published a Green paper entitled "Towards a European strategy for the security of energy supply" which initiated years of debate, culminating in the inclusion of energy security as a goal in the 2007 Lisbon Treaty. EU enlargement, which saw more Eastern European countries join, also put energy security higher on the agenda as these countries heavily relied on energy imports from Russia. When the European Commission published its Second Strategic Energy Review in 2008 entitled "An EU Energy Security and Action Plan," it specifically named both the United States and Canada as potential partners for closer collaboration in the field of energy, including on energy security matters (Baumann and Simmerl 2011). In 2014, the Ukraine crisis brought energy security to the fore again. It was discussed within NATO, the G7, and the European Union. The EU Commission's European Energy Security Strategy of May 2014 explicitly called for strategies to lower its dependency on energy imports from Russia. At the same time, as a result of the shale revolution, in which hydraulic fracturing and horizontal drilling (fracking) enabled oil production from shale rock formations, domestic production in the United States picked up again and completely reversed its energy paradigm, turning its decade-long import dependence into abundance and diverging significantly from the energy position of the European Union (Conley et al. 2016).

The United States

Energy relations between the European Union and the United States constitute only a small part of one of the largest bilateral trade relationships worldwide. Covering two of the most significant energy markets, together the two sides represent a large share of global energy consumption and carbon emissions. Since the end of the Cold War,

US-EU energy relations have gone through three distinct phases. The 1990s were mostly dominated by questions of international trade. The decade, which began with the implosion of the Soviet Union and stretched into the new millennium, when the events of 9/11 put security on the top of the agenda, saw the official commencement of the World Trade Organization (WTO) in 1995 after the conclusion of the Uruguay trade round replacing the General Agreement on Tariffs and Trade (GATT), which had been in place since 1948. Not surprisingly, discussions between the United States and its European counterpart were equally driven by questions of market liberalization and possible free trade agreements. In 1990 the Transatlantic Declaration was announced, followed by the New Transatlantic Agenda and US-EU Action Plan (1995), which floated the idea of a New Transatlantic Marketplace, and the Transatlantic Economic Partnership (1998). None of these agreements were particularly dedicated to energy issues. However, as oil prices steadily rose in the 2000s and global demand peaked later in the decade, both the United States and the European Union needed to address their import dependencies. Two years after the Transatlantic Economic Council was launched in 2007, the EU-US Energy Council was established at the November 2009 EU-US Summit. Both partners pledged to collaborate on strategies to address their vulnerabilities. A third phase began when the United States underwent a complete reversal of its energy situation and policy priorities due to the shale revolution which began in the late 2000s and led to distinctly diverging transatlantic economic and energy outlooks. US oil production more than doubled between 2007 and 2019. Its newly restored fossil fuel abundance allowed Washington to use its natural gas exports strategically to lessen EU dependence on Russian exports. In addition, the United States was less concerned about the competitiveness of clean energy technologies, although recent political commitments to net-zero emission goals have brought this green strategy back to the table.

All three phases point toward a structural constant. EU-US energy relations follow political and technological developments, but they do not actively shape the transatlantic relationship. Unlike other commodities, disagreement over energy resources has not led to a transatlantic trade war, which is not to say that there have not been tensions related to energy, as shown by US criticism of the gas pipeline deal between West Germany and the Soviet Union in the early 1980s and the more recent controversy over Nord Stream 2. These phases also highlight how different energy mixes and policy environments impact US-EU energy relations. For a long time, the European Union prioritized market mechanisms to address its energy dependence, while the United States securitized energy, resorting to (geo)political and even military approaches (Herranz-Surrallés 2016). Finally, both energy markets are interconnected and changes in one market will impact the other. As could be seen with the redirection of Middle Eastern oil exports from the United States to Europe in the 1950s and 1960s, other substitution processes also connected North America and Europe. For example, cheaper US coal entered European markets during the coal sales crises in West Germany and Belgium in the late 1950s (Dolata-Kreutzkamp 2006). More recently, in the early 2010s, US coal found new markets in Europe, when increasing production from shale in the United States displaced coal demand in the Eastern Seaboard region of the United States (Conley et al. 2016). Equally, the shale revolution led to an upsurge in liquefied natural gas (LNG) deliveries from the United States to Europe, exerting pressure on natural gas prices and substituting a small share of Russian gas deliveries.

First attempts at institutionalized energy talks in the mid-2000s were not particularly successful and short-lived. Even though there was agreement on the necessity to discuss energy security and climate change beyond the transatlantic summits in 2006 and 2007, the mechanisms that were set up did not last long, nor did they transform the energy relationship. They included an annual strategic review of energy cooperation, a climate change dialogue, and an EU-US Energy CEO Forum (Conley et al. 2016). These ineffective attempts were followed by the 2009 decision to establish a high-level EU-US Energy Council, co-chaired by the US Secretaries of Energy and State and the EU High Representative of the Union for Foreign Affairs and Security Policy and Vice-President for a Stronger Europe in the World, and the EU Commissioner for Energy. Scheduled to meet annually, the joint council aims to "deepen the dialogue on strategic energy issues of mutual interest, foster cooperation on energy policies and further strengthen research collaboration on sustainable and clean energy technologies" (European Commission 2009). It operates through three working groups dedicated to energy technology, energy policy, and energy security respectively. Created at a time when the world had seen prices for crude oil surge close to a record $150 per barrel, fueling discussions on peak oil and depletion of global supplies, the Energy Council's mandate connected traditional challenges of energy security with emerging debates on the energy and climate change nexus. While both sides pledged to collaborate, the range of topics also showed the different weighing of policy priorities at the time. Because the United States was on the verge of its shale revolution, which soon after led to a surge in unconventional gas and oil production, transforming the United States into a net producer after almost 50 years, Washington was much more focused on the strategic challenge of energy security. The EU, depending on imports for more than half of its energy consumption, resorted to a different approach and was already working on greening its energy policies.

By 2021 the Energy Council had met eight times, first every year (2009–2014) and then only twice in 2016 and 2018. Energy collaboration shifted toward LNG, which arrived for the first time from the United States in the European Union (Portugal) in April 2016. Two years later, in a joint statement, the European Union and United States agreed to strengthen their "strategic cooperation" in energy matters, especially for facilitating trade in LNG, which the European Union pledged to import from the United States to diversify its own energy supply and ensure its energy security (European Commission 2018). In 2019, the EU-US Energy Council organized its first Business-to-Business Energy Forum on the topic of LNG. Entitled "Towards large-scale U.S. LNG exports to the EU's gas market: competitive pricing, infrastructure investments and technological innovation," the forum brought together government and business representatives to promote closer LNG trade and investment links. After 2018 the transatlantic LNG trade grew significantly and by 2020 more than 24 billion cubic meters had been imported from the United States. In 2019 more than a third of US LNG exports were destined for the European

Union. This successful energy trade expansion remained the only noteworthy development during the Trump administration, which was otherwise characterized by a hiatus of energy diplomacy. The recent June 2021 EU-US Summit marked the beginning of a new phase of transatlantic energy relations under President Biden. The summit statement "Towards a Renewed Transatlantic Partnership" reinvigorated the Energy Council, which now explicitly includes questions of climate neutrality, sustainable energy supply chains, and the circular economy. The two sides even announced that they would work together on establishing a Transatlantic Green Technology Alliance collaborating on designing, deploying, and scaling to markets green technologies (White House 2021).

As this recent reset of energy relations indicates, differences between US and EU approaches to energy are not only driven by distinct energy mixes and divergent roles as net producers or consumers but also by policy priorities of changing US governments. The Trump administration championed fossil fuels, in particular shale oil and gas, as well as coal. When President Biden took office in early 2021, he immediately initiated a switch toward a greener energy future by rejoining the Paris Agreement, which President Trump had left, and committing to net-zero carbon dioxide emissions by 2050, realigning US energy policy with the European Union and its 2019 Green Deal legislation. He also convened a Leaders' Summit on Climate in Washington in April 2021, at which the United States and the European Union committed to cutting emissions by 50–52% and 55% by 2030 respectively. These necessary but ambitious goals were reiterated at a G7 meeting in June 2021, when leaders pledged to limit the rise in global temperatures to 1.5 °C and to "phase out new direct government support for carbon-intensive international fossil fuel energy" (G7 2021).

Following the creation of the Transatlantic Economic Council in 2007 and motivated by the slowdown of international trade and economic activities in the wake of the 2008 global financial crisis, negotiations over an EU-US trade agreement continued and officially launched in 2013. The EU was particularly pushing for the inclusion of an energy chapter, which the United States was less interested in since it had re-emerged as an oil and gas producer which did not need dedicated transatlantic support to find markets. However, these talks to reach a Transatlantic Trade and Investment Partnership (TTIP) ended without a conclusion in 2016 (Conley et al. 2016). While the EU-US negotiations failed, EU-Canadian talks, which had been launched in 2009, were successfully completed in 2016, creating the Comprehensive Economic and Trade Agreement (CETA), which is currently provisionally applied awaiting ratification through various EU member states.

Canada

The EU considers Canada "a key, and like-minded, energy partner" (European Commission 2021). As a net exporter of both conventional and unconventional oil and natural gas, it has played and still plays a significant role in helping the European Union to diversify its fossil fuel energy needs. In contrast to the United States and the

European Union, which are in themselves large energy consumer markets, Canada is much smaller, and its GDP depends to a large extent on exports, including energy exports. A large share of these, whether oil, natural gas, or hydropower, are supplied to its neighbor to the South. The EU is Canada's second-largest trade and investment partner, but the United States is its primary export destination by a wide margin. However, when the shale revolution made the United States a significant producer of unconventional oil and gas in the 2010s, Ottawa had to redirect its attention toward new markets both in Europe and Asia. Like the United States in the first two decades of the twenty-first century, Canada began to actively position itself as a secure supplier of energy to the European Union. Prime Minister Harper touted Canada as an energy superpower that could supply Europe with alternative deliveries of oil and especially natural gas through LNG. Not surprisingly, EU-Canada summits in the first two decades included discussions on energy and energy security.

With a few notable exceptions, Canada-EU energy relations have gone through various phases that mirror the development of US-EU relations over the last three decades, but because Canada is a much smaller economy and middle power, it often plays the role of the junior partner in transatlantic relations. At other times, closer relations with Europe were welcomed in Canada as a counterweight against the country's unequal relationship with its southern neighbor (Barry 2004). It can also get caught up in US-EU relations, especially when Canada is sidelined in more important discussions on direct US-EU free trade proposals. For the European Union, the United States figures as one of the most important partners. However, because Canada is a net exporter of energy, at times it can play a distinct role in transatlantic energy relations. As outlined above, Canada played a unique role as a supplier of uranium and as the first industrialized country to sign an agreement with EURATOM (1959) as well as a framework agreement with the European Community in 1976. It also clashed with the European Union on energy-related issues in the late 1970s when the Canadian government instituted its uranium export embargo and more recently when the European Union instituted a Fuel Quality Directive which Ottawa interpreted as targeting Canadian oil sands production. Adopted in 2009, the directive required that the carbon intensity of petrol, diesel, and biofuels used for transport be reduced by 6% between 2010 and 2020. After a lengthy discussion in 2010 and 2011, it was proposed that the directive, which uses life cycle assessments to calculate emissions intensity, consider oil sands production as five times more carbon-intensive than conventional oil and thus de facto disallow oil from Canadian oil sands production to enter the European Union. However, member states could not agree, and Canada began a successful lobbying effort in Brussels and European capitals arguing that the directive unfairly targeted Canadian oil sands production, overstating its carbon footprint. So, when the fuel quality rules were finally adopted in 2014, Canadian unconventional oil was treated no differently than conventional oil. In 2016, after the Brexit vote in the United Kingdom, the worsening US-EU relations and the signing of the Paris Agreement in 2015 had highlighted the necessity to collaborate with like-minded third countries to address global challenges such as climate change and energy security, and Canada and the European Union signed a Strategic Partnership Agreement (Bendiek et al. 2018).

Despite the broader nature of the 1976 Framework Agreement, Canada's engagement with the EC/European Union was dominated by economic matters, since strategic and security questions were the remit of NATO. The Framework Agreement itself was more important for trust-building and symbolic collaboration than directly addressing trade between the two partners. It failed in diversifying Canada's trade flows away from the US market. It was, however, followed by several agreements that were intended to deepen existing transatlantic ties. In 1988, the two sides established a Political Dialogue and in 1990 they signed a Declaration on Transatlantic Relations, just 1 day before the United States signed a similar agreement with the European Union, which was followed 6 years later by the Joint Political Declaration on EU-Canada Relations and the Joint EU-Canada Action Plan. In 1998 the EU-Canada Trade Initiative was launched at the EU-Canada summit. During the 1990s a number of these agreements were reached in tandem with US-EU agreements and embedded in a larger attempt by the European Union to liberalize trade multilaterally across the Atlantic. Canada's strategy changed from diversification to actively seeking economic opportunities after the end of the Cold War (Barry 2004). However, Ottawa's attempts were not always successful. Even though the European Union wanted to avoid bilateral agreements, Canada was not included in US-EU talks because Washington feared that Canada would side with Brussels. Ottawa repeatedly failed to trilateralize economic talks in the 1990s, including during talks over the creation of a Transatlantic Marketplace, emphasizing Canada's junior role in transatlantic relations. Unlike the United States, these talks were mainly between governments and did not include sizeable input from business. At the same time, Canada obtained its own Transatlantic Declaration and its bilateral dialogue with the European Union was increasingly institutionalized, although it produced few tangible results at the time (Barry 2004; Potter 1999). Although the Transatlantic Marketplace did not become a reality in the 1990s, by the early twenty-first century, Canada and the European Union had concluded several sectoral agreements, some of which address scientific cooperation (Agreement for Scientific and Technological Cooperation 1996), including in energy-related research areas such as nuclear research (Agreement between Canada and the European Atomic Energy Community for Cooperation in the Area of Nuclear Research 1998).

In 2004, Canada and the European Union announced a Partnership Agenda and a year later they agreed on establishing a framework for the participation of Canada in the European Union crisis management operations. As energy questions took on more urgency in the mid-2000s, Canada and the European Union established a High-Level Energy Dialogue in 2007, which was revitalized in the wake of the Ukraine crisis in 2014 and incorporated into the Strategic Partnership Agreement, which the European Union and Canada signed in 2016. In the same year, EU-Canadian talks on a Comprehensive Economic and Trade Agreement (CETA) were finally concluded. Due to increased US protectionism, this time around negotiations did result in an agreement on trade and economic collaboration. Covering a broad range of trade and investment areas, joint and specialized committees, as well as dialogues, have been set up to facilitate the implementation of the agreement. In addition, with the Strategic Partnership Agreement, the two sides committed to political and strategic cooperation addressing global challenges including international peace and stability as well as economic and sustainable development. In the agreement Canada and the European Union "recognise the importance of the energy sector to economic prosperity and international peace and stability" (European Union 2016), formalizing the High-Level Energy Dialogue, which meets annually to discuss energy policy issues. Its key areas reflect the dual challenges of planetary climate change and geopolitical energy dependence. The dialogue focuses on renewable energy and energy efficiency but also energy security and more specifically LNG trade. Starting in 2015, Canada and the European Union held various joint energy-related workshops culminating in a series of five Canada-EU exchange webinars. The second EU-Canada workshop on CETA opportunities in late March 2021 was dedicated to the clean technology sector. Targeted at industry leaders and clean technology experts, this workshop focused on promising technology areas including hydrogen and carbon, capture, and utilization (CCUS), which Canada is specifically interested in, as well as zero-emissions vehicles and the circular economy. Finally, the two sides promised collaboration in international energy institutions such as the IEA and the International Renewable Energy Agency (IRENA), founded in 2009.

The United States, Canada, the European Union, and Multilevel Energy Governance

Beyond the various direct bilateral and trilateral transatlantic energy relations described above, in energy matters the European Union is often engaging with both Canada and the United States through global energy governance. Here, they are partners exhibiting similar interests and values pushing for more cohesive global energy governance. The United States and European Union are two of the largest energy markets in the world, and together with Canada they share a mutual interest in ensuring global energy governance. However, ever since the founding of the IEA in 1974, international energy governance has remained fragmented. Regional regimes with energy competencies including NAFTA and the European Union overlap with international institutions dedicated to energy matters such as the IEA (Leal-Arcas 2016). As the founding of the IEA has illustrated, international energy relations are partly determined through the competition between producers and consumers but also between state and market (Florini 2011). With the increasing significance of the international LNG trade and, more importantly, the energy-climate nexus and emerging climate change regimes, energy governance has become even more complex and less cohesive (Goldthau and Witte 2010). The linkage with climate change regimes has also exhibited differences between the European Union and its transatlantic partners. The European Union considers itself a normative power and leader in climate policies. As a supranational actor, it is a rather unique actor in regional and global energy governance.

With the exception of the International Atomic Energy Agency (IAEA), which was founded in 1957 and governs the use of nuclear technologies both for military and civilian purposes, and OPEC, there were only a few dedicated international organizations governing energy until the founding of the International Energy Agency in 1974. Within the United Nations and under the GATT regime committees dealt with coal and increasingly with oil trade, but as the example of the regional OEEC/OECD and its Oil Committee has shown, these were ill-prepared to deal with the effects of the transformative energy transition from coal to oil, as well as the emerging resource nationalism in producing countries and the changing oil order. The IEA itself was only made up of consumer countries in the West to coordinate emergency responses. Attempts in the 1970s to create an institution or a framework that would bring together producers and consumers, especially the IEA and OPEC, came to nothing at the time. Only in 1991, after the first Gulf War, was the intergovernmental International Energy Forum (IEF), which includes IEA and OPEC member states accounting for most of the global oil and gas demand and supply, founded in Paris. Dedicated to providing a space for global energy dialogue, the IEF mainly fosters the exchange of information and views on energy developments and possible conflicts. Since 2005 it also coordinates the Joint Organisations Data Initiative to share energy market data among its members. Unlike the IEA, the IEF is a soft institution lacking decision-making powers. Equally, while setting up investment and trade rules for oil and natural gas, the Energy Charter Treaty, which was concluded in 1994, struggles with non-ratification by important energy players such as Russia (Goldthau and Witte 2010).

In principle, questions of energy trade are dealt with by the WTO. However, trade institutions do not really have an interest in comprehensive energy governance, and some oil-rich countries have not even joined these organizations. More importantly, due to the geopolitical nature of oil and gas, the strategic goal of energy security has at times dominated international energy relations and shifted the discussion to institutions that do not primarily deal with energy, including NATO or the G7/G8. At the same time, while energy security has become an important shared concern for the European Union, the United States, and Canada since the 1970s, there is no global campaign for energy security. There is, however, global concern for climate change, as demonstrated by the 1997 Kyoto Protocol and the 2015 Paris Agreement (Leal-Arcas 2016). The founding of IRENA in 2009 highlights how existing energy governance regimes were considered insufficient in dealing with the newly emerging emphasis on renewable energy, clean technologies, and energy efficiency. Germany, which was instrumental in pushing for an institution focusing on renewable energy, was disillusioned with the focus of the IEA, which Berlin perceived as unsupportive of the energy transition. Instead of expanding the remit of the IEA, a separate institution was established, IRENA. However, contrary to German plans, it was not housed in Bonn but Abu Dhabi (Florini 2011). There have also been attempts within the G20, which was first initiated in 1999 and includes a diverse group of members – producer and consumer countries and states from the Global South and Global North – to put energy on its agenda and cooperate with the IEA and IRENA on facilitating sustainable energy regimes globally (Röhrkasten and Westphal 2016). Apart from the IEA and IRENA, there are currently a few other multilateral energy forums that allow the European Union, Canada, and the United States to cooperate. These include the annual Clean Energy Ministerial meetings, a global forum which began in 2009 and focuses on energy efficiency and clean energy technologies and the more specific Carbon Sequestration Leadership Forum established in 2003. They are also all members of CDP, formerly the Carbon Disclosure Project, which focuses on climate change data collection and assessment.

Future Directions

As renewable energy takes up an increasing share of global energy consumption and decarbonization leads to decreasing importance of oil and natural gas, global energy markets will undergo significant transformation in the future. New geopolitics of renewable energy will emerge, and electricity grids will become one of the most important pieces of energy infrastructure. In such a changing world, the European Union, Canada, and the United States will share many interests, although changes in government could jeopardize their agreement on net-zero goals to address climate change. Republicans in the United States and Conservatives in Canada are questioning these climate and energy policies. These energy transformations may also lead to increased transatlantic tensions as the United States and even more so Canada depend to a certain degree on their oil and gas industries for jobs and revenue. What made them once complementary partners for a fossil fuel-hungry Europe may now begin to sour their relations with a greening European Union.

Cross-References

▶ Energy Governance in Germany
▶ European Union Energy Policy: A Discourse Perspective
▶ EU-Russia Energy Relations
▶ The Energy Charter Treaty: Old and New Dilemmas in Global Energy Governance
▶ The EU in Global Energy Governance

References

Abbasov, F. G. (2014). EU's external energy governance: A multidimensional analysis of the southern gas corridor. *Energy Policy, 65*(3), 23–36.

Andoura, S., & Vinois, J.-A. (2015). *From the European energy community to the energy union: A policy proposal for the short and the long term*. Jacques Delors Institute. https://institutdelors.eu/en/publications/from-the-european-energy-community-to-the-energy-union-a-new-policy-proposal/

Axelrod, R. S. (1996). The European energy charter treaty: Reality or illusion? *Energy Policy, 24*(6), 497–505.

Baev, P. K., & Øverland, I. (2010). The south stream versus Nabucco pipeline race: Geopolitical and economic (Ir)rationales and political stakes in mega-projects. *International Affairs, 86*(5), 1075–1090.

Barry, D. (1998). The Canada-European Union turbot war. *International Journal, 53*(2), 253–284.

Barry, D. (2004). Toward a Canada-EU Partnership? In P. M. Crowley (Ed.), *Crossing the Atlantic comparing the European Union and Canada* (pp. 35–58). Routledge.

Baumann, F., & Simmerl, G. (2011). *Between conflict and convergence: The EU member states and the quest for a common external energy policy*. Center for Applied Policy Research.

Bendiek, A., Geogios, M., Nock, P., Schenuit, F., & von Daniels, L. (2018). *EU-Canada relations on the Rise: Mutual interests in security, trade and climate change*. Stiftung Wissenschaft und Politik. https://www.swp-berlin.org/publications/products/arbeitspapiere/1_WP_Bendiek_etal_EU-Canada_relations_final_01.pdf

Boardman, R. (1981). Canadian resources and the contractual link: The case of uranium. *Journal of European Integration, 4*(3), 299–325.

Bösch, F. (2014). Energy diplomacy: West Germany, the Soviet Union and the oil crises of the 1970s. *Historical Social Research, 39*(4), 165–185.

Bratt, D. (2006). *The politics of CANDU exports*. De Gruyter.

Buchan, D. (2009). *Energy and climate change: Europe at the crossroads*. Oxford University Press.

Chaban, N., & Knodt, M. (2015). Energy diplomacy in the context of multistakeholder diplomacy: The EU and BICS. *Cooperation and Conflict, 50*(4), 457–474.

Cherp, A., Jewell, J., & Golthau, A. (2011). Governing global energy: Systems, transitions, complexity. *Global Policy, 2*(1), 75–88.

Conley, H., Ladislaw, S. & Hudson, A. (2016). The US–EU Energy Relationship. In Godzimirski, J. M. (Ed.), *EU Leadership in Energy and Environmental Governance*. Palgrave Macmillan.

Deni, J. R., & Smith Stegen, K. (Eds.). (2014). *Transatlantic energy relations: Convergence or divergence*. Routledge.

Diebold, W. (1959). *The Schuman plan: A study in economic cooperation, 1950–1959*. Praeger.

Dolata-Kreutzkamp. (2006). *Die deutsche Kohlenkrise im nationalen und transatlantischen Kontext*. VS-Verlag.

Dubash, N. K., & Florini, A. (2011). Mapping global energy governance. *Global Policy, 2*(1), 6–18.

Duffield, J. S., & Birchfield, V. L. (2011). Introduction: The recent upheaval in EU energy policy. In V. L. Birchfield & J. S. Duffield (Eds.), *Toward a common European Union energy policy: Problems, progress, and prospects* (pp. 1–9). Palgrave Macmillan.

European Commission. (2009). *The EU-U.S. Energy Council*. https://ec.europa.eu/energy/sites/ener/files/documents/2009_energy_council_joint_press_statement.pdf

European Commission. (2018). *Joint U.S.-EU statement following President Juncke's visit to the White House*. https://ec.europa.eu/commission/presscorner/detail/en/STATEMENT_18_4687

European Commission. (2021). *Energy: Canada*. https://ec.europa.eu/energy/topics/international-cooperation/key-partner-countries-and-regions/canada_en

European Union. (2012). *Consolidated version of the treaty on the functioning of the European Union*. Official Journal of the European Union. https://eur-lex.europa.eu/LexUriServ/LexUriServ.do?uri=CELEX:12012E/TXT:en:PDF

European Union. (2016). *Strategic Partnership Agreement between the European Union and its Member States, of the one part, and Canada, of the other part*, 3 December 2016. Official Journal of the European Union. https://eur-lex.europa.eu/legal-content/EN/TXT/?uri=uriserv:OJ.L_.2016.329.01.0045.01.ENG&toc=OJ:L:2016:329:FULL

Florini, A. (2011). The international energy Agency in Global Energy Governance. *Global Policy, 2*(1), 40–40.

Florini, A., & Sovacool, B. (2009). Who governs energy? The challenges facing global energy governance. *Energy Policy, 37*(12), 5239–5248.

Focken, H. (2015). Between National Interests and the greater good: Struggling towards a common European Union energy policy in the context of climate change. *Journal of International Affairs, 69*(1), 179–191.

G7. (2021). *Climate and Environment Ministers' Communiqué, 21 May 2021*. https://www.g7uk.org/g7-climate-and-environment-ministers-communique/

Georgiou, N. A., & Rocco, A. (2017). The energy union as an instrument of global governance in EU-Russia energy relations. *Geopolitics, History, and International Relations, 9*(1), 241–268.

Goldthau, A., & Witte, J. M. (2010). The role of rules and institutions in global energy: An introduction. In A. Goldthau & J. M. Witte (Eds.), *Global energy governance: The new rules of the game* (pp. 1–21). Brookings Institution.

Gretz, J., Baselt, J. P., Ullmann, O., & Wendt, H. (1990). The 100 MW euro-Quebec hydro-hydrogen pilot project. *International Journal of Hydrogen Energy, 15*(6), 419–424.

Haglund, D. (2012). On the road to Lisbon: Canada, the U.S., and the transatlantic Alliance. In J.-M. Lacroix & G. Mace (Eds.), *Politique étrangère comparée:Canada-Etats-Unis* (pp. 35–48). Peter Lang.

Herranz-Surrallés, A. (2016). An emerging EU energy diplomacy? Discursive shifts, enduring practices. *Journal of European Public Policy, 23*(9), 1386–1405.

Kander, A., Malanima, P., & Warde, P. (2013). *Power to the people: Energy in Europe over the last five centuries*. Princeton University Press.

Khakova, O. (2019). *A transatlantic agenda for the new European Commission*. Atlantic Council.

Leal-Arcas, R. (2016). *Energy security, trade and the EU: Regional and international perspectives*. Edward Elgar.

Lesage, D., Van de Graaf, T., & Westphal, K. (2010). *Global energy governance in a multipolar world*. Ashgate.

Lovett, A. W. (1996). The United States and the Schuman plan. A study in French diplomacy 1950-1952. *The Historical Journal, 39*(2), 425–455.

Lundestad, G. (2012). *The rise and decline of American "empire": Power and its limits in comparative perspective*. Oxford University Press.

Maltby, T. (2013). European Union energy policy integration: A case of European Commission policy entrepreneurship and increasing supranationalism. *Energy Policy, 55*(4), 435–444.

McDermott, R. (1998). The Suez crisis. In *Risk-taking in international politics: Prospect theory in American foreign policy* (pp. 135–164). University of Michigan Press.

Miller, R. (2014). The euro-Arab dialogue and the limits of European external intervention in the Middle East, 1974-77. *Middle Eastern Studies, 50*(6), 936–959.

Nemeth, T. (2014). A brief history of transatlantic energy security relations: The pursuit of balance and stability through interdependence. In J. R. Deni & K. Smith Stegen (Eds.), *Transatlantic energy relations: Convergence or divergence*. Routledge.

Neuss, B. (2000). *Geburtshelfer Europas? Die Rolle der Vereinigten Staaten im europäischen Integrationsprozess 1945–1958*. Nomos.

Noor, S. (2004). European Union and the Middle East: A historical analysis. *Pakistan Horizon, 57*(1), 23–46.

Painter, D. S. (2009). The Marshall plan and oil. *Cold War History, 9*(2), 159–175.

Potter, E. H. (1999). *Transatlantic partners: Canadian approaches to the European Union*. McGill-Queen's University Press.

Risse-Kappen, T. (1995). *Cooperation among democracies. The European influence on U.S. foreign policy*. Princeton University Press.

Röhrkasten, S., & Westphal, K. (2016). The G20 and its role in global energy governance. In S. Röhrkasten, S. Thielges, & R. Quitzow (Eds.), *Sustainable energy in the G20: Prospects for a global energy transition* (pp. 12–18). IASS.

Stingelin, P. (1975). Europe and the oil crisis. *Current History, 68*(403), 97–100. 132–134.

The White House. (2021). *U.S.-EU Summit statement: Towards a renewed transatlantic partnership, June 15, 2021*. https://www.whitehouse.gov/briefing-room/statements-releases/2021/06/15/u-s-eu-summit-statement/

Türk, H. (2014a). The European Community and the founding of the international energy agency. In C. Hiepel (Ed.), *Europe in a globalizing world: Global challenges and European responses in the "long" 1970s* (pp. 357–372). Nomos.

Türk, H. (2014b). The oil crisis of 1973 as a challenge to multilateral energy cooperation among Western industrialized countries. *Historical Social Research, 39*(4), 209–230.

Tuschhoff, C. (2006). Manifestations of (Mis)understanding. A transatlantic value community in historical perspective. In I. Peters (Ed.), *Transatlantic tug-of-war: Prospects for US-European cooperation* (pp. 53–76). Lit-Verlag.

Van der Linde, C. (2007). External energy policy: Old fears and new dilemmas in a larger union. In A. Sapir (Ed.), *Fragmented power: Europe and the world economy* (pp. 266–307). Bruegel.

Venn, F. (1999). International cooperation versus national self-interest: The United States and Europe during the 1973–1974 oil crisis. In K. Burke & M. Stokes (Eds.), *The United States and the European Alliance since 1945* (pp. 71–98). Berg.

Venn, F. (2002). *The oil crisis*. Longman.

Vogler, J. (2013). Changing conceptions of climate and energy security in Europe. *Environmental Politics, 22*(4), 627–645.

Wurster, R. (1990). The Euro-Quebec hydro-hydrogen pilot project (EQHHPP). *Erdoel, Erdgas, Kohle, 106*(11), 449–452.

Youngs, R. (2020). EU foreign policy and energy strategy: Bounded contestation. *Journal of European Integration, 42*(1), 147–162.

Energy Relations in the EU Eastern Partnership

13

Katharina Kleinschnitger, Michèle Knodt, Marie Lortz, and Anna K. Stöckl

Contents

Introduction	288
The European Neighbourhood Policy and the Eastern Partnership	289
Energy Relations Between the European Union and the Eastern Partnership Countries	291
Armenia	291
Azerbaijan	294
Belarus	296
Georgia	298
Republic of Moldova	300
Ukraine	303
Conclusion	307
Cross-References	309
References	309

Abstract

Within the framework of the European Neighbourhood Policy, the Eastern Partnership, established in 2009, aims to strengthen the relations between the European Union and the six neighboring countries: Armenia, Azerbaijan, Belarus, Georgia, Moldova, and Ukraine. So far cooperation has taken place both bilaterally and multilaterally in areas such as governance, economic development, energy efficiency, environmental protection, and civil society. However, the shape of these relations between the European Union and the individual Eastern Partnership countries varies widely, not just formally, but also within the specific policy areas. With regard to the area of energy and the related climate actions of the European Green Deal which the president of the European Commission presented

---

K. Kleinschnitger (✉) · M. Knodt · M. Lortz · A. K. Stöckl
Institute of Political Science, Technical University of Darmstadt, Darmstadt, Germany
e-mail: kleinschnitger@pg.tu-darmstadt.de; knodt@pg.tu-darmstadt.de; lortz@pg.tu-darmstadt.de

© Springer Nature Switzerland AG 2022
M. Knodt, J. Kemmerzell (eds.), *Handbook of Energy Governance in Europe*,
https://doi.org/10.1007/978-3-030-43250-8_57

in 2019, this chapter descriptively examines the specific and different relationship arrangements of the EU with its six Eastern neighbors. Thereby, the analysis follows the central questions of how the relationship between the European Union and each of the six Eastern Partnership countries has developed since the initiative's launch in 2009 until today and what the current state of these relations is in the field of Energy policy.

Keywords

ENP · Eastern Partnership · External relations · Armenia · Azerbaijan · Belarus · Georgia · Moldova · Ukraine · Energy policy

Introduction

On June 18 2020, following the video conference of the European Union and the Eastern Partnership (EaP) leaders, President Ursula von der Leyen stated that one of five priorities for post-2020 cooperation with the Eastern partners would be to shape a sustainable partnership and the European Green Deal (European Council/Council of the European Union 2022a) which envisions a climate-neutral European economy and society by 2050. She pointed out: "We need to focus on climate resilience. It is only natural that the green transition is at the centre also of the new Eastern Partnership framework as it is at the centre of the political agenda in the European Union" (European Commission 2020). In this respect, von der Leyen lifted the issues of climate and energy resilience to a new level within the framework of the European Neighbourhood Policy (ENP), which the EU has been conducting with its southern and eastern neighboring countries since 2004. From the Commission's point of view, resilience in this context means "economic prosperity, so stability and security, even in times of crisis, such as the one that we are facing now" (European Commission 2020).

In her statement, the President explicitly refers to the relations with the six EaP countries, Armenia, Azerbaijan, Belarus, Georgia, the Republic of Moldova, and Ukraine, which are the focus of this chapter. In order to achieve and "to build a resilient eastern neighbourhood" (European Commission 2020) within the EaP framework, it is important to analyze the current state of relations between the EU and these six countries to the European east. In the following, we focus on one single strand of EU-EaP relations, namely, the area of energy policy, and ask the central question of how the relationship between the EU and each of the six EaP countries has developed to date within the field of energy since the initiative's launch in 2009.

In order to achieve this, the following section "The European Neighbourhood Policy and the Eastern Partnership" provides a brief, introductory insight into the general relationships between the EU and the EaP countries, before turning in detail to the specific energy relations of the EU with the six EaP countries in section "Energy Relations Between the European Union and the Eastern Partnership Countries" (see sections "Armenia," "Azerbaijan," "Belarus," "Georgia," "Republic of

Moldova," and "Ukraine"). The conclusion (see section "Conclusion") summarizes the results and provides an outlook for the EU's external relations with the EaP countries within the framework of energy.

The European Neighbourhood Policy and the Eastern Partnership

In 2009, the influential German daily newspaper Süddeutsche Zeitung published an article entitled "Aufbruch ins Ungewisse" ("Departure into the Unknown"; own translation, SZ 2009) describing the launch of the EaP in November 2009 as being an extension of the EU's ENP started in 2004. The title hints at the question of the character of this new policy of the ENP, which is neither an instrument of enlargement policy nor can clearly be assigned to a type of "classical" European foreign policy. Thus, it is characterized as an expression of a "paradigm shift" in European enlargement policy, which is switching "from an enlargement policy to expansion without enlargement" (own translation: Vobruba 2010, p. 48) (Gaedtke 2009, p. 160; Bicchi and Lavenex 2015; Börzel and van Hüllen 2014).

The EU already established relationships with the former Soviet countries of the later EaP before the dissolution of the Soviet Union (USSR) in 1991. The instrument used was the transformation assistance program, later officially named "Technical Assistance to the Commonwealth of Independent States" program (TACIS). TACIS aimed to create structures for a market economy and democracy after the collapse of the Soviet Union (European Commission 1992; Commission of the European Communities 1999, pp. 2–3, 11–12; Doinjashvili 2017, pp. 59–62).

In 2004, the ENP resulted from the eastern enlargement of the EU toward former Soviet space and the following major reframing of EU policies and the TACIS program. Already in August 2002, the then-Commissioner for External Relations, Christopher Patten, the then-High Representative for Common Foreign and Security Policy, Javier Solana turned toward to the former Soviet countries and in a letter on the "Wider Europe" addressed "the dual challenge of avoiding new dividing lines in Europe while responding to needs arising from the newly created borders of the Union." The letter can be interpreted as being the starting point of the ENP, as Patten and Solana (2002) stated that, "at the same time, we should fully exploit the new opportunities created by enlargement to develop relations with our neighbours."

Initially, it was intended that the ENP was to consist of Ukraine, Belarus, the Republic of Moldova and Russia. The European Security Strategy of December 2003 then additionally shifted the focus toward the Southern Caucasus. "We should now take a stronger and more active interest in the problems of the Southern Caucasus, which will in due course also be a neighbouring region" (Council of the European Union 2003a). Thus, the Commission's Strategy Paper of May 2004 included Armenia, Azerbaijan, and Georgia in the ENP (Commission of the European Communities 2004). The strategy of the ENP published by the EU Commission on 12 May 2004 states: "The European Neighbourhood Policy's vision involves a ring of countries, sharing the EU's fundamental values and objectives, drawn into an increasingly close relationship, going beyond co-operation to involve a significant measure of economic and political integration" (Commission of the European Communities 2004, p. 5; Nervi Christensen 2011).

Accordingly, the goals of this rather new EU policy included the establishment of democracy and human rights, but above all aimed to strengthen the rule of law and the economies of the partner countries through political and economic reforms and related financial support from the EU (Gaedtke 2009, p. 162). To realize these goals, the ENP focuses on the development of "special" and "privileged" relations of the EU – as enshrined in Article 8(1) of the Treaty on European Union – with its neighboring countries. The ENP initially achieved only limited impact in the target countries. For this reason, the EU reformed the ENP several times. In view of the Georgian-Russian war in 2008, the EU began to adapt its neighborhood policy to specific circumstances and founded the Union for the Mediterranean (UfM) for the southern neighborhood and the EaP for the eastern neighborhood, also to strengthen regional, multilateral cooperation. In 2011, in the wake of the Arab Spring, the EU refocused its neighborhood policy on economic and political transformation. The reorientation also focused on democratization in the partner countries and cooperation with the new elites (Lippert 2020, p. 208). As part of an extensive consultation process by the European Commission and the EEAS, the "20 Deliverables for 2020" (European Council/Council of the European Union 2021) were published at the end of 2016 to measure concrete progress on four, rather new priorities: economic development; good governance and security cooperation; environment and climate; and mobility and people-to-people contacts (European Council/Council of the European Union 2022a). Currently, the success of the ENP, and the EaP respectively, is measured according to these formulated objectives (Böttger 2020, p. 487; Langbein and Börzel 2014).

Within the framework of the ENP, the EaP was established in 2009 to strengthen the EU's relations with Armenia, Azerbaijan, Belarus, Georgia, the Republic of Moldova, and Ukraine. Cooperation has been both bilateral and multilateral in the areas of governance, economic development, energy efficiency, environmental protection, and civil society (EPRS 2018, p. 10; Kratochvíl and Tulmets 2010). The EU's bilateral approach builds on various instruments. These include the Commission's strategy papers, country reports and progress reports, action plans, association and free trade agreements, and, finally, financing instruments such as the European Neighbourhood and Partnership Instrument (ENPI), which consists of National Indicative Programmes (NIP) and accounts for a significant part of the ENP assistance funding schemes (EPRS 2018) and the European Neighbourhood Instrument (ENI), which has replaced the ENPI since 2014. According to Böttger (2020, pp. 488–489), the instruments for promoting privileged relations with the EaP countries can be divided into two generations: Generation (1) includes Partnership and Cooperation Agreements (PCA) as a contractual basis, Country Reports, and Action Plans; Generation (2) comprises the Association Agreement (AA) and the Comprehensive and Enhanced Partnership Agreement (CEPA) – in the specific case of Armenia – as the contractual basis, concrete Association Agendas as the former Action Plans, the Deep and Comprehensive Free Trade Agreement (DCFTA), and visa regulations such as readmission agreements or visa facilitation agreements.

So to date, AAs with DCFTAs were completed with the Republic of Moldova and Georgia in July 2016, as well as with Ukraine in September 2017. The EU and Armenia, a member of the Russian-led Eurasian Economic Union (EAEU), signed a CEPA adapted to these conditions in November 2017. So far, no comparable agreement exists with either Azerbaijan or Belarus. With Belarus in particular, there will be no deepened bilateral relationship in the near future (Böttger 2020, pp. 488–489). Due to the tense situation in Belarus in 2021 and the resulting strengthening of EU restrictive sanctions, Belarus suspended its participation in the EaP as of 28 June 2021.

Multilateral cooperation between the EaP countries and the EU is organized through various bodies (EPRS 2018, p. 10). According to the Joint Declaration of the Prague EaP Summit on 7 May 2009, four thematic platforms representing the main areas of multilateral cooperation were identified, including: "Democracy, good governance and stability; Economic integration and convergence with EU sectoral policies; Energy security; and Contacts between people" (Council of the European Union 2009, p. 9).

From the beginning, energy has been a central topic in the EaP – multilaterally in the declaration of the EaP or in the bilateral agreements with several EaP countries, such as in the AAs with Ukraine, Georgia, and Moldova and in the CEPA between the EU and Armenia. Within the EaP, energy has been dedicated as one platform of cooperation between the EU and the EaP countries. The platform provides an opportunity for the EU and EaP countries to discuss questions of energy security, connectivity, renewable energy, energy efficiency, climate change, and nuclear safety. Especially at the beginning, the focus was very much on energy security, reflecting the EU's interest in focusing on energy transit and supply to the EU. Hence this implies stability of the regions, as well as cooperation. The following chapter provides an in-depth look at the current state of bilateral relations between the EU and the six partner countries in the field of energy.

Energy Relations Between the European Union and the Eastern Partnership Countries

Armenia

From 1991 on, Armenia and the EU established a bilateral relationship and Armenia received aid from the EU under TACIS (Commission of the European Communities 1999, pp. 2–3, 11–12). The strategy of the European Commission's External Relations Directorate and the former European Cooperation Office (EuropeAid) focused on political reforms, building up market economy, environmental protection and agriculture, and regional cooperation (Doinjashvili 2017, pp. 60–61). TACIS was expanded 2 years later to include the "Europe-Caucasus-Asia Transport Corridor" program (TRACECA) and the "Interstate Oil and Gas Transport to Europe" energy technical assistance program (INOGATE). While the first project focuses on the promotion of transport corridors and trade, the second project promotes cooperation in energy infrastructure systems. In 1994, the "European Instrument for Democracy and Human Rights" (EIDHR) was added, initiated by the European Parliament. EIDHR envisaged to (financially) promote human rights and democratization measures in cooperation with international organizations and NGOs.

The coming into force of the PCA in 1999 was of great significance. The partnership agreement stated that Armenia, in cooperation with the EU, should work on democratic transition, economic relations, trade (in goods), rule of law, and other sectors such as technology and culture in the 10 years that followed. Furthermore, a Country Strategy Paper (CSP) (2002–2006) were drawn up, which included the strategic priorities of cooperation, goals, and expectations. Joint institutions, such as the Cooperation Council, the Cooperation Committee, and the Parliamentary Cooperation Committee, were formed within the PCA. The former being responsible for monitoring the establishment of the agreement and includes representatives of the EU Council and the Commission, as well as the Armenian government. Delegates of the Council and the Commission, as well as representatives of the Armenian government, sit on the Cooperation Committee, which serves to support the Cooperation Council. The Parliamentary Cooperation Committee is composed of representatives of the European Parliament and the Armenian Parliament (Pataraia 2015, pp. 1–2; Doinjashvili 2017, pp. 60–61; Schrötter and Ghulinyan-Gerz 2017, p. 97).

In 2004, Armenia became part of the ENP and the first Country Report which resulted was adopted by the EU Commission in 2005. While under the PCA, the relations mainly consisted of an Armenian-EU dialog in areas of common interest, especially in economic terms. The ENP however, brought a focus on democracy and human rights issues (Smith 2012). Thus, the ENP Action Plan (2006) classified a broader range of areas as short- and medium-term priorities: political reform, economic/social cooperation, development, trade and market, justice and home affairs, infrastructure, energy supply, environment, research, education, and health. Instruments for the implementation, which, for example, regulated the EU financial support, were laid down in a CSP (2007–2013). The amount of financial assistance was based on the fulfillment of the Action Plan objectives. The CSP also included a NIP, which concerned itself with the national allocation of funds from the ENPI. The NIPs are a large and essential part of the ENP's assistance programs. In addition to these, there are still other bilateral projects, such as Germany's financial support for the development of renewable energies, increased energy efficiency, and agriculture. In 2009, Armenia was in the process of becoming a member of the EaP and thus benefited from further EU assistance under the EU neighborhood policy (Schrötter and Ghulinyan-Gerz 2017; European Council/Council of the European Union 2020a).

In the year 2013, Armenia became a member of the Eastern Europe Energy Efficiency and Environment Partnership (E5P). The partnership aims to expand measures to improve energy efficiency and reduce emissions. To this end, it was favored by the international donor community at a donor conference with the sum of 60 million euros. NGOs, local authorities, and governments participate in such individual projects. These aim to compensate the insufficient goals of European development policy and to achieve the goals of the EU Lisbon Treaty (Doinjashvili 2017, pp. 82–83). As all countries of the EaP, Armenia is also taking part in Phase 1 and Phase 2 of the energy program "EU4Energy" of the International Energy Agency (IEA), funded by the EU, which started in 2016 and besides data collection, provides technical assistance on legislative and regulatory frameworks, and key energy infrastructure investments (EU Neighbours 2021).

The third EU EaP Summit, at which the EU was to sign AAs with various states, took place in Vilnius in 2013. However, the AA, which focused primarily on visa facilitation and free trade agreements, was rejected by the government in Yerevan because the Armenian government was attempting to join the Russian-led Eurasian Customs Union (EACU), the former EAEU (Giragosian 2014). After 4 years of negotiations, including talks on a DCFTA, this withdrawal from the AA came as a surprise to the EU. The reason for this decision may have been Armenia's continued high level of dependency on Russia, geopolitical concerns, its dependence on Russian security guarantees (including Russian support in the conflict with Azerbaijan), and pressure from Russia, trying to institutionalize its influence over the former Soviet countries and form a buffer zone between Russia and the West.

The case of Armenia should serve as a sign, not only to the EU but also in the direction of Kiev. Energy policy played a crucial role in Armenia's decision to join the EACU. At that time Armenia used Russian natural gas for up to 40% of its electricity production and 70% of cars used natural gas as fuel. At the end of the AA negotiations, Gazprom threatened the country with a significant increase in gas prices. After the decision to join the EACU, Armenia signed a gas agreement with Russia on fixed gas prices. The deal came with a transfer of 20% of shares of the Armenian gas network operator ArmRosGazprom to Gazprom. With this transfer, these last 20% of shares transformed the operator into the 100% Gazprom owned company, Gazprom Armenia (Konrad Adenauer Stiftung 2020). In 2015, with the entry of Armenia under then President Serzh Azati Sargsyan into the EAEU, as successor of the EACU, the long-standing negotiations for a new EU AA had to be suspended (Smolnik 2018, pp. 2–5). Nevertheless, both the EU and Armenia aimed to consolidate cooperation in a cooperation agreement (Schrötter and Ghulinyan-Gerz 2017, pp. 98–99).

In November 2017, the EU and Armenia signed the CEPA to strengthen relations between the EU and Armenia at the fifth EaP Summit in Brussels, which was fully ratified by March 2021. In addition to the alignment with EU standards, economy, research, and democracy, the agreement also provides for development in the field of environmental protection and energy (European Commission 2021; Smolnik 2018, pp. 2–3). It included the topics of energy strategy, an expanded energy security, competitive markets, the promotion of energy efficiency, renewable energy, and energy savings, as well as the encouragement of regional market integration, tariff policies, cooperation in the field of nuclear energy, and scientific and technical cooperation (CEPA 2017).

Armenia's energy policy has gone through a deep transition since the country's independence in 1991. It has changed from a unified all-union energy system of the then Soviet Union, to a market-oriented system (Minasyan in this handbook). Unlike

Azerbaijan, Armenia cannot draw on natural energy resources. Accordingly, the landlocked country is primarily dependent on Russia for its energy supply. Around 80% of Armenia's natural gas is imported from Russia through Georgia, and a small amount from the Islamic Republic of Iran. Refined petroleum is imported primarily from Russia but also from Central Asian Countries, Greece, and Iran (Minasyan in this handbook). Russian companies own a large share of Armenia's energy sector, such as the natural gas infrastructure and essential power plants (Aslanidze 2016; Opitz 2015; Weaver 2016). Nevertheless, the electricity transmission network in the country needs extensive modernization, as many transmission networks, distribution networks, and facilities are outdated and need to be upgraded. There is a risk of supply interruptions, power outages, and price fluctuations (Baur 2015, pp. 66–67).

The most important Armenian energy source within the country is nuclear energy, which is produced by the nuclear power plant of Medzamo. The country relied on the reopening of this reactor to overcome the energy crisis at the beginning of the 1990s, especially in the period of upheaval after the collapse of the Soviet Union. Nevertheless, the location of the reactor in a seismically active – e.g., the major earthquake in 1988 – and geopolitically strongly contested region – e.g., the war over Nagorno Karabakh and the economic blockade of Azerbaijan and Turkey – remains controversial, especially in neighboring countries.

However, the country has great potential in terms of renewable energies. The many sunny days, hydropower, wind power, and geothermal energy are an ideal starting point for the development of renewable energies (OECD 2018, pp. 68–69). The Armenian government aims to improve energy efficiency in the country and promote renewable energy beyond hydropower (Opitz 2015, pp. 196–200).

Azerbaijan

The EU is of prominent economic importance for Azerbaijan in the South Caucasus. Similarly, the EU is Azerbaijan's largest trading partner. However, trade is almost exclusively based on fossil energies. In this context, the country plays a key role for Europe in oil exports from the Caspian Sea. This includes Azerbaijan's own oil and gas reserves, and the avoidance of Russian networks in providing an export route, a role it also serves for other Caspian oil producers such as Kazakhstan and Turkmenistan.

After the breakdown of the Soviet Union, the EU-Azerbaijan relationship was based on the PCA of 1999. This agreement focuses on the areas of political dialog and economic cooperation and already comes with a strong focus on energy policy. The PCA was accompanied by the support programs TACIS, INOGATE, and TRACECA. Together with the Energy Charter Treaty, which entered into force in 1998, it gave energy policy a strong focus in the EU-Azerbaijan relationship. Azerbaijan is especially important for the EU due to energy diversification. For Azerbaijan, the interest of a close relationship lies primarily in support measures for modernization, diversification, and financial assistance (Pataraia 2015). The accession of Azerbaijan to the ENP in 2004 was accompanied by a Country Report adopted by the EU Commission in 2005, and an Action Plan (2006), which focused on democracy, the rule of law, market developments but also the environment, as well as the strengthening EU-Azerbaijan bilateral energy cooperation and regional cooperation in the field of energy and transport. In the same year, Azerbaijan launched a state program to reduce greenhouse gas emissions and increase energy efficiency. The program allocated $60 million for the development of alternative energy sources (Baur 2015, pp. 111–112). In 2006, an EU-Azerbaijan Strategic Energy Partnership was set up and a "Memorandum of Understanding on a Strategic Partnership in the Field of Energy" was signed to enhance energy-cooperation between the partners. It focused on diversification and the security of energy supplies, the deepening of the market reforms, the development and modernization of energy infrastructures, energy efficiency, energy savings, and the use of renewable energies (European Council/Council of the European Union 2020b; Guliyev 2015).

In 2009, Azerbaijan became part of the EaP. Negotiations on an AA between the EU and Azerbaijan began in June 2010, but were never concluded. Negotiations have repeatedly stalled, particularly due to political and economic tensions in Azerbaijan (Simão 2018a), as well as disagreements in areas such as justice and human rights, and democracy. The authoritarian government of Azerbaijan wanted to focus mainly on issues of politics and security, trade and investment, and sector-specific cooperation, while the EU insisted on political reforms (European Parliament/Directorate-general for External Policies – Policy Department 2017, pp. 21–23). In 2018, EU and Azerbaijan agreed on their new partnership priorities. The agreement is based on the common political and economic interests of the EU and Azerbaijan, and aims to strengthen and expand relations in this regard. In this context, partnership priorities have been defined, of which connectivity, energy efficiency, environment, and climate activities are some of the priorities (European Council/Council of the European Union 2020b). In addition, initiated by the European Commission, it was agreed that the Southern Gas Corridor of Azerbaijan would be put into operation and long-standing plans would be realized. The gas corridor, which consists of the South Caucasus Pipeline, TANAP, and TAP pipelines, is intended to ensure the infrastructure for gas transport from the Caspian region and the Middle East to Europe. The gas corridor is thus an alternative to the Russian supply route and contributes to the desired diversification of energy exports (DGAP Research Institute 2014, pp. 3–5). Oil is transported to Europe via the main oil pipeline Baku-Tbilisi-Ceyhan.

Oil, however, has played a central role in Azerbaijan's energy supply since the beginning of the twentieth century and this role was even enlarged during the Soviet era (Nasibov in this handbook). Oil (onshore as well as offshore) and gas exports are still an essential economic factor, as a large share of the country's government revenue depends on exports. For example, Azerbaijan exported 2.5 million tons of crude oil to Germany in 2020. In total, the country produced approximately 37.5 million tons of crude oil and 24.5 billion cubic meters of natural gas in 2019 (Feyziyeva 2021, pp. 55–58). This makes Azerbaijan a significant energy producer and exporter of crude oil and natural gas (Karimli and Aghayev 2020; Baur 2015; Souleimanov 2004). The dependence of the Azerbaijani economy on export levels poses a risk of external shocks but is also the basis for the wealth of the country's economic elite. Due to its energy resources and strategic location, Azerbaijan plays a central role as an energy supplier and actor for European energy security and has a great interest in expanding onto the European market. Given Azerbaijan's geopolitical situation and the European Union's needs, both actors cooperate closely in the field of energy security (DGAP Research Institute 2014, pp. 3–5; Halbach and Musayev 2011). Nevertheless, many European countries still require fossil fuels, which is why Azerbaijan will continue to export crude oil and natural gas in the future (Feyziyeva 2021, pp. 55–58). The impact of this dependency was evident in 2015 when, after years of economic growth, the country saw a decline of around 15% in its GDP compared to 2014, due to lower demand for oil and gas and the subsequent fall in world market prices.

One threat for the cooperation of the country with the West is the frozen, but also recurrently flaring, conflict between Azerbaijan and Armenia over the Nagorno-Karabakh region. Between 1992 and 1994, the renewed conflicts over the Nagorno-Karabakh region led to the "Contract of the Century," which was signed with Western (primarily USA and British) oil companies over the use of Azerbaijani oil resources. The signing immensely increased the importance of Azerbaijani energy supplies to the West (Karimli and Aghayev 2020; Feyziyeva 2021). Due to this threat and the dependence on oil and gas, Azerbaijan has also developed abundant solar and wind resources, as well as biomass, geothermal, and hydropower. As the country has sufficient potential for the development of renewable energy, the development of alternative energy sources could contribute to the achievement of environmental goals, such as the reduction of greenhouse gas emissions. The expansion and use of alternative energy sources are planned by a medium-term national strategy of the country (OECD 2018, pp. 107–110.; Karimli and Aghayev 2020; Pataraia 2015). For this reason, Azerbaijan's government has reached out for energy resources beyond oil and gas since 2015. Like Armenia, Azerbaijan has had good prerequisites for the expansion of renewable energies in the area of wind, sun, biomass, and hydropower sources for a couple of years (Nasibov in this handbook).

Belarus

After the collapse of the Soviet Union, Belarus and the EU initially started a cooperative relationship in the early 1990s. As a comparatively well-developed state in the East with a well-developed processing industry, highly skilled workers and a noteworthy technology sector, Belarus was certainly a potentially interesting economic partner (Timmermann 2003, p. 16). This relationship deteriorated rapidly, however, when Alyaksandr Lukashenka took office in 1994. The development of Belarus into an authoritarian state has hindered further rapprochement with the EU until today and has turned this into the most complicated relationship within the EaP.

Under Lukashenka, the regime cultivated a stronger relationship with Russia. Both states signed a treaty creating a Union State of Russia and Belarus in 2000, laying the foundation for a common economic space (Nice 2012, p. 5). This bond was strengthened in 2010, when Belarus was one of the founding members of the EACU; a principal task of the EACU together with Kazakhstan, Russia, and the "Single Economic Space" created in 2012 (Schrötter and Ghulinyan-Gerz 2017, pp. 83–86). In January 2015, membership in the EAEU, as the successor of the EACU, followed. While Russia hopes for integrational effects, for Belarus, the interest of this closer cooperation lies especially in the heavy discounts on Russian oil and gas supplies. These indirect subsidies account for a decisive share of Belarusian economic power, which indicates a strong dependence. Due to its geographic location, Russia is also dependent on Belarus for oil and gas exports to the European Union, since the shortest, and thus cheapest, transport route passes through Belarus (Nuti 2005).

For the EU, the relationship between Russia and Belarus is crucial when it comes to the security of energy supply, as the Jamal pipeline from the Siberian oil fields runs through Belarus. The outcome of conflict between both states was witnessed in 2009. Despite granted discounts, oil and gas prices have been rising steadily over the years, confronting the Minsk government with economic problems. Unpaid bills then led to conflicts with Russia, which resulted in a shutdown of the gas pipeline through Belarus (▶ Chap. 7, "European Union Energy Policy: A Discourse Perspective" in this handbook).

In view of these interconnections between Russia and Belarus, the relations between the EU and Belarus are mainly limited to attempts to influence the normative shaping of Belarusian domestic policy and to support civil society and the respect for human rights (Nice 2012, p. 8; Haukkala 2008). As part of the ENP, the EU put forward proposals for improved cooperation with the government in 2006 (European Council/Council of the European Union 2022b). A speech by Deputy Foreign Minister Valery Voronetsky at a conference in Brussels initially raised hopes that Belarus would want to cooperate more closely with the EU on energy security issues in the future.

In May 2009, Belarus officially became part of the EaP, allowing cooperation, at least in a multilateral context. Nevertheless, cooperation remained difficult, as the Minsk government did not meet European demands for basic democratic values and the principles of international cooperation. As a result, the EU has increasingly distanced itself from the authoritarian government, thus failing to intensify relations or conclude a PCA. Due to increasing tensions between the Lukashenka government and the opposition, the EU imposed sanctions against government representatives for the first time after the presidential elections in 2010, which ultimately led to a "diplomatic impasse" (Nice 2012, p. 9).

However, the Belarus-Russia relationship also fluctuates between rapprochement and conflict. Russia's efforts to enter into a full union with Belarus failed, as the Belarusian government was not eager to endanger the sovereignty and retention of power of its country. Nevertheless, Belarus is still highly dependent on Russia. The dependence of Belarus on Russian energy resources and low energy prices is shown by a dependency of over 90% of Belarusian food exports and 70% of industrial exports to Russia (Schrötter and Ghulinyan-Gerz 2017, p. 86). In 2016, tensions between Russia and Belarus erupted again over oil and gas prices. Lukashenka paid less than contractually agreed, which ended in a dispute between the two economic partners. As a result of this conflict, there was another short-lived rapprochement with the EU in 2017, when the Belarusian president reached an agreement with the European Commission for a refugee center and adopted relaxations regarding the entry of foreigners. However, Lukashenka's announcement that he would pursue a more "multivectoral" foreign policy in the future remained more of a provocation toward Russia (Schrötter and Ghulinyan-Gerz 2017, p. 92).

With the Belarusian presidential elections in August 2020, relations with the EU reached an all-time low. The elections have not been recognized by EU member states, and several calls to end the violence and repression by Belarusian authorities against peaceful protesters and opposition figures have also been ignored by the Lukashenka regime. The result has been a series of sanctions, the end of which is currently not in sight due to continued repression (European Council/Council of the European Union 2022c).

Belarus's vulnerability to Russia is particularly evident regarding its energy system. This is characterized by high energy consumption with, at the same time, hardly any resources of its own (Novikau 2019; Gerasimov 2010; Balmaceda 2006). Consequently, a large share of Belarus' energy supply is imported from Russia. Natural gas accounted for 62% of Belarusian primary energy supply in 2017, and crude oil for 26% (IRENA 2017). The status of being a transit country for Russian energy cannot counteract this dependence. To reduce the dependence on Russian energy, Belarus is trying to become more independent in its energy policy (IEA 2015, p. 94). Central to this goal is the increase in energy efficiency and the expansion of renewable energies. Due to its significant potential, especially in the solar, wind, and biomass sectors, the country managed to at least reach a share of 7% in 2017 (IEA 2020a). The completion of Belarus' first post-Chernobyl nuclear power plant in 2020 is also an expression of the desire for energy independence (Valynets 2021). The entire Belarusian energy sector is a state monopoly and operators are organized hierarchically under the government. All strategic decisions within energy policy are made exclusively by the president (IEA 2015, p. 93). For this reason, it is difficult for Belarus to convince foreign economic actors to invest in the country's energy market.

Georgia

Georgia, together with Ukraine and Moldova, is one of the most EU friendly countries. Georgia strongly and steadily insists on its European vocation. It expects the EU to recognize it by accepting at least a general and long-term perspective of eventual membership (Knodt et al. 2018, pp. 9–27). In March 2022, Georgia applied for EU membership in the face of the Russian invasion of Ukraine. Relations between Georgia and the EU began with the recognition of Georgia as an independent state in 1992. Cooperation was initially based on humanitarian, economic, and technical support, as well as various aid programs. In 1996, the PCA was signed and entered into force in 1999. In the same year, the Caucasian Summit also agreed upon an intensified joint cooperation in favor of democratization, respect for human rights, and economic and social development.

Since the Georgian "Rose Revolution" and the resignation of President Eduard Shevardnadze in 2003, the country has become increasingly oriented toward the West (Halbach 2015; Schrötter and Ghulinyan-Gerz 2017). The European Union supported Georgia's development process after the Rose Revolution and thus hoped for democratization (Jafarova 2011; Darchiashvili and Bakradze 2019). The European Commission, together with the World Bank, supported Georgia financially, with a sum of about 850 million euros in 2004–2006 (Doinjashvili 2017, pp. 68–69). In 2004, Georgia was included in the ENP and the first Country Report was adopted by the EU Commission in 2005 as part of the following Action Plan, listing the measures needed to achieve the ENP goals. One year later, the ENP Action Plan (2006) came into force, setting out the strategic points of cooperation between the EU and Georgia. Key points were democratization, rule of law, the respect for human rights, the fight against corruption, and reform of the judiciary. In the framework of the ENP, Georgia was also supported by the ENPI and the NIP. The focus lay on the priorities of the ENP: the development of politics, economy, and society in the country (Whitman and Wolff 2010, p. 88; Doinjashvili 2017, pp. 70–71). In addition, individual projects and other programs were supported in the areas of agriculture, justice, regional development, conflict resolution, and public financial management (Doinjashvili 2017, pp. 70–73).

Meanwhile Georgia's relationship with Russia has deteriorated after separatist conflicts in Abkhazia and South Ossetia, putting it in conflict with Russia, the patron and protector of the two separatist powers. As an outcome of the war in South Ossetia and Abkhazia, the EU devoted special attention toward Georgia from 2008 onward. The EU and former French President Nicolas Sarkozy played a special role in resolving the conflict by setting up an EU Monitoring Mission (Council of the European Union 2008a) and creating the post of EU Special Representative for the crisis in Georgia (Council of the European Union 2008b). In 2011, the post of Special Representative was combined with the one of EU Special Representative for the South Caucasus (established in 2003, Council of the European Union 2003b), thus creating the post of an EU Special Representative for the South Caucasus and the crisis in Georgia (Council of the European Union 2011; Knodt et al. 2018, p. 41).

In 2014, the AA between the EU and Georgia was signed, representing a "signpost to modernization" for Georgia. It replaced the old PCA and the ENP Action Plan from 2006. The AA has been in full force since July 2016. It includes an expansion of relations between the EU and Georgia, development of the country's territorial integrity, a DCFTA, visa liberalization, and conflict resolution between Abkhazia and South Eastern Georgia (European Council/Council of the European Union 2020c). Georgia is also a recipient of financial resources from EU bilateral programs. The funds contribute significantly to the modernization of the country (Simão 2018b). The establishment of the DCFTA increases Georgian exports of goods into the EU and thus, its political and economic integration with the EU. For the AA, Georgia also committed itself to the respect for human rights, democracy, the rule of law, market economy, and sustainable development (Halbach 2015).

Thus, in the South Caucasus, relations between the EU and Georgia are the most consolidated and advanced (Simão 2018b; Delcour 2019; Schrötter and Ghulinyan-Gerz 2017). This can also be seen by Georgia's decision to join other EU energy and climate initiatives. It is part of the "EU4Energy," the IEA program financed by the EU, aiming to improve energy data capabilities and enhance data collection and monitoring. In addition, it provides technical assistance on legislative and regulatory frameworks, and key energy infrastructure investments (EU Neighbours 2021). Furthermore, Georgia has joined the EU Covenant of Mayors on Climate and Energy and declared its commitment to a voluntary reduction of greenhouse emissions by 2030, as well as an energy and climate action plan (Aslanidze 2016; Nabiyeva 2018). Georgia, like Armenia, has also joined the Partnership for Energy Efficiency and Environmental Protection in Eastern Europe and is pursuing projects to improve energy efficiency and CO_2 reduction (Doinjashvili 2017, pp. 82–83).

In principle, Georgia has no fossil energy resources of its own, such as natural gas or oil. However, it serves as a transit country for oil and gas from Russia to Armenia, as well as from Azerbaijan to Turkey. In this position, Georgia receives revenue for the respective oil and gas transport routed through the country, such as the oil pipelines coming from Azerbaijan and gas exports via the South Caucasus Pipeline (SCP) (Aslanidze 2016). Unlike Azerbaijan and Armenia, the country derives 80–90% of its electricity from renewable energy sources. The largest share is obtained from hydropower plants (Aslanidze 2016, p. 8). However, fluctuations in hydropower and the aging energy infrastructure can lead to seasonal power outages (Nabiyeva 2018, p. 17). Yet, the expansion of renewable energy is concentrated on hydropower and has picked up momentum, as Georgia seeks both to meet its domestic needs and to export more electricity. The EU is an important supporter and cooperation partner of Georgia on the path to renewable energy. Both bilateral agreements and regional, as well as international, initiatives play a role in this regard (Baur 2015). Thus, Georgia is part of the Energy Community, which aims to create a sustainable energy market, increase energy security, improve energy efficiency, and promote the use of renewable energy. Its member states have agreed to implement the EU energy legislation. They follow national energy and climate plans, and endorse the set targets to reduce greenhouse gas emissions by 2030. Despite the commitment of the initiatives, there are no enforcement mechanisms and sanctions available, which is why the progress of the member countries, including Georgia's, is comparatively low (Nabiyeva 2018).

Republic of Moldova

The government in Moldova has been in favor of cooperation with the EU since gaining independence from the Soviet Union in 1991 (Całus and Kosienkowski 2018, p. 3). The Republic of Moldova has strong ties to the EU through its common history with Romania. Between the first and second world wars the two countries were united. Moldovans automatically gain a Romanian passport if they prove that their ancestors were Romanian before the split of the two countries. Nevertheless, public opinion is divided into pro-European and pro-Russian communities.

In 1994, the PCA was established as a legal framework for bilateral relations and came into force in 1998 (Gabanyi 2005, p. 12). Regarding cooperation in the field of energy, the PCA laid down general market economy rules and specified areas of cooperation such as environmental impact, promotion of energy conservation and modernization, development and diversification of the energy infrastructure. As with all EaP countries, Moldova accessed the ENP in 2004. Accession was accompanied by a Country Report adopted by the EU Commission in 2004, and an ENP Action Plan (2005), which focused on democracy, the rule of law, market developments but also the environment. Moldova was also able to have funds allocated to it from the ENPI.

In the years 2001–2009 there was a significant increase not only in EU aid for Moldova but also in exports to the EU market, whereas trade to the "Commonwealth of Independent States" (CIS) region declined sharply (Całus and Kosienkowski 2018, pp. 7–8). However, the EU's involvement in Moldova was rather hesitant due to the country's instability and its affinity with Russia. The conflict over Transnistria in particular has contributed to the latter (Gabanyi 2005). Transnistria split from Moldova in 1992 after armed internal conflicts between the Moldovian government and Transnistrian Separatists, and the stationing of Russian troops in the territory of Transnistria. Although de facto independent from the central government of Moldova (in terms of administration, currency, and government), Transnistria is not recognized as an independent state (Schrötter and Ghulinyan-Gerz 2017). Only with the eastward enlargement of the EU and the accession of Romania in 2007, has Moldova, as a new EU neighboring state, become of greater importance to the EU. In 2009, Moldova officially became part of the EaP (Całus and Kosienkowski 2018).

Since 2009, the pro-European government in Moldova intensified its relationship with the EU, striving for greater independence from Russia. An important step in energy policy cooperation was Moldova's accession to the Energy Community in 2010, aiming to expand the existing rules and principles, and establish them in a domestic legal framework (IEA 2020a; Energy Community 2022a). In addition, the Energy Community provides financial incentives and organizational support for the development of Moldova's energy infrastructure and measures to achieve security of supply (IEA 2020b).

As a member of the EaP, Moldova is also part of a multilateral cooperation that discusses energy security issues in addition to economic and security issues. Moreover, the Moldovan government's EU-friendly course led to a bilateral AA in 2014, which established a legal basis, and strengthened the relationship between Moldova and the EU (Schrötter and Ghulinyan-Gerz 2017). Included in the AA was a DCFTA on economic integration (Całus and Kosienkowski 2018). Moldova is also taking part in the "EU4Energy" programme of the IEA, financed by the EU, which besides data collection, provides technical assistance on legislative and regulatory frameworks, and key energy infrastructure investments.

Russia has reacted to Moldova's intensification of its pro-European relations by imposing drastic sanctions on Moldova's agricultural sector (especially wine), which has especially caused anger in the country's pro-Russian camp. Since 2015 Moldova has been facing a governmental and constitutional crisis. In 2018 there was a severe incident of embezzlement of EU funds, which led to an almost completely suspension of support for the period from mid-2018 to July 2019. The resumption of payments followed only after Moldova's promise to fully clarify the incident and draw consequences. After a year of continuing unrest, public pressure led to the first direct election of a Moldovian president since 1997 and brought a swing to a more pro-Russian government (Schrötter and Ghulinyan-Gerz 2017). Currently the country has returned to a more pro-European policy with the election of the acting president, the pro-EU Maia Sandu. Together with the victory of her pro-European party in the parliamentary elections of 2021 the political course will, at least for the time being, continue in the direction of intensifying EU relations (Deutsche Welle 2021). After the Russian invasion of Ukraine, Moldova submitted its application for membership to the EU on 3 March 2022 (European Council/Council of the European Union 2022d).

With the rapprochement to the European West, it is even more important for Moldova to become as independent as possible from Russian Energy resources. In 2018, the energy mix in Moldova consisted of 19% biomass, 23% oil, and 53% natural gas (IEA 2020b, p. 6). Moldova had to import almost 80% of its energy needs due to a lack of domestic resources such as oil, gas or coal (Nabiyeva 2018). Only biomass energy production could be self-produced. Rising prices and conflicts with Russia have always posed a threat to the country's energy security and economy. Similar to Belarus and Ukraine, the Republic of Moldova is a transit country for gas exports from Russia, through Ukraine to Turkey and the Trans-Balkan Corridor. However, Moldova does not play a large role in exports to the EU, Russia's main market.

To gain greater independence from Russia in energy policy, Moldova is trying to diversify energy imports. As one of the measures for independence from Russian energy, the EU supported, with over seven million euros, the infrastructural measure to connect the Ukrainian power network Ukrenergo and the Moldovan power network Moldelectrica with the Continental European Network of the "European Network of Transmission System Operators for Electricity" (ENTSO-E). Moldova intends to fully synchronize its power network with ENTSO-E and connect to the European electricity market (IEA 2020b; ENTSO-E 2017). A second very significant project is the Ungheni-Chișinău gas interconnector to Romania, commissioned in 2015, which will provide Moldova with access to the European gas market and was expected to ensure Moldova's entire gas supply at full capacity in 2020. As early as 2015, one year after the pipeline was put into operation, 31.2% less gas was imported from Russia (Gazprom). The increased synchronization with ENTSO-E will also contribute to the diversification and higher stability of the Moldovan electricity grid. For technical compatibility, however, the outdated infrastructure and technology must be renewed and expanded, for which financial resources are needed from the EU (OECD 2018; IEA 2020b; EU Neighbours 2020).

The Moldovan energy policy is based on the National Energy Strategy 2030 which includes the National Renewable Action Plan (NREAP) and the National

Energy Efficiency Action Plan (NEEAP), formulated on the basis of the Energy Community Treaty (IEA 2020b; Energy Community 2022b). With a share of around 20% renewables in the energy mix, consisting almost entirely of solid biofuels, the Republic of Moldova could meet the given renewable energy targets, mainly due to the greater availability of biomass resulting from its large agricultural sector (IEA 2020b, p. 7). Although Moldova is comparatively less developed than other states in the region, its attractiveness has increased for renewable technologies such as hydro, wind or solar, with the "Law on Promotion of the Use of Energy from Renewable Source" of 2016. In addition to the targeted diversification and synchronization with the EU energy market, security of supply is also to be achieved by increasing energy efficiency (Energy Community 2022b).

Ukraine

Since the first years of its independence from the Soviet Union, Ukraine has had an interest in joining the EU as a member. In fact, with the signing of the PCA in 1994, which came into force in 1998, the country was among the first of the post-Soviet states to institutionalize its relationship with the EU and has been part of the ENP since 2004. The political divide between pro-European and pro-Russian interests in the country, as well as corruption, a lack of transparency and deficits in the rule of law have impacted negatively on the accession path for many years (Timmermann 2003). The election of Russian-backed Viktor Yanukovych as Ukrainian president in 2004 sparked the Orange Revolution, a protest movement that criticized not only the fraudulent election results but also Russian influence in Ukraine (Grund 2008, p. 80). The election after the Revolution brought the victory of the pro-European President Viktor Yushchenko. When Yushchenko took office in 2005, one of his first steps was to declare the political goal of EU membership. Although the EU deemed Ukrainian membership for less likely, early on the ENP and later the EaP considered Ukraine to be a "frontrunner" for relations with the EU (Trabandt 2012, p. 78; Stratenschulte 2009, p. 33).

The new, more explicit pro-European foreign policy prompted Brussels to readily allow development aid to flow to the struggling Ukrainian economy, which was also intended to help curb its dependence on Russia. As the largest country in the EaP, with a population of over 40 million, Ukraine also represents a large potential market. This may also have favored the rapprochement by the EU. Based on the ENP Country Report (2004), on 25 February 2005, Ukraine and the EU signed a bilateral Action Plan that was valid until 2008. The plan did not offer the prospect of accession but included the convergence of the Ukrainian legal system with EU law, the respect for human rights, promotion of democratic and market-economy principles, as well as a stable political development. In March 2007, the EU and Ukraine started talks on an enhanced agreement that would include a free trade area and increased cooperation in the field of energy. The war between Russia and Georgia in the separatist regions of Abkhazia and South Ossetia 2008 accelerated the start of negotiations on a far-reaching AA, which was originally to be signed already by the end of 2009. The negotiations were first delayed by political changes which brought Victor Yanukovych back to power. Then, in 2011, the EU suspended further negotiations due to the unlawful imprisonment of opposition member Yulia Tymoshenko, and finally, in 2013, Yanukovych refused to sign the agreement due to pressure from Russia (European Parliament/Directorate-general for External Policies – Policy Department 2015, p. 13). The halt of the AA acted as an accelerant on the already polarized society (Schrötter and Ghulinyan-Gerz 2017, p. 49). The pro-European Euromaidan movement mobilized against the corrupt regime and Russia's influence, ending in a violent conflict and the overthrow of the government. In reaction to the development in Ukraine, Russia illegally annexed the Crimea and provided military support to the separatist movements in the Donbas.

The Russia-Ukraine conflict is marked by humanitarian, social, economic, and political crises. The violent conflict had a fundamental impact on the EU (Davis Cross and Karolewski 2017, p. 4), with the EU being linked to Ukraine in all critical junctures of this conflict (Chaban et al. 2018). The EU in pre-Maidan times had failed to understand that Russia viewed the EU and NATO enlargements as an interference into its "zone of privileged interests" (e.g., Klein 2019, p. 7). The annexation caused a major shift in the EU's foreign policy, introducing the first tranche of sanctions against the Russian Federation in April 2014 and intensifying them after July 2014 when the MH17 flight carrying almost 300 people (many EU citizens) was downed over eastern Ukraine. In addition, the EU cancelled several high-level meetings with Russia and forced the suspension of Russia's entry to the Organisation for Economic Co-operation and Development (OECD) and the IEA. The EU also engaged in mediation talks with Russia and Ukraine starting with the Geneva Format: Ukraine, Russia, the EU, and the USA negotiating within the framework of G8 and G20 summits in April 2014; the Normandy Format: Ukraine, Russia, Germany, and France, without US involvement (Germany and France participated as single players, but also as the voices of the EU); and the Minsk Protocol (Minsk I): Ukraine, Russia and the Organization for Security and Co-operation in Europe (OSCE). With three earlier formats failing, the fourth format (Minsk II) included Ukraine, Russia, Germany, and France and brought a ceasefire, which, however, was also repeatedly broken.

In June 2017, the EU activated a no-visa entry into Schengen for Ukrainian citizens, after long negotiations with Ukraine. Finally, in October 2017, the EU signed the AA including the DCFTA with Ukraine (Chaban et al. 2018). In March 2018, the then High Representative (HR)/Vice-President Federica Mogherini, commenting on the benefits of the AA and a wider EU-Ukraine partnership, stressed that the EU is "there to support you step by step and we will continue to be at your side in the most consistent way we can. The European Union is Ukraine's partner and strongest supporter in striving to build a stable, prosperous democracy and economy" (EEAS 2018). These comments are in line with the strong focus on the ENP and EaP within the central strategic Foreign Policy document of the EU, "The Global Strategy for the European Union's Foreign and Security Policy," published in 2016. Russia's invasion of Ukraine on 24 February 2022 prompted the EU to reimpose strong sanctions against Russia and to support Ukraine in the war against the Russian aggression with military aid. However, the EU is reluctant to extend sanctions to the energy sector because of its heavy dependence on Russian energy resources. In March 2022, Ukraine applied for membership to the EU (European Council/Council of the European Union 2022e).

The energy policy relationship between the EU and Ukraine has always been influenced by the fact that a large share of Russian gas imported into the EU passes through Ukraine (Grošelj 2009). Ukraine is thus, along with Belarus, the most important transit country. As such, on one hand, they benefited from the compensation payments for Russian exports to Europe as well as from the discounted gas prices for its imports. But on the other hand, dependence on Russian gas and the transit status have always been an instrument for Russian pressure. Many scholars therefore interpret Russia's threat of increasing gas prices in 2005 as a way of putting pressure on the then Yushchenko government, as it would have decisively weakened Ukraine's already struggling economic power (e.g. Weaver 2016, p. 112). After long disputes, Russia and Ukraine failed to reach an agreement and Gazprom curtailed gas supplies for the first time in January 2006. In 2009 a similar process was witnessed due to the next Russian Ukrainian gas conflict, with serious impact on the economies of several EU member states (Grošelj 2009, p. 5). Thus, Russia demonstrated not only its power toward Ukraine but also toward the EU with regard to how much European energy security relies on the relationship between Ukraine and Russia (Goda 2017; ▶ Chap. 11, "EU-Russia Energy Relations").

As a result, the pipeline project Nord Stream 1, with a direct link from Russia to Germany, was realized (▶ Chap. 7, "European Union Energy Policy: A Discourse Perspective" in this handbook). While the alternative pipelines entail an increased security of supply for the EU, Russia's interest is to create routes for Russian gas directly to key consumer states in the EU, reducing dependence on difficult transit states (Weaver 2016, p. 107). For Ukraine, on the other hand, the commissioning of alternative gas pipelines implies the loss of a significant source of income. At the same time, Ukraine is also trying to become less dependent on Russian gas and oil and therefore wishes to further expand its relationship with the EU – even after the election of Yanukovych in 2010, who has since turned his political course more toward the EU than during his first election campaign in 2004. In the same year, Ukraine became an Observer in the Energy Community, before officially joining in 2011, one year after Moldova. This step was undoubtedly the most significant in energy relations between the EU and Ukraine (Goda 2017, p. 96). The tense situation with Russia combined with the two gas crises certainly contributed to Ukraine's attempt to become a part of the EU energy market.

In the wake of the annexation of Crimea and the conflict in the Donbas region, Ukraine stopped importing gas from Gazprom and instead purchased only from European suppliers (IEA 2020c). The conflicts also destroyed existing energy and transport infrastructure. The Donbas region, one of the most important coal and industrial locations in Ukraine, was particularly affected (IEA 2020c). Together with the loss of access to its own onshore gas deposits off the Crimean Peninsula, this led to serious threats to energy supply security (Chumak and Prokip 2018, pp. 75–76). Since the 2014 conflict, there have been several changes in the Ukrainian energy system, which have gradually reduced dependence on Russia and strengthened ties with the EU energy market (Goda 2017, p. 94). Specifically, and in accordance with the Energy Community Treaty, Ukraine drafted a new Energy Strategy in 2017, which emphasized for example, energy efficiency, renewables development, and market integration with the EU (Chumak and Prokip 2018, p. 76). Like Moldova, Ukraine is also planning to integrate its electricity system with ENTSO-E and to modernize its infrastructure. A significant step in this direction for Ukraine was the agreement with ENTSO-E to connect its electricity network to the EU in the coming years, as well as the introduction of an ownership unbundling model (Energy Community 2022c). To support modernization and integration processes, Ukraine also benefits from EU4Energy as all EaP countries do.

A threat to the EU-Ukraine relationship was Germany's Nord Stream 2 project, which build a second direct connection from Russia to Germany. Ukraine in particular has since feared losing its all-important strategic transit status, and with it, an important source of revenue. But Ukraine's security strategy (as well as those of other eastern EU member states) is also threatened, because the gas transport system functions as a protective shield against Russia. The new Ukrainian President Volodomyr Zelensky views "[...] this project exclusively through the prism of security and consider[s] it a dangerous geopolitical weapon of the Kremlin" (The Guardian 2021). Since fall 2021, Russia has almost exclusively supplied gas to Europe through the Nord Stream 1 pipeline, leaving the pipeline through Belarus (Yamal) and the pipelines through Ukraine almost unused. Moreover, Gazprom has let its European gas storage facilities run dry.

Ukraine is also able to produce a relatively high share, more than 60%, of its energy demand itself, through nuclear, fossil, and renewable energy. In 2018, the energy mix was composed of 30% coal, 28% natural gas, 24% nuclear and 5% renewables (IEA 2020c). This can be explained, on the one hand, by the fact that it has abundant coal and gas reserves as well as stocks of oil, which, moreover, have been heavily subsidized by the government in the past. Secondly, Ukraine is one of the world's largest producers of nuclear energy and, within the EaP, one of the only producers, along with Armenia (Chumak and Prokip 2018, p. 75). As part of Ukraine's nuclear fuel supply diversification policy, the country now imports almost half of its nuclear fuel from a US company (Westinghouse), replacing the previous traditional provider, the Russian company TVEL.

In accordance with the Energy Community Treaty, but also to increase independence, Ukraine aims to achieve higher energy efficiency. Especially due to energy-intensive industry and an old infrastructure, as well as the heating of old residential buildings, Ukraine has a large deficit in energy efficiency. Therefore, another key strategy is the expansion of renewable energy, which will be pushed even more in the coming years. For example, the Law on Promotion of Heat Production from Alternative Sources reduces subsidies for the private use of gas and makes biomass competitive (Schön-Chanishvili 2021). In recent years, investments have also been made in the supply of other renewable energy sources to generate electricity, such as solar and wind. These renewables were able to achieve a share of almost 7% by 2020 (IEA 2020c). However, Ukraine will continue to need investments from EU to modernize the existing energy system and reduce the high energy consumption (Goda 2017, p. 95). All these developments are now subject to the outcome of the war.

Conclusion

The analysis of the EU's energy relations with the EaP countries draws a very heterogeneous picture. The shape of the EU's relations to its eastern partners is currently changing at a rapid pace; from the attempt to further deepen relations in the case of Georgia, Moldova, and Ukraine by submitting EU membership applications in 2022, to the apparent secession of Belarus from the EU, which has suspended participation in the EaP in 2021 and has taken a further clear pro-Russia stance following the Russian invasion of Ukraine in February 2022. The domestic, political, and geographical conditions could not be more different. Combined with the frozen but also open conflicts between and within the EaP countries, and the related influence of Russia, not only the political autonomies of the countries are weakened but so is the development of reliable energy infrastructure systems that enable investments from the EU and other foreign economic actors.

Currently, Armenia's most important energy source is nuclear energy which is produced by the nuclear power plant of Medzamo, located in a seismically active and geopolitically strongly contested region. The war over Nagorno-Karabakh and the economic blockade by Azerbaijan and Turkey further weaken the country's abilities not only to develop alternative energy sources but also to modernize the electricity transmission network in the country thereby reducing the risk of supply interruptions and power outages. Nevertheless, the Armenian government is eager to improve energy efficiency and promote renewable energies beyond hydropower (Opitz 2015). Similar to Azerbaijan, the country has great potential to expand renewable energies. The numerous sunny days, hydropower, wind power, and geothermal energy are an optimal starting point for the development of renewable energies in the future (OECD 2018).

In the case of Azerbaijan, the EU is of prominent economic importance. Similarly, the EU is Azerbaijan's largest trading partner. However, trade is almost exclusively based on fossil energies. In this context, the country plays a key role for Europe in oil exports from the Caspian Sea. Several European countries still require fossil fuels, which is why Azerbaijan will continue to export crude oil and natural gas in the future (Feyziyeva 2021). Due to lower demand for oil and gas and the subsequent fall in world market prices since 2015 together with the recurrently flaring conflict between Azerbaijan and Armenia over the Nagorno-Karabakh region, Azerbaijan began to invest in extensive solar and wind power resources as well as biomass, geothermal and hydropower.

Belarus' vulnerability to Russia is particularly evident with regard to its energy system. This is characterized by high energy consumption with hardly any resources of its own (Novikau 2019; Gerasimov 2010), which leads to the import of a large part of Belarus' energy supply from Russia. Its status as a transit country for Russian energy cannot counteract this dependence. In addition, the entire Belarusian energy sector is a state monopoly and operators are organized hierarchically under the government. All strategic decisions within energy policy are made exclusively by the president (IEA 2015) hindering the EU and foreign economic actors to invest in the country's energy market.

In contrast to Armenia and Azerbaijan, the two other South Caucasus countries, Georgia derives 80–90% of its electricity from renewable energy sources. The largest share is obtained from hydropower plants (Aslanidze 2016). However, fluctuations in hydropower and the aging energy infrastructure can lead to seasonal power outages (Nabiyeva 2018). Yet, the expansion of renewable energy is concentrated on hydropower and has picked up momentum as Georgia seeks both to meet its domestic needs and to export more electricity. The EU is an important supporter and cooperation partner on Georgia's path to renewable energy. Both bilateral agreements and regional, as well as international, initiatives play a role in this regard (Baur 2015).

The government in Moldova has been in favor of cooperation with the EU (Całus and Kosienkowski 2018) and has strong ties to the EU through its common history with Romania. With a share of 20% renewables in the energy mix in 2018, Moldova could meet the given renewable energy targets, mainly due to the greater availability of biomass resulting from its large agricultural sector (IEA 2020b). Although Moldova is comparatively less developed than other states in the region, its attractiveness for renewable technologies such as wind or solar has increased over time. In addition to the targeted diversification and synchronisation with the EU energy market, security of supply is to be achieved in the future by increasing energy efficiency.

Finally, the energy relations between the EU and Ukraine have always been influenced by the fact that a large share of Russian gas imported into the EU passes through Ukraine (Grošelj 2009). Ukraine is thus, along with Belarus, the most important transit country. As such, on one hand, Ukraine benefited from the compensation payments for Russian exports to Europe, as well as from the discounted gas prices for its imports. But on the other hand, dependence on Russian gas and its transit status have always been instruments for Russian pressure. This tense situation with Russia combined with two gas crises contributed to Ukraine's efforts to increase liberalization and harmonization with the EU energy market. Since 2014, several changes in the Ukrainian energy system have led to a reduced dependence on Russia and a stronger connection to the EU energy market (Goda 2017). The expansion of renewable energies is also an important strategy in Ukraine, which will be pushed more strongly in the coming years. Thus, in recent years, investments have been made in the supply of other renewable energy sources for electricity production, such as solar and wind energy. However, Ukraine will still need EU investments to modernize the existing energy system and reduce high energy demand (Goda 2017). All these developments now depend on the outcome of the war.

From the 1990s onward, EU policy in Eastern Europe and the South Caucasus seemed reactive and inconclusive. In the post-Soviet region, no common goals and measures could be developed for long periods, despite the establishment of the EaP (Schrötter and Ghulinyan-Gerz 2017). The strategy papers of the ENP stated that sustainable ecological development within the EaP countries was of great importance and could only be realized through close cooperation with the countries. Although issues of environmental protection as well as energy security were hardly considered in the ENPI's NIPs and did not constitute an independent development program, the EU nevertheless subsidized various ecological development projects. For example, European development cooperations supported projects for the expansion of renewable energies, the increase of energy efficiency, and measures regarding sustainable management in agriculture. The instruments of the ENP and the EaP, not only by means of financial grants and budget support, but also by consultations and the development of strategies, are crucial for progress in energy supply (Doinjashvili 2017).

Almost all the countries of the EaP have great potential to further develop renewable energies within the framework of the energy transition. Yet, concrete measures for the deployment of such technologies have remained largely absent in recent years. To accelerate energy transition in the countries, specific regional and domestic energy initiatives, regional cross-border cooperation, financial support, research, and promotion programs are needed. Although the EU's relations with the EaP countries, with the exception of Belarus, have strengthened in recent years, the set goals are far from being achieved. Due to Russia's influence and impact, the institutional and infrastructural weakness of the countries and the protracted conflicts, the potential that exists has not yet been realized.

Cross-References

► Energy Governance in Armenia
► Energy Governance in Azerbaijan
► Energy Governance in Germany
► Energy Governance in Russia: From a Fossil to a Green Giant?
► Energy Relations of the EU and its Southern Neighborhood
► European Union Energy Policy: A Discourse Perspective
► EU-Russia Energy Relations

References

Aslanidze, A. (2016). *The role of the energy charter in promoting electricity cooperation in the south Caucasus* (Occasional paper series). Brussels: Energy Charter Secretariat.

Balmaceda, M. M. (2006). *Belarus: Oil, gas, transit pipelines and Russian foreign energy policy*. London: GMB.

Baur, B. (2015). Die Energieinteressen der EU im Südkaukasus und die Rolle der Europäischen Nachbarschaftspolitik. *TAIF*, (10), 3–37.

Bicchi, F., & Lavenex, S. (2015). The European neighbourhood: Between European integration and international relations. In K. E. Jörgensen, A. K. Aarstad, E. Drieskens, K. Laatikainen, & B. Tonra (Eds.), *The SAGE handbook of European foreign policy: Two volume set* (pp. 868–882). London: Sage Publishers.

Börzel, T. A., & van Hüllen, V. (2014). One voice, one message, but conflicting goals: Cohesiveness and consistency in the European neighbourhood policy. *Journal of European Public Policy, 21*(7), 1033–1049.

Böttger, K. (2020). Östliche Partnerschaft. In W. Weidenfeld, W. Wessels, & F. Tekin (Eds.), *Europa von A bis Z: Taschenbuch der europäischen Integration* (pp. 485–491). Wiesbaden: Springer VS.

Całus, K., & Kosienkowski, M. (2018). Relations between Moldova and the European Union. In P. Flenley & M. Mannin (Eds.), The European Union and its eastern neighbourhood: Europeanisation and its twenty-first-century contradictions (pp. 99–113). Manchester: Manchester University Press.

CEPA (The Comprehensive & Enhanced Partnership Agreement between the European Union & Armenia). (2017). Bruxelles, 24/11/2017. https://eeas.europa.eu/sites/eeas/files/eu-armenia_comprehensive_and_enhanced_partnership_agreement_cepa.pdf. Accessed 14 May 2021.

Chaban, N., Knodt, M., & Elgstroem, O. (2018). Perceptions of the EU's role in the Ukraine-Russian and the Israeli-Palestinian conflicts: A biased mediator. *Cooperation and Conflict, 23*(2), 299–318. https://doi.org/10.1163/15718069-23021154.

Chumak, D., & Prokip, A. (2018). Regional stability through energy cooperation: The case of the EU and Ukraine. *European View, 17*(1), 74–81.

Commission of the European Communities. (1999). Communication from the Commission to the Council and the European Parliament. The European Union's relations with the South Caucasus, under the Partnership and Cooperation Agreements. COM(l999) 272 final.

Commission of the European Communities. (2004). Communication from the Commission, European Neighbourhood Policy, Strategy Paper. COM(2004) 373 final.

Council of the European Union. (2003a). A secure Europe in a better world. European Security Strategy. http://www.consilium.europa.eu/uedocs/cmsUpload/78367.pdf. Accessed 11 Nov 2019.

Council of the European Union. (2003b). Council Joint Action 2003/496/CFSP of 7 July 2003 concerning the appointment of an EU Special Representative for the South Caucasus. 2003/496/CFSP.

Council of the European Union. (2008a). Council Joint Action 2008/736/CFSP of 15 September 2008 on the European Union Monitoring Mission in Georgia, EUMM Georgia. 2008/736/CFSP.

Council of the European Union. (2008b). Council Joint Action 2008/760/CFSP of 25 September 2008 appointing the European Union Special Representative for the crisis in Georgia. 2008/760/CFSP.

Council of the European Union. (2009). Joint Declaration of the Prague Eastern Partnership Summit, Prague, 7 May 2009. 8435/09 (Presse 78).

Council of the European Union. (2011). Council Decision 2011/518/CFSP of 25 August 2011 appointing the European Union Special Representative for the South Caucasus and the crisis in Georgia. 2011/518/CFSP.

Darchiashvili, D., & Bakradze, D. (2019). The EU eastern partnership initiative and Georgia. *Politejy, 62*, 117–140.

Davis Cross, M., & Karolewski, I. (2017). What type of power has the EU exercised in the Ukraine–Russia crisis? A framework of analysis. *Journal of Common Market Studies, 55*(1), 3–19.

Delcour, L. (2019). Armenia's and Georgia's contrasted positioning vis-à-vis the EU: Between vocal centrality and strategic marginality. *Journal of Contemporary European Studies*. https://doi.org/10.1080/14782804.2019.1608815.

Deutsche Welle. (2021, July 11). Moldova election: Pro-EU party headed to victory. https://www.dw.com/en/moldova-election-pro-eu-party-headed-to-victory/a-58228907. Accessed 9 Oct 2021.

DGAP Research Institute (Forschungsinstitut der Deutschen Gesellschaft für Auswärtige Politik e. V.). (2014). Energy security in the South Caucasus. The Southern Gas Corridor in its geopolitical environment. https://dgap.org/system/files/article_pdfs/2014-02_dgapkompakt_meister_engl_www.pdf. Accessed 2 Feb 2022.

Doinjashvili, G. (2017). *Die Wirksamkeit der EU-Entwicklungspolitik in Georgien und Armenien – Vergleichende Fallstudie*. Magdeburg: Bamberger Geographische Schriften.

EEAS (European External Action Service). (2018). Remarks by High Representative/Vice-President, Federica Mogherini at the joint press point with Mr Volodymyr Groysman, Prime Minister of Ukraine. https://eeas.europa.eu/headquarters/headquarters-homepage/41162/remarks-high-representativevice-president-federica-mogherini-joint-press-point-mr-volodymyr_en. Accessed 11 Nov 2020.

Energy Community. (2022a). Who we are. https://www.energy-community.org/aboutus/whoweare.html. Accessed 1 March 2022.

Energy Community. (2022b). Action plans, reports and statements. Moldova. https://energy-community.org/implementation/Moldova/reporting.html. Accessed 20 Feb 2022.

Energy Community. (2022c). Ukraine. https://www.energy-community.org/implementation/Ukraine.html. Accessed 20 Feb 2022.

ENTSO-E. (2017). Electricity transmission system operators of the ENTSO-E Continental Europe Region sign agreements on the Conditions for Future Interconnections with Ukraine and Moldova. https://www.entsoe.eu/news/2017/07/07/entsoe-ce-agreement-conditions-future-grid-connections-with-ukraine-moldova/. Accessed 2 Mar 2022.

EPRS (European Parliamentary Research Service). (2018). Association agreements between the EU and Moldova, Georgia and Ukraine. European implementation assessment. https://www.europarl.europa.eu/RegData/etudes/STUD/2018/621833/EPRS_STU(2018)621833_EN.pdf. Accessed 1 Feb 2022.

EU Neighbours. (2020). How the Ungheni–Chișinău gas pipeline will help Moldova to gain the energy independence. https://www.euneighbours.eu/en/east/eu-in-action/stories/how-ungheni-chisinau-gas-pipeline-will-help-moldova-gain-energy. Accessed 6 Jan 2022.

EU Neighbours. (2021). EU4Energy Programme. https://www.euneighbours.eu/en/east/stay-informed/projects/eu4energy-programme. Accessed 6 Jan 2022.

European Commission. (1992). EC technical assistance to the Commonwealth of Independent States and Georgia: The TACIS programme, 14 September 1992. https://ec.europa.eu/commission/presscorner/detail/en/MEMO_92_54. Accessed 19 April 2020.

European Commission. (2020). Statement by President von der Leyen at the joint press conference with President Michel following the Eastern Partnership Leaders' videoconference. 18 June 2020 Brussels. https://ec.europa.eu/commission/presscorner/detail/en/STATEMENT_20_1131. Accessed 8 Oct 2021.

European Commission. (2021). The EU and Armenia Comprehensive and Enhanced Partnership Agreement enters into force, 28 February 2021, Press release. https://ec.europa.eu/commission/presscorner/detail/en/ip_21_782. Accessed 1 Feb 2022.

European Council/Council of the European Union. (2020a). EU relations with Armenia. https://www.consilium.europa.eu/en/policies/eastern-partnership/armenia/. Accessed 4 Jan 2022.

European Council/Council of the European Union. (2020b). EU relations with Azerbaijan. https://www.consilium.europa.eu/en/policies/eastern-partnership/azerbaijan/. Accessed 4 Jan 2022.

European Council/Council of the European Union. (2020c). EU relations with Georgia. https://www.consilium.europa.eu/en/policies/eastern-partnership/georgia/. Accessed 4 Jan 2022.

European Council/Council of the European Union. (2021). 20 Deliverables for 2020. https://www.consilium.europa.eu/en/policies/eastern-partnership/20-deliverables-for-2020/. Accessed Jan 2022.

European Council/Council of the European Union. (2022a). Eastern Partnership policy beyond 2020. https://www.consilium.europa.eu/en/policies/eastern-partnership/eastern-partnership-policy-beyond-2020/. Accessed 9 Feb 2022.

European Council/Council of the European Union. (2022b). EU relations with Belarus. https://www.consilium.europa.eu/en/policies/eastern-partnership/belarus/. Accessed 21 Mar 2022.

European Council/Council of the European Union. (2022c). Restrictive measures against Belarus. https://www.consilium.europa.eu/en/policies/sanctions/restrictive-measures-against-belarus/. Accessed 21 Mar 2022.

European Council/Council of the European Union. (2022d). EU relations with the Republic of Moldova. https://www.consilium.europa.eu/en/policies/eastern-partnership/moldova/. Accessed 21 Mar 2022.

European Council/Council of the European Union. (2022e). EU relations with Ukraine. https://www.consilium.europa.eu/en/policies/eastern-partnership/ukraine/. Accessed 25 Mar 2022.

European Parliament/Directorate-general for External Policies – Policy Department. (2015). The eastern partnership after five years. Time for deep rethinking. https://www.europarl.europa.eu/RegData/etudes/STUD/2015/536438/EXPO_STU(2015)536438_EN.pdf. Accessed 27 Dec 2021.

European Parliament/Directorate-general for External Policies – Policy Department. (2017). In-depth analysis: EU relations with Armenia and Azerbaijan. https://www.europarl.europa.eu/RegData/etudes/IDAN/2017/603846/EXPO_IDA(2017)603846_EN.pdf. Accessed 27 Dec 2021.

Feyziyeva, G. (2021). Energiebeziehungen zwischen Aserbaidschan und Deutschland. *German International Journal of Modern Science, 9*, 55–58. https://doi.org/10.24412/2701-8369-2021-9-2-55-58.

Gabanyi, A. U. (2005). Die Republik Moldau im Kontext der Neuen EU-Nachbarschaftspolitik, SWP-Studie (S 46), November 2004, Stiftung Wissenschaft und Politik, Deutsches Institut für Internationale Politik und Sicherheit, Berlin. https://www.files.ethz.ch/isn/118613/2004_Moldavia_D.pdf. Accessed 1 Mar 2022.

Gaedtke, J-C. (2009). Europäische Außenpolitik, Stuttgart: UTB.

Gerasimov, Y. (2010). Energy sector in Belarus: Focus on wood and peat fuels. Working papers of the Finnish Forest Research Institute 171. https://jukuri.luke.fi/bitstream/handle/10024/536080/mwp171.pdf?sequence=1&isAllowed=y. Accessed 5 Feb 2022.

Giragosian, R. (2014). Armenia's strategic U-turn, European council of Foreign Relations (ECFR), ECFR/99, April 2014. https://ecfr.eu/wp-content/uploads/ECFR99_ARMENIA_MEMO_AW.pdf. Accessed 27 Dec 2021.

Goda, S. (2017). EU and Ukraine – State of Affairs in Energy Security. *International Issues & Slovak Foreign Policy Affairs, 26*(1–2), 81–100.

Grošelj, K. (2009). Energy security in Russia-EU partnership. *Politics in Central Europe, 5*(1), 5–19.

Grund, M. (2008). Die Ukraine nach der Parlamentswahl 2007: neue Aussichten für die Integration? *Integration, 31*(1), 80–84.

Guliyev, F. (2015). After us, the deluge – Oil windfalls, state elites and the elusive quest for economic diversification in Azerbaijan. *Caucasus Analytical Digest, 69*, 2–20.

Halbach, U. (2015). Georgien im Assoziierungsprozess mit der EU. *SWP-Aktuell, 30*, 1–4.

Halbach, U., & Musayev, K. (2011). EU-Aserbaidschan: Nicht nur Energiepartner: Politische Reformen und friedliche Konfliktbearbeitung sollten mehr Gewicht bekommen. *SWP-Aktuell, 11*, 1–4.

Haukkala, H. (2008). The European Union as a regional normative hegemon: The case of European Neighbourhood Policy. *Europe-Asia Studies, 60*(9), 1601–1622.

IEA (International Energy Agency). (2015). Belarus energy profile Country report. https://iea.blob.core.windows.net/assets/63aaa8a4-d16d-4ff4-84a8-387f440304be/IDR_EasternEurope Caucasus_2015.pdf. Accessed 14 Oct 2021.

IEA (International Energy Agency). (2020a). Belarus energy profile. https://iea.blob.core.windows.net/assets/a9233b70-ee3e-4a0c-8cde-7a174760b3e2/BelarusEnergyProfile.pdf. Accessed 14 Oct 2021.

IEA (International Energy Agency). (2020b). Moldova energy profile. https://www.iea.org/reports/moldova-energy-profile. Accessed 14 Oct 2021.

IEA (International Energy Agency). (2020c). Ukraine energy profile. https://www.iea.org/reports/ukraine-energy-profile/energy-security. Accessed 14 Oct 2021.

IRENA (International Renewable Energy Agency). (2017). Energy profile Belarus. https://www.irena.org/IRENADocuments/Statistical_Profiles/Europe/Belarus_Europe_RE_SP.pdf. Accessed 4 Jan 2022.

Jafarova, E. (2011). EU conflict resolution policy towards the South Caucasus. *Connections, 10*(3), 59–80.

Karimli, A., & Aghayev, A. (2020). The economic opportunities of renewable energy resources in Azerbaijan: Major challenges and scenarios. *Business & IT*. https://doi.org/10.14311/bit.2020.03.06.

Klein, M. (2019). Russia's Military Policy in the Post-Soviet Space: Aims, Instruments and Perspectives, German Institute for International and Security Affairs, SWP Research Paper 1, January 2019, Berlin.

Knodt, M., Urdze, S., Nodia, G., & Paramonov, V. (2018). *EU's policy of democracy promotion. Strategies and impact in Central Asia and the South Caucasus*. Baden-Baden: Nomos.

Konrad-Adenauer-Stiftung. (2020). Armenia's precarious balance: The European Union and the Eurasian Economic Union. https://www.kas.de/documents/269781/0/Armenia%E2%80%99s+Precarious+Balance+The+European+Union+(EU)+and+The+Eurasian+Economic+Union+(EAEU).pdf/68995f77-79e5-0efe-633d-1b13bb8eee90?version=1.0&t=1613112266994&fbclid=IwAR36-IpxADXzQyI-NW3sPF302z_JPpjrn1FPH7-ykhP4B7qxX7eTVV0k4I4. Accessed 11 Dec 2021.

Kratochvíl, P., & Tulmets, E. (2010). *Constructivism and rationalism in EU external relations: The case of the European Neighbourhood Policy*. Baden-Baden: Nomos.

Langbein, J., & Börzel, T. (Eds.). (2014). *Explaining policy change in the European Union's Eastern neighbourhood*. London/New York: Routledge.

Lippert, B. (2020). Europäische Nachbarschaftspolitik. In W. Weidenfeld, W. Wessels, & F. Tekin (Eds.), *Europa von A bis Z: Taschenbuch der europäischen Integration* (pp. 207–213). Wiesbaden: Springer VS.

Nabiyeva, K. (2018). *Energy transition in South East and Eastern Europe, South Caucasus and Central Asia – Challenges, opportunities and best practices on renewable energy and energy efficiency*. Berlin: Friedrich-Ebert-Stiftung.

Nervi Christensen, A. (2011). *The making of the European Neighbourhood Policy*. Baden-Baden: Nomos.

Nice, A. (2012). *Playing Both Sides: Belarus between Russia and the EU, DGAP-Analyse*, 2. Berlin: Forschungsinstitut der Deutschen Gesellschaft für Auswärtige Politik e.V. https://nbn-resolving.org/urn:nbn:de:0168-ssoar-350228. Accessed 1 Nov 2021.

Novikau, A. (2019). Conceptualizing and achieving energy security: The case of Belarus. *Energy Strategy Reviews, 26*(2019). https://doi.org/10.1016/j.esr.2019.100408.

Nuti, D. M. (2005). The Belarus economy: Suspended animation between state and markets. In S. White, E. Korosteleva, & J. Löwenhardt (Eds.), *Postcommunist Belarus* (pp. 92–122). Oxford: Rowman & Littlefield.

OECD (Organisation for Economic Co-operation and Development). (2018). *Inventory of energy subsidies in the EU's eastern partnership countries, green finance and investment*. Paris: OECD. https://doi.org/10.1787/9789264284319-en.

Opitz, P. (2015). Erneuerungsbedarf: Energiewirtschaft in Armenien, Aserbaidschan und Georgien. *Osteuropa, 7*, 191–209.

Pataraia, T. (2015). Energy transit and security imbalance in South Caucasus: The road between Russia and the European Union. Heinrich Böll Stiftung South Caucasus. https://ge.boell.org/sites/default/files/uploads/2015/03/energy_eng-final_1.pdf. Accessed 10 Mar 2022.

Patten, C., & Solana, J. (2002). Joint Letter on Wider Europe, 07.08.2002.

Schön-Chanishvili, M. (2021). Analyse: Erneuerbare Energien und Mittelstand statt Kohle und Stahl. https://www.bpb.de/internationales/europa/ukraine/327498/analyse-erneuerbare-energien-und-mittelstand-statt-kohle-und-stahl. Accessed 10 Mar 2022.

Schrötter, H. J., & Ghulinyan-Gerz, I. (2017). *Die Europäische Union und ihre östlichen Nachbarn – Neue Partner, die Rolle Russlands und Armeniens gescheiterte Assoziierung*. Baden-Baden: Nomos.

Simão, L. (2018a). *The EU's neighbourhood policy towards the South Caucasus. Expanding the European Security Community.* Coimbra: Palgrave Macmillan.

Simão, L. (2018b). The European neighbourhood policy and the South Caucasus. In T. Schumacher, A. Marchetti, & T. Demmelhuber (Eds.), *The Routledge handbook on the European neighbourhood policy* (pp. 312–323). Abingdon/New York: Routledge.

Smith, N. R. (2012). The EU's two-track promotion of democracy in its eastern neighbourhood examining the case of Armenia. *Asia-Pacific Journal of EU Studies, 10*(1), 19–43.

Smolnik, F. (2018). CEPA im 'Neuen Armenien' – Armeniens Reformkurs unter der Regierung Paschinjan und das neue Partnerschaftsabkommen mit der EU. *SWP-Aktuell, 42,* 1–4.

Souleimanov, E. (2004). Der Konflikt um Berg-Karabach. In IFSH (Ed.), *OSZE-Jahrbuch 2004* (pp. 217–236). Baden-Baden: Nomos.

Stratenschulte, E. D. (2009). Planquadrat Osteuropa, Die Östliche Partnerschaft der EU. *Osteuropa, 5,* 29–43.

SZ (Süddeutsche Zeitung). (2009, May 7). Aufbruch ins Ungewisse: Die EU lädt sechs östliche Länder zur Partnerschaft ein, 07.05.2009.

The Guardian. (2021, August 22). Nord Stream 2 'dangerous geopolitical weapon'. https://guardian.ng/news/nord-stream-2-dangerous-geopolitical-weapon/. Accessed 23 Sept 2021.

Timmermann, H. (2003). Die EU und die 'Neuen Nachbarn' Ukraine und Belarus, SWP-Studie (S 41), Stiftung Wissenschaft und Politik, Deutsches Institut für Internationale Politik und Sicherheit, Berlin. https://nbn-resolving.org/urn:nbn:de:0168-ssoar-262095. Accessed 1 Nov 2020.

Trabandt, V. (2012). *Neue Nachbarn, gute Nachbarschaft? Die EU als internationaler Akteur am Beispiel ihrer Demokratieförderung in Belarus und der Ukraine 2004–2009.* Stuttgart: ibidem-Verlag.

Valynets, H. (2021). The new nuclear power plant in Belarus and reminders of Chernobyl, Heinrich Böll Stiftung, 26.04.2021, Brussels. https://eu.boell.org/en/2021/04/26/new-nuclear-power-plant-belarus-and-reminders-chernobyl. Accessed 23 Sept 2021.

Vobruba, G. (2010). Das politische Potential der Europäischen Nachbarschaftspolitik. Zur Überwindung des Widerspruchs zwischen Integration und Erweiterung der Europäischen Union, in: Leviathan, 38, S. 45–63.

Weaver, C. (2016). *The politics of the Black Sea region – EU neighbourhood, conflict zone or future security community?* London/New York: Routledge.

Whitman, R., & Wolff, S. (2010). The EU as a conflict manager? The case of Georgia and its implications. *International Affairs, 86*(1), 87–107.

Energy Relations of the EU and its Southern Neighborhood

14

Britta Daum

Contents

Introduction	316
Current Research and New Research Directions	317
EU Cooperation with the Southern Neighborhood	319
Multilateral Cooperation: From the Euro-Mediterranean Partnership (EMP) to the Union for the Mediterranean (UfM)	320
Bilateral Cooperation: The European Neighborhood Policy (ENP)	320
The Role of Energy in the EU's Partnership with the Southern Neighborhood	323
EU-Southern Neighborhood Energy Relations in a Historical Perspective	323
Recent Developments and Challenges	327
Current Focus	328
Fossil Fuels Oil and Gas	329
Renewables	332
Outlook for Relations	337
Nuclear	338
Conclusion	340
Cross-References	341
References	341

Abstract

Energy has always been a key topic in the EU's relations with the southern neighborhood whose importance in this regard lays above all in its role regarding energy supplies, both for fossil fuels and potentially for renewables. Past efforts at building a fruitful energy relationship between the EU and the region have been rather disappointing though, with (geo) political events such as the European financial crisis or the Arab Spring, for example, having further revealed the limits or weaknesses of the partnership. Against this background, the COVID-19

B. Daum (✉)
Paris, France

© Springer Nature Switzerland AG 2022
M. Knodt, J. Kemmerzell (eds.), *Handbook of Energy Governance in Europe*,
https://doi.org/10.1007/978-3-030-43250-8_58

disease outbreak undoubtedly serves as another test case and eventually shifting interests, may lead to a readjusting of the partnership's strategic focus: while the pandemic certainly represents a challenge as it may destabilize the region both politically and from an economic point of view and may thus question existing energy patterns, notably as regards to the oil and gas sectors, it is also an opportunity, because it may provide the prospect for the region to rethink its energy strategies and policies and accelerate their transition towards a clean energy system.

This chapter deals with the exploration of the EU's energy relations with the southern neighborhood and illustrates the EU's energy approach towards the region. It considers both past and current developments and lays a special focus on the different energy sources oil, gas, renewables, and nuclear.

Keywords

European Union · Southern neighborhood · Euro-Mediterranean Partnership (EMP) · European Neighborhood Policy (ENP) · Union for the Mediterranean (UfM) · MENA · Oil · Gas · RES · Nuclear

Introduction

Various documents of the European Union (EU) such as the **European Energy Security Strategy** of 2014 (COM/2014/0330 final) or the Communication for a European Energy Union of 2015 (COM/2015a/080 final) present the southern neighborhood or the Mediterranean as a top priority for EU energy policies. This is not surprising given that energy has always been a key topic in the EU's relations with the region whose importance in this regard lays above all in its role regarding energy supplies, both for fossil fuels and potentially for renewables (COM/2011b/ 0539 final). However, past efforts at building a fruitful energy relationship between the EU and the region have been rather disappointing, with (geo) political events such as the European financial crisis or the Arab Spring, for example, having further revealed the limits or weaknesses of the partnership. Against this background, the COVID-19 disease outbreak undoubtedly serves as another test case, and eventually shifting interests, may lead to a readjusting of the partnership's strategic focus.

This chapter deals with the exploration of the EU's energy relations with the southern neighborhood and illustrates the EU's energy approach towards the region: for this purpose, and building on the main scholarly debate, it begins with a background section aimed at sharing some contextual information on the general EU-southern foreign policy cooperation framework. Building on this, it undertakes an examination of the status-quo of EU-southern energy links and their historical milestones, considering both multilateral and bilateral aspects. It then examines and evaluates recent and current energy developments and challenges, whereby the relations in the field of fossil fuels, renewables, and nuclear energy are separately investigated and discussed.

Current Research and New Research Directions

Although energy has been a driver of the European idea (Momete 2015), it has also often been a source of division and the literature acknowledges that European energy policy is far from being complete (Morata and Solorio Sandoval 2012). This is particularly true for external energy policy where "[...] cooperation of EU institutions and member states has proven to be weak [...]" (Leal-Arcas and Wouters 2017). The reason for this is that external energy policymaking is a particularly complex issue and involves a wide range of different actors which makes it difficult to achieve any harmony. Despite this, the literature hardly focused on the external dimension of EU energy policymaking though. This shortcoming has only begun to be addressed in the context of recurrent concerns over energy supply security. Indeed, academic output as regards EU external energy governance has only increased in recent years and is, as a rule, either generic, i.e., focusing, for example, on its challenges and limitations (cf. Godzimirski 2016) or centered around the issue of supply security (cf. Prontera 2017; Youngs 2009). In this context, research has been driven by (a) global energy-related geopolitical changes and (b) repeating energy supply security threats occurring above all in the EU's eastern neighborhood, whereby a great focus has been led on the influence of external actors like Russia (Blockmans et al. 2017). Energy sustainability-related aspects have also started to move up the academic agenda, notably given the threat of climate change (cf. Morata and Solorio Sandoval 2012; Youngs 2014; Herranz-Surrallés 2015; Looney 2016), however, they have been given less importance.

While the literature's focus on the eastern neighborhood seems to be logical given the sheer importance this region plays for the EU's energy supply, it by no means reflects current energy geopolitical developments. Although external events and conflicts like the Arab Spring and the concomitant migration crisis, as well as the rise of terrorism in the region have led to a shift of focus in the literature towards the southern neighborhood, this does only apply to some extent to the energy sphere. It must be noted here that researchers have generally rather focused on the energy relations with big supplier countries, whereas the relations with less important supplier or transit countries have received less attention. For example, main southern gas supplier Algeria has received considerable attention (cf. Darbouche 2010; Tagliapietra and Zachmann 2015; Weber 2016; Escribano 2016; Grigorjeva 2016); by contrast, other fossil fuel suppliers like Libya, Egypt, and since recently Israel and Lebanon have not yet been covered in depth (cf. Hancher 2018), whereas transit countries like Tunisia or Morocco have almost not been dealt with at all which is surprising given the important role these countries play in ensuring the security of the EU's energy supply and the fact that they share similar energy challenges as the EU. The same is true for non-supplier or transit countries like Jordan and Palestine which have been completely neglected by the research sphere to the author's best knowledge.

The relatively sparse existing literature on the southern neighborhood has primarily examined energy relations from a political science and International Relations (IR), an International Political Economy (IPE) (cf. Tagliapietra 2016), or European integration (e.g., multilevel governance, supranationalism, intergovernmentalism) (cf. Knodt et al. 2015) perspective. It has above all investigated Euro-Mediterranean energy cooperation in the context of regional dynamics (cf. Sartori 2014) or from a regional point of view (i.e., from the perspective of the Union for the Mediterranean (UfM), for example) (cf. Cambini and Rubino 2014; Tagliapietra 2016) with a focus on technical aspects (cf. Rubino et al. 2015). In this context, there has been a clear focus on the security of energy supply (cf. Haghighi 2007), however, and given its impact on political stability, recent years have also seen a rising interest in climate change and environmental concerns (cf. Roehrkasten et al. 2016; Moore 2018). Researchers have thus addressed important topics, nonetheless, some aspects have been neglected. For example, bilateral energy relations have hardly been investigated which is astonishing given that the privileged focus on bilateral cooperation in EU-Mediterranean relations has been clearly outlined in the literature (Tagliapietra and Zachmann 2016). Likewise, as regards the influence of external actors, the literary focus is, other than in the case of the eastern neighborhood, not on one actor (Russia) but rather takes into consideration regional dynamics as a whole (Blockmans et al. 2017). Overall, the literature on the EU's southern neighborhood displays an EU-centric bias as it primarily investigates EU external energy governance from a single-level point of view, focusing on the EU *sui generis* (in fact, while the focus is on the supranational level, the national level is hardly considered). Indeed, outside the multilevel governance framework, bilateral relations involving the EU member states are, with some exceptions (cf. Knodt et al. 2015), barely considered. In this context, there is also a lack of southern perspectives, i.e., the existing literature does not sufficiently investigate these countries' perceptions of European energy policies towards them.

As regards the nature of the relationship between the EU and the southern neighborhood, numerous authors have adopted a rather critical stance towards the EU's approach towards the region over the years, reproaching it to lack a unified strategic (Thaler 2015) or coherent approach (Hoebink 2005). Added to this, scholars like Escribano (2017) have observed a "growing sense of Euro-Mediterranean fatigue" on both sides of the Mediterranean in recent years, whereby notably the European financial crisis and the Arab Spring revealed a "lack of EU strategic vision for the Mediterranean." According to these scholars, the result is a lack of integration and an asymmetric relationship that follows a top-down logic (Rubino et al. 2015) and misses "consideration of local needs" and "local ownership" (Blockmans et al. 2017). For example, they blame the EU for using a "one-size fits all" approach (Herranz-Surrallés 2018) and for not having been able to properly consider the interests of the region and accuse it of unrealistic target-setting, at least as regards to certain (big-scale) projects like Desertec or the Mediterranean Solar Plan (MSP) (Tagliapietra and Zachmann 2016). Criticism is particularly pronounced in discussions related to the establishment of a regional framework, with Escribano (2017) claiming that the UfM has not provided any "added value" and that none of its projects have succeeded in "taking off," an opinion that is shared by Aliboni (2012) who affirms that "the UfM proved to be a non-starter before the Arab Spring and has since lost any residual credibility." Overall, there is awareness within the literature regarding the limitations of regional projects and the reservations on the part of both some of the target countries and the member states against fostering multilateral exchange. However, and similarly, the set-up of bilateral policies has been equally heavily criticized and some scholars go as far as to claim that the Arab uprisings even reflected a failure of the European Neighborhood Policy (ENP), notably with respect to democracy and human rights promotion. In this context, Escribano (2017) argues that the ENP had already been rendered "obsolete years ago," i.e., long before the Arab turmoils. Although in response to the geopolitical changes of 2011 and intending to put a greater focus on security, the economy, and migration, the ENP was reviewed twice, in May 2011 (COM (2011a) 303 final) and in November 2015 (JOIN (2015b) 50 final), Delcour (2015) as well as other scholars like Escribano criticize that the revision has fallen short "of sketching out a real and much-needed strategic vision" and "failed to extricate" the EU from its "identity crisis." Accordingly, and as this also impacts energy, there is scholarly consensus on the need to reform the EU's approach towards its neighborhood and to extend its geographical scope.

EU Cooperation with the Southern Neighborhood

Similarly to other neighboring regions and countries like Eastern Europe or Russia, the EU has developed specific partnership patterns with its Mediterranean neighborhood. Being tied to each other by strong (geo) political, economic, and commercial links, cooperation with the southern neighborhood has been a key priority area for the EU since the 1970s. The neighborhood comprises the partner countries Algeria, Egypt, Israel, Jordan, Lebanon, Libya, Morocco, Palestine, Syria, and Tunisia, and takes place in both a multilateral and bilateral context (Table 1).

Table 1 EU-southern cooperation framework

		MA	DZ	TN	LY	EG	IL	PS	LB	JO	SY
Multilateral	**Policy framework/instruments** *Date of entry; creation*										
	Union for the Mediterranean (UfM)	2008	2008	2008	/*	2008	2008	2008	2008	2008	/**
	Euro-Mediterranean Partnership (EMP)	1995	1995	1995	/	1995	1995	1995	1995	1995	1995
	*Libya is an observer state. **The EU suspended cooperation in 2011.*										
Bilateral	**Policy framework/instruments** *Date of entry; creation*										
	Association Council (most recent)	2019	2018	2019	/	2017	2012	/	2017	2019	/
	Rev. European Neighborhood Policy (ENP)					2011, 2015					
	Advanced Status	2008	/	2012	/	/	/	/	/	2010	/
	Action Plans (APs)	2013	/	2013	/	2007	2005	2013	2007	2012	/
	European Neighborhood Policy (ENP)	2004	2004	2004	/	2004	2004	2004	2004	2004	2004
	Association Agreement (AA)	2000	2005	1998	/	2004	2000	1997	2006	2002	/

Source: Own elaboration based on data from the EU

Multilateral Cooperation: From the Euro-Mediterranean Partnership (EMP) to the Union for the Mediterranean (UfM)

Early attempts to establish relations within a regional framework date back to the 1970s when the European Economic Community (EEC) started addressing development concerns with some of the Mediterranean countries. Relations were strengthened in 1976, with notably France having pushed for the launch of the Global Mediterranean Policy (GMP) on commerce and the economy (Mahncke et al. 2004; Sartori 2014). However, this policy format had little success globally, primarily because priority was given to internal European integration issues (Colombo and Abdelkhaliq 2012; Sartori 2014). Other than that, regional cooperation also suffered severe setbacks in the aftermath of the oil shocks in 1973 and 1979, as well as during the debt crisis of the 1980s (Behr 2010). In 1990, and driven by the 1986 enlargement of the EEC by Spain and Portugal (Hoebink 2005), it was followed by the Renovated Mediterranean Policy (RMP), which introduced some new ideas (for example, regarding environmental protection) but was equally of "limited impact," in part because the EU was increasingly distracted with problems at its eastern borders (e.g., Yugoslav wars) (Mahncke et al. 2004). Finally, and in parts as an answer to increasing security threats in the Mediterranean (Hoebink 2005), the Euro-Mediterranean Partnership (EMP) – a general foreign policy framework that includes a political and security, economic and financial, and sociocultural chapter – was launched in 1995 under the so-called Barcelona Process.

Aspiring to political and economic reform in the Mediterranean by providing an institutionalized framework, the EMP called upon its 12 partner countries to pursue both horizontal and vertical integration (Fernandez-Molina 2016), with one sub-aim here having been the establishment of the Euro-Mediterranean Free Trade Area (EMFTA) by 2010 (Behr 2010). However, practically none of its ambitions have been fulfilled, with several structural, institutional, and political factors that have limited its (and the EMFTA's) efficacy, and most importantly the fact that it tried to bring countries under one umbrella without considering their bilateral relationships (Fernandez-Molina 2016). For this reason, and to replace the EMP, the Union for the Mediterranean (UfM), an intergovernmental organization headquartered in Barcelona was launched in 2008. In fact, by including more co-ownership and excluding political conditionality (such as any references to democracy and human rights) (Youngs 2009), the aim of this Pan-Mediterranean policy initiative, which like the GMP was strongly pushed by French diplomacy, was to enhance cooperation between the member countries by better taking into account their specific policy interests (Diez and Tocci 2017). However, as with the EMP, and although meant to be a bottom-up organization (Herranz-Surrallés 2018), the UfM brings together countries that are hostile to or in conflict with each other.

Bilateral Cooperation: The European Neighborhood Policy (ENP)

The bilateral basis of the EU-Mediterranean partnership are the so-called Association Agreements (AAs) which aim to provide a suitable framework for political dialogue and seek to promote regular exchange on political and security matters, economic and financial cooperation, as well as social and cultural cooperation and educational matters. So far, the EU has signed AAs with most of the countries of the southern neighborhood, except for Libya and Syria. While negotiations with the two countries were initiated in 2008, they were subsequently suspended in the context of the outbreak of the civil wars in 2011. Some southern countries such as Morocco (2008), Jordan (2010), and Tunisia (2012) have equally been granted a so-called advanced status and thus obtained the status of a privileged partner with the EU, entailing, among other things, a closer political relationship and increased financial support.

As of the mid-2000s, the AAs have been strengthened by the European Neighborhood Policy (ENP) which initially launched in 2003 in the context of the upcoming wave of enlargement of 2004 to support the EU's eastern neighbors in their political and economic transitions, finally, and upon insistence from France, Italy, and Spain, also included the EU's southern neighbors (Colombo and Abdelkhaliq 2012). While the ENP does not give any prospect to membership, it does, however, pursue a principle of *more for more*, built on the values of democracy, the rule of law, human rights, and social cohesion, whereby progress primarily depends on the target countries' efforts. In other words, the more the target countries implement (democratic) market reforms, the more the EU grants financial support or other concessions such as access to its internal market or visa facilitation.

Based on the AAs, the ENP seeks to strengthen the EU's bilateral relations with its neighbors through more tailor-made nonbinding Action Plans (APs), which serve as the main operative instrument and cover all areas of cooperation. Without the APs, which extend over a timeframe of 3–5 years and define "a series of social, economic and political reforms with short- and medium-term priorities" (EU Neighbours 2020), the AAs cannot be fully implemented. For example, despite having signed an AA with the EU, Algeria has not signed any AP until today: in fact, it took 3 years and a renewed ENP policy to convince Algeria to agree on elaborating an AP in 2011. Negotiations took place in 2012 (first round) and 2013 (second round), with progress having particularly been made in trade and science; however, in recent years, Algeria has increasingly shown dissatisfaction with certain EU-backed actions just as the North Atlantic Treaty Organization (NATO) intervention in Libya and negotiations are on hold.

While cooperation under the ENP has become overall more substantial (Boening et al. 2013), the EU's neighborhood has, contrary to what was planned, not turned into a more secure, stable, prosperous, and democratic region. On the contrary, the EU's partnership with the region has increasingly become challenged and strained by conflicts, insecurity, and instability which is why the EU decided to review the ENP twice, first in 2011 in the aftermath of the Arab Spring, and second in 2015 in the context of the outbreak of the migration crisis. As an outcome, the EU revitalized its strategy to make more additional funds available (*more for more* principle) and to include more differentiation and joint ownership (Bouris and Schumacher 2016), as is for example reflected in the 2017 Association Councils with Algeria, Tunisia, Jordan, Lebanon, and Egypt.

In the same spirit, and to eliminate trade barriers and enhance the neighboring countries' integration into the single market, the EU announced the start of negotiations for a Deep and Comprehensive Free Trade Area (DCFTA) with Morocco, Tunisia, Egypt, and Jordan in 2011. However, so far, negotiations have only started with Morocco (2013) and Tunisia (2015) – Algeria, for its part, is currently in the process of renegotiating the terms of its Free Trade Agreement with the EU of 2005 – and since 2014, little news on their status have been brought forward (EC 2020f). In the case of Morocco, one explanatory reason here is the country's unilateral suspension of any contact with the EU between December 2015 and January 2019 in the context of fights over some trade agreements and the Moroccan/Western Sahara question.

Overall, the EU's efforts as regards the southern neighborhood have not borne fruits yet so far and this despite the various multilateral and bilateral cooperation initiatives mentioned before. Therefore, and following the outbreak of the COVID-19 disease, the EU has recognized the need to reassess its relationship with its Middle East and North Africa (MENA) neighbors, the context in which the Commission presented a Joint Communication on a Renewed Partnership with the Southern Neighborhood in September 2020 (EC 2020a).

The European Neighborhood Instrument (ENI)

The European Neighborhood Instrument (ENI) which strives to support the European Neighborhood Policy (ENP) is the European Commission's most important European financial instrument to boost cooperation with the southern neighborhood. The ENI replaced the European Neighborhood and Partnership Instrument (ENPI) in 2014 and ran until 2020, with one of its objectives being the achievement of progressive integration into the EU internal market. Aid under the ENI does comprise both policy and technical support and mainly takes the form of bilateral assistance programs, but the instrument may also cover or finance regional programs. Total assistance for the period 2014–2020 stood between € 7.5 billion and € 9.2 billion (EC 2020c).

Overall, support is given through Twinning/Technical Assistance and Information Exchange Instrument (TAIEX), Cross-Border Cooperation (CBC), or the Neighborhood Investment Facility (NIF), an important instrument of donor coordination which, in September 2017, was transformed into the Neighborhood Investment Platform (NIP), becoming an integral part of the European Fund for Sustainable Development (EFSD) (EC 2020). The NIP is a so-called *blending* instrument which combines EU grants with loans from third public and private funders (which otherwise might not invest, as too risky), to achieve the EU's external policy objectives. The rationale behind this is that, as an EU mechanism, the NIP has much easier access to loans from the European Financing Institutions (EFIs), which it then redistributes to partner countries eligible for funding. Recognized EFIs and the main donors, in general, are apart from the European Investment Bank (EIB) and the European Bank for Reconstruction and Development (EBRD), the French Agency for Development (AfD), and the German Reconstruction Loan Corporation (KFW). As this suggests, the projects to be financed under the NIP – which spans across all kinds of sectors, including energy – are generally quite capital-intensive. The NIP not only funds projects via grants but also provides technical assistance (TA). Other possibilities include investment grant and interest rate subsidy, risk capital, or guarantees. Its funding comes primarily from the EU budget, or the ENI, as well as from contributions from the EU member states (via the NIP Trust Fund) which are managed by the EIB.

The Role of Energy in the EU's Partnership with the Southern Neighborhood

Energy trade has been a long-standing pillar of the EU's partnership with the southern neighborhood whose importance lies above all in its role regarding energy supplies, both for fossil fuels and potentially for renewables (COM/2011b/0539 final). The southern neighborhood is a fundamental energy supplier that holds considerable amounts of the world's oil and natural gas reserves, providing around 9% of the EU's oil and 12% of its gas needs (EUROSTAT 2019). Moreover, it has a vast renewable energy potential and is an important and strategic maritime transit passage for oil and gas supplies from the Middle East, Russia, and the Caspian Sea to Europe and the USA (Suez Canal, Tanger-Med...), as well as for intra-regional trade (Sartori 2014).

In this light, and in view of the past deterioration of diplomatic relations with Russia due to the wars in Syria and Ukraine and recurrent discords over human rights, numerous were those who assumed that closer energy cooperation with the southern neighborhood would become indispensable for the securing of the EU's energy and climate interests. However, past efforts at building a fruitful energy relationship with notably the southern Mediterranean have been rather disappointing. Relations do mainly occur at the bilateral level, where they are led by individual member states, and the few multilateral initiatives that have taken place, including the Desertec project and the Mediterranean Solar Plan (MSP), have only shown limited success so far (Tagliapietra and Zachmann 2016). Against this background, calls have become loud to take the COVID-19 crisis as an opportunity to rethink the EU's foreign policy towards neighboring countries and to rebuild its relationship with the southern neighborhood, including regarding energy.

EU-Southern Neighborhood Energy Relations in a Historical Perspective

Given the increasing global energy challenges ahead and the magnitude of its internal energy problems, the EU has increasingly sought to integrate energy into its foreign policy relations with third countries over the last couple of years (Youngs 2007) (Table 2), whereby it relies on external energy governance, an approach that is closely linked to its three main internal energy policy objectives, namely energy security, competitiveness, and sustainability (Neframi 2012). Its ultimate aim hereby

Table 2 EU-southern energy cooperation framework

		MA	DZ	TN	LY	EG	IL	PS	LB	JO	SY
Multilateral	**Policy framework/instruments** *Date of entry, creation*										
	European Energy Charter (signature)	2012	/	/	/	/	/	2014	/	2018	/
	Energy Platforms Union for the Mediterranean (UfM)	2015	2015	2015	/*	2015	2015	2015	2015	2015	/**
	Mediterranean Solar Plan (MSP)	2008	2008	2008	/*	2008	2008	2008	2008	2008	2008
Bilateral	**Policy framework/instruments** *Date of entry, creation*										
	Strategic Energy Partnership	/	2015	/	/	2018	/	/	/	/	/
	MoU on Strategic Energy Partnership	/	2013	/	/	2008	/	/	/	/	/

* Libya is an observer state. ** The EU suspended cooperation in 2011.

Source: Own elaboration based on data from the EU

is the integration of third countries in its internal energy market through energy sector reforms in the partner countries, whereby it has identified its eastern and southern neighborhoods as being equally important, seeking for both regions to become "full, important and equal players" in its "internal gas and electricity markets" (COM (2003) 262 final). There is consensus in the literature that increased energy cooperation between the EU and the southern neighborhood will not only be advantageous for Europe but also for the target region. Both regions face similar energy challenges such as a high dependence on conventional energy sources or climate change and right from the beginning, energy has been a pivotal aspect of EU-Mediterranean relations: for example, a feasibility study for the construction of a gas pipeline connecting Algeria to Italy, the Trans-Mediterranean Natural Gas Pipeline, was first conducted in 1969 and the first Euro-Arab Dialogue was launched in the context of the oil crisis in 1973. Further, due to the proximity to Portugal, Spain, and Greece, and interdependence to and with the southern shore of the Mediterranean, energy also became a key aspect of cooperation in the context of these countries' accession to the European Economic Community (EEC) (Colombo and Abdelkhaliq 2012). Indeed, with energy representing the bulk of trade within this region, the EU was very keen to establish a common energy market from early on, notably through the harmonization of policies. The key concepts here were and are market framework, liberalization, and regulation (Rubino et al. 2015; Herranz-Surrallés 2018).

The general legal basis of EU multilateral external energy governance is the Energy Charter Treaty (ECT) of 1998, with its political foundation being the European Energy Charter which was signed in 1991 in The Hague and whose early focus was on the EU's eastern neighborhood. Energy relations with the southern neighborhood were, as of 1995, rather framed by the Euro-Mediterranean Partnership (EMP) whose aim was to ensure consistency and which was supposed to cover all energy sources, be it conventional or renewable, and expand across the entire energy supply chain. However, and as shown before, the EMP has shown overall limited success, and until the establishment of the Union for the Mediterranean (UfM), was not followed by any significant or more specific energy policy initiative (Colombo and Abdelkhaliq 2012). Attempts to extend the ECT to the southern neighborhood were reiterated in the mid-2000s and in reaction to the Arab Spring in 2011 (Rubino et al. 2015) and while they resulted in Morocco signing the European Energy Charter in 2012, Palestine in 2014, and Jordan in 2018, both Algeria and Libya have never formally committed to adopting the *energy acquis* (Boening et al. 2013). Against this background, and in the absence of any legal leverage, the EU has sought to achieve the extension of its *energy acquis* and the convergence of markets by other means, namely through outward Europeanization (Escribano 2017). In this context, since the 2000s, the integration of for example the Maghreb gas and electricity markets with the EU internal market has been identified as a priority energy goal, resulting in 2004 in the launch of the Rome Euro-Mediterranean Energy Platform (REMEP), whose priority action plan spawned a relatively advanced set of common energy goals. Three years later, in 2007, the - Euro-Mediterranean Energy Ministers Conference held in Limassol launched the priority action plan for Euro-Mediterranean Energy Cooperation. However, the Limassol initiative was not very fruitful and most of the proposals remained largely "confined at the declaratory level" (Sartori 2014). It was followed suit in 2008 by the UfM under which energy was defined as a key priority area. The focus was hereby on alternative energies or the "mass-scale production of renewable energy sources (RES) with view to creating a vast Euro-Mediterranean green energy market" (Herranz-Surrallés 2018). The EU has sought to reinforce cooperation in this matter through several policy initiatives, including the Mediterranean Solar Plan (MSP) which was the UfM's flagship project and a common initiative of the Commission (financed by the Neighborhood Investment Platform (NIP), the European Investment Bank (EIB), the French Agency for Development (AfD), and the German Reconstruction Loan Corporation (KFW)) (European Commission 2020p).

The goal of the MSP was or is to support the development of RES and energy efficiency within the southern Mediterranean countries by developing 20 GW of renewables production capacities and achieving significant energy savings by 2020 and to strengthen regional electricity connections through the development of integrated regional markets. However, the MSP and similar initiatives have all shown only limited success so far, among other things, because of "their lack of realism or inadequacy to the region's dynamics" (Escribano and Lazaro 2020), as well as because of disagreement between the EU member states (Sartori 2014). In fact, while initially, it was believed that these projects would be crowned by success, since 2013, little news on the status of the MSP has been brought to the public. The same is true for the work of Medgrid, another industrial consortium, whose implementation strongly depended upon or was connected to the advancements of the plan (Sartori 2014). Several problems also contributed to the discontinuation of Dii, a consortium made up of around 40 large multinational and international energy companies, and with this to the provisional collapse of the Desertec project. Although many factors have played a role here, the failure of these projects was in large parts because of disagreement among the different EU member states (Box 1) (Daum 2020). Struggling with its electricity overcapacities at that time, Spain vetoed a master plan for the implementation of the MSP in 2013 (Rubino et al. 2015), leading to its de facto dissolution. In 2015, and partly in reaction to the Arab Spring (Herranz-Surrallés 2018), the UfM started a new initiative, a high-level political dialogue on energy matters, setting up three energy platforms on gas, electricity and RES, and energy efficiency, with the overall goal of achieving gas and electricity supply security, as well as to enhance climate change mitigation and adaptation. Supported by a different set of regional institutions such as the Mediterranean Energy Regulators (MedReg) or the Mediterranean Transmission System Operators (Med-TSO), the UfM platforms foresee an overall stronger role for the EU member states and the Mediterranean target countries, as well as for the energy industry actors. However, the platforms which had a relative bumpy start (for example, the platform on RES and energy efficiency was launched with 1 year of delay) (Daum 2020), have been dubbed as "weak" by some scholars such as Escribano and Lazaro (2020) and their overall success remains yet to be seen.

> **Box 1 Past EU – Southern Neighborhood Energy Initiatives**
> **Desertec**: Created in 2009 and comprising a large network of politicians, economists, and scientists in the Middle East and North Africa region (MENA), the Desertec Foundation is a nonprofit organization whose aspiration is to develop renewable energy sources (RES), above all solar, in the world's desert regions – for local use, but also to export part of this green energy to Europe. In this context, the Sahara was, given its size, as well as its geographical proximity to the European continent, identified as an ideal location (Desertec 2020). After its creation, a group of industrialists picked up the vision of the Desertec Foundation and together formed the Desertec Industrial Initiative (Dii), a consortium made up of around 40 large multinational and international integrated energy groups. The mission of this initiative was to develop solar and wind energy in North Africa in order to provide the EU with 15% green electricity by 2050, as well as to cover a substantial part of the North African green power demand (Dii Desertenergy 2020).
> **Medgrid**: In line with the Euro-Mediterranean Gas and Electricity Link and inspired by the Desertec vision, 2010 saw also the launch of Medgrid, another industrial consortium created under French initiative and uniting 21 companies active in the production, transmission, and distribution of electricity, infrastructure financing, and climate change. Medgrid's ultimate aim is to provide renewable electricity to the countries of both the northern and southern shores of the Mediterranean. More specifically, its mission is to design and promote a transmission network between Europe and North Africa that has a generation capacity of 20 GW and an export capacity of 5 GW in order to "facilitate large-scale electricity trading between the north and south, in addition to inter-grid trading throughout the region." Just as the MSP, Medgrid was also set up within the framework of the UfM; in fact, it was originally conceived to complement the MSP, as well as Dii (Medgrid PSM https://www.medgridpsm.com/en/).

Recent Developments and Challenges

Notwithstanding the beforementioned attempts to institutionalize Euro-Mediterranean energy cooperation through the Energy Charter Treaty (ECT) and the acceleration of corresponding initiatives such as the Union for the Mediterranean (UfM) platforms, the EU's multilateral energy policy towards the Mediterranean is regularly met with heavy criticism for its low perceptibility and its lack of concrete impact (Tagliapietra and Zachmann 2016; Diez and Tocci 2017; Cebeci 2019). This reproach is based on the fact that plans to establish a common energy market have never materialized and that the integration of the gas and electricity markets has "remained a distant perspective" (Herranz-Surrallés 2018), reflecting the EU's general "limited capacity to engage" the North African countries (Sartori 2014). According to the literature, this is largely due to a lack of international legally binding rules and effective institutionalization which stems from an erroneous vision of the complexities of the region (Boening et al. 2013; Escribano and Lazaro 2020). As a result, energy cooperation has, until today, above all been bilateral, whereby failures on both sides of the Mediterranean can be denounced. For example, on the EU side, and as for the realization of the integrated electricity market, the idea of importing green electricity from the energy-rich south has become less appealing owing, among other things, to the long-lasting effects of the economic crisis and a projected decrease in energy demand. Moreover, corresponding projects were increasingly perceived as a neo-colonialist attempt of the European countries to gain control over Middle Eastern and North African energy resources, especially since the European stakeholders did not manage to properly address the question of access to or transfer of technology. Finally, the credibility of the EU in that regard has been increasingly damaged, as the Union itself does not serve as a prime example of regional electricity integration (Herranz-Surrallés 2018). On the Mediterranean side, one often cited reason why regional energy initiatives do not deliver is the low level of political and economic integration (Rubino et al. 2015), caused, among other things, by political instabilities, a lack of economic complementarity, and tariff barriers leading to high trade costs. A good example here is the Arab Maghreb Union (AMU), an intergovernmental organization created by Morocco, Algeria, Tunisia, Libya, and Mauritania in 1989 to formulate a common approach in diverse policy areas, including energy. Yet, negotiations have regularly failed, with the last Presidential Council meeting having taken place in 1994 (Worrall 2017).

In the current economic and political context, this undoubtedly poses new challenges, all the more so, as the region had already been confronted with major geopolitical challenges in recent years, above all the Arab Spring which has introduced "a series of dramatic political, socio-economic and security changes across the region" and led to destabilization (Libya, Syria) and a shifting geopolitical focus. In fact, the geostrategic consequences of the Arab Spring have favored "the emergence of new international actors in the Mediterranean energy game" (Sartori 2014) or a new actor constellation: firstly, because the Mediterranean's outstanding energy resources attract an ever-increasing number of countries seeking new energy partnerships and investment opportunities and secondly, because the region itself is seeking to increasingly diversify its energy portfolios and relations (Daum 2020).

In this context, there is a "rising dynamism of Gulf Arab state and non-state actors in the southern Mediterranean" (Zoubir and White 2015), while "Russia has also extended its cooperation with North African countries to the energy sector" (Ghanem and Kuznetsov 2018). Another key actor is Turkey which, aspiring to become a regional energy power, is increasingly focusing its diplomatic attention on Africa, trying to carve out a new role for itself not only in Libya but on the entire continent (Saddiki 2020). Likewise, the region itself is changing with its countries having begun to demonstrate a strong appetite for developing their networks of international energy relations and partners, with for example especially the North African countries (above all, Morocco) increasingly turning their attention towards sub-Saharan Africa (Daum 2020; Werenfels 2020).

Adding to this, the COVID-19 disease crisis and occasional disasters like the Beirut explosion put additional pressure on the already aching economies of the region and will undoubtedly impact the EU's relations with them. Indeed, while the EU itself is likely to struggle with internal problem-solving and reduced spending capacity, the impact of these events on the southern partners is expected to be even more profound, including among other things economic and social consequences like a fall in foreign direct investments (FDI), unemployment, or even food crisis which, in turn, could lead to a new migration crisis, requiring for a recalibration of foreign policies, for example.

At the same time, the coronavirus-related impacts could accelerate the transformation of the region towards greater self-sufficiency and, in combination with global trends such as reshoring, bring new business opportunities, including renewables.

Current Focus

Despite the EU's early focus on energy in its relations with the southern neighborhood, energy cooperation was very broad in this initial phase and at the beginning of the European Neighborhood Policy (ENP), the Action Plans (APs) applied a rather generalist approach to energy, not reflecting the existing real energy problems and issues within the region. This only changed over the years, when priorities were further extended, now requiring the southern partners to implement energy strategies compatible with those of the EU (AP of 2013–2017). In this context, and compared with the previous APs, objectives have become far more ambitious, touching upon areas like renewable energies, energy efficiency, and even oil shale and shale gas, as well as nuclear safety cooperation and regional energy cooperation (notably in the field of infrastructure) (Table 3). For example, and with the Neighborhood Investment Platform (NIP) supposed to support the partner countries' national energy goals and to contribute to projects that enhance both these countries' and the EU's energy security (ideally in coherence with other aid), the facility pursues strategic objectives such as the diversification of energy supplies, the establishment of sustainable energy interconnections, the improvement of energy efficiency, or the promotion of renewables and the fight against climate change. The ultimate objective is the integration of the southern energy markets into the EU internal market,

Table 3 EU-southern energy cooperation focus

EU focus of cooperation	MA	DZ	TN	LY	EG	IL	PS	LB	JO	SY
Oil					x			x		
Gas		x			x			x		
Nuclear										
Renewables	x	x	x		x	x	x	x	x	
Energy efficiency	x	x	x		x	x	x	x	x	
Electr. generation	x		x		x	x	x			
Market integration	x	x			x					
Regional cooperation		x			x	x				
Technical, scientific, industrial cooperation	x				x	x			x	

Source: Own elaboration based on data from the EU

with the overall aim of deepening and accelerating the convergence of energy policies, as well as legislative, institutional, organizational, and technical settings within the EU framework (NIF Strategic Orientations 2014–2020). Moreover, and having often been criticized for being too vague in its energy approach towards the southern partners, the EU started to develop more tailored energy cooperation tools as of the mid-2010s. In this light, it entered for example into a so-called Strategic Energy Partnership with both Algeria (2013) and Egypt (2018) (EC 2015, 2018a). The agreement with Egypt replaces the existing energy cooperation that had been in place since 2008.

Fossil Fuels Oil and Gas

The southern neighborhood is an important supplier of fossil fuels, holding considerable amounts of the world's oil and natural gas reserves and providing around 12% of the EU's gas and 9% of its oil needs in 2018, with several pipeline connections to Spain and Italy (Maghreb-Europe, Transmed) (EUROSTAT 2019). Accordingly, around 60% of the loans (in financial terms) granted by the European Investment Bank (EIB) to the Mediterranean region between 1956 and 2020 went to natural gas and LNG projects (EIB 2020). Especially Algeria functions as a key actor here, with the EU considering the country a strategic partner able to provide for a reliable energy supply – indeed, despite some ups and downs between the country and some of its southern European clients, Algeria never interrupted the supply of gas, be it for political, commercial, or technical reasons. Therefore, when relations between the EU and Russia deteriorated in the context of the wars in Ukraine and Syria, the idea came up for Algerian gas to replace Russian supplies in the future (COM/2014/330 final; COM/2015a/80 final); however, this plan has been abandoned in recent years. While the turmoils of the Arab Spring did certainly play a role here, this is also because Russia, in order to compete with cheap liquefied natural gas (LNG) from Australia and the USA and to gain global shares, has reviewed its gas contracts, adapted pricing, and invested in infrastructure. This made its gas (again) highly attractive to European buyers.

While according to scholars like Escribano and Lazaro (2020), the "Mediterranean as diversification from Russia narrative" has thus got lost, the region, above Algeria, nonetheless continues to be a top priority for the EU and this both as regards to gas and energy in general. Trade relations date back to the 1970s and Algeria is the EU's third-largest supplier of gas, after Russia and Norway, exporting the equivalent of around 11% of the Union's entire imports, whereby the southern EU countries Italy, Spain, and France account for most of the total (EC 2020g). Moreover, Algeria's conventional and unconventional gas reserves are among the largest in the world and the country is equally a dominant supplier of LNG. However, Algerian gas production has been in decline in recent years, the context in which one aim of EU-Algerian energy cooperation is to improve the legislative and regulatory framework to make the country more attractive for investors; another one is to support infrastructure (EC 2020j).

Contrary to Algeria, Libya is an important supplier of oil to the EU, accounting for around 6% of the Union's total oil imports (supplying notably Italy, Germany, and France) (EC 2020i). Apart from this commercial dimension, relations have been either limited or nonexistent though, with the country not being bound to the EU by neither an Association Agreement (AA) nor free trade agreement. Relations have also suffered severed backsets in the context of the civil war of 2011, another example of the inconsistency of which the EU came out divided. Actually, the EU has left a gap and outside players like Russia and Turkey have entered the conflict, involving the regional powers in a contest for energy resources and commercial transport routes. In this context, Libya has increasingly come to the fore of political attention and as a result, since April 2019, the EU has again been intensifying its efforts to serve as a meditator to calm down the conflict. However, European assistance has primarily centered around non-energy-related areas so far and foreign influence remains strong.

Compared to Libya, Egypt only supplies some marginal quantities of oil (making up for around 0.7% of the total); however, recent discoveries of gas in the eastern Mediterranean have sparked hope to significantly alter energy supply dynamics in the region, with the offshore Levant Basin comprising the waters of Cyprus, Egypt, Greece, Israel, Lebanon, Palestine, and Turkey, estimated to contain enormous gas reserves. Potentially providing for new export options, among other things to the EU (through the planned EastMed pipeline connecting the basin to Greece), the finds have, however, exacerbated regional territorial disputes, rendering the viability of such projects uncertain. The stakes are not only high for the countries of the region but also for commercial players like France and Italy whose national energy companies Total and Eni operate various licensing blocks in Libya and Egypt (for instance, Eni discovered the giant Zohr gas field, however, sold its stakes to Russian Rosneft in 2017). In this light, the aim for EU-Egyptian energy cooperation remains to attract new investors through reforms (e.g., the modernization of the

Egyptian gas sector) and to transform the country into an energy hub (EC 2018b). While the diversification away from oil and a shift towards cleaner energies do emphasize the region's importance in this regard, its exact role going forward remains, given the current context of declining energy demand and gas oversupplies, yet to be seen though.

Outlook for Relations

The southern neighborhood is not only an important supplier of oil and gas to the EU but very much depends on these energy resources itself, with most of its energy systems being fossil-fuel based. In Algeria, the energy sector accounts for around 85% of total export earnings, whereas in Libya, oil roughly makes up for around 69% of the county's total export income (OPEC 2020). Likewise, the Egyptian oil sector accounts for around 27% of the country's total gross domestic product (GDP).

Against this background, the world market's overabundance of American, Australian, and Russian gas constitutes a serious threat especially for Algeria's conventional gas exports to the EU, as well as for the exploitation of Eastern Mediterranean gas, a threat that has been further intensified by the COVID-19 pandemic-driven depression of demand. For example, Spanish gas imports from Algeria dropped by around −56% in April 2020 compared to the same month in the previous year (CORES 2020), as the country turned to cheaper LNG supplies from the USA and Russia. Likewise, exports to Italy and Portugal (which did not import any Algerian gas in April at all) were equally hit. However, Algeria will most probably continue to serve as an important gas supplier to the EU, firstly, because gas is considered an important transition fuel towards cleaner energy supply and secondly, because eastern supplies via Nord Stream II to Germany continue to remain uncertain in the context of the Navalny affair and ongoing pressure by newly imposed US sanctions.

The outbreak of the COVID-19 disease, together with oil price volatility, represents a tremendous challenge for the countries of the region, not only because their economies are largely dependent on oil and gas exports (which is a problem in the context of overall declining demand), but also because many of them strongly rely on the oil-rich Gulf countries for foreign exchange and investments. In this light, it is therefore highly likely that these countries, in an attempt to compensate for the sharp fall in energy export revenues (Algeria's energy revenues declined by around 10$ billion in 2020) and to reduce spending, will undergo massive reforms, open-up for greater private investments, and choose the path of diversification (both of the non-energy sector and within the energy sector). Having been struggling with stagnating gas output and insufficient investment for some time, Algeria, for example, had already tried to change the wheel before the health crisis. To attract foreign investors and modify its contractual terms, it passed a Hydrocarbon Law in 2020 and plans to launch a new international tender in 2021. In this context, looming peak oil demand will most probably force it and other countries to rethink further their national energy strategies.

While this will of course create new business opportunities for the EU, it will also entail changes for its relations with these countries, even more as they have been primarily centered around gas so far. Indeed, with both its own and the neighborhood's political priorities having started to shift during the crisis, the EU will have to readjust its European Neighborhood Policy (ENP) instruments accordingly. For example, as there has been a greater political focus on renewables in the context of the European Green Deal, it is perfectly conceivable that it will lay a special emphasis on this type of energy in its future relations with the region (Escribano and Lazaro 2020). Another issue is the fact that, as indicated before, the EU's energy cooperation with the region has generally been intergovernmental for the past decade and this despite the potential collaboration pillars proximity, interdependence, and complementarity. Cooperation has above all been based on strong bilateral links between notably the southern EU member states (France, Italy, and Spain) and the big energy-producing countries Algeria, Libya, and Egypt. Indeed, although the region can hardly be considered homogeneous, energy dynamics and challenges are similar; however, so far, the regional exchange has been rather limited. In the current crisis mode and with increasing geopolitical outside interference from external actors in the region, this lack of unity could pose a serious threat going forward.

Renewables

Despite oil and gas being at the heart of the EU's energy relations with the southern neighborhood, the region does also have a potential role in clean energy sources, with its biomass, geothermal, hydro, wind, and solar energy resources being among the best in the world. The EU's interest in this regard has been reflected in various strategies such as The EU Energy Policy: Engaging with Partners beyond Our Borders (COM/2011b/539 final), as well as in projects such as the Mediterranean Solar Plan (MSP), Desertec, and Medgrid.

Although these projects do no longer exist in their initial form, they do, however, show the importance the EU and its member states attach to the topic. In fact, while there was a high level of enthusiasm for close cooperation on renewables in the early 2010s, the logic of the beforementioned endeavors has changed over time, away from their initial purpose of *importing* green energy to the idea of *exchanging* electricity (Daum 2020). While such bilateral cooperation already exists (see between Morocco and Spain) or is currently being planned (see between Algeria and Spain), the set-up of an integrated regional grid has, as reflected in the MSP, Desertec, and Medgrid examples turned out to be more difficult to realize than what was initially thought.

Nonetheless, there has been a revival of interest in the initial essence of these plans in recent years, suggesting that the Desertec idea continues to persist: for example, at the margin of the COP21 in 2015 in Paris, TuNur Limited, a British solar plant developer, announced plans to import 4.5 GW of solar power from Tunisia to Italy from where the electricity would then be transmitted to other European countries (Nur Energie 2020). Similarly, in 2019, the Tunisian Company of Electricity and Gas (STEG) and Italian transmission system operator Terna signed an agreement for the construction of a 600 MW undersea connection between Tunisia and Italy, an undertaking which, known as the Elmed project, figures on the Union's list of Projects of

Common Interest (PCI). Likewise, under the Commission's Climate Action and Energy initiative, and in the context of the COP22 in 2016, a joint declaration to establish a roadmap for facilitating sustainable renewable electricity trade between the European energy market and northern Africa was signed between Germany, France, Spain, Portugal, and Morocco (Set 2016). However, there have been little news on this project and voices have become loud that downplay the political relevance of this agreement, arguing that it was signed in a context of high international pressure and media coverage and was thus not backed by any real interest.

From 2013 onwards, projects have largely focused on *supporting* renewables and energy efficiency initiatives in the context of the Neighborhood Investment Platform (NIP), be it at the bilateral or regional level. For example, bilaterally, the EU has supported various sustainable energy projects in Egypt, Jordan, Morocco, Palestine, and Tunisia through the platform (Table 4), whereas multilaterally, one aim has been the enhancement of the financing of renewable energy and energy efficiency investments through the extension of credit lines to financial institutions in Morocco, Jordan, and later Egypt (SEMED Sustainable Energy Financing Facility), the context in which both the European Investment Bank (EIB) and the European Bank for Reconstruction and Development (EBRD) do play an important role.

Indeed, other than the Commission, the EIB has equally been an early supporter of energy initiatives addressing regional environmental and climate issues in the Mediterranean region, particularly in Morocco (Fig. 1). For example, in 2002, it created the Facility for Euro-Mediterranean Investment and Partnership (FEMIP) which, aiming at opening-up the Mediterranean economies, soon developed into the

Table 4 Renewables investments granted to the southern neighborhood under the NIP from 2013 to 2019

Renewables investments granted under the NIP 2013–2019			
Country	Project	Year	Total cost (€ m)
Egypt	Suez Oil Processing Company Energy Efficiency	2018	172
Egypt	200 MW Wind Farm Project Gulf of Suez	2015	344
Jordan	NEPCO Green Corridor	2015	146
Jordan	Support for the Sustainable Credit Facility	2013	39
Morocco	Noor Mideld I and II Solar Power Plants	2018	2137
Morocco	Creation of Training Institutes (Renewable Energies and Energy Efficiency)	2014	26
Morocco	Support to the Ouarzazate Solar Complex - Phase II	2014	1000
Morocco	Support to the Ouarzazate Solar Complex - Phase III	2014	855
Morocco	Integrated Wind Energy Programme	2013	859
Palestine	Sustainable Use of Natural Resources and Energy Finance (SUNREF)	2017	42
Tunisia	Sustainable Use of Natural Resources and Energy Financing in Tunisia	2015	133
Tunisia	Centrale Photovoltaique Tozeur	2015	16

Source: Own elaboration based on data from the EU

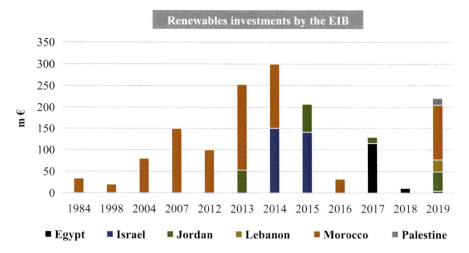

Fig. 1 Renewables investments granted to the southern neighborhood by the EIB from 1959 to 2019. (Source: Own elaboration based on data from the EIB. Note: Renewables investments refer to investments in solar, wind, and hydropower technology projects, as well as to projects related to energy efficiency)

bank's financial arm in the region and contributed significantly to the financing of the MSP, for example. The bank also manages the FEMIP Trust Fund (FFT), which was set up in 2004 and serves to carry out climate actions through Climate Action in the Middle East and North Africa (CAMENA). At the COP22 in Marrakech, the bank announced plans to strengthen its support for the Green for Growth Fund (GGF) (EIB 2020). The GGF seeks to promote renewables and energy efficiency across North Africa, Lebanon, Jordan, and Palestine (GGF https://www.ggf.lu/). Finally, together with the EU and the European Bank for Reconstruction and Development (EBRD), the EIB is involved in the setup of a €50 million program to boost renewable energy investments in Ukraine, but also in its south, particularly in Jordan, Lebanon, and Tunisia. The program is expected to add 340 MW of additional installed renewable energy capacity in these countries (EC 2020d).

Overall, in recent years, both the EU and the southern neighborhood – which as a whole is one of the most vulnerable regions when it comes to climate change and thus committed to reaching carbon neutrality – have been increasingly enlarging the thematical focus to include more green energies and sustainability-related topics in their agenda (UN 2020):

- **Energy exporters**: with their entire economies depending on oil and gas revenues, the development of renewable energy sources offers an opportunity for diversification.
  - **Algeria** has set a conditional (e.g., dependent on external financial and technical support) CO_2 emissions reduction target of 7–22% by 2030

(compared to a business as usual scenario) and plans to reach 27% of electricity generated from renewable sources of energy by 2030.
 – **Egypt** has not yet set any formal reduction target, however, is committed to mitigation policies.
 – Both **Libya and Syria** have not submitted any Nationally Determined Contribution (NDC).
• **Energy importers**: the energy situation of energy importers being above all characterized by nonavailability of natural resources and high energy dependence, the context in which renewable energy sources do not only offer the opportunity to lower emissions but are above all a means to enhance energy security and economic development.
 – **Israel**: seeks to reduce its per capita greenhouse gas emissions (GHG) emissions by 26% by 2030 (compared to 2005) and 17% of its electricity generated in 2030 is supposed to come from renewable sources.
 – **Jordan** aims to reduce its GHG emissions by 1.5% by 2030 (compared to a business as usual scenario) and has a 20% renewable electricity production target for 2025.
 – **Lebanon**: intends to lower its GHG emissions by 15% by 2030 (compared to 2011) and at achieving 15% of its power and heat demand to be generated by renewables by 2030.
 – **Morocco**: is committed to reducing its CO_2 emissions by 32% by 2030 (compared to a business as usual-scenario) and its Noor Solar plan and the Integrated Wind program foresee to install 52% of renewable energy capacity by 2030, a goal that includes the development of solar, wind, and hydro capacity; it is to be achieved through as projects like the Ouarzazate solar power plants, for example.
 – **Palestine**: has set a conditional CO_2 emissions reduction target of 12.8% by 2040 (relative to a business as usual scenario) and of 24.4% should it gain independence from Israel.
 – **Tunisia**: plans to decrease its carbon intensity by 46% by 2030 (on 2010 levels) in the energy sector and in the context of the Tunisia Solar Plan of 2016, targets for 30% of installed electricity capacity by 2030 to come from renewables. This is to be achieved through projects like the development of a 30 MW wind farm in Sidi Mansour.

While the southern neighborhood's climate and renewables commitments differ from each other in terms of timeframe and ambition, they do nonetheless all go in the direction towards a low-carbon world. Against this background, and in the context of their Strategic Energy Partnership of 2015, the EU and **Algeria** agreed to not only cooperate on natural gas but also on renewable energies, energy efficiency, energy market integration, and energy infrastructure (EC 2015). For the period 2018–2020, the bilateral assistance to Algeria under the European Neighborhood Investment (ENI) amounted to €125 million, whereby one main focus was on energy/environment and climate actions (EC 2020m). With the Sahara Desert occupying more than four-fifths of its territory, Algeria has substantial solar potential but also disposes of other resources like wind, hydro, biomass, and geothermal energy. The decline in gas production, as well as gas price volatility, provide an impetus for the country to increasingly invest in clean energies and many efforts have already been undertaken by the state in this regard. Yet, numerous political, legislative, and institutional challenges related to subsidies and tenders, for example, remain, negatively impacting the country's attractiveness for investors (Bouraiou et al. 2020). Other hurdles are of administrative and fiscal nature (Jalilvand and Westphal 2017) which is why one aim of common initiatives has been the improvement of the sector's regulatory environment. However, so far, cooperation on this matter has been perceived as rather disappointing by Algerian key stakeholders who reproach the EU to not propose any new solutions. Consequently, various authors like Escribano (2016) or Grigorjeva (2016) call on the EU to come up with a more appealing energy narrative for the country (one that considers the country's interests). Likewise, the Energy Partnership with **Egypt** not only aims at modernizing Egypt's gas sector but also at accelerating its energy transition and transforming the country into an energy hub by sharing experience and providing financial and technical assistance (EC 2020e). Indeed, the Memorandum of Understanding (MoU) signed in 2018 for strategic cooperation in energy until 2022 lays a greater emphasis on sustainable development and the transition to low carbon economies. A particular focus is hereby on the country's massive solar and wind resources and energy efficiency actions, an area whose development keeps struggling with various investment challenges (IRENA 2018). One priority for the 2017–2020 period in this context was to cooperate on the update of the country's integrated energy strategy (Consilium 2017).

A major focus in the cooperation of the EU with **Morocco** and **Tunisia** – both net energy importers – is the improvement of energy security, the diversification of energy sources and the promotion of renewables and energy efficiency (EC 2020l). For example, the EU's External Investment Plan (EIP) which seeks to attract private investments into the neighboring countries has greatly benefitted Morocco, notably in the context of the Noor Midelt solar plant (EFSD Operational Report 2018). But Tunisia also regularly benefits from EU aid; for example, in the context of the NIP, the EU supported the completion of Tunisia's first solar power plant Tozeur with around €16 million. Overall, both countries are highly advanced in terms of renewables penetration and energy efficiency; however, their solar and wind energy potentials are not yet fully exploited and various difficulties persist. One hurdle is the lack of capacity to store and integrate electricity generated from these sources into the national power grid; another one may be local involvement/opposition in the Western Sahara (Hochberg 2016). Just as Morocco and Tunisia, **Jordan** heavily relies on expensive energy imports and although the country is deeply committed to the energy transition and disposes of high renewable energy potential (wind and solar), the share of renewables in its total power generation capacity is only at around 14%. Factors slowing down the transition to renewables are, among other things, a lack of a long-term strategy, regulatory changes, and concerns about grid stability (Franceschini 2019). In this context, EU support concentrates on the strengthening of the country's institutional framework and the implementation of its renewable energy policy, as well as on the transfer of technology (EEAS 2012). **Lebanon**'s renewable energy potential remains equally largely untapped and the country suffers from recurrent power cuts, with inefficiencies of the national grid impeding the growth of renewables (Qudrat-Ullah and Kayal 2019). And although there has been the political will to speed up the energy transition in recent years, most of the country's power stations still run on fuel oil (which is heavily subsidized) and a lot of power is illegally generated (Mehmet and Yorucu 2020). Progress towards using cleaner energy, which has also been driven by the EU (2018a), has been stalled by the crippling economy as a result of the COVID-19 crisis, as well as the Beirut port explosion in August 2020. The latter has not only further revealed the lack of stable electricity (Peritz 2020) but also triggered anti-government manifestations, which is why current EU aid primarily focuses on the revitalization of the economy and socioeconomic development. Similarly, **Palestine**, which is highly reliant on energy imports from Israel, Egypt, and Jordan, has huge renewables potential, particularly solar energy. However, alternative energies are still in their early stages in the country, and overall, the Palestinian energy transition is considered to be in a "pre-development phase" (Khaldi and Sunikka-Blank 2020). For example, so far, only solar and wind energy are being exploited, whereas other sources like geothermal or biomass are neglected. Hampering factors are land availability, regulation, and technical capabilities, for example (Hamed et al. 2012). Therefore, one key aspect of the EU's bilateral assistance to Palestine under the ENI for the 2017–2020 period was to strengthen the institutional framework and the access to self-sufficient energy services. A second was to foster cooperation between Israel and Palestine (EC 2020m). Cooperation with **Israel** equally focuses on the deployment of renewables and the promotion of energy efficiency, the context in which the recent gas discoveries in the Eastern Mediterranean may serve as an accelerator for developing a closer partnership and for establishing more essential regional links (EP 2020). Indeed, one angle of collaboration is regional electricity integration, with one Project of Common Interest (PCI) being the 1,208 km subsea interconnection between Crete, Cyprus, and Israel (EuroAsia Interconnector) (EC 2020n).

Outlook for Relations

While the southern neighborhood has begun the transition to sustainable development, its renewables sector has, however, been greatly impacted by the COVID-19 disease outbreak, with investments and solar and wind additions having considerably slowed down in the first half of 2020 (IEA 2020). However, this development is expected to be temporary and the idea of putting climate change and sustainability at the center of the post-pandemic recovery will, together with corresponding EU initiatives like the European Green Deal, most probably lead to a greater focus on renewables in the EU's (multilateral and bilateral) cooperation with the southern neighborhood (COM/2020b/301 final). In this context, this cooperation focus will likely be extended to Africa (in fact, already before the crisis, the EU had begun to lay greater emphasis on Africa in its Africa Strategy), all the more so as the current crisis may set back the fight against climate change as it severely threats the economies of many countries.

The EU's post-pandemic green focus already becomes clear with the example of hydrogen – a fuel that the EU seeks to upscale decisively in the framework of the Green Deal – with actors like Dii promoting the set-up of a green hydrogen system connecting the two regions (Hydrogen Europe 2020). In this light, and following the adoption of a national hydrogen strategy in June 2020, Germany signed an agreement with Morocco on the development of the green hydrogen production sector (BMWI 2020). Likewise, Spain adopted a hydrogen roadmap in October 2020 and equally seeks to develop a partnership in this field with Morocco and so does Portugal. Whereas Europe seeks to develop and use hydrogen to notably decarbonize CO_2 intensive areas like the maritime or truck sectors, as well as the steel and cement industries, North African countries like Morocco, dispose of ideal topographic and economic conditions for green and affordable H2 production to be used to stabilize the grid or to be exported to Europe. However, the hydrogen market is still in its infancy and there are various challenges and risks to such endeavors: indeed, as mentioned before, the investment framework is, due to both political and economic insecurity, still unstable and the North African region may have to compete with other hydrogen-producing regions for market shares (whereas Europe may have to compete with other interested stakeholders). Moreover, a lack of mutual understanding and/or equality may lead to distrust and undermine any large-scale project right from the beginning (see, for example, accusations of colonialism).

Overall, politics constitute a general threat to energy ties and as for fossil fuels, the political debate remains unpredictable, with structural problems such as a lack of regional dialogue and integration continuing to persist which is not only a problem as regards intra-southern or Mediterranean relations but does also affect EU-southern relations. For example, while Spain and Morocco are connected via two submarine cables with a capacity of 1,400 MW and de facto exchange electricity, in 2019, Spain filed a complaint to the Commission as regards the issue of carbon leakage. In fact, in the absence of any carbon emissions regulation in Morocco, coal-fired power generation in Morocco had undercut Spanish renewables production (which must comply with the EU's Emissions Trading System). Going forward, carbon competition from neighboring countries may be an issue of concern and discussion in EU-southern energy relations.

Nuclear

Despite recurrent concerns about the development of weapons of mass destruction (WMD), almost all the countries of the EU's southern neighborhood are bound by the United Nation's Treaty on Non-Proliferation of Nuclear Weapons (NPT) and maintain strong cooperation links with the International Atomic Energy Agency (IAEA). The only exception is Israel which has remained rather ambiguous on the matter, refusing, for example, to confirm or deny the possession of such weapons.

Nuclear energy is not yet part of the energy mix in the southern neighborhood, however, and with steadily rising energy and electricity needs and the looming threat of climate change, there is great interest among the countries of the MENA region in developing and using nuclear power for peaceful purposes. Indeed, the advantages of nuclear power are numerous, ranging from affordability to reliability, resilience, and high energy intensity. Moreover, nuclear power can improve a country's energy security and thus contribute to its energy independence. Finally, nuclear power is – factoring out nuclear waste – a clean energy source and does therefore contribute to the achievement of the UN's 7th Sustainable Development Goal, namely, to ensuring access to affordable, reliable, sustainable, and modern energy.

The MENA countries' nuclear interest is reflected in various nuclear power programs aimed at decarbonizing electricity production: **Algeria**, where uranium exploration and discovery occurred as early as the 1970s (World Nuclear Association 2020b), has two research reactors, one at the Draria nuclear complex (built by Argentina), around 20 km east of Algiers and one at Birine (built by China). And while the country does not yet have any nuclear power plant under construction, the government is currently looking into the possibility of constructing the first plant by 2022 (1,200 MW) and a second one by 2027 (IAEA 2020). Likewise, **Egypt** pursues plans to construct four 1,200 MW reactors near the city of El Daaba in the north for which it agreed with the Russian State Atomic Energy Corporation Rosatom in 2015. The project is planned for completion by the end of the 2020s (World Nuclear News 2020). Planning to build a 2,000 MW nuclear power plant in Al Amra by 2023, and disposing of some uranium reserves, **Jordan** (which already has one research reactor) equally signed an agreement with Rosatom in 2015. While this initial deal was canceled in 2018 over discordances as regards financing and costs, a new agreement was signed shortly after which still foresees the construction of the plant but with less power (World Nuclear Association 2020a). Finally, **Tunisia** has been considering the introduction of nuclear power in its electricity system since the 1980s and has also been planning to construct a light water reactor in the 1990s, however, corresponding plans have been abandoned. As for **Morocco**, the country has been seeking to develop nuclear energy (in addition to fossil fuels and renewables) to construct a first nuclear center by 2030, the context in which it has demonstrated interest in collaborating with Russia and Rosatom and has also already carried out a pre-project study with China for the construction of a 10 MW reactor at Tan-Tan, which is supposed to provide power for a desalination plant. Morocco's nuclear ambitions already date back to the early 1980s, when French and Russian geologists first carried out nuclear studies according to which the country disposes of vast resources of uranium, notably unconventional uranium, i.e., uranium to be recovered from phosphoric acid. Since 2000, the country disposes of the Maamora Nuclear Research Centre (CENM), located 22 km to the northeast of Rabat where the first research reactor was built in 2003 with assistance from the USA and France (World Nuclear Association 2020b). However, and given its great renewables potential and its progress in this regard, there are doubts among the scientific community that Morocco will go down the nuclear lane (either in the short- or long-term) but rather chose to focus on the expansion of its wind and solar resources, as well as the development of an export-oriented hydrogen economy.

In fact, with renewables becoming more and more cost-competitive, researchers presume that Morocco's future foreign cooperation will increasingly focus on this angle (including with the EU). Even more so in the context of a post-COVID-19 energy system transformation. The same is likely to happen to other "renewables countries" which, confronted with the choice of either developing renewables or nuclear, may, given the cost, safety, and environmental challenges going along with nuclear, rather opt for the first possibility. Other, not insignificant hurdles to nuclear power development in the region are the tense geopolitical environment and public opposition. For example, following the Fukushima nuclear incident of 2011, Jordan temporarily paused its nuclear program amid public backlash and there have also been regular calls for canceling Egypt's nuclear plans. Moreover, the nuclear ambitions of the southern countries also open the way for geopolitical or nuclear competition and the wrestling for influence and power. Indeed, and as shown before, both Russia and China play a nuclear power game in the region, a reality that, in return, may not please France which used to traditionally assert control over this domain and used to be the go-to partner in this regard, in particular for the North African countries.

Overall, and in view of enhancing energy security and independence and achieving the climate change goals, the countries of the southern neighborhood are making huge steps towards nuclear energy use, with various large-scale nuclear power plants being currently under construction. However, most of the nuclear programs are still in an exploratory phase, and to push forward the nuclear energy agenda and make it wildly acceptable, a greater commitment to safety, security, and regional cooperation would be necessary. Moreover, and given that renewables are increasingly on the rise across the region, nuclear energy will most probably rather serve as a bridge fuel to a low-carbon future in the region in the long-term. Against this background, it is rather unlikely for nuclear energy to be deployed on a large scale going forward.

Conclusion

The EU's southern neighborhood has long played a key role in the Union's energy relations, above all thanks to its role as an important supplier of oil and gas and its potential for renewables. Geopolitical developments like the Arab Spring and the reconfiguration of alliances in the region have increasingly put a strain on the region's relationship with the EU in recent years. Adding to this, the COVID-19 pandemic and the oil market collapse of 2020, as well as the corresponding calls for a green recovery represent a further challenge, as they destabilize the region not only politically but also from an economic point of view and question existing energy patterns, notably as regards the carbon-intensive oil and gas sectors. Going forward, volatile oil markets will, in combination with the low-carbon transition, force investors to redirect capital towards green financing goals – all the more so as the region is highly vulnerable to the impacts of climate change – and the fossil fuel industry to reconfigure their operating models accordingly. However, these events may also be an opportunity because they provide the prospect for the southern neighborhood to rethink its energy strategies and policies and accelerate transitions towards clean energy systems. While several of the southern oil and gas producer countries had already engaged in climate change action before the onset of the health crisis, they have been stepping up their efforts towards diversification of their economies, laying now an even greater focus on the green energy shift. Here, and with sustainable development expected to gain importance in EU policies, the region may have a greater role in green energy cooperation with the Union, notably when it comes to renewable electricity or hydrogen. To ensure enduring success in this regard though, the EU will need to adapt to current market circumstances and take a more balanced approach towards the region, one that is based on equality and mutuality and that considers common goals.

Cross-References

▶ Energy Governance in Germany
▶ Energy Governance in Italy
▶ Energy Governance in Spain
▶ Energy Relations in the EU Eastern Partnership
▶ European Union Energy Policy: A Discourse Perspective
▶ EU-Russia Energy Relations
▶ The Energy Charter Treaty: Old and New Dilemmas in Global Energy Governance
▶ The EU in Global Energy Governance

References

Aliboni, R. (2012). *EU multilateral relations with southern partners: Reflections on future prospects*. Retrieved from: https://www.iss.europa.eu/content/eu-multilateral-relations-southern-partners-reflections-future-prospects

Behr, T. (2010). Regional integration in the Mediterranean: Moving out of the deadlock? Institut Jacques Delors, 77, 100.

Blockmans, S., Kostanyan, H., Remizov, A., Slapakova, L., & Van der Loo, G. (2017). *Assessing European Neighbourhood Policy: Perspectives from the literature* (p. 171). Brussels: CEPS.

BMWI. (2020). Retrieved from: https://www.bmwi.de/Redaktion/DE/Pressemitteilungen/2020/20200610-globale-fuehrungsrolle-bei-wasserstofftechnologien-sichern.html

Boening, A., Kremer, J.-F., & Van Loon, A. (2013). *Global Power Europe – Vol. 2: Policies, actions and influence of the EU's external relations* (p. 344). Heidelberg: Springer Science & Business Media.

Bouraiou, A., Necaibia, A., Boutasseta, N., Mekhilef, S., Dabou, R., Zidane, A., Sahouane, N., Attoui, I., Mostefaoui, M., & Touaba, O. (2020). Status of renewable energy potential and utilization in Algeria. *Journal of Cleaner Production, 246*, 1–16.

Bouris, D., & Schumacher, T. (2016). *The revised European Neighbourhood Policy: Continuity and change in EU Foreign Policy*. London: Springer.

Cambini, C., & Rubino, A. (2014). *Regional energy initiatives: MedReg and the energy community*. London: Routledge.

Cebeci, M. (2019). Problematizing effectiveness and potential of EU policies in the Mediterranean, MEDRESET, n°8, April 2019.

Colombo, S., & Abdelkhaliq, N. (2012). The European Union and multilateralism in the Mediterranean: Energy and Migration Policy, Mercury Papers, n°18, 42.

Consilium. (2017). Association Council between the European Union and Egypt, EU-Egypt Partnership Priorities 2017–2020. Retrieved from: https://www.consilium.europa.eu/media/23942/eu-egypt.pdf

CORES. (2020). Estadisticas. Retrieved from: https://www.cores.es/es/estadisticas

Darbouche, H. (2010). Energising EU-Algerian relations. *The International Spectator, 45*(3), 71–83.

Daum, B. (2020). (In)consistency in European External Energy Governance in the EU's Southern Neighbourhood: The Case of Morocco. Ph.D., Technische Universität Darmstadt.

Delcour, L. (2015). The 2015 ENP Review: Beyond stocktaking, the need for a political strategy, College of Europe Policy Brief CEPOB, December 2015.

Desertec. (2020). Retrieved from: https://www.desertec.org/

Diez, T., & Tocci, N. (2017). *The EU, promoting regional integration, and conflict resolution*. Berlin: Springer.

Dii Desertenergy. (2020). Retrieved from: https://dii-desertenergy.org/

EEAS. (2012). EU/Jordan ENP Action Plan. Retrieved from: https://eeas.europa.eu/archives/delegations/jordan/documents/eu_jordan/jordan_enp_ap_final_en.pdf

Escribano, G. (2016). The EU-Algeria Energy Forum: A new Narrative in the Making or just another Missed Opportunity? Real Instituto Elcano Royal Institute, Expert Comment 21/2016.

Escribano, G. (2017). The Shrinking Euro-Mediterranean Policy Space, Real Instituto Elcano, ARI 69/2017.

Escribano, G., & Lazaro, L. (2020). Balancing geopolitics with green deal recovery: In search of a comprehensive Euro-Mediterranean energy script, Real Instituto Elcano Royal Institute, ARI 95/2020.

EU Neighbours. (2020). Retrieved from: https://www.euneighbours.eu/en/policy/european-neighbourhood-instrument-eni#plans

European Commission. (2003). On the Development of Energy Policy for the Enlarged European Union, its Neighbours and Partner Countries. Retrieved from: http://aei.pitt.edu/39124/1/COM_(2003)_262.pdf

European Commission. (2011a). A new Response to a Changing Neighbourhood, COM (2011) 303 final. Retrieved from: http://aei.pitt.edu/39626/1/COM_(2011)_303.pdf

European Commission. (2011b). On Security of Energy Supply and International Cooperation - The EU Energy Policy: Engaging with Partners beyond our Borders, COM (2011) 539 final. Retrieved from: https://eur-lex.europa.eu/legal-content/EN/TXT/PDF/?uri=CELEX:52011DC0539&from=EN

European Commission. (2014). European Energy Security Strategy, COM (2014) 330 final. Retrieved from: https://eur-lex.europa.eu/legal-content/EN/TXT/PDF/?uri=CELEX:52014DC0330&from=EN

European Commission. (2015). Dialogue Energétique de Haut Niveau entre l'Algérie et l'Union Européenne. Retrieved from: https://ec.europa.eu/energy/sites/ener/files/documents/dialogue.pdf

European Commission. (2015a). A Framework Strategy for a Resilient Energy Union with a Forward-Looking Climate Change Policy, COM (2015) 80 final. Retrieved from: https://eur-lex.europa.eu/resource.html?uri=cellar:1bd46c90-bdd4-11e4-bbe1-01aa75ed71a1.0001.03/DOC_1&format=PDF

European Commission. (2015b). Review of the European Neighbourhood Policy, JOIN (2015) 50 final. Retrieved from: http://eeas.europa.eu/archives/docs/enp/documents/2015/151118_joint-communication_review-of-the-enp_en.pdf

European Commission. (2016). Roadmap for Sustainable Electricity Trade Between Morocco and the European Internal Energy Market. Retrieved from: https://ec.europa.eu/energy/sites/ener/files/documents/2016_11_13_set_roadmap_joint_declaration-vf.pdf

European Commission. (2018a). Memorandum of Understanding on a Strategic Partnership on Energy between the European Union and the Arab Republic of Egypt 2018–2022. Retrieved from: https://ec.europa.eu/energy/sites/ener/files/documents/eu-egypt_mou.pdf

European Commission. (2018b). Retrieved from: https://ec.europa.eu/commission/presscorner/detail/en/ip_20_96

European Commission. (2020a). Letter of Intent to President David Maria Sassoli and to Chancellor Angela Merkel. Retrieved from: https://ec.europa.eu/info/sites/info/files/state_of_the_union_2020_letter_of_intent_en.pdf

European Commission. (2020b). A Hydrogen Strategy for a Climate-neutral Europe, COM (2020) 301 final. Retrieved from: https://ec.europa.eu/energy/sites/ener/files/hydrogen_strategy.pdf

European Commission. (2020c). Retrieved from: https://ec.europa.eu/neighbourhood-enlargement/neighbourhood/southern-neighbourhood_en#:~:text=EU%20cooperation%20with%20the%20Southern,Palestine*%2C%20Syria%20and%20Tunisia

European Commission. (2020d). Africa-Europe Alliance: Four New Financial Guarantees Worth €216 Million Signed under the EU External Investment Plan, Press Release. Retrieved from: https://ec.europa.eu/commission/presscorner/detail/en/ip_20_96

European Commission. (2020e). Memorandum of Understanding on a Strategic Partnership on Energy between the European Union and the Arab Republic of Egypt 2018–2022. Retrieved from: https://ec.europa.eu/transparency/regdoc/rep/3/2018/EN/C-2018-1764-F1-EN-ANNEX-1-PART-1.PDF

European Commission. (2020f). Retrieved from: https://ec.europa.eu/trade/policy/countries-and-regions/negotiations-and-agreements/

European Commission. (2020g). Retrieved from: https://ec.europa.eu/eurostat/statistics-explained/index.php?title=File:Extra_EU-27_imports_of_natural_gas_from_main_trading_partners,_2018_and_2019_v2.png

European Commission. (2020h). Retrieved from: https://ec.europa.eu/commission/presscorner/detail/fr/SPEECH_16_1898

European Commission. (2020i). Retrieved from: https://ec.europa.eu/eurostat/cache/infographs/energy/bloc-2c.html

European Commission. (2020j). Retrieved from: https://ec.europa.eu/info/news/european-union-and-algeria-strengthen-their-energy-partnership-2018-nov-19_lt

European Commission. (2020l). Retrieved from: https://ec.europa.eu/neighbourhood-enlargement/news_corner/news/eu-tunisia-partnership-also-helps-boost-tunisia%E2%80%99s-economy_en

European Commission. (2020m). Retrieved from: https://ec.europa.eu/neighbourhood-enlargement/neighbourhood/countries/palestine_en

European Commission. (2020n). Retrieved from: https://ec.europa.eu/energy/infrastructure/transparency_platform/map-viewer/main.html

European Commission. (2020o). Retrieved from: https://ec.europa.eu/neighbourhood-enlargement/neighbourhood/countries/algeria_en

European Commission. (2020p). Barcelona Process: Union for the Mediterranean ministerial conference, Marseille, 3-4 November 2008, Final Declaration. Retrieved from: https://ufmsecretariat.org/wp-content/uploads/2015/10/Marseille-Declaration.pdf

European Investment Bank. (2020). Retrieved from: https://www.eib.org/de/projects/loans/index.htm?q=&sortColumn=loanParts.loanPartStatus.statusDate&sortDir=desc&pageNumber=0&itemPerPage=9&pageable=false&language=DE&defaultLanguage=DE&loanPartYearFrom=1959&loanPartYearTo=2019&countries.region=5&orCountries.region=true&orCountries=true&sectors=1000&orSectors=true

European Parliament. (2020). Draft Joint Statement following the Meeting between the Delegations of the European Parliament and of the Knesset. Retrieved from: https://www.europarl.europa.eu/cmsdata/215787/20201130_joint-statement.pdf

EUROSTAT. (2019). Retrieved from: https://ec.europa.eu/eurostat/cache/infographs/energy/bloc-2c.html

Fernandez-Molina, I. (2016). *Moroccan foreign policy under Mohammed VI, 1999–2014*. London: Routledge.

Franceschini, B. (2019). Scaling-up Renewable Energy Development in Jordan, Position Paper, RES4MED.

Ghanem, D., & Kuznetsov, V. (2018). *Moscow's Maghreb Moment*. Carnegie Middle East Center. https://carnegie-mec.org/diwan/76572

Godzimirski, J. M. (2016). *EU leadership in energy and environmental governance: Global and local challenges and responses*. London: Palgrave Macmillan.

Grigorjeva, J. (2016). *Starting a new chapter in EU-Algeria energy relations: A proposal for a targeted cooperation* (p. 173). Berlin: Jacques Delors Institute Berlin.

Haghighi, S. S. (2007). *Energy security: The external legal relations of the European Union with major oil and gas supplying countries*. Portland: Hart Publishing.

Hamed, T. A., Flamma, H., & Azraq, M. (2012). Renewable energy in the Palestinian territories: Opportunities and challenges. *Renewable and Sustainable Energy Reviews, 16*(1), 1082–1088.

Hancher, L. (2018). *Transformation of EU and East Mediterranean Energy Networks: Legal, regulatory and geopolitical challenges*. Deventer: Claeys & Casteels Law Publishing.

Herranz-Surrallés, A. (2015). European external energy policy: Governance, diplomacy and sustainability. In K. E. Jorgensen, A. K. Aarstad, E. Drieskens, K. Laatikainen, & B. Tonra (Eds.), *Sage handbook of European Foreign Policy*. London: Sage.

Herranz-Surrallés, A. (2018). Thinking energy outside the frame? Reframing and misframing in Euro-Mediterranean energy relations. *Mediterranean Politics, 23*(1), 122–141.

Hochberg, M. (2016). Renewable energy growth in Morocco: An example for the region, Middle East Institute, MEI Policy Focus 2016-26.

Hoebink, P. (2005). *The Coherence of EU Policies: Perspectives of the North and the South*. Nijmegen: Centre for International Development Issues.

Hydrogen Europe. (2020). Green Hydrogen for a European Green Deal–A 2×40 GW Initiative. Retrieved from: https://hydrogeneurope.eu/sites/default/files/Hydrogen%20Europe_2x40%20GW%20Green%20H2%20Initative%20Paper.pdf

IAEA. (2020). Retrieved from: https://www-pub.iaea.org/MTCD/Publications/PDF/P1500_CD_Web/htm/pdf/topic1/1S02_B.%20Meftah.pdf

IEA. (2020). Retrieved from: https://www.iea.org/reports/renewables-2020/covid-19-and-the-resilience-of-renewables

IRENA. (2018). Renewable Energy Outlook Egypt, Based on Renewables Readiness Assessment and Remap Analysis. Retrieved from: https://www.irena.org/publications/2018/Oct/Renewable-Energy-Outlook-Egypt

Jalilvand, D. R., & Westphal, K. (2017). *The political and economic challenges of energy in the Middle East and North Africa*. London: Routledge.

Khaldi, Y. M., & Sunikka-Blank, M. (2020). Governing renewable energy transition in conflict contexts: Investigating the institutional context in Palestine. *Energy Transitions, 4*, 69–90.

Knodt, M., Müller, F., & Piefer, N. (2015). *Challenges of European external energy governance with emerging powers*. London: Routledge.

Leal-Arcas, R., & Wouters, J. (2017). *Research handbook on EU Energy Law and Policy*. Cheltenham: Edward Elgar Publishing.

Looney, R. E. (2016). *Handbook transitions to energy and climate security*. London: Routledge.

Mahncke, D., Ambos, A., & Reynolds, C. (2004). *European Foreign Policy: From rhetoric to reality?* Brussels: Peter Lang.

Mehmet, O., & Yorucu, V. (2020). *Modern geopolitics of Eastern Mediterranean hydrocarbons in an age of energy transformation*. Cham: Springer.

Momete, D. C. (2015). Towards a better European integration through a common energy planning. *Procedia Economics and Finance, 22*, 463–469.

Moore, S. (2018). *Sustainable energy transformations, power, and politics: Morocco and the Mediterranean*. London: Routledge.

Morata, F., & Solorio Sandoval, I. (2012). *European energy policy: An environmental approach*. Cheltenham: Edward Elgar Publishing.

Neframi, E. (2012). Panorama des Relations Extérieures de l'Union Européenne dans le Domaine de l'Energie. In C. Blumann (Ed.), *Vers une Politique Européenne de l'Energie*. Paris: Bruylant.

Neighbourhood Investment Facility. (2020). Strategic Orientations 2014–2020. Retrieved from: https://ec.europa.eu/neighbourhood-enlargement/sites/near/files/neighbourhood/pdf/key-documents/nif/20150731-nif-strategic-orientations-2014-2020.pdf

Nur Energie. (2020). TuNur files for authorisation for 4.5 GW solar export project. Retrieved from: http://www.nurenergie.com/index.php/news/123/66/TuNur-files-for-authorisation-for-4-5-GW-solar-export-project

OPEC. (2020). Retrieved from: https://www.opec.org/opec_web/en/index.htm

Peritz, A. (2020). Beirut's Port Explosion Reveils Underlying Problems in Energy Supply. Atlantic Council.

Prontera, A. (2017). *The new politics of energy security in the European Union and beyond: States, markets, institutions.* London: Routledge.

Qudrat-Ullah, H., & Kayal, A. A. (2019). *Climate change and energy dynamics in the Middle East: Modeling and simulation-based solutions.* Cham: Springer.

Roehrkasten, S., Quitzow, R., Auktor, G., & Westphal, K. (2016). *Advancing an International Energy Transition Policy in North Africa and Beyond.* IASS.

Rubino, A., Ozturk, I., Lenzi, V., & Costa Campi, M. (2015). *Regulation and investments in energy markets solutions for the Mediterranean.* London: Academic Press.

Saddiki, S. (2020). The New Turkish Presence in North Africa: Ambitions and Challenges, Konrad Adenauer Stiftung, n°33.

Sartori, N. (2014). The Mediterranean energy relations after the Arab spring: Towards a new regional paradigm? *Cahiers de la Méditerranée, 89*, 145–157.

Tagliapietra, S. (2016). *Energy relations in the Euro-Mediterranean: A political economy perspective, Business & Economics.* Cham: Springer.

Tagliapietra, S., & Zachmann, G. (2015). Reinvigorating EU-Algeria Energy Cooperation, Blog Post. Retrieved from: https://www.bruegel.org/2015/06/reinvigorating-the-eu-algeria-energy-cooperation/

Tagliapietra, S., & Zachmann, G. (2016). Energy across the Mediterranean: A Call for Realism, Bruegel Policy Brief, n°3, 8.

Thaler, P. (2015). Unpacking 'Coherence' in EU Foreign Policy: How Policy Setting and Policy Content shape EU External Relations towards Russia. Ph.D., Doctoral School of Political Science, Public Policy and International Relations, Central European University.

The European Fund for Sustainable Development (EFSD). (2018). Promoting Investment in the EU Neighbourhood and Africa. Retrieved from: https://ec.europa.eu/commission/sites/beta-political/files/eip_operational_report.pdf

UN. (2020). Retrieved from: https://www4.unfccc.int/sites/NDCStaging/Pages/All.aspx

Weber, B. (2016). The EU External Energy Governance and the Neighbouring Gas Suppliers Azerbaijan and Algeria: Ensuring European Gas Supply Security at the Borderline between Markets and Geopolitics. Ph.D., Sciences Po – Institut d'Etudes Politiques de Paris.

Werenfels, I. (2020). Maghrebi Rivalries Over Sub-Saharan Africa: Algeria and Tunisia Seeking to Keep Up with Morocco, SWP Comment. Retrieved from: https://www.swp-berlin.org/fileadmin/contents/products/comments/2020C54_MaghrebiRivalries.pdf

World Nuclear Association. (2020a). Retrieved from: https://www.world-nuclear.org/information-library/country-profiles/countries-g-n/jordan.aspx

World Nuclear Association. (2020b). Retrieved from: https://www.world-nuclear.org/information-library/country-profiles/others/uranium-in-africa.aspx

World Nuclear News. (2020). Retrieved from: world-nuclear-news.org

Worrall, J. (2017). *International institutions of the Middle East: The GCC, Arab League, and Arab Maghreb Union.* London: Routledge.

Youngs, R. (2007). Europe's external energy policy: Between geopolitics and the market, CEPS, n°278, 17.

Youngs, R. (2009). *Energy security: Europe's new foreign policy challenge.* London: Routledge.

Youngs, R. (2014). *Climate change and European security.* London: Routledge.

Zoubir, Y. H., & White, G. (2015). *North African politics: Change and continuity.* London: Routledge.

The Energy Charter Treaty: Old and New Dilemmas in Global Energy Governance

15

Anna Herranz-Surrallés

Contents

Introduction	348
Origins and Ratification (1990s): A Special Creature in the Energy Governance Landscape	350
The ECT to Test (2000s): Gas Transit Disputes and the Decoupling of Legal Orders	353
Modernization and the International Energy Charter (Early 2010s): Crisis or Relaunch?	355
New Contestation Fronts (Late 2010s): Politicization of ISDS and Climate Change	358
Future Directions	361
Cross-References	363
References	363

Abstract

The Energy Charter Treaty (ECT) is a rare example of rules-based international energy governance, joining consumer, producer, and transit countries. Besides extending the multilateral trade rules to the energy domain, the ECT has also become the most often invoked international investment agreement. However, the evolution of the ECT has remained particularly susceptible to changing international power balances and ideational struggles. In reviewing the main scholarly and practical debates on the ECT, this chapter walks through three decades of European and global energy governance, addressing the emergence, transformation, and the recent mixed signs of modernization and decline of the ECT. The chapter touches on several core debates across disciplines, from the factors explaining the emergence of international regimes, the problem of overlapping regional and international legal orders, or the consequences of politicization of international economic institutions. The chapter concludes with a forward-looking reflection on the main challenges facing the ECT in a context of crisis

A. Herranz-Surrallés (✉)
Faculty of Arts and Social Sciences, Maastricht University, Maastricht, The Netherlands
e-mail: anna.herranz@maastrichtuniversity.nl

© Springer Nature Switzerland AG 2022
M. Knodt, J. Kemmerzell (eds.), *Handbook of Energy Governance in Europe*,
https://doi.org/10.1007/978-3-030-43250-8_65

of the liberal world order and growingly relevant concerns such as climate change and the security implications of foreign investment.

Keywords

Energy Charter Treaty · Dispute settlement · Global energy governance · Foreign investment · Energy transit · EU energy policy

Introduction

Although largely unknown outside the energy policy community, the Energy Charter Treaty (ECT) has a prominent place in the architecture of global energy governance. With its origins in the immediate post-cold war period, the ECT is still a unique international regime in a domain characterized by institutional fragmentation and weak governance (Van de Graaf 2013, pp. 44–65). Some of the ECT's particularities include its diverse membership, aimed at bridging energy producer, transit, and consumer countries. Besides a core of 48 countries having ratified the 1994 ECT, the so-called Energy Charter Conference also encompasses an outer circle of 91 countries and regional organizations that signed the nonbinding 2015 International Energy Charter (IEC). The ECT is also unique in extending the World Trade Organisation (WTO) multilateral binding rules to the energy sector and, owing to its dispute settlement mechanism, currently considered "one of the most important investment protection agreements in our modernized and globalized economy" (Hobér 2018, p. 201).

However, the ECT has not been free from controversy, among states, EU institutions and, more recently, also the wider public. Following Robert Cox's famous description of international institutions as "particular amalgams of ideas and material power" (Cox 1981, p. 137), the ECT's evolution has been particularly susceptible to changing power balances and international ideational shifts. Therefore, the study of the ECT requires examining wider developments, such as East-West relations, the evolution of European integration, the rise of emerging economies, or the politicization of international institutions and climate change. In reviewing the main practical and theoretical debates surrounding the ECT, this chapter touches on such wider material and ideational international shifts (see Table 1).

The chapter begins discussing the origins of the ECT, negotiated between 1991 and 1994, amidst high hopes for the expansion of (neo)liberal economic ideas and institutions, but also turmoil and uncertainty following the dissolution of the Soviet Union. Section "Origins and Ratification (1990s): A Special Creature in the Energy Governance Landscape" discusses different explanations for the emergence of this remarkable multilateral institution in such a volatile context. However, despite the low energy prices and the favorable winds for liberalization initiatives, negotiations were complex and several times at the verge of collapse. Therefore, the section examines both the drivers of the ECT and the tensions reflected in its design.

The deployment of the ECT provisions and first major hiccups during the 2000s is the focus of section "The ECT to Test (2000s): Gas Transit Disputes and the Decoupling of Legal Orders." The tightening of global energy markets in the mid-2000s prefigured the growing leverage of producer countries, putting the

Table 1 Overview of key international trends and theoretical/practical debates over the ECT

Period	Material power	Ideational trends	Main debates and questions
1990s	Dissolution of Soviet Union Low energy prices	Ascendancy of neoliberal ideas Tendency towards liberalization of energy sector	What explains the ECT's creation and institutional design? What are the lessons learned from the difficult ECT negotiations?
2000s	Rising non-Western powers Growing energy prices EU Eastern enlargement	Acceleration of EU internal energy market Roll-back of liberalization in producer countries	Why did the Transit Protocol negotiations fail? Why did Russia abandon the ECT?
Early 2010s	Economic crisis hitting the EU and West High energy prices High instability around the EU	Crisis of neoliberal ideas Deterioration of EU-Russia relations, esp. following annexation of Crimea	Did the EU accommodate or entrench into previous positions? To what extent does the 2015 IEC provide the basis for the ECT's relaunch?
Late 2010s	Ascendancy of China and non-Western FDI Moderation in energy prices	Public backlash to integration/globalization Crisis of multilateralism	Are the EU and ECT law compatible? How can the ECT respond to public contestation of ISDS and rising climate activism?

Source: Own elaboration

ECT and its implementation under stress. At the same time, the deepening and widening of the EU also started to impact on the ECT, since the EU focused on the acceleration of its internal energy market and launched more ambitious frameworks to "export" its regulatory model to the countries of its proximity. This section investigates how these tensions played out in the negotiations of the transit protocol and the eruption of the first serious gas crises in 2006 and 2009, as well as the different interpretations for the unexpected move by the Russian government to abandon the ECT.

The 2010s set off amidst a confluence of crises in and around the EU: internally, the EU was absorbed by the fallout of the global financial crisis; and externally, the security environment deteriorated, with new focuses of conflict in both Southern and Eastern neighborhoods and mounting tension in EU-Russia relations. In this context, the ECT launched a reform process, which finalized with the signature of the 2015 IEC. Section "Modernization and the International Energy Charter (Early 2010s): Crisis or Relaunch?" addresses how scholars and commentators interpreted the response by the ECT and the EU to Russia's withdrawal as well as the prospects of the IEC in re-invigorating the Energy Charter process.

By the mid-2010s, the ECT became object of yet another form of contestation, this time related to the politicization of international trade and, particularly, the so-called Investor State Dispute Settlement (ISDS). Even if the criticism towards

ISDS clauses emerged in the context of mega-trade agreements such as the Transatlantic Trade and Investment Partnership (TTIP), demands for reform eventually reached the ECT, which is by far the world's most litigated international treaty. Moreover, the growing public salience of climate change also placed the ECT under closer public scrutiny. Therefore, section "New Contestation Fronts (Late 2010s): Politicization of ISDS and Climate Change" examines those debates and its consequences on the legitimacy and further reforms undertaken by the ECT.

Finally, the chapter concludes with a discussion on the main challenges at the turn of the 2020s, which anticipates as one of the most delicate phases the ECT has experienced so far. Again, developments in the EU and Russia take center stage. The intra-EU discussion on the competences in foreign investment and the first ever case of arbitration against the EU, in relation to the Nord Stream 2 pipeline, have turn the ECT into a complex legal and (geo)political battleground. The final section concludes with a review of the possible paths the ECT might take and their consequences for global energy governance.

Origins and Ratification (1990s): A Special Creature in the Energy Governance Landscape

The signing of the European Energy Charter declaration in December 1991 by 48 states (plus the European Community and the Interstate Economic Community) and its relatively quick evolution into a binding Treaty in December 1994 is a remarkable achievement. At that time, the governance of international energy was very limited and split into two camps: The Organisation of Petroleum Exporting Countries (OPEC) on the side of producer countries and the International Energy Agency (IEA) created by Western countries highly dependent on energy imports. The ECT was therefore a novelty in that, for the first time, it bridged consuming and producer countries. Moreover, energy policy had remained largely outside liberal trade and investment regimes. Even within the European Community (EC), energy policy remained a strict national competence, despite the repeated efforts by the European Commission to gather support for an Internal Energy Market (McGowan 1989). Therefore, the significance of binding provisions on energy trade and investment including countries emerging out of a planned economy can hardly be exaggerated. It is also remarkable that the Energy Charter was the very first multilateral treaty signed after the end of the Cold War (Axelrod 1996, p. 467).

Studies examining the *creation* of the ECT have emphasized different aspects of this puzzle. On the one hand, some scholars highlighted the economic and geopolitical drivers of the ECT. First proposed by the Dutch government in 1990, the idea of a sectoral agreement on energy with the countries of the Eastern bloc was quickly taken up as a potential win-win solution for all parties. On the West-European side, the initiative was, first, an opportunity for investment in a region that had remained closed to foreign companies for decades and where political risks remained high (Doré 1996). Secondly, boosting energy supplies from Russia and the Caspian Region would increase Europe's energy security in times of severe instability in the Persian Gulf (ibid.). More broadly, a multilateral economic agreement could also help stabilize East-West relations and serve as a "geopolitical instrument to shape the transition" in the Soviet Union and Eastern Europe (Basedow 2018, p. 132). On the side of a Soviet Union in process of dissolution, the prospect of attracting foreign capital and Western technology was also attractive, given the depressed state of the Soviet energy sector, severely hit by a decade of divestment and plummeting oil prices (Konoplyanik 1996).

On the other hand, ideational and institutional factors seem to have played an equal or even more important role. In a detailed account of the birth of the ECT, Basedow (2018, pp. 131–132) argues that the energy business did not push for the initiative. On the contrary, energy companies in the distribution business were against steps towards liberalizing the sector in Europe; and major gas and oil exploration companies remained rather skeptical about the chances of the agreement to improve the investment climate in the Soviet Union (ibid.). The economic rationale of the ECT is better explained by the dominant policy paradigm guiding economic policy at that time. In that regard, the ECT coincided with the ascendancy of neoliberal ideas and the EC's push for the Single Market program. The European Commission thus readily supported the ECT initiative, as a tool to advance the liberalization of the EU electricity and gas sectors (Matlary 1996, p. 265). Moreover, the Commission's entrepreneurship in the ECT can also be explained by the institutional goal of asserting its role and competences in international affairs (Basedow 2018, p. 129). More broadly, the ECT was also imbued with Western functionalist ideas about the relevance of sectoral cooperation as a first step for regional political cooperation and for "socializing" the countries emerging from a planned economy system into the institutions and rules of market economies (Lubbers 1996, p. xiv).

The confluence of these propitious economic, geopolitical, and ideational factors explains well the swift adoption of the European Energy Charter declaration in December 1991, just a few days before the formal dissolution of the Soviet Union. The *negotiations* for the fully fledged binding Treaty were more protracted, both due to resistance from Russia and the newly independent states and disagreements within the OECD block. On the Eastern side, negotiations were delayed due to the turmoil accompanying the creation of new states and their respective energy policies. Substantively, Russia and other non-EU countries (notably Norway) opposed the liberalization of investment in the form of National Treatment (NT) on the pre-establishment phase. At the most, Russia was open to consider a transition period, which would allow granting only Most-Favored Nation (MFN) treatment, something that was rejected by the EC and the USA as a "blank cheque for investment liberalisation" (Basedow 2018, p. 124).

On the Western side, there were notable disagreements within the OECD itself. First, some EC member states were highly suspicious of the possibility that the ECT would mean the liberalization of the energy sector through the back door. One of the most contentious issues in that regard was the idea of "freedom of transit" (art. 7 ECT), as some member states saw it as the precursor of an obligation of Third Party Access (TPA), which the member states had already rejected in the context of the discussions on the liberalization of the EC gas market (Anders-Speed 1999, p. 127).

Second, the Member States were not eye to eye on the geographical reach of the Treaty. For example, France and Belgium were not in favor of opening the agreement to non-European OECD countries. It was only at the insistence of the USA that the EC extended the invitation to all OECD economies (Doré 1996, p. 140). Finally, this led to frequent transatlantic disagreements, since the USA defended strict liberalization obligations, whereas the EC Member States favored a more flexible and gradual approach that would better accommodate the preferences of Russia and other producer countries (Herranz-Surrallés 2016a, p. 53).

The *outcome* of the negotiation was closer to the flexible option defended by the EC, which still included legally-binding investment protection provisions, if only for the postestablishment phase (art. 13 ECT). More specifically, the ECT provided for a dispute settlement mechanism (art. 26 ECT) that included the possibility of investor-state arbitration. The provisions on preestablishment phase were not included in the ECT and were postponed to a later stage, envisaging a negotiation on a "supplementary protocol." However, this flexible approach also prompted the withdrawal of the USA, in disagreement with the limited character of the Treaty. Moreover, the outcome of the negotiation and ensuing ratification process was an indication of the difficulties soon to come.

To begin with, the Treaty came into force in 1998 without the ratification of two of the key producing countries involved in the ECT process (Russia and Norway). As foreseen in art. 45 of the ECT, Russia accepted to provisionally apply the Treaty and hence to remain bound by all its obligations. However, the provisional application would become a bone of contention in later stages and was an indication of Russia's cautious stance on the ECT. Similarly, the negotiations for the Supplementary Protocol on investment liberalization also collapsed (Basedow 2018). According to some key observers at the time, there was some sense that the ECT was coming even ahead of its time, since it reflected more the Western liberal economic ideas than the actual practice, which was still of limited liberalization within the EU. In that sense, Wälde (1996, pp. xix–xx) raised the question "will these 'Western' models work in 'Eastern' practice?" or in the words of Axelrod (1996), was the ECT "reality or illusion?"

More retrospectively, the birth of the ECT episode has also raised debate about the EU's international actorness. On the one hand, the sponsorship of such a special international regime has been interpreted as a case of institutional entrepreneurship from the Commission (Basedow 2018) and a paradoxical case of significant international leadership despite the internal divisions and limited sophistication of intra-EU internal market rules (Herranz-Surrallés 2012, p. 166). Conversely, other studies have suggested that the divisions in the OECD block led the EU to miss the window of opportunity of the early 1990s when the most reformist sectors in Russia were receptive to international commitments as a tool to shape the reorganization of domestic interests (Grätz 2011, p. 67). Either way, the European Commission remained the main driving force behind the ECT and the international organization created to support it, with a secretariat in Brussels. This support, however, would start to become more ambiguous already during the 2000s.

The ECT to Test (2000s): Gas Transit Disputes and the Decoupling of Legal Orders

The turn of the millennium was characterized by contradictory trends that soon started to leave a mark on the ECT. On the one hand, the first decade of the 2000s coincided with the gradual tightening of world energy markets, among others due to a growing energy demand by new emerging economies. In just one decade, oil prices went from historical lows (15 USD/barrel in 1998) to the record price spikes (147 USD/barrel in mid-2008). This context of growing economic and strategic importance of the energy sector gave strong leverage to the producer countries, which in many cases halted, or even reversed, the liberalization reforms initiated during the 1990s (Goldthau and Witte 2009). This is the case of Russia, where the newly elected President Putin in 2000, embarked on a process of regaining control of the oil and gas sectors, after a decade of privatizations and investment-friendly measures (Belyi 2014, p. 322). On the other hand, the first decade of the 2000s is also when the recently enlarged EU started making substantial progress in the liberalization of its internal electricity and gas markets, as well as the development of an external energy policy (Herranz-Surrallés 2016b). This section presents the debates on how these two opposite trends impacted on the development of the ECT, particularly on the failure of "Transit Protocol" negotiations and on Russia's withdrawal from the ECT in 2009.

The initiative of the Transit Protocol was the response to the deterioration of the transit governance in the former Soviet space. During the early 2000s, frequent supply and transit disputes started to occur between Russia and the new transit countries (most notably, Ukraine), due to the lack of transparency of gas prices and transit fees, the poor state of the pipeline systems, and the worsening of political relations in the region (Westphal 2009). However, the negotiations for the Transit Protocol became tangled into broader disagreements between Russia and the EU. In fact, in 2001 Putin's government made the ratification of the ECT, pending since 1994, conditional to the successful adoption of the Transit Protocol (Belyi 2012, p. 265). The clash of views has been explored in different aspects of the negotiations.

First, the parties disagreed over the very *principles of the transit regime*. For Russia, the main goal of the ECT was to ensure long-term supply stability, which in the view of Moscow, demanded vertically integrated companies (ibid.). Conversely, the emerging rules of the EU internal energy market were based on the principle of competition and hence required TPA, the separation between supply and transit (the so-called "unbundling") as well as a move away from long-term contracts. In this context, one of the main hurdles in the Transit Protocol negotiations was Russia's request to include a Right of First Refusal (ROFR) clause, namely, the right of exporters to prolong an existing transit contract before the pipeline capacity is offered to other competitors. Russia considered the inclusion of a ROFR as a red line in the negotiations, given that many of its transit contracts were expiring before its supply contracts. Conversely, the EU opposed the inclusion of such a clause, as it was deemed incompatible with TPA and the principle of nondiscrimination in the internal energy market (Yafimava 2011, p. 304). By the mid-2000s, the European

Commission even suggested that Russia should also adopt the TPA model and open its infrastructure network for transit of hydrocarbons from other producers in the Caspian and Central Asia (Herranz-Surrallés 2016a, p. 60). Such demands were totally dismissed by Russia, for which the ECT was understood as a mechanism to ensure the transit of Russian gas to Europe – and in no way an obligation to liberalize its gas and oil transit networks, under the monopoly of Gazprom and Rosneft, respectively.

A second obstacle in the Transit Protocol negotiations was the *legal status of the EU*. The development of the EU internal energy market had led to a growing gap between the minimum standards of the ECT and the much deeper liberalization rules introduced by the Second and Third Energy Directives (Talus 2013, p. 243). In view of the limited prospects that Russia would follow on a liberalized energy model, the EU demanded instead to introduce a Regional Economic Integration Organisation (REIO) clause in the Transit Protocol. The reasoning behind this request was that the 2003 Gas Directive had de facto abolished the categories of transit and distribution within the EU. Accordingly, the Transit Protocol should only apply between the EU and third states, and not to the relations between the EU Member States. However, Russia plainly opposed to introducing such a REIO clause and even suspended the negotiations for almost a year as a reaction (Yafimava 2011, p. 286). According to Russia, the recognition of the EU as a REIO in the Transit Protocol would give instruments to the EU to hinder Russian companies' access to the EU market (Belyi 2008, p. 212). In that sense, it could be argued that the "rapid evolvement of regional institutions inside the EU created a stumbling block to negotiations for an international Transit Protocol" (Bonafé and Mete 2016, p. 180).

Third, the Transit Protocol negotiations were also tainted by broader *geopolitical considerations*. Already since the early 1990s, the EU's technical assistance in the energy sector in the Former Soviet Union, with programs such as INOGATE, had been perceived by Russia as a threat to its influence in the region as well as its dominant position in the European gas markets (Belyi 2012). This sentiment aggravated with the gradual development of EU external energy policy. Since the mid-2000s, the EU started supporting the strategic diversification of gas supplies away from Russia, via legal, political, and financial means (Herranz-Surrallés 2016b). Mistrust grew stronger with the EU's creation of the Energy Community (EnC) in 2005, a new international institution aimed at the integration of candidate countries into the EU's energy regulatory space ahead of their accession (Prange-Gstöhl 2009). The Western Balkans's adoption of the EU internal energy market rules was another challenge to Gazprom's influence in the region and Russian-sponsored diversification projects, such as the South Stream. Moreover, while initially the EnC was designed only for candidate countries, it would soon be open to the countries of the European Neighbourhood Policy (ENP). Therefore, the attempt to create a multilateral transit governance in the ECT, while in parallel, both Russia and the EU were seemingly trying to reduce their mutual interdependence, fits well a classical prisoners' dilemma situation, where no side could trust the intentions of the other (Krikovic 2015).

Finally, the *transit dispute settlement* provisions of the ECT revealed of limited use during the first serious gas crises of 2006 and 2009. The worsening of relations between Russia and Ukraine in the context of the "orange revolution" aggravated the commercial dispute on gas prices between the two countries, leading to a major interruption of gas supplies to Ukraine and Europe in January 2009. The transit dispute settlement measures foreseen in article 7(7) of the ECT envisaged the intervention of a mediator, which would set the tariffs and volumes during a 90-day period. However, these provisions were not used, given that the dispute was more on the supply agreement, rather than the transit (Belyi 2012, pp. 266–267). At the same time, the ECT's bystander role in this dispute also reflects the lack of political will as well as mistrust on the mediation provisions, since none of the parties notified the ECT Secretary General or raised the possibility to use the conciliatory settlement mechanism (Pominova 2014, p. 16).

In this context of growing gap between EU and Russia's expectations, in August 2009 the Russian government decided to formally terminate its provisional application of the ECT. This decision was justified on Russia's disappointment with the limited use of the ECT during the 2009 gas crisis as well as the stalemate of the Transit Protocol negations (Yafimava 2011, p. 289). However, the decision took many experts by surprise and was seen with some perplexity, as Russia did not seem to gain much from such a withdrawal. First, Russian companies would lose the ECT rights to challenge the EU or its Member States in case of disputes arising from the application of the EU third energy package. At the same time, in application of a so-called sunset or survival clause, foreign investments in Russia would remain under the protection of the Treaty for another 20 years following the withdrawal notification (Konoplyanik 2009, pp. 2–3). Moreover, Russia's disengagement with the Energy Charter was ambiguous, since it did not abandon the Conference of the Energy Charter and continued seconding the Vice-Secretary General of the ECT. In that sense, some observers initially interpreted Russia's move as a manoeuver to re-establish a reform agenda more in line with Russian preferences (Belyi et al. 2011; Herranz-Surrallés 2012). However, at the turn of the decade, Russia's withdrawal became clearer, opening a soul-searching period in the ECT.

Modernization and the International Energy Charter (Early 2010s): Crisis or Relaunch?

The opposition of Russia to the ECT became more frontal when in November 2009 an UNCITRAL arbitral tribunal announced its jurisdiction to hear the *Yukos v. Russia* case, which could end up with the obligation by Russia to compensate Yukos with around $50bn. The arbitral case had been filed in 2005 by the oil company Yukos, following the Russian government's seizure of its assets amidst a complex political saga against the company's CEO, Michail Chodorkovski. The decision of the arbitral tribunal to proceed with the case was a backlash to Putin's government, which had sustained that the ECT dispute settlement provisions were not applicable to Russia, given that the country had never ratified the Treaty (Konoplyanik 2005; Gazzini

2015). In this context, in late 2010 the Russian government launched the initiative of a "Convention on International Energy Security" as an alternative to the ECT. The Convention resembled the ECT in terms of subject matters and pretension of universality, but was clearly less market-centric. For instance, the Convention advocated for a more protectionist investments regime, favored long-term contracts as the centerpiece of market stability, and opposed any REIO clause (Belyi et al. 2011; Selianova 2012). The Convention initiative thus made clear Russia's intention to eschew any obligations arising from the ECT, thus putting "the ball on the European court" (Westphal 2011).

The unambiguous withdrawal by Russia placed the focus on the EU and ECT's response. Given its central position in the ECT, Russia's departure amounted to leave the ECT "like Hamlet without the Prince" (Buchan 2009, p. 84). This situation was puzzling also because it meant that the ECT had "violated the first rule of effective institution building: it alienated the most important player" (Van de Graaf 2013, p. 58). Therefore, this raised the question of whether the EU and ECT responses to this setback would be a shift towards accommodation to Russia's interests and that of other producer countries, or on the contrary, further entrenchment into previous positions (Herranz-Surrallés 2016a).

One the one hand, some scholars and practitioners emphasized the tendency towards *accommodation*. Most notably, the ECT launched a "modernization process," with the adoption of a Roadmap for reform in November 2010, and the EU agreed to cancel the negotiations on the Transit Protocol, in order to open a broad consultation process (Belyi et al. 2011; Westphal 2011). Similarly, the Secretary General of the ECT expressed on many occasions the willingness to find ways "to more equally balance out the interests of energy consuming and producing nations" in the ECT and to "strengthen its legitimacy" (Rusnák 2013). The goal was also to bring Russia back on board and to position the institution as a "neutral platform" to deal with transit disputes and to facilitate EU-Russia dialogue (Rusnák 2014). Similarly, with the deterioration of the political situation following Russia's annexation of Crimea in March 2014, the ECT also established an Energy Security Contact Group, presented again as a neutral platform to exchange information and foster trust (Pominova 2014, p. 16).

The modernization process finalized with the adoption of the political declaration of the IEC in May 2015, aimed at boosting the global character of the Energy Charter. Currently signed by around 90 states and regional organizations, the IEC has been object of mixed assessments. On the bright side, the IEC has been praised for its ability to attract countries outside Europe and Central Asia, with new entrants from East Asia, Middle East, Latin America, and Africa (Bonafé and Piebalgs 2017, p. 5). The signature of China and the USA also added political value and global character, despite some important absences, including fossil fuel producers such as Argentina, Australia, Brazil, Canada, India, Indonesia, Mexico, Russia, and Saudi Arabia (Aalto 2016, p. 94). Content-wise, the IEC has been assessed as a balanced declaration, catering for the consumer, producer, and transit countries, as well as recognizing the simultaneous importance of market principles, national sovereignty, and climate change. Yet, its lack of legal value leads to different assessments. While for some, the added value of the IEC is its "capability to reveal long-term political commitment and therefore to build trust in the global energy business" (Bonafé and Piebalgs 2017, p. 3); for others, the IEC is a loose political declaration, which offers "few building blocks for a more precise roadmap or eventual Treaty" (Aalto 2016; see also De Jong 2017).

On the other hand, despite these signs of reform and relaunch, there are also more skeptical analyses regarding the EU's commitment to the ECT process and its reform. Some of the signs of EU *entrenchment* into previous positions include, first, a renewed focus on the internal energy market, with the coming into force of the Third Gas Directive in 2009, and a more pro-active stance to expand the internal energy market towards the Eastern neighboring countries. Internally, the more stringent requirements on unbundling and the third country clause introduced by the new directive led to further clashes between the EU and Russia (Grätz 2011; Romanova 2016). Externally, the EU prioritized the expansion of the EnC, with the accession of Moldova (2010), Ukraine (2011) and Georgia (2017). Therefore, the growing overlap between the ECT and EnC memberships was, quite inevitably, an element of marginalization of the ECT (Herranz-Surrallés 2016a, p. 63).

Secondly, the EU's position in the negotiations and adoption of the IEC in 2015 is also an indication of entrenchment, at least on the side of the European Commission. Despite the nonbinding character of the IEC, the Commission showed its determination to be recognized as a REIO. Even defying the Council of the EU, the Commission submitted a statement to the IEC conference arguing that, due to the nature of the EU internal legal order, the ECT could not create legally binding effects upon the Member States inter se (ibid.). This generated an interinstitutional conflict over the limits of competence in the IEC negotiations and ended up with the Council submitting a counter-statement to discredit the European Commission (ibid.). This episode shows how the ECT became growingly tangled with broader debates on the external competences of the EU following the Lisbon Treaty and the legality of intra-EU investment treaties (see next section).

Finally, and relatedly, the ambiguity of the EU's position in the ECT is also reflected in the decision of Italy to abandon the regime in December 2014 – the first case of withdrawal from a full contracting party. The Italian government justified the decision on financial grounds as well as a way to fulfill the European Commission's request to terminate intra-EU bilateral investment agreements (MENA Chambers 2015; Dreyer 2015). Indeed, in view of the growing number of intra-EU arbitration cases, the relation between the EU and ECT law started to generate real tensions (see next section). Therefore, in contrast to the initial phase of the ECT, when the new international rules were fully in line with the incipient energy liberalization process within the EU, by the mid-2000s a gap had grown between the minimum standards of the ECT and a the much deeper liberalization rules introduced by the Second and Third Gas Directives (Talus 2013, p. 243; see also Hadfield and Amkhan-Bayno 2012, p. 9). As explained in the next section, investment provisions have become a growing source of concern from the legal point of view, as well as for broader political reasons.

New Contestation Fronts (Late 2010s): Politicization of ISDS and Climate Change

Since the mid-2010s, the ECT has been object of further controversies, particularly surrounding its ISDS mechanism, in a context of sharp increase and changing pattern of arbitration cases. With an overall number of 128 known cases until 2019, the ECT has become the world's most often invoked international treaty. Moreover, contrary to the initial purpose of ISDS, which was to protect investors' rights in countries with weak judicial systems, most arbitration cases in recent years are intra-EU, meaning that they involved an EU investor as claimant against an EU member state as respondent (see Fig. 1). This revived the debate on the compatibility between ECT and EU law. However, the adequacy of ISDS in general has also been under discussion, in view of the unprecedented levels of public contestation towards investor-state arbitration. Given the growing concern with the effects of ISDS on the right of states to regulate, for example, in the context of climate change, the ECT has also come under scrutiny on environmental grounds.

The legal discussion about the *compatibility between EU and ECT law* took up another notch after the judgment of the Court of Justice of the EU (CJEU) on the *Slovak Republic v. Achmea* case (6 March 2018). In this landmark judgment, the CJEU Grand Chamber supported the Commission's view that international arbitral courts had no jurisdiction in the concerned intra-EU dispute, ruling that any compensation by Slovakia to Achmea would amount to state aid. Although this judgment concerned an arbitration case in the context of a Bilateral Investment Treaty (BITs), it sparked the discussion on whether the ban of intra-EU BITs also applies to intra-EU cases in the framework of the ECT. While the Commission has for several years been arguing that the ECT does not apply to intra-EU cases (Verburg 2019, p. 433),

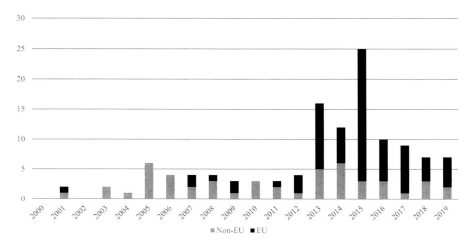

Fig. 1 Evolution in the number of arbitration cases in the ECT (by type of respondent state). (Source: Own elaboration from databases of UNCTAD (2019) and Energy Charter (2019))

legal scholars and practitioners have argued differently. For example, from a historical perspective, Basedow (2020) examined the *travaux preparatoires* of the ECT negotiations during 1990s to demonstrate that, even if reluctantly, the EU eventually accepted the intra-EU applicability of the ECT's dispute settlement provisions. Therefore, in absence of a formal "disconnection clause," the Commission's argument has so far not been successful in ECT arbitral judgments.

The discussion on the relation between EU and ECT law has also become more complicated, as the jurisprudence of the growing number of cases points to different, and sometimes contradictory interpretations. For example, Verburg (2019, p. 432) indicates that in certain cases the arbitral tribunals argued that EU law had precedence over the ECT (e.g., *Electrabel v. Hungary*), whereas in others, the ECT provisions were said to prevail (e.g., *RREEF v. Spain*). While acknowledging the tensions, other legal scholars argue that there are no real normative conflicts between the two legal orders. For instance, Álvarez (2018) argues at length that there should not be debates about the jurisdiction of the ECT in intra-EU disputes, since EU law does not contain any explicit prohibition of investor-state arbitration. Moreover, the ECT deals with substantive protections of investors that are not envisaged in EU law, for example, in cases of expropriation or regarding the notion of Fair and Equitable Treatment (ibid.). However, there is a broad agreement that the different paces of market convergence in the EU and elsewhere generate "regulatory tensions" and risk "loosening the bridge between different regions" (Bonafé and Mete 2016, p. 188). The *Nord Stream 2 AG v. European Union* case filed in September 2019 means yet another step in the legal escalation between the EU and the ECT (see next section).

Beyond the EU-ECT relations, reform of the ECT dispute settlement provisions also became politically urgent given the *public and political mobilization against ISDS*. Within the EU, anti-ISDS campaigns gathered more than three million signatures in the context of the TTIP negotiations, and the Comprehensive Economic and Trade Agreement (CETA) almost derailed following the negative vote in the regional Parliament of Wallonia (De Ville and Gheyle 2019; Magnette 2017). The list of criticisms of ISDS is a long one, from a principled opposition to give foreign companies special rights to sue states, to a wide array of procedural concerns, such as the lack of transparency and consistency of arbitration (Herranz-Surrallés 2020). Although the ECT remained for long outside the public radar, anti-ISDS campaigns finally came to target it as "the world's most dangerous investment treaty" (CEO 2018). Besides being the most litigated international treaty, the ECT has been criticized for its vague and broad investment protection provisions, which are more likely to lead to expansive and inconsistent interpretations (Verbrug, 2019). Indeed, already in the 1990s, legal experts expressed concern that "open-ended formulations of the Treaty provide extensive opportunity for individuals to complain and litigate against governments" and that "the more open-ended such obligations, the more interpretation may create considerable surprise for the original negotiators and signatories of the Treaty" (Wälde 1996, p. xx).

Yet another growing source of public contestation and scholarly debate concerns the degree to which the ECT is the right instrument to foster the transition towards renewable forms of energy. In defense of the ECT, some experts have noted that

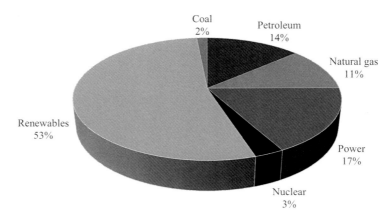

Fig. 2 ECT arbitration cases by sector. (Source: Own calculation from database of the Energy Charter (2019))

rules-based energy governance and strong investment protection mechanisms are necessary for fostering investment confidence in renewable energies, which are particularly susceptible to regulatory risks (Bonafé and Piebalgs 2017, p. 10). The fact that most of the recent arbitration cases within the ECT concern the renewable energy sector (see Fig. 2) seems to back this argument. On the other hand, however, some ECT cases also illustrate the clash between investment protection and the right of states to regulate on environmental matters. Some of the most notorious cases in that regard are the 2012 *Vattenfal v. Germany*, where a Swedish company sued Germany for the decision to phase out nuclear energy, or the 2018 *Rockhopper v. Italy*, whereby a UK-based gas and oil company brought Italy to arbitration for the withdrawal of a drilling concession in the Adriatic Sea (CEO 2018). More broadly, other experts have questioned the contribution of the ECT to fostering renewable energy investment, arguing that political risks are likely to decrease with the gradual phase-out of subsidies and that there is no hard evidence suggesting ISDS' positive effect on investment (Tienhaara and Downie 2018, p. 462).

In view of this public mobilization against ISDS, the ECT Secretariat launched a second modernization process in late 2018 to discuss the reform of its dispute settlement provisions. While most contracting parties are in favor of modernizing ISDS (e.g., via including specific safeguards on the right to regulate and other measures to enhance transparency and participation of third parties), the outcome of the process is still uncertain. To begin with, the reform of dispute settlement provisions in the ECT is difficult to address in isolation, given the wider ISDS reform at the EU and global levels (Herranz-Surrallés 2020). In response to domestic contestation, the EU has been advocating a reformed system of investor-state arbitration with permanent judges, an appeal mechanism, and stronger safeguards against corporate abuse. Since 2016, the EU has advanced the so-called Investment Court System (ICS) in its bilateral agreements and the Multilateral Investment Court (MIC) at a global level (ibid.). The outcome of global ISDS reform might therefore affect the ECT as well, even if options such as an appellate facility or a roster of arbitrators for ECT disputes are not currently on the table of the modernization discussions (Verburg 2019, p. 437). At the same time, the modernization process has been criticized for not paying enough attention to climate change and the need to align investment provisions with UNFCCC Paris Agreement and UN Sustainable Development Goals (Keay-Bright and Defilla 2019). The unclear contribution of the ECT to climate change mitigation has even been considered as a factor that should tip the balance of the EU's position towards terminating or withdrawing from the ECT (Voon 2019).

Future Directions

At the turn of the 2020s, the ECT is at a crossroads. While on the one hand, the ECT modernization process is underway and efforts to gather new signatories for the IEC continue, on the other, the commitment from the EU institutions and its Member States to the success of these endeavors appears, at best, uncertain. This delicate impasse also raises broader questions about the EU's international actorness as well as the future of global energy governance.

Regarding the EU's role in the ECT, the *Nord Stream 2 AG v. European Union* arbitration case filed in September 2019 brings the legal and political tensions between the EU and the ECT to a new level. Although the resolution of this case might take years, the fact that for the first time the EU as whole is the respondent party in an arbitration case is a significant new development. Quite ironically, despite Russia's withdrawal from the ECT, partly in disagreement with arbitration provisions, the ECT is now being used by a Russian-funded company (Nord Stream 2 AG is a subsidiary of Gazprom registered in Switzerland) to challenge EU regulations on grounds of discriminatory treatment (Gotev 2019). Therefore, as some legal scholars already anticipated, the EU has become a "frontline actor in the international investor-state regime" (Berman 2018, p. 220). This opens a new legal game, since so far, the European Commission was only indirectly involved in intra-EU arbitration cases via *amicus curiae*, arguing for the hierarchical precedence of EU Law to free Member States from liability on ECT provisions. However, in a case where the EU itself is challenged, EU law cannot be used anymore as a defense, as the parties cannot refer to their domestic laws as a reason for not observing international obligations (ibid., p. 205). This is therefore an interesting case for the EU international actorness and its relation to International Law. While the EU has usually been one of the standard-bearers of a rules-based multilateral order, the ECT case reveals that, when international and EU law collide, the EU may opt for defending the latter.

The *Nord Stream 2 AG v. European Union* arbitration case as well as other controversial legal measures in the context of the Nord Stream 2 pipeline, such as Denmark's amendment of its Continental Shelf Act (Schill 2017), bring to the front another rising debate: how to balance investment protection and security concerns. In both cases, the amendments were motivated by security and geopolitical considerations – indirectly in the case of the EU and more directly in the case of Denmark, where the amendment introduces a new procedure to deny a permit for the construction of a pipeline in case it is deemed incompatible with "national foreign-, security-, and defence policy interests" (ibid., p. 3). Yet, security-related restrictions, regardless of their proportionality and political justifiability, risk violating investment protection obligations. With the rise of sovereign investment, via State-Owned Enterprises (SOEs) or Sovereign Wealth Funds (SWFs), the debate on the security implications of foreign investment has taken up speed (Wehrlé and Pohl 2016). Given its strategic character, foreign control of energy infrastructure is particularly susceptible to generate this type of concerns. Infrastructure diplomacy by China in the context of the Belt and Road Initiative (BRI) is a case in point. Therefore, the role of economic statecraft and investment arbitration will continue to generate debate for the foreseeable future (Boute 2019).

In view of the uncertain commitment from the EU in the ECT, future analyses will have to gauge a broad range of possible scenarios and their consequences for global energy governance. For example, some experts have called for a discussion on the options of termination of the ECT or withdrawal from the treaty by one or more parties (Voon 2019). Such an option, however, would raise questions about the possibility to modify or derogate the applicability of the 20-year survival clause (ibid.). Less drastic scenarios would be, for example, an inter se modification of the ECT, whereby the EU and its Member States would modify the investment provisions among them, without affecting their obligations towards non-EU investors (Verburg 2019, p. 447). However, it is not clear whether the ECT provisions allow for an elimination of intra-EU ECT protections and whether all contracting parties (including some EU Member States) would support such an option (Beham and Prantl 2020). Moreover, any scenario where the EU could include a carve-out for intra-EU applicability would certainly open a wider debate on the added value of the ECT, as well as the IEC, compared to other international energy institutions, most notably the IEA, which has for a long time considered widening its membership, or the International Renewable Energy Agency (IRENA), which already encompasses 161 members.

Going back to Robert Cox's (1981) definition of institutions as amalgams of material power and ideas, the uncertainty over the Energy Charter's future can be seen as part of the wider erosion of the liberal world order (Alcaro 2018; Ikenberry 2018). Just as in other domains, the epicenter of global energy dynamics continues to shift East-wards, with the centrality of China as both consumer, producer, and investor in energy infrastructure. Therefore, quite interestingly, while the EU is on the defensive regarding the ECT, China has taken some interest in its investment protection provisions. At the same time, with the ideational backlash to globalization in Western countries and ascendancy of state-capitalist ideas elsewhere, the context has become growingly unpropitious for binding trade and investment provisions in the energy sector and beyond. The success of the Energy Charter process is therefore more likely to hinge on its ability to become a testing ground for flexible arrangements, for example, a focus on mediation and conciliation, and its ability to adapt investment arbitration to both climate imperatives and new geopolitical concerns.

Cross-References

▶ Energy Relations in the EU Eastern Partnership
▶ European Union Energy Policy: A Discourse Perspective
▶ EU-Russia Energy Relations
▶ Extending Energy Policy: The Challenge of Sector Integration
▶ The EU in Global Energy Governance

References

Aalto, P. (2016). The new International Energy Charter: Instrumental or incremental progress in governance? *Energy Research & Social Science, 11*, 92–96.

Alcaro, R. (Ed.). (2018). The liberal order and its contestations. *International Spectator, Special Issue, 53*(1). https://doi.org/10.1080/03932729.2018.1397878.

Álvarez, G. M. (2018). Redefining the relationship between the Energy Charter Treaty and the treaty of functioning of the European Union: From a normative conflict to policy tension. *ICSID Review, 33*(2), 560–581.

Anders-Speed, P. (1999). The politics of petroleum and the Energy Charter Treaty as an effective investment regime. *Journal of Energy Finance & Development, 4*, 127.

Axelrod, R. S. (1996). The European Energy Charter Treaty. Reality or illusion? *Energy Policy, 24*(6), 497–505.

Basedow, J. R. (2018). *The EU in the global investment regime*. London: Routledge.

Basedow, J. R. (2020). The Achmea judgment and the applicability of the Energy Charter Treaty in intra-EU investment arbitration. *Journal of International Economic Law*. https://doi.org/10.1093/jiel/jgz025.

Beham, M., & Prantl, D. (2020). Intra-EU investment reform: What options for the Energy Charter Treaty?. *Kluwer Arbitration Blog*. Retrieved from: http://arbitrationblog.kluwerarbitration.com/2020/01/07/intra-eu-investment-reform-what-options-for-the-energy-charter-treaty/

Belyi, A. V. (2008). EU external energy policies: A paradox of integration. In J. Orbie (Ed.), *Europe's global role. External policies of the European Union* (pp. 203–216). Aldershot: Ashgate.

Belyi, A. V. (2012). The EU's missed role in international transit governance. *Journal of European Integration, 34*(3), 261–276.

Belyi, A. V. (2014). International energy governance: Weaknesses of multilateralism. *International Studies Perspectives, 15*, 313–328.

Belyi, A., Nappert, S., & Pogoretskyy, V. (2011). Modernizing the Energy Charter process? The Energy Charter Conference Road Map and the Russian Draft Convention on Energy Security. *Oil, Gas & Energy Law Intelligence, 5*, 78. Retrieved from: https://www.ogel.org

Berman, G. A. (2018). ECT and European Union law. In M. Scherer (Ed.), *International arbitration in the energy sector* (pp. 203–220). Oxford: Oxford University Press.

Bonafé, E., & Mete, G. (2016). Escalated interactions between EU energy law and the Energy Charter Treaty. *Journal of World Energy Law and Business, 9*, 174–188.

Bonafé, E., & Piebalgs, A. (2017). *The new International Energy Charter: Sustainable energy transition, investment dispute resolution and market regulation*. Policy brief 33, Robert Schuman Centre for Advanced Studies/European University Institute.

Boute, A. (2019). Economic statecraft and investment arbitration. *University of Pennsylvania Journal of International Law, 40*(2), 383–418.

Buchan, D. (2009). *Energy and climate change: Europe at the crossroads*. Oxford: Oxford University Press/Oxford Institute for Energy Studies.

Corporate Europe Observatory. (2018). One treaty to rule them all: The ever-expanding Energy Charter Treaty and the power it gives corporations to halt the energy transition. *Corporate Europe*

Observatory. Retrieved from: https://corporateeurope.org/en/international-trade/2018/06/one-treaty-rule-them-all

Cox, R. W. (1981). Social forces, states and world orders: Beyond international relations. *Millennium: Journal of International Studies, 10*(2), 126–155.

De Jong, S. (2017). The International Energy Charter: A new impetus for global energy governance? In R. Leal-Arcas & J. Wouters (Eds.), *Research handbook on EU energy law and policy* (pp. 179–191). Northampton: Edward Elgar.

De Ville, F., & Gheyle, N. (2019). The unintended consequences of the Transatlantic Trade and Investment Partnership negotiations. *The International Spectator, 54*(1), 16–30.

Doré, J. (1996). Negotiating the Energy Charter Treaty. In T. Waelde (Ed.), *The Energy Charter Treaty. An East–West gateway for investment and trade* (pp. 137–155). London/The Hague/Boston: Kluwer Law International.

Dreyer, I. (2015). Brussels moves against bilateral investment treaties within EU, undermines Energy Charter. *Borderlex*, 7 September. Retrieved from: http://www.energypost.eu/brussels-moves-intra-eu-investor-state-arbitration-puts-pressure-energy-charter/

Energy Charter. (2019). Investment dispute settlement cases. Retrieved from: https://www.energycharter.org/what-we-do/dispute-settlement/all-investment-dispute-settlement-cases/

Gazzini, T. (2015). Yukos Universal Limited (Isle of Man) v The Russian Federation: Provisional application of the ECT in the Yukos case. *ICSID Review, 30*(2), 293–302.

Goldthau, A., & Witte, J. M. (2009). Back to the future or forward to the past? Strengthening markets and rules for effective global energy governance. *International Affairs, 85*(2), 373–390.

Gotev, G. (2019). Nord Stream 2 seeks arbitration in dispute with EU Commission. *Euractiv*, 1 October. Retrieved from: https://www.euractiv.com/section/energy/news/nord-stream-2-seeks-arbitration-in-dispute-with-eu-commission/

Grätz, J. (2011). Common rules without strategy: EU energy policy and Russia. In V. L. Birchfield & J. S. Duffield (Eds.), *Toward a common European Union energy policy* (pp. 61–86). Basingstoke: Palgrave Macmillan.

Hadfield, A., & Amkhan-Bayno, A. (2012). From Russia with cold feet: EU–Russia energy relations, and the Energy Charter Treaty. *International Journal of Energy Security and Environmental Research, 1*, 1–16.

Herranz-Surrallés, A. (2012). La UE y el Tratado de la Carta Energética: la política energética europea en el limbo de la (in)coherencia. In E. Barbé (Ed.), *Cambio mundial y gobernanza global: La interacción entre la Unión Europea y las instituciones internacionales*. Madrid: Tecnos.

Herranz-Surrallés, A. (2016a). An upstream battle: The EU and the reform of the Energy Charter Treaty. In E. Barbé, O. Costa, & R. Kissack (Eds.), *EU policy responses to shifting multilateral system* (pp. 49–66). Basingstoke: Palgrave.

Herranz-Surrallés, A. (2016b). An emerging EU energy diplomacy? Discursive shifts, enduring practices. *Journal of European Public Policy, 23*(9), 1386–1405.

Herranz-Surrallés, A. (2020). "Authority shifts" in global governance: Intersecting politicizations and the reform of investor–state arbitration. *Politics and Governance, 28*(1). https://doi.org/10.17645/pag.v8i1.2651.

Hobér, K. (2018). Overview of Energy Charter Treaty cases. In M. Scherer (Ed.), *International arbitration in the energy sector* (pp. 175–202). Oxford: Oxford University Press.

Ikenberry, G. J. (2018). The end of liberal international order? *International Affairs, 94*(1), 7–23.

Keay-Bright, S., & Defilla, S. (2019). Energy Charter Treaty review should end protection for fossil fuels. *Energy Post EU*, 20 March. Retrieved from: https://energypost.eu/energy-charter-treaty-review-should-end-protection-for-fossil-fuels

Konoplyanik, A. A. (1996). The Energy Charter Treaty: A Russian perspective. In T. Wälde (Ed.), *The Energy Charter Treaty. An East–West gateway for investment and trade* (pp. 156–178). London/The Hague/Boston: Kluwer Law International.

Konoplyanik, A. A. (2005). ECT and the Yukos case. *Petroleum Economist*, June, pp. 35–36.

Konoplyanik, A. A. (2009). Russia: Don't oppose the Energy Charter, help to adapt it. *Petroleum Economist*, July, pp. 2–3.

Krikovic, A. (2015). When interdependence produces conflict: EU–Russia energy relations as a security dilemma. *Contemporary Security Policy, 36*(1), 3–26.

Lubbers, R. (1996). Foreword. In T. Wälde (Ed.), *The Energy Charter Treaty. An East–West gateway for investment and trade* (pp. i–xvii). London/The Hague/Boston: Kluwer Law International.

Magnette, P. (2017). *CETA, Quand l'Europe déraille*. Namur: Luc Pire.

Matlary, J. H. (1996). Energy policy: From a national to a European framework? In H. Wallace & W. Wallance (Eds.), *Policy making in the European Union* (3rd ed.). Oxford: Oxford University Press.

McGowan, F. (1989). The single energy market and energy policy: Conflicting agendas? *Energy Policy, 17*(6), 547–553.

MENA Chambers. (2015). Italy's withdrawal from the Energy Charter Treaty, Note 12, 5 May. Retrieved from: http://www.menachambers.com/expertise/energy-charter-treaty/MCET_ECT_Note-12_05052015.pdf

Pominova, I. (2014). *Risks and benefits for the Russian Federation from participating in the Energy Charter. Occasional paper*. Brussels: Energy Charter Secretariat.

Prange-Gstöhl, H. (2009). Enlarging the EU's internal energy market: Why would third countries accept EU rule export? *Energy Policy, 37*(12), 5296–5303.

Romanova, T. (2016). Is Russian energy policy towards the EU only about geopolitics? The case of the Third Liberalisation Package. *Geopolitics, 21*(4), 857–879.

Rusnák, U. (2013). Modernization of the Energy Charter, Russia in global affairs, December. Retrieved from: http://eng.globalaffairs.ru/number/Modernization-of-the-Energy-Charter-16294

Rusnák, U. (2014). Reinforcing the EU's external energy policy: Views from the Energy Charter Secretariat, Brussels, 21 May. Retrieved from: https://www.energycharter.org/media/news/article/reinforcing-eu-external-energy-policy-energy-charter-secretariat-perspective/

Schill, S. (2017). Memorandum on possible implications under Denmark's Investment Treaty Commitments of the Draft Bill to amend the Danish Continental Shelf Act (submitted for public consultation on 23 June 2017). Retrieved from: https://www.ft.dk/samling/20171/lovforslag/L43/bilag/3/1805330/index.htm

Selianova, Y. (2012). The Energy Charter and the International Energy Governance. In Y. Selianova (Ed.), *Regulation of energy in international trade law* (pp. 373–406). New York: Kluwer Law International.

Talus, K. (2013). *EU energy law and policy: A critical account*. Oxford: Oxford University Press.

Tienhaara, K., & Downie, C. (2018). Risky business? The Energy Charter Treaty, renewable energy and investor-state disputes. *Global Governance, 24*, 451–471.

UNCTAD. (2019). Investment dispute settlement navigator. Retrieved from: https://investmentpolicy.unctad.org/investment-dispute-settlement

Van de Graaf, T. (2013). *The politics and institutions of global energy governance*. New York: Palgrave.

Verburg, C. (2019). Modernising the Energy Charter Treaty: An opportunity to enhance legal certainty in investor-state dispute settlement. *The Journal of World Investment & Trade, 20*(2–3), 425–454.

Voon, T. (2019) Modernizing the Energy Charter Treaty: What about termination?. *IISD Analysis*, 2 October. Retrieved from: https://iisd.org/itn/

Wälde, T. (1996). Foreword. In W. Wälde (Ed.), *The Energy Charter Treaty: An East–West gateway for investment and trade* (pp. xiii–xvii). London/The Hague/Boston: Kluwer Law International.

Wehrlé, F., & Pohl, J. (2016). *Investment policies related to national security: A survey of country practices* (OECD working papers on international investment). Paris: OECD Publishing.

Westphal, K. (2009). *Russian gas, Ukrainian pipelines, and European supply security. Lessons of the 2009 controversies* (SWP research paper 11). Berlin: Stiftung Wissenschaft und Politik.

Westphal, K. (2011). *The Energy Charter Treaty revisited* (SWP comments, no. 8). Berlin: Stiftung Wissenschaft und Politik.

Yafimava, K. (2011). *The transit dimension of EU energy security* (p. 117). Oxford: Oxford University Press/Oxford Institute for Energy Studies.

Sustainable Europe: Narrative Potential in the EU's Political Communication

16

Natalia Chaban and Jessica Bain

Contents

Introduction	368
Outlining Strategic Narratives for the EU: Sustainable Europe?	369
Narrators and Receivers	370
Content and Levels	371
Case Study: "Sustainable Energy Europe"	373
Structure	373
Life-Cycle of Narratives	375
Conclusions	378
Cross-References	380
References	381

Abstract

This chapter explores the potential of the strategic narrative "Sustainable Europe" to secure the EU's appeal to European and international audiences by examining the potential of one concrete issue-specific narrative "Sustainable Energy Europe" to support the broader strategic narrative. "Sustainable Energy Europe" provides an example of a narrative that demonstrates the promising flow between the projection of sustainability-focused objectives and priorities by the EU's official formulations to the communication of these through a range of media to their reception by the public. The chapter examines one case study: the EU's Sustainable Energy Week events communicated through Twitter to explore this

N. Chaban (✉)
Department of Media and Communication, University of Canterbury, Christchurch, New Zealand
e-mail: natalia.chaban@canterbury.ac.nz

J. Bain
School of Media, Communication and Sociology, University of Leicester, Leicester, UK
e-mail: jessica.bain@leicester.ac.uk

© Springer Nature Switzerland AG 2022
M. Knodt, J. Kemmerzell (eds.), *Handbook of Energy Governance in Europe*,
https://doi.org/10.1007/978-3-030-43250-8_52

narrative's potential. The chapter argues that the narrative of "Sustainable Europe" has a potential to exist on systemic, identity, and issue-specific levels and appeal to European and global audiences on all levels.

Keywords

European Union · Sustainability · Strategic narratives · Social media · Strategic communication

Introduction

The new leadership of the European Union (EU) has marked a clear priority for the Union – Europe must lead in tackling the climate and ecological crisis. Ursula von der Leyen, President of the European Commission, announced the European Green Deal at the end of 2019, a new EU growth strategy. It stated that Europe will be "the world's first climate-neutral continent by 2050..." by implementing the package of ambitious measures that "should enable European citizens and businesses to benefit from sustainable green transition" (European Commission 2019a). This is one of the first broad visions of how to address the existential threat of the climate catastrophe in one geopolitical region: "The comprehensive nature of the European Green Deal ... encompasses the air we breathe to how food is grown, from how we travel to the buildings we inhabit" (Harvey et al. 2019). Importantly, the formulation of the Green Deal is a strategic projection of the EU's role and know-how to the rest of the world, with the concept of sustainability at its core. Reflecting on this daring vision, this chapter explores the potential of the strategic narrative "Sustainable Europe" to secure the EU's appeal to European and international audiences. Strategic narrative is defined here as a "tool for political actors to extend their influence, manage expectations, and change the discursive environments in which they operate" (Miskimmon et al. 2013, p. 2). Through strategic narratives, a polity seeks to be an actor "other nations listen to, rely on and emulate out of respect and admiration" (Slaughter 2011, p. 4).

The narrative of "Sustainable Europe" is not entirely new. Manners and Murray (2016) referenced "Green Europe" as one of the alternative narratives for the EU to keep in view, after arguing the demise of the "Europe of peace" narrative. Hajer (1995) also considered narratives in the works on environmental politics. Our chapter builds on these works (and especially Manner and Murray 2016) adding a novel perspective – by engaging with strategic narrative theory (Miskimmon et al. 2013). Our chapter asks: Does the narrative "Sustainable Europe" possess an overarching strategic potential to produce a consistent and coherent message for internal and external receivers, and project the EU's influence? Assuming this narrative's relation to other narratives argued by the relevant literature, we argue a range of European narrators to contribute to the formulation and projection of this narrative. How might the differentiated consideration of receivers facilitate the narrative's flow and its function on different levels of communication – systemic, identity, and issue-specific? Do novel methods of delivery count?

The chapter tests its conceptualizations of the "Sustainable Europe" narrative on the materials of one case-study – an issue-specific narrative "Sustainable Energy Europe" (detailed in an earlier work by Bain and Chaban 2017). *Issue-specific* narrative is defined as the one "seeking to shape the terrain on which policy discussions take place" (Miskimmon et al. 2013, p. 7). Using the most recent theorization of strategic narratives (Miskimmon et al. 2013; Roselle et al. 2014), the case-study answers the questions: How is the narrative formulated? How is it projected? And, how is it received? The definition of a narrative also suggests the presence of an actor, an action, a goal or intention, a scene, and instrument. Bain and Chaban (2017) identified those for the narrative "Sustainable Energy Europe" and tested the flow of the narrative in an empirical analysis of Twitter communications surrounding the EU Sustainable Energy Week (EUSEW). A total of 2,560 English language tweets using the hashtag #EUSEW13 were gathered and analyzed by a trained team of coders examining their frames, the energy issues discussed, as well as the overall sentiment (Bain and Chaban 2017). Social media communications presented a unique opportunity to trace intertwined phases of *formulation, projection* and *reception* in action as social media possesses a two-pronged nature – evidence of media framing of the content as well as evidence of the public opinion. This chapter considers the empirical results of the issue-specific case-study in application to a broader narrative of "Sustainable Europe."

This chapter starts with a conceptual delineation of the "Sustainable Europe" narrative. It continues with an empirical consideration of the issue-specific narrative "Sustainable Energy Europe" in terms of its structure and life-cycle of *formation, projection* and *reception*. The chapter ends with a discussion about growing appeal and potential pitfalls of the strategic narrative "Sustainable Europe" and proposes an outline of the future research directions based on the results of the case-study.

Outlining Strategic Narratives for the EU: Sustainable Europe?

Entering the third decade of the twenty-first century, the EU is facing a challenge of disequilibrium – changing Europe in the changing world. To cope with the former, Europe must balance multiple internal crises of a political, economic, social, and environmental nature – from an irregular migration crisis and the rise of nationalist, nativist and openly far-right sections in EU member states, to the lasting impacts of the euro debt crisis, a prolonged Brexit drama, and tragedy of the Covid pandemic. The latter dimension confronts Europe with a need to counterbalance the moves to upset – or put an end to – the multilateral world order. A determined champion of multilateralism (see the inauguration speech by Ursula von den Leyen, new President of the European Commission (European Commission 2019b)), the EU may have to learn to act and survive in a changing world of political "bullies."

Overshadowing these immediate internal and external challenges is the looming global environmental catastrophe. An environmental crisis aggravated by climate change means that the EU has to act and enlist allies regionally and globally to tackle this unprecedented threat. Europe has a global reputation as an environmental champion and advocate against climate change (see research on EU external perceptions by Chaban and Holland 2008, 2014, 2018; Killian and Elgström 2010; Lucarelli and Fioramonti 2009). This reputation may help the EU to secure the position of a global leader who can propose solutions how to balance economic security, secure fair, and just access to key life-sustaining resources in a socially responsible way, and foster the transition to sustainable practices and outlooks to secure future for Europe and the world. While Europe cannot choose to ignore these urgent problems, it can choose to lead or not to lead the world in setting global landmarks, demonstrating on its own example that change is possible, and proactively correcting negative environmental effects. This chapter argues that a new successful narrative for Europe – shared by EU citizens and global audiences – can be "Sustainable Europe." To support this potential, the most recent release of the European Green Deal announced by von der Leyen in December 2019 is one of the latest powerful messages from Europe to the world. The EU is announcing it is setting out on a new "path for a transition" pledging to change its economy "supported by investments in green technologies, sustainable solutions and new businesses" (European Commission 2019b). This is a course of actions with global repercussions. How does this new message resonate with existing strategic formulations and projections? Does it have a potential to impact receivers both inside the EU and beyond its borders? According to Schmidt and Radaelli (2004, p. 201), a narrative becomes successful when it evokes existing ideas and suggests a compelling way to address a current challenge facing policymakers.

The EU has had systemic problems in formulating, disseminating, and securing the reception of appealing narratives. For Miskimmon (2017, p. 86), the problem lies with the hybrid nature of the EU as a political body: "The EU's structure and inner workings have often made it very difficult to maintain and deploy a consistent narrative." Yet, from its launch post-WWII and until present day, the project of European integration has always needed a narrative. And not just a story of where the EU came from and where it is going, but a *strategic* narrative: "a means by which political actors attempt to construct a shared meaning of international politics to shape the behaviour of domestic and international actors" (Miskimmon et al. 2013, p. 2). Relevant literature argues a lack of consistent and coherent narrative for the EU – internally and externally. This lingering deficit is problematic: it "potentially hampering the EU's strategic impact" (Miskimmon 2017, pp. 85–86).

This chapter advocates the strategic narrative "Sustainable Europe" as a frontrunner (for discussion on the EU's alternative narratives see Manners and Murray 2016). Keeping in mind the scale of the problem it addresses, this strategic narrative has the potential to overcome the key challenges that have beset previous attempts – either in terms of narrators and receivers, or content that has a potential to address global/systemic, identity/polity-specific, and issue-specific levels.

Narrators and Receivers

The EU as a *narrator* who formulates and projects strategic narratives is a challenged one. On the one hand, its hybrid structure and internal mechanics are so complicated that it is difficult to keep up with a consistent and coherent narrative by all its parts. On the other, this ongoing inconsistency translates from internal to external relations. A plethora of works talks about the lack of a unified EU voice on the global stage, using the term "polyphony" to describe many voices that speak for the EU internationally (see, for e.g., Bain et al. 2017). Yet, the scale of unsustainable practices is such that it cannot be a task for one actor or department. It means an existential crisis for humanity. As an issue, sustainability has the potential to appeal to different levels in the EU's structure (supranational, national, and regional) and produce a coherent vision. Beyond EU institutions, it has the chance to present a more unified and strategic vision of the EU *with* its own citizens, fostering the emergence of shared European interests the lack of which are widely lamented in the relevant literature on European integration. As Longo and Murray argue, the EU has shown an "inability or unwillingness...to provide the conditions for informed public deliberation on the need for further integration" (Longo and Murray 2011, p. 669). As for the global dimension, polyphony should be expected for such a hybrid polity. Arguably, polyphony is beneficial when it is produced in resonance. Cacophony, on the other hand, is detrimental.

Turning now to the *receivers*, we note the recurrent problem of the dual objective when it comes to conveying the EU's influence through a narrative. The EU's narratives aim to "build support within Europe for deeper integration" as well as seek to "forge influence internationally" (Miskimmon 2017, p. 85). This duality comes with two different target receiver groups. Often the two dimensions mis-align or even clash (e.g., a narrative of "transformative power Europe" worked for the internal EU constituencies, but clashed with the vision of Russia when it came to the shared neighborhood (see for e.g., Headley 2018)). In the case of the "Sustainable Europe" narrative, sustainability has a real potential to integrate member states and their citizens on a new level of economic, social, and political interactions. This narrative also has a chance to strike a chord with international receivers: the planet cannot be saved in isolation.

According to Miskimmon (2017, p. 86), "the EU struggles to project an effective strategic narrative because it struggles to communicate in areas where existing narratives have already taken hold." As such, one solution is to look to areas where the competition with other narrators is minimal. Sustainability – in the context of climate change, environmental challenges and energy transition – is an enormous issue-area with vague core and blurred boundaries with plenty of space for maneuver. The increasing pressure to save the planet suggests that there is a space for several key narratives, and the EU has a potential to formulate a powerful strategic narrative with the EU as a leader in it, and project it with strategic impact.

Content and Levels

The changing equilibria inside and outside Europe push the EU to update old or create new narratives. The relevant literature argues that the narrative of peace is now outdated (see Manners and Murray (2016) reflecting on mixed emotions to the EU being awarded a Nobel Prize for Peace). Other narratives seem to capture attention of the scholars and practitioners, yet each of them receives its share of criticisms: normative Europe (Manners 2002), market power Europe (Damro 2012)/economic Europe (Manners and Murray 2016), ethical Europe (Aggestam 2008), social Europe (van Hamm 2010; see also Manners and Murray 2016), transformative Europe (Börzel and Risse 2009), human security Europe (Kaldor et al. 2007), global Europe (Manners and Murray 2016) or a force for good Europe (Nicolaïdis and Howse 2002) (see Miskimmon 2017 for discussion of strategic narratives for the EU, as well as Manners and Murray 2016). This is in addition to "civilian power" Europe (Duchêne 1972) and even "metrosexual power" Europe (Khanna 2009) (this last vision argues a clever combination of "hard" and "soft" power characteristics). The sheer diversity of the narratives is often criticized by scholars: the lack of an overarching narrative is seen as a weakness, either of theorization or the project.

Manners and Murray (2016), analyzing the potential of "Green Europe" narrative came to the conclusions that for this narrative "Europe's narrative norms are not powerful enough, when placed in competition with economic Europe or global Europe, to sustain a convincing and legitimating story of the EU" (195). In contrast, our argument states that "Sustainable Europe" has the potential to absorb many of the narratives listed above as sub-narratives, or "sub-plots" into a "new story" of Europe that faces the complex and evolving problem of an unsustainable world. With environment protection listed by Manners (2002) as one of the key norms of the EU's international identity, there is a firm link of the narrative of "Sustainable Europe" to the narrative of "normative power" (NPE). The NPE narrative also stresses the ideas of solidarity and justice – critical norms when contemplating socially equitable and sustainable access to the basics of life in unsustainable world. With the need to balance economic security when revising non-sustainable practices and ensure protocols in energy transition, there is a potential to engage with "market power" and "economic" narratives. With climate change and environmental disaster affecting individual citizens and presenting non-traditional security challenges, "ethical power Europe" and "human security Europe" are logical sub-narratives. This also resonates with the three pillars of sustainability: economy, environment, and social issues. With climate change threatening the planet's population, "global" Europe narrative is a necessary storyline. The EU can revisit "a force for good" narrative in this quest to forge influence and explore the "social power" narrative: the ability to establish norms and rules that other actors can converge around. Arguably, the strategic narrative "Sustainable Europe" has a chance to facilitate the revisiting of established narratives and deploying them innovatively, to "pursue [the EU's] preferences and shape the expectations of third parties" (Miskimmon 2017, pp. 88–89).

Temporality and dynamics are key features of narratives which unfold from the past to present to future – narratives feature a "causal transformation which take actors from one status quo to another" (Miskimmon et al. 2013, p. 7). Many strategic narratives are anchored more heavily in the past and present, when circumstances and outcomes already known and visible, thus are easier to "weave" into a storyline. Arguably, many of Europe's narratives listed above have been focused on the past and present when selectively communicating Europe. In contrast, the EU of the twenty-first century – aiming to secure a certain status inside Europe and outside its borders – needs to formulate and project an appealing future-oriented shared narrative. In this regard, sustainability is about the future – it is about hope, solution, shared contribution and transition to new energy, practices and outlooks. As such, it has a constructive potential.

We should also expect that the content of the strategic narrative "Sustainable Europe" will be a narrative of uncertainty, able to trigger contestation. An unsustainable world needs a collective EU response, yet a coherent response will remain a challenge facing EU member states (see e.g., Leonard 2019). If the EU steps up and takes more responsibility in the crisis management, counter-narratives of contestation between and inside EU member states may appear, in addition to the contestations by external actors. Yet, with the EU's aspiration to lead Europe and, by example, the world (consider the European Green Deal 2019 mentioned above), a consistent narrative "Sustainable Europe" has a strong potential on the *system, identity* and *issue* levels (Miskimmon et al. 2013). More specifically (and following definitions of the levels by Miskimmon et al. 2013, p. 7), *system* narrative "Sustainable Europe" may tell a story of Europe as an actor to can influence how the world is arranged. As an *identity* narrative, it can highlight norms and values of the EU as a sustainable actor in international affairs and boost the EU's confidence to engage with negotiations and contestations. Finally, the "Sustainable Europe" narrative may provide a space for a number of *issue*-specific narratives – the ones that "seek [...] to shape the terrain on which policy discussions take place" (Miskimmon et al. 2013, p. 7).

This chapter argues that the *issue-specific* narratives may serve a powerful level in the life-cycle of the complex narrative "Sustainable Europe." The issue-specific narratives are typically more concrete and focused than *systemic* narratives on the macro level and less controversial than often ideologically-loaded *identity* level narratives. This chapter invites to consider one such narrative – "Sustainable Energy Europe." Its case-study, elaborated below, assesses if this issue-specific narrative possesses the *structure* argued by the relevant literature to underlie a successful narrative and enjoys a *life-cycle* of an effective strategic communication in terms of being constructed, disseminated, and received. The case-study is informed by the results of the Jean Monnet Project "External Images of the EU: Images of the EU as a Global Energy Actor" (EXIE) (main results are reported in Chaban et al. 2017), and specifically by research on EU communications via Twitter conducted by Bain and Chaban (2017).

Case Study: "Sustainable Energy Europe"

Structure

Research in the field of strategic narratives argues a set of structural elements needed for an impactful narrative: an actor, an action, a goal or intention, a scene and instrument (Miskimmon et al. 2013). In addition, Roselle et al. (2014), proposed a character or actors; setting, environment, or space; conflict or action; and resolution or suggested resolution. According to Bain and Chaban (2017), all above listed elements are in place for the issue-specific narrative "Sustainable Energy Europe."

While the EU itself is of course the principal actor, the story of "Sustainable Energy Europe" also features a plethora of other EU *actors* possessing agency and a set of unique characteristics, interests, and behaviors (see Table 1). Multiple stakeholders are responsible for communicating and executing the strategic vision of sustainability globally and within the EU. Perhaps unsurprisingly, a concerted unified voice is an undertaking. Despite this challenge, for the broader narrative of "Sustainable Europe," these actors have established and tested instruments, mechanisms, and structures of communication.

Bain and Chaban (2017), informed by the EU's official texts (including the Treaty of Lisbon (2009)), suggested that energy-related *actions* by these actors are framed by a set of norms – security of supply, competitiveness, and sustainability defined by the Treaty of Lisbon (Title XXI, Art.194 TFEU) (2009, online) (see also ▶ Chap. 7, "European Union Energy Policy: A Discourse Perspective" in this Handbook). Chaban et al. (2017, 8), referencing the Treaty, noted that the sustainability vision aims to "promote energy efficiency and energy saving and the development of new and renewable forms of energy," and includes the EU's emphasis on renewable energies; the reduction of CO_2 emissions; sustainable development; and alleviation of energy poverty. Security of supplies is interpreted as the goals to ensure the security of energy supply in the EU. This interpretation of the EU's understanding of the security of supplies suggests that energy access, energy efficiency, and resource governance are priorities. Finally, competitiveness is defined as "ensur[ing] the functioning of the energy market" and the promotion of the "interconnection of energy networks." It covers notions of economic and industrial competitiveness, investments, market access, financing, infrastructure, networks, research and development of technologies, technology transfer, and energy efficiency (Chaban et al. 2017, p. 8).

Table 1 Actors communicating sustainability in the energy sector

EU institutions	EU member states	Business actors	NGOs and civil society
European Commission with its Commissioners EC's Directorates-General on Energy, DevCo, Clima, Enterprise, Environment, Research and Trade European External Action Service (EEAS); European Parliament; Council of the EU; EU Delegations	Individual EU member states with governments, parliaments, ministries of energy, national diplomatic missions, etc.	Corporations Transnational companies Business chambers Business associations	Non-governmental organizations Experts and think tanks Academia General public

Source: Bain and Chaban 2017 (revisited)

Arguably, with the EU's foundational text locking the notion of *sustainability* in a central position, there is a solid foundation to continue framing the EU's actions in this vein.

As for the *settings* of the *actions*, the EU's is seen to act in multiple "arenas" – some are EU-bound (within the EU supranational discourses as well as among member states) and others are international (either when the EU interacts with third countries (typically through EU Delegations) or partakes in multilateral fora). These *"arenas"* are realistic options for the "Sustainable Europe" narrative formulations.

This "storyline" also features a major *conflict* – according to Bain and Chaban (2017, p. 138) "unsustainable production of energy will lead to strategic and ecological risks, bearing in mind the future impacts of climate change and resource scarcity." The *conflict* is not static, and the EU – as a protagonist – is sometimes framed as a champion (e.g., its role in Kyoto Protocol in 2005) and or an actor who underperforms (e.g., UN Climate Conventions in Copenhagen in 2009). This analysis extends the original argument. The European Green Deal 2019 is a strong contribution into the narratives of the EU as a global leader who looks into the future, ready to search for solutions to battle the climate and ecological crises, solutions that are "designed in such a way as to leave no individual or region behind in the great transformation ahead" (European Commission 2019a). Three pillars of sustainability – economy, environment, and social issues – are seen as three arenas where *conflicts* may emerge.

The final element in setting the effective narrative is the possession of *instruments* to carry out the *actions*. For Bain and Chaban (2017), the EU frames itself as an able actor who targets and interacts with state and non-state actors on bilateral and multilateral levels with a number of instruments ranging from EU's Energy Dialogues, summits, sectoral dialogues on the ministerial levels to negotiations during the major multilateral meetings. Following Bain and Chaban (2017), this chapter chooses the case of EU Sustainable Energy Week (EUSEW) as one of the *instruments* in the EU's arsenal addressing the execution of the sustainable energy policies.

Life-Cycle of Narratives

In their study of EU communications on EUSEW 2013 via Twitter Bain and Chaban (2017) have demonstrated that the "Sustainable Energy Europe" narrative already exists in the inter-connected phases of *formulation* and *projection* eliciting positive *reception*. Their choice of the medium of communication was instrumental to profile the three phases: Twitter, as any social media platform, is both a media product and evidence of public engagement. In its former aspect, Twitter may be analyzed for content and framing of it (thus enabling the tracing of *formulation* and *projection*). The latter aspect reveals *reception* of the posts on Twitter, including through replies to and reposts. Bain and Chaban (2017) chose to focus their analysis on the Twitter account "EU Energy Week," username @euenergyweek. According to Bain and Chaban (2017, p. 141) "The data used was a set of Twitter posts from the EU's Sustainable Energy Week 2013, which ran from 24–28 June. Tweets were included in the sample according to their use of the EU's official EUSEW hashtag #EUSEW13. A total of

2560 English language tweets were gathered. The decision to restrict the sample to English was made in order to remove the complications arising from translation to and from multiple languages."

Formulation

The *formulation* of the narrative focuses on tracing the process in order to understand "domestic political pressures evident when studying policy narratives' (Roselle et al. 2014, p. 78). According to the EU's official formulations, the EUSW is an annual event intended to promote "energy efficiency and renewable energy sources in an engaging, accessible and interactive way" (European Union, Sustainable Energy Week 2013). Sustainability is central to the EUSEW's stated priorities – Energy Week was conceived as a platform to profile and reward excellence in the field of sustainable energy. Bain and Chaban (2017, p. 143) noted that in the official formulations the benefits of *sustainability* in the energy sector are linked in the EU's official rhetoric to economic growth and competitiveness, while alternative energy sources can help secure Europe's energy future (see http://europa.eu/rapid/press-release_MEMO-13-596_en.htm). The EU's official discourse formulates that "one of the EU's priorities in all policy areas is to facilitate the sharing of ideas and best-practices, and to encourage networking and exchange, to support the replication of successful projects across Europe" (European Union 2013, np., cited in Bain and Chaban 2017, p. 143). In the EUSEW's focus are businesses, civil society organizations, policy-, decision- and opinion-makers, as well as the general public – primarily from inside the EU, but also internationally. For Bain and Chaban (2017, p. 143), the EUSEW initiative "was organised by the EU to 'encourage a bottom-up approach', in line with the EU's broader goals of making itself more accessible and transparent to its citizens and stakeholders."

Projection

According to Roselle et al. (2014, p. 78), *projection* of the narrative involves communication of the positions. To study this element involves tracing the narrative flow. Focusing on the EUSEW13, Bain and Chaban (2017) studied the flow of the narrative between the EU actors and other non-EU actors (state, non-state, and individuals), analyzing data "in terms of actors speaking (authors of the tweets) and selective information highlights (frames) present in the texts" (141).

In terms of *authors*, Bain and Chaban (2017) found a range of actors. While active, the EU's "authors" were not among the most vociferous. Lobbyists, think tanks, and consultancies were the most active, followed by the ordinary citizens. The leading position of interest groups in the Twitter conversations is hardly a surprise. These groups are typically savvy in social media communications. In contrast, individual journalists and media organizations were among the least active commentators. Arguably, high volume of contributions by "ordinary citizens" commenting on the EU's positions on sustainable energy demonstrates a potential for public interest and engagement with the EU in in the sustainability issue-area (Bain and Chaban 2017, p. 142).

In terms of *content* on the EU energy issues – and frames of this content – multiple frames were observed in individual examples. Research by Bain and Chaban (2017, p. 145) coded for thematic frames of EU actions in economic, political, social, environmental, and climate change issue-areas. Economic and political themes dominated in the framing, leading over climate change and environmental themes. Bain and Chaban (2017, p. 144) concluded that "the political and economic advantages or challenges posed by its energy actions strongly shape the conversation" – "a normative strength emerges, but it uses economic pragmatism as the driver."

Reception

To answer the key question of *reception* "how is the EU recognized?", and treating Twitter posts as evidence of opinion shared publicly, Bain and Chaban (2017) identified the EU's most visible *actors*, dominant *norms*, the EU's top agenda *issues* and the most frequent *sentiments* that guided the perceptions toward the EU as sustainable energy actor. The most visible *actor* in the eyes of the Twitters users was "the EU" itself, with two Commissioners (for energy and climate change) following in visibility. For Bain and Chaban (2017, p. 146), this shows a "growing recognition of the EU and its actors as the protagonists in the narration of the strategic story 'Sustainable Energy Europe'." The *norm* of sustainability led in the visions of the EU highlighting the EU's profile "linked with sustainability concerns" (Bain and Chaban 2017, p. 147). Predictably, the tweets about the events on the EUSEW13 program were the most topical during the period of observation. However, the next two most visible topics that shaped the Twitter discussion during the EUSEW were sustainable development and energy efficiency. These were followed by specific energy *issues* of energy policies/governance, energy investment, and energy infrastructure. Conversations on sustainable energy were also linked to the issues of urbanization and emissions. Arguably, visibility of these issues resonates with a broader sustainability agenda the EU is seeking to project in Europe and globally, and with an issue-specific narrative of "Sustainable Energy Europe." Bain and Chaban (2017, p. 148) observed how "the EU's own energy security is often seen to be intertwined with a plan for sustainable development and cutting energy wastage that seems to resonate with the EUSEW Twitter audience."

The sentiment analysis conducted by Bain and Chaban (2017) pointed to the predominant neutrality towards the EU's projections of its positions/policies on sustainable energy. A human-led qualitative protocol assessed the tweeter texts for linguistic metaphors and underlying conceptual metaphors, and this technique allowed researchers to track more nuances in the sentiments expressed. The volume of neutral-to-positive and positive tweets was significantly higher than the volume of negative ones (Bain and Chaban 2017, p. 149). This positive image of the EU as an actor involved in sustainable (energy) issues may serve yet another support that narrative of "Sustainable Energy Europe" in general is able to elicit positive attitudes from the participants in communication. Arguably, these positive sentiments in reception may feed into an emerging broader narrative of "Sustainable Europe."

With metaphors "trigger[ing] and/or shap[ing] narratives" (Miskimmon et al. 2013, p. 7), the dominant positive metaphorical images employed personifications, i.e., compared the EU to a human being. This image points to a particular vision in reception – the EU as a protagonist in the strategic story of "Sustainable Energy Europe," as the metaphors

> compared the EU with an able athlete who is kicking off sports games and leaping over barriers. It was even described as a champion. In a related set of images, the EU was constructed as an energetic, adventurous, and strong individual – a pioneer, seizing opportunities, buzzing with excitement, and providing support. (Bain and Chaban 2017, p. 149)

To assess *reception*, Bain and Chaban (2017) also examined the patterns of connectivity. For this purpose, they assessed the sample for one-directional messages, dialogic messages, and re-tweets (RTs). Retweeting was interpreted as a "form of information diffusion and participation ... and an important way of validating the messages (boyd et al. 2010) and potentially engaging with others (who receive but may not distribute the messages themselves)." In general, Bain and Chaban (2017, p. 144) found a significant share of RTs (over 900 in a 2560 size sample). Importantly, the EU was not observed to engage in discussion in this particular case – most of the tweets by the EU actor were one-off comments that were communicated and sometimes shared (retweeted). For Bain and Chaban (2017, p. 145), this constitutes a "promotional, shouting or sharing type of conversation" on Twitter around EUSEW.

Conclusions

This chapter explored a potential of one concrete *issue-specific* narrative "Sustainable Energy Europe" to support a broader strategic narrative "Sustainable Europe" currently projected by the EU globally and to the EU citizens. "Sustainable Energy Europe" provides an example of a narrative that demonstrates a promising flow between the projection of sustainability-focused objectives and priorities by the EU's official formulations to the communication of these through a range of media (through a social platform of Twitter in this chapter's case-study) to reception (tracked in the sample of public opinion through Twitter conversations around one particular EU-facilitated event – EUSEW – in the analysis presented above). The EU formulates its position as a leader and facilitator of a dialogue and collaboration in the field of sustainable energy aiming at European and international audiences. The EU's goals are seen as achievable and normatively desirable, with audience reaction demonstrating support to sustainability. The Twitter communications frame the EU as an actor who carries out sustainability-focused actions, with ordinary citizens being among the most prolific "authors" revealing a wider appeal of the EU in this action. A frame of economic benefits arising from participation in the EUSEW, engagement in sustainable energy field in general, and with Europe in particular, was observed. The EU and its leaders are subsequently recognized as the most visible actors who proclaim and exercise the norm of sustainability and elicit positive reactions from the commenting public.

Yet, the constructions, communication, flow, and effect on this *issue-specific* narrative reveals several potential challenges which this study translates for a more encompassing strategic narrative "Sustainable Europe." Formulation of an *issue-specific* narrative benefits from a pointed focus. The analysis of how the EU is recognized pointed to the public's awareness of a number of concrete sustainable energy policy issues. In them, the EU was seen to have a role and authority. In contrast, the pitfall for a "grand" narrative like "Sustainable Europe" on *systemic* and *identity* levels may be in its lack of a more precise focus. Importantly, since "strategic narratives employed at one level may affect narratives on the other levels" (Roselle et al. 2014, p. 77), the resonance between a well-chosen *issue-specific* narrative with the narratives on *identity* and *systemic* levels will be instrumental to counterbalance contestations inside and outside Europe effectively.

The case-study also demonstrated a certain deficit of the EU voices as "narrators" of the Union's "story." If the goal of the EU is to "conquer hearts and minds" inside and outside the EU and win over the strategic narratives of other international actors (see also Roselle et al. 2014, p. 71), then reliance on other groups of "narrators" puts the EU in a vulnerable position. As the case-study demonstrated, mainstream media organizations and professionals were reluctant participants in the Twitter communications around the EUSEW13 event. This group of opinion-makers may have increased its activity over the next years of the EUSEW initiative and more analysis is needed of these future events to compare. However, the lack of media interest in the observed case may be of a more systemic nature. It may be linked to the character of the EUSEW news – good, positive, and non-scandalous, as well as complex and even supranational. News media is infamous for its preference for negative and dramatic news and simpler storylines. Both characteristics are often seen by newsmakers as instrumental to "sell the news." Finally, the supranational news is seen as difficult to report to domestic audiences in EU member states or third countries. Future "narrators" of the EU will have to manage a similar character of news stories about "Sustainable Europe," especially if the news is reporting the EU's successes in this area. Future studies will have to approach the newsmakers from the EU member states and third countries to explore their views and positions on communicating the EU as a champion of sustainability. Insight into *who* communicates the EU's position is argued by the relevant literature to be one of the key elements in the analysis of the projection element of a strategic narrative (Chaban et al. 2019).

The annual EUSEW event has a dual target of reaching diverse groups inside Europe (the top priority of the initiative) as well as outside Europe. The case-study pointed to a dominance of the European commentators vis-à-vis external ones. In this light, if the EU enters a global competition on "whose story wins" (Nye Jr. 2014), and auditions "Sustainable Europe" narrative for this purposes, then the EU needs to consider effective tools how to increase global reaction and reception. In addition, most of the reactions came from a small number of interest groups. Bain and Chaban (2017, p. 151) citing Bruns and Stieglitz (2013, p. 171) noted that "Twitter 'conversations' are most often shaped by a 'dedicated in-group'– a small, but vocal minority who dominate the dialogue." Yet, engaging broader audiences – both state and non-state actors as well as the general public – is crucial for a successful narrative, if

"Sustainable Europe" is ever considered as a promising new narrative. On the other hand, a complex profile of the receivers will remain a challenge in successful communication of "Sustainable Europe" messages and visions.

The results of the case-study showed that the public are engaged and interested in EU affairs when it comes to sustainable energy issues to the degree that non-EU actors talk to each other about the EU's positions often bypassing the EU. Here lies a challenge – the connectivity between the public and the EU as a producer of the narrative was found to be low. The Twitter-focused study demonstrated that while the EU "authors" are among the audible voices, their messages are often one-directional, not eliciting dialogues or discussions. Such a "promotional" character of EU communication has its value. A "monologue" mode and advocacy of a position have a chance to educate, raise awareness about the EU and influence audience's attitudes towards a more positive stance. Bain and Chaban (2017, p. 151) argued that "For the 'Sustainable Energy Europe' narrative... all parts of this shared conversation are contributing to heightened salience of the message and therefore potentially greater engagement with it." This chapter, however, argues that true engagement suggests dialogue and conversation as a pathway to a shared consensus. This would concern the narrative of "Sustainable Europe." In the increasingly multipolar world, competition for global appeal and dominance of strategic narratives is severe. Shared consensus is highly sought after (Roselle et al. 2014, p. 72).

Future studies may trace the "echo" of the European Green Deal 2019 as one of the powerful formulations and projections by the EU. These studies may look into diverse methods to study formation, communication, and reception of the EU's narratives about "sustainable Europe," as well as examine political communication around other initiatives (the EUSEW remains a rather unique event) and look into a range of digital channels in their projection and reception of this narrative in different locations. This chapter argued that the narrative of "Sustainable Europe" has a potential to exist on *systemic, identity,* and *issue-specific* levels and appeal to European and global audiences on all levels. Future studies may also explore other *issue-specific* narratives under a wider "umbrella" of the "Sustainable Europe" narrative. Importantly, a frame of economic benefits arising from engagement in sustainable energy field in general, and with Europe in particular traced in the case of "Sustainable Energy Europe" parallels the emphasis on economic and business actions by EU actors to tackle the climate crisis articulated by the European Green Deal 2019 – "the biggest overhaul of policy since the foundation of the modern EU" (Harvey et al. 2019). This coupling of a pragmatic approach with a normative agenda may become a subject for future critical investigations.

Cross-References

▶ Energy Governance in Europe: Introduction
▶ European Union Energy Policy: A Discourse Perspective
▶ The EU in Global Energy Governance

References

Aggestam, L. (2008). Introduction: ethical power Europe? *International Affairs, 84*(1), 1–11.

Bain, J., & Chaban, N. (2017). An emerging EU strategic narrative? Twitter communication during the EU's sustainable energy week. *Comparative European Politics, 15*(1), 135–155.

Bain, J., Greenland, B., Knodt, M., & Nielsen, L. (2017). A polyphonic marketplace: Images of EU external energy relations in British, French and German media discourses. *Comparative European Politics, 15*(1), 115–134.

Börzel, T., & Risse, T. (2009). *The transformative power of Europe: The European Union and the diffusion of ideas.* Available at: https://nbn-resolving.org/urn:nbn:de:0168-ssoar-364733

boyd, D., Golder, S., & Lotan, G. (2010). Tweet, tweet, retweet: Conversational aspects of retweeting on Twitter, *43rd Hawaii International Conference on System Sciences*, 1–10.

Bruns, A., & Stieglitz, S. (2013). Towards more systematic Twitter analysis: metrics for tweeting activities. *International Journal of Social Research Methodology, 16*(2), 91–108.

Chaban, N., & Holland, M. (Eds.). (2008). *The European Union and the Asia–Pacific: Media, public and elite perceptions of the EU.* London/New York: Routledge.

Chaban, N., & Holland, M. (Eds.). (2014). *Communicating Europe in the times of crisis: External perceptions of the European Union.* Houndmills: Palgrave-McMillan.

Chaban, N., & Holland, M. (Eds.). (2018). *Shaping the EU's global strategy: Partners and perceptions.* Basingstoke: Palgrave-McMillan.

Chaban, N., Knodt, M. and Verdun, A. (Eds.). (2017). Special issue "external images of the EU – Energy power across the globe", Comparative European Politics 15(1).

Chaban, N., Knodt, M., Liekis, S., & NG, I. (2019). Narrators' perspectives: Communicating the EU in Ukraine, Israel and Palestine in times of conflict. *European Security, 28*(3), first on line https://doi.org/10.1080/09662839.2019.1648256.

Damro, C. (2012). Market power Europe. *Journal of European Public Policy, 19*(5), 682–699.

Duchêne, F. (1972). Europe's role in world peace. In R. Mayne (Ed.), *Europe tomorrow: Sixteen Europeans look ahead.* London: Fontana.

European Commission. (2013). EU Sustainable Energy Week 2013: FAQ and main features. Available at: http://europa.eu/rapid/press-release_MEMO-13-596_en.htm

European Commission. (2019a). A European green deal: Striving to be the first climate-neutral continent. Available at: https://ec.europa.eu/info/strategy/priorities-2019-2024/european-green-deal_en

European Commission. (2019b). Opening statement in the European Parliament Plenary Session by Ursula von der Leyen, Candidate for President of the European Commission. Available at: https://ec.europa.eu/commission/presscorner/detail/en/SPEECH_19_4230

European Union. (2013). Sustainable Energy Week 2013. Available at: http://www.eusew.eu/

Hajer, M. A. (1995). *The politics of environmental discourse: Ecological modernization and the policy process.* Oxford: Oxford University Press.

Harvey, F., Rankin, J., & Boffey, D. (2019). European Green Deal will change economy to solve climate crisis, says EU. *The Guardian.* Available at: https://www.theguardian.com/environment/2019/dec/11/european-green-deal-will-change-economy-to-solve-climate-crisis-says-eu?CMP=share_btn_link

Headley, J. (2018). Perceptions of the Ukraine crisis: A clash between a Modern Russia and a Postmodern European Union? *European Foreign Affairs Review, 23*(1), 101–117.

Kaldor, M., Martin, M., & Selchow, S. (2007). Human security: A new strategic narrative for Europe. *International Affairs (Royal Institute of International Affairs), 83*(2), 273–288.

Khanna, P. (2009). The metrosexual superpower. *Foreign Policy.* Available at: https://foreignpolicy.com/2009/10/27/the-metrosexual-superpower/.

Killian, B., & Elgström, O. (2010). Still a green leader? The European Union's role in international climate negotiations. *Cooperation and Conflict, 43*(3), 255–273.

Leonard, M. (2019). The Green Deal Will Make or Break Europe. *Project Syndicate.* December 13. Available at: https://www.project-syndicate.org/commentary/european-green-deal-von-der-leyen-by-mark-leonard-2019-12

Longo, M., & Murray, P. (2011). No ode to joy? Reflections on the European Union's legitimacy. *International Politics, 48*(6), 667–690.
Lucarelli, S., & Fioramonti, L. (2009). *External perceptions of the European Union as a global actor.* London: Routledge.
Manners, I. (2002). Normative power Europe: a contradiction in terms? *Journal of Common Market Studies, 40*(2), 235–258.
Manners, I., & Murray, P. (2016). The end of a noble narrative? European integration narratives after the Nobel Peace Prize. *Journal of Common Market Studies, 54*(1), 185–202.
Miskimmon, A. (2017). Finding a Unified voice? The European Union through a strategic narrative lens. In A. Miskimmon, B. O'Loughlin, & L. Roselle (Eds.), *Forging the world: Strategic narratives and international relations* (pp. 85–109). Ann Arbor: University of Michigan Press.
Miskimmon, A., O'Loughlin, B., & Roselle, L. (2013). *Strategic narratives, communication power and the new world order.* New York: Routledge.
Nicolaïdis, K., & Howse, R. (2002). This is my EUtopia . . .': Narrative as power. *Journal of Common Market Studies, 40*(4), 767–792.
Nye, J. S. (2014). The Information Revolution and Soft Power. *Current History, 113*(759), 19–22.
Roselle, L., Miskimmon, A., & O'Loughlin, B. (2014). Strategic narrative: A new means to understand soft power. *Media, War & Conflict, 7*(1), 70–84.
Schmidt, V., & Radaelli, C. (2004). Change and discourse in Europe: Conceptual and methodological issues. *West European Politics, 27*(2), 183–210.
Slaughter, A.-M. (2011). Preface. In W. Porter & M. Mykleby (Eds.), *A national strategic narrative* (pp. 2–4). Washington, DC: Woodrow Wilson International Centre for Scholars. Available at: http://www.wilsoncenter.org/sites/default/files/A%20National%20Strategic%20Narrative.pdf.
The Treaty of Lisbon. (2009). Title XXI, Art. 194 TFEU.
Van Ham, P. (2010). *Social power in international politics.* London: Routledge.

Clean Energy in the European Green Deal: Perspectives of European Stakeholders

17

Nils Bruch, Marc Ringel, and Michèle Knodt

Contents

Introduction	384
Material and Methods	385
Qualitative Review	387
Quantitative Review	390
Results	391
Qualitative Review	391
Survey Results	393
Comparison of Stakeholder and Public Salience	398
Discussion	400
Clean Energy Components of the Green Deal	400
Assessment of Salience	401
Limitations of This Study and Need for Further Research	402
Conclusion and Policy Implications	403
Cross-References	403
Supplementary Material	403
References	403

Abstract

The Fit-for-55 Package of the European Commission is a key element to implement the European Green Deal and thus for the decarbonization of the European Union's economies by 2050. Major elements of the package are legislative proposals to support both renewable energy and energy efficiency. In these two domains, the body of EU law has been changed multiple times during the last years. These changes raise the question of stakeholder support for more ambitious

N. Bruch (✉) · M. Knodt
Institute of Political Science, Technical University of Darmstadt, Darmstadt, Germany
e-mail: nils.bruch@tu-darmstadt.de; knodt@pg.tu-darmstadt.de

M. Ringel
Nuertingen Geislingen University, Geislingen, Germany
e-mail: marc.ringel@hfwu.de

© Springer Nature Switzerland AG 2022
M. Knodt, J. Kemmerzell (eds.), *Handbook of Energy Governance in Europe*,
https://doi.org/10.1007/978-3-030-43250-8_79

policies. To assess such support, we apply the concept of salience to four core European stakeholder groups. We use a mixed-method design, testing external issue salience through a qualitative read-out of 182 stakeholder position papers and 198,128 Twitter messages, and then testing internal salience through quantitative analysis of an in-depth survey of 20 key European stakeholders. We find stakeholders closely align with the European Commission in demanding binding energy efficiency and renewable energy policies. Strong focus can be expected on energy efficiency targets and measures, less on the further development of the framework for renewable energies. These findings confirm earlier studies on salience in different policy fields.

Keywords

European Union · Green Deal · Stakeholder · Interest groups · Renewable energy · Energy efficiency · Salience

Introduction

The European Commission published the Fit-For-55 Package on 14 July 2021 to align the EU's key energy and climate change legislation with the EU's new 2030 climate target of a 55% reduction in greenhouse gas emissions compared to 1990. Among other things, the package includes proposals for a revision of the Energy Efficiency Directive, an expansion of carbon pricing through a new emissions trading scheme for buildings and road transport, the proposal to establish a new social climate fund, and higher targets for renewable energy and energy savings. The package is thus central to the implementation of the European Green Deal, which is the European Commission's key policy strategy for transforming the European Union into a fully decarbonized economy by 2050 (European Commission 2019). The Green Deal, as well as the measures of the Fit-for-55 Package aim at combining decarbonization with green economic growth (Krail et al. 2016; Knodt et al. 2020) through policy actions in the fields of the circular economy, mobility, agriculture, and, notably, energy. The energy sector stands out because it represents 80% of the EU's greenhouse gas emissions, making it pivotal for decarbonization (European Commission 2016a, 2018a). The Green Deal's ambitions for the energy sector build on the "Energy Union" strategy (European Commission 2016b) pursued by the previous Juncker Commission.

The Juncker strategy led to the revision of almost the entire body of European legislation in the energy domain through the "Winter Package" of 2016 (Knodt and Ringel 2018, 2019a). Also known as "Clean Energy for All Europeans" (European Commission 2016b), the Winter Package systematically updated renewable energy and energy efficiency policies with a view to 2030. Negotiations were sometimes thorny, but the outcomes were: (i) an updated Renewable Energy Directive (RED II; European Commission 2018b); (ii) an updated Directive on Energy Performance of Buildings (EPBD; European Commission 2018c); (iii) a recast Energy Efficiency

Directive (EED; European Commission 2018d); and (iv) a new Governance Regulation (European Commission 2018e), which introduced a harder form of soft governance (Knodt and Ringel 2019b) to coordinate national energy policies through National Energy and Climate Plans (NECPs) (European Commission 2016c, 2016d; Lopez et al. 2016; Bayer et al. 2017; European Commission 2017, 2018f; Höh et al. 2017; Sajn 2017; Wilson 2017; Knodt and Ringel 2019a).

The clean energy legislation was negotiated on the basis of the EU commitment to the Paris Agreement of reducing greenhouse gas (GHG) emissions by 40% by 2030. The new ambition, to increase this level to at least 50% through a European "Climate Law" (European Commission 2020), implies that the clean energy legislation just adopted will need to be strengthened again. This raises the question of political readiness to again reopen the key clean energy dossiers. After a first "notice" (European Council 2019), the Council is currently dealing with both legislative proposals. Observers expect that more ambitious policy efforts for renewable energy and energy efficiency will largely depend on stakeholder pressure (Claeys et al. 2019; Garabetian et al. 2019).

Our contribution aims to assess stakeholder readiness to support (yet again) upgraded European clean energy policies and to take on the issues which would arise. To this aim, we apply a mixed-methods approach, comprising a qualitative read-out of 182 stakeholder position papers and 198,128 Twitter messages, complemented by a quantitative analysis of in-depth survey data from 20 key European stakeholders. Our results advance insights into energy policy in two ways: (i) on a policy level, our results offer insights for policy-makers into how key stakeholders are likely to position themselves in the upcoming negotiations on the Green Deal's energy pillar; (ii) on a theoretical level, we test the application of the concept of "salience" to the European energy and climate fields. A central concept in political science, salience, broadly defined as "the importance actors attribute to a political matter" (Beyers et al. 2018), has yet to be applied to evaluate actors in the EU energy and climate fields.

Material and Methods

Figure 1 presents an overview of our methodology. Due to a lack of information on the Green Deal by the European Commission at the beginning of the process, our analysis is based on a comprehensive screening of peer-reviewed papers (Scopus), grey literature, and primary sources such as the public consultations on the clean energy dossiers. In addition, we identified core European stakeholders and political issues that could emerge in the re-opened negotiations.

To assess stakeholder sentiments, we chose the mixed-methods approach shown in Fig. 1. A qualitative analysis reviewed online channels (press releases, website content, and newsletters) and Twitter messages from stakeholders in topic areas ("hashtags") related to the energy issues raised by the Green Deal. This yielded information about the external agenda of core stakeholders. Quantitative analysis used a survey of key European energy and climate policy stakeholders to investigate

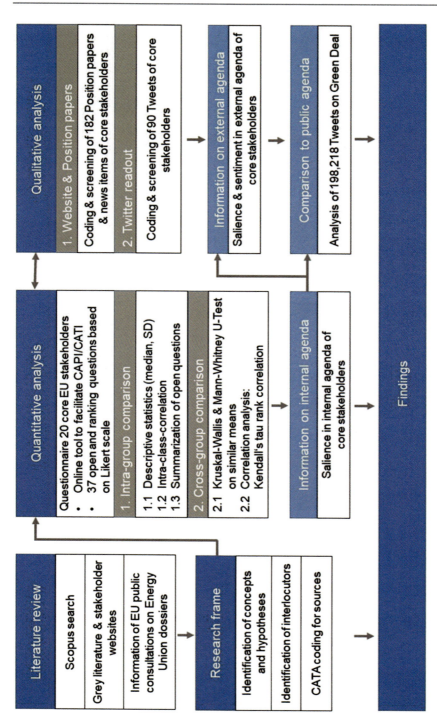

Fig. 1 Methodology overview

the internal agenda of core stakeholders. Finally, we compared our findings to the broad public discussion on social media of the Green Deal. The following sections describe this methodology in more detail.

Qualitative Review

In this review, we sought a qualitative characterization of the issues important to key stakeholders in European energy policy. We identified four core stakeholder groups: Industry, NGOs, Consultancy/Think Tanks, and Mixed Stakeholders. These groups were identified based on feedback from earlier climate and energy regulations, notably the Clean Energy Package. In this way, 20 European associations were identified as "core stakeholders."

Our review method rests on the theoretical concept of *salience*. Salience is hereby defined as *"the relative importance actors attribute to a specific political matter"* (Beyers et al. 2018). It is both actor-specific and issue-specific, which means that actors can perceive the salience of a particular issue differently (Warntjen 2012). Or, said the other way around, a particular issue can elicit widely different perceptions of salience.

We used this concept to identify which elements of the Green Deal are particularly *salient* to the core stakeholders. To gauge the likely interactions between these actors, we compared the differences in salience among the four core stakeholder groups. A fifth group – the general public – was consulted in the closing part of our analysis to assess their salient concerns against those of the core stakeholders.

With regard to issues, we tested the salience of specific clean energy issues set out in the Green Deal rather than the overall concept of the Green Deal. These issues were identified based on stakeholder consultations and Impact Assessment works in the Clean Energy Package. We translated the energy-relevant issues into a codebook, which is presented in the supplementary material A.1.

The literature review necessary to create the research framework yielded 93 articles by searching Scopus, Researchgate.net, academia.edu, and Google Scholar. This led to the identification of further interview partners.

Table 1 lists the categorization of identified papers and shows that out of the 93 papers, 47 addressed topics relevant for this assessment, notably energy and climate policy, as well as governance. The categories "General Climate Policy" (7 papers), "Multi-Topic" (6 papers), and "General Energy Policy" (4 papers) include research and assessments about multiple aspects of the respective dimension of the Green Deal, while the other categories summarize papers covering more specific segments of the Green Deal. The remaining 46 papers identified in the literature review either cover issues irrelevant to the analysis or mention the Green Deal only briefly without further inquiry. These were categorized as "Others."

Our source of data for salience assessment among stakeholders comprised two primary communication channels: (1) online communications via press releases, website content, newsletters, and the like; and (2) Twitter messages. The latter also provided data to investigate the general public's assessment of salient clean energy issues in the Green Deal.

Table 1 Categorization of identified papers in the grey literature review

Category	Number of Papers	References
Competitiveness and Carbon Border Tax	10	(Abbas 2020; Cano 2019; Dias et al. 2020; Krenek et al. 2020; Kontovas and Psaraftis 2020; Sartori 2019; Simola 2020; Stefano 2020; McWilliams and Zachmann 2020)
General Climate Policy	7	(Claeys et al. 2019; Catuti et al. 2020; Hughes 2020; Allenbach et al. 2019; Löschel 2020; Neuhoff 2020; Giuli et al. 2020)
Just Transition and Financing	6	(Bergamaschi 2020; Cameron et al. 2020; Claringbould et al. 2019; Landesmann and Stöllinger 2020; Rehn 2019; Tesche 2020)
Multi-Topic	6	(Dullien et al. 2020; EuroMemo Group 2020; Lucchese and Pianta 2020; Lucchese et al. 2020; Ciot et al. 2019; Watt 2020)
General Energy Policy	4	(Bianchi and Colantoni 2020; Goldthau 2019; Kemfert 2019; Fischedick and Lechtenböhmer 2020)
Renewable Energies	4	(Agora Energiewende et al. 2020; Brodny and Tutak 2020; Jäger-Waldau 2020; Thaler 2020)
Climate Target	4	(Ålander et al. 2020; Geden and Schenuit 2019; Hainsch et al. 2019; Schenuit 2019)
Climate Law	3	(Cittadino 2019; Fairbrass et al. 2020; Kingston 2020)
Natural Gas	3	(Belyi and Piebalgs 2020; Bros 2020; Olczak and Piebalgs 2020)
Others	46	Not included

To process online channel communications, we applied computer-aided content analysis (CATA) provided by MaxQDA software. To calibrate our search, we did a manual screening of the stakeholder websites, blogs, and social media for the period 15 December 2019 to 21 February 2020. This returned expert opinions and statements from 13 of the 20 core stakeholders. These 13 stakeholders had been following the negotiations closely and provided commentary on ambition level and weak points in the new legislation. The seven remaining stakeholders offered no expert opinions or statements on the Green Deal in their online communications.

Retrieved materials were coded using two broad categories with several sub-categories to tag content:

Category 1. Stakeholder policy background: Here, the possibilities were Industry; NGOs; Mixed Stakeholders (comprising both NGO and industry representatives); and Consultancy/Think Tanks

Category 2. Theme(s) covered. These included Climate Elements of the Green Deal (8 issues); Governance and Impacts (16 issues); Clean Energy (33 issues); Just Transition (10 issues)

The number of mentions of an issue in the collected statements was used as an indicator of issue salience. This allowed us to compare issue saliences in the external agendas of the four stakeholder groups. While different measurements of salience are still debated in the literature, this type of text analysis is an established method of measurement (Warntjen 2012).

The above categories and codings were retained in our second data source, Twitter messages. We used tweet analysis first to supplement the screening of website content and help refine our assessment of external issue salience among the core stakeholders. Using Twitter's advanced search, tweets were compiled manually by applying the search string "#GreenDeal OR #EUGreenDeal OR #ClimateLaw OR #EUClimateLaw" to the accounts of the 20 identified associations. These tweets were analyzed together with statements gathered in the screening of website content.

The second use we made of Twitter as a data source was to provide means to assess the salience of clean energy issues in the Green Deal to the public. The analysis of Twitter messages as evidence of public opinion regarding energy and climate policy issues set out by the European Union was already used by Chaban and Bain (see ▶ Chap. 16, "Sustainable Europe: Narrative Potential in the EU's Political Communication" in this Handbook). Furthermore, Tweet traffic can be considered a proxy for public salience, as case study research indicates that public salience is echoed in social media (Bode et al. 2010; Southwell and Weeks 2010). Accordingly, we performed a comprehensive screening of all Twitter accounts mentioning the Green Deal from 21 February 2020 to 27 April 2020. The automated search was conducted using the Data Scraping Tool "Social Media Observatory," developed by the Department of Computer Science at TU Darmstadt. The search string used was "Green Deal OR Climate Law OR Just Transition Fund." This found 198,218 tweets, which we analyzed using our coding system and the MaxQDA software.

In assessing public salience, we followed the same practice used in assessing stakeholder salience, namely taking the number of mentions as an indicator of salience. Table 2 summarizes the tweets found per search string. The explosion in tweets on the relevant issues after the special meeting of the European Council on 20–21 February 2020 is apparent.

Table 2 Search strings applied in Twitter Advanced Search and Social Media Observatory to identify relevant Tweets

Search type	Population	Period	Number of Tweets
Manual Search	Core stakeholder Accounts	15 December 2019 to 21 February 2020	90
Automated Search	All Twitter Accounts, including core stakeholders as subset	21 February 2020 to 27 April 2020	198,128
Total			198,218

Source: Authors, based on website research

Quantitative Review

A survey approach was used to collect quantitative data from our focus group of 20 core stakeholders. As several of these organizations serve as a "bundling organization," acting as a platform for several other organizations with shared interests, the number of associations represented by our survey covers some 70 individual stakeholders.

A questionnaire was developed in English, comprising eight banks of questions and taking from 10 to 15 min to complete. To facilitate comparisons with earlier studies of climate and energy policy stakeholder assessments, the questionnaire followed a four-part semi-structured design:

Part 1. Assess the concept and key elements of the Green Deal as compared to the Energy Union strategy
Part 2. Assess the governance elements and the stringency of the energy pillar of the Green Deal
Part 3. Rate additional measures to promote renewable energies as well as energy efficiency
Part 4. Rate elements for a "just transition mechanism" to remedy transitional damages in the energy sector

The questionnaire used six-point Likert scales to quantify items and sub-items. An even number of points (1 through 6) allowed for clear conclusions and avoided an "average choice bias" (Scholl 2009). In all scales, one ranked the lowest and six the highest. The questionnaire was pretested with two stakeholders to check understandability, logic, and ease of answering the questions before it was launched to the whole target group.

We used IBM's SPSS Data Analysis Software on the questionnaire data. For each group of stakeholders, descriptive and inferential statistics were calculated to (1) examine stakeholders' views of the Green Deal as policy framework compared to the Energy Union concept of the Juncker Commission; (2) assess governance and stringency of the available coordination and compliance options; and (3) survey options for additional measures in the field of energy policy. These items were analyzed both intra- and inter-group. We also explored correlations between components to identify whether similar combinations were present in the four groups.

Intra-group comparisons capture similarities and differences in issue salience within a group. Comparisons were made on the basis of descriptive statistics (median, standard deviation). We also ran Intra-Class correlation coefficient (ICC) tests to check consistency among surveyed stakeholders from the same group.

Inter-group comparisons looked at the aggregated characteristics between the four core stakeholder groups to identify potential areas of cooperation. This analysis comprised:

- Kruskal-Wallis Test: to check for statistically significant differences among the four core stakeholder groups.

- Mann-Whitney-U-Test: to deepen understanding of comparisons between any two significantly different groups found by the Kruskal-Wallis Test.
- Correlations analysis: items for governance, technology use, drivers, and barriers were tested against each other at aggregate and detailed levels using Kendall's tau rank, preferred over Spearman's rank for small sample sizes (Field 2018).

Results

Our findings identify points of contrast and agreement – areas suitable for consensus-building – regarding stakeholders' initial assessment of and positioning toward the Green Deal and its key energy and climate policy elements.

Qualitative Review

Following the approach presented in section "Materials and Methods - Qualitative Review," we retrieved 182 press releases, policy papers, and social media/blog postings from 20 stakeholders, together with their Twitter communications. We applied our codebook (see Supplemental Material A.1) to this literature pool to retrieve issues of external salience to our four stakeholder groups.

Of the 182 press items retrieved, 114 addressed issues included in our codebook: 28 communications by Industry; 52 by NGO; 34 by Mixed Stakeholders, but none by the group of Consultancy/Think Tanks. Of these 114 items, 33 focused on technology-related details: 8 by Industry; 7 by NGO; 18 by Mixed Stakeholders, and none by Consultancy/Think Tanks. The remaining 68 press items addressed issues not listed in the codebook and yielded no hits at all. The analysis also identified 20 aspects identified in the codebook not present in stakeholder communications and therefore seemed to have been of lesser importance in shaping and influencing the content of the Green Deal during our evaluation period.

The top 10 issues by salience identified by our codebook are presented in Table 3, which lists the results of the coding and the importance (absolute counts) of the 10 most prominent aspects raised by stakeholders regarding the European Green Deal.

Several results in Table 3 merit highlighting. First, and most noteworthy, is the complete absence of external communications about the top-ranked items from the group of Consultancy/Think Tanks. This is in stark contrast to the numerous hits generated by the groups of NGOs and Mixed Stakeholders. Whether this contrast in issue salience pertains only to external communications or also represents a contrast in internal issue salience will be addressed in section "Survey Results."

Second, we can identify six prominent issues that emerge from the overview in Table 3 of the most salient aspects in external stakeholder communications:

1. Energy efficiency
2. Decarbonization and climate policy
3. Finance

Table 3 Overview of 10 most salient aspects in stakeholder communication with regard to Green Deal

Issue raised	Coding	Incidence (overall)	Industry	NGOs	Mixed	Consultancies
Energy efficiency	Energy Efficien*	529	68	216	245	0
Energy Efficiency Directive	Energy Efficiency Directive; EED	128	19	21	88	0
Financing	Financ*; Finance; Financing; Financial Support	121	18	73	30	0
Decarbonization	Decarboni*ation	121	51	48	22	0
Innovation	Innovation; innovative	62	20	35	7	0
Climate Law	Climate Law	61	11	5	45	0
Renewable energy	Renewable Energ*; Renewable Energy, Renewable Energies	61	10	30	21	0
Competitiveness	Competitiveness; competitive	59	23	11	25	0
National Energy and Climate Plans	National Energy and Climate Plans; NECPs; NECP	58	8	1	49	0
Article 7 EED	Article 7	54	9	3	42	0

Source: Authors
*wildcard search

4. Renewable energies
5. Innovation and competitiveness and
6. Governance (National Energy and Climate Plans)

The numbers found can be explained partly by the prevalence of topical issues circulating in the press during our sample period. Press coverage of the Climate Law and its financing remained a topical issue, as reporting continued on the debate over the multiannual financial framework of the European Commission.

A third point to note concerns the energy-related issues, which are core elements of the Fit-for-55 Package: our counting shows a strong divergence between the salience of energy efficiency issues and that of renewable energies. This might be interpreted to mean that although stakeholders seemed comfortable overall with the results of the updated Renewable Energy Directive, they contrastingly believed that the energy efficiency side still needs improvement. The detailed mentioning of the Energy Efficiency Directive and its Article 7 on energy efficiency obligations stand out strongly in this respect. This point, in particular, is likely to become a major topic of discussion in the Council under the Slovenian and French Presidencies, as the negotiations on the recast of the Energy Efficiency Directive fall within the period from the end of 2021 to the beginning of 2022.

Finally, the Mixed Stakeholders stand out in their apparent need for publicly accompanying the national implementation of European policies by commenting on the governance mechanisms such as the NECPs (Meyer-Ohlendorf 2015; Umpfenbach 2015; Ringel 2016). Here again, these issues merit a follow-up when assessing stakeholder perception of internal salience. We now turn to this assessment in considering the quantitative results of our study.

Survey Results

Here we report on data from the survey questionnaire given to 20 core EU stakeholders. Featuring a mix of open-ended and ranking questions, the survey gives insight into issue salience on the internal agendas of these stakeholders. We subject survey data to both intra-group and inter-group comparisons.

We applied intra-class correlation (ICC) to test whether the opinions and ratings sampled for each core stakeholder group internally converged. Table 4 presents our results. Almost all groups show very high convergence among their members, with coefficients close to or greater than 0.7 and strong significance ($p > 0.05$). Compared to other stakeholder groups, the group of Consultancy/Think Tanks shows tightly aligned results, combined with an especially strong significance level. This seems to suggest that this group could be extremely influential in shaping the discussions, as it can be expected to speak with one voice.

In our questionnaire, we asked core stakeholders to respond to several items that allowed us to assess the internal salience of central elements in the Green Deal. A first bank of questions assessed stakeholder readiness to adapt to the new framework, which integrates clean energy issues into the broader concept of climate neutrality. Results are shown in Table 5. Scores are from 1 to 6, with 1 the lowest and 6 the highest rating.

Table 4 Intra-class correlation coefficients (ICC) for respondents (all items)

	Intra-Class Correlation Coefficient	95% confidence interval		F-test with value 0			Significance (p-value)
		upper	lower	F-value	df1	df2	
Industry	0.896	0.732	0.983	10.772	5	185	0.000
NGO	0.795	0.463	0.966	4.894	5	185	0.000
Consultancy/Think Tanks	0.995	0.980	1.000	196.160	2	74	0.000
Mixed Stakeholders	0.733	0.090	1.000	6.245	1	37	0.017

Table 5 Items to assess readiness to switch to the Green Deal as framework for clean energy policies

Core groups		Climate neutrality as overall target	A Climate Law with enforceable targets	Clean and secure energy as part of a larger concept	Focus on growth and jobs	Increased EU financial support	Broader focus of research and development
Industry	M	5.00	5.00	4.00	4.00	5.00	5.00
	SD	0.535	0.787	1.069	1.345	1.069	0.951
NGO	M	6.00	5.50	4.50	3.00	4.00	4.00
	SD	0.816	0.816	1.211	1.211	0.408	0.632
Consultancy/Think Tanks	M	6.00	4.00	4.00	4.00	5.50	4.00
	SD	1.155	0.577	0.577	1.155	0.707	0.577
Mixed Stakeholders	M	5.50	4.50	3.50	3.50	3.50	3.50
	SD	0.707	0.707	0.707	0.707	0.707	0.707

Legend: M – median, SD – standard deviation

All core groups supported the overall goal of climate neutrality, with the group of Consultancy/Think Tanks being the most positive (M = 6, SD = 1.155). Still, this group proved to be the most skeptical about supporting a Climate Law with enforceable targets (M = 4, SD = 0.577). All groups also seemed wary about clean energy policies becoming part of a larger array of policies. Here, only the NGOs score higher than 4 (M4.50, SD = 1.211), while Mixed Stakeholders (M = 3.5, SD = 0.71) stand out as being the least convinced.

Next, to assess the internal salience of the overall energy policy topics, core stakeholders were asked where they saw the need to step up European action and/or increase coordination between the European member states. Table 6 reports our results.

The roughly equal salience ratings for the different policy fields by three of the core groups – Industry, NGO, and Mixed – suggests no clear positioning on anyone focus issue. This contrasts sharply with the positioning of the Consultancy/Think Tank group, which favored more policy action in the field of renewable energies (M = 5, SD = 0.577) and energy efficiency (M = 5, SD = 0.577), but was, interestingly, less convinced about coordinating security of supply via a more integrated EU energy policy (M = 2.0, SD = 1.73).

Finally, we asked core stakeholders to focus on the clean energy directives and rate the importance of additional measures in the (i) Renewable Energy Directive, (ii) Energy Efficiency Directive, and (iii) the Energy Performance of Buildings Directive. The items presented to stakeholders were derived from earlier proposals made during negotiations for the Clean Energy Package, proposals that had not been retained in the final political compromise or were criticized as not being ambitious enough (Table 7).

Table 6 Role of more integrated European energy policy and coordination via the NECPs

Grouping		Security of supply	Internal energy market	Energy infrastructure	Energy efficiency	Renewable energies	Research and innovation
Industry	M	4.00	4.00	4.00	4.00	4.00	3.00
	SD	1.95	1.35	1.25	1.39	0.95	1.78
NGO	M	4.00	4.50	4.00	4.00	4.00	3.5
	SD	1.10	1.17	1.33	1.03	1.41	1.05
Consultancy/Think tank	M	2.00	4.00	3.00	3.00	5.00	4.00
	SD	1.732	1.000	0.577	0.577	0.507	0.55
Mixed Stakeholders	M	4.50	5.00	5.00	5.00	5.00	4.50
	SD	0.71	0.00	0.00	0.00	0.00	0.71

Legend: M – median, SD – standard deviation

The results suggest that in the energy efficiency field, all core stakeholder groups support binding national targets. This issue was dropped in the 2018 recast of the EED and is also not on the agenda of the EED recast of the Fit-for-55 Package. Moreover, especially Mixed (M = 6, SD = 0.0) and NGO (M = 6, SD = 1.21) supported more stringent target values in the framework of the national energy efficiency obligation schemes (Article 7 EED). Interestingly, more technical options (management systems, combined heat, and power, smart metering) received less support than the overall framing of policies through targets. This also holds for items related to the EPBD, where stakeholders rated renovation strategies and roadmaps higher than the more technical option to replace heating systems. Note also the relatively low rating for energy efficiency coordination via the NECPs (Table 6) in comparison to the support for binding targets (Table 7). This might be interpreted as limited trust in the "hard soft governance" (Knodt et al. 2020) installed with the Clean Energy Package and shown already in earlier stakeholder feedback (Knodt and Ringel 2019a; Knodt et al. 2021).

This result is mirrored in the renewable energy field, where stakeholders rated binding national targets as extremely important (M = 6 for Industry and Mixed, SD = 1.45 and SD = 0.0, respectively) or very important (M = 5 for NGO and Consultancies/Think Tanks with SD = 0.837 and 2.082, respectively). This, too, was not considered in the Commission's proposal presented in the Fit-For-55 Package. Note also the importance that three out of the four groups attributed to binding targets at the sector level. In contrast, respondents took a somewhat more cautious stance on harmonizing support schemes and measures in the heating/cooling and transport sectors.

We applied the Kruskal-Wallis test to check for similarities and differences between the four stakeholder groups. The test allows the comparison of groups containing independent scores by ordering rankings from lowest (rank 1) to highest, first ignoring group membership. After ranking, the scores are sorted back into their group and added, yielding a group rank R. The test statistic H for the Kruskal-Wallis test is calculated as:

Table 7 Rating of options to step up clean energy policies

Core groups			Energy Efficiency Directive				
			Binding national targets	Higher saving target for article 7	Mandatory energy management systems	Further measures to foster CHP	Stronger regulation for metering & billing
Industry	M		6.00	5.00	3.00	3.00	3.00
	SD		1.732	2.059	1.254	1.380	0.816
NGO	M		6.00	6.00	4.50	4.00	4.00
	SD		1.211	1.211	1.049	1.033	0.837
Consultancy/ Think tank	M		5.00	5.00	5.00	4.00	4.00
	SD		1.000	1.000	1.000	1.155	1.528
Mixed Stakeholders	M		6.00	6.00	5.00	4.00	5.00
	SD		0.000	0.000	0.000	1.414	0.000

Core groups			Renewable Energy Directive & EPBD					
			Mandatory replacement of heating systems	Mandatory renovation roadmaps	Binding national targets	Binding sectorial targets	Harmonized EU support scheme	Stronger integration of RES in heating/ cooling and mobility
Industry	M		4.00	6.00	6.00	4.00	4.00	4.00
	SD		1.215	1.215	1.464	1.528	1.272	0.756
NGO	M		4.50	6.00	5.00	6.00	4.00	5.00
	SD		1.862	0.516	0.837	2.191	1.140	1.000
Consultancy- Think tank	M		3.00	3.00	5.00	6.00	3.00	4.00
	SD		0.000	1.732	2.082	1.155	2.517	0.577
Mixed Stakeholders	M		4.50	6.00	6.00	6.00	4.00	4.50
	SD		0.707	0.000	0.000	0.000	1.414	0.707

Legend: M – median, SD – standard deviation

$$H = \frac{12}{N(N+1)} \sum_{i=1}^{k} \frac{R_i^2}{n_i} - 3(N+1)$$

with N being the total number of samples and n the number of samples per group.

The results of the Kruskal-Wallis test show that 36 of 38 cases tested were not significant. This means in 36 cases the alternative hypotheses must be rejected and the null hypothesis retained. The null hypothesis states that the groups have similar score orders in the items on the survey, while the alternative hypothesis is true when a significant ($p \leq 0.05$) difference between the groups in the scores of the items exists. Therefore, the results show that the stakeholder groups do not differ significantly in their positions on the Green Deal. Only "Finance" and "Smart metering" are significant cases in the Kruskal-Wallis test, but a closer inquiry into which specific groups differ in their scores through pairwise comparison of all combinations of stakeholders shows no significant result. In conclusion, the Kruskal-Wallis test shows a strong coherence between all stakeholder groups in our survey results.

As the Consultancy/Think Tank-group stood out against the other groups in terms of internal coherence, we additionally applied the Mann-Whitney-Test to compare the perceptions of this group against the set of all other stakeholders as a test group. The test compares the two groups by ranking the individual choices and comparing the median ranks (Field 2018). We report the test statistic U, calculated based on the sample sizes n_1 and n_2 of groups 1 (Consultancy and Think Tanks) and 2 (all other stakeholders), with R_1 is the sum of ranks for group 1:

$$U = n_1 n_2 + \frac{n_1(n_1 + 1)}{2} - R_1$$

In Table 8 we report the median ranks, p values, and effect sizes for the items specifying our four research questions, in case p values are statistically significant, implying $p \leq 0.05$. Effect size r is calculated as

$$r = \frac{z}{\sqrt{N}}$$

where z is the z-score that SPSS produces, and N is the size of the study, that is, of the total observations on which z is based. Effect sizes should be 0.5 or higher to demonstrate a strong effect, aka. the "Cohen benchmark" (Field 2018).

The Mann-Whitney-U-Test shows similar results to those from the Kruskal-Wallis test. In 36 of 38 cases, the items are in similar order when comparing the group Consultancy/Think Tank with the other three stakeholder groups. Again only two items show significant differences in the item order: "Finance" and "Requalification" (i.e., training and re-qualifying employees from "old" energy industries such as coal to adapt to structural changes), both with a strong effect size (see Table 8). Despite the differences in the ranking of the two items, it should be noted that similarities and coherence between the stakeholder groups largely prevail

Table 8 Significant Items of the Mann-Whitney-U-Test comparing "Consultancy/Think Tank" and other stakeholder groups

	Finance	Requalification
Mann-Whitney-U	4.500	9.000
SPSS Z-Score	−2.219	−2.264
Exact significance (p) - two -sided	0.027	0.037
Reject null hypothesis	X	X
Effect size	0.509	0.519

as the results of the Kruskal-Wallis and the Mann-Whitney-U-Test indicate: Stakeholders overall speak with one voice.

To assess the interplay between key factors identified in earlier stakeholder consultations, we applied correlation analysis, seeking to detect patterns of interactions that help explain stakeholder positioning. To appropriately address the small sample size, Kendall's tau rank correlation was applied rather than the more common Spearman rank correlation coefficient. Where correlations showed strong significance (*$p < 0.05$; **$p < 0.01$; ***$p < 0.001$), bias-corrected and accelerated-bootstrap 95% confidence intervals were computed. A complete read-out of the correlations for the items of the questionnaire is given in section A.2 of the supplementary material.

The correlation analysis shows a high number of correlations at the lowest significance level (*$p < 0.05$) between items in the stakeholder groups of Industry and NGOs. While correlations with apparently stronger significance did occur in our analysis, we choose not to report these, as they could have been caused by the low case numbers, making an interpretation of these numbers suspect, especially between "Consultancy/Think Tanks" and "Mixed." Nevertheless, there are still 40 correlations in the Industry group and 93 correlations in the NGO group, albeit all at the lowest significance level.

In the Industry group, the highest number of correlations occurs between items regarding technology use, especially "Internal Energy Market & Regional Integration," "Energy Infrastructure," and "Energy Efficiency." These correlations show unity in the standpoints among the industry stakeholders regarding future technology use. Correlations of items regarding "Governance" and" Climate Policy" also occur in the Industry group, but not to the extent of technology use items.

The item "Clean and Secure Energy as Part of a Larger Concept" correlates ($p = 0,022*$) positively with the item "Focus on Growth and Jobs" which shows how industry stakeholders connected the Green Deal to economic opportunities. In the NGO group, more correlations between "Governance" and "Climate" items occur than in the Industry group, which indicates more unity among the NGO stakeholders. However, the NGO group also shows the most correlations between items regarding technology use, especially "Energy Infrastructure" and "Internal Energy Market & Regional Integration." These are similar to those seen in the Industry group.

A notable difference can be observed in correlations with items regarding renewable energies. While renewable energy items were not prominent in the Industry group, indicating less unity among the stakeholders, NGOs seemed to have more unity on this issue. They viewed renewable energies as a more salient issue than do Industry stakeholders, who were more focused on energy efficiency.

Comparison of Stakeholder and Public Salience

Having assessed core stakeholder salience along both external and internal dimensions, we next consider what elements of the Green Deal's clean energy package are most salient to the general public. The assessment is based on a computer-aided read-out of 198,128 Twitter messages. Table 9 and Table 10 present the results of this analysis.

As can be seen in Table 9, the core topics in Twitter mass media discussions broadly followed the lines of the overall Green Deal strategy. They are aligned around: (1) decarbonization and Climate Law with 21,344 hits; (2) jobs and growth with 2575 hits; (3) finance, innovation, and infrastructure with 1,602 hits; (4) just transition and social aspects with 1428 hits; and (5) research with 412 hits. These overriding, rather general topics roughly mirrored the Commission's communication activities during the observation period.

Our core stakeholders' Twitter communication mirrored this overall picture for decarbonization and economic aspects, reflecting the two key strands of the European Green Deal (Table 10). The individual clean energy aspects however only played a marginal role in their overall communication.

Table 9 Overview of 10 most raised aspects in public Twitter communication with regard to Green Deal

Issue	Incidence	Share of total (%)
Climate Law	20,916	10.56
Jobs	1811	0.91
Growth	764	0.39
Social	740	0.37
Just Transition Fund	688	0.35
Financ*	628	0.32
Innovation	546	0.28
Infrastructure	436	0.22
Decarboni?ation	428	0.22
Research	412	0.21

Legend: * and ?wildcard searches

Table 10 Rank of the 10 most raised aspects of stakeholders in the public Twitter communication

Issue raised	Coding	Incidence (overall)	Share of total (%)
Energy efficiency	Energy Efficien*	68	0.03
Energy Efficiency Directive	Energy Efficiency Directive; EED	0	0.0
Financing	Financ*; Finance; Financing; Financial Support	628	0.32
Decarbonization	Decarboni*ation	428	0.22
Innovation	Innovation; innovative	546	0.28
Climate Law	Climate Law	20,916	10.56
Renewable energy	Renewable Energ*; Renewable Energy, Renewable Energies	161	0.08
Competitiveness	Competitiveness; competitive	195	0.10
National Energy and Climate Plans	National Energy and Climate Plans; NECPs; NECP	7	0.0
Article 7 EED	Article 7	0	0.0

Discussion

Our analysis has a twofold aim: first, to assess stakeholder readiness to support upgraded European clean energy policies and, second, to identify the salient issues the new policies are likely to bring up. We use a mixed-method approach combining qualitative analysis of external communications from core stakeholders with quantitative analysis of their responses to survey questions about issues in the EU Green Deal. Our results provide insight into the political positioning of key stakeholders in the upcoming negotiations on the Green Deal's energy pillar. These results also permit testing the concept of "salience" as applied to the European energy and climate fields.

Clean Energy Components of the Green Deal

Our qualitative review and survey of core stakeholder positions showed strong internal coherence in each of the four stakeholder groups, most notably in the group of Consultancy/Think Tanks. This suggests a potentially strong influence from this group in the upcoming process of agenda-setting and policy formulation. Typically, members of this stakeholder group – consultants – prepare the background studies commissioned by the European Commission to underpin their policy impact assessments. As such, certain confidentiality would be expected, which might explain our results that found this group silent in terms of external communications on Green Deal issues.

Regarding the other core stakeholder groups, our results suggest overall alignment in relative salience on the issues raised in external communications with the general public's Twitter topics: renewable energy capacities and targets are to be increased; energy efficiency is to be given greater priority in legislation.

As far as renewable energies are concerned, there is not much difference between the internal and external positioning of core stakeholders: renewable energy is important, but it is not the focus of the Green Deal debate. Social media communications underpin the importance of renewable energies for decarbonization and industrial competitiveness, thereby linking this specific topic to the leitmotif of the Green Deal. The majority of stakeholder tweets on renewable energy call for a robust industrial policy for renewable energy, including increased investment support. This mirrors assessments of the Clean Energy Package in the literature (Adedoyin et al. 2020; Hobbs et al. 2020).

Both internal and external communications focus on (re-)installing national renewable energy targets or sector targets. This concept was part of the 2009 Renewable Energy Directive but was dropped in the revised 2018 Directive due to opposition from the member states. This leaves a certain regulatory gap, inter alia as the EU legal framework lacks a clear policy for using renewables for heating and cooling purposes (Bosselaar et al. 2019). Our results suggest that strong stakeholder pressure will emerge to reengage in the discussion of national targets for renewable energies with a time horizon of 2030 and 2050. This confirms earlier findings on stakeholder assessments of the outcomes of the Clean Energy Package (Knodt and Ringel 2019a).

The situation is different for energy efficiency. Here, our results suggest a significant difference between internal and external salience. In the social media tweets from the public, energy efficiency seems to lack salience; it is a rather minor topic discussed in the context of the Climate Law. However, in stakeholder tweets, energy efficiency has a very high salience and is the focus of the Green Deal debate. Stakeholder demands are also more detailed and include technical details of the legislation, which is (naturally) not the case with the tweets of the general public. The focus on energy efficiency is even greater when analyzing internal salience, where energy efficiency scores high ratings.

First and foremost, the stakeholder groups align strongly around the demand for national energy efficiency targets to underpin the European 2030 objective. Second, they suggest stepping up the EED's energy efficiency obligation schemes (Article 7 EED; see Bertoldi et al. 2019), as a sort of quasi-national target. Only after these steps do demands for further detailed measures arise. This internal call for a more binding framework aligns with external communications that ask for making energy efficiency the core of the refocused European climate policy, especially given the history of moderate policy results so far (Capros et al. 2018; Knodt and Ringel 2019a; Bertoldi 2020; Bertoldi and Mosconi 2020). As the most cited and shared tweet sequence among the core stakeholders reads, the call is to "Enlighten the climate law with energy efficiency first!".

Summing up these findings, our analysis suggests that stakeholders are willing to take up the debate on re-opening the Clean Energy Directives. Their positioning is strongly influenced by the earlier debates over the Winter Package. Whereas the debates in the renewable energy field seem to be less contentious, the multiple internal communications on energy efficiency show a stronger will to engage in a more binding framework. This can be interpreted as a cautious view of the effectiveness of the "harder soft governance" (Knodt and Ringel 2019b; Knodt et al. 2020) installed in the Governance Regulation of the Clean Energy Package (Knodt et al. 2021).

Assessment of Salience

A further important finding of our study concerns the concept of *salience* and its applicability to the energy and climate policy fields. Issue salience can be influenced by multiple factors. The four factors observed in the literature are *governmental agenda, stakeholder strategy, type of stakeholder group,* and *divisiveness of issue.* If the *governmental agenda* and activity changes to a certain subject, for example, a new legislative proposal, stakeholder groups tend to prioritize the subject highlighted by the government, and hence salience of certain issues rises (Baumgartner et al. 2011; Fraussen et al. 2018). This can be seen clearly in the external communications of our core stakeholders that called for more ambitious clean energy policies to anchor both decarbonization efforts and the Climate Law.

Differences in issue salience can also occur because stakeholder groups pursue different goals that require different *stakeholder strategies.* Stakeholders that pursue more general interests are more likely to address the general public with statements about broader subjects or problems. Stakeholders that pursue technical goals are more likely to address bureaucrats and policy-makers directly with detailed statements on a subject, like a legislative proposal (Binderkrantz and Krøyer 2012). Here again, these findings may explain differences in internal and external communications that we observed, notably in the energy efficiency field.

Regarding the *type of stakeholders,* a reciprocal relationship between stakeholder and issue salience exists. NGOs need public support to survive. Therefore, they tend to support issues that are already salient to the public to attract more members. Industry associations have firms as members and do not depend on the public directly, so industry associations are more likely to focus on issues less salient to the public than those worked on by NGOs (Dür and Mateo 2014).

The public *divisiveness of issue* refers to a high public salience and divisiveness of an issue resulting in a divide between industry associations and NGOs. Industry stakeholders tend to withdraw from the public sphere if an issue gets too divisive; they then use more discreet channels of communication or a change of strategy to maintain their ability to influence (Woll 2013). In contrast, high public salience is an opportunity for NGOs to win public support and increase the level of their influence. In theory, a divisive issue should therefore lead to differences in issue salience between different stakeholder groups, though this assumption is contested in the literature (Carroll et al. 2014). By comparing industry and NGO salience, our study tends to confirm the theory. We show that Clean Energy in the Green Deal is not a particularly divisive issue for the stakeholder groups or the public. Stakeholder views on issues are closely aligned as the intergroup comparison shows and the public issue salience also aligns with these views. The industry stakeholders, therefore, do not need to change their strategy to more discreet channels of communication because of the alignment with NGOs and the other stakeholder views regarding the non-divisive issues.

Limitations of This Study and Need for Further Research

As with all stated-preference studies, self-report and selection biases are potential weaknesses of our study instrument. The questionnaire, however, was constructed to mitigate these biases. Firstly, it used neutral language from historical decisions and experiences rather than focusing on options per se. Secondly, topics susceptible to bias, especially in the assessment of target settings, were verified and reliability was validated by applying open-ended questions (i.e., the test-retest approach). Third, the questions were carefully ordered to avoid bias.

A further limitation is the small number of interviews. This should be considered in perspective: The population of European stakeholders covering the energy and climate fields is small. Having said that, our survey covers "bundling organizations" with a significant outreach and significant power for opinion shaping. We also took steps to validate results with stakeholders by sharing the survey results via email and retrieving individual feedback from interested parties. An overall majority of stakeholders (re-)contacted confirmed that the findings mirrored their view of the overall stakeholder perception or "what is in the Brussels' air," as one respondent put it.

Next, our study was limited to an observation period that was largely characterized by political uncertainty about detailed policy actions in the clean energy field. It would be worthwhile to follow up on this study once the detailed Commission proposals are tabled.

Conclusion and Policy Implications

Our study sought insight into stakeholder readiness to pressure for upgraded European clean energy policies. We applied a mixed-methods approach, comprising a qualitative read-out of 182 stakeholder position papers, 198,128 Twitter messages, and an in-depth survey of 20 key European stakeholders. Regarding the development of European energy policy, we find that core stakeholders will push for more action regarding energy efficiency, less so with renewable energies. Our core group argues strongly for a framework of national targets in both policy fields. This suggests that on a general level, stakeholders are wary about the "harder soft governance" installed in the framework of the Clean Energy Package and would prefer more binding governance.

On a conceptual level, our study serves to test the notion of salience in the energy and climate policy fields. We find our results tend to confirm findings on actor and issue salience, as witnessed in other studies on different policy fields.

Cross-References

▶ Sustainable Europe: Narrative Potential in the EU's Political Communication

Acknowledgments Funding from the Kopernikus-Projekt Ariadne (FKZ 03SFK5LO) by the German Federal Ministry of Education and Research is gratefully acknowledged.

Supplementary Material

The supplementary material can be accessed via https://www.politikwissenschaft.tu-darmstadt.de/media/politikwissenschaft/ifp_bilder/arbeitsbereiche_bilder/vergleich_integration/projekte_vergleich_integration/ariadne/Supplementary_material_2021.pdf.

References

Abbas, M. (2020). Decarbonizing trade policy. *Policy Options to Build a European Decarbonized Trade Policy*. Montreal: Centre d'études sur l'intégration et la mondialisation (CEIM). https://doi.org/10.13140/RG.2.2.23887.84646.

Adedoyin, F. F., Alola, A. A., & Bekun, F. V. (2020). Growth impact of transition from non-renewable to renewable energy in the EU: The role of research and development expenditure. *Renewable Energy, 159*(2020), 1139–1145. https://doi.org/10.1016/j.renene.2020.06.015.

Ålander, M., Bendiek, A., Bossong, R., Geden, O., Ondarza, N. von, & Tokarski, P. (2020). Neue Initiativen für eine gelähmte Union. Nach der Ankündigungswelle braucht die EU einen politikfeldübergreifenden Reformansatz. *SWP-Aktuell, 2020/A07*, p. 8. Stiftung Wissenschaft und Politik (SWP). https://doi.org/10.18449/2020A07.

Allenbach, K., Bentz, J., Coninx, I., Leitner, M., Lourenço, T. C., Rohat, G. T., & Swart, R. (2019). Foresight promotion report for policy & decision-makers: Work package 4 – Institutional Strenghtening task 4.3 – Promote foresight activities. Placard Network. https://www.researchgate.net/publication/324223229_Foresight_for_policy_decision-makers_Work_Package_4-institutional_strengthening_Task_43-Promote_Foresight. Accessed 05 Nov 2021.

Baumgartner, F. R., Larsen-Price, H. A., Leech, B. L., & Rutledge, P. (2011). Congressional and presidential effects on the demand for lobbying. *Political Research Quarterly, 64*(1), 3–16. https://doi.org/10.1177/1065912909343578.

Bayer, E., Cowart, R., Fabbri, M., & Rosenow, J. (2017). Assessing the European Union's energy efficiency policy: Will the winter package deliver on 'Efficiency First'? *Energy Research & Social Science, 26*(2017), 72–79. https://doi.org/10.1016/j.erss.2017.01.022.

Belyi, A., & Piebalgs, A. (2020). Towards bottom-up approach to European Green Deal: Lessons learned from the Baltic Gas Market. *Policy Brief 4*, p. 12. Florence School of Regulation. https://cadmus.eui.eu/bitstream/handle/1814/66149/PB_2020_04_FSR_Energy.pdf?sequence=1&isAllowed=y. Accessed 05 Nov 2021.

Bergamaschi, L. (2020). There is no Green Deal without a just transition. IAI Commentaries, 20, p. 5. https://www.academia.edu/41716127/There_Is_No_Green_Deal_without_a_Just_Transition. Accessed 05 Nov 2021.

Bertoldi, P. (2020). Overview of the European Union policies to promote more sustainable behaviours in energy end-users. In M. Lopes, C. Henggeler Antunes, & K. B. Janda (Eds.), *Energy and behaviour. Towards a low carbon future* (pp. 451–477). Cambridge: Academic.

Bertoldi, P., & Mosconi, R. (2020). Do energy efficiency policies save energy? A new approach based on energy policy indicators (in the EU Member States). *Energy Policy, 139*(2020), 111–320. https://doi.org/10.1016/j.enpol.2020.111320.

Bertoldi, P., Fawcett, T., & Rosenow, J. (2019). Energy efficiency obligation schemes: Their future in the EU. *Energy Efficiency, 12*(1), 57–71. https://doi.org/10.1007/s12053-018-9657-1.

Beyers, J., Dür, A., & Wonka, A. (2018). The political salience of EU policies. *Journal of European Public Policy, 25*(11), 1726–1737. https://doi.org/10.1080/13501763.2017.1337213.

Bianchi, M., & Colantoni, L. (2020). Energy Union Watch: What future for Europe's climate and energy policy? *Energy Union Watch, 16*, p. 34. Istituto Affari Internazionali. https://www.academia.edu/41841687/Energy_Union_Watch_No._16_Special_Issue_January_2020_. Accessed 05 Nov 2021.

Binderkrantz, A. S., & Krøyer, S. (2012). Customizing strategy: Policy goals and interest group strategies. *Interest Groups and Advocacy, 1*(1), 115–138. https://doi.org/10.1057/iga.2012.6.

Bode, L., Sayre, B., Shah, C., Shah, D., & Wilcox, D. (2010). Agenda setting in a Digital Age. Tracking attention to California proposition 8 in social media, Online News, and Conventional News. *Policy & Internet, 2*(2), 7–32. https://doi.org/10.2202/1944-2866.1040.

Bosselaar, L., Braungardt, S., Bürger, V., & Zieger, J. (2019). How to include cooling in the EU renewable energy directive? Strategies and policy implications. *Energy Policy, 129*(2019), 260–267. https://doi.org/10.1016/j.enpol.2019.02.027.

Brodny, J., & Tutak, M. (2020). Analyzing similarities between the European Union Countries in terms of the structure and volume of energy production from renewable energy sources. *Energies, 13*(4), 913. https://doi.org/10.3390/en13040913.

Bros, A. (2020). What should the EU do regarding Decarbonization? *Gas Lighthouse, 1*, p. 5. Energy Project. https://www.academia.edu/42069694/Gas_Lighthouse_1_What_Should_the_EU_Do_Regarding_Decarbonization. Accessed 05 Nov 2021.

Cameron, A., Claeys, G., Midões, C., & Tagliapietra, S. (2020). How good is the European Commission's just transition fund proposal? *Policy Contribution, 4*, 11. http://aei.pitt.edu/102554/1/PC%2D04_2020%2DV2.pdf. Accessed 05 Nov 2021.

Cano, M. C. (2019). Global tax 50 2019: Ursula von der Leyen. *International Tax Review*. https://www.internationaltaxreview.com/article/b1jdvlg51cytt7/global-tax-50-2019-ursula-von-der-leyen. Accessed 05 Nov 2021.

Capros, P., DeVita, A., Evangelopoulou, S., Kannavou, M., Petropoulos, A., Siskos, P., Tasios, N., & Zazias, G. (2018). Outlook of the EU energy system up to 2050: The case of scenarios prepared for European Commission's "clean energy for all Europeans" package using the PRIMES model. *Energy Strategy Reviews, 22*(2018), 255–263. https://doi.org/10.1016/j.esr.2018.06.009.

Carroll, B. J., Lowery, D., & Rasmussen, A. (2014). Representatives of the public? Public opinion and interest group activity. *European Journal of Political Research, 53*(2), 250–268. https://doi.org/10.1111/1475-6765.12036.

Catuti, M., Egenhofer, C., Elkerbout, M., Kustova, I., Núñez Ferrer, J., Rizos, V. (2020). The European Green Deal after Corona: Implications for EU climate policy. *CEPS Policy Insights, No 2020-06* / March 2020. Centre for European Policy Studies. http://aei.pitt.edu/102671/. Accessed 05 Nov 2021.

Ciot, M.-G., Franțescu, D., Popescu, M.-F., & Volintiru, C. (2019). Political support at EU level for energy and environmental policies. *Romanian Journal of European Affairs, 19*(2).

Cittadino, F. (2019). There's a climate emergency! A bit more than a warning, a bit less than a fully-fledged commitment. https://www.eurac.edu/en/blogs/eureka/theres-a-climate-emergency-a-bit-more-than-a-warning-a-bit-less-than-a-fully-fledged-commitment. Accessed 5 Nov 2021.

Claeys, G., Tagliapietra, S., & Zachmann, G. (2019): How to make the European Green Deal work. *Bruegel Policy Contribution,* 13/2019.

Claringbould, D., Koch, M., & Owen, P. (2019). Sustainable finance: The European Union's approach to increasing sustainable investments and growth – Opportunities and challenges. *Vierteljahreshefte zur Wirtschaftsforschung, 88*(2), 11–27. https://doi.org/10.3790/vjh.88.2.11.

de Stefano, G. (2020). Measurable environmental protection as a necessity for competition law. https://doi.org/10.2139/ssrn.3533499.

Dias, A., Nosowicz, A., & Seeuws, S. (2020). EU border carbon adjustment and the WTO: Hand in hand towards tackling climate change. *Global Trade and Customs Journal, 15*(1), 15–23.

Dullien, S., Gechert, S., Herzog-Stein, A., Rietzler, K., Stein, U., Tober, S., & Watt, A. (2020). Wirtschaftspolitische Herausforderungen 2020: Im Zeichen des Klimawandels. *IMK Report Nr. 155*. Düsseldorf: Hans-Böckler-Stiftung, Institut für Makroökonomie und Konjunkturforschung (IMK). https://www.econstor.eu/handle/10419/213413. Accessed 05 Nov 2021.

Dür, A., & Mateo, G. (2014). Public opinion and interest group influence. How citizen groups derailed the Anti-Counterfeiting Trade Agreement. *Journal of European Public Policy, 21*(8), 1199–1217. https://doi.org/10.1080/13501763.2014.900893.

Energiewende, A., Verkehrswende, A., & Max-Planck-Institute for Biogeochemistry, Technical University of Denmark. (2020). Making the most of offshore wind: Re-evaluating the potential of offshore wind in the German North Sea. https://static.agora-energiewende.de/fileadmin/Projekte/2019/Offshore_Potentials/176_A-EW_A-VW_Offshore-Potentials_Publication_WEB.pdf. Accessed 05 Nov 2021.

EuroMemo Group. (2020). A Green New Deal for Europe. Opportunities and Challenges: EuroMemorandum 2020. http://www2.euromemorandum.eu/uploads/euromemorandum_2020.pdf. Accessed 05 Nov 2021.

European Commission. (2016a). Clean energy for all Europeans. Website overview. https://ec.europa.eu/energy/en/news/commission-proposes-new-rules-consumer-centred-clean-energy-transition. Accessed 05 Nov 2021.

European Commission (2016b). *Clean energy for all Europeans. Communication. COM/2016/860 final* (pp. 13). Brussels: European Commission.

European Commission (2016c). *Proposal for a regulation on the governance of the Energy Union.* COM/2016/759 final (pp. 89). Brussels: European Commission.

European Commission. (2016d). *New energy union governance to deliver common goals.* Memo (pp. 5). Brussels: European Commission.

European Commission. (2017). Commission welcomes agreement on energy performance of buildings. Press release. http://europa.eu/rapid/press-release_IP-17-5129_en.htm. Accessed 05 Nov 2021.

European Commission. (2018a). A clean planet for all. A European long-term strategic vision for a prosperous, modern, competitive and climate neutral economy. https://ec.europa.eu/energy/sites/ener/files/documents/2_dgclima_rungemetzger.pdf. Accessed 05 Nov 2021.

European Commission. (2018b). Directive (EU) 2018/2001 of the European Parliament and of the Council of 11 December 2018 on the promotion of the use of energy from renewable sources. PE/48/2018/REV/1. https://eur-lex.europa.eu/legal-content/EN/TXT/?uri=CELEX%3A32018L2001. Accessed 05 Nov 2021.

European Commission. (2018c). Directive (EU) 2018/844 of the European Parliament and of the Council of 30 May 2018 amending Directive 2010/31/EU on the energy performance of buildings and Directive 2012/27/EU on energy efficiency. https://eur-lex.europa.eu/legal-content/EN/TXT/?uri=uriserv%3AOJ.L_.2018.156.01.0075.01.ENG. Accessed 05 Nov 2021.

European Commission. (2018d). Directive (EU) 2018/2002 of the European Parliament and of the Council of 11 December 2018 amending Directive 2012/27/EU on energy efficiency. https://eur-lex.europa.eu/legal-content/EN/TXT/?uri=uriserv%3AOJ.L_.2018.328.01.0210.01.ENG. Accessed 05 Nov 2021.

European Commission. (2018e). Regulation (EU) 2018/1999 of the European Parliament and of the Council of 11 December 2018 on the Governance of the Energy Union and Climate Action, amending Regulations (EC) No 663/2009 and (EC) No 715/2009 of the European Parliament and of the Council, Directives 94/22/EC, 98/70/EC, 2009/31/EC, 2009/73/EC, 2010/31/EU, 2012/27/EU and 2013/30/EU of the European Parliament and of the Council, Council Directives 2009/119/EC and (EU) 2015/652 and repealing Regulation (EU) No 525/2013 of the European Parliament and of the Council. https://eur-lex.europa.eu/legal-content/EN/TXT/?uri=uriserv:OJ.L_.2018.328.01.0001.01.ENG&toc=OJ:L:2018:328:FULL. Accessed 05 Nov 2021.

European Commission. (2018f). The Energy Union gets simplified, robust and transparent governance: Commission welcomes ambitious agreement. http://europa.eu/rapid/press-release_IP-18-4229_en.htm. Accessed 05 Nov 2021.

European Commission. (2019). Communication from the Commission to the European Parliament, the European Council, the Council, the European Economic and Social Committee and the Committee of the Regions. The European Green Deal. COM/2019/640 final. https://eur-lex.europa.eu/resource.html?uri=cellar:b828d165-1c22-11ea-8c1f-01aa75ed71a1.0002.02/DOC_1&format=PDF. Accessed 05 Nov 2021.

European Commission. (2020). Proposal for a Regulation establishing the framework for achieving climate neutrality and amending Regulation (EU) 2018/1999 (European Climate Law). COM/2020/80 final. https://eur-lex.europa.eu/legal-content/EN/TXT/?qid=1588581905912&uri=CELEX:52020PC0080. Accessed 05 Nov 2021.

European Council. (2019). European Council meeting (12 December 2019). Conclusions. EUCO 29/19. Brussels: European Council.

Fairbrass, J., Herranz-Surrallés, A., & Solorio, I. (2020). Renegotiating authority in the energy union: A framework for analysis. *Journal of European Integration, 42*(1), 1–17. https://doi.org/10.1080/07036337.2019.1708343.

Field, A. (2018). *Discovering statistics using IBM SPSS statistics*. Los Angeles: SAGE.

Fischedick, M., & Lechtenböhmer, S. (2020). Integrierte Klima-Industriepolitik als Kernstück des europäischen Green Deal. *In Brief - Wuppertaler Impulse zur Nachhaltigkeit, No 9*. Wuppertal Institut für Klima, Umwelt, Energie. https://epub.wupperinst.org/files/7482/7482_klima-industriepolitik.pdf. Accessed 05 Nov 2021.

Fraussen, B., Halpin, D. R., & Nownes, A. J. (2018). The balancing act of establishing a policy agenda: Conceptualizing and measuring drivers of issue prioritization within interest groups. *Governance, 31*(3), 215–237. https://doi.org/10.1111/gove.12284.

Garabetian, T., Palmer, P., & Sahin, G. (2019). European stakeholders call upon the new Commission to make 2030 climate target a priority. http://www.caneurope.org/publications/press-

releases/1857-european-stakeholders-call-upon-the-new-commission-to-make-2030-climate-target-a-priority. Accessed 05 Nov 2021.
Geden, O., & Schenuit, F. (2019). Konfliktfeld Klimaneutralität. Ausgestaltung des EU-Nullemissionsziels und Folgen für Deutschland. *Energiewirtschaftliche Tagesfragen, 69*(11), 28–31.
Giuli, M., Hedberg, A., & Piqueres, S. L. (2020). Adapting to change: Time for climate resilience and a new adaptation strategy. *EPC Issue Paper 5* March 2020. Issue Paper – Sustainable Prosperity for Europe Programme. European Policy Centre. http://aei.pitt.edu/102572/. Accessed 05 Nov 2021.
Goldthau, A. (2019). Global energy in transition: How the EU should navigate new realities and risks. *Policy Brief, 4*, pp. 8. German Council on Foreign Relations. https://www.academia.edu/41825701/Global_Energy_in_Transition._How_the_EU_Should_Navigate_New_Realities_and_Risks. Accessed 05 Nov 2021.
Hainsch, K., von Hirschhausen, C., Holz, F., Kemfert, C., Löffler, K., & Oei, P.-Y. (2019). Neues Klima für Europa: Klimaschutzziele für 2030 sollten angehoben werden. *DIW-Wochenbericht, 86*(41), 753–760. https://doi.org/10.18723/diw_wb:2019-41-1.
Hobbs, B. F., van Hout, M., Koutstaal, P. R., & Özdemir, Ö. (2020). Capacity vs. energy subsidies for promoting renewable investment: Benefits and costs for the EU power market. *Energy Policy, 137*(3), 111–166. https://doi.org/10.1016/j.enpol.2019.111166.
Höh, A., Schwan, G., & Treichel, K. (2017). Die Governance der europäischen Energieunion. Zwischen nationalen Energiestrategien und Pariser Klimazielen. Humboldt Viadrina Governance Platform. Bericht ETR/02-2017. https://www.governance-platform.org/wp-content/uploads/2017/11/HVGP_ETR_sb6-Bericht_Energieunion.pdf. Accessed 05 Nov 2021.
Hughes, K. (2020). Smaller States' strategies and influence in an EU of 27: Lessons for Scotland. Policy paper. UCL European Institute; Scottish Centre on European Relations. https://www.ucl.ac.uk/european-institute/sites/european-institute/files/small_states_policy_paper.pdf. Accessed 05 Nov 2021.
Jäger-Waldau, A. (2020). Snapshot of photovoltaics – February 2020. *Energies, 13*(4), 930. https://doi.org/10.3390/en13040930.
Kemfert, C. (2019). Green Deal for Europe: More climate protection and fewer fossil fuel wars. *Intereconomics, 54*(6), 353–358. https://doi.org/10.1007/s10272-019-0853-9.
Kingston, S. (2020). The polluter pays principle in EU climate law. An effective tool before the Courts? *Climate Law, 10*(1), 1–27. https://doi.org/10.1163/18786561-01001001.
Knodt, M., & Ringel, M. (2018). The governance of the European Energy Union: Efficiency, effectiveness and acceptance of the Winter Package 2016. *Energy Policy, 112*(2018), 209–220. https://doi.org/10.1016/j.enpol.2017.09.047.
Knodt, M., & Ringel, M. (2019a). EU 2030 energy policies: A review of the clean energy package from a stakeholder perspective. *Zeitschrift für Umweltpolitik und Umweltrecht, 4*(2019), 445–467.
Knodt, M., & Ringel, M. (2019b). Creating convergence of National Energy Policies by increased cooperation: EU energy governance and its impact on the German energy transition. In E. Gawel (Ed.), *The European dimension of Germany's energy transition: Opportunities and conflicts* (pp. 123–145). Cham: Springer International Publishing.
Knodt, M., Müller, R., & Ringel, M. (2020). 'Harder' soft governance in the European Energy Union. *Journal of Environmental Policy & Planning, 2*(1), 1–14. https://doi.org/10.1080/1523908X.2020.1781604.
Knodt, M., Müller, R., & Schlacke, S. (2021). (Un)Fit for 55? Lehren aus der Implementation der Governance-Verordnung. Ariadne-Analyse, https://ariadneprojekt.de/publikation/analyse-unfit-for-55/. Accessed 05 Nov 2021.
Kontovas, C. A., & Psaraftis, H. N. (2020). Influence and transparency at the IMO. The name of the game. *Maritime economics and logistics, 22/2020*, 211. https://doi.org/10.1057/s41278-020-00149-4.
Krail, M., Ringel, M., Rohde, C., & Schlomann, B. (2016). Towards a green economy in Germany? The role of energy efficiency policies. *Applied Energy, 179*(2016), 1293–1303. https://doi.org/10.1016/j.apenergy.2016.03.063.

Krenek, A., Schratzenstaller, M., & Sommer, M. (2020). A WTO-compatible border tax adjustment for the ETS to finance the EU Budget. *WIFO 596*. WIFO. https://econpapers.repec.org/repec:wfo:wpaper:y:2020:i:596. Accessed 05 Nov 2021.

Landesmann, M., & Stöllinger, R. (2020). The European Union's industrial policy: What are the Main challenges? *Policy Notes and Reports, 36*. Wiener Institut für Internationale Wirtschaftsvergleiche. https://wiiw.ac.at/the-european-union-s-industrial-policy-what-are-the-main-challenges-dlp-5211.pdf. Accessed 05 Nov 2021.

Lopez, P., Nuffel, L. van, Post, M., Rademakers, K., & Yearwood, J. (2016). Energy union: Key decisions for the realisation of a fully integrated energy market. Study for the ITRE Committee, DG IPOL, Policy Department A. IP/A/ITRE/2015-01 (pp. 136). Brussels: European Parliament.

Löschel, A. (2020). European Green Deal und deutsche Energiewende zusammen denken! *Wirtschaftsdienst, 100*(2), 78–79. https://doi.org/10.1007/s10273-020-2566-x.

Lucchese, M., & Pianta, M. (2020). Europe's alternative: A Green Industrial Policy for sustainability and convergence. *MRPA papers 98705*, pp. 17. Scuola Normale Superiore; Istat. https://mpra.ub.uni-muenchen.de/98705/1/MPRA_paper_98705.pdf. Accessed 05 Nov 2021.

Lucchese, M., Nascia, L., & Pianta, M. (2020). The policy space for a novel industrial policy in Europe. *Industrial and Corporate Change, 29*(3), 779–795. https://doi.org/10.1093/icc/dtz075. 10.1093/icc/dtz663.

McWilliams, B., & Zachmann, G. (2020). A European carbon border tax: Much pain, little gain. *Bruegel Policy Contribution, 5/2020*. http://aei.pitt.edu/102592/1/PC%2D05%2D2020%2D050320v2.pdf. Accessed 05 Nov 2021.

Meyer-Ohlendorf, N. (2015). An effective governance system for 2030 EU climate and energy policy: Design and requirements. Discussion Paper. *Ecologic Discussion Paper Series*, 1–25.

Neuhoff, K. (2020). Ein europäischer grüner Deal mit vielen Facetten: Kommentar. *DIW-Wochenbericht, 5*. DIW. https://www.econstor.eu/bitstream/10419/214221/1/1690052961.pdf. Accessed 05 Nov 2021.

Olczak, M., & Piebalgs, A. (2020). Methane emission reduction: An important step in strengthening the sustainability dimension in gas network companies. *Policy Briefs, 13*. Florence School of Regulation - Energy. https://cadmus.eui.eu/handle/1814/66751. Accessed 05 Nov 2021.

Rehn, O. (2019). Sustainable finance: A road towards a climate neutral Europe. Bank of Finland Articles on the Economy. Bank of Finland. https://helda.helsinki.fi/bof/bitstream/handle/123456789/16383/bofbulletin_blog_20191029_rehn.pdf?sequence=1. Accessed 05 Nov 2021.

Ringel, M. (2016). Energy efficiency policy governance in a multi-level administration structure. *Energy Efficiency, 10*(3), 1–24. https://doi.org/10.1007/s12053-016-9484-1.

Sajn, N. (2017). Revised energy efficiency directive. European Parliamentary Research Service, pp. 1–8.

Sartori, N. (2019). Five pillars for a CO2-free industry in Europe and Italy. *IAI Commentaries, 60*, 6. Istituto Affari Internazionali. https://www.academia.edu/40732360/Five_Pillars_for_a_CO2-Free_Industry_in_Europe_and_Italy. Accessed 05 Nov 2021.

Schenuit, F. (2019). Lichtblick EU? Internationale Politik und Gesellschaft (IPG-Journal). https://www.ipg-journal.de/rubriken/nachhaltigkeit-energie-und-klimapolitik/artikel/lichtblick-eu-3952/. Accessed 05 Nov 2021.

Scholl, A. (2009). *Die Befragung*. Konstanz: UVK/UTB.

Simola, H. (2020). CO2 emissions embodied in EU-China trade and carbon border tax. *BOFIT Policy Brief, 4*. https://helda.helsinki.fi/bof/handle/123456789/16561. Accessed 05 Nov 2021.

Southwell, B., & Weeks, B. (2010). The Symbiosis of news coverage and aggregate online search behavior: Obama, rumors, and presidential politics. *Mass Communication and Society, 13*(4), 341–360. https://doi.org/10.1080/15205430903470532.

Tesche, T. (2020). Why 'greening' the EU's institutions remains far from straightforward. LSE European Politics and Policy (EUROPP) Blog. https://blogs.lse.ac.uk/europpblog/2020/01/17/why-greening-the-eus-institutions-remains-far-from-straightforward/. Accessed 05 Nov 2021.

Thaler, P. (2020). Energy cooperation between the EU and Switzerland: Partners by destiny in search of a new model. GovTran Policy Brief 01. GovTran Network. https://www.alexandria.unisg.ch/259117. Accessed 05 Nov 2021.

Umpfenbach, K. (2015). Streamlining planning and reporting requirements in the EU Energy Union framework. http://ecologic.eu/sites/files/publication/2015/planning_reporting_ecologic_institute_final_20150908_2.pdf. Accessed 05 Nov 2021.

Warntjen, A. (2012). Measuring salience in EU legislative politics. *European Union Politics, 13*(1), 168–182. https://doi.org/10.1177/1465116511428495.

Watt, A. (2020). The European Green Deal: Will the ends, will the means? https://www.socialeurope.eu/the-european-green-deal-will-the-ends-will-the-means. Accessed 05 Nov 2021.

Wilson, A. B. (2017). Briefing: Governance of the Energy Union. European Parliamentary Research Service, pp. 1–8.

Woll, C. (2013). Lobbying under pressure: The effect of salience on European Union Hedge Fund Regulation. *Journal of Common Market Studies, 51*(3), 555–572. https://doi.org/10.1111/j.1468-5965.2012.02314.x.

Cities in European Energy and Climate Governance

18

Jörg Kemmerzell

Contents

Introduction	412
Cities in Energy Sector Development	413
Cities in European Energy and Climate Governance	414
Vertical Governance	415
Horizontal Governance	417
Integration of Vertical and Horizontal Governance	419
The Covenant of Mayors for Climate & Energy	420
Foundation and Instruments of the Covenant of Mayors	420
Membership Patterns of the Covenant of Mayors	421
Governance Achievements and Shortcomings of the Covenant of Mayors	423
Conclusion	424
Cross-References	425
References	425

Abstract

With the growing awareness of climate change, cities have increasingly become the focus of energy policy, as they are not only considered the main originators of global climate change but particularly places where innovations toward low carbon transitions take place. Notably in the European context, municipal policies are embedded in a dense structure of multilevel governance arrangements establishing a unique political opportunity structure of energy and climate policy. This chapter gives, firstly, a general overview of the role of cities in the development of the energy sector in Europe. Secondly, it concentrates on their current position in European energy and climate policy and distinguishes three forms of governance: vertical governance, horizontal governance, and an integrated type of governance that conflates the vertical and the horizontal dimension. Thirdly,

---

J. Kemmerzell (✉)
Institute of Political Science, Technical University of Darmstadt, Darmstadt, Germany
e-mail: kemmerzell@pg.tu-darmstadt.de

© Springer Nature Switzerland AG 2022
M. Knodt, J. Kemmerzell (eds.), *Handbook of Energy Governance in Europe*,
https://doi.org/10.1007/978-3-030-43250-8_69

the chapter pays closer attention to a specific organization of the latter type, the Covenant of Mayors for Climate & Energy. Finally, it provides an outlook of the role of cities in European energy governance, particularly in the context of the European Union's Fit for 55 package.

Keywords

Multilevel governance · Cities · Energy governance · Climate policy · Covenant of mayors · European Union · Orchestration · Trans-local action

Introduction

With the growing awareness of climate change, cities have increasingly become the focus of energy policy, as they are not only considered the main originators of global climate change but particularly places where innovations toward low carbon transitions take place (Bulkeley et al. 2011). Notably in the European context, municipal policies are embedded in a dense structure of multilevel governance arrangements (Hofmeister 2022; Busch et al. 2018; Benz et al. 2015; Bouteligier 2013; Andonova et al. 2009; Kern and Bulkeley 2009) establishing a unique political opportunity structure of energy and climate policy.

From the perspective of the European Union (EU), municipalities were hardly considered as relevant actors in energy governance for a long time. However, the establishment of sustainability in the context of climate change as a particular goal of energy policy increased the importance of the local level and led to its stronger recognition in multilevel governance (Hooghe and Marks 2003). Since the 1990s, the EU has addressed climate change and the linked transition of the European energy sector by various instruments. Sustainable energy and climate policies are usually part of general long-term strategies, like the *Climate and Energy Package* of 2008 (European Commission 2008a, b) its successor, the *Climate and Energy Framework* of 2014 (European Commission 2014), and the recently proposed *European Green Deal* (European Commission 2019). European secondary law-making takes place under these general frameworks and use both regulatory and non-regulatory policy instruments. Examples of non-regulatory instruments are programs providing funding opportunities for different actors, such as municipalities. As a unique innovation solely targeting cities, the European Commission launched the *Covenant of Mayors* in 2008.

While multilevel governance *in Europe* cannot be properly understood without paying attention to the intermediate, national, and subnational levels, this chapter concentrates on the European dimension of local energy and climate policy. Therefore, we distinguish two analytic dimensions of multilevel governance: the involvement of cities in vertical climate governance and their participation in horizontal structures of climate governance, particularly transnational municipal networks.

This chapter gives, firstly, a general overview of the historical role of cities in the development of the energy sector. Secondly, I concentrate on current energy and climate policy and distinguish three forms of governance; *vertical* governance, *horizontal* governance, and a particular *integrated type* that conflates the vertical and the horizontal dimension (Kern 2019; Kemmerzell 2018; Kern 2014). Thirdly, the chapter pays closer attention to a specific organization of the latter type, the *Covenant of Mayors for Climate & Energy*. Based on a literature review and data provided by the organization, both achievements and shortcomings of this kind of orchestrated governance will be analyzed. Finally, I will provide an outlook of the role of cities in European energy governance, particularly in the context of the *European Green Deal,* resp. the *Fit for 55* package, launched by the European Commission in December 2019 (European Commission 2019).

Cities in Energy Sector Development

Municipalities played a major role in the development of centralized power and heat distribution in Europe. The electrification of the city (Schott 2014) on a broad scale, apart from isolated applications, emerged as an answer to multiple challenges of the industrial age and was often immediately managed by local authorities. Therefore, it is no surprise that in many countries power as well as gas networks came on a municipal scale "before nationalization" (Hannah 1979). In Britain, municipal utilities provided not only the networks but also energy supply (Berka 2018; Hannah 1979). A similar pattern developed in Germany, where industrial cities were the first to develop integrated energy networks. However, the energy law of 1935 established a structure of a few energy corporations responsible for energy supply and transmission, and many small local utilities responsible for energy distribution. The different actors were bonded by long-term contracts (Sack 2018). This system provided for an effective nationalization of the energy sector, which excluded the emerging regional monopolies from competition and stabilized the dominance of powerful corporate actors. However, e.g., Denmark displays a different pattern, as municipalities and local cooperatives were not only the nucleus of the energy sector but maintained a stronger position even in the era of widespread nationalization policies (Eikeland and Inderberg 2016). Therefore, Danish municipalities uphold their dominance in the heating sector, while cooperatives remained the most important actors in energy supply (Dyrhauge 2020).

However, the European picture displays a widespread trend toward centralization, nationalization, and corporatism in the energy sector, which emerged independently of the particular political-economic regime. Instead, technological innovations, like nuclear power or structural constraints of the industrial mass-society, particularly the claim to get access to energy any time in any place to constant and affordable prices, sustained this long-term development. Until the 1990s, energy policy of the European Community/European Union mainly concentrated on fair competition on a national market scale and later on the security of supply by restraining the dependence on energy imports. The subnational and municipal levels were not much considered by the European institutions in this era (Knodt 2016).

Two developments raised the importance of the local level in European energy governance. First, market liberalization led to a weakening of the entrenched corporatist structures in the energy sector with, however, double-edged effects on municipalities. On the one hand, municipalities gained new opportunities to become strategic actors in many areas of the energy sector, including energy supply. On the other hand, many financially burdened municipalities privatized utilities and lost political influence in energy policy. Secondly, the European Commission added sustainability to the still existing energy policy goals of competitiveness and security (European Commission 1995). In the White Paper *An Energy Policy for the European Union,* the Commission not only mentioned climate change and other environmental concerns of energy policy but also stressed the role of regions and municipalities in addressing the new challenges. The Commission paid attention to the rising awareness that cities play a crucial role in the mitigation of climate change and the related transition of energy systems. On a global scale, around 50% of the world population live in urban regions, cities have a share of about 75% of the world's energy consumption, and are responsible for roughly 80% of greenhouse gas emissions (Bulkeley et al. 2011; OECD 2010; Schreurs 2008). For Europe, the numbers are quite higher. Cities were at the same time main originators of climate change, victims of climate change, but also places where innovations toward a low carbon transition and climate experiments take place (Evans et al. 2016; Castán Broto and Bulkeley 2013; Bulkeley et al. 2011). In this regard, cities became a kind of *incubator* of policies, institutions, and governance arrangements that has the potential for *diffusion* and *upscaling* to peer cities as well as to upper jurisdictions (Kern 2019).

Cities in European Energy and Climate Governance

In the period after the adoption of the *United Nations Framework Convention on Climate Change* in 1992, climate change became a political issue in many European policy fields, particularly in energy policy. In the White Paper on Energy (s. a.), the Commission claimed that the EU should "encourage energy consumers through their local authorities to develop a more active role." The White Paper considers subnational entities as important actors to strengthen energy efficiency and promote renewable energy production, and it emphasizes "exchanges between the different regions or cities" as a "powerful catalyst" for technology and knowledge transfer (European Commission 1995). It declares that the Commission intends to facilitate such exchanges, particularly outside the confines of regional funding; an early notice of *vertical governance* and *orchestration* (see below). In its Green Paper *A European Strategy for Sustainable, Competitive and Secure Energy,* published 11 years after the White Paper, the Commission suggested an integrated approach "to tackling climate change" that addressed the scope of action and responsibilities in more detail. Local authorities were addressed, inter alia, to integrate the expansion of renewable energies in urban planning (European Commission 2006).

In common with the Commission's Communication *An Energy Policy for Europe* (European Commission 2007), the Green Paper served as the basis of the comprehensive *Climate and Energy Package* that was adopted by the European Council in

2008 (European Commission 2008a). Under the umbrella *Climate and Energy Package,* the EU adjusted several laws like the Directive on Energy Efficiency or the Directive on Renewable Energy to the *2020 goals.* It determined the goals of a 20% cut in greenhouse gas emissions, an increase in the share of renewable energy by 20%, and a 20% improvement of energy efficiency (based on 1990 numbers). While largely relying on familiar regulatory policy, the package also capitalized on incentive-based instruments and soft governance (Knodt and Ringel 2018). The EU Commission explicitly emphasized the importance of the local level in the debate on the package, as could be read in the quote by the then Energy Commissioner Andris Piebalgs who declared that "the approach to tackle the climate crisis can only be holistic (...). This complex picture is best managed at local level." Therefore, Piebalgs continues, "cities must become leading actors for implementing sustainable energy policies, and must be supported" (European Commission 2008b). In this context, subnational and municipal entities were included in large-scale European funding schemes like *Intelligent Energy Europe,* they were granted access to apply for funding within the European research program Horizon 2020, and a particular initiative was launched to facilitate municipal engagement in sustainable energy, the *Covenant of Mayors* (CoM). In the subsequent section, I will go into detail about the Covenant, since it represents the particular EU tool for integrating cities into the European Energy strategy. However, I will first outline the general patterns of cities' integration into the European multilevel system: *vertical governance, horizontal governance,* and *integrated governance,* a type of governance combining features of the former.

Vertical Governance

Vertical governance has been described as an "interplay between institutions" on different levels of authority that create interdependencies (Kern 2014, p. 114). In the EU these interdependencies result from the specific institutional structures of the EU and its member states. Most of the decisions are only feasible if different actors on different levels with diverging interests agree or cooperate. Consequently, the European multilevel governance system shapes institutional arrangements and specific political opportunity structures for municipalities (Princen and Kerremans 2008). The vertical relation of municipalities to upper governmental levels can take different forms. From the bottom-up perspective, cities can attempt to influence political decisions by lobbying and by up-loading of their policies. However, such options seem only relevant to a few major cities that have direct access (Liefferink and Wurzel 2018). More relevant in this regard became the strategies of municipal networks that create a transnational space in which municipal interests can be collectively voiced. From a top-down perspective, upper governmental authorities can develop collaborative programs, like funding schemes, to mobilize municipalities to contribute to the attainment of European (or national) goals.

On the European level, the EU Commission regularly set up funding schemes for research and development, or collaborative action that are open to municipalities, like the *Horizon* schemes. However, research data suggests that participation in such programs depends on particular structural and financial prerequisites. A survey on climate change mitigation in German major cities shows, e.g., that less than half of the cities with more than 100,000 inhabitants participated in at least one European-funded project. The picture is somewhat different if national and state-funded programs are concerned, where the vast majority of cities attained at least one program (Kemmerzell 2018, p. 50). This indicates that vertical energy and climate governance in the European multilevel system cannot be properly understood without paying attention to the intermediate levels. In some countries, national governments set up funding schemes that support local energy planning. Kern (2014, p. 119) points to the Dutch *BANS Agreement* and its successor, *SLOK*, which connected access to funding with the introduction of municipal climate action plans. Another example was the Swedish *Sustainable Municipalities Program* that supported networking on different sustainability-related topics like energy efficiency and provided financial resources for municipalities after their application for a particular project has been approved (Schaefter et al. 2013). In France, national law required local climate action plans from municipalities with more than 50.000 inhabitants by 2012 (Bendlin 2020). In Germany, the federal government 1997 already provided guidelines on the adoption of local climate protection and founded a federal service agency to support municipalities. While these guidelines can be coined as a soft governance approach concentrating on the spread of information and the distribution of knowledge, the *National Climate Initiative* in 2008 extended the merely consultative approach with a funding instrument, the *Climate Protection Directive* that has been updated several times. Under this directive, local authorities can apply for the co-funding of sustainable energy and climate plans, financial support for infrastructural modernization, and receive a partial refund for the employment of municipal climate and energy advisors. A closer look at the adoption of climate and sustainable energy concepts reveals an upturn after 2008, which indicates a strong influence of the *Climate Protection Directive* (Kemmerzell 2018, p. 49).

Kristine Kern further identified hierarchical governance as a unique form of governance that forces municipalities to comply with standards set by the EU or national governments. While vertical governance considered so far largely encompass voluntary action, hierarchy is characterized by strict top-down relations and the competence to superimpose policies on subordinate jurisdictions (Kern 2014). In European multilevel governance, hierarchy plays a rather limited role if it comes to the relation of the EU and municipalities. Even if European regulations, like the Energy Efficiency Directive, the Renewable Energy Directive, or the Emissions Trading System, have an indirect effect on the local level, they do not require compliance in a sense of *command and control.* Examples of hierarchical governance are restricted to national regulations that require particular municipal activities. Kern (2019, p. 135) mentions regulations in France and Britain, which require municipal authorities to develop local energy and climate plans or to regularly integrate climate mitigation into local planning processes. Those approaches differ from the German practice, as they do not make offers that a municipality can accept or not, but define mandatory standards.

Horizontal Governance

As already mentioned, municipalities may refer to collective action to get their voice heard at the European scale. Horizontal governance in energy and climate policy emerged in the early 1990s after climate change and sustainable energy transition became global issues. Among cities, a horizontal sphere of action emerged, facilitated by a variety of *transnational municipal networks* (TNM), such as the *Climate Alliance, Energy Cities,* or *Cities for Climate Protection,* an initiative within the broader ICLEI (*Local Governments for Sustainability*) network (Kern and Bulkeley 2009). Such networks aim to connect like-minded municipalities and provide several benefits (Table 1). These cover information exchange assistance in the setup of energy and climate plans by providing a common methodology, or the organization of benchmarking and certification schemes. They also establish policy-specific working groups on specific topics like greenhouse gas inventories, energy efficiency in buildings, or smart traffic infrastructures, which address local policy specialists and allow them to establish regular contacts with peers. Also, non-thematic networks are important in the policy area, e.g., *Eurocities*, a network of European major cities that aims at "turning EU policies and ambitions into reality" (Eurocities 2020) and has climate change and energy transition as one priority.

It is useful to distinguish between *corporative* organizations and *networks*. Corporative organizations represent the generalized collective interests of a broad membership, particularly on a national scale. Examples are the *German Association of Cities* (Deutscher Städtetag) or the *Austrian Association of Cities* (Österreichischer Städtebund). With respect to networks, Heinelt and Niederhafner (2008) specify cooperative and coordinative networks. Cooperative networks as *associations of associations,* e.g., the *Council of European Municipalities and Regions* (CEMR), mainly concentrate on conventional interest mediation and are hardly able to put their individual members' preferences into account. As the opposite, Heinelt and Niederhafner (2008, p. 181) consider *Eurocities* as an example of a coordinative network, which organizes individual members immediately around common "basic demands and crucial interests." In the following, I will concentrate on such specific coordinative energy and climate networks.

Table 1 Transnational Municipal Networks

Network	Members	Members in Europe	Foundation
CCP	185	165	1994
Climate Alliance	1909	1909	1990
Energy cities	207	203	1990
Eurocities	201	201	1986
C 40	97	20	2005
Covenant of mayors	10,880	10,600	2008

Own compilation, numbers retrieved from the organizations' websites and updated January 31, 2022

The early stage of transnational horizontal governance up to the 2000s has been coined "municipal voluntarism" (Bulkeley and Betsill 2013, p. 139). It was mainly characterized by individuals within local authorities that act as pioneers toward sustainable municipal energy in the context of global climate change. The participation in networks particularly had a focus on the dissemination of knowledge, mutual learning, or just getting in touch with like-minded peers. Within the network organizations, functional networks or epistemic communities of local policy entrepreneurs emerged that enabled also an exchange on an informal base (Kern 2019; Kern and Bulkeley 2009). During the formative stage of horizontal governance, activities usually were committed to a self-governing approach, which includes the monitoring and reduction of GHG emissions in municipal properties and infrastructures as well as agenda-setting for issues of sustainable energy in the local society, and promoting an evidence-based approach to planning within the administration (Benz et al. 2015). However, activities in TNMs not only had an internal governing function but also addressed the external dimension, which was hardly accessible for most cities. Kern and Bulkeley (2009, pp. 323) highlight influence, interdependence, and intermediation as external governance functions. *Influence* enables cities to appear as collective actors in the exchange with governmental actors and to get access to different kinds of resources provided by upper jurisdictions. While influence pertains to relations with governmental actors, *interdependence* points to exchange between networks. *Intermediation* covers the relationship between networks and single actors. If these are influential in their local policy network, this may have positive feedback on the TNM, since its activities and initiatives will be more effective on the ground. This highlights the importance of policy entrepreneurs. If they are absent, it seems almost impossible for a network to stimulate action on the ground. Similarly, if such *success*, which is embodied by exemplary leading cities and their representatives (Kern 2019, p. 132), is lacking, networks may be weakened in achieving other governing functions.

Empirical work on the effects of TNMs suggests that local actors are aware of both internal and external dimensions of horizontal governance. However, a survey on major and medium-sized German cities on the functions of networking points to the dominance of internal factors. Most frequently the respondents named *enabling internal mobilization, formulating emission reduction goals, institutionalizing climate trajectories, enabling direct exchange*, and *offering project support* as the most important benefits of network participation. External governance characteristics like *advocacy and lobbying* occur to a much lesser extent in the survey (Busch et al. 2018, pp. 225).

These findings largely correspond to qualitative research results that refer to in-depth interviews with local politicians and civil servants in three German metropolises (Kemmerzell 2019, Benz et al. 2015). *Policy learning* and *safeguarding through self-commitment* were the most prominent effects of TNM membership perceived by local actors. Learning takes place in the view of the actors both on an individual and an organizational level. Individual learning occurs in epistemic communities of experts (s.a.), organizational learning comprises the diffusion of best practices if cities get affected by policy models established elsewhere.

However, because of context-specific constraints diffusion usually does not lead to the imitation or emulation of best practices, policy learning rather happens in the mode of inspiration. Safeguarding comes to the fore if a municipality commits itself, by joining a TNM, to particular goals or common standards. Such a commitment can strengthen the position of policy specialists in debates with the city council or the political leaders. Therefore, safeguarding aims at the lock-in of programmatic or institutional change, once a certain policy has been established. While learning and safeguarding are typical assets of horizontal governance, local actors assign *achieving fiscal co-benefits* and *compliance* rather to the vertical dimension. However, empirical evidence suggests that local actors mostly conflate the vertical and horizontal dimensions and consider them as elements of a coherent *trans-local action space* that encompasses every action and communication that transcends the municipal boundaries (Benz et al. 2015).

The voluntary nature of horizontal governance defines the boundaries of the approach. Since it depends on the availability of local resources, it remained most relevant for "leading cities," which are "relatively wealthy and powerful" and "highly integrated into the European economy" (Kern 2019, p. 131). Therefore, pure horizontal networks can be regarded as organizations of pioneers for pioneers. At best, those pioneering cities may serve as models influencing the policies of *followers*, but there is also the danger of widening the gap between the *leaders* and *laggards*.

Integration of Vertical and Horizontal Governance

As already mentioned, the differentiation between vertical and horizontal governance often remains analytical, since local actors do not strictly distinguish between bot spheres of action. They rather understand all kinds of activities beyond the formal boundaries of their authority as activities within a rather unified *trans-local action space*, in which they deliberately combine different kinds of governance. Benz et al. (2015, p. 325) emphasize that "more often than not, municipalities cooperate on a horizontal level when they bid for project funding (...) and become involved in vertical structures of multi-level governance."

Regarding the effectiveness and outreach of transnational governance, researchers emphasized particular shortcomings of horizontal governance (Kern 2014) and the voluntary approach (Bulkeley and Betsill 2013). They stressed the need for integrated approaches to correct the split between leaders and laggards but likewise observed the emergence of a "more overtly political approach" of "strategic urbanism" (Bulkeley and Betsill 2013, p. 140). Bulkeley and Betsill (2013) refer to the US Mayors Climate Protection Agreement, the C 40 Network of world-leading cities, and the European Covenant of Mayors for Climate & Energy (CoM) (see next section) as examples of a mixed governance approach that integrates both dimensions. Kern (2019, p. 136) referred to the integrated approach as a hybrid form of governance with the potential of "embedded upscaling." It means that the typical features of horizontal governance, task-specific activities by intersecting members, become embedded in the vertical dimension, and even get backing by hierarchical elements. Embedded governance is intended to reach out from pioneers to follower cities and even to address the specific needs of often structurally disadvantaged laggards (Kern 2019, p. 140). In the case of the CoM, integration depends on an attempt of *orchestration* (Hale and Roger 2014), i.e., by exploiting the merits of horizontal governance through an upper jurisdiction, the European Commission (Bendlin 2020). With the purpose to commit municipal authorities to the European energy and climate policy, the Commission launched the network-like CoM as a unique European approach.

The Covenant of Mayors for Climate & Energy

With the purpose to commit municipal authorities to the European energy and climate policy, the EU Commission launched the network-like *Covenant of Mayors for Climate & Energy* (CoM) in 2008 as a unique European approach that goes beyond pure voluntary networking. The CoM combines a vertical mode of governance, attracting cities to contribute to the EU goals, with a horizontal layer related to network building, mutual learning, and the spread of best practices among the members. Therefore, it aims to provide a more robust pattern of mutual exchange between and interest aggregation of cities. Additionally, the CoM intends to allow for a stronger commitment to the organizations' goals than common in TNMs (Domorenok et al. 2020). In the remainder of this section, I will take a closer look at the CoM and ask, how far it delivers on the promises of orchestration.

Foundation and Instruments of the Covenant of Mayors

The foundation of the CoM took place in the context of the expansion of the European energy and climate policy. The CoM as a kind of *orchestration* (Bendlin 2020) in an *experimental governance architecture* (Domorenok et al. 2020) indicates a strategic approach to the local level differing significantly from the older voluntary networks. The CoM goes beyond the voluntary network, as it provides a basis for the aggregation of interests of cities toward the European level. Membership in this specific network requires a stronger commitment to the network goals through several compliance mechanisms that could be understood as, albeit cautious, variants of "harder soft governance" (Knodt and Ringel 2018). Network goals were first the *2020 goals* described above. They were later replaced by the stepped-up goals of the *Climate and Energy Framework* of 2014. In 2021, the CoM adopted the goals of the *Fit for 55* package, a 55% greenhouse gas reduction target by 2030 and climate-neutrality by 2050 (CoM 2022a). Additionally, the CoM broadened its focus in 2014 and integrated the climate adaptation initiative *Mayors Adapt*. It changed its name from *Covenant of Mayors* to *Covenant of Mayors for Climate & Energy*. In the wake of the relaunch, the CoM enabled membership from non-EU and non-European countries and joined forces with the global initiative *Global Compact of Mayors* as *Global Covenant of Mayors for Climate and Energy*.

While municipalities are the major addressees of the CoM, the organization also promotes multilevel activities and partnerships, in that it introduced the special membership categories of *Covenant Coordinators* and *Covenant Supporters*. Administrative jurisdictions as regions, provinces, or states, as well as local and regional agencies can join the CoM and support the ordinary members in policymaking and capacity building (Domorenok et al. 2020).

Members of the CoM commit themselves to apply the *Covenant Methodology* that comprises the implementation of four major steps. Membership starts with the signing of the covenant program by the mayor or a representative of the municipal council, after the council adopted a resolution expressing the will of the municipality to become a member. Within 2 years following the signature, municipalities must submit the two core documents, *Baseline Inventories* of GHG emissions and *Sustainable Energy and Climate Action Plans* (SECAP). In the follow-up of the submission of a SECAP comes monitoring. Two years after submission of the first SECAP, members should monitor and report their achievements in a *Progress Report*. Both the core documents and the progress report should meet the standards defined by the Covenant Methodology and are reviewed by the Joint Research Centre (JRC) of the European Commission. Part of the monitoring process is the reporting of good practices, or *benchmarks*, which are available from the CoM database. The benchmarks include a summary of the activities, the indication of the sector (e.g., residential buildings, transport, or industry among 16 categories), timing, and costs (Domorenok et al. 2020, p. 133). The Covenant of Mayors Office in Brussels coordinates the whole program. In a fourth step, municipalities should validate the results of the monitoring process and update the SECAPs respectively.

Membership Patterns of the Covenant of Mayors

In overall numbers of membership, the CoM can only be called a success. As of January 31, 2022, the CoM Office reported 10,880 signatories from 54 countries, 7761 SECAP, and 7350 Baseline Inventory submissions. Among the submitted plans, 4981 were accepted, 628 were rejected, and the remaining are in process. 2544 municipalities (about 23% of all signatories) completed the whole process and finished the monitoring process. Besides, the CoM has 231 Covenant Coordinators and 238 Covenant Supporters (CoM 2022b). The CoM represents roughly 340 million inhabitants. The expansion becomes visible by comparing with data from 2016. As of December 31, 2016, 7190 signatories were reported, 5674 SECAP submissions (4433 accepted, 130 rejected, and 1105 plans under review), and 1263 monitoring/progress reports (Kemmerzell 2018, p. 43).

However, while overall numbers are impressive, membership is unevenly distributed among regions and countries, and therefore remains asymmetric (Domorenok 2019). The bulk of signatories comes from three countries, Italy, Spain, and Belgium, which account for roughly 77% of the member municipalities. Strongholds of the

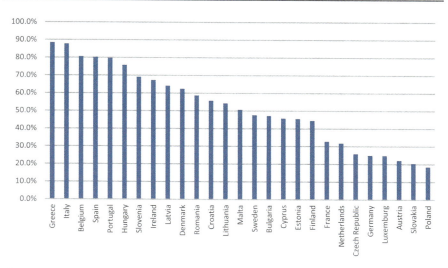

Fig. 1 Share of national population living in Covenant of Mayors Municipalities in 2021. (CoM 2022b; Statistisches Bundesamt 2022)

CoM are located in Southern European countries, like Greece or Portugal, and some countries from Eastern and South-Eastern Europe, e.g., Hungary, Croatia, and Slovenia. Membership is rather weak in Western and Central Europe. A meaningful indicator for the outreach of the CoM might be the share of national populations living in CoM municipalities (Fig. 1). It indicates that in about half of the EU member states more than 50% of the population lives in those communities.

This variance might partly be explained by the availability of domestic support structures. In countries where domestic programs for local sustainable energy and climate activities are widely absent or insufficient, the CoM seems to be a welcome opportunity to build up capacities, both in major cities and small communities (Domorenok et al. 2020, p. 130). Otherwise, in countries that established domestic support structures early, as in Germany, the Netherlands, or the United Kingdom, the CoM failed to spread among a broad range of municipalities (Heidrich et al. 2016). Research on German members of the CoM indicates that "signing the covenant seems to be rather an add-on within an already established climate protection portfolio" (Kemmerzell 2018, p. 55). France shows a specific pattern, as accession to the CoM was attractive as long as no effective national support scheme existed. As soon as the national energy agency provided assistance tools, many French municipalities perceived CoM-related obligations as overlapping and redundant and stopped compliance to the *Covenant Methodology* or withdrew membership (Bendlin 2020).

These findings suggest different functions of membership in different settings. While particularly municipalities from Southern Europe perceive the importance of the CoM for establishing and adjusting sustainable energy strategies from the very beginning (Domorenok et al. 2020), members from Western and Northern Europe rather emphasize opportunities to raise the visibility of cities or to safeguard already existing climate policies internally against competing claims (Kemmerzell 2019).

Uneven updating of the municipal plans indicates another problem for the CoM. Particularly many early members failed to adopt the European 2030 goals and still maintain the outdated 2020 targets. According to the CoM office, only 18% of signatory countries have committed to the 2030 targets, and only 2% have submitted plans for climate adaptation, which still plays a secondary role. The experience of the reluctance of the CoM members to review their plans regularly points to a second issue besides regional fragmentation of membership, namely, the problems in keeping pace with European energy and climate policy dynamics.

Governance Achievements and Shortcomings of the Covenant of Mayors

Following the descriptive findings on the membership and adherence to the methodology of the CoM, I will discuss its governance functions. Therefore, I will briefly evaluate how far the CoM meets the achievements theorized in the approaches on *orchestration*, *experimental governance*, and *upscaling*.

Orchestration takes place in settings where hierarchical governance by regulation is not feasible because of lacking competencies or according to the complex nature of a policy problem (Hale and Roger 2014). In energy policy, the former is the case as most decisions fall into the competency of the member states. Therefore, the European Commission must apply different modes of soft and indirect governance to steer the concerned actors and jurisdictions *in the desired direction*. The theory of experimental governance architecture claims that its advantage compared to traditional forms of governance is the establishment of recursive processes of provisional goalsetting and revision, which enables the adoption of common goals to specific contexts (Domorenok et al. 2020). Finally, (embedded) upscaling is supposed to link a variety of municipalities, including pioneers and laggards, and provide favorable conditions for policy transfer (Kern 2019).

The rationale of orchestration is the empowerment of autonomous units to contribute to a common good, namely, the network goals in case of the CoM. The findings in the literature on success display a mixed picture. The most seminal paper on the CoM by Domorenok et al. (2020, p. 131) shows that commitment to the Covenant Methodology unfolds as a "multispeed process." The timeframe of completing the full cycle of the methodology strongly varies across countries and types of cities. Additionally, many cities failed to update their plans to the 2030 goals of the EU, which means that the promises of orchestration are not effectively fulfilled. This shed also a light on recursiveness, the main feature of experimental governance. Since the bulk of members maintained the 2020 goals, the circular process of *submission and review* only unfolded in a minority of CoM municipalities. Diffusion of the CoM goals remains limited due to the fragmented membership (Fig. 1). Finally, fragmented membership affects the achievements in upscaling. While these are remarkable in countries with a significant membership, in many countries diffusion through the CoM hardly takes place, as membership is restricted to cities with a well-developed climate policy portfolio.

If we look for causes for these deficiencies, two aspects, in particular, stand out. First, a lack of experience and capacity among the signatories is only inadequately addressed by the network organization. Notwithstanding the manifold information provided by the CoM Office, activities mainly depend on scarce municipal (financial and human) resources and the offers of the CoM seem too weak to enhance the capacities of its members materially. Additionally, membership in the CoM does not even provide privileged access to European project funding, as has been conceived by member cities in the early days of the CoM (Benz et al. 2015). Secondly, asymmetric membership hampers the reach-out of good practices from many countries with long-term experiences in local climate action. Particularly, the opportunities of cross-border peer-to-peer learning seem to be underexplored in this regard (Domorenok et al. 2020, p. 139).

However, it would be short-sighted to concentrate on the *external* network goals of the CoM. Besides, it provides *internal* governance functions (Benz et al. 2015) or internal co-benefits (Bendlin 2016). At an early stage of local climate policy development, membership in the CoM may establish authoritative constraints for climate action, provides benchmarks for local programs, and supports the establishment of a methodology for climate and energy planning. Particularly at a mature stage of municipal climate policy, local politicians and bureaucrats can make strategic use of the membership. It creates a lock-in for pursuing local action and safeguards policies and institutional settings through external commitment. Moreover, cities perceive membership in the CoM as a means to strengthen their international visibility. The following quote from an official council proceeding of the German city Frankfurt is very revealing in this regard. It has been argued that an "abstention from the CoM would weaken Frankfurt's position because it would be much more difficult to demonstrate the (city's) achievements at the European level" (Benz et al. 2015, p. 329).

Conclusion

This chapter has demonstrated that municipalities, as other subnational jurisdictions, play an important role in European energy governance. Particularly the European Commission is aware of the weight of cities and introduced various attempts to tie municipalities stronger to the European energy and climate goals in absence of robust compliance mechanisms. These attempts depend on orchestration like in the *Covenant of Mayors* (CoM), vertical governance instruments like project funding, and voluntary action from single cities and particular municipal networks. In the context of the *European Green Deal*, both the orchestrated CoM (CoM 2022a) and voluntary networks like Eurocities (Eurocities 2021) engage in contributing to the *Fit for 55* package.

However, the most significant attempt of orchestration, the CoM displays mixed results. On a meta-governance level, it provides cities with the opportunity to become active on a global scale because the CoM not only constitutes a municipal network but also a meta-network that becomes active as a transnational actor by itself. Membership of non-European municipalities and organizations characterize this meta-network quality of the CoM. When it comes to signatories, attendance in some countries is impressively high. Otherwise, the CoM failed to reach out to all EU countries in a similar way, which diminishes the potential of upscaling in two ways. First, as CoM membership remains a matter among pioneering cities in countries like Germany, the "gap between leaders and laggards" will not be closed but probably widened. In that regard, the CoM differs not that much from voluntary networks. Secondly, asymmetric membership reduces the opportunity of cross-border learning, which is still rather limited to pioneering cities that are active on a transnational scale anyway. It will be therefore a challenge for the EU, if the Commission stays engaged in this kind of multilevel politics, to improve incentives for cities to commit to the full *Covenant Methodology*. Such commitment would be also a prerequisite to capitalize on the opportunities of experimental governance.

Outside the EU framework in the narrower sense, however, it is to be expected that municipalities will gain further importance in energy and climate policy. This has to do in particular with the changing structure of energy supply, which is becoming much more decentralized with a higher share of renewable energies. In this context, those structural factors are likely to increase cooperation between municipalities, because the establishment of efficient monitoring systems and the preparation of effective energy and climate plans likely depends on the ability of municipalities to adopt good practices and make use of opportunities for mutual exchange.

Cross-References

▶ Energy Governance in Denmark
▶ Energy Governance in Germany
▶ Energy Governance in the United Kingdom
▶ European Union Energy Policy: A Discourse Perspective

Acknowledgments I would like to thank Anne Hofmeister for a thorough review and helpful comments on the first draft of the chapter. Funding by the German Federal Ministry of Education and Research (Kopernikus-Projekt ENavi (FKZ 03SFK4P0) and the Kopernikus-Projekt Ariadne (FKZ 03SFK5LO)) is gratefully acknowledged.

References

2020 to 2030. COM. (2014). *final* (Vol. 15). Brussels: European Commission.
Andonova, L. B., Betsill, M., & Bulkeley, H. (2009). Transnational climate governance. *Global Environmental Politics, 9*(2), 52–73.
Bendlin, L. (2016). Cities' views and ownership of the covenant of mayors. In J. Kemmerzell, M. Knodt, & A. Tews (Eds.), *Städte und Energiepolitik im europäischen Mehrebenensystem. Zwischen Energiesicherheit, Nachhaltigkeit und Wettbewerb* (pp. 103–124). Baden-Baden: Nomos.

Bendlin, L. (2020). *Orchestrating local climate policy in the European Union: Inter-municipal coordination and the covenant of mayors in Germany and France*. Wiesbaden: Springer. https://doi.org/10.1007/978-3-658-26506-9_5.

Benz, A., Kemmerzell, J., Knodt, M., & Tews, A. (2015). The trans-local dimension of local climate policy. Sustaining and transforming local knowledge orders through trans-local action. *Urban Research & Practice, 8*(3), 319–335. https://doi.org/10.1080/17535069.2015.1051380.

Berka, A. L. (2018). Community renewable energy in the UK. A short history. In L. Holstenkamp & J. Radtke (Eds.), *Handbuch Energiewende und Partizipation* (pp. 1013–1036). Wiesbaden: Springer.

Bouteligier, S. (2013). *Cities, networks, and global environmental governance. Spaces of innovation, places of leadership*. London: Routledge.

Bulkeley, H., & Betsill, M. (2013). Revisiting the urban politics of climate change. *Environmental Politics, 22*(1), 136–154. https://doi.org/10.1080/09644016.2013.755797.

Bulkeley, H., Castán Broto, V., Hodson, M., & Marvin, S. (2011). Cities and the low carbon transition. *The European Financial Review*, 24–27.

Busch, H., Bendlin, L., & Fenton, P. (2018). Shaping local response – The influence of transnational municipal climate networks on urban climate governance. *Urban Climate, 24*, 221–230. https://doi.org/10.1016/j.uclim.2018.03.004.

Castán Broto, V., & Bulkeley, H. (2013). A survey of urban climate change experiments in 100 cities. *Global Environmental Change, 23*(1), 92–102. https://doi.org/10.1016/j.gloenvcha.2012.07.005.

Covenant of Mayors for Climate & Energy (CoM). (2022a). *Objectives and scope*. Brussels. https://www.covenantofmayors.eu/about/covenant-initiative/objectives-and-scope.html

Covenant of Mayors for Climate & Energy (CoM). (2022b). *Covenant in figures*. Brussels. https://www.covenantofmayors.eu/about/covenant-initiative/covenant-in-figures.html

Domorenok, E. (2019). Voluntary instruments for ambitious policies? The covenant of mayors of the European Union. *Environmental Politics, 28*(2), 293–314. https://doi.org/10.1080/09644016.2019.1549777.

Domorenok, E., Acconia, G., Bendlin, L., & Ruiz Campillo, X. (2020). Experiments in EU climate governance: The unfulfilled potential of the covenant of mayors. *Global Environmental Politics, 20*(4), 122–142. https://doi.org/10.1162/glep_a_00563.

Eikeland, P. O., & Inderberg, T. H. (2016). Energy system transformation and long-term interest constellations in Denmark: Can agency beat structure? *Energy Research & Social Science, 11*, 164–173. https://doi.org/10.1016/j.erss.2015.09.008.

Eurocities. (2020). *About us*. Brussels. https://eurocities.eu/about-us/

Eurocities. (2021). *A mayors Alliance for the European Green Deal*. Brussels. https://eurocities.eu/latest/a-mayors-alliance-for-the-european-green-deal/

European Commission. (1995). *White paper. An energy policy for the European Union. COM (95) 682 final*. Brussels: European Commission.

European Commission. (2006). *Green paper. A European strategy for sustainable, competitive and secure energy. COM(2006) 105 final*. Brussels: European Commission.

European Commission. (2008a). *20 20 by 2020. Europe's climate change opportunity. COM(2008) 30 final*. Brussels: European Commission.

European Commission. (2008b). *Sustainable energy cities take the lead on climate change: The European Commission launches the covenant of mayors. IP/08/103*. Brussels: European Commission.

European Commission. (2014). A policy framework for climate and energy in the period from.

European Commission. (2019). *The European green Deal. COM(2019) 640 final*. Brussels: European Commission.

Evans, J., Karvonen, A., & Raven, R. (Eds.). (2016). *The experimental city*. London & New York: Routledge.

Hale, T., & Roger, C. (2014). Orchestration and transnational climate governance. *Review of International Organization, 9*, 59–82. https://doi.org/10.1007/s11558-013-9174-0.

Hannah, L. (1979). *Electricity before nationalisation: A study of the development of the electricity supply industry in Britain to 1948*. London & Basingstoke: Macmillan.

Heidrich, O., Reckien, D., Olazabal, M., Foley, A. M., Salvia, M., De Gregorio Hurtado, S., & Hans Orru, H. (2016). National Climate Policies across Europe and their impacts on cities strategies. *Journal of Environmental Management, 16*(8), 36–45. https://doi.org/10.1016/j.jenvman.2015.11.043.

Heinelt, H., & Niederhafner, S. (2008). Cities and organized interest intermediation in the EU multi-level system. *European Urban and Regional Studies, 15*(2), 173–187. https://doi.org/10.1177/0969776408090023.

Hofmeister, A. (2022). *Der Einfluss der Europäischen Union auf städtische Klimapolitik. Eine Analyse der Rolle motivationaler Faktoren.* Darmstadt, Technische Universität, https://doi.org/10.26083/tuprints-00020636, [Dissertation].

Hooghe, L., & Marks, G. (2003). Unraveling the central state? Types of multi-level governance. *American Political Science Review, 97*(2), 233–243.

Kemmerzell, J. (2018). Innovations in European climate governance and their impact on local climate policy: An analysis of German major cities. In S. Hughes, E. Chu, & S. Mason (Eds.), *Climate change in cities. Innovations in multi-level governance* (pp. 39–57). Cham: Springer.

Kemmerzell, J. (2019). Bridging the gap between the local and the global scale? Taming the wicked problem of climate change through trans-local governance. In N. Behnke, J. Broschek, & J. Sonnicksen (Eds.), *Configurations, dynamics and mechanisms of multilevel governance* (pp. 155–172). Cham: Palgrave Macmillan.

Kern, K. (2014). Climate governance in the European Union multilevel system: The role of cities. In I. Weibust & J. Meadowcroft (Eds.), *Multilevel environmental governance. Managing water and climate change in Europe and North America* (pp. 111–130). Cheltenham: Edward Elgar.

Kern, K. (2019). Cities as leaders in EU multilevel climate governance: Embedded upscaling of local experiments in Europe. *Environmental Politics, 28*(1), 125–145. https://doi.org/10.1080/09644016.2019.1521979.

Kern, K., & Bulkeley, H. (2009). Cities, Europeanization and multi-level governance: Governing climate change through transnational municipal networks. *Journal of Common Market Studies, 47*(2), 309–332.

Knodt, M. (2016). Die Energiepolitik der Europäischen Union und Städte. In J. Kemmerzell, M. Knodt, & A. Tews (Eds.), *Städte und Energiepolitik im europäischen Mehrebenensystem. Zwischen Energiesicherheit, Nachhaltigkeit und Wettbewerb* (pp. 23–43). Nomos: Baden-Baden.

Knodt, M., & Ringel, M. (2018). The European Commission as a policy shaper – Harder soft governance in the energy union. In M. W. Bauer, J. Ege, & S. Becker (Eds.), *The European Commission in turbulent times* (pp. 181–204). Wiesbaden: Nomos.

Liefferink, D., & Wurzel, R. (2018). Leadership and pioneers. Exploring their role in polycentric governance. In A. Jordan, D. Huitema, H. van Asselt, & J. Foster (Eds.), *Governing climate change: Polycentricity in action?* (pp. 135–151). Cambridge: Cambridge University Press.

OECD. (2010). *Cities and climate change.* Paris: OECD Publishing.

Princen, S., & Kerremans, B. (2008). Opportunity structures in the EU multi-level system. *West European Politics, 31*(6), 1129–1146. https://doi.org/10.1080/01402380802370484.

Sack, D. (2018). Zwischen europäischer Liberalisierung und Energiewende – Der Wandel der Governanceregime im Energiesektor (1990–2016). In L. Holstenkamp & J. Radtke (Eds.), *Handbuch Energiewende und Partizipation* (pp. 83–100). Wiesbaden: Springer.

Schaefter, S., Mohns, T., Hemmati, M., & Offenmueller, S. (2013). *Promoting local climate mitigation (scoping study).* Berlin: Adelphi.

Schott, D. (2014). *Europäische Urbanisierung (1000–2000). Eine umwelthistorische Einführung.* Köln: Böhlau.

Schreurs, M. A. (2008). From the bottom up. Local and subnational climate change politics. *The Journal of Environment & Development, 17*(4), 343–355.

Statistisches Bundesamt. (2022). *Europa: Bevölkerung.* Wiesbaden. https://www.destatis.de/Europa/DE/Thema/Basistabelle/Bevoelkerung.html.